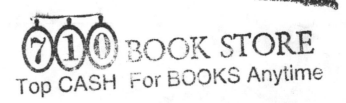

Public Administration

UNDERSTANDING MANAGEMENT, POLITICS, AND LAW IN THE PUBLIC SECTOR

Public Administration

UNDERSTANDING MANAGEMENT, POLITICS, AND LAW IN THE PUBLIC SECTOR

FOURTH EDITION

David H. Rosenbloom
American University

With the assistance of
Deborah D. Goldman, J.D., M.P.A.
Member of the New York State, District of Columbia, and Maryland Bars

The McGraw-Hill Companies, Inc.

New York   St. Louis   San Francisco   Auckland   Bogotá   Caracas   Lisbon
London   Madrid   Mexico City   Milan   Montreal   New Delhi
San Juan   Singapore   Sydney   Tokyo   Toronto

McGraw-Hill

A Division of The McGraw-Hill Companies

PUBLIC ADMINISTRATION
Understanding Management, Politics, and Law in the Public Sector

This book is printed on acid-free paper.

1 2 3 4 5 6 7 8 9 0   DOC   DOC   9 0 9 8 7

ISBN 0-07-053972-3

This book was set in Janson by Graphic World, Inc.
The editors were Lyn Uhl and Larry Goldberg;
the production supervisor was Paula Keller.
The cover was designed by Christopher Brady.
Project supervision was done by Graphic World Publishing Services.
R. R. Donnelley & Sons Company was printer and binder.

Library of Congress Cataloging-in-Publication Data

Rosenbloom, David H.
   Public administration: understanding management, politics, and
law in the public sector / David H. Rosenbloom with the assistance
of Deborah D. Goldman. — 4th ed.
      p. cm.
   Includes bibliographical references and index.
   ISBN 0-07-053972-3 (alk. paper)
   1. Public administration.   2. United States—Politics and
government.   I. Goldman, Deborah D.   II. Title.
JF1351.R56   1998
351—DC21   96–53404

Chapter-Opening Photo Credits:
Chapter 1: NASA; *Chapter 2:* Library of Congress; *Chapter 3:* Paul S. Conklin; *Chapter 4:* HUD; *Chapter 5:* Library of Congress; *Chapter 6:* Michael Dwyer/Stock, Boston; *Chapter 7:* George Gardner/The Image Works; *Chapter 8:* Anthony Yarns/Impact Visuals; *Chapter 9:* National Archives; *Chapter 10:* Bureau of Census; *Chapter 11:* Library of Congress; *Chapter 12:* Ron Bennett/Bettmann Newsphotos; *Chapter 13:* Jeff Albertson/Stock, Boston.

http://www.mhhe.com

About the Author

David H. Rosenbloom is Distinguished Professor of Public Administration in the School of Public Affairs at American University. He received his Ph.D. in political science from the University of Chicago in 1969. In 1970–1971 he was an American Society for Public Administration Fellow in the U.S. Civil Service Commission. Professor Rosenbloom was elected to the National Academy of Public Administration in 1986. He served as editor-in-chief of *Public Administration Review* from 1991 through 1996. In 1992 he received the Distinguished Research Award of the National Association of Schools of Public Affairs and Administration and the American Society for Public Administration. In 1993 he received the Charles Levine Memorial Award for Excellence in Public Administration from the same organizations. In 1996 he was corecipient of the Thomas Dye Award for Outstanding Service to the Policy Studies Organization. He was appointed to the Clinton-Gore Presidential Transition in 1992, with responsibilities for the U.S. Office of Personnel Management. In 1993 he testified before the U.S. Senate Governmental Affairs Committee with regard to revisions of the Hatch Act. His international consulting on civil service systems includes China, Costa Rica, Hong Kong, Israel, South Africa, and Japan.

Professor Rosenbloom's published work focuses on the politics, law, and personnel of public bureaucracy. His first title was *Federal Service and the Constitution* (Cornell University Press, 1971) and his most recent is *Public Administration and Law*, second edition (Marcel Dekker, 1997; with Rosemary O'Leary). He is coeditor of *Contemporary Public Administration* (McGraw-Hill, 1994; with Deborah Goldman and Patricia Ingraham).

Contents in Brief

Preface to the Fourth Edition   *xv*
Acknowledgments   *xvii*
Preface to the First Edition   *xix*

PART ONE   INTRODUCTION: DEFINITIONS, CONCEPTS, AND SETTING   1

1 *The Practice and Discipline of Public Administration: Competing Concerns*   *3*
2 *The American Administrative State: Development and Political Environment*   *45*
3 *Federalism and Intergovernmental Relations: The Structure of the American Administrative State*   *99*

PART TWO   CORE FUNCTIONS   139

4 *Organization: Structure and Process*   *141*
5 *Public Personnel Administration and Collective Bargaining*   *207*
6 *Budgeting*   *275*
7 *Decision Making*   *323*
8 *Policy Analysis and Implementation Evaluation*   *361*

PART THREE   THE CONVERGENCE OF MANAGEMENT, POLITICS, AND LAW IN THE PUBLIC SECTOR: AN ILLUSTRATION   405

9 *Regulatory Administration: An Illustration of Management, Politics, and Law in the Public Sector*   *407*

PART FOUR   PUBLIC ADMINISTRATION AND THE PUBLIC   451

10 *Public Administration and the Public*   *453*
11 *Public Administration and Democratic Constitutionalism*   *493*
12 *Accountability and Ethics*   *529*
13 *The Future*   *561*

Glossary   *573*
Index   *581*

Contents

Preface to the Fourth Edition   xv

Acknowledgments   xvii

Preface to the First Edition   xix

PART ONE   INTRODUCTION: DEFINITIONS, CONCEPTS, AND SETTING   1

1   *The Practice and Discipline of Public Administration: Competing Concerns*   *3*

Some Definitions   4

Emphasizing the *Public* in Public Administration   6
     Constitutions / The Public Interest / The Market/ Sovereignty

Regulation and Service   14

Managerial, Political, and Legal Approaches   15
     The Managerial Approach to Public Administration /
     Traditional Managerial Approach to Public Administration /
     The New Public Management (NPM) / The Political Approach
     to Public Administration / The Legal Approach to Public
     Administration

Conclusion: Public Administration Reconsidered   39

Notes   40 / Additional Reading   42 / Study Questions   43

2   *The American Administrative State: Development and Political Environment*   *45*

The Rise of the American Administrative State   46
     The Political Roots of the American Administrative State /
     The Legal Origins of American Public Administration /
     The Managerial Origins of the Contemporary American
     Administrative State

Administrative Authority and Responsibility   59

Responses to the Rise of the Administrative State   64
     The President and Public Administration / Congress and the
     Administrative State / The Courts: A Judicial Response to Contemporary
     Public Administration / Interest Groups / The Public / Political Parties

State and Local Governments   90

Conclusion   92

Notes   93 / Additional Reading   96 / Study Questions   97

3   Federalism and Intergovernmental Relations: The Structure
of the American Administrative State   *99*

Why Federalism?   100
Administrative Decentralization   104
The Quest for Uniformity among the States   106
Mixes of Federalism   108
American Government: The Building Blocks   109
Intergovernmental Relations   123
    Federal and State Relations / Interstate Relations/
    Relationships among Local Governments
Conclusion   135
Notes   136 / Additional Reading   138 / Study Questions   138

PART TWO   CORE FUNCTIONS   139

4   Organization: Structure and Process   *141*

Organization Theory   142
Commonalities in Public Administrative Organization   144
    Bureaucracy / Scientific Management / The Human Relations
    Approach / Leadership / Motivation / Contemporary Approaches
    to Organization Theory
Managerial Perspectives on Public Organization   172
    Contemporary Managerial Perspectives
The Political Approach to Public Organization   183
    Pluralism / Autonomy / The Legislative Connection / Decentralization /
    A Checklist of Political Questions on Administrative Organization
The Legal Approach to Public Organization   189
    Independence / The Commission Format / Insulation from Ex Parte
    Influences / Independent Hearing Examiners–Administrative Law
    Judges / Staffing for Adjudication / ADR
The Future   194
    Fundamental Assumptions / Democratic Organization / Market-Based
    Organization
Notes   200 / Additional Reading   204 / Study Questions   204

5   Public Personnel Administration and Collective Bargaining   *207*

Historical Background   208
    Public Personnel Administration According to "Gentlemen" / Public
    Personnel Administration According to "Spoils" / Public Personnel
    Administration According to "Merit"
Management, Politics, and Law in Public Personnel Administration   219
    Civil Service Reform, 1978

Managerial Public Personnel Administration   226
   Position Classification / Recruitment, Selection, and Promotion /
   Performance Appraisal / Pay / Cutbacks / Political Neutrality
The Political Approach to Public Personnel Administration   244
   Responsiveness/ Representativeness
The Legal Approach to Public Personnel Administration   254
   The Constitutional Rights of Public Employees and Applicants /
   The Liability and Immunity of Public Employees
Collective Bargaining   261
Conclusion: Change Is Inevitable   269
Notes   270 / Additional Reading   273 / Study Questions   273

6   *Budgeting*   275

The Size and Growth of Budgets   276
   Sources of Revenues / Countercyclical Governmental Fiscal Policy /
   Supply-Side Economics
The Federal Budgetary Process   288
   Stages in the Budgetary Process / The Continuing Saga of the Budget:
   Execution / Constant Problem Areas
A Budget Theory, or Theories about Budgeting?   302
   The Managerial Approach to Public Budgeting / The Political Approach
   to Public Budgeting / The Legal Influence on Budgeting
Conclusion: The Search for a Synthesis   317
Notes   318 / Additional Reading   320 / Study Questions   321

7   *Decision Making*   323

The Traditional Managerial Approach to Decision Making   324
   Specialization / Hierarchy / Formalization / Merit / The Rational-
   Comprehensive Model / Critique of the Rational-Comprehensive Model
The New Public Management and Decision Making   335
   Market Criteria / Employee Empowerment
The Political Approach to Decision Making: The Incremental Model   338
   A Critique of the Incremental Model
The Legal Approach to Decision Making   344
The Case of Benzene in the Workplace   348
Synthesizing Decision-Making Approaches   352
   What to Avoid / Computers and Information Systems
Notes   357 / Additional Reading   358 / Study Questions   358

8   *Policy Analysis and Implementation Evaluation*   361

The Growing Concern with Policy Analysis   362
Approaches to Analyzing Public Policy   364
   Impact Analysis / Process Analysis and Implementation Studies
Implementation Evaluation   372

Managerial Perspectives on Implementation   373
   *Traditional Management / The New Public Management / Monitoring and
   Measuring Performance*
The Political Perspective on Implementation   389
   Representation / Responsiveness / Accountability
The Legal Perspective on Implementation   393
   *Constitutional Integrity / Equal Protection / Procedural Due Process
   and Protection of Individual Rights / Estoppel*
Utilizing Analysis and Evaluation   398
Conclusion: The Complexity of Policy Design   399
Notes   400 / Additional Reading   402 / Study Questions   403

**PART THREE   THE CONVERGENCE OF
   MANAGEMENT, POLITICS, AND LAW IN
   THE PUBLIC SECTOR: AN ILLUSTRATION   405**

*9   Regulatory Administration: An Illustration of Management,
   Politics, and Law in the Public Sector   407*

The Development and Growth of Regulatory Administration   408
   Political Patterns / Social Factors
The Structure and Process of Regulatory Administration   419
Problems in Regulatory Administration   424
   *Regulation Is Expensive / Regulation Dampens Economic Performance /
   Regulation Produces Delay and Extravagant Red Tape / Incompetence /
   Corruption / The Ever-Increasing Inclusiveness of Regulation /
   The Regulatory Process Is Out of Control / Determining Success*
Deregulation and Regulatory Reform   431
Perspectives toward Regulatory Administration   434
   *The Traditional Managerial Perspective / The New Public Management
   Approach to Regulation / The Political Approach to Regulatory
   Administration / The Legal Approach to Regulatory Administration*
Synthesis   444
Notes   447 / Additional Reading   450 / Study Questions   450

**PART FOUR   PUBLIC ADMINISTRATION
   AND THE PUBLIC   451**

10   Public Administration and the Public   453

The Public's Interaction with Public Administration   454
The Individual in the Administrative State   456
   *The Individual in Society / The Individual in the Political System /
   The Individual in the Economy*

The Public's Evaluation of Public Administration   467
Clients and Customers Are Satisfied / Regulation Is Opposed /
A Look at Local Government Services
Public Administrative Perspectives on the Public   474
The Traditional Managerial Approach to the Public / The New Public
Management Approach to the Public / The Political Approach to the Public /
The Legal Approach to the Public
Synthesis: Putting the *Public* Back in Public Administration   483
Notes   487 / Additional Reading   489 / Study Questions   489

11   *Public Administration and Democratic Constitutionalism*   *493*

Why Public Administrators Must Understand the Constitution   494
Administrative Structure and Constitutional Structure   498
Constitutional Values   501
Legitimacy / Diversity among the Citizenry / Freedom and Liberty /
Property Rights / Procedural Due Process / Equal Protection /
Individuality / Fourth Amendment Privacy Rights / Equity / State Action
Synthesis: An Ongoing Partnership   524
Notes   525 / Additional Reading   526 / Study Questions   527

12   *Accountability and Ethics*   *529*

Why the Guardians Need Guarding   530
Misconception of the Public Interest / Corruption / Subversion
Why It Is Difficult to Guard the Guardians   539
Perspectives on Accountability and Ethics   542
The Traditional Managerial Perspective / The New Public Management /
The Political Perspective / The Legal Perspective
Conclusion: Personal Responsibility   554
Notes   557 / Additional Reading   559 / Study Questions   559

13   *The Future*   *561*

Complexity Is Here to Stay   562
Dominant Public Administration Will Be Defined by Politics   563
Law will Continue to Be Central to Public Administration   564
Performance   565
Disaggregation of Public Administration   565
Decomposition of the Civil Service   566
The Changing Face of Management   567
Personal Responsibility   568
A New Administrative Culture   569
Notes   570 / Additional Reading   570 / Study Questions   571

Glossary   573
Index   581

Preface to the Fourth Edition

In many respects, the Fourth Edition of *Public Administration: Understanding Management, Politics, and Law in the Public Sector* is a *new* book rather than an update. It continues to describe, explain, and analyze public administration from the point of view of three well-established perspectives: management, politics, and law. These perspectives are related to the constitutional separation of powers and are ingrained in the American political culture. Our public administration cannot be understood comprehensively without paying full attention to each of them. However, the orthodox or classical managerial approach is currently under significant challenge by an infusion of ideas and new energy from the "reinventing government" movement, the federal National Performance Review, and the vast administrative reforms taking place abroad. Consequently, the book now provides full treatment of the new public management (NPM), as a distinctive approach alongside traditional management and the other perspectives. Setting forth the NPM perspective on such core areas as organization, personnel, budgeting, decision making, policy analysis and implementation evaluation, regulatory administration, dealing with the public, and accountability is highly instructive and better prepares students for administrative practice. The book makes it clear that the NPM, which often appears to be a hodgepodge of theoretical and pragmatic prescriptions for improving public administration, is really quite coherent and comprehensive. It has the potential to become a dominant new managerial paradigm. However, like all approaches to the complex enterprise of contemporary public administration, it also has limitations. It does not speak sufficiently to the values and administrative arrangements favored by the political and legal approaches, such as group representation, citizen participation, constitutional rights, procedural fairness, and ethics. While it emphasizes performance, it may lack the traditional managerial approach's ability to promote accountability and limit corruption. Therefore, at present, the NPM is best viewed as contesting, as opposed to replacing, the other perspectives.

   Providing full consideration of the NPM has refreshed and energized the book. The treatment of management is now more comprehensive and forward looking. Other changes include complete updating, providing the book with a more generic feel by shedding some of the earlier detailed discussion of federal administrative processes, greater recognition of the developments taking place in state and local administration, and much rewriting with a view toward clearer explanation and simplification. The book strives hard to capture the rapid changes occurring in public administration and the excitement associated with them. I have listened carefully to faculty who use the book and to students who have read it. The book has proven to be eminently "teachable," but the text has been adjusted throughout to make it even more so.

Public Administration: Understanding Management, Politics, and Law in the Public Sector is unique. It combines comprehensive treatment of public administration in all its complexity with an analytic framework that organizes the material to generate an enduring understanding of the field. The three perspectives it uses as lenses for analyzing and describing public administrative concerns are linked to the separation of powers in the American context, but they also have a universal quality. In addition to being widely adopted in the United States, the book is used in many places abroad, including China, The Georgian Republic, Hong Kong, The Netherlands, Singapore, and Taiwan. I very much hope it works well for you.

David H. Rosenbloom

Acknowledgments

Naming all the colleagues and students who have contributed directly and indirectly to this book would require several pages. I hope it is enough to say that I have benefited greatly from the warm collegiality and generosity that characterizes those who are dedicated to the study and reflective practice of public administration. I am particularly thankful to my colleagues in the School of Public Affairs at American University, who have provided a wonderful intellectual environment and great reservoir of knowledge of public management. Among them, I am especially grateful to Robert Boynton for very helpful suggestions regarding revisions for this edition. Finally, thanks go to those reviewers who aided in the development of this fourth edition: Barbara Adams, Grand Valley State University; Thomas Barth, University of Memphis; Robert Bartlett, Purdue University; Hugh Hinton, University of Toledo; and David Winder, Valdosta State University.

Preface to the First Edition

Public Administration: Understanding Management, Politics, and Law in the Public Sector appears sixty years after the publication of the first major American public administration textbook, Leonard D. White's *Introduction to the Study of Public Administration* (1926). White viewed public administration as "the heart of the problem of modern government."[1] He tried not only to explain and cover his subject matter comprehensively but also to frame the discipline of public administration and its discourse. I have sought to remain within the tradition of public administration texts begun by White. *Public Administration: Understanding Management, Politics, and Law in the Public Sector* agrees with White that public administration is central to modern government. It also presents an intellectual framework that can be a device for developing a deep and comprehensive understanding of contemporary public administration in all its complexity. I believe that this framework can provide a basis for further fruitful discourse and development in the discipline and practice of public administration. Ironically—but not really surprisingly—the most succinct description of the intellectual framework employed here is Dwight Waldo's, rather than my own. With reference to my essay introducing the framework,[2] Waldo remarked:

> . . . David Rosenbloom has set forth the structure of the problem before us. For each of the three constitutional branches, he points out, there is a body of doctrine, set of values, collection of instruments, and repertoire of procedures. For the executive branch this "cluster" is administrative, managerial, bureaucratic, and the emphasis is upon effectiveness and efficiency. For the legislative branch the cluster is political and policy making, and the emphasis is upon the values of representativeness and responsiveness. For the judicial branch the cluster is legal, and the emphasis is on constitutional integrity on one side and substantive and procedural protections for individuals on the other.
>
> Realistically our public administration does consist of varying mixtures of these three approaches or clusters. It is not just undesirable, it is impossible to narrow the concerns of public administration to any one of them. Our task is to find the proper way to put the three together.[3]

These clusters (I call them *approaches* or *perspectives*) are an outgrowth of the constitutional separation of powers; they are inherent in our political culture and institutions. As public administration is central to contemporary American government, these approaches are central to our contemporary public administration.

Waldo called this framework "both an excellent analysis and an excellent prescription."[4] *Public Administration: Understanding Management, Politics, and*

Law in the Public Sector engages the task of putting the three approaches together. I hope the reader will find this effort worthwhile and participate in it. Together we may be able to help resolve the problem of modern government; certainly we can improve our understanding and practice of public administration.

The book is divided into four parts. Part One introduces the book's intellectual framework and discusses the development of public administration in the United States. Part Two considers public administration's core functions: organization, personnel, budgeting, decision making, and policy analysis and evaluation. Each of these areas is analyzed from the perspectives of management, politics, and law. Efforts are made to synthesize these three perspectives with regard to each core function. Part Three analyzes regulatory administration as an illustration of the interplay of management, politics, and law in the public sector. Part Four focuses on the place of the "public" and the "public interest" in public administration. Chapters are devoted to public administration and the public, public administration and democratic constitutionalism, and accountability and ethics. The concluding chapter is devoted to the prospects for building a new "administrative culture."

The book is accompanied by an instructor's manual, which includes a test bank.

In many respects, *Public Administration: Understanding Management, Politics, and Law in the Public Sector* differs from other texts in the field. It addresses the complexity of public administration in theory and practice. It provides a comprehensive intellectual framework. It emphasizes *understanding* public administration in its presentation of information, description, theory, and interpretation. It is an ambitious book. I hope you find it rewarding.

NOTES

1. Leonard D. White, *Introduction to the Study of Public Administration* (New York: Macmillan, 1926), preface.
2. David H. Rosenbloom, "Public Administrative Theory and the Separation of Powers," *Public Administration Review* 43 (May/June 1983): 219–227.
3. Brack Brown and Richard J. Stillman, "A Conversation with Dwight Waldo: An Agenda for Future Reflections," *Public Administration Review* 45 (July/August 1985): 463–464.
4. Ibid., 464.

David H. Rosenbloom

Public Administration
UNDERSTANDING MANAGEMENT,
POLITICS, AND LAW
IN THE PUBLIC SECTOR

| PART ONE | *Introduction: Definitions, Concepts, and Setting* |

Introduction:

Definitions, Concepts, and Setting

Chapter 1 The Practice and Discipline of Public Administration: Competing Concerns

Chapter 2 The American Administrative State: Development and Political Environment

Chapter 3 Federalism and Intergovernmental Relations: The Structure of the American Administrative State

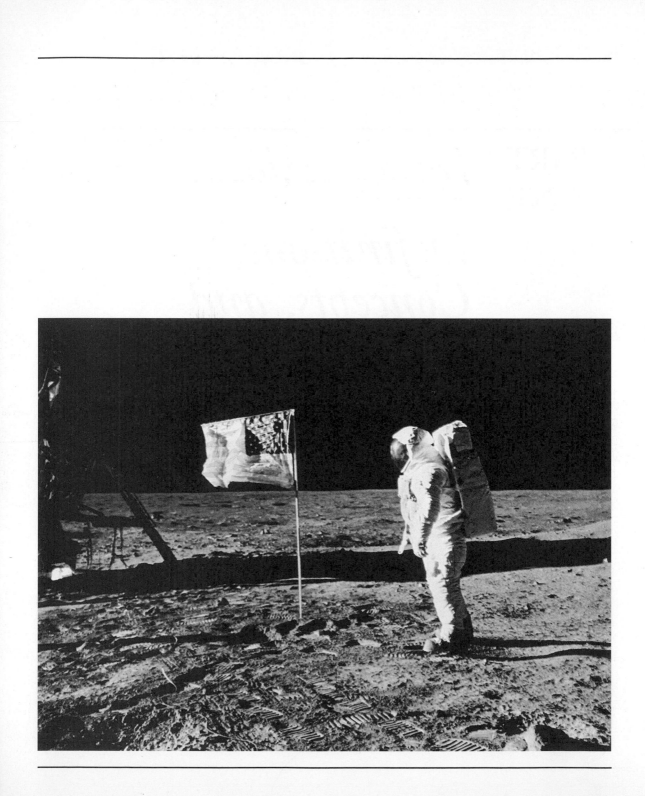

CHAPTER 1 | *The Practice and Discipline of Public Administration: Competing Concerns*

This chapter develops a definition of public administration. It considers what distinguishes *public* administration from the administration and management of private enterprises, focusing on the roles of the Constitution, the public interest, economic market forces, and sovereignty. The tendency for public administration to provide both *service* and *regulation* is explored. The bulk of this chapter discusses three general and competing approaches to public administration. One sees public administration as essentially management, another emphasizes its political nature, and the third, its legalistic concerns and processes. The managerial approach currently has two subsets: traditional and the new public management (NPM). Each perspective favors a different set of values, offers distinctive organizational approaches for maximizing these values, and each considers the individual in different ways.

Public administration, like many human endeavors, is difficult to define. Nonetheless, we all have a sense of what it is, though we may disagree profoundly about how it should be carried out. In part, this is because public administration covers such a vast amount of activity. Public administrative jobs range from the exploration of outer space to sweeping the streets. Some public administrators are highly educated professionals, who may be at the forefront of their fields of specialization; others possess few skills that differentiate them from the mass of the citizenry. Some public administrators make policies that have a nationwide impact and may benefit millions of people; others have virtually no responsibility for policy making at all and simply carry out mundane governmental tasks like word processing, filing, and record keeping. Public administrators are doctors, lawyers, scientists, engineers, accountants, budgeters, policy analysts, personnel officers, managers, clerks, keyboarders, manual laborers, and individuals engaged in a host of other occupations and functions. But knowing what public administrators *do* does not resolve the problem of defining what public administration *is*.

At first glance, one might be inclined to ignore the problem of defining public administration. It was pointed out some time ago that any one-paragraph or even one-sentence definition of public administration is bound to prove temporarily mind-paralyzing.[1] This is because public administration as a category is so abstract and varied that it can only be described in vague, general, amorphous, and somewhat competing terms. Yet some attention to definition is important. First, it is necessary to establish the general boundaries and to convey the major concerns of the discipline and practice of public administration. Second, the definition of public administration helps to place the field in a broader political, economic, and social context. Third, consideration of the leading definitions of public administration reveals that there are three distinct underlying approaches to the field. For years the tendency of scholars and practitioners to stress one or another of these approaches has promoted confusion, because each approach tends to emphasize different values, different organizational arrangements, different methods of developing information, and radically distinct views of the individual citizen.

SOME DEFINITIONS

One can find a wide variety of definitions of public administration, but the following are among the most serious and influential efforts to define the field.

1. "Public administration . . . is the action part of government, the means by which the purposes and goals of government are realized."[2]
2. "Public administration as a field is mainly concerned with the means for implementing political values. . . ."
3. ". . . Public administration can be best identified with the executive branch of government."

4. "Public administration differs from political science in its emphasis on bureaucratic structure and behavior and in its methodologies. Public administration differs from administrative science in the evaluative techniques used by nonprofit organizations, and because profit-seeking organizations are considerably less constrained in considering the public interest in their decision-making structures and the behavior of their administrators."

5. "The process of public administration consists of the actions involved in effecting the intent or desire of a government. It is thus the continuously active, 'business' part of government, concerned with carrying out the law, as made by legislative bodies (or other authoritative agents) and interpreted by the courts, through the processes of organization and management."

6. Public administration: (a) is a cooperative group effort in a public setting; (b) covers all three branches—executive, legislative, and judicial—and their interrelationships; (c) has an important role in the formulation of public policy, and is thus part of the political process; (d) is different in significant ways from private administration; and (e) is closely associated with numerous private groups and individuals.

What conclusions can be drawn from the variety of definitions of public administration and their myriad nuances? One is that definitions of public administration are indeed mind-paralyzing. Another conclusion is that there is really no such subject as "public administration," but rather that public administration means different things to different observers and lacks a significant common theoretical or applied meaning. However, this perspective has limited appeal because the problem is certainly not that there is no public administration—we not only know it's there, but also are often acutely aware of its contributions or shortcomings. The fact that we cannot neatly define the substance and process of public administration is hardly an excuse for concluding that the phenomenon is nonexistent, especially at a time when almost every society is seeking to improve its public sector operations.

Ironically, another conclusion that can be drawn from the multiplicity of definitions is that, on the contrary, public administration is everywhere. Some have argued that there is no field or discipline of public administration per se because the study of public administration overlaps a number of other disciplines, including political science, sociology, economics, psychology, and business administration. Although this approach contains a great deal of truth, in practical terms it is unsatisfactory because it leaves us without the ability to analyze coherently a major aspect of contemporary public life—indeed, one that is clearly a central political development of the twentieth century, namely, the emergence of large and powerful governmental agencies.

This book develops a less extreme approach to the problem of defining public administration. We conclude that all the above definitions are helpful. Public administration does involve *activity*, it is concerned with *politics* and *policy-making*, it tends to be concentrated in the *executive* branch of government, it does differ from private administration, and it is concerned with *implementing the law*. But we can be much more specific by offering a definition of our own: *Public administration is the use of managerial, political, and legal theories and processes to fulfill legislative, executive, and judicial governmental mandates for the provision of regulatory and service functions for the society as a whole or for some segments of it.* There are several points here that require further elaboration.

EMPHASIZING THE PUBLIC IN PUBLIC ADMINISTRATION

First, public administration differs from private administration in significant ways. The lines between the public and private sectors are often blurred, and several aspects of management are generic to both sectors. However, on balance, public administration remains a separate enterprise. The reasons for this are outlined in the following pages.

Constitutions

In the United States, the federal and state constitutions define the environment of public administration and place constraints on it. First, constitutions fragment power and control over public administration (see Box 1–1). The separation of powers places public administration under three "masters." We have become accustomed to thinking of governors and presidents as being in control of public administration, but in practice legislatures possess as much or more constitutional power over administrative operations. This is clearly true at the federal level, where Congress has the constitutional authority to create agencies and departments by law; fix their size in terms of personnel and budget; determine their missions and legal authority, internal structures, and locations; and establish personnel procedures. Congress has also enacted a large body of **administrative law** to regulate administrative procedures. The courts often exercise considerable power and control over public administration. They help define the legal rights and obligations of agencies and those of the individuals and groups upon whom public administrators act. They also define the constitutional rights of public employees and the nature of their liabilities for breaches of law or the Constitution. In recent years, the judiciary has also been active in the restructuring of school systems, public mental health facilities, public housing, and prisons in an effort to make certain they comply with constitutional standards. Judicial review of agency activities is so extensive that one federal judge has written that the courts and public administrators are now "partners."[3] The extent of legislative and judicial authority over public administration leaves chief executives with only limited control over the executive branch, and far less authority than is commonly found in the hands of chief executive officers of private organizations, whether profit-seeking or not. In fact, the federal Constitution grants the president only two specifically mentioned pow-

BOX 1–1 *Morrison v. Olson* (1988)*: Whose Executive Branch Is It, Anyway?

The Ethics in Government Act of 1978, which expired in 1992, provided for the appointment of an independent counsel to investigate and prosecute certain high-ranking government officials for federal crimes. The independent counsel was located in the Department of Justice and had "full power and independent authority to exercise all investigative and prosecutorial functions and powers of the Department, . . . the Attorney General, and other department [personnel]." The independent counsel was appointed by a special court, called the Special Division, and could not be removed by the attorney general except for "good cause, physical disability, mental incapacity, or any other condition that substantially impairs the performance of such independent counsel's duties." The key question before the U.S. Supreme Court in *Morrison v. Olson* was whether these arrangements violated the constitutional separation of powers. The Court, per Chief Justice William Rehnquist, held that they did not. First, the appointment of an executive officer by a court under these circumstances was not "incongruous" because it did not have "the potential to impair the constitutional functions assigned to one of the branches" of the government. Second, the Court noted that in its "present considered view . . . the determination of whether the Constitution allows Congress to impose a 'good cause'-type restriction on the President's power to remove an official cannot be made to turn on whether or not that official is 'purely executive.'" Rather, ". . . the real question is whether the removal restrictions are of such a nature that they impede the President's ability to perform his constitutional duty . . ." to take care that the laws be faithfully executed. The Court concluded that although "[i]t is undeniable that the Act reduces the amount of control or supervision that the Attorney General and, through him, the President exercises over the investigation and prosecution of a certain class of criminal activity," the executive branch retained "sufficient control over the independent counsel to ensure that the President is able to perform his constitutionally assigned duties."

Justice Antonin Scalia heatedly dissented:

> There are now no lines. If the removal of a prosecutor, the virtual embodiment of the power to "take care that the laws be faithfully executed," can be restricted, what officer's removal cannot? This is an open invitation for Congress to experiment. What about a special Assistant Secretary of State, with responsibility for one very narrow area of foreign policy, who would not only have to be confirmed by the Senate, but could also be removed only pursuant to certain carefully designed restrictions? . . . Or a special Assistant Secretary of Defense for Procurement? The possibilities are endless. . . . As far as I can discern from the Court's opinion it is now open season upon the President's removal power for all executive officers. . . . The Court essentially says to the President: "Trust us. We will make sure that you are able to accomplish your constitutional role." I think the Constitution gives the president— and the people—more protection than that.

So an executive official with law enforcement duties can be appointed by a court and dismissed only for limited reasons specified by Congress. Whose executive branch is it, anyway?

*487 U.S. 654.

ers that can be exercised on his own—*specific* powers over public administrators to ask department heads for their opinions in writing on various subjects and to make temporary appointments to vacant offices when Congress is in recess. In practice, of course, chief executives in the public sector now often exercise statutory powers given to them by legislatures—but it is unusual for legislative bodies to be altogether uninterested in matters of public administration.

The separation of powers not only provides each branch with somewhat different authority over public administration but may also frustrate coordination among them. Basic political science tells us that chief executives, legislatures, and courts are responsive to different constituencies, political pressures, and time constraints. All three branches have legitimate interests in public administration. However, they often differ with regard to what they think agencies should do and how they ought to do it.

The federal constitutional framework also creates a system of federalism that places serious constraints on public administration at the state and local levels. Often the federal government will create a program and rely on the states to implement it. Funding and authority may be shared. In practice, state agencies may be responsible to federal departments to a greater extent than they are to state governors or state legislatures. The same may be true of local governments.

The federal courts also have a substantial impact on state and local administration. They define the constitutional or legal rights of citizens as they are affected by governmental activity. Over the years the federal courts have ordered extensive reforms in state and local prisons, mental health facilities, schools and personnel systems.[4]

The separation of powers and federalism creates a very complex environment for contemporary public administration in the United States. This complexity of fragmented authority is generally not matched in the private sector. Legal restrictions and requirements affect private management, but they do not fragment authority over it in the same way or to the same extent, nor do they provide so many parties with a legal right to participate in private firms' policy decisions and other affairs.

Constitutional concerns are important in another way as well. They establish values in the public sector that frequently run counter to the values embodied in private management. Efficiency in government is often subordinated to political principles such as representativeness, or to legalistic considerations like due process. Remember that, with the exception of the Thirteenth Amendment, which prohibits slavery and involuntary servitude, the Constitution does not regulate relationships between private parties. Rather, it applies to relationships among units of government, such as Congress and the president or the federal and state governments, and to those between the public and its governments. Further, in most of the public sector, there is no genuine equivalent to the profit motive, which is so central to private enterprise. This brings us to a second aspect of the "publicness" of public administration.

The Public Interest

The governmental obligation to promote the public interest distinguishes public administration from private management. In a moral and basic sense, it must serve "a higher purpose."[5] Even though it is often difficult to say precisely what is in the public interest, there can be no dispute about the obligation of public administrators to consider it as a general guide for their actions. When they fail to do so, public administrators may rightly be criticized for placing personal or agency interests above those of the people as a whole. A central issue presented by public administration is assuring that public administrators represent and respond to the interests of the citizenry.[6] Otherwise, democracy may not prevail. Various regulations have been enacted over the years in an effort to assure that those exercising public power will not use it for narrow partisan or purely private gain or engage in subversion. Many public personnel systems in the United States and abroad place restrictions on the political activities of civil servants, some have very comprehensive conflict-of-interest regulations, and all are concerned with the political loyalty of their employees.

By contrast, private firms are thought to best serve the general interest by vigorously pursuing their own economic interests. Their task is to be highly efficient and competitive in the marketplace. Profit not only is the bottom line, but also is viewed as a positive social and economic good. Of course, private companies should not damage the health and safety of their workers or that of the general community. Nor should they damage or destroy the environment. By and large, however, it is assumed to be government's role to assure, through proper regulation, that the private sector does not harm society at large.

One way of summarizing this different perspective on the public interest is to think in terms of **externalities**—or aspects of the productive or service operations of organizations that do not enter into the agreement between buyer and seller. Pollution is a classic example of an externality. It is not accounted for in the sale of the product itself; that is, it is external to the market. Historically, in the United States private firms have not always felt a moral or other nonlegal obligation to avoid creating harmful externalities. Pollution, damage to the environment, and social damage caused by such practices as sweatshops, child labor, or abusive conditions in migrant labor were all viewed as costs to be passed off on society as a whole. Eventually, governments took steps to regulate such practices. More recently, there has been pressure on governments to regulate plant closings because of their devastating impact on communities. The main point, however, is that in contemporary public administration, there are few harmful practices that, once recognized, government is not called upon to deal with in some fashion. When one government agency creates a problematic condition, the public interest will almost inevitably demand that it or another governmental unit be empowered to combat it. Public administrators are called upon to take a wider view of their responsibilities, recognizing that harmful practices or by-products should not simply be "someone else's problem." This is partly why it is plausible to hold that "public administration is not a kind of technology but a form of moral endeavor."[7]

The Market

A closely related distinction between public and private administration concerns the market. It is generally true that public agencies do not face free, competitive markets in which their services or products are sold.[8] For the most part, the price tags attached to governmental operations are established through budgetary routines rather than fixed at the market through free transactions between buyer and seller. Revenues are largely generated through taxation, although in some cases user fees are a substantial source of operating budgets and bonds are sold to pay for capital projects. Even where user fees are important, however, the governmental agency may be operating as a legal monopoly or be under a mandate to provide service to everyone at a fixed cost, no matter how difficult or expensive it may be to reach them. The U.S. Postal Service's mission regarding delivery of first-class mail is an example: the cost of sending a letter from Miami to North Miami is the same as sending one to Honolulu or Nome.

The market is less constraining in the public than in the private sector. In fact, the market becomes most salient for public agencies when governments, primarily cities, are under severe fiscal constraints. In the long run, excessive taxation of the public in support of undesired or inefficient governmental operations can erode tax bases to the extent that certain market pressures begin to develop. Individuals (the consumers or customers of public administrative operations) may opt out of the system by moving to another jurisdiction. They may also seek to privatize some services, such as trash collection. The federal, state, and local governments also face market forces when they borrow money. And the worse their financial shape, the more expensive borrowing is likely to be. But the governments in question are likely to remain in some form.

In recent years, the "public choice" movement has held that government agencies will be more responsive and efficient if they can be compelled to react to marketlike forces. For instance, public schools might be made to compete with one another by allowing parents the opportunity to choose which schools to send their children within a general geographic area.

Except when government operations are "marketized," private firms typically face markets in a far more direct fashion. Under free-market conditions, if they fail to produce products or services at competitive prices, consumers turn to alternate sources and the company's income declines. Eventually the noncompetitive private firm will go out of business. In between the typical public agency and private firm is a gray area in which not-for-profit organizations and highly regulated industries, such as utilities, operate.

The remoteness of market forces from most public administrative operations has profound consequences. First, it enables government to provide services and products that could not profitably be offered by private firms, which is another way of saying would not be provided by private enterprise at all. Some of these services and products are referred to as **public goods** or quasi-public goods. Broadly speaking, these are goods, like nuclear defense, that individuals cannot be excluded from using, that are not exhausted or significantly diminished as more individuals use them, and for which individuals do not compete. Because it would be impossible to provide such goods to one person only, individuals lack the incentive to purchase the goods, no matter how desirable they are. Why would anyone seek to protect his or her home from nuclear attack, for instance, when it would be necessary to shield the entire neighborhood (or even state)? Such defense might be in everyone's self-interest, but it would also be in everyone's self-interest to obtain it free by letting someone else in the neighborhood provide the protection. Under these conditions, especially if the costs are significant, everyone may be apt to be a "free rider" on a neighbor's defense system. The net result would most likely be that no one would invest in nuclear defense.

Much public sector activity is addressed to the production and maintenance of public goods and quasi-public goods. Roads and public education are examples. Society as a whole benefits from a good network of modern highways and from a better educated population. Therefore, society as a whole should bear some of the costs of these goods. Moreover, it would not be feasible to make only direct users pay for the building and maintenance of all roads, because the fees would be too high. If only those who had children in public schools bore the cost, funding levels would surely drop and the quality of education would fall, perhaps drastically.

Historically, some public goods, like education and public welfare (called "charity" in an earlier time), were provided primarily by nongovernmental organizations, often of a religious nature. Eventually, however, they were "secularized," with government taking the leading role in their provision on the theory that it was in the general public interest to do so, and that universal public education or welfare could not be provided successfully solely by private groups. When universal access to a good, such as health care or day care, becomes viewed as an essential ingredient of the kind of society the political system wants to foster, it is likely to be considered a public good.

The remoteness of market forces in the public sector also makes it difficult to assess or evaluate the worth and efficiency of public administrative operations. If government agencies produce a product that is not sold freely in open markets, then it is hard to determine what the product is worth. Proxy measures such as opinion surveys that try to determine what the public is willing to pay for a good or a service can help. But they can be too expensive to develop and are approximations at best. In any case, it is very difficult to determine the value of any given public administrator's contribution to the worth of a government good or service. This means that measuring performance and efficiency can be extremely difficult in the public sector. One way that governments try to get around this problem is to contract out some of their functions to private organizations. Theoretically, at least, private companies will compete against one another to obtain the public sector's business.[9] But the range of activity that the public and their governments deem appropriate for contracting out is limited. Nor are the long-term economic and political implications of contracting out some traditional governmental functions, such as prison management, clear. Accordingly, for the most part, when taken together, its relationship to markets makes public administration substantially different from private enterprise.

Sovereignty

Sovereignty is the concept that somewhere in a political community there is an ultimate repository of supreme political power and authority. In the United States, sovereignty resides in the people, as a whole, who exercise it through a representative government. Public administration and public employment, in particular, are consequently considered to be a "public trust." As representatives of the sovereign people, public administrators are also placed in a position that differs considerably from that of managers and employees in the private sector. *Public administrators are engaged in the formulation and implementation of policies that allocate resources, values, and status in a fashion that is binding on the society as a whole.* They are agents of the sovereign, which means that the actions of public administrators have the force of law and the coercive power of the government behind them. Private firms also make policies and are engaged in activities that affect the lives of individuals in the society as a whole, but their actions are not binding in the same sense and they cannot be enforced through legitimate coercive physical power. Rather, the private sector must turn to the public sector's courts and police power for the enforcement of contracts.

Public administrators, being agents of the sovereign, are inevitably engaged in matters of public policy making and implementation. From the 1880s to the late 1940s, public administrative theory in the United States held that administration and politics should be almost separate from one another. Perhaps this dichotomy between politics and administration was primarily concerned with eliminating partisan or electoral politics from the public service. But today it is broadly accepted that public administrators do have a legitimate role in all phases of the public policy cycle.* In other words, theory and practice now support the idea that the political system should take advantage of public administrators' expertise when it is appropriate to the identification of problems to which public policy ought to be addressed (agenda setting) and to the formulation, analysis, evaluation, and revision of policies. It is now also recognized that public administrators are often re-

---

*The notion of the public policy cycle is a conceptual tool that views public policy as moving through the following stages: agenda setting (identification of an issue), policy formulation, implementation, analysis/evaluation of impact or implementation process, and revision of some sort, including termination and succession.

quired to make policy choices while implementing statutes and executive orders. They exercise discretion because their mandates from legislatures are general (rather than specific) and/or because of a scarcity of resources that virtually requires the selective enforcement of the law. Of course, to say that public administrators *participate* in policy making is not to say that *all* policy is made by them or that all they do is make policy.

Public administrators' involvement in the public policy cycle makes politics far more salient in the public sector than in private enterprise. Public administrators are perforce required to build and maintain political support for the policies and programs they implement. They must try to convince members of the legislature, chief executives, political appointees, interest groups, private individuals, and the public at large that their activities and policies are desirable and responsive. This involves far more than the kind of advertising done in the private sector. It may involve the trading of political support or the modification of public policies and activities to win over the support of some particularly important group or individual.

Involvement in policy making and politics raises the question of how it can be assured that those exercising a public trust will in fact be representative, in some sense, of the people as a whole. For instance, federal policy has sought to make federal administration representative by assuring that its work force is drawn from all social segments of the society. It also provides formal processes through which interested parties can express their views on the adoption of administrative policies and rules.[10] In the past, the representative principle was applied to the public service through the widespread use of partisan patronage, which allowed the political party in power to select the vast majority of public employees. Once again, it is evident that concerns of this nature are less relevant in the private sector. Private enterprise is built around the principle of the profit motive, not that of providing representation to different groups and political parties. It would be ludicrous to think that a private company would institute a spoils system along the lines of that used in the federal government in the 1840s and 1850s, where just about every four years almost the entire work force would be fired and replaced by supporters of another political party or faction. Yet, when practiced in the public sector, spoils systems have some beneficial effects, such as enabling the growth of strong, competitive, and representative political parties.

Sovereignty also dictates that much of public administrative business involves formulation and implementation of public policies that are very broad, ambitious, and sometimes rather amorphous and oriented toward change in the long run. Analyzing the effectiveness and costs of these policies is generally possible, but it is often much more difficult to evaluate the operations of public agencies than to assess those of private firms. Politics may require that the objectives of public programs be rather ill defined and vague. Often Congress will empower a federal agency to formulate policies affecting some area of public life with little more direction than to require that the agency promote the public interest. It is frequently easier to build a consensus around very general principles than around specifics, as is apparent in the typical political party platform. For instance, there has been very little disagreement over the objective of establishing equal employment opportunity, but the technique of affirmative action—that is, the use of goals for hiring and promoting members of minority groups and women—has been extremely controversial for over two decades. Moreover, evaluating the full impact of public policies dealing with such matters as equality, nutrition, the environment, eliminating the federal budget deficit, and promoting world peace may require years of observation.

In sum, any definition of public administration must lay heavy stress on the *public*. There are similarities between public and private administration, but these are often relatively unimportant in conveying the essence of each. Public administration is concerned with administration of the public interest, it is constrained by constitutions and relatively unconstrained by market forces, and it is considered a public trust exercised on behalf of the sovereign. Private administration, on the other hand, generally has a narrower concept of the public interest; profit-making firms are heavily constrained by market forces, not by constitutions. Moreover, private administration is not connected to the issue of sovereignty and is rarely considered to be a public trust of any kind. The lines between public and private administration may become blurred when government contracts out essentially public functions to not-for-profit organizations or other third parties. The same is sometimes true when public agencies are run like corporations. But the private sector is not dominated or characterized by not-for-profit organizations, nor is the public sector largely organized in corporate form. Substantial differences between the public and private sectors remain and, importantly, they promote reliance on different values and processes.

REGULATION AND SERVICE

In the discussion of sovereignty, it was mentioned that the activities of public administrators have a binding quality and that, in general, they have the force of law and can rely on the coercive physical power of the government for enforcement. This raises another point that is crucial to a satisfactory definition of public administration. Although we often think of public administration in terms of providing services to the public, it is also true that public administrators are engaged in *regulation* of the public. In fact, political conservatives opposed to governmental administration have long charged that the public service or the civil service is not a "service" at all, but rather an authoritarian regulatory force used to place constraints on the public. In truth, one person's service often turns out to be another's constraint, and it is common to find regulation and service intertwined in governmental programs. For instance, welfare programs undeniably provide a service, but at the same time they place constraints on the behavior of the recipients. Benefits can be denied to recipients who do not allow social workers to inspect their homes and to a mother who does not identify her child's father.

One could go down the list of government functions and find that service after service turns out also to be a constraint. Public transportation services often preclude direct competition from private companies. Occupational licenses serve the public by assuring that doctors, hairdressers, and plumbers are competent, but they also regulate entry into those occupations. Driver's licensing and vehicle inspections promote highway safety, but they also regulate the use of the roads. Food and drug regulations certainly constrain producers and serve consumers. It is sometimes true that agencies with the word "service" in their title are the most directly engaged in regulation. The Internal Revenue *Service* and the Selective *Service* System (former military drafting agency) are examples. Similarly, public *service* commissions are involved in the regulations of utilities.

In many cases, however, governmental regulation is billed as such. Thus, there is a Nuclear Regulatory Commission and a variety of other commissions to deal not only with utilities but also with consumer safety, securities and stocks, transportation, radio and television, and many other aspects of contemporary life. Regulatory activities also provide a service when they promote the public interest. The student of public administration should be continually cognizant of the fact that by exercising public power on behalf of the sovereign people, public *servants* are also frequently engaged in the business of placing constraints on the behavior of individuals or corporations. The acceptability and constitutionality of these constraints are often a matter to be decided by the courts, bringing legal processes directly to bear on public administration.

MANAGERIAL, POLITICAL, AND LEGAL APPROACHES

It is evident that public administration involves a number of complex concerns and functions. Not surprisingly, therefore, as an intellectual discipline or body or theory, public administration lacks coherence. It is the overall view of this book that public administration contains three relatively distinct approaches that grow out of different perspectives on its functions. Some have viewed it as a managerial endeavor, similar to practices in the private sector. Others, stressing the "publicness" of public administration, have emphasized its political aspects. Still others, noting the importance of sovereignty, constitutions, and regulation in public administration, have viewed it as a distinctly legal matter. Each of these approaches tends to stress different values and procedural and structural arrangements for the operation of public administration, each views the individual citizen in a remarkably different way, and each adopts a different perspective on how to develop knowledge. A further complexity is that the managerial approach has two subsets: traditional (or orthodox) public management and a contemporary reform-oriented new public management (NPM). It is very important to bear in mind that these approaches are embedded in our political culture. They reflect the constitutional separation of powers and assignment of functions to different branches.

The managerial approach is associated with the executive branch's interest in faithful execution or implementation of the law. The political approach is associated with legislative policy-making concerns. The legal approach focuses on government's adjudicatory function, commitment to maintaining constitutional rights (the "blessings of liberty"), and the rule of law.

Once we have presented the gist of these three broad approaches to public administration, we will have completed our definitional discussion. Then we can turn to an explanation of how each of them is present in the various central activities of contemporary public administration.

The Managerial Approach to Public Administration

Those who define public administration in managerial terms and take a businesslike approach to it tend to minimize the distinctions between public and private administration. In their view, public administration is essentially the same as big business and ought to be run according to the same managerial principles and values. This outlook is strongly entrenched in some segments of American society and is frequently found among elective political leaders who tend to resent the political influence exercised by civil servants. It is unusual for a presidential election campaign not to stress the candidates' purported abilities to "manage" the "huge" federal bureaucracy and to make it more efficient. Gubernatorial and mayoral candidates often tout their managerial skills as well.

Today, those who look at public administration as management fall into two main groups. Traditionalists are being challenged by reformers who call for "reinventing government" and developing an NPM. At this point it is not clear whether the NPM will supplant the traditional approach, and, if so, whether it will be successful. Today's public administration students should be familiar with both. Each is currently of great importance in some organizations.

Traditional Managerial Approach to Public Administration

The roots of the traditional managerial approach go back to the nineteenth-century civil service reformers who first promoted the approach as a means of organizing the public service. The reformers' chief complaints were that political patronage appointments to the public services at all levels of government led to corruption, inefficiency, and the emergence of a class of politicians— "spoilsmen," as they were frequently called—who were fundamentally unfit to lead the nation. In fact, one well-known historian of the 1850s insisted that the federal service had become staffed by the nation's "refuse" (garbage).[11] In the reformers' view, "What civil service reform demand[ed], [was] that the business part of the government shall be carried on in a sound businesslike manner."[12] In order for it to become businesslike, it had to become nonpolitical. Consequently, appointments were to be made on the basis of "merit" and "fitness" rather than political partisanship. Many reformers thought that public employees should be prohibited from taking an active part in electoral politics, other than voting. Once politics was rejected as the basis for hiring and firing public administrators, the reformers believed that the selection and tenure of public servants could be based on their efficiency and performance.

In order to sustain this logic, the reformers had to insist that the vast majority of public administrators had no legitimate political or policy-making functions. Much of their thinking and the logic of the traditional managerial approach depended on the existence of a dichotomy between politics and administration. Woodrow Wilson (1856–1924) was a strong supporter of civil service reform in the 1880s and is often considered the founder of self-conscious American public administrative thought. In his famous 1887 essay, "The Study of Administration," Wilson wrote, "Administration lies outside the proper sphere of *politics*. Administrative questions are not political questions."[13] Rather, they are managerial questions because, as Wilson expressed it, public administration is "a field of business."

Just as politics involves certain values, such as representativeness, so does business or management. Wilson was also influential in his straightforward articulation of these: "It is the object of administrative study to discover, first, what government can properly and successfully do, and, secondly, how it can do these proper things with the utmost possible efficiency and at the least possible cost either of money or of energy."[14] In other words, according to the traditional managerial approach, public administration is to be geared toward maximizing effectiveness, efficiency, and economy.

The advocacy of businesslike public administration eventually became the orthodox or classical view of how the public service should be run. Managers, not politicians, were to be in control, and efficiency was to be considered the ultimate "good," the "axiom number one in the value scale of administration."[15] Politics was to be eliminated because it produced inefficiency. Moreover, despite the growing regulatory activities of the public service, law was deemphasized because, as Leonard White's influential *Introduction to the Study of Public Administration* (1926) contended, "the study of administration should start from the base of management rather than the foundation of law, and is therefore more absorbed in the affairs of the American Management Association than in the decisions of the courts."[16] In fact, from the 1910s to the 1940s, a worldwide "scientific management" movement, based on the work of Frederick Taylor (1856–1915),[17] developed and advocated the premise that effective, efficient management could be reduced to a set of scientific principles. In the view of critics of this approach, the net result in terms of administrative values was that "the 'goodness' or 'badness' of a particular organizational pattern was a mathematical relationship of 'inputs' to 'outputs.' Where the latter was maximized and the former minimized, a moral 'good' resulted. Virtue or 'goodness' was therefore equated with the relationship of these two factors, that is, 'efficiency' or 'inefficiency.' Mathematics was transformed into ethics."[18] Wastefulness, through inefficiency, was considered immoral.

Organizational Structure   In an effort to maximize the attainment of these values, the traditional managerial approach promotes an organizational structure that is universally identified as *bureaucratic*. This may strike the contemporary reader as odd, since today *bureaucratic* is often used as a synonym for *inefficient*. In Chapter 4, we will consider the complex reasons why bureaucratic organizations often develop inefficiencies. Nevertheless, it remains true that many of their organizational principles are *intended* to maximize the amount of output per unit of input. Bureaucracies stress the need for a division of labor that enables employees to specialize in the accomplishment of a given set of tasks. Specialization enables each worker to become expert at what he or she does, although the work of any individual may be only a small part of the organization's total activity. *Specialization* requires coordination, and bureaucracy relies on *hierarchy* for this purpose. Hierarchy creates a chain of authority to manage and coordinate the work divided according to the principle of specialization. Hierarchy, in turn, requires that programs and functions be clearly assigned to specific organizational units. Otherwise there will be overlapping authorities that are likely to promote conflicts. Bureaucratic organizations are also organized along *formalistic* lines, which spell out the functions and responsibilities of each employee. Positions are classified according to "scientific" principles and are organized into a rational scheme. The selection of employees is based on their ability to perform the tasks at hand, that is, on their merit. Other factors, such as political affiliation, race, or sex, should not be taken into account.

View of the Individual   The traditional managerial approach to public administration promotes an impersonal view of individuals. This is true whether the individuals in question are the employees, clients, or "victims" of public administrative agencies.[19] One need not go so far as Max Weber (1864–1920), perhaps the foremost analyst of bureaucracy, in considering "dehumanization" to be the "special virtue" of bureaucracy or to view the bureaucrat as a "cog" in an organizational machine over which he or she has virtually no control.[20] Weber saw this as an advantage of bureaucracy because it meant that "irrational" emotions would not interfere with the bureaucrat's job performance. This perspective was promoted by the Scientific Management Movement and the traditional managerial approach, which tend to turn the individual worker into an appendage to a mechanized means of production. The worker has to adapt to the machine; the machine is not engineered to suit an *individual* worker's physical, mental, social, and emotional idiosyncrasies (see Box 1–2). By 1920, this view of the employee was clearly embodied in the principles of position classification (that is, the description of duties and rank) in the public sector: "The individual characteristics of an employee occupying a position should have no bearing on the classification of the position." The strong "position orientation" of the traditional managerial approach to public administration, which views organization in formalistic structural rather than human terms, diminishes the importance of the individual employee to the organization.

Clients, too, have been depersonalized and turned into cases in an effort to promote the traditional managerial values of efficiency, economy, and effectiveness. Ralph Hummel explains:

BOX 1–2 Scientific Management from Shoveling to Baseball

Shoveling: "There is a scientific fact. A first-class shoveler ought to take twenty-one and one-half pounds on his shovel in order to work to the best possible advantage. You are not giving that man a chance unless you give him a shovel which will hold twenty-one pounds. . . .

"There is only one way to do it right. Put your forearm down onto the upper part of your leg, and when you push into the pile, throw your weight against it. That relieves your arm of work. You then have an automatic push, we will say, about eighty pounds, the weight of your body thrown on to it."

Baseball: ". . . I think this instance represents one of the best illustrations of the application of the principles of scientific management. I refer to the management of a first-class American baseball team. In such a team you will find almost all of the elements of scientific management.

"You will see that the science of doing every little act that is done by every player on the baseball field has been developed. Every single element of the game of baseball has been the subject of the most intimate, closest study of many men, and, finally, the best way of doing each act that takes place on the baseball field has been fairly well agreed upon and established as a standard throughout the country. The players have not only been told the best way of making each important motion or play, but they have been taught, coached, and trained to it through months of drilling. And I think that every man who has watched first-class play, or who knows anything of the management of the modern baseball team, realizes fully the utter impossibility of winning with the best team of individual players that was ever gotten together unless every man on the team obeys the signals or orders of the coach and obeys them at once. . . ."

SOURCES: Frederick Winslow Taylor, "The Principles of Scientific Management," in Jay Shafritz and Philip Whitbeck, eds., *Classics of Organization Theory* (Oak Park, Ill.: Moore, 1978), 18–19; and "Scientific Management," in Jay Shafritz and Albert Hyde, eds., *Classics of Public Administration* (Oak Park, Ill.: Moore, 1978), 20.

Bureaucracy is an efficient means for handling large numbers of people. "Efficient" in its own terms. It would be impossible to handle large numbers of people in their full depth and complexity. Bureaucracy is a tool for ferreting out what is "relevant" to the task for which bureaucracy was established. As a result, only those facts in the complex lives of individuals that are relevant to that task need to be communicated between the individual and the bureaucracy.

To achieve this simplification, the modern bureaucrat has invented the "case." At the intake level of the bureaucracy, individual personalities are converted into cases. Only if a person can qualify as a case, is he or she allowed treatment by the bureaucracy. More accurately, a bureaucracy is never set up to treat or deal with persons: it "processes" only "cases."[21]

"Victims" of public administrators' activities may be depersonalized to such an extent that they are treated as subhuman, especially where physical force or coercion is employed, as, historically, in public mental health facilities, prisons, and police functions.

Other approaches to organization argue that reliance on impersonality tends to be counterproductive because it generates dysfunctions. These matters will be discussed in Chapters 4 and 10. Nevertheless, the impersonal view of individuals is deeply ingrained in the traditional managerial approach and is considered essential to the maximization of efficiency, economy, and effectiveness.

Cognitive Approach The traditional managerial approach emphasizes a scientific method in developing knowledge. The kernel of the idea that public administration could be a science was contained in Woodrow Wilson's 1887 essay.[22] By 1926, Leonard White noted that public administration was being transformed from an art into a science and, in 1937, Luther Gulick and L. Urwick could publish, most influentially, *Papers on the Science of Administration*.[23] The commitment to developing a science of public administration remains very strong—in fact, dominant—in contemporary American public administrative research and scholarship.

In practice, treating public administration as a science has promoted an effort to develop generalizations about administrative behavior. This involves the formulation of hypotheses that can be tested empirically. Data are gathered, aggregated, and statistically analyzed. The basic orientation is deductive; knowledge consists of statistically verifiable generalizations that can be applied, with caution, to specific cases.

Budgeting The traditional managerial approach's commitment to the values of efficiency, economy, effectiveness, and science leads it to favor rational budgeting systems (see Chapter 6). Such systems emphasize the need to build cost-effectiveness considerations into the formulation of budgets. Ideally, under this approach, how to allocate funds among the multitude of governmental functions and at what levels could be determined by the projected "bang for the buck," or benefit for the cost.

Decision Making The traditional managerial approach also favors rational decision making, as explored in Chapter 7. Essentially, it holds that in making decisions public administrators should consider all plausible alternatives comprehensively and choose the one that is most cost-effective. Relying on scientific expertise, including that of social scientists, this approach does not favor broad public participation.

The New Public Management (NPM)

In the early 1990s, a new managerial approach to public administration began to take hold in the United States. Like the traditional managerial approach at its inception, the new approach is reform-oriented and seeks to improve public sector performance. It starts from the premise that traditional, bureaucratically organized public administration is "broke" and "broken," and consequently the public has lost faith in government.[24] After years of antigovernment political rhetoric, "bureaucrat bashing," and negative press coverage, public administration was broadly viewed as incredibly inept and wasteful. Public opinion polls revealed that in 1993 only 20 percent of the public trusted the federal government to do the right thing most of the time—a steep drop from 76 percent in 1963.[25] Americans thought the federal government wasted 48 cents of every tax dollar collected! The image of state and local governments also fared badly. Taxpayer revolts broke out from California to Massachusetts. By 1991, nineteen states had enacted limits on taxes and expenditures—up from two in 1978 when California's tax-limiting Proposition 13 first captured a great deal of public attention. A majority of the states had also placed tax limits of one kind or another on their local governments.[26] Governments throughout the United States were viewed as needing drastic reforms, even "reinvention," as David Osborne and Ted Gaebler put it in the title of their best selling 1992 book, *Reinventing Government*.[27]

Fortunately for the new managerial reformers, some models for improvement were already available. In the English-speaking world abroad, New Zealand, Australia, and the United Kingdom had been undertaking drastic administrative reforms.[28] As Osborne and Gaebler reported, several cities and states in the United States had successfully done the same. Taken as a whole, these reforms embrace the following premises:

1. Public administration should focus on achieving results rather than primarily on conforming with processes.
2. To achieve results, public administration should make better use of marketlike competition in the provision of goods and services. This may be accomplished in several ways. Privatization can enable government to buy services that it once produced itself from private firms that can provide them at lower prices. Agencies can be reorganized to more closely resemble private corporations that obtain revenues through the sale of goods and services (the U.S. Postal Service, for instance). Agencies can be made to compete with each other and/or nongovernmental organizations. For example, a central personnel agency can be transformed into a service center that competes with private consulting firms in selling training and other services to administrative agencies and bureaus.
3. A corollary of making public administration more marketlike is to make it customer-driven. The public and agency clients are viewed as customers to whom the government should be responsive. Where an agency sells a product or service in competition with private firms, the logic of responding to customers is obvious. But even when government provides service and regulation on a monopoly basis or without charging fees, treating the public and clients like customers can enhance public administration's service ethic and efficiency. Customer service initiatives have produced such changes as emulating best practices in the private sector; providing satellite offices in shopping centers

for renewing drivers' licenses and vehicle registrations; mobile services like library bookmobiles; "one-stop shopping" for social services such as welfare, food stamps, and public housing; quicker responses to telephone inquiries; and case management changes that reduce the number of government employees an individual has to deal with to obtain what he or she is seeking. Overall, agencies should use their resources to create valued services for customers.

4. Also related to the market idea and privatization is that government should "steer, not row," in Osborne and Gaebler's phrase. Government's job is to assure that public goods and services are provided, not necessarily to produce them itself. In other words, governments may appropriately rely on third parties, such as other governments, not-for-profit organizations, and corporations to implement their policies and enforce some of their regulations.

5. Government should be deregulated. Traditional bureaucracy's emphasis on centralized control of staffing, personnel administration, budgeting, auditing, procurement, and allocation of agency resources is inappropriate to results-oriented public administration. Agency managers will be driven by competition, customers, and accountability for results to make the best use of their employees and budgets.

6. An extension of deregulation is that employees should be empowered to use their creativity in serving customers and doing their jobs. Empowerment is not only possible, it is highly desirable because today's public sector workers are well educated and because computerization makes a great deal more information available to them—information of the kind that was previously held mostly by managers who used it to determine what employees should do. Empowerment, as opposed to hierarchy, promotes teamwork.

7. Overall, public administrative culture should change to be flexible, innovative, problem solving, entrepreneurial, and enterprising as opposed to rule-bound, process-oriented, and focused on inputs rather than results.

At the national level, the NPM approach is employed in Vice President Al Gore's National Performance Review (NPR). Its 1993 Report, *From Red Tape to Results: Creating a Government That Works Better & Costs Less*, explicitly seeks "a new customer service contract with the American people, a new guarantee of effective, efficient, and responsive government."[29] It calls for the following steps, among others: putting customers first, making service organizations compete, creating market dynamics, using market mechanisms to solve problems, empowering employees to get results, decentralizing decision making power, streamlining the budget process, decentralizing personnel policy, and streamlining procurement.

The NPR report explicitly relies on the traditional managerial approach's insistence that there can be a dichotomy between politics and administration. In the Preface, Gore admonishes:

> This performance review is not about politics. Programs passed by both Democratic presidents and Republican presidents, voted on by members of Congress of both parties, and supported by the American people at the time, are being undermined by an inefficient and outdated bureaucracy, and by our huge debt. For too long the basic functioning of the government has gone unexamined. We want to make improving the way government does business a permanent part of how government works, regardless of which party is in power.[30]

The view that public administration is largely apolitical and businesslike is essential to the NPM more generally. To work in democracies and to maintain accountability, deregulated, empowered, results-oriented public administrators must stick to achieving the policy goals established by elected and politically appointed officials. Market mechanisms as construed by the NPR and the NPM are not substitutes for public participation in politics. Employees and agencies are not empowered to make public policy.

Several states and local governments have consciously adopted NPM measures. In the mid-1980s, Minnesota developed a Striving Toward Excellence in Performance (STEP) program for administrative reform. According to Michael Barzeley's book, *Breaking Through Bureaucracy*, STEP "focused on improving the quality and cost-effectiveness of government rather than on producing cuts in expenditures";[31] it had broad participation, drawing on unions, business, and government; and it placed the initiative for change with state employees themselves. STEP was innovative in forging ahead with much that is now familiar: customer orientation, market dynamics, personnel and procurement systems reforms, and information management improvement.

Oregon began a highly innovative benchmark program in 1989. Under the direction of the Oregon Progress Board, "Oregon Benchmarks" established clear, quantified goals for improving health, family life, education, civic participation, equal opportunity, social harmony, the environment, housing, transportation, public safety, per capita income, industrial diversification, economic growth, and public sector performance.[32] The benchmark approach is explained in Box 1–3. It promotes results-oriented public administration and, as used in Oregon, encourages experimentation by local governments. It also permits much greater flexibility in implementing federally funded programs. The Progress Board explains:

> . . . the federal government has become a partner in using benchmarks. Oregon has signed a first-in-the-nation agreement to design and test a new approach to delivering federally funded public services through state and local governments [called the Oregon Option] . . .
>
> The typical federal approach to domestic programs carried out by state and local governments is to structure and manage service delivery from the top down. Officials in Washington define problems and solutions, prescribe service activities, impose complex but often conflicting and wasteful regulations, and measure program success on the basis of client contacts and other activities rather than true results. Under the Oregon Option, federal, state, and local partners work together to

BOX 1–3 **What Are Benchmarks?**

Benchmarks, the individual measures that collectively make up Oregon Benchmarks, are indicators of the progress that Oregon has set out to achieve in its strategic vision. Oregon wants to be a state of well-educated, competent people living in thriving communities, working in a well-paying, competitive economy, and enjoying a pristine environment. Just as blood pressure, cholesterol levels, and other such indicators serve as signs of a patient's health, benchmarks serve as signs of Oregon's social, economic, and environmental well-being. Benchmarks measure progress toward Oregon's vision of well-being in such terms as family stability, early childhood development, K–12 student achievement, air and water quality, housing affordably, crime, employment, and per capita income. Benchmarks keep Oregon's leaders, state and local government agencies, service institutions, and citizens focused on achieving those results. By staying focused on outcomes, and by keeping track of results, leaders in Oregon life can reset priorities and adapt and modify programs as they learn what works.

	Historical		Target		
Typical Benchmarks	1980	1990	1995	2000	2010
Percentage of children living above poverty	88%	84%	88%	92%	100%
Miles of assessed Oregon rivers and streams not meeting state and federal in-stream water quality standards		1,100	723	75	0
Real per capita income of Oregonians as a percentage of U.S. real per capita income	99%	92%	95%	100%	110%

Historical data is used to establish a baseline for various target benchmark measures. In response to each benchmark, Oregon's institutions—public, nonprofit, and private—take periodic data measures that are then collected and compiled by the Progress Board in biennial reports such as this one. This compilation of benchmarks attainment forms a foundation for determining Oregon's progress and for making policy recommendations.

SOURCE: Oregon Progress Board, *Oregon Benchmarks: Standards for Measuring Statewide Progress and Institutional Performance* (Salem: Oregon Progress Board, 1994), 2.

define outcomes—in the form of benchmarks—that they want to achieve with federal dollars. State and local service providers then have the latitude to determine how best to achieve those outcomes. In exchange for this discretion, state and local agencies agree to measure progress toward benchmarks and to be held accountable for results. This approach unburdens Oregon's state and local service providers from thousands of hours of paperwork and frees their time and energy to deliver more services to clients. And it makes them far more accountable for outcomes that really matter.[33]

Benchmarking also facilitates setting priorities. Some benchmarks, such as reducing teen drug use and protecting wild salmon runs, are considered "urgent." They may overlap "core" benchmarks, which are especially good indicators of progress. Among these are increasing student achievement and the percentage of the state's population with college degrees.

The NPM certainly holds great promise. But it is still too soon to know whether it will replace or substantially modify traditional public administration and, if so, what new problems it may generate. To date, there have been both success stories and failures. We will analyze the NPM's potential advantages and limitations in several of the chapters that follow. For the sake of comparison with the traditional managerial, political, and legal approaches, here it is desirable only to offer the following summary.

Organizational Structure   The NPM favors organizing administrative activities to maximize the extent to which administrative units can act like firms in a market serving customers. From its perspectives, this should create cost-effectiveness and responsiveness. It relies on decentralization to enable individual units to act as service centers. Consequently, overall agency organizations should become flatter (less hierarchical) and subunits more autonomous. Coordination should be through competition rather than hierarchy. Employee empowerment also diminishes the need for hierarchy because it makes command and control management inappropriate. Teams consisting of employees and managers will become more common. Information systems can be used to monitor service activity and results, much as supermarkets use scanners to track sales and inventory. The boundaries between agencies and their environments will become less distinct as administrators become more responsive to customers' needs and as privatization requires them to devote more attention to negotiating with and monitoring private service providers.

View of the Individual   The NPM views individuals as customers. As the NPR puts it,

> Effective, entrepreneurial governments insist on customer satisfaction. They listen carefully to their customers—using surveys, focus groups, and the like. They restructure their basic operations to meet customers' needs. And they use market dynamics such as competition and customer choice to create incentives that drive their employees to put customers first.
>
> By "customer," we do not mean "citizen." A citizen can participate in democratic decisionmaking; a customer receives benefits from a specific service. All Americans are citizens. Most are also customers: of the U.S. Postal Service, the Social Security Administration, the Department of Veterans Affairs, the National Park Service, and scores of other federal organizations.
>
> In a democracy, citizens and customers both matter. But when they vote, citizens seldom have much chance to influence the behavior of public institutions that directly affect their lives; schools, hospitals, farm service agencies, social security offices.[34]

Customers can also be other agencies, governments, and private organizations. Customers within the same governments are called "internal" customers. For instance, a central personnel agency, such as a civil service commission can recruit, test, investigate, and train employees for other agencies.

It can also design positions for them and regulate some of their practices to assure that they comport with equal opportunity, labor, and other legal requirements. Service agencies are frequently used to provide internal customers with vehicle and building maintenance, protection, and equipment. Customer relations among different governments are also common because so much public policy involves more than one government. For example, federal environmental law regulates subnational governments, state and local governments often use services provided by the Federal Bureau of Investigation (FBI), the federal government relies on state agencies for implementation of a wide array of policies, and local governments may obtain services from states and, sometimes, from one another. Consider the number of governmental units involved in a typical local public school system.

The idea that public administrative agencies have customers is not new. As early as 1936, administrative theorist Marshall Dimock advised, "The customer-satisfaction criterion applies with as much force to government as to business. . . . If the administrator keeps his eyes constantly on the end result, namely customer satisfaction, then the steps which need to be taken in order to improve the internal administration are usually self-apparent."[35] However, the NPM's emphasis on organizing public administration to be responsive to customers—or even driven by them—has evoked concern. Customers in a market differ from citizens in a community. Customers seek to maximize their individual welfare; so do citizens, but public participation in politics is aimed at solving common problems and defining governmental (rather than personal) objectives. Public policy driven by customer demand and/or satisfaction may differ from that based on political agreement or administrative expertise. Because resources are limited, allocating them according to customer preferences is not necessarily the same as basing them on electoral outcomes. Should public schools satisfy their customers even when it may weaken public education and national economic competitiveness? Should social service agencies be more responsive to welfare recipients than to voters in general? Should agencies stratify price (discounts) and service (priority) according to the importance of their individual customers, as businesses sometimes do, or treat everyone equally? To the extent that the NPM succeeds, the appropriate boundaries of customer responsiveness will have to be worked out in the future.

Cognitive Approach   The NPM is largely driven by theory but it can be pragmatic in determining what works and what does not. It borrows heavily from the "public choice" approach to public policy. Public choice posits the individual as a consumer of government services and theorizes that both consumer choice and administrative efficiency will be enhanced if governments can be made to compete for individuals' purchases of goods and services like firms in a market. Public choice also argues that, generally speaking, government should not supply a service or apply a regulation unless it cannot be done as well by the private sector. Markets are viewed as typically superior to administrative operations in satisfying individual preferences, developing technical efficiency, and operating in cost-effective ways. But in the United States, the NPM is pragmatic. In testing its theories, it relies on observation and measurement. Hard measures like the Oregon Benchmarks can often be used to see whether changes in administrative operations are associated with such things as declining crime, teenage pregnancy, infant mortality, and dropout rates, or with improvement in nutrition and education. Even where it is not possible to use quantitative indicators of performance, surveys can be used to determine levels of customer satisfaction. Costs are scrutinized to locate inefficiencies and opportunities for effective privatization. The NPR has also been relying on experimentation, in the form of "reinvention labs" to try to isolate the impact of administrative changes on service delivery and costs.

Budgeting   NPM budgeting focuses on the production of services and regulatory enforcement (outputs) and results (outcomes) rather than on inputs such as personnel and equipment. If feasible, it prefers that agencies or administrative units generate their own revenues, or some share of them, by charging user fees. Legislative appropriations should be based on performance and the creation of value for customers, the public, and the national interest. Lack of output should be investigated to see whether greater investment in the function is warranted or it should be terminated, privatized, or shifted to some other level or unit of government. Agencies should have great flexibility in handling their budgets as long as they produce results. Centralized controls on the number of staff that can be employed, the equipment or travel that can be purchased, and so forth, should be minimized. The ideal is (1) to allow agencies to "manage to budget," that is, to be able to use allocations as they think best to achieve results; and (2) to be entrepreneurial in developing markets for services they can produce at competitive costs. Budgets are viewed as an inappropriate way of controlling agency actions.

Decision Making   Decisions should be based on responsiveness to customers, performance levels, and cost-effectiveness. Generally, decision making should be decentralized. As the NPR puts it, "In fact, it's the people who work closest to problems who know the most about solving them."[36] However, decisions regarding missions and entrepreneurial opportunities should be made by agency leaders, generally with input from rank and file employees. NPM decision making is cost-conscious. Box 1–4 presents an example of NPR's decision approach for determining whether and how federal programs should be continued.

The Political Approach to Public Administration

The political approach to public administration was perhaps most forcefully and succinctly stated by Wallace Sayre:

Public administration is ultimately a problem in political theory: the fundamental problem in a democracy is responsibility to popular control; the responsibility and

BOX 1-4 **Sample Decision Tree for Analyzing Agency Programs**

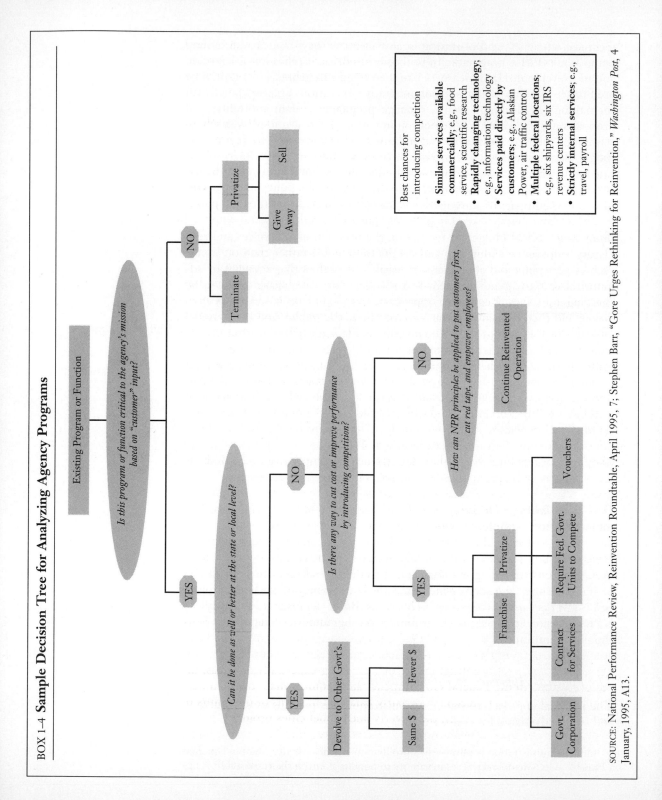

SOURCE: National Performance Review, Reinvention Roundtable, April 1995, 7; Stephen Barr, "Gore Urges Rethinking for Reinvention," *Washington Post*, 4 January, 1995, A13.

responsiveness of the administrative agencies and the bureaucracies to the elected officials (the chief executives, the legislators) is of central importance in a government based increasingly on the exercise of discretionary power by the agencies of administration.[37]

This approach grew out of the observations of scholars, such as Paul Appleby, that public administration during the New Deal and World War II was anything but devoid of politics. Appleby considered administration to be a "political process,"[38] and numerous others have since called attention to the extent to which public administrators participate in public policy making. Unlike the origin of the managerial approach, which stressed what public administration ought to be, the political approach developed from empirical observation.

Once public administration is considered a political endeavor, emphasis is inevitably placed on a different set of values than those promoted by the managerial approach. Efficiency, in particular, becomes highly suspect, because it has little to do with the larger questions of government (see Box 1–5). As Supreme Court Justice Louis Brandeis pointed out in dissent in *Myers v. United States* (1926):

> The doctrine of the separation of powers was adopted by the Convention in 1787, not to promote efficiency but to preclude the exercise of arbitrary power. The purpose was, not to avoid friction, but, by means of the inevitable friction incident to the distribution of governmental powers among these three departments, to save the people from autocracy.[39]

The political approach to public administration stresses the values of representativeness, political responsiveness, and accountability through elected officials to the citizenry. These are viewed as requirements of constitutional democracy, and incorporating them into all aspects of government, including public management, is considered necessary.

Many governmental reforms have been aimed at maximizing the political values of representativeness, responsiveness, and accountability within public administration. For instance, the Federal Civil Service Reform Act of 1978 seeks representativeness by making it "the policy of the United States . . . to provide a . . . Federal work force reflective of the Nation's diversity" by endeavoring "to achieve a work force from all segments of society." The Federal Advisory Committee Act of 1972 tries to make administrative advisory committees more representative. It declares that such committees "are frequently a useful and beneficial means of furnishing expert advice, ideas, diverse opinions to the Federal Government" and requires that "the membership of advisory committee(s) . . . be fairly balanced in terms of the points of view represented. . . ." Earlier, the poverty and model cities programs of the 1960s sought to use citizen participation to promote political responsiveness in administrative operations. In addition, the quest for responsiveness has blended into a wide variety of attempts to promote public administration ac-

BOX 1–5 **The Supreme Court on "Efficiency"**

In *Immigration and Naturalization Service v. Jagdish Rai Chadha* (1983),* Chief Justice Warren Burger, on behalf of the Supreme Court, had occasion to observe:

> [I]t is crystal clear from the records of the [Constitutional] Convention, contemporaneous writings and debates, that the Framers ranked other values higher than efficiency. . . .
>
> The choices we discern as having been made in the Constitutional Convention impose burdens on governmental processes that often seem clumsy, inefficient, and even unworkable, but those hard choices were consciously made by

men who had lived under a form of government that permitted arbitrary governmental acts to go unchecked. There is no support in the Constitution or decisions of this Court for the proposition that the cumbersomeness and delays often encountered in complying with explicit Constitutional standards may be avoided, either by the Congress or by the President. . . . With all the obvious flaws of delay, untidiness, and potential for abuse, we have not yet found a better way to preserve freedom than by making the exercise of power subject to the carefully crafted restraints spelled out in the Constitution.

*462 U.S. 919, 958–959

countability to the public and their elected officials, including the use of "sunshine" and "sunset" provisions.

The political approach to public administration is frequently in tension with the managerial approach. For instance, efficiency in the managerial sense is not necessarily served through sunshine regulations that open aspects of public administration to public scrutiny and can dissuade public administrators from taking some courses of action, though they may be the most efficient. They can divert time and resources from program implementation to the deliverance of information to outsiders. Consultation with advisory committees and "citizen participants" can be time-consuming and costly. Civil service regulations aimed at creating a socially representative work force add complexity to public personnel systems. Public managers have long complained that their effectiveness is hampered by centralized budgetary and personnel controls, the large congressional role in public administration, and the need to consult continually with a variety of parties having a legitimate concern with their agencies' operations. The NPM seeks to promote effectiveness by eliminating many of the accountability mechanisms traditionally used to regulate administrative operations.

Organizational Structure   Public administration organized around the political values of representativeness, responsiveness, and accountability also tends to be at odds with the managerial approaches to organization. The political approach stresses the extent and advantages of political **pluralism** within public administration. In its view, "[e]xecutive branch structure is in fact a microcosm of our society. Inevitably it reflects the values, conflicts, and competing forces to be found in a pluralistic society. The ideal of a neatly symmetrical, frictionless organization structure is a dangerous illusion."[40] Overlapping programs and authority, broad, general missions, and multiple field offices are common when politics dominates administrative organization. Roger Davidson finds a political virtue where the managerially inclined might see disorder: "In many respects, the civil service represents the American people more comprehensively than does Congress."[41]

The basic concept behind pluralism within public administration is that because the administrative branch is a policy-making center of government, it must be structured to enable competing groups to counteract each other by providing political representation to a comprehensive variety of the organized political, economic, and social groups that are found in society at large. To the extent that the political approach's organizational scheme is achieved, the structure of public administration becomes politicized, with different groups continually seeking representation. Overlapping missions and programs become common as the administrative structure comes to resemble a political party platform that promises something to almost everyone without establishing clear priorities for resolving conflicts among them. Agency becomes adversary of agency and the resolution of conflict is shifted to the legislature, the office of the chief executive, interagency committees, and the courts. Moreover, the number of bureaus and agencies tends to grow over time, partly in response to the political demands of organized interests for representation. This approach to administrative organization has been widely denounced as making government "unmanageable," "costly," and "inefficient," but, as Seidman argues, it persists because administrative organization is frequently viewed as a political question heavily emphasizing political values.

View of the Individual   The political approach to public administration tends to aggregate the individual into a broad social, economic, or political group. It does not depersonalize the individual by turning him or her into a "case" or treat him or her as a customer. Rather it identifies the individual's interests as being similar or identical to those of others considered to be within the same group or category. Once grouped, individuals are viewed as the targets or beneficiaries of public policies.

For example, affirmative action within the government service is aimed at specific groups, such as African-Americans and women, without inquiry as to the particular circumstances of any individual member of these broad and diverse groups. Similarly, farmers growing the same crops and/or located in the same national geopolitical subdivisions are considered alike, despite individual differences among them. The same is true in any number of areas of public administration that are engaged in implementing public policies. This is a tendency, of course, that fits the political culture well—politicians tend to think in terms of groups, for example, the "black" vote, the "farm" vote, the "urban" vote, the "labor" vote, and so forth. In the political approach, individuals are aggregated into communities of interest.

Cognitive Approach   The political approach views science as an appropriate way of developing factual knowledge. However, it is so concerned with representativeness and responsiveness that it looks for consensus or the development of broad coalitions in determining what is correct. It often bases decisions on the opinions of the public, interest groups, and the media. Elections, public opinion surveys, content analysis of constituents' letters and news coverage, and review of citizens' views expressed at hearings or in other ways are among the political approach's prime techniques for gaining the information it finds relevant.

Political discussion and debate are viewed as methods for developing knowledge and finding truth. Consequently, the "proper" approach to serving the public interest through administration is not necessarily a question for resolution by experts or science. Nor is it treated as the outcome of individual customer demand. Rather, the public, or organized segments of it, ought to have a large role in determining what is in the collective interest. Informed public administration reflects public choice,[42] which may or may not coincide with generalizations that are scientifically derived.

Budgeting   The political perspective on public administration views budgets as political, rather than business, documents. Allocations are formal statements of how the political system ranks competing values, not necessarily of how the money will be used most effectively or best satisfies customer demand. Budgeting itself is a contest among a plethora of groups competing for the public's money. The outcome of the competition is likely to shift over time, roughly in conjunction with changes in the relative strength of different groups, political actors, and points of view held by the public.

Historically, this approach has contributed to **incrementalism,** a budgetary process that tends to accept agencies' current budgets as a base to which next year's allocations will be made. More recently, as the federal deficit became an important political concern, the reverse of incrementalism, or **decrementalism,** has become significant. Here, attention is paid to the relative decrease in budgetary funds allocated to competing purposes, programs, and organizations.

Decision Making   The political approach tends to favor an incremental style of decision making that is often called "muddling through" (see Chapter 7). It assumes that political pluralism, limited rationality, and time and resource pressures on public administrators are significant constraints on decision making. Consequently, administrators typically can take only small steps toward some general policy objective. This political fact of life is reflected in the succession of limited decisions that administrators tend to make. The test of the desirability of a decision tends to be measured in terms of political support or opposition, rather than cost-effectiveness or scientific analysis.

The Legal Approach to Public Administration

In the United States, the legal approach to public administration historically has been eclipsed by the other approaches, especially the orthodox managerial. Nevertheless, it has a venerable tradition and has recently emerged as a full-fledged way of defining public administration. It views public administration as applying and enforcing the law in concrete circumstances. As such, it is infused with legal and adjudicatory concerns.

This approach is derived primarily from three interrelated sources. The first is administrative law, which can be defined as the body of law and regulations that control generic administrative processes. It consists of statutes; executive orders; the binding directives of central personnel, budget, service, and related agencies; and constitutional law decisions. Because the latter have had a great and relatively distinctive impact on American public administration, constitutional law is given separate treatment below. The federal and typical state administrative procedure acts address the handling of information (e.g., freedom of information), rule making, adjudication, enforcement, and "sunshine" (open government).

A second source of the legal approach has been the movement toward the **judicialization** of public administration. Judicialization is the tendency for administrative processes increasingly to resemble courtroom procedures designed to safeguard individual rights. Dimock succinctly captured the essence of judicialization:

> Before the Administrative Procedure Act (1946) came into existence, decisions were made by the regular administrative staff, with the ultimate decision being entrusted to the head of the agency. Characteristically, it was a collective or institutional decision, each making his contribution and all checking each other. The decisions were made on the basis of statutory law, plus agency sublegislation, plus decided court cases. The system worked, and in most cases worked well. Then the idea arose of using "hearing examiners" in certain cases where hearings were long and technical, as in railroad cases coming under the Interstate Commerce Commission. . . .
>
> When the Administrative Procedure Act . . . was enacted, however, judicialization was speeded up, and now, like a spreading fog, it has become well-nigh universal. It began with hearing officers who were recruited by the U.S. Civil Service Commission and put in a pool, from which they were assigned to various agencies. . . . The idea of courtroom procedure was still further enlarged when [the government] created the office of "Administrative [Law] Judge," this being one who operates inside the agency instead of outside it, as in the case of the European administrative courts.
>
> . . . In actual practice . . . the longer the system has been in existence, the more frequently the [hearing examiner's] recommended decision becomes the final decision.[43]

Judicialization brings not only law, but also legal procedure to bear on administrative decision making. Agencies begin to function more like courts, and consequently legal values come to play a greater role in their activities. In 1992, thirty-two federal agencies employed 1,185 administrative law judges (ALJs). Another twelve or so agencies "borrowed" ALJs under a program operated by the Office of Personnel Management. Seventy-three percent of all ALJs were employed by the Social Security Administration.[44]

Constitutional law provides a third source of the contemporary legal approach to public administration. Since the 1950s, the federal judiciary has virtually redefined the procedural, equal protection, privacy, and substantive rights and liberties of the citizenry vis-à-vis public administrators. Public employees were given a wide array of new constitutional rights. There was a vast expansion in the requirement that public administrators afford constitutional procedural due process, such as trial-like hearings, to the specific individuals whose governmental benefits, including welfare, public employment, and public education were terminated through administrative action. A new stringency was read into the Eighth Amendment's prohibition of cruel and unusual punishment. Wholly new rights, including the rights to treatment and habilitation, were created, if not fully ratified by the Supreme Court, for those confined to public mental health facilities. The right to equal protection was vastly strengthened and applied in a variety of administrative matters ranging from public personnel recruitment systems to the operation of public schools and prisons. Individuals involved in encounters with **"street-level" administrators,** such as housing or health inspectors, were afforded stronger Fourth Amendment protection against unreasonable searches and seizures. Privacy rights involving matters such as marriage and family were also afforded clearer protection. (These developments are addressed throughout the book. The place of constitutional values in public administration is the subject of Chapter 11.)[45]

The expansion of the constitutional rights of individuals vis-à-vis public administrators has been enforced primarily in two ways, both of which enhance the relevance of the legal approach to contemporary public administration. The courts have sought to force public administrators scrupulously to avoid violating individuals' constitutional rights by reducing public officials' once absolute immunity from civil suits for damages to a qualified immunity. In a remarkable development, discussed further in the next chapter, many public administrators are now liable for monetary damages if they reasonably should have known that their actions abridged someone's constitutional rights. This is one reason why the student and practitioner of public administration must have an understanding of several aspects of constitutional law. Public administrators who violate someone's constitutional rights may well find themselves personally responsible for paying damages to the injured individual. In the Supreme Court's view, this approach, "in addition to compensating victims, serves a deterrent purpose" that "should create an incentive for officials who may harbor doubts about the lawfulness of their intended actions to err on the side of protecting citizens' constitutional rights."[46] Consequently, the concept of administrative competence is expanded to include reasonable knowledge of constitutional law. In addition, in suits challenging the constitutionality or legality of public institutions such as schools, prisons, and mental health facilities, the courts have frequently decreed ongoing relief requiring institutional reforms that place courts in the role of supervising public administrators. In some instances of remedial law, judges have revamped entire public school, prison, and state mental health systems. They have even established such detailed administrative standards as the number of mental patients there should be per shower or toilet and how hot or cold mental health facilities should be.

The constitutional law affecting public administration is continually changing as the judiciary applies the Constitution to new situations and revises its interpretations of older ones. Some rights that have not yet been established will be declared; the scope of others will be reduced. But constitutional law, and therefore the courts, will continue to define the rights of individuals vis-à-vis public administrative activity.

The legal approach to public administration emphasizes the rule of law. It embodies several central values. One is **procedural due process,** which is hard to define precisely because it has long been recognized that this value cannot be confined to any single set of requirements or standards. Rather, the term stands for the value of fundamental fairness and is viewed as requiring procedures designed to protect individuals from malicious, arbitrary, erroneous, capricious, or unconstitutional deprivation of life, liberty, or property at the hands of government. A second value concerns individual *substantive rights* and equal protection of the laws as embodied in evolving interpretations of the Bill of Rights and the Fourteenth Amendment. In general, the judiciary views broad individual rights and liberties as a positive good and a necessary feature of the United States political system. Limitations of these rights may be tolerated by the courts when, on balance, some essential governmental function requires their abridgment. However, the usual presumption is against the government in such circumstances; consequently, judicial doctrines place a heavy burden on official administrative action that infringes upon the substantive constitutional rights of individuals. Third, the judiciary values *equity*, a concept that, like due process, is subject to varying interpretation. In terms of public administration in general, equity is probably now most central in empowering judges to fashion remedies for individuals or groups whose constitutional or statutory rights have been violated by public administrators. Additionally, the legal approach values constitutional integrity and opposes efforts to take shortcuts, such as the legislative veto, to get around the strict application of constitutional procedures (see Box 1–5).

One of the major features of the values of the legal approach to public administration is the downgrading of the cost-effectiveness reasoning associated with the managerial approaches. The judiciary is not oblivious to the costs of its decisions, but its central focus tends to be on the nature of the individual's rights, rather than on the costs to society of securing those rights. This is especially evident in cases involving the reform of public institutions.

As one court said, "Inadequate resources can never be an adequate justification for the state's depriving any person of his constitutional rights."[47]

Organizational Structure   As suggested in the discussion of judicialization, the preferred structure of the legal approach to public administration is adversary procedure. The full-fledged judicial trial is the clearest model of this structure. Adversary procedure calls up two opposing parties to marshal facts and arguments in support of their positions. These are brought before an impartial referee (e.g., a judge or a jury) who weighs them and ultimately decides which side is sufficiently persuasive. In public administration, however, adversary procedure is generally modified to allow greater flexibility in the presentation of "evidence" and interpretation. Juries are not used and hearing examiners often play a more active role than traditional judges in bringing out relevant information. Although this structure is often associated with regulatory commissions, it has broad presence in public administration. For example, it is heavily relied on in contemporary public personnel administration, especially in the areas of dismissals and disciplinary actions against employees, equal employment opportunity, and labor relations. It is also common in instances where governmental benefits, such as welfare or public school education, are being withheld or withdrawn from individuals. The precise structure varies from context to context, but the common element running through it is the relative independence and impartiality of the hearing examiner. To a large extent, this independence undermines the traditional managerial approach's reliance on hierarchy, especially in the sense of "unity of command." Hearing examiners stand outside administrative hierarchies in an important sense. Although they can be told what to do, that is, which cases to hear, they cannot be told how to rule or decide, where cases turn on matters of judgment. Moreover, for all intents and purposes, their rulings may be binding on public agencies. This may introduce serious limitations on administrative coordination because the hearing examiner's interpretation of law and agency rules may differ from that of the agency's managerial hierarchy. Dimock summarized the impact of the adjudicatory structure as follows:

> The hearing officers and administrative judges are on a different payroll. Moreover, unlike other officials in his department or agency, the executive is expressly forbidden to fire, discipline, or even communicate with the administrative judge except under very special circumstances, which usually means when the judge submits his proposed order. Under the old system, the entire resources of the agency could be relied upon in making an institutional decision. Under the new system, the judge is isolated in the same manner as a judicial judge, for fear that improper influence will be brought to bear upon him.[48]

To a considerable extent, therefore, this model is at odds with all the values embodied in the other approaches: it turns customer service into a legal procedure; it militates against efficiency, economy, and managerial effectiveness, but also against representativeness, responsiveness, and political accountability. It is intended, rather, to afford maximum protection of the rights of private parties against illegal, unconstitutional, or invidious administrative action. However, because it is so cumbersome and time-consuming, interest in alternative dispute resolution (ADR) has been growing. ADR typically involves negotiation, mediation, and/or arbitration. It is discussed further in Chapter 9.

View of the Individual   The legal approach's emphasis on procedural due process, substantive rights, and equity leads it to consider the individual as a unique person in a potentially unique set of circumstances. The notion that every person is entitled to a "day in court" is appropriate here. Adversary procedure is designed to enable an individual to explain his or her unique and particular circumstances, thinking, motivation, and so forth to the governmental decision maker. A decision may turn precisely upon such state-of-mind considerations, which become part of the "merits" of the case. There are some outstanding examples of this in the realm of public administration. The Supreme Court has ruled that before a mandatory maternity leave could be imposed on a pregnant public school teacher, she was entitled to an individualized medical determination of her fitness to continue on the job.[49] In *Wyatt v. Stickney* (1971),[50] a federal district court required that an individual treatment plan be developed for each person involuntarily confined to Alabama's public mental health facilities. Whether an individual's right to equal protection has been violated may depend not only on the administrative action taken, but also on the public administrators' *intent* or purpose in taking it.[51] Emphasis on the individual as an individual does not preclude the aggregation of individuals into a broader group, as in the case of class-action suits. Although such a suit may be desirable to obtain widespread change, it does not diminish the legal approach's focus on the rights of specific individuals.

Cognitive Approach   The legal approach favors adjudication as the method of developing knowledge. Facts are established through adversary procedure and rules of evidence that screen the information that can be considered by the decision maker. Individuals' intentions or states of mind are treated as objective facts rather than as subjective conditions. Science is not rejected, but the legal approach is very wary about applying generalizations to individual cases. The adjudicatory method is frequently inductive. It relies on the specific elements of the case at hand to develop broad, general legal principles. The whole inquiry may be normative in seeking to choose between competing values. Because individual constitutional rights are intended to protect political, economic, and social minorities from a majoritarian government, the results of public opinion polls and elections are not necessarily of immediate import to adjudicators.

One of the most striking differences between the intellectual orientation of the legal approach and the others concerns the use of social classifications for the sake of analyzing and predicting individual behavior. The traditional managerial approach's reliance on social science may involve the use of such categories as race or sex in analyzing behavior. The customer and entreprenurial emphasis on marketing may do the same. The political approach, being concerned with representation and responsiveness in the distribution of governmental benefits and burdens, is frequently intensely interested in how programs affect women, African-Americans, and members of other social groups. By contrast, the legal approach views some social classifications as "suspect" because they are presumed to threaten the constitutional requirement of equal protection. Racial classifications are the preeminent example. Such classifications may be constitutional, depending on a number of factors (discussed in Chapter 11), but the courts review them with strict scrutiny to ensure that the government has a compelling need for their use.

Budgeting   The legal approach to budgeting emphasizes constitutional integrity and the need to protect constitutional rights, even though those exercising them may be an unpopular minority. In recent years, as political concern with the federal budget deficit and the national debt intensified, Congress and the president adopted a number of steps to reform the budgeting process (budgeting is discussed in Chapter 6). In one case, *Bowsher v. Synar* (1986),[52] the Supreme Court overturned a promising reform on the grounds that it violated the separation of powers by vesting an executive function in an official, the comptroller general, who is subordinate to Congress. In a broad range of other cases, the federal courts have required states either to fund activities, such as incarceration and public mental health care, at levels that assure the protection of constitutional rights or, alternatively, to release prisoners and mental patients. In one case, *Missouri v. Jenkins* (1990),[53] a federal district court even required increases in local taxation to pay for court-ordered public school desegregation. Eventually, however, the court's remedy was found to be too broad an exercise of equity powers.[54]

Decision Making   Judicial decision making is generally incremental. The facts of each new case are evaluated in light of the applicable principles of law derived from past decisions. Even where cases present wholly new issues (cases of "first impression"), the courts are apt to analogize to more familiar circumstances. Decisions are likely to be framed in narrow terms or as a balance between competing concerns. This enables the courts to adjust their rulings in future cases while applying the concepts and language of those of the past. It also lends stability to judicial doctrines and may generally yield better decisions. Precedential incrementalism probably also bolsters the judiciary's legitimacy because it structures their decisions and, to some degree, binds them to past tradition.

Box 1–6 summarizes the varying approaches to public administration. In analyzing the chart, it is useful to consider the ways in which the three approaches are sometimes in tension and sometimes in harmony with one another.

BOX 1–6 **Perspectives on Public Administration**

Characteristic	Perspectives			
	Traditional Management	NPM	Politics	Law
Values:	Economy, efficiency, effectiveness	Cost-effectiveness, responsiveness to customers	Representation, responsiveness, accountability	Constitutional integrity, procedural due process, robust substantive rights, equal protection, equity
Structure:	Ideal-typical bureaucracy	Competitive, firmlike	Organizational pluralism	Adjudicatory (adversary)
View of individual:	Impersonal case, rational actor	Customer	Member of group	Individual and/or member of class, reasonable person
Cognitive approach:	Rational-scientific	Theory, observation, measurement, experimentation	Agreement and public opinion, debate	Inductive case analysis, deductive legal analysis, normative reasoning, adversary process
Budgeting:	Rational (cost-benefit)	Performance-based, market-driven	Incremental (distribution of benefits and burdens)	Rights funding
Decision making:	Rational-comprehensive	Decentralized, cost-minimizing	Incremental muddling through	Precedential incrementalism
Governmental function characterized by:	Execution	Execution	Legislation	Adjudication

---

CONCLUSION: PUBLIC ADMINISTRATION RECONSIDERED

Public administration is an extremely complex endeavor. It embodies at least the major approaches just discussed. Each of these approaches emphasizes values, organizational arrangements, views of the individual, and intellectual orientations that are sometimes at odds with those of the others. The public administrator is called upon to be a manager, policy maker, and constitutional lawyer. He or she is stuck between the proverbial rock and a hard place when called upon to act in a fashion that will integrate administrative approaches that may defy successful integration. This is one reason why politicians and the society generally have become so critical of public administration. It is virtually impossible to satisfy frequently all the managerial, political, and legal/constitutional demands placed upon public agencies and public administrators. Efficient management may preclude political representation and constitutional due process. Emphasizing one approach is certain to provoke criticisms from those who think the others are more important. No doubt this is discouraging in some respects, but it also makes public administration challenging and even fascinating. Public administrators are called upon to help solve the nation's problems and improve its quality of life. However, there is little consensus on how they should proceed. They are both blessed and cursed by living in "interesting times."

NOTES

1. Dwight Waldo, "What Is Public Administration?" in Jay Shafritz and Albert Hyde, eds., *Classics of Public Administration* (Oak Park, Ill.: Moore, 1978), 171.

2. This and the next five definitions can be found in *Public Administration: Concepts and Cases*, ed. Richard Stillman (Boston: Houghton Mifflin, 1978), 2–4. They are offered by John J. Corson and J. P. Harris; John Pfiffner and Robert Presthus; James W. Davis, Jr.; Nicholas Henry; Dwight Waldo; and Felix and Lloyd Nigro, respectively.

3. David Bazelon, "The Impact of the Courts on Public Administration," *Indiana Law Journal* 52 (1976): 101–110. See also David H. Rosenbloom, "Public Administrators and the Judiciary: The 'New Partnership,'" *Public Administration Review* 47 (January/February 1987): 75–83.

4. See David H. Rosenbloom and Rosemary O'Leary, *Public Administration and Law*, 2d ed. (New York: Marcel Dekker, 1997).

5. David K. Hart, "The Virtuous Citizen, the Honorable Bureaucrat, and 'Public' Administration," *Public Administration Review* 44 (March 1984): 112.

6. Frederick Mosher, *Democracy and the Public Service*, 2d ed. (New York: Oxford University Press, 1981).

7. Hart, "The Virtuous Citizen," 116.

8. See Anthony Downs, *Inside Bureaucracy* (Boston: Little, Brown, 1967).

9. But private firms are not always interested in doing business with the government. See Susan A. MacManus, "Why Businesses Are Reluctant to Sell to Governments," *Public Administration Review* 51 (July/August 1991): 308–316.

10. These goals are embodied in the Civil Service Reform Act of 1978 (PL 95–454) and the Federal Advisory Committee Act of 1972 (PL 92–463).

11. James Parton, *The Life of Andrew Jackson*, vol. 3 (Boston: Houghton Mifflin, 1887), 220.

12. Carl Schurz, *The Necessity and Progress of Civil Service Reform* (Washington, D.C.: Good Government, 1894), 3.

13. Woodrow Wilson, "The Study of Administration," *Political Science Quarterly* 56 (December 1941): 494 (originally published in 1887).

14. Ibid., 481.

15. See Luther Gulick and L. Urwick, eds., *Papers on the Science of Administration* (New York: Institute of Public Administration, 1937), 10, 192. See also Alan Altshuler and Norman Thomas, eds., *The Politics of the Federal Bureaucracy* (New York: Harper & Row, 1977), 2–17.

16. Leonard D. White, *Introduction to the Study of Public Administration* (New York: Macmillan, 1926), vii–viii. See also Herbert J. Storing, "Leonard D. White and the Study of Public Administration," *Public Administration Review* 25 (March 1965): 38–51.

17. Frederick Taylor, *The Principles of Scientific Management* (New York: Harper & Bros., 1917).

18. Robert Simmons and Eugene Dvorin, *Public Administration* (Port Washington, N.Y.: Alfred Publishing, 1977), 217.

19. See Eugene Lewis, *American Politics in a Bureaucratic Age: Citizens, Constituents, Clients, and Victims* (Cambridge, Mass.: Winthrop, 1977).

20. Max Weber, *From Max Weber: Essays in Sociology*, in H. H. Gerth and C. W. Mills, trans. and eds. (New York: Oxford University Press, 1958), 196–244.

21. Ralph Hummel, *The Bureaucratic Experience* (New York: St. Martin's, 1977), 24–25.

22. Wilson, "The Study of Administration," 481–482. Wilson noted that "the eminently practical science of administration is finding its way into college courses. . . ." He also maintained that "the science of administration is the latest fruit of that study of the science of politics."

23. White, *Introduction to the Study of Public Administration*, vii–viii, 4; Gulick and Urwick, *Papers on the Science of Administration*.

24. Al Gore, *From Red Tape to Results: Creating a Government That Works Better & Costs Less: The Report of the National Performance Review* (Washington, D.C.: Government Printing Office, 1993), 1.

25. Ibid.

26. Philip Joyce and Daniel Mullins, "The Changing Fiscal Structure of the State and Local Public Sector: The Impact of Tax and Expenditure Limitations," *Public Administration Review* 51 (May/June 1991): 240–253.

27. Reading, Mass.: Addison-Wesley.

28. R.C. Mascarenhas, "Building an Enterprise Culture in the Public Sector: Reform of the Public Sector in Australia, Britain, and New Zealand," *Public Administration Review* 53 (July/August 1993): 319–328.

29. Gore, *From Red Tape to Results*, i.

30. Ibid., iv.

31. Michael Barzeley, *Breaking Through Bureaucracy* (Berkeley: University of California Press, 1992), 39.

32. Oregon Progress Board, *Oregon Benchmarks: Standards for Measuring Statewide Progress and Institutional Performance* (Salem: Oregon Progress Board, 1994).

33. Ibid., 2.

34. Gore, *From Red Tape to Results*, 6.

35. Quoted in Laurence Lynn, Jr., *Public Management as Art, Science and Profession* (Chatham, N.J.: Chatham House, 1996), 82, note 4.

36. Gore, *From Red Tape to Results*, 69

37. Wallace Sayre, "Premises of Public Administration: Past and Emerging," in Jay Shafritz and Albert Hyde, eds., *Classics of Public Administration* (Oak Park, Ill.: Moore Publishing, 1978), 201. Dwight Waldo, *The Administrative State* (New York: Ronald Press, 1948), demonstrates how the basic value choices of manage-

rial public administration are ultimately statements of political preference.

38. Paul Appleby, *Policy and Administration* (University, Ala.: University of Alabama Press, 1949). See also Theodore J. Lowi, *The End of Liberalism* (New York: Norton, 1969).

39. *Myers v. United States*, 272 U.S. 52, 293 (1926).

40. Seidman, *Politics, Position, and Power* (New York: Oxford University Press, 1970), 13.

41. Roger Davidson, "Congress and the Executive: The Race for Representation," in A. DeGrazia, ed., *Congress: The First Branch of Government* (New York: Anchor, 1967), 383.

42. See Gordon Tullock, *The Politics of Bureaucracy* (Washington, D.C.: Public Affairs Press, 1965); and Vincent Ostrom, *The Intellectual Crisis in American Public Administration* (University, Ala.: University of Alabama Press, 1973).

43. Marshall Dimock, *Law and Dynamic Administration* (New York: Praeger, 1980), 113. According to Charles Dullea, "Development of the Personnel Program for Administrative Law Judges," *Administrative Law Review* 25 (Winter 1973): 41–47, the title "administrative law judge" was created by the U.S. Civil Service Commission rather than by Congress.

44. Jeffrey Lubbers, "Management of Federal Agency Adjudication" in David H. Rosenbloom and Richard Schwartz, eds., *Handbook of Regulation and Administrative Law* (New York: Marcel Dekker, 1994), 291.

45. See also Rosenbloom and O'Leary, *Public Administration and Law*.

46. *Carlson v. Green*, 446 U.S. 14, 21 (1980); *Owen v. City of Independence*, 445 U.S. 622, 652 (1980); *Harlow v. Fitzgerald*, 457 U.S. 800, 819 (1982).

47. *Hamilton v. Love*, 328 F. Supp. 1182, 1194 (1971). See Rosenbloom and O'Leary, *Public Administration and Law*, for an extended discussion.

48. Dimock, *Law and Dynamic Administration*, 114.

49. *Cleveland Board of Education v. LaFleur* and *Cohen v. Chesterfield Co. School Board*, argued and decided together, 414 U.S. 632 (1974).

50. *Wyatt v. Stickney*, 325 F. Supp. 781 (1971); 334 F. Supp. 387 (1972).

51. *Washington v. Davis*, 426 U.S. 229 (1976); *Baker v. St. Petersburg*, 400 F.2d 294 (1968).

52. *Bowsher v. Synar*, 478 U.S. 714 (1986).

53. *Missouri v. Jenkins*, 495 U.S. 33 (1990).

54. *Missouri v. Jenkins*, 115 S.Ct. 2038 (1995).

ADDITIONAL READING

BARZELEY, MICHAEL with the collaboration of Babak Armajani. *Breaking Through Bureaucracy*. Berkeley: University of California Press, 1992.

COHEN, STEVEN, AND WILLIAM EIMICKE. *The New Effective Public Manager*. San Francisco: Jossey-Bass, 1995.

OSTROM, VINCENT. *The Intellectual Crisis in American Public Administration*, 2d ed. Tuscaloosa, Ala.: University of Alabama Press, 1989.

ROSENBLOOM, DAVID H., AND ROSEMARY O'LEARY. *Public Administration and Law*, 2d ed. New York: Marcel Dekker, 1997.

SIMON, HERBERT. *Administrative Behavior*, 3d ed. New York: Free Press, 1976.

THOMPSON, FRANK, ED. *Revitalizing State and Local Public Service*. San Francisco: Jossey-Bass, 1993.

WALDO, DWIGHT. *The Administrative State*, 2d ed. New York: Holmes and Meier, 1984.

STUDY QUESTIONS

1. Consider public administrative operations with which you have recently dealt or are familiar. List all their functions that (a) provide services, (b) enforce regulations, or (c) provide a mix of service and regulation.

2. Think about some public administrative issue that has recently been in the news. Consider whether the three perspectives emphasized in this chapter are present in the general discussion of the issue. If so, are the proponents and opponents addressing each other's concerns?

3. What do you consider to be the chief advantages and disadvantages of the NPM? How would you gauge its prospects for success? Why?

CHAPTER
2

The American Administrative State:

Development and Political Environment

The chapter begins by addressing how and why public administration became so important in the United States. It considers the authority and responsibilities of public administrative agencies. It addresses the ways in which various other political actors have tried to cope better with the emergence of public administration as a central feature of government: the presidency, Congress, the judiciary, interest groups, the politically involved public, and political parties. These actors are part of public administration's political environment and affect the scope and nature of public administrators' activity.

Public administration in the United States is currently under great challenge—some might even say, siege. Political rhetoric rings with denunciation of bureaucracy and calls to cut back drastically the size, cost, and intrusiveness of public administration. But much of this rhetoric notwithstanding, the modern administrative state fulfills a variety of highly valued functions. Understanding its development and political environment is a prerequisite to evaluating it sensibly and prescribing sound reforms.

THE RISE OF THE AMERICAN ADMINISTRATIVE STATE

Today, there are roughly 18 million civilian public employees in the United States (see Boxes 2–1 and 2–2). The vast majority work for state and local gov-

---

BOX 2–1 **Growth of Federal Employment**

Year	Number of Employees
1791	4,479
1821	6,914
1831	11,491
1841	18,038
1851	26,274
1861	36,672
1871	51,020
1881	100,020
1891	157,442
1901	239,476
1911	395,905
1921	561,143
1931	609,746
1941	1,437,682
1951	2,482,666
1961	2,435,808
1971	2,862,926
1981	2,865,000
1991	3,111,912
1994	2,971,357

SOURCES: Richard Stillman, *The American Bureaucracy* (Chicago: Nelson-Hall, 1987), 13, Fig. 1.4. Through 1951, U.S. Bureau of the Census and Social Science Research Council, *Statistical History of the United States from Colonial Times to the Present* (Stamford, Conn.: Fairfield Publishers, 1965), 10. Figures for 1961 and 1971 are from U.S. Civil Service Commission, *Annual Report*, 78, 88, App. A. The U.S. Bureau of the Census is the source for 1981, 1991, and 1994.

BOX 2–2 **State and Local Government Employment (Full- and Part-Time), 1980–1992**

Type of Government	Employees (1,000)			
	1980	1985	1990	1992
State	3,753	3,984	4,503	4,595
County	1,853	1,891	2,167	2,253
Municipal	2,561	2,467	2,642	2,665
School districts	4,270	4,416	4,950	5,134
Townships	394	392	418	424
Special districts	484	519	585	627
Total	13,315	13,669	15,265	15,698

SOURCE: Department of Commerce, *Statistical Abstract of the United States* (Washington, D.C.: Government Printing Office, 1995), 322, table 506.

ernments, which have grown far more rapidly than the federal government in recent years. Approximately 6 out of every 100 people in the nation work for state or local governments, while another 1 per 100 is a civilian employee at the federal level. The growth of public employment in the twentieth century and the development of large administrative components in governments at all levels are generally referred to as the "rise of the administrative state" (see Box 3–3). The term "administrative state" is intended to convey several realities of contemporary government: that a great deal of the society's resources flow through public agencies; that public administrators are crucial to the operation of contemporary government; that, as a whole, they are politically central; and that the nation has decided on a course of attempting to solve its problems and achieve its aims through the use of administrative action. The growth of administrative power is a worldwide phenomenon that affects government in virtually all nations. The traditional managerial, political, and legal approaches discussed in the previous chapter have contributed to the expansion of public administration in the United States.

The Political Roots of the American Administrative State

The constitutional government of the United States came into existence in 1789 with some clearly stated formal goals. These are found in the Preamble to the Constitution, which reads:

> WE THE PEOPLE of the United States, in Order to form a more perfect Union, establish Justice, insure domestic Tranquility, provide for the common defence, promote the general Welfare, and secure the Blessings of Liberty to ourselves and our Posterity, do ordain and establish this CONSTITUTION for the United States of America.

In this passage can be found some of the classic purposes of almost all contemporary nations: the desire to provide for the defense of the political community, for law and order, and for the general welfare. The latter may seem too vague to convey anything of a specific nature, but generally it includes a commitment to economic development and to the provision of services by the government for the purpose of advancing the common good. The idea that the state should provide such services did not begin to develop in western Europe until the 1660s, but now it is perhaps the most prominent feature of the administrative state. Thus, governments in the United States provide educational services, child care services, transportation services, communications services, and many other services intended to promote health, social, and economic well-being in general.

The decision to pursue these purposes in the first place is political. So is the choice of a means for achieving them. Several alternatives to government sponsorship of such services exist. Governments could rely heavily upon private resources and incentives to serve their purposes. For example, private armies of mercenaries were once a common means of waging war or promoting national defense. Education was once a private or church-related endeavor. Taking care of individuals' health and welfare needs was once left up to families and religious institutions. Private action has frequently been augmented by the provision of governmental financial assistance to those individuals whose actions promote general national goals. Governmental subsidies and grants to promote a broad variety of private activities—including research, health care, training, education, sound agricultural practices, and technological development—are common. Today, some economists argue that education should be supplied by private organizations through a scheme in which the parents of school children would receive tuition vouchers from the government. These could be used at any school the parents felt best suited their children's educational needs. Such an approach, it is argued, would create a greater incentive for schools to operate efficiently and effectively and would also maximize the freedom of parents to choose among competing educational services. In the early 1980s, the Department of Housing and Urban Development tested a voucher system as a means of aiding people to obtain housing. Rather than build more housing units directly, the department's policy assumed that vouchers would make some housing units already available more affordable. It might also stimulate some growth in the number of housing units by increasing the demand for them. Similarly, various incentives can be built into the government's system of taxation to promote individual behavior deemed in the common interest. The federal tax structure has used deductions and differential rates to promote investment and home owning by private individuals.

There are now so many federal purposes sought through grants, direct loans, loan guarantees, tax provisions, contracts, and other indirect means that the United States has a great deal of "third-party government." In other words, "many of the newer or most rapidly growing tools of government action share a common characteristic: they are *indirect*, they rely upon a variety of non-federal 'third parties'—states, cities, banks, industrial corporations, hospitals, nonprofit organizations, etc.—for their operation."[1] But because the total scope of government activity has grown so dramatically, during the twentieth century governments have also sought to achieve many of their goals through direct public action. For instance, in addition to encouraging home ownership through the tax code, governments have also sought to assure that everyone is adequately housed by building and running public housing projects. They may also maintain shelters for those who remain homeless.

The essence of the administrative state and reliance on large-scale public administration lie in the policy choice of governments to undertake organizational action themselves to achieve their ultimate political goals. In the language of the new public management (NPM), the administrative state both *steers* and *rows*. The Constitution itself indicates the preference for public action in some areas. For instance, it authorizes the federal government to establish post offices and post roads and to raise and direct an army and a navy. Even a brief review of the development of large-scale public administration in the United States during the past two centuries indicates the extent to which such direct administrative action has become increasingly commonplace.

In a thoughtful and succinct analysis, James Q. Wilson identified several primary roots of the development of the contemporary American administrative state.[2] One was to provide a reliable postal service. The U.S. Post Office was not viewed as an end in itself but rather as a means of promoting economic development and national cohesion. It was also spurred by a desire for political patronage. Wilson observes that "from 1816 to 1861, federal civilian employment in the executive branch increased nearly eightfold (from 4,837 to 36,672), but 86 percent of this growth was the result of additions to the postal service."[3]

A second source of administrative growth has been the desire to promote economic development and social well-being through governmental action in various sectors of the economy. The Department of Agriculture was created in 1862 and the Departments of Commerce and Labor came into existence in 1913. More recently, the Department of Health, Education, and Welfare (now Health and Human Services) and the Departments of Housing and Urban Development, Transportation, Energy, and Education were created to promote governmental goals in these economic and social areas of American life. The Veterans Administration was made the Department of Veterans Affairs in the late 1980s.

Departments such as Agriculture, Labor, Veterans Affairs, and Commerce are often called **clientele departments** because they deal largely with a relatively well-defined category of people who are generally assumed to have common economic interests. Clientele departments are often directly engaged in supplying services. For example, the Department of Agriculture tries to educate farmers in improved agricultural techniques and to provide direct economic assistance to them in a variety of ways. It has also undertaken projects to conserve soil, and it manages a system of national forests.

Departments such as Health and Human Services, having a broader mission, also engage in direct action, such as research and disease control.

Another source of administrative growth has been defense. The Departments of War and Navy were created in the eighteenth century, but the military establishment did not emerge as the federal government's largest administrative operation until after World War II. Since that time, the Department of Defense has often employed one-third or more of all civilian federal workers. The Department of Veterans Affairs, which is functionally related to Defense, is also large (about 260,000 civilian employees). Interestingly, this means that roughly two-thirds of all federal civilian employees are employed in three agencies—Defense, Veterans Affairs, and the Postal Service. The creation of a standing army, navy, and air force, and a large civilian administrative component to manage the military reflects the government's view that providing for the common defense requires centralized planning for the procurement and deployment of weapons and personnel. No longer is it believed that private individuals can be trained quickly for military service at the outbreak of war, or that private industry can be rapidly converted for military defense. Here, as in other areas, the government has increasingly moved away from relying on private action alone.

In sum, the political roots of development of contemporary public administration in the United States lie primarily in two political choices made by the government and society. First was that government would exist to promote such objectives as the common defense, economic development, and the general welfare. At the national level, this was a choice first made back in the late 1780s and reinforced subsequently on many occasions. Second has been the more recent choice of placing heavy reliance on direct provision of services and functions by government as opposed to reliance solely on the manipulation of subsidies for private action. The state and local governments have been especially active in providing education, public safety, and transportation services.

The Legal Origins of American Public Administration

Political communities seek to promote law and order within their jurisdictions. Otherwise, political, economic, and social conditions become chaotic. Contracts and property rights become difficult or impossible to enforce. Governmental stability and the achievement of purposes such as defense and economic development are threatened. Again, it is possible to promote law and order through private means. Private religious groups, social leaders, and private schools can imbue individuals with the sense of a moral and civic obligation to obey the law and avoid violating the rights of others. Social sanctions—such as excommunication, ostracism, and shunning—can act as powerful controls on individual behavior. However, governments have typically played a large role in promoting law and order through the creation and enforcement of criminal and civil law. These bodies of law establish the obligations of individuals toward one another and toward the government. In less complex societies, law and order centers largely on the character of direct interaction between individuals and can be enforced by police, courts, and moral suasion. However, as societies become more complex, that is, as large organizations and institutions emerge as potential threats to the stability and welfare of society, governments typically strengthen their regulatory activities as a means of securing law and order. To do so, they create new administrative units to oversee the activities of these large organizations in an effort to protect the public from them and to protect the organizations from each other. Donald Warwick has explained this source of administrative growth as follows: As the concentration of power increases, "governmental bureaucracies arise to: (a) provide the political and economic stability needed to protect the investments of the corporate giants; (b) protect the interests of society against the corporations; (c) prevent political chaos by mediating between corporations and organized labor; or (d) act as agents to stimulate economic activity by corporations and channel it in constructive directions."[4]

Regulation   James Q. Wilson also points to regulatory activity as a source of administrative growth in the United States.[5] He indicates that regulatory agencies were created mainly during four periods, each having a common set of political features. The first period was 1887 to 1890, when the Interstate Commerce Commission (1887) was created to regulate transportation (primarily railroads) and the Sherman Act (1890) was passed as a rudimentary means of controlling the development of economic monopolies. During the second period, which was from 1906 to 1915, some of these regulatory activities were strengthened and the Pure Food and Drug Act (1906) and the Meat Inspection Act (1907) were passed to regulate the quality of these products being offered to consumers. Banks were regulated by the Federal Reserve Act (1913). Additional economic and trade practices were brought under regulatory administration by the Clayton and Federal Trade Commission Acts (1914). During the 1930s, a third period, a host of industries were added to the list of the federally regulated, including cosmetics, utilities, securities, airlines, and communications. Private sector labor relations also came under federal regulation at this time. Finally, during the 1960s and early 1970s, federal regulatory activities focused on environmental and workplace safety concerns (in the Environmental Protection Agency and the Occupational Safety and Health Administration, respectively) and the protection of racial and ethnic minorities and women from discrimination in employment (in the Equal Employment Opportunity Commission).

Wilson points out that the political circumstances prevailing during each of these periods were relatively unusual:

Each of these periods was characterized by progressive or liberal Presidents in office (Cleveland, T. R. Roosevelt, Wilson, F. D. Roosevelt, Johnson); one was a period of national crisis (the 1930s); three were periods when the President enjoyed extraordinary majorities of his own party in both houses of Congress; . . . and only the first period preceded the emergence of the national mass media of communication. These facts are important because of the special difficulty of passing any genuinely regulatory legislation. . . . Without special political circumstances . . . the normal barriers to legislative innovation . . . may prove insuperable.[6]

A major political problem with governmental regulatory activities is that although they do tend to promote domestic tranquility, they are also widely viewed as a breach of the government's commitment to secure the "blessings of liberty." Traditionally in the United States, liberty included the freedom to pursue one's economic interests free of wide-ranging governmental control. To a large extent, regulation was through the common law, if at all. However, by the 1890s, it was evident that the common law would have to be augmented by administrative regulation. A major stimulus for change was conceptual and biological, as legal historian Lawrence Friedman explains:

> The discovery of germs, insidious, hidden in every spot of filth, had a profound effect on the legal system. To a much greater extent than before [the 1890s], goods—including food—were packaged and sent long distances, to be marketed impersonally, in bulk, rather than to be felt, handled, and squeezed at the point of purchase. This meant that a person was dependent on others, on strangers, on far-off corporations, for necessities of life, that society was more than ever a complex cellular organism; these strangers, these distant others had the capacity to inflict catastrophic irreparable harm.[7]

Society as a whole also needed protection against industrial pollution of the environment, such dangers as unsafe vehicles, and a host of products that could not sensibly be evaluated by the public. Harmful products and production practices, it was agreed, could best be controlled through governmental regulation.

To some extent, the political conflict over regulation is related to a much wider historical political tension between liberty and equality. This conflict has been a characteristic political problem in the United States since its founding. Liberty to pursue one's economic interests results in differences in individual wealth. These economic disparities can be translated into inequalities in terms of political influence and economic and social power. Government intervention, often generated by populist opposition to the practices of big business, inevitably reduces economic liberty. Minimum wage and hours legislation and regulation of child labor are excellent examples of this phenomenon. Fearing the exploitation of workers by large corporations that can exercise great power over labor markets, government stepped in and limited how little a worker can be paid, how long he or she may be required to work per week, and how young or old he or she may be. Originally, such legislation was opposed by many, including the U.S. Supreme Court, on the grounds that it limited workers' liberty to contract out their services at their discretion, but nowadays the Fair Labor Standards Act is generally viewed as an important constraint on employers. Equal employment opportunity legislation presents another example of the tension between liberty and equality found in regulatory legislation. In the absence of statutes barring discrimination against members of minority groups, individuals with disabilities, and women, private employers would be free to exclude them from their work forces. But this would, and did, promote economic, social, and political inequality. At the same time, requiring nondiscrimination interferes with an employer's liberty to hire and fire as it pleases.

Because governmental regulation of economic practices is in tension with the stated constitutional goal of securing the blessings of liberty, far-reaching efforts have been made to ensure that such governmental intervention is not arbitrary, capricious, or unduly violative of the economic liberty of individuals and businesses. These efforts have generally used law and legal processes as a check upon the activities of public administrators in this realm. Consequently, regulatory activities become law-bound, and the agencies engaging in regulation are structured to emphasize the values of the legal approach to public administration. In fact, they are heavily regulated themselves by administrative law.

Many federal and state regulatory agencies are structured as commissions. Typically, they differ from other administrative agencies in the extent to which they combine legislative, executive, and judicial functions. In other words, they make rules for the regulation of some aspect of economic life, such as radio and television broadcasting or the fares and rates charged by public utilities (a legislative function); they enforce these rules (an executive function); and they adjudicate issues arising out of the adoption or enforcement of these rules (a judicial function). The combination of these functions in single agencies seems to ignore the constitutional commitment to a system of checks and balances and to the separation of powers. Consequently, there has been a long-standing crisis of legitimacy associated with the operations of regulatory commissions.[8] To some extent efforts have been made to mitigate this crisis by placing a bipartisan group of commissioners at the head of each such agency. But this raises another problem: The commissioners are often people familiar with the industries being regulated, sometimes having been employed in them. These appointments reduce the opposition of businesses to regulation, but they promote a situation in which the regulatory commissions may speak more for industry interests than for the public. In fact, some industries, such as the airlines in the 1930s, actively sought to be regulated to save themselves from the chaos of uncontrolled competition. (And some chaos in the form of widespread bankruptcies and mergers followed deregulation in 1978.)

The original idea behind the creation of regulatory commissions was that, as administrative bodies, they could develop a great deal of expertise in the area they were assigned to regulate. This expertise could be used to define the public interest, which could be refined incrementally over time through adjudication. Regulatory commissions could use adversary procedure to determine the interests of all parties to disputes and to develop a body of precedent that would assure a relatively high degree of continuity in regulatory policies.

The Administrative Procedure Act   By the mid-1940s, however, Congress had come to believe that the regulatory process should afford greater protection to economic liberty from encroachments by administrative agencies. It enacted the Administrative Procedure Act (1946). Although the act, as amended, contains many exceptions, basically it affords the following protections to private parties being regulated:

- An agency must publish in the *Federal Register* descriptions of its organization, general method of operation, and procedural and substantive rules.

- Proposed changes in substantive rules (also called "legislative rules") must be published in the *Federal Register;* an opportunity for response by interested parties must be granted, and such responses are to be taken into account by the agency before adopting its final rule on the matter. The final rule must be published in the *Federal Register,* and not less than thirty days must elapse between its publication and its initial application. In some cases, called "formal rule making" or "rule making on the record," a judicial-like hearing is held before an administrative law judge or agency officials to determine the desirability of a new rule or rule change. (Box 2–3 on pages 56 and 57 presents an example of a proposed rule, though one that is shorter and simpler than most.)

- Adjudicatory procedures within the agency must include the opportunity for aggrieved parties to be heard, to submit information and arguments on their behalf, and to have an initial recommendation for disposition of the case made by an impartial hearing examiner (administrative law judge).

- A right to judicial review is required for a person suffering legal wrong or adversely affected by agency actions. Judicial review is intended to check arbitrary or capricious abuses of discretion, violations of constitutional rights and statutes, breaches of procedural regularity, and agency decisions that are unwarranted by the facts of the case.

About two-thirds of the states also have administrative procedure acts (APAs). There are two main models, a 1961 state model APA and a 1981 version. Over half the state APAs were enacted between 1955 and 1980, but the 1981 model law has attracted some attention. It reflects the more contemporary approach calling for greater openness and public participation in the administrative process. It also calls for cost-benefit analysis in regulatory rule making and for systematic efforts to coordinate rules. Neither model applies directly to local governments.[9]

Clearly, governmental regulatory activities have not only promoted the growth of public administration, but also infused it with a legalistic character. A great deal of administrative time and resources at all levels of government are now devoted to regulatory hearings for setting utility rates, issuing licenses, controlling a host of economic endeavors, and monitoring practitioners of a wide variety of occupations. Many view regulation as going too far in diminishing economic liberty and as too greatly increasing the costs of providing regulated services. During the early 1980s, there was a broad move toward *deregulation*, as in the banking, trucking, and airline industries. Much of the deregulation was considered "procompetitive"; that is, it was intended to allow markets rather than administrative agencies to establish price and service levels. However, there has been little support for deregulation of safety, as in the case of the Federal Aviation Administration or the Food and Drug Administration. By the early 1990s, as several major airlines and banks failed, some calls for "reregulation" of deregulated industries could be heard. Even earlier, economists Walter Adams and James Brock urged the Reagan administration to enforce the antitrust laws to stimulate competition among the airlines. They were also among many calling for greater regulation of flight safety.[10] We will have more to say about the operation of regulatory agencies in Chapter 9.

The Managerial Origins of the Contemporary American Administrative State

Public administration has developed and expanded in pursuit of broad political goals, including the provision of defense, infrastructure, economic development and stability, education, health, and the protection of the environment, workers, and consumers. The administrative activities of agencies assigned to achieve these substantive goals should not just follow a reasonably standardized and relatively fair set of procedures; they should also comply with the standards of good management. Goals and legal constraints aside, the day-to-day organizational operations of administrative agencies should be managed well, meaning they should be efficient, effective, and economical in their operations. Perhaps surprisingly, this too has been a source of the growth of the American administrative state.

Good management may immediately suggest getting more done for less money—a government "that works better and costs less," as Vice President Al Gore's National Performance Review (NPR) puts it[11]—which in turn might mean that fewer people would be employed in the public sector. Certainly it is true that well-managed agencies may realize such savings. However, it may also be desirable to rely on **overhead agencies.** Such administrative units perform services for other agencies and/or exercise oversight over some of their operations.

The traditional managerial approach relies heavily on overhead agencies for supplying government with materials and personnel. In its view, centralization promotes expertise and economies of scale. For example, a central procurement agency may be able to buy office products in huge quantities at substantial discounts. A central personnel agency can develop highly specialized knowledge regarding selection and promotion examinations. By contrast, the NPM contends that centralization costs too much in terms of lost flexibility. In its view, overhead agencies promote red tape, delay, rigid and

BOX 2–3 **Proposed Rule Regarding Treatment for Veterans with Substance Dependency**

Department of Veterans Affairs
38 CRF Part 17
RIN 2900–AH77
Contract Program for Veterans with Alcohol and Drug Depedence Disorders

AGENCY: Department of Veterans Affairs.

ACTION: Proposed rule.

SUMMARY: This document proposes to amend 38 CRF Part 17 by modifying eligibility criteria for veterans participating by contract in the Department of Veterans Affairs' program of alcohol and drug dependence or abuse treatment and rehabilitation in residential and nonresidential facilities. Current regulations stipulate that, prior to participation in contract care under this program, veterans must be provided hospital care in facilities over which the Secretary has direct jurisdiction. It is proposed to change the regulations to stipulate that, prior to participation in contract care, veterans must have been or must be receiving care (regardless of whether it was or is hospital care) by professional staff over whom the Secretary has jurisdiction (regardless of whether it is direct jurisdiction). The proposed elimination of the requirement of "hospital care" appears to be necessary to address changed clinical practices and continue the intended program. In the past, substance abuse treatment generally was provided in a hospital setting. Now, much substance abuse treatment also is provided in an ambulatory care or residential setting. Also, the proposal to change "direct jurisdiction of the Secretary" to "jurisdiction of the Secretary" would allow for continuation of any cases in which VA has had involvement (including, among other things, fee basis care) and thereby help ensure that a complete course of treatment is provided.

DATES: Comments must be received on or before July 22, 1996.

ADDRESSES: Mail written comments concerning these proposed regulations to: Director, Office of Regulations Management (02D), Department of Veterans Affairs, 810 Vermont Avenue, NW., Washington, DC 20420; or hand deliver written comments to: Office of Regulations Management, Room 1176, 801 Eye Street, NW., Washington, DC 20001. Comments should indicate that they are submitted in response to "RIN 2900-AH77." All written comments are available for public inspection in the Office of Regulations Management, Room 1176, 801 Eye Street, NW., Washington, DC 20001 between the hours of 8:00 a.m. and 4:30 p.m., Monday through Friday (except holidays).

FOR FURTHER INFORMATION CONTACT: Karen G. Boies, Ph.D., Deputy Associate Director for Addictive Disorders and Psychiatric Rehabilitation, Veterans Health Administration, Department of Veterans Affairs, (202) 565-7316.

SUPPLEMENTARY INFORMATION: This proposed rule is authorized under provisions of 38 U.S.C. 501 and 38 U.S.C. 1720A.

The Secretary hereby certifies that the provisions of the proposed rule would not have a significant economic impact on a substantial number of small entities as they are defined in the Regulatory Flexibility Act, 5 U.S.C. 601–612. There does not appear to be

---

BOX 2–3 *Continued*

---

a basis for considering special provisions for small entities since, in all likelihood, only entities that are small entities would conduct activities affected by this rule. Also, because of budgetary constraints and the high utilization of this program, we anticipate no change in the total number of bed days of care paid by VA to participating small entities. Therefore, pursuant to 5 U.S.C. 605(b), this rule is exempt from the initial and final regulatory flexibility analyses requirements of sections 603 and 604.

List of Subjects in 38 CRF Part 17

Alcoholism, Claims, dental health, Drug abuse, Foreign relations, Government contracts, Grant program—health, Health care, Health facilities, Health professions, Medical devices, Medical research, Mental health programs, Nursing homes, Philippines, Veterans.

　　Approved: February 29, 1996.

Jesse Brown,
Secretary of Veterans Affairs.

For the reasons set out in the preamble, 38 CRF Part 17 is proposed to be amended as follows:

PART 17—MEDICAL

1. The authority citation for Part 17 continues to read as follows:
Authority: 38 U.S.C. 501, 1721, unless otherwise noted.

2. In section 17.80, paragraph (a)(1) is revised to read as follows:
§ 17.80   Alcohol and drug dependence or abuse treatment and rehabilitation in residential and nonresidential facilities by contract.

(a) * * *
(1) Veterans who have been or are being furnished care by professional staff over which the Secretary has jurisdiction and such transitional care is reasonably necessary to continue treatment.

SOURCE: *Federal Register*, vol. 61, 21 May 1996, 25428.

---

sometimes bizarre requirements, as well as unnecessary expense. They frustrate results and customer-oriented public administration by emphasizing procedures rather than effective outcomes. At the federal level, the NPM has encouraged some overhead agencies to redefine their missions.

　　The following are examples of classic overhead agencies.

- The General Services Administration (GSA) supplies other agencies' needs, ranging from rubber bands to the most sophisticated office technologies. It is involved in building facilities for agencies and renovating and altering them. It provides maintenance and policing functions for agency buildings and operates various food services within them. Although scandals involving kickbacks and corrupt contracting have sometimes rocked the GSA, it can buy products in huge quantities at significant discounts. If each agency had to worry about procuring supplies directly from manufacturers or having its buildings built, the agencies would not only be distracted from their substantive missions but also lack the expertise to obtain the supplies economically or efficiently. However, as the NPM contends, overcentralization occurs when the paperwork and delay in using an agency like the GSA outweigh the costs of making direct purchases.

- The *Government Printing Office* (GPO) is officially part of Congress. It publishes government documents, such as the *Federal Register, Congressional Record*, and a massive variety of administrative reports. These range over everything from tips on controlling common garden insects to elaborate reports on substantive policy areas such as civil rights. The Government Printing Office also publishes the *Government Manual*, which describes each federal agency's function and organization, making it an invaluable tool for students and practitioners of public administration. Traditionally, the GPO was viewed as reliable and cost-effective. However, contemporary computerized printing technology may enable private firms to produce government documents faster and at a lower cost than the GPO. There was some irony in the fact that the first NPR report cost $14 from the GPO, but only $9 in the Penguin version at local bookstores. The Penguin book was more conveniently sized and included an exclusive Foreword by management guru Tom Peters.

- The *General Accounting Office* (GAO) is also a part of the legislature. It was established in 1921 to facilitate Congress's ability to monitor the use of governmental funds by administrative agencies. In more recent years it has added to its concern with fiscal accountability an effort to evaluate the general quality of management of specific administrative agencies. It also evaluates the policies agencies are pursuing. For the most part, GAO serves core governmental functions that are unlikely to be privatized.

- The *Office of Management and Budget* (OMB) is part of the Executive Office of the President. It works with the president, his advisers, and federal agencies to prepare the annual budget submitted by the chief executive to the legislature. In formulating the budget, the OMB evaluates agency requests for funding and evaluates their activities. It also makes recommendations to the president when agencies seek new legislation or the issuance of presidential executive orders to aid them in fulfilling their functions. In practice, the OMB exercises a veto over such requests. It plays a similar role in overseeing the proposed regulatory rules of some executive branch agencies. Although less developed than its budgeting activities, the OMB also tries to advise agencies on good management practices and to evaluate their managerial operations. The NPR recommends that the OMB provides agencies with greater flexibility as part of the effort to deregulate federal administration.

- The *Office of Personnel Management* (OPM) is an executive branch agency that once policed much of the federal personnel system, but that is now redefining its role as part of the NPR. It broadly regulated the way agencies recruited, selected, trained, promoted, transferred, classified, paid, and generally treated federal employees. It also developed centralized merit examinations. For the most part, these functions were previously performed by a Civil Service Commission, which was created in 1883 and abolished in 1979, when the OPM was established. Following the NPR report in 1993, many of the OPM's responsibilities were given directly to the various agencies and departments. In 1994, the Clinton administration created a media event by having OPM director, James King, use a wheelbarrow to throw out the *Federal Personnel Manual.* The voluminous, 10,000-page, highly detailed, compendium of often arcane federal personnel regulations symbolized much of the NPR's critique of traditional management. OPM still administers federal retirement and health programs, operates the Federal Executive Institute for training high-level career employees, and enforces some remaining governmentwide regulations.

- The *Merit Systems Protection Board* (MSPB), the *Federal Labor Relations Authority* (FLRA), and the *Equal Employment Opportunity Commission* (EEOC) also regulate limited aspects of the federal personnel system. MSPB is the legal successor of the Civil Service Commission. It is charged with ensuring that the federal merit system is not violated, and it hears appeals involving employee discipline and dismissal. The FLRA oversees the federal labor-management relations program and adjudicates charges of unfair labor practices. The EEOC is primarily concerned with combating illegal discrimination in private employment, but it also has responsibilities for ensuring equal opportunity in the public sector at all governmental levels.

- The *Bureau of the Census* and the *Bureau of Labor Statistics* are examples of the classic managerial administrative function of gathering information as an aid to policy planning. Both of these agencies supply invaluable information to other agencies as well as to members of the public.

State and local governments typically make use of overhead agencies as well. Budget and civil service agencies are particularly common.

In sum, the quest for good management as well as the desire to promote various political, social, and economic goals, while protecting the rights of private parties, has contributed to the growth of public administration in the United States. However, the essence of the administrative state is not characterized by the large number of administrative units and public employees alone. Its fundamental importance lies instead in the extent to which public administrative agencies are responsible for much of the nation's welfare.

ADMINISTRATIVE AUTHORITY AND RESPONSIBILITY

We have been discussing the rise of the administrative state in terms of the development and growth of administrative units. But the phenomenon of the administrative state and what makes public administration so interesting goes well beyond simply counting the number of units, employees, or money spent. Contemporary public administration is of fundamental concern not only because it is large and expensive, but also because of its authority and responsibilities. It is sometimes difficult to imagine that public employees have emerged as major—perhaps in some policy areas, the major—actors in complex political systems such as the United States. After all, what does a postal letter carrier, a government accountant, a personnel official, a record-keeping clerk, or a typist have to do with the exercise of governmental power? What kind of impact can even high-level officials have in administrative systems that are dominated by organizations rather than individuals, that are rule-bound, and that place major constraints on individual action? These questions hint at a paradox of contemporary public administration. Cumulatively, public administrators have a great deal of authority, but individually they are often likened to cogs in a machine over which they have very little control.[12] Each administrator's discretion is constrained by many rules, procedures, and checks, yet public administration has become a center for the development of policy choices for American society as a whole. The French writer Honoré de Balzac captured this irony by referring to bureaucracy as "giant power wielded by pygmies."[13]

One place to begin a consideration of the nature of administrative authority is with a consideration of what public administrators do. As was discussed earlier, public administrators have become a vehicle through which society has chosen to carry out public action aimed at securing political objectives, such as economic development and regulation to promote law and order. The scope of their activities is truly astounding. It is difficult to find more than a few interests or concerns in the society that are not in some way addressed through administrative action (see Box 2–4). Births and deaths are recorded by administrators; so are marriages and divorces. They inspect food and drugs and regulate radio and television broadcasting. Entrance into a very wide variety of occupations—from the most manual to the most cerebral—requires an administrative stamp of approval. Transportation, housing, education, health service, banking, wages and hours for work, employment, and many, many more aspects of daily life are subject to some kind of administrative action. There is no denying that the contemporary administrative state is characterized by a high degree of penetration of the daily life of society. This is true whether it steers, rows, or both.

The centrality of public administration does not automatically make it powerful. It is at least theoretically possible that public administrative action could be wholly directed by law and political arrangements to the extent that it simply carried out the will of the elected legislative and executive officials. But in practice administrative organizations have considerable independence, for at least two reasons.

First, public administrators develop a great deal of expertise upon which the society becomes dependent. All the functional specialization, record keeping, and information gathering that goes on in public administration enable public administrators to develop expertise on some matters that cannot be matched elsewhere in society. Who else but an administrator is likely to know how much of a particular crop was produced in any given year, or how much of

BOX 2–4 **The Reach of the Federal Bureaucracy—"Touching You, Touching Me"**

The *U.S. Government Manual* indicates that bureaucratic agencies deal with the following areas of American life: Abaca production and sale; adult education; the arts; consumer affairs; historic preservation; economic growth and stability; aeronautics; age discrimination and aging (there is an Office of Aging); agriculture, including the subsidization and regulation of the production of specific crops, marketing, and farmers in general; welfare; maintenance of an air force; various Alaskan projects; alcohol; drug abuse; mental health; tobacco; firearms; aliens; allergies and infectious diseases; battle monuments; Indians; Mexicans; the blind; transportation, technology; armed forces and defense, including the procurement of manpower and weaponry; astronomy; building of dams; reclamation of land; conservation of soil; arthritis; metabolism and digestive diseases; athletics; atomic energy; automobiles; Coast Guard; aviation; banks; standards and measures; biology; birds; bituminous coal; blood; boating safety; bonds; school breakfast and lunch programs; broadcasting; business; cable television; campaign financing; census; (Center for) Short-Lived Phenomena; chemistry; child development; children; environmental quality; cities; civil defense; civil rights; coins; colleges and community development; conservation; construction; corporations; cosmetics; cost of living; cotton; crime; dairy industry; day care; the deaf; Delaware River basin; disadvantaged persons; disaster assistance; discrimination; docks; earthquakes; economic development; the economy; education; electric power; emergencies; employment; unemployment; underemployment; the handicapped; energy; engineering; equal opportunity; exports; families; highways; radiation; railroads; fertilizer; fish, wildlife; fitness; fabrics; floods; food; gas; geographic names; patents; copyrights; grain; grazing; Great Lakes; hazardous substances; health; hospitals; housing; nutrition; hydroelectric power; ice-breakers; immigration; imports; insects; intergovernmental relations; international affairs; irrigation; justice; juvenile delinquency; labeling; labor; land; law enforcement; libraries; livestock; loans; mail; manpower; maps; maritime activities; mediation; medical matters; minoirities; Mississippi River; Missouri basin; motor vehicles; narcotics; outer space; national parks; water quality; national forests; naval matters; occupational health and safety; oceans; oil; minority business; outdoor recreation; passports; plants; police; pollution; postal service; power; prices; rat control; reading; refugees; rents; retirement; rivers; rubber; rural areas; safety; savings; scholarships; schools; science; screw threads; securities; small business; social security; subversive activities; sugar; tariffs and taxes; Tennessee Valley; textiles; trade; trademarks; veterans; visual disorders; vocational affairs; wages; war; water; waterways; weather; women; youth.

SOURCE: David Nachmias and David H. Rosenbloom, *Bureaucratic Government, USA* (New York: St. Martin's, 1980), 59.

some product was imported, or how many people took an occupational licensing examination? Sometimes one is puzzled by the kind of information collected by public bureaucracies, but, in the end, the cumulative information held by public administrators becomes an important source of political authority and influence. Organizational and policy specialization compound this situation. Not only do public administrators often know more about many aspects of national life than does anyone else, they also know more about how to accomplish programmatic ends than do legislators or elected officials. (Take a careful look at the information sought by the form reproduced in Box 2–5.)

Second, elected officials frequently delegate decision-making authority to public administrators. In part this delegation flows from deference to administrative expertise. It also stems from recognition that public administrative directives are actually more flexible than legislation in the sense that they can be redrafted or abolished through a far less elaborate process than enacting a statute. Where the legislature believes that standards for regulation or for eligibility for various governmental benefits will have to be changed frequently, or applied in a great variety of circumstances, it may be apt to delegate power to administrative agencies. For instance, the Occupational Safety and Health Administration Act (1970) mandates that "so far as possible every working man and woman in the Nation [shall have] safe and healthful work conditions." Among other issues, implementing this mandate requires that somebody determine which levels of which substances used in manufacturing and other sectors are toxic. Given the vast number of production practices and potentially toxic chemicals used (not to mention their combination), it is unlikely that Congress *could* address every such danger through specific legislation. Instead, it has delegated its legislative authority to the Occupational Safety and Health Administration to make and enforce rules regarding workers' safety.

Another example is the National Labor Relations Board. Charged with enforcing federal law against unfair labor practices, it has adjudicated thousands of cases since its creation in 1935. It is inconceivable that Congress could have written a statute that either specified all the unfair labor practices the board has thus far declared or was so precise that it eliminated all controversy regarding the distinctions between fair and unfair practices.

Delegations of legislative authority can contain clear and forceful legislative guidance. Frequently, however, the legislature places only the vaguest of conditions on the exercise of powers it delegates to public administrators. For example, the Federal Communications Commission (FCC), which regulates radio and television broadcasting, is supposed to exercise the powers granted to it by Congress in "the public convenience, interest, or necessity." If you were chairperson of the FCC, what kind of guidance would you find in these words? Confronted with an equally unspecific charge, a chairman of the Civil Aeronautics Board (CAB), which regulated the airline industry, once said that the "philosophy of the [CAB] changes from day to day,"[14] something that could not occur if its authority was constrained by strict standards laid down by Congress. Delegations with little guidance often result from the legislature's inability or unwillingness, for political reasons, to set clear standards

BOX 2–5 Bureaucracy at Birth

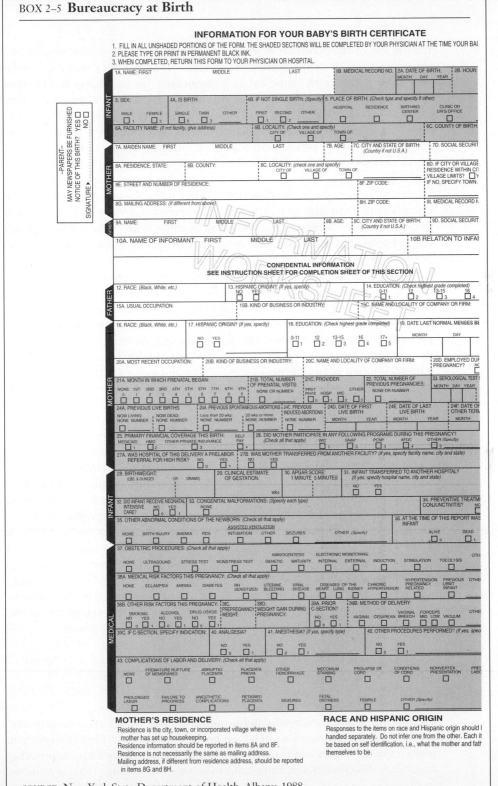

INFORMATION FOR YOUR BABY'S BIRTH CERTIFICATE

1. FILL IN ALL UNSHADED PORTIONS OF THE FORM. THE SHADED SECTIONS WILL BE COMPLETED BY YOUR PHYSICIAN AT THE TIME YOUR BAI
2. PLEASE TYPE OR PRINT IN PERMANENT BLACK INK.
3. WHEN COMPLETED, RETURN THIS FORM TO YOUR PHYSICIAN OR HOSPITAL.

MOTHER'S RESIDENCE

Residence is the city, town, or incorporated village where the mother has set up housekeeping.
Residence information should be reported in items 8A and 8F.
Residence is not necessarily the same as mailing address.
Mailing address, if different from residence address, should be reported in items 8G and 8H.

RACE AND HISPANIC ORIGIN

Responses to the items on race and Hispanic origin should l handled separately. Do not infer one from the other. Each it be based on self identification, i.e., what the mother and fatl themselves to be.

SOURCE: New York State Department of Health, Albany, 1988.

for the use of the powers it delegates to administrative agencies. Sometimes the subject matter of the agency's jurisdiction is so complex that the legislature does not have the time or staff resources truly to master it. At other times, political expediency dictates that the legislature will not take a firm stand on an issue, which may be politically controversial, divisive, and lead to a loss of support among segments of the electorate. The net result of reliance on the expertise of public administrators, and the scope and frequency of vague delegations is that public administrators, as a group, become influential policy makers. They are consulted by committees and subcommittees in Congress, by officials in the Executive Office of the President, and by the politically appointed department heads and their staffs. Moreover, despite the denunciations of "bureaucratic power" at election times, political officials often acknowledge the legitimacy of including agency administrators in the policy-making process.

Public administrators are even more influential when it comes to choosing the means through which public policies will be implemented. The choice of means and the pace and regularity of enforcement can be as much as policy-making exercise as the choice of ends. In many cases, universal enforcement is precluded by inadequate resources. Consequently, selective enforcement and nonenforcement are very common. Where selective enforcement manifests a pattern—aimed at large firms rather than small ones, for example, or poorer neighborhoods rather than richer areas—administrative decisions have clear political consequences because they determine the distribution of benefits and/or burdens created by public policies.

Public administrative authority in the United States today is also evidenced in the volume of rule making by administrative agencies, which far exceeds the volume of legislation passed by the nation's legislatures; in the fact that even with very crowded judicial dockets, more adjudication, such as hearings, takes place in administrative agencies; and in the fact that despite the vast publicity given to presidential and gubernatorial policy initiatives, public administrative agencies remain a main source of ideas for new legislation. The power of individual agencies and officials varies with a variety of factors, a topic generally called *bureaucratic politics*. But, overall, administrative influence has developed to such an extent that it has had a major impact on the nature of the other branches of government. The rise of the administrative state is perhaps the most important governmental development in this century: it transforms the nature of the political system as a whole.

RESPONSES TO THE RISE OF THE ADMINISTRATIVE STATE

Over the long run, a successful public administrator must have a deep understanding of the environment in which he or she operates. That environment includes many actors and the managerial, political, and legalistic approaches and values discussed in the first chapter. Among the leading actors are elected chief executives, legislatures, courts, interest groups, and the public at large. In some jurisdictions, where there are a large number of elected and/or politically appointed administrative officials, political parties are important as well. The successful practitioner of public administration may come to develop a feel for the way these actors influence public administration, for their values and objectives. The student of public administration, on the other hand, may not have the opportunity for daily interaction with the environment of public administration and consequently finds it necessary to rely on accounts of others. In this section we will explain how the president, Congress, the federal judiciary, interest groups, the public, and, to a lesser extent, political parties have responded to the rise of the administrative state. Related developments at the state and local levels are summarized on pages 90–92.

The President and Public Administration

The office of the president of the United States is surrounded by so much myth that it is sometimes very difficult even to begin to figure out what really goes on in the White House, much less in the president's mind. For some reason—a psychological need for a hero figure, perhaps—Americans have built up the image of the president in a way that simply does not correspond to reality. It has been claimed that "the President of the United States of America is, without question, the most powerful elected executive in the world";[15] and "there is virtually no limit to what the President can do if he does it for democratic ends and by democratic means."[16] But the experience of recent presidents has often been characterized by an inability to achieve their stated goals and deliver on their promises to the public. At least some modern presidents might well have been the topic of a famous nineteenth-century essay, "Why Great Men Are Not Chosen Presidents."[17] More to the point, why have so many presidents come into office promising that they could do something constructive to control "the bureaucracy," only to leave office with questionable accomplishments and a sense of defeat. Even Jimmy Carter, who did introduce major reforms in the federal personnel system, eventually admitted that he was unable to overcome the entrenched force of the federal bureaucracy. Although his reforms were hailed as equal in importance to the adoption of a merit system in the 1880s and called the "centerpiece" of his efforts to reform government and make it more efficient and effective, Carter hardly mentions civil service reform in his memoirs, *Keeping Faith*. In some important ways, discussed later on in this section, President Ronald Reagan's administration was more successful than most in influencing federal administration. But it also faced serious frustrations. Despite Reagan's vows to cut the federal bureaucracy's size, toward the end of his second term the budget deficit was larger than ever and, although some agencies had been shrunk, overall levels of federal employment were higher than when he took office. Not only were no federal departments eliminated during Reagan's presidency, but the Department of Veterans Affairs was created. At times, the Reagan administration was mired in bureaucratic politics, as was true of the scandal-rocked Environmental Protection Agency in the first term and during the Iran-Contra affair in the second. Perhaps even more telling government spending continued to rise as a proportion of the gross domestic product (GDP). President George Bush, a man with much Washington experience, avoided challenging federal administration head on. But he did vow to cut the budget deficit, which nevertheless continued to grow.

The Clinton administration's NPR, spearheaded by Vice President Gore, promised drastic administrative reforms and a massive cutback in the number of federal employees. It succeeded in formally deregulating much federal personnel management and in reforming procurement. Whether it will eventually bring about a culture change that makes federal administration more results- and customer-oriented remains moot. Even after the *Federal Personnel Manual* met its highly celebrated demise, many agency field offices continued to use it because doing otherwise required difficult and, perhaps, risky changes. After the 1994 elections brought Republican majorities to both houses of Congress, the NPR faced great frustration. Congress preferred cutting programs and agencies to reforming them, much of the government was temporarily shut down twice for lack of a federal budget, and as the 1996 election drew near, several legislators showed a distinct preference for micromanagement over deregulating agencies and empowering their employees. The administration's "body counts" showed reductions in personnel, but not necessarily the desired impacts. Most of the reductions were in the Department of Defense, which was slated for downsizing earlier when the Soviet Union collapsed and the Cold War ended. In many cases, cutbacks left remaining employees demoralized and with little enthusiasm for the NPR. The cuts were aimed at ". . . the structures of overcontrol and micromanagement that . . . bind the federal government: supervisors, headquarters staffs, personnel specialists, accountants, and auditors."[18] However, because of the very personnel rules detested by the NPR, these employees often remained while those more directly involved in the delivery of services left.[19]

It is obvious that the gap between the imaginary presidency and the real powers and influence available to the president is vast. Virtually all presidential administrations since the days of Franklin D. Roosevelt (1933–1945) have noted how difficult it is for the president to get things done. President Harry S. Truman may have conveyed the limits of presidential power best when he mused about General Dwight D. Eisenhower, president-elect, taking over: "He'll sit here, and he'll say, 'Do this! Do that!' *And nothing will happen.* Poor Ike—it won't be a bit like the Army. He'll find it very frustrating."[20] Years later, Richard Cheney, chief of staff in the Ford administration and subsequently secretary of defense under Bush, commented on the same phenomenon:

There's a tendency before you get to the White House or when you're just observing it from outside to say, "Gee, that's a powerful position that person has." The fact of the matter is that while you're here trying to do things, you are far more aware of the constraints than you are of the power. You spend most of your time trying to overcome obstacles getting what the President wants done.[21]

President Carter once exclaimed, "I can't even get a damn mouse out of my office," after its removal was delayed by a jurisdictional dispute between the Department of the Interior (White House grounds) and the General Services Administration (White House building)! President Reagan's secretary of state, George Schultz, summed up the political environment in Washington, D.C., best: "Nothing ever gets settled in this town. You have to keep fighting every inch of the way."[22]

Presidential powers over public administration are particularly limited. It is customary to view the president as the chief executive, but almost all of his powers over the executive branch are shared with Congress and the courts. The presidential appointment of principal officers is shared with the Senate. Dismissals, even of some presidential appointments such as the chair of the Federal Trade Commission, have been constrained by constitutional and statutory law.[23] Funding for agencies and salaries must be authorized by Congress. Likewise, agencies must either be created by law or pursuant to a congressional delegation of power to the president. In either case, their creation requires at least the tacit approval of the legislature. Agency missions are rarely if ever established or significantly formally modified by the president alone. The federal personnel system is based on statute and consequently requires congressional involvement. Collective bargaining arrangements also place constraints on what the president can do in terms of managing people in the executive branch. Presidential executive orders are subject to challenge in the federal courts. They may not be legally binding on the independent regulatory commissions.[24] Nor can presidents refuse to spend money allocated by Congress without congressional approval. During the Reagan, Bush, and Clinton administrations, the problem of presidential control of administration was complicated by "divided government," that is, the White House and one or both houses of Congress controlled by different political parties.

So what are these presidential powers of which so many have so long been in awe? Some would point to the president's duty to faithfully execute the laws. Yet this and other significant powers are shared with the legislature and the courts—and that presents the crux of the president's problem vis-à-vis large-scale federal public administration. Stated concisely, the president is held responsible and accountable for the performance of the executive branch, but does not have the powers necessary to control its performance. This has led presidents to augment their constitutional authority with "tools" for better management.

The **Executive Office of the President (EOP),** created in 1939 is one of the more formidable of these managerial tools—a veritable tool kit, really. It was originally designed to be relatively small and compact. It was intended to strengthen the president's ability to provide executive branch agencies with policy direction and to control their budgets. It has since grown substantially and taken on something of a life of its own. Today its main units are the following:

1. *White House Office*, which provides staff and managerial assistance to the president. Basically it serves to coordinate the activities of the executive

branch, enable the president to exert greater influence on the executive branch, generate ideas for solutions to pressing problems, and deal with outsiders such as Congress, interest groups, and the media. The White House Office has grown from 45 full-time employees in 1939 to more than 400 under recent presidents.

2. *Office of Management and Budget* (OMB) was discussed earlier. Created in 1970, it encompassed the old Bureau of the Budget, which was established in 1921, as an independent unit within the Treasury Department and moved to the EOP in 1939. OMB has been very strong in dealing with executive branch agencies and has provided the presidential office with a strong tool for coordinating budgets and policy. It has sometimes been used to blunt congressional influence on agencies and administrative processes. OMB has housed about 570 or more employees in recent years.

3. *National Security Council* (NSC) was established in 1947. The NSC seeks to advise the president on the integration of domestic, foreign, and military policies as they relate to national security. However, the NSC has sometimes been a competitor of the Departments of State and Defense in defining policy.

When viewed in organizational terms, these three units can be seen as "superagencies" intended to make it possible to run a great deal of the executive branch directly out of the presidential office. The OMB deals with policy coordination, budgets, economic matters, and management. The National Security Council deals with foreign affairs. The operations of these specialized units are coordinated by the White House Office, which controls access to the president. Thus, the standard managerial principles of specialization and hierarchy are present, and the whole Executive Office of the President is intended to serve as a presidential tool for management and policy making in the executive branch.

From the administrative side, the EOP increases the number of actors to whom attention must be paid. No longer does the chain of command reach from the president to the career public administrators through the politically appointed agency heads and their assistants. Rather, the agency heads are for the most part in fact responsible and subordinate to people in the EOP. They rarely have direct access to the president, but rather must go through functionaries in the White House Office.

This arrangement *might* enable the president to gain authority more commensurate with thrust upon or self-imposed responsibilities. The president has great freedom to make appointments to the White House Office, because these functionaries do not require senatorial approval. Many of the operations of the Executive Office of the President can be cloaked in the secrecy afforded by the principle of executive privilege, which limits congressional inquiry into its affairs. But in practice the EOP has not wholly solved the presidential dilemma, primarily because it has grown too large to serve, in any simple sense, as a direct arm of the president. As Stephen Wayne summed up the problem:

The growth of presidential policy making has encouraged the development of a large, specialized and highly structured White House, one that has become capable of assisting the president in more of his duties but one that also has become less amenable to his direct, personal control. . . .

In the process of expansion, the White House aggregated considerable power. By the 1970s, it had clearly become more than the president's personal office.[25]

Political executives—that is, department heads, assistant secretaries, and other political appointees to executive agencies—are a means of bringing presidential policy direction to the bureaucracy. The president appoints about 650 top political executives to positions in the Executive Office and executive branch agencies. These include the cabinet members and about fifteen to twenty other individuals in each of the departments as well as approximately eleven appointees in each of the independent agencies, including their heads. Additionally, there are some 2,400 political appointees scattered throughout the upper and middle levels of the executive branch. These appointees are exceptions to the nonpartisan career service that overwhelmingly comprises these ranks. About 700 such political appointees are in the Senior Executive Service (SES) positions at the top of federal service and about 1,700 are in Schedule C slots in the middle levels.

Traditionally, political executives and appointees have had a dual allegiance. On the one hand, they are presidential appointments and consequently are expected to express loyalty to the chief executive. On the other, political executives must be able to work with the top-ranking career staffs of the agencies to which they are assigned. This job is complicated by the likelihood that the political executive's tenure will be relatively short—2.1 years was the governmentwide median from 1981 to 1991, but it was less in each of the cabinet departments.[26] Consequently, political executives often depend considerably on the expertise of the career staffs to achieve policy objectives. Too often it is assumed that the hierarchy of an organizational chart actually conveys the authority necessary to manage a federal agency. Those public administrators who make it to the top career positions in their agencies necessarily develop a considerable network of supporters in the legislature and among interest groups. They are politically influential and cannot be effectively ordered around without considerable managerial and political skill. The politically appointed secretary depends on them to a certain extent. Consequently, he or she not only represents the president's will to the agency, but must also represent the agency to the president. The fact that most political executives no longer enjoy direct access to the president complicates their jobs considerably. Let's take a look at what two political executives have observed about the problems they faced:

- In a real sense, delegation of authority to the operating manager of an entirely unfamiliar field means that the Secretary serves the bureau chiefs [career bureaucrats managing bureaus] rather than vice versa.

- The White House attitude is often bafflingly ambivalent. Thus, the staffer who is charged with relaying his own or the President's instructions to a cabinet officer usually expects unquestioning obedience. On the other hand, the President, when and if he has occasion to call on the Secretary to help, often expects him to enjoy at least the public image of independence.

- [The Secretary's] judgment on budget items is, of course, the most important decision he will make in his term in office and is the decision he is usually least well-equipped to make intelligently.

- The traditional answer of the busy executive to excessive workload—delegation of authority—is often a high-risk business in a political organization.[27]

The Reagan administration is generally credited with excelling in the use of political executives. The following were among his strategies.

1. "[T]he appointment to top government positions of men and women who share my economic philosophy. We will have an administration in which the word from the top isn't lost or hidden in the bureaucracy."[28]
2. Appointees that would be "the managers of the national administration—not the captives of the bureaucracy or the special interests they are supposed to direct."[29]
3. A willingness to appoint individuals who were opposed to the programs being managed by the agencies to which they were appointed, as in the Departments of Labor and Housing and Urban Development, the Commission on Civil Rights, the Equal Employment Opportunity Commission, and, in the early 1980s, the Environmental Protection Agency.
4. Considerable care in making appointments to political positions in the SES and to Schedule C.

An interesting aspect of Reagan's relative success in relying on political appointees to control the career service indicated how varied the patterns of influence and styles of management were. Similar political ideologies among his appointees did not necessarily yield parallel managerial styles. Some political executives were almost ruthless in their treatment of career civil servants, who were downgraded, transferred, dismissed in cutbacks, and prompted to resign. But others adopted a managerial style imbued with greater respect for the talent of the career staffs and more open to their participation in decision making.[30] More systematic information is contained in Boxes 2–6 and 2–7. Box 2–6 indicates that Reagan's political executives generally held the career service in high regard, but less so than did political executives in other recent administrations.

A more probing analysis reveals several deep divisions between the views of former political appointees and career members of the SES. (The SES is comprised mainly of top-level career managers, but up to 10 percent of its members can be politically appointed. See Chapter 5 for a further discussion.)

BOX 2–6 **Presidential Appointees Rate the Career Bureaucrats**

Administration	Competence*	Responsiveness*
Johnson	92%	89%
Nixon	88%	84%
Ford	80%	82%
Carter	81%	86%
Reagan	77%	78%

*Positive ratings

SOURCE: National Academy of Public Administration, Presidential Appointees Project, *Leadership in Jeopardy: The Fraying of the Presidential Appointments System* (Washington, D.C.: NAPA, 1985). The survey was mailed to all living presidential appointees in these administrations whose addresses were known. The response rate was 56 percent.

The information in Box 2–7 shows that career administrators are much less likely than political appointees to believe that the latter bring valuable experience to the job, have good leadership and managerial abilities, or view their jobs as opportunities to make long-term improvements in government. Further, only 15 percent of the career SES members thought that the political appointees supported merit principles, which are central to the federal civil service's career personnel system. Overall, the chart shows that career and political appointees have strikingly different worldviews regarding the value of political appointments in the SES.

BOX 2–7 **Career and Noncareer Former Senior Executive Servants' Evaluations of Noncareer Executives**

	Percent Agreeing/Disagreeing	
Item	Career	Noncareer
Noncareer executives:		
■ Bring valuable experience to the job	25/42	62/12
■ Have good leadership qualities	18/41	54/17
■ Have good management skills	15/44	39/17
■ View job as opportunity to make long-term improvements in government	27/42	70/17
■ Support merit principles	15/45	46/20

SOURCE: U.S. Merit Systems Protection Board, *The Senior Executive Service* (Washington, D.C.: MSPB, 1989), 20.

The overall effectiveness of political executives has been increasingly questioned in recent years. The National Commission on the Public Service (known as the Volcker Commission, after its chair, Paul Volcker) argued that there were too many political appointees and that their number should be reduced by about one-third.[31] Paul Light argues that the number of political executives is less important than their tendency to "thicken" government by constituting new administrative layers beneath assistant secretaries, undersecretaries, and other higher-level appointees.[32] Thickening can diffuse and obscure the very accountability political executives are supposed to promote. It can also lead to inertia, the distortion of information, and disunity.

Several additional presidential tools bear mention. The president can often block administrative actions sought by Congress and/or agencies. Political executives can be especially adroit at getting agencies to do less—that is, initiate fewer regulations and enforcement actions. But the president can also use the veto power to block legislative initiatives for administrative change or action, and can also try to block agencies from using funds for purposes to which the president is opposed through impoundments and recisions (see Chapter 6 on budgeting). However, these tools are crude and subject to congressional override. The line-item veto, which many state governors have and the president will gain in 1997, offers a more finely honed instrument for vetoing legislative efforts to fund agencies and programs at levels above those desired by the chief executive. Finally, under various statutes enacted since 1939, the president has sometimes had considerable power to initiate extensive agency and departmental reorganizations, subject ultimately to congressional assent.

The NPR and many observers view these tools as inadequate. The NPR has called for the following reforms:

1. *A biennial budget.* Budgeting for two years rather than annually would presumably reduce congressional oversight and involvement in federal administration. Coupled with other NPR recommendations, it would also enhance agencies' flexibility in using funds. Twenty states use biennial budgeting.
2. *A line-item veto.* As noted above, this will be operative in 1997 and will enable the president to cut items from spending bills more effectively.
3. *Fifty percent rollover.* Permit agencies to retain 50 percent of unspent authorizations for internal operations each year. This would encourage agencies to save money and potentially reduce their dependence on legislative appropriations.
4. *Service fees and debt collection.* Provide agencies greater freedom to set fees for their services and to use the revenues collected. Allow them to use private debt collectors and to keep a portion of debts collected. As above, these reforms would give agencies more independence from congressional funding.
5. *Reduce congressional micromanagement.* Congress should stop trying to regulate agencies by earmarking funding for highly specific actions (such as locating offices in specified legislative districts). It should also

eliminate staffing floors for programs and drastically reduce the number of reports it requires of agencies.

6. *Performance agreements.* The president should enter into written performance agreements with the heads of departments and agencies. This would clarify expectations and, perhaps, reduce the tendency for these political executives to fall under the influence of congressional committees and subcommittees.

7. *Alternative dispute resolution.* Agencies should try to avoid litigation—and therefore, the courts—by resolving disputes through negotiation, mediation, and other approaches.

As this list suggests, from managerial perspectives the president needs more authority and tools to run the executive branch. But other perspectives are also built into the nation's constitutional separation of powers.

Congress and the Administrative State

The response of legislatures to the rise of the contemporary administrative state has been complex and somewhat convoluted. Typically, unlike chief executives, their problem is not the lack of adequate constitutional or legal authority to control the actions of public administrative agencies. Rather, the problem is one of technical ability to exercise *oversight* (review) of public administrators and the political interest or will to do so. The U.S. Congress presents an excellent and well-researched example of how the growth of public administration affects the operation of legislatures.

Institutional Responses   It is sometimes said that it takes one bureaucracy to control another. This could be the motto of Congress, except that it is uncertain whether it really desires systematically to control the actions of public administrators at all. Beginning with a legislative reorganization in 1946, Congress has sought to deal with the burgeoning federal bureaucracy primarily with three tools. First, it has added a vast number of new staff. In 1947, there were 182 committee staff in the House and 222 in the Senate. In the mid-1990s, the number of committee staff stood at about 2,150 in the House and 1,000 in the Senate.[33] Committee staff are attached to congressional committees and subcommittees. Their primary tasks are to aid in the drafting of legislation, assist the members of Congress during committee hearings, and engage in the oversight of administrative agencies in the executive branch. Although committee staff hold no formal tenure, many of them remain in office for long periods of time and develop working relationships with bureau chiefs in the executive branch. Committee staff often write the reports that accompany bills, and these provide useful guidance for administrators seeking to understand the legislature's intent.

The personal staffs of members of Congress have also grown immensely—from 590 in the Senate and 1,449 in the House in 1947 to about 4,000 and 7,400, respectively, in the mid-1990s. Personal staff are attached to members of Congress and can be used as the member sees fit. In practice, most members of Congress organize them according to similar functions, including administrative assistance, legislative assistance, and clerical. Personal staff assist the members of Congress in developing legislation, responding to constituents, and engaging in oversight. The combined total of personal and committee staff has been relatively constant for a decade, at more than 14,900, or almost 28 per member.

Second, Congress has strengthened its own administrative units for dealing with federal administration. Although there is nothing new in the use of legislative administrative agencies for this purpose, in recent years Congress has placed greater reliance upon them by establishing the Congressional Budget Office and strengthening the General Accounting Office. There is also a Congressional Research Service, which has some importance vis-à-vis the executive branch. To an extent, the growth in size and importance of Congress's administrative units matches the expansion of the Executive Office of the President, and presents similar problems. All told, the combined staff of Congress—personal, committee, and administrative—is close to 30,000. Given the influence of committee staff, personal staff, and administrative staff, it is not the least bit implausible to ask of Congress, "Who's in charge here?"[34]

The third tool employed by Congress as a response to the growth of federal administration has been to strengthen committee and subcommittee specialization in an effort to improve oversight of federal agencies. In 1996, there were 36 standing committees and 147 subcommittees of these in the legislature. Their subject matter jurisdiction covers virtually all the areas of life with which government deals. These range from matters of nationwide importance, such as economic policy and defense, to highly specialized areas, such as the production of specific crops. In fact, as Harold Seidman observes, the committee structure of Congress tends to match the administrative specialization found in the executive branch.[35]

Political Responses   These tools, along with Congress's legal, constitutional authority, could place the legislature in a position to exercise a great deal of direction over executive branch agencies. But such direction has not been exercised in any consistent manner because, individually and collectively, most members of Congress have little incentive to engage in forceful oversight. Generally, oversight can be conceptualized as responding to fire alarms more than engaging in routine police patrols.[36] Crises and scandals such as the savings-and-loan debacle receive a great deal of attention, while the day-to-day activities of agencies receive only cursory attention. The issue is largely one of incentive, not authority.

Somewhere along the line members of Congress came to realize that the executive branch bureaucracy could be used to promote their own incumbency. Although turnover in Congress has been very substantial in the 1990s, **pork barrel,** or the spending of federal funds in the member of Congress's home district, has long been a staple of American politics.

Such funds are often used for a number of capital improvement and public works (infrastructure) programs as well as for federal facilities. Roads, bridges, river and harbor improvement, new postal facilities, and defense installations are some classic examples. To a large extent, these are "gifts" that Congress as a whole gives to each of its members. But the gifts, delivered through the executive branch administrative agencies, may be provided with more or less vigor, depending in part on a member of Congress's stance on something the agency is seeking. After an exhaustive analysis, R. Douglas Arnold reported in a somewhat overly cautious tone that

> . . . bureaucrats appear to allocate benefits strategically in an effort both to maintain and to expand their supporting coalitions. When it furthers their purposes, they broaden their program's geographic scope and increase the number of shares of benefits so that more congressmen can be brought into their supporting coalitions. When necessary, they allocate extra shares of benefits to leaders and to those who are crucial coalition members.[37]

It was no surprise that in 1993 the first choice of a majority of the 110 new members in the House was a seat on the Public Works and Transportation Committee. The desire was bipartisan—twenty-nine Democratic and twenty-seven Republican first-termers sought a seat on the sixty-three-member committee. When one new member was asked whether critics might label his pet projects, "pork," he replied "there ain't much beef up here." Even intense concern with budget deficits and the cost of government has not eliminated the quest for pork.[38]

Casework, or constituency service, is another way Congress uses the federal bureaucracy to promote its own incumbency. "Casework" refers to the service rendered by members of Congress to constituents having some sort of problem with a federal agency or with filling out forms and the like for federal grants or benefits. In essence, casework is used to cut through bureaucratic red tape. It has emerged as a major congressional activity. Members of Congress handle tens of thousands of cases each year. They may actually advertise their willingness and ability to engage in this function. The proportion of personal staff assigned to the home district has grown partly in accordance with the increasing casework activities of members of Congress. Casework is important to the member's desire to be reelected because it provides a favor that may presumably be repaid with a vote. For example, when a member of Congress helps someone receive social security benefits, he or she is likely to win at least one vote—perhaps more, depending upon the recipient's garrulousness and the size of the recipient's family and circle of friends and acquaintances. (See Box 2–8 for a congressman's solicitation of casework and Box 2–9 for a representative's effort to keep them happy back home.) Boxes 2–10 and 2–11 show the top fifty counties in per capita federal spending and some examples of federal spending on agricultural pork in the states.

BOX 2–8 **A Congressman's "Dear Postal Patron" Letter**

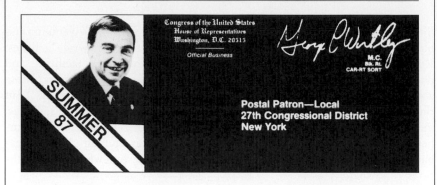

Need Assistance? Have an Opinion?
I'm Eager to Listen and Help

Besides voting in Congress, one of my most important responsibilities is to help constituents solve problems that they encounter with any federal agency. . . .

Whenever you, members of your family, or friends have an opinion on any legislative issue or federal policy or program, please express your views in a letter to me and send it to my Washington office. **I'll give it my personal attention.**

Send your letter to:
Congressman George C. Wortley
229 Cannon House Office Building
Washington, D.C. 20515

Because my legislative duties require my presence in Washington on most weekdays throughout the year, the quickest way to get my help when experiencing any federal problem is to telephone, visit or write my district office in Syracuse. Should you experience a problem with the Internal Revenue Service, an undue delay in receiving a benefit check, or any difficulty with a federal agency, the members of my district staff are eager to try and solve your problems as quickly as possible.

Each member of my staff, in the 27th district and in Washington, is an authority in dealing with specific agencies. My staff helps constituents who encounter bureaucratic difficulties obtaining education grants, Social Security, pension and disability benefits. They help to resolve medicare, medicaid and workers' compensation claims. They provide advice to applicants seeking federal jobs, and assist veterans who are eligible for home loans and educational benefits. They help constituents in the military services to obtain emergency leaves and reassignments under certain hardship circumstances. Planning a visit to Washington? My staff can arrange White House and FBI tours. We fulfill requests for flags that have been flown over the U.S. Capitol as well as requests for federal documents. We also assist persons who seek small business loans and federal contracts.

If you live in Onondaga County and need assistance, please telephone or write my Syracuse district office. The telephone number is 423-5657. The office address is:

1269 Federal Building
Clinton Square
Syracuse, New York 13260

If you reside in Madison County, telephone 687-5027 or toll free, 1-800-462-8080. The address of my Madison County office is:

601 Lake Port Road
Chittenango, New York 13037

BOX 2–9 **Olives for the Troops**

The 1993 funding bill for the military included a directive by the House Appropriations Committee ordering the Defense Procurement Agency to buy more jumbo, colossal, and super colossal olives. No doubt they're tasty, but what could possibly explain the depth of the committee's solicitude in the troops' gustatory welfare? It turned out that Representative Vic Fazio, a central figure on both the appropriations Committee and the Campaign Committee that funds Democrats, was elected by an olive-rich California district. Its classic (vegetarian) pork leaves one wondering how many pecks of packed pimentos public procurement personnel are pressured to procure as well.

SOURCE: Based on an item in the *New York Times*, 3 October 1993.

Congressional efforts at pork barreling and casework are sometimes called micromanagement. Adherents to both the NPM and traditional managerial approaches to public administration generally denounce such legislative involvement because it places politics ahead of sound, universalistic administrative practices and values, such as efficiency and economy. From the political perspective, however, these practices are viewed as ways of making government more responsive to elected officials and their constituents. In fact, many members of Congress may view administrative agencies as more or less an extension of the legislature and its committees. The Administrative Procedure Act of 1946 clearly looks toward agencies to supplement legislation with rules. The more recently enacted Government Performance and Results Act of 1993 requires federal agencies to consult with Congress (read, committees and subcommittees) in establishing strategic plans that contain specific objectives and performance indicators.

The Courts: A Judicial Response to Contemporary Public Administration

The federal and state judiciaries have also reacted to the rise of public administrative power. It is common to find judges heavily involved in public administrative matters, such as equal opportunity in personnel administration and the management of prisons, public mental health facilities, and schools. Judges have also begun to question public administrators' expertise and to second-guess their decisions with some frequency. To a very large extent, **judicial activism** of this kind has been decried as inappropriate, undemocratic, a threat to federalism, and a breach of the separation of powers.[39] Yet it arises as a direct response to the growth of authority in the hands of public agencies.

One of the chief constitutional problems of the contemporary administrative state is that the separation of powers tends to collapse as more and more legislative and judicial activity takes place in public administrative

BOX 2–10 **Sweet and Sour Pork, County Style: The Top 50 Counties and Localities in Per Capita Federal Spending, Fiscal 1994**

	Per Capita Federal Spending		
Counties and Localities	*Per Capita*	*Counties and Localities*	*Per Capita*
1. Los Alamos County, N.M.	$63,014	26. Albany County, N.Y.	14,957
2. Falls Church, Va.	59,652	27. Prince George County, Va.	14,937
3. Fairfax city area, Va	47,701	28. Calhoun County, Ark.	14,652
4. Bryan County, Ga.	42,539	29. Jackson County, Miss.	14,503
5. Anderson County, Tenn.	38,843	30. Yukon-Koyukuk area, Alaska	14,095
6. Washington, D.C.	36,536	31. Clark County, Idaho	13,816
7. King George County, Va.	30,308	32. Hughes County, S.D.	13,615
8. Arlington County, Va.	30,130	33. Tooele County, Utah	13,552
9. Sagadahoc County, Maine	27,451	34. Houston County, Ga.	13,078
10. Bristol Bay Borough, Ark.	25,429	35. Juneau, Alaska	13,002
11. Geary County, Kan.	24,025	36. Greene County, Ohio	12,811
12. St. Louis, Mo.	23,278	37. Richmond, Va.	12,731
13. Martin County, Ind.	22,940	38. Williamsburg, Va.	12,460
14. Benton County, Wash.	18,815	39. Sacramento County, Calif.	12,441
15. Alexandria, Va.	18,703	40. Tishomingo County, Miss.	12,333
16. Rhea County, Tenn.	17,777	41. Pulaski County, Mo.	12,259
17. Franklin County, Ky.	16,638	42. Coffee County, Tenn.	12,156
18. Cole County, Mo.	16,623	43. Bonneville County, Idaho	11,868
19. Christian County, Ky.	16,510	44. Suffolk County, Mass.	11,864
20. Norfolk, Va.	16,179	45. Bent County, Colo.	11,744
21. Aiken County, S.C.	15,994	46. Camden County, Ga.	11,738
22. Madison County, Ala.	15,990	47. Bethel, Alaska	11,720
23. Box Elder County, Utah	15,786	48. Sangamon County, Ill.	11,713
24. Pike County, Ohio	15,124	49. Brevard County, Fla.	11,597
25. Manassas, Va.	14,976	50. Portsmouth, Va.	11,548

SOURCE: U.S. Bureau of the Census, Economics and Statistics Administration, as reprinted in the *Washington Post*, 18 April 1995, A15.

BOX 2–11 **Examples of Agricultural "Pork"—Sonar Catfish Counters, Grackle Control, Potatoes, Chickens, Beaver Damage, and More, Fiscal 1988: How'd Your State Do?**

State	Purpose	Appropriation
Arizona	Biotech lab	$13.3 million
Arkansas	Agricultural law center, University of Arkansas	493,000
Connecticut	Food marketing policy center	300,000
Florida	Sugarcane research	300,000
Georgia	Poultry lab addition	2.5 million
Hawaii	Damage control, sugarcane and macadamia nuts	240,000
Idaho	Common crupina eradication	121,000
Illinois	High-acid fertilizer	4.2 million
Iowa	National food center, University of Iowa	8.5 million
Kansas	World trade center, Wichita	5 million
Kentucky	Fruit and vegetable production	142,000
Louisiana	Commercial crawfish and red drum research, Louisiana State University	200,000
Maine	Potato breeding studies	36,000
Maryland	Avian flu research	150,000
Massachusetts	Belgian endive research	60,000
Michigan	Blueberry shoestring virus	92,000
Minnesota	Organic and low-cost farming	200,000
Mississippi	Sonar catfish counters	500,000
Missouri	Soybean cyst nematode studies	285,000
North Dakota	Chernobyl disaster impact, University of North Dakota	600,000
Ohio	Center for new uses for agricultural products	133,000
Oklahoma	International trade development center, Oklahoma State University	100,000
Oregon	Agricultural research center, Oregon State University	2.5 million
Pennsylvania	Milk consumption study	285,000
South Carolina	Peach tree short-life study	183,000
Texas	Grackle (blackbird) control	300,000
Vermont	Combating squirrel and rat damage to maple sap lines	60,000
Virginia	Equine critical care unit	483,000
Washington	Planning replacement of Yakima fruit laboratory	1 million
West Virginia	Poultry research center	3.7 million
Wisconsin	Study of beaver damage to trees	150,000

SOURCE: Kerry Koritsas, "The '88 Agriculture Appropriations: Where's the Pork?" *Washington Post*, 10 November 1987.

agencies in the executive branch. In the abstract, to say that these agencies make rules, enforce their rules, and adjudicate challenges to those rules may hardly sound like a matter of grave constitutional concern. But when these powers are exercised over specific individuals or corporations, a sense of unfairness and injustice may occur. For example, suppose an agency makes rules for eligibility to receive welfare benefits, enforces these by holding predawn raids on the homes of recipients, and then adjudicates challenges to this method of enforcement.[40] Or suppose an agency makes rules for licensing cable TV, denies a license to a would-be broadcaster, and upon challenge holds that the agency does in fact have the authority to do exactly what it did.[41] Or, to take a final example, suppose a personnel agency refuses to hire a member of a minority group, who then challenges its personnel rules on the grounds that they are racially discriminatory, only to be told by the agency itself after it holds a hearing that the rules are valid and have been properly followed.[42] These are all based on actual cases, and when public administrators act as legislature, prosecutor, judge, and jury in ways that are harmful to individuals or businesses, the judiciary, which is often viewed as the constitutional guardian of individuals' rights, may find it difficult to sit idly by.

Yet, from the late 1930s until the 1950s, this is largely what the courts did.[43] The federal judiciary, in particular, had been politically weakened by its opposition to the New Deal in the 1930s. After President Franklin D. Roosevelt threatened to "pack" the Supreme Court with justices more favorable to his approaches, the judiciary as a whole began to ignore the genuine constitutional problems posed by the vesting of legislative and judicial authority in executive branch administrative agencies. By the 1950s, however, neither the power of public administrators over individual citizens nor the injustices they perpetrated could be ignored. For example, during the "Red scare" of the late 1940s and 1950s, there were cases of federal employees losing their jobs, accused of "disloyalty" for having been readers of the *New York Times*, favoring racial integration, believing in the desirability of sex before marriage, or even having intelligent or clever friends.[44] Until the 1960s and 1970s, welfare recipients were subject to all manners of harassments, and anyone seeking an occupational license seemed to be almost completely at the mercy of petty administrative tyrants.

Since the 1950s, when the federal courts rekindled their interest in the actions of public administrators, the judiciary as a whole has responded to the rise of administrative power primarily in four ways. These have a great deal to do with the contemporary legal approach and legal constraints on public administration, and they also explain how the courts have become a full-fledged partner in seeking to control the direction of the administrative state.[45]

The Strengthening and Articulation of Constitutional Rights   The federal judiciary has "created" or had occasion to declare new constitutional rights for individuals as they come into contact with public administrators in some contexts, and it has strengthened individuals' rights in others. Although trea-

tises could be (and have been) written on these subjects, basically what the
courts have done is to provide individuals greater constitutional protections
when assuming the role of public employee or that of client or customer of
public administrative agencies. In both instances, the substantive, equal protection, and procedural constitutional rights of the individual have been
strengthened considerably. Prior to the 1950s, clients' and public employees'
rights were governed by the constitutional doctrine of privilege, which had
the effect of denying them virtually any protections against administrative infringements upon the civil rights and liberties normally held by United States
citizens. If they wanted a public sector job or a benefit, such as public housing, they had to accept virtually any and all conditions attached to it. Individuals can no longer be denied welfare benefits because they do not meet an
extended residency test, nor can they be denied unemployment compensation
because their religious beliefs preclude their acceptance of work on Satur-
days. They are also often entitled to due process when benefits are being
withdrawn or denied. Similarly, the right of public employees to speak out in
nonpartisan fashion on matters of political or administrative concern has
been upheld, as has their right to belong (or not belong) to associations, including political parties and labor unions. Public employees also enjoy extensive constitutional procedural protections when facing dismissals for causes
that would seriously damage their reputations, future employability, or infringe upon a property interest, such as tenure, that they hold in their jobs.
The courts have also afforded greater protection to prisoners and to people
confined to public mental health facilities. Indeed, the latter now have a constitutional right to treatment or training.[46] Street-level administration has
also been brought under some constitutional constraints.

Stricter Scrutiny of Administrative Decisions Although this policy is
somewhat haphazardly applied, the federal judiciary has begun to require
public administrators to explain the basis of their policy-making decisions
with greater precision. From the late 1930s until the 1970s, the courts tended
to pay great deference to the expertise of public administrators and consequently rarely questioned their decisions on technical or policy matters.
More recently, however, the judiciary has demanded that the substance of
agency decisions be logical. For instance, the United States Supreme Court
followed this approach in *FTC v. Sperry & Hutchinson* (1972), when it set aside
an FTC decision on the grounds that the agency's reasoning was illogical—
one could not rationally proceed from its premise to its conclusion. The
Court adhered to the same approach more recently in *Motor Vehicle Manufacturers Association v. State Farm* (1983).[47] Other important cases in this line, often called the "hard look" approach, include *Citizens to Preserve Overton Park
v. Volpe* (1971) and *Industrial Union Department, AFL-CIO v. American Petroleum Institute* (1980, discussed in Chapter 9).[48] By contrast, the Supreme
Court has decisively told the federal judiciary to grant agencies considerable
flexibility in their choice of rule-making procedures, statutory interpretation,
and enforcement decisions.[49]

Public Law Litigation or Remedial Law   In a far more complex development, the federal judiciary has altered the model of the traditional lawsuit in a fashion that makes it far easier for the courts to intervene in public administration. The new model is often called *public law litigation* or *remedial law.*[50] Roger Cramton is among many who have noted its significance for public administration. He asks us to "consider in the context of the Leviathan [administrative] State two models of judicial review of administrative action."[51] One is "the traditional model . . . of a restrained and sober second look at what government has done that adversely affects a citizen. The controversy is bipolar in character, with two parties opposing each other; the issues are narrow and well-defined; and the relief is limited and obvious."[52] He views judicial review in this model as an essential corrective to the "tunnel vision in which particular values are advanced and others are ignored" by public administrators socialized into particular organizations and charged with implementing some possibly very narrow aspect of public policy. However, this model has been viewed by the judiciary as a whole as too limiting because it does not enable the courts to be proactive in their influence on public administration.

Consequently, as Cramton observes, a newer attitude toward public administration developed. As one federal judge expressed it, "If there is a serious problem, and the legislature and executive don't respond, the courts have to act."[53] In Cramton's words, this approach leads to

> a second model of judicial review that is growing in acceptance and authority. This model of the judicial role has characteristics more of general problem-solving than of dispute resolution. . . . [There is] a modern tendency to view courts as modern handymen—as jacks of all trades available to furnish the answer to whatever may trouble us. "What is life? When does death begin? How should we operate prisons and hospitals? Shall we build nuclear power plants, and if so, where? Shall the Concorde fly to our shores?"[54]

Three major features of the remedial law model should be emphasized. First, it was developed by the courts themselves as a means of intervening in administrative operations.

Second, remedial law enables the judiciary to become directly involved in public management. For instance, in decreeing that public mental health facilities and prisons be brought up to constitutional standards, federal judges have used their powers to provide equitable relief to specify the maximum number of inmates or patients there can be per toilet and per shower; they have established minimum standards for square footage of space per individual in various rooms in such facilities; they have established permissible temperature ranges; they have directed the placement of guards; and, in one case, a judge even "ordered" that the management of the prison be improved immediately. The courts have also been heavily involved in public administration in other areas, including public schools.

Third, judicial involvement in public administration has budgetary ramifications. Consequently, the remedial law model enables judges to have an expanded impact on budgeting. For instance, in 1980, 48 percent of Boston's budgetary appropriations were "presided" over by federal and state judges seeking to reform aspects of public education, public housing, public personnel administration, jails, and care of the mentally retarded.[55]

The remedial law model of judicial review is a powerful tool for enabling the judiciary to assume direction of many aspects of public administration. Consequently, public administrators are likely to find themselves working with the judiciary in a way that was virtually unheard of only three decades ago.

Liability and Immunity   A final and equally dramatic aspect of the judiciary's response to the rise of the contemporary administrative state has been to reduce drastically public administrators' immunity from civil suits for money damages for breaches of individuals' constitutional rights. Traditionally, under American common law and with some broad general support from constitutional law, public administrators were absolutely immune from such suits. Under the doctrine of absolute immunity, a public administrator who abridged someone's constitutional rights, through racial discrimination, for instance, could not be sued for money damages by the injured individual. Or, as happens with some frequency, police, FBI, narcotics agents, and other law enforcement personnel might act in an overzealous manner, violating an individual's Fourth Amendment rights against unreasonable searches and seizures. Under the doctrine of absolute immunity, however, there would be virtually no effective recourse available to the injured party.

During the 1970s, the Supreme Court abandoned the prevailing approach of *absolute* immunity and substituted a *qualified* immunity. Although some public administrative actions—primarily those involving adjudicatory functions—still enjoy absolute immunity, today most public employees are potentially *personally* liable for any actions within the scope of their official duties that abridge the constitutional or federally protected legal rights of other individuals. In other words, the public administrator who unconstitutionally or illegally injures another person can be sued for damages, and if awarded, the public administrator is personally responsible for the settlement. It is important to grasp the connection between the changing presumption from immunity to liability and the creation of new constitutional rights for individuals vis-à-vis public administration, as discussed above. The Supreme Court has stated flatly that the greater liability of public administrators is a means of assuring that these officials will scrupulously avoid violating individuals' constitutional rights.[56] The Court has sought to assure that when in doubt, public administrators will err on the side of protecting constitutional rights. This approach is contained in the current standard for determining the scope of qualified immunity: in plain language, the public administrator is very likely to be personally liable if he or she violated constitutional or federal statutory rights of which a reasonable person would have known.[57]

The switch from a presumption of absolute immunity to a presumption of potential liability touched off a flurry of activity among public administrators.

Nobody likes to be sued, or to pay damages out of his or her pocket. Many sought legal insurance. Some probably quit their jobs and sought private sector employment. Others have complained bitterly that this aspect of the judicial response to the administrative state has made their jobs almost impossible. They are afraid to take action and they are afraid to remain inactive. The problem is compounded by the severe economic plight of many agencies and political jurisdictions, which is coupled with the continuing requirement that they meet their obligations to various groups under federal law, whether these be schoolchildren, prisoners, mental patients, the handicapped, members of disadvantaged minority groups, or others.

The Supreme Court is not oblivious to the problems involved, but it remains committed to the new standard of liability. Although the Court has held that state governments and agencies cannot be sued for money damages under federal law, officials at all governmental levels remain vulnerable to such suits and local governments may even be sued for failure to train their employees to protect individuals' constitutional rights.[58]

The public administrator is potentially liable if he or she violates someone's constitutional rights. But constitutional rights, as they now exist, are not simply engraved in the Constitution. As former Supreme Court Justice Lewis Powell has pointed out, constitutional law is "what the courts say it is."[59] At any given time, individual constitutional rights are a reflection of the judiciary's values and interpretation of constitutional history. Standards of individual civil rights and liberties, equal protection, and due process are forever undergoing change. Prior to 1954, racial segregation in public schools was permissible, pupils could be expelled without any established or fair procedure, public employees could be fired for "wrong thoughts," mental patients and prisoners could be "warehoused" under incredibly harsh and brutal conditions, and citizens generally had little or no legal protection against public administrative action denying them various benefits or occupational licenses. Today, the picture has radically changed as a result of newer judicial views of what the Constitution requires. The courts have created the present standard of public administrators' liability to force public administrators to be responsive not only to declared constitutional law, but also to constitutional values as well. The fact that there may be no specific precedent in the constitutional case law does not afford protection from liability today. The facts surrounding a public administrator's actions may never have arisen before.[60] They may never have been previously litigated. Or they may have been litigated at a time when the content of the constitutional law was clearly different. In such circumstances, the smart public administrator will not look simply to the most recent case, but rather will consider how the next one—the one he or she may be involved in— is likely to be decided. In order to do this effectively, public administrators must have a broad understanding of constitutional values and contemporary judicial philosophies. Public administrators must now be responsive to the judiciary's values, and therefore, the judiciary gains greater ability to exercise influence on the activities of the administrative state. (The relevance of constitutional values to public administration is discussed in Chapter 11.)

It should be evident that the judicial response to the rise of the contemporary administrative state considerably strengthens the legalistic approach to public administration. Public administrators find themselves working as partners with judges. They are under greater pressure to explain their decisions and actions to the courts. Knowledge of constitutional values, as expressed by the judiciary, becomes a positive job requirement for many public administrators. All this while members of the chief executive's establishment are demanding sound management and members of the legislature may be seeking favorable treatment for their constituents and districts. The job of the public administrator probably has never been more complicated.

Interest Groups

Organized interest groups have long been an important feature of American politics.[61] These organizations typically are established to represent the economic or social interests of a relatively well-defined group of people such as cotton farmers or sugar growers. There are literally thousands of such groups, representing everything from A (American Civil Liberties Union) to Z (zinc producers). A quick check of the Washington, D.C., phone book yields examples of groups representing bankers, bikers, physician's assistants, baseball fans, corngrowers, ornithologists, nonsmokers, sugarbeet growers, association executives, and many, many others.

Traditionally, interest groups lobbied in the legislature in an effort to convince its members to sponsor or vote for a bill that would be of benefit to the group's members. Conversely, they might try to convince a legislator to oppose a policy that might be harmful to their interests. Although much criticism has been levied at lobbyists, essentially they exercise First Amendment rights to freedom of speech and association, and to petition the government for a redress of grievances. As long as bribery and other corruption does not take place, the activities of pressure groups can be viewed as valuable in informing policy makers of where important interests stand on any given matter. In fact, despite much criticism of interest group politics, many Americans find such groups an efficient means for representing their points of view—more efficient in some cases than seeking to promote their policy objectives through electoral politics.

Naturally, as public administrators became more involved in agenda setting and policy formulation, interest group lobbying became more common in the executive branch. Nowadays, public administrators interact with representatives of perhaps a thousand or so interest groups. The number of "advisory committees" and the size of their overall membership have remained relatively stable since the early 1980s. In 1990, 60 federal departments and agencies supported 1,071 advisory committees totaling 22,391 members. The committees held 3,774 meetings and issued 972 reports. Whereas some committees have fairly broad concerns, the majority have a narrow focus.[62] Advisory committees frequently deal with specific geographic places, crops and foods (such as peanuts and raisins), diseases, and chemicals.

By 1972, the role of interest groups in pressing for their policy preferences was fully legitimized by the Federal Advisory Committee Act. This statute started from the premise that such committees are a useful source of opinion and information. The main purpose of the act was to improve the quality of interest group interaction with public administrative agencies by assuring that the lobbying process was representative. An important part of this act was the requirement that the official meetings between advisory committees and public administrators be open to the public.

The evidence to date is inconclusive, but it suggests that the Federal Advisory Committee Act of 1972 has fallen short of its goals of ensuring that the interaction of interest groups with public administrators be representative and open.[63] But the truly significant point is Congress's readiness to recognize that public administration should promote representativeness in its dealings with interest groups and, presumably, in its policy making. Traditionally, representation was the function of legislative bodies, such as the House of Representatives, not of executive branch agencies. This change captures the essence of the political approach to public administration that we discussed in the previous chapter. The lines between politics and administration become hopelessly blurred because "advisory committees are connected to administrative agencies, but they are established as frequently by Congress as by the agencies involved."[64] Moreover, as Henry Steck explains, "Congress and agencies look to advisory groups to introduce representational and participatory legitimacy into the administrative process."[65] Accordingly, "Advisory committees become a technique for reducing political uncertainty vis-à-vis clientele groups, stabilizing existing political relations, deflecting group opposition, securing group cooperation, and mobilizing political support."[66]

Interest groups not only interact with public administrators through the use of the advisory committees, they also lobby outright and work indirectly through the legislature. Their influence is greatest when for all practical purposes "The function of policy-making is often turned over to the private group in what amounts to a delegation [of administrative power to it]."[67]

Private interest groups can influence public power by gaining an informal veto power over appointments to the political executive positions in administrative agencies. In practice, this means that the leadership of many agencies, especially regulatory commissions, may come directly from the industry being regulated. In some ways, this is necessary if the appointees are to be familiar with the industry in question, but it also tends to turn would-be regulation into "collusion." In recent years, there has been concern that career civil servants and political appointees will be influenced in their decision making and enforcement activities by the opportunity to join private firms represented by interest groups and by the sometimes lavish hospitality and honoraria the latter provide at their annual or other general meetings. At the federal level, ethics legislation has sought to close the "revolving door" through which federal administrators or appointees and corporate executives change positions and to outlaw the acceptance of substantial job-related hospitality and honoraria.

Contemporary research points to several models of interest group influence.[68] The "iron triangle," also known as the "cozy triangle," is perhaps the classic model. Here, interest groups interact with agency bureaus and congressional (sub)committees. Relationships are generally mutually supportive and harmonious. The three corners of the triangle share a similar worldview. A second model contends that to the extent that iron triangles were once dominant, they are now much more permeable to competing interests and outside expertise in recent years. This is largely because public policy issues, such as environmental protection, have become denser in the sense that they are more complex and likely to affect a large number of interests. Where participants in these more open systems of influence are relatively limited, homogeneous, and stable, the pattern of interaction is called a "policy network." There is no common term for policy making involving a large number of groups and individuals who are heterogeneous and only weakly linked to one another. "Hollow cores" exist where "no interest groups, individual freelance lawyers or lobbyists, or government officials [are] providing much connective tissue across the [policy] domain."[69]

In all the models, interest groups track agency activity, seek access, provide administrators with information and perspectives, and try to influence their decision making, especially in the context of regulatory rule making. Jeffrey Berry, a leading analyst of interest group politics, summarizes the overall relationship between administrators and group representatives as follows:

> Agency officials have strong incentives . . . to cooperate with groups that share at least some of their policy objectives. . . . Strong clientele support can help them win larger budgets in Congress or protect them from would-be budget cutters at the Office of Management and Budget. It can also help them win approval for new policy initiatives. . . . Interest group representatives approach a potentially receptive agency from much the same perspective. They want to build an enduring tie and not one that is issue-specific. Administrators, however, also value autonomy and balance their desire for outside support with their desire to make decisions themselves.
>
> As in congressional advocacy, lobbyists know that their effectiveness is only as good as their credibility. In their personal presentations to administrators, many lobbyists see their approach being much the same as with legislators or their staffs. . . . Some indicate, however, their presentations are even more factual, with more data for administrators than for those on Capitol Hill.[70]

Grant McConnell points out that the overall system of interaction with interest groups leads to discrimination against two types of interests. One is that of weak minorities, who are unable to organize and gain access to the system of representation through interaction with public administrators. Nonunionized, minimum, or subminimum wage employees are an example. The other is the general public interest, which is too diffuse and not salient enough to any particular group to gather sufficient support to be actively promoted in this fashion.[71]

The latter problem has been the target of public interest groups. A public interest group has been defined as "one that seeks a collective good, the achievement of which will not selectively and materially benefit the membership or activists of the organization."[72] Yet when discussing public interest groups, it should not be forgotten that traditional interest groups often promote what they believe to be in the public interest. Therefore the distinction is not perfect. Among the organizations generally considered to be public interest groups are the Consumers Union, Common Cause, the League of Women Voters, and a variety of public interest research groups.

Since the 1970s, public interest groups have gained influence, often by working with public administrative agencies or for reform of administrative processes. They have employed the provisions of the Administrative Procedure Act of 1946 to gain access to bureaucratic decision making by filing views, data, and opinions concerning proposed agency rules and policy changes. They have also used the Freedom of Information Act of 1966 and the National Environmental Policy Act of 1969 as vehicles to influence and challenge the actions of public administrators. Although much of the process is technical, obscure, and highly legalistic, it is precisely through the day-to-day monitoring of the *Federal Register*, the submission of opinions, and the participation in public agency decision making that public interest groups can have a significant impact.

The Public

Promotion of the public interest is certainly a prime goal of contemporary public administration in the United States. But defining the public interest is often difficult. Public administrators, like all human beings, are limited in their ability to foresee all the immediate and long-term consequences of their policy choices. They are subject to a number of influences that may distort their perception and definition of the public interest. Public interest groups may come forth in an effort to correct this tendency, but they may also represent a rather select perspective. Their membership appears to be overwhelmingly composed of middle-class activists. So, the question arises, how can the public respond to the growth of administrative power?

To date the public's reaction to the rise of the administrative state appears to lack overall coherence. It involves elements of opposition, satisfaction, support for specific programs, and interest in reforms. Chapter 10 is devoted to this subject. Here, it should be pointed out that public opinion regarding public administration is complex, divided, and perhaps even inconsistent. Despite political rhetoric that would suggest otherwise, public bureaucracy is by no means universally or consistently opposed. The public is aware that administrative agencies are now a central component of government and it recognizes that the citizenry is dependent upon them. Politically, the public seems to demand candidates who can "manage" bureaucracy. Sometimes it favors cutting back on public administrative activities. However, there is limited support for abandoning a host of regulatory functions intended to protect the public's safety, including aircraft and food and drug inspection, for example. As a practical matter, public administrators may accurately view public opinion as both a constraint on and a stimulus for a variety of administrative actions. This is precisely a point made by Woodrow Wilson, more than a century ago, in his famous essay entitled "The Study of Administration": "In order to make any advance at all we must instruct and persuade a multitudinous monarch called public opinion."[73]

Political Parties

Historically, there has been a strong link between political parties and public administration.[74] In many countries, including the United States, political parties promoted the growth of large-scale public administration as a means of creating and securing patronage positions for their members. During the nineteenth century, this **spoils system** was instrumental in both the development of American political parties and in the increasing size of several public agencies. However, patronage politics led to widespread political corruption and administrative inefficiency and mismanagement. In the effort to remove the pernicious effects of partisan politics from public administration through civil service reforms, political parties were weakened in an organizational sense.

Civil service reforms mandating the use of merit systems were instituted in the federal government and some states and cities in the 1880s. The rationale behind these was that public administration was essentially a field of business, and consequently ought to be run according to businesslike, managerial principles. Whoever heard of a business firing its employees every four years on the grounds that they held their places long enough and ought to give someone else a turn, the reformers asked with indignation and derision. There is no doubt that merit-oriented reforms vastly improved the honesty, morality, efficiency, economy, and administrative effectiveness of public agencies. But they also weakened the political parties.

The parties' first response was to turn to the rising industrial sector for support. It seemed that patronage could be replaced by large-scale financial donations—in return for various policy and other considerations, of course. Soon the Senate became known as the millionaires' club, and the politics associated with patronage and the "common man" of President Andrew Jackson's day rapidly receded. Yet reliance on large monetary contributions also caused corruption, and from the turn of the century until the 1920s, several political reforms were inspired by the Progressive movement. Especially important among these was the institution of the primary election and the promotion of restrictions on the political activities of public employees. Further, cities were reorganized under the city management model of urban government created during this period. Many other administrative operations were depoliticized by being organized as "public authorities" for the management of bridges, parks, ports, and other functions. Such reforms were aimed at destroying political machines and political bossism. Although largely successful in this regard, they also further weakened the parties. By the 1930s and 1940s, when the federal government passed the Hatch Acts, regulating the political activities of federal and some categories of state and local public employees, some members of Congress argued that limiting the participation of such employees in political conventions would lead to the total destruction of political parties.

Reforms along these lines have had the impact not only of weakening the political parties, but also of freeing public administration from their influence and control. Merit systems prevent partisan intrusion in the selection, assignment, promotion, dismissal, and general treatment of public employees. It is actually illegal to ask a federal civil servant or an applicant for such a position what political party he or she belongs to. Political officials have long complained of the inability to take charge of administrative operations that result from the lack of power to make civil service assignments on a partisan basis. They feel that members of the opposition party are forever subverting their electoral mandates. In at least one sense, though, public administrators may be nonpartisan, as former president Gerald Ford explained: "There are bureaucratic fiefdoms out in the states or in various regions [that] have been disregarding Presidents for years, both Democratic and Republican."[75] Sometimes this leads politicians to engage in illegal maneuvers or questionable practices to get around "all the civil service restrictions." On balance, however, the political community has opted for politically neutral public personnel administration as opposed to pronounced partisan intrusion in public administration. The Supreme Court has even held that patronage dismissals from the public service can be unconstitutional infringements upon the public employee's First and Fourteenth Amendment rights and that the government bears the burden of showing that partisanship is positively related to on-the-job performance when seeking to make such dismissals. Partisanship in transfers, promotions, and other ordinary personnel actions has also been found to be unconstitutional (see Box 2–12). In this area, then, we see both the conflict and the congruence of managerial, political, and legal considerations pertaining to public administration.

Are the political parties totally powerless to influence public administration under these conditions? The answer is no, as the 1994 Republican "Contract with America" demonstrated. A unified party in control of the legislature can do much to change agencies' directions and to reorganize administrative operations. Political executives also exercise influence over top-level career public administrators. But when all is said and done, where strong merit systems prevail, political parties are a relatively limited channel for exercising control over public administration. Of course, in places where political machines and bossism still prevail, parties continue to maintain a heavy presence in administrative affairs despite laws and general constitutional decisions to the contrary.

State and Local Governments

It would take at least a large volume to discuss comprehensively the impact of administrative growth on the structure and policy making of state and local

---

BOX 2–12 **The "Unconstitutionalizing" of Political Patronage**

In *Elrod v. Burns* (1976), the Supreme Court held that patronage dismissals of rank-and-file employees of the Cook County, Illinois, Sheriff's Office were unconstitutional. Justice Brennan announced the judgment of the Court. He expressed the view that "patronage dismissals severely restrict political belief and association. Though there is a vital need for government efficiency and effectiveness, such dismissals are on balance not the least restrictive means for fostering that end. There is also a need to insure that policies which the electorate has sanctioned are effectively implemented. That interest can be fully satisfied by limiting patronage dismissals to policy-making positions. . . . [A]ny contribution of patronage dismissals to the democratic process does not suffice to override their severe encroachment on First Amendment freedoms." In dissent, Justice Powell admonished that "history and long prevailing practice across the country support the view that patronage hiring practices make a sufficiently substantial contribution to the practical functioning of our democratic system to support their relatively modest intrusion on First Amendment interests. The judgment today unnecessarily constitutionalizes another element of American life. . . ." *Branti v. Finkel* (1980) went even further in making patronage dismissals unconstitutional. A majority of the Supreme Court held that because such dismissals infringe on First Amendments rights, "the ultimate inquiry is not whether the label 'policymaker' or 'confidential' fits a particular position; rather, the question is whether the hiring authority can demonstrate that party affiliation is an appropriate requirement for the effective performance of the public office involved."

Patronage was made even tougher, if not altogether impossible, in *Rutan v. Republican Party of Illinois* (1990). There the Court held that "the rule of *Elrod* and *Branti* extends to promotion, transfer, recall, and hiring decisions based on party affiliation and support. . . ." Together, these decisions essentially constitutionalize the goal of the nineteenth-century civil service reformers, who sought to take partisan politics out of the civil service and the civil service out of partisan politics.

SOURCES: *Elrod v. Burns*, 427 U.S. 347 (1976); *Branti v. Finkel*, 445 U.S. 506 (1980); *Rutan v. Republican Party of Illinois*, 110 S. Ct. 2729 (1990).

---

governments. Although there are clear parallels to the responses to the federal administrative state, as outlined in this chapter, there are also differences. And there is remarkable variation. More space is devoted to state and local governments in the next chapter. In general, the following observations seem pertinent here.[76] First, the gubernatorial office has been strengthened as a means of providing governors with greater managerial and policy direction over administrative agencies. In over forty states, governors possess a line-item veto, as noted previously. Many also make appointments to 50 to 100 or so top administrative posts, often subject to legislative confirmation, and hundreds, if not thousands, more appointments to citizen boards and commissions.

The governorship has also become increasingly institutionalized and professionalized.[77] Second, state governments have been reorganized, largely with a view toward the consolidation of functions and reduction in the number of administrative units. However, as in the case of the federal government, a great deal of fragmentation remains. Third, the extent of legislative oversight of administration and delegation of authority to it varies widely. Only a handful of states continue to hold biennial rather than annual legislative sessions. However, in some states, sessions are relatively brief and legislatures tend to leave administrative matters to the governor and his or her appointees. In about a dozen states, however, legislative committees can veto agency rules, which strengthens their involvement in administrative matters. Fourth, there are also considerable differences in the impact of state courts on administration. Strong state supreme courts, as in New Jersey, for example, have been deeply engaged in large-scale educational and/or prison reform. Finally, the overall context of administration differs, as noted by Bonfield and Asimow:

> Federal agencies are, in general, much larger and better financed and staffed than state agencies. On the whole, state agencies deal with less affluent, less influential, and less well educated people than federal agencies, and handle matters of smaller economic value than those handled by federal agencies. Persons dealing with state agencies are also less likely to be represented by a lawyer than persons dealing with federal agencies. State agencies are closer to the people and usually have smaller constituencies that can more easily communicate with them than federal agencies. In addition, state constitutions often differ significantly from the federal Constitution in important particulars that relate to their respective administrative processes. State and federal constitutions often differ in the way in which they create administrative units within governments, allocate authority among units, and impose procedural or substantive limits on those units. For example, some state agencies are created directly by their state constitution; and some state agency heads are directly elected by the people.[78]

Some state constitutions also create rights in the administrative context, including a right to public education.

It is more hazardous to generalize about local governmental responses to large-scale administration because they vary extensively. For the most part, these governments are becoming more executive-oriented and professional, though not necessarily in response to administrative pressures alone. It is now common to rely on county executives and city managers to act as the chief administrative officers of these governments.

CONCLUSION

The American administrative state has developed in response to a host of factors, including political, managerial, and legalistic concerns. There is no doubt that the growth of public administration has enabled governments to exercise greater influence over the society and the economy. However, contemporary public administration poses several problems. One is the question of according to which principles public administration should be organized—political, managerial, legal, or in what combination of these? Another problem is whether the administrative state can be adequately controlled by elected public officials or political processes in general. Yet another concerns the proper role of the judiciary in public administration and whether contemporary public administrators can harmoniously incorporate the judiciary's constitutional values. The presidential, legislative, and judicial responses to the rise of the administrative state have certainly enhanced their influence over it. But they have also promoted the development of a large Executive Office of the President that is hard to manage effectively, a proliferation of subcommittees and staff in Congress that has fragmented the legislative process and made it difficult for the institution to act in a coordinated fashion, and a judiciary that is often heavily involved in the thicket of administrative micromanagement. Overarching all of these concerns is the major issue of the public's relationship to government in the contemporary administrative age. Finally, although not stressed here, the cost of running the administrative state has become increasingly problematic—hence the widespread desire to reduce taxes and deficits and to balance budgets.

If the political community knew how to solve some of these problems and were willing to do so, American politics would be considerably different. In truth, however, lasting solutions have been elusive and some of the problems consequently appear intractable. The constitutional separation of powers places most public administration in the United States under three sometimes competing branches with different institutional and political interests. It complicates public administration immensely and makes fundamental reforms difficult. Federalism and intergovernmental relations, the topics of the next chapter, add further to the challenges public administrators face.

NOTES

1. Lester Salamon, "The Rise of Third Party Government: Implications for Public Management," in Donald Kettl, *Third Party Government and the Public Manager* (Washington, D.C.: National Academy of Public Administration, 1987), 12.
2. James Q. Wilson, "The Rise of the Bureaucratic State," *The Public Interest* 41 (Fall 1975): 77–103.
3. Ibid., 82.
4. Donald Warwick, *A Theory of Public Bureaucracy* (Cambridge, Mass.: Harvard University Press, 1975), 7–8.
5. Wilson, "The Rise of the Bureaucratic State," 89–91, 95–96.
6. Ibid., 96–97.
7. Lawrence Friedman, *A History of American Law* (New York: Simon & Schuster, 1973), 458.
8. James Freedman, *Crisis and Legitimacy* (New York: Cambridge University Press, 1978).

9. Arthur Bonfield and Michael Asimow, *State and Federal Administrative Law* (St. Paul, Minn.: West, 1989), chap. 1.

10. Walter Adams and James Brock, "Why Flying Is Unpleasant," *New York Times*, 6 August 1987.

11. Al Gore, *From Red Tape to Results: Creating a Government That Works Better & Costs Less: The Report of the National Performance Review* (Washington, D.C.: Government Printing Office, 1993).

12. Max Weber, *From Max Weber: Essays in Sociology*, trans. and ed. by H. H. Gerth and C. W. Mills (New York: Oxford University Press, 1958), 228.

13. Honoré de Balzac, *Les Employées*, 1836. Quoted in Martin Albrow, *Bureaucracy* (New York: Praeger, 1970), 18.

14. Quoted in Grant McConnell, *Private Power and American Democracy* (New York: Knopf, 1966), 286.

15. Thomas E. Cronin, *The State of the Presidency* (Boston: Little, Brown, 1975), 27.

16. Ibid., 28.

17. James Bryce, *The American Commonwealth* (New York: Putnam, 1959 [originally published in 1888]).

18. Gore, *From Red Tape to Results*, iii.

19. Discussion with John Kamensky, NPR Deputy Project Director, April 1995.

20. Richard Neustadt, *Presidential Power* (New York: Wiley, 1969), 9.

21. Quoted in George C. Edwards III and Stephen J. Wayne, *Presidential Leadership* (New York: St. Martin's, 1985), 351.

22. Robert Pear, "The Policy Wars: Those to Whom 'Battle Royal' Is Nothing New," *New York Times*, 28 July 1987.

23. *Humphrey's Executor v. U.S.*, 295 U.S. 602 (1935), is the classic example.

24. Mareno, Angel, "Presidential Coordination of the Independent Regulatory Process," *Administrative Law Journal of the American University* 8 (1994): 461–516.

25. Stephen Wayne, *The Legislative Presidency* (New York: Harper & Row, 1978), 59–60.

26. Stephen Barr, "When the Job Gets Old after 2 Years," *Washington Post*, 2 June 1994, A21.

27. Joseph W. Bartlett and Douglas N. Jones, "Managing a Cabinet Agency: Problems of Performance at Commerce," *Public Administration Review* 34 (January/February 1974): 63–64.

28. Richard Nathan, "The Reagan Presidency in Domestic Affairs," in *The Reagan Presidency: An Early Assessment*, ed. Fred I. Greenstein (Baltimore: Johns Hopkins University Press, 1983), 71.

29. Ibid.

30. Ibid., 48–81. See also Laurence Lynn, Jr., "The Reagan Administration and the Renitent Bureaucracy," in *The Reagan Presidency and the Governing of America*, ed. Lester Salamon and Michael Lund (Washington, D.C.: Urban Institute Press, 1985), 339–370, especially 345–348.

31. National Commission on the Public Service, *Leadership for America* (Lexington, Mass.: Lexington Books, 1990), 16–19.

32. Paul Light, *Thickening Government* (Washington, D.C.: Brookings Institution, 1995).

33. See Burdett Loomis, *The Contemporary Congress* (New York: St. Martin's Press, 1996), chaps. 5–6, for recent and historical statistics on Congress.

34. Michael Malbin, "Congressional Committee Staffs: Who's in Charge Here?" *The Public Interest* 47 (Spring 1977): 36.

35. Harold Seidman and Robert Gilmour, *Politics, Position, and Power*, 2d ed. (New York: Oxford University Press, 1975), 38–68.

36. Matthew McCubbins and Thomas Schwartz, "Congressional Oversight Overlooked: Police Patrols versus Fire Alarms," *American Journal of Political Science* 28 (1984): 165–179.

37. R. Douglas Arnold, *Congress and the Bureaucracy* (New Haven, Conn.: Yale University Press, 1979), 207.

38. Kenneth Cooper, "The House Freshmen's First Choice," *Washington Post*, 5 January 1993, A13.

39. See David H. Rosenbloom and Rosemary O'Leary, *Public Administration and Law*, 2d ed. (New York: Marcel Dekker, 1997); and James D. Carroll, "The New Juridical Federalism and the Alienation of Public Policy and Administration," *American Review of Public Administration* 16 (1982): 89–105.

40. See *Parrish v. Civil Service Commission*, 425 P.2d 233 (1967).

41. *United States v. South Western Cable Co.*, 392 U.S. 157 (1968).

42. See Robert Vaughn, *The Spoiled System* (New York: Charterhouse, 1975), for an analysis of this problem.

43. Martin Shapiro, *The Supreme Court and Administrative Agencies* (New York: Free Press, 1968).

44. See David H. Rosenbloom, *Federal Service and the Constitution* (Ithaca, N.Y.: Cornell University Press, 1971), chap. 6.

45. For a full discussion, see Rosenbloom and O'Leary, *Public Administration and Law*.

46. See Rosenbloom and O'Leary, *Public Administration and Law*, and the following cases: *Shapiro v. Thompson*, 394 U.S. 618 (1969); *Sherbert v. Verner*, 374 U.S. 398 (1963); *Hobbie v. Appeals Commission*, 480 U.S. 136 (1987); *Goldberg v. Kelly*, 397 U.S. 254 (1970); *Pickering v. Board of Education*, 391 U.S. 563 (1968); *Rankin v. McPherson*, 483 U.S. 378 (1987); *Cleveland Board of Education v. Loudermill*, 470 U.S. 532 (1985); *Wyatt v. Stickney*, 325 F. Supp. 781 (1971); *Youngberg v. Romeo*, 457 U.S. 307 (1982).

47. *FTC v. Sperry & Hutchinson Co.*, 405 U.S. 233 (1972); *Motor Vehicle Mfg. Ass'n. v. State Farm*, 463 U.S. 29 (1983).

48. *Citizens to Preserve Overton Park v. Volpe*, 401 U.S. 402 (1971); *Industrial Union Department, AFL-CIO v. American Petroleum Institute*, 448 U.S. 607 (1980).

49. *Chevron v. NRDC*, 467 U.S. 837 (1984); *Vermont Yankee Nuclear Power Corporation v. NRDC*, 435 U.S. 519 (1978).

50. See Abram Chayes, "The Role of the Judge in Public Law Litigation," *Harvard Law Review* 89 (1976): 1281–1316; and Robert Wood and Clement Vose, *Remedial Law* (Amherst, Mass.: University of Massachusetts Press, 1990).

51. Roger Cramton, "Judicial Lawmaking and Administration in the Leviathan State," *Public Administration Review* 36 (September/October 1976): 552.

52. Ibid.

53. Ibid., 554.

54. Ibid., 552.

55. Robert Turner, "Governing from the Bench," *The Boston Globe Magazine*, 8 November 1981, 12 ff.

56. *Carlson v. Green*, 446 U.S. 14, 21 (1980).

57. See Rosenbloom and O'Leary, *Public Administration and Law*, chap. 8, for a more detailed discussion.

58. Among the key cases are *City of Canton v. Harris*, 489 U.S. 387 (1989), *Will v. Michigan Department of State Police*, 109 S. Ct. 2304 (1989); and *Hafer v. Melo*, 502 U.S. 21 (1991).

59. *Owen v. City of Independence*, 445 U.S. 622, 669 (1980).

60. See *Pembaur v. Cincinnati*, 475 U.S. 469 (1986), for an example.

61. See Jeffrey Berry, *The Interest Group Society*, 2d ed. (Glenview, Ill.: Scott, Foresman, 1989). See also Samuel Krislov and David H. Rosenbloom, *Representative Bureaucracy and the American Political System* (New York: Praeger, 1981).

62. Henry J. Steck, "Politics and Administration: Private Advice for Public Purpose in a Corporatist Setting," in *Politics and Administration*, ed. Jack Rabin and James Bowman (New York: Marcel Dekker, 1984), 158, 160; and Mary Palladino, "Ensuring Coverage, Balance, Openness, and Ethical Conduct for Advisory Committees under the Federal Advisory Committee Act," *Administrative Law Journal of the American University* 5 (1991): 231–274.

63. Krislov and Rosenbloom, *Representative Bureaucracy*, 93–97.

64. Steck, "Politics and Administration," 159.

65. Ibid., 161.

66. Ibid.

67. McConnell, *Private Power and American Democracy*, 162–163.

68. See Robert Salisbury, John Heinz, Robert Nelson, and Edward Laumann, "Triangles, Networks, and Hollow Cores: The Complex Geometry of Washington Interest Representation," in Mark Petracca, ed., *The Politics of Interests* (Boulder, Co.: Westview, 1992), 130–149; and Robert Hrebener and Ruth Scott, *Interest Group Politics in America*, 2d ed. (Englewood Cliffs, N.J.: Prentice-Hall, 1990), chap. 8.

69. Salisbury et al., "Triangles, Networks, and Hollow Cores," 149.

70. Berry, *Interest Group Society*, 150.

71. McConnell, *Private Power and American Democracy*, Chap. 4.

72. Jeffrey Berry, quoted in Krislov and Rosenbloom, *Representative Bureaucracy*, 170.

73. Woodrow Wilson, "The Study of Administration," *Political Science Quarterly* 56 (December 1941): 491 (originally published in 1887).

74. A thoughtful discussion in the U.S. context can be found in Herbert Storing, "Political Parties and the Bureaucracy," in *Political Parties, USA*, ed. Robert A. Goldwin (Chicago: Rand McNally, 1964).

75. Edwards and Wayne, *Presidential Leadership*, 360.

76. For a general discussion of state and local administration see Frank J. Thompson, ed., *Revitalizing State and Local Public Service* (San Francisco: Jossey-Bass, 1993).

77. Larry Sabato, *Goodbye to Good-Time Charlie: The American Governorship Transformed*, 2d ed. (Washington, D.C.: CQ Press, 1983).

78. Bonfield and Asimow, *State and Federal Administrative Law*, 3.

ADDITIONAL READING

ARON, CINDY. *Ladies and Gentlemen of the Civil Service*. New York: Oxford University Press, 1987.

PATTERSON, BRADLEY. *The Ring of Power*. New York: Basic Books, 1988.

SKOWRONEK, STEPHEN. *Building a New American State*. New York: Cambridge University Press, 1982.

STILLMAN, RICHARD. *The American Bureaucracy*. Chicago: Nelson-Hall, 1996.

WHITE, LEONARD D. *The Federalists; The Jeffersonians; The Jacksonians; The Republican Era*. New York: Free Press, 1965.

WILSON, JAMES Q. *Bureaucracy*. New York: Basic Books, 1989.

STUDY QUESTIONS

1. The current reach of public administration is considered too broad by some people. Can you identify public administrative functions and programs that you think deal with matters that should be left up to private individuals, families, and/or private groups? What distinguishes these activities from those you think are appropriately dealt with through public administration?

2. Are there areas of social or economic life that you believe require more governmental involvement through public administration?

3. Think about a recent political campaign with which you are familiar. Did the candidates express concern with matters of public administration? If so, from what perspectives? How might a practicing public administrator respond to their campaign statements?

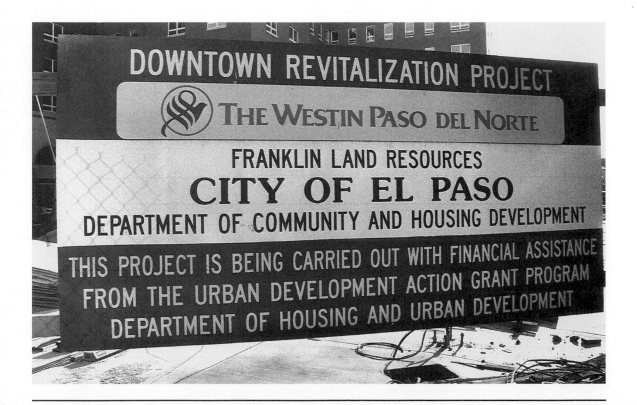

CHAPTER 3

Federalism and Intergovernmental Relations:

The Structure of the American Administrative State

Governing the United States is one of the most complicated activities in the world. The nation has some 87,000 governments within its boundaries. Their relationships are sometimes cooperative, sometimes competitive, and sometimes even conflictual. Public administrators often face the challenging task of coordinating the programs of several governments with one another in a variety of related policy areas. This chapter explores federalism, intergovernmental relations, and the administrative structure of the major forms of governments found in the United States. The maze of governments form a substantial part of the political and legal environments in which public administrators work.

The complicated and fragmented nature of the American administrative state is partly a response to the growing complexity of economic and social life but also has roots in the system of federalism itself. Patriotic spirits are fond of referring to the United States as the "land of the free and the home of the brave." But by generally accepted count, the land of the free is regulated and served by some 87,000 governments—and it does indeed take some bravery to support these governments financially and to find one's way through the maze of complicated interrelationships. Although we sometimes think of the separation of powers as being manifested in the division of governmental authority among legislative, executive, and judicial branches, authority and jurisdiction are also divided up among a national government, 50 state governments, over 3,000 counties, about 19,000 municipalities, 17,000 townships, 15,000 school districts, and more than 33,000 special districts.[1] The management, politics, and laws of federalism and intergovernmental relationships are so perplexing that they have emerged as areas of activity and study to which some have devoted their working lives. The typical citizen escapes with a lesser burden—on average he or she works five months a year just to pay for federal, state, and local governments.[2] Obviously, governmental decentralization and fragmentation are key areas of concern for public administrators and a feature of governance that they sometimes find quite frustrating.

WHY FEDERALISM?

Federalism is a common feature of contemporary nation-states. It is the division of political authority between a central government and state or provincial governments. Canada, Australia, Nigeria, and the United States are leading examples. In each of these nations, there are states or provinces that have a substantial measure of legal or constitutional sovereignty, (supreme political authority). However, in each case, these units of government are also subordinate in many major legal/constitutional respects to a central government. Federalism stands in contrast to "unitary" political systems in which there are not quasi-sovereign governmental units coexisting with the national government. England and Israel are examples. In such nations, all sovereignty is exercised by the national government, which in democracies is viewed as the agent of the people, who are the sovereign. Unitary governments may delegate administrative and political authority to municipalities or other governmental bodies, but these bodies have no inherent sovereignty or any authority other than that which is given to them by the national government. Delegations of this type constitute political and administrative "decentralization," but not federalism.

Federalism represents a political solution to a vexing political problem. There are obvious advantages to the formation of *large* nation-states, such as the United States. Such nations are likely to be powerful economically and militarily. They will be more likely to mobilize effectively large-scale human effort to pursue their vision of "the good life" and the just society. They are likely to have a greater human and physical resource base than smaller nations. Their large scale may also enable them to develop more vigorous economies within their territories. There is likely to be less internal strife among the units of a single nation than there would be if that nation were divided into separate countries having full sovereignty and autonomy. These points can be illustrated by imagining for a moment that the United States were not "one nation, indivisible," but rather fifty separate, fully autonomous, and fully sovereign nations, each with its own armed forces and system of tariffs. Clearly our economic, military, and civic lives would be radically different under such circumstances.

But for all the advantages that large size can bring to nation-states, it can also have some important drawbacks. The main ones concern representation and keeping the parts together. These two concerns are often related. Many federal nations are "compound" political communities, that is, they are made up of *territorially based* and heterogeneous ethnic, tribal, racial, religious, linguistic, or other social groups imbued with different cultural values. Before its breakup and reorganization in the early 1990s, the Soviet Union was an example. There, a plethora of ethnic and religious groups are involved, including Russians, Ukrainians, Latvians, Lithuanians, Estonians, Georgians, and several Central Asian and Turkish populations. A multitude of languages is spoken and, although the Soviet national government opposed it, a number of religions are practiced. To a large extent, these diverse groups were organized into Soviet Republics, which were the political subunits of the Soviet Union as a whole.

Federalism in compound nations provides a measure of representation and political autonomy for ethnic and other territorially based cultural groups. Yet a large nation might also turn to federalism as a means of providing representation to a homogeneous population or one whose heterogeneity is not territorially based. The United States is a leading example here. In large part the United States relies on federalism because of the historical pattern of its early settlement by Europeans. Thirteen colonies were carved out and chartered. Initially there was some important religious and linguistic diversity among them. But soon English became the common language and a sense of being "American" developed. During the Revolutionary War, a *confederal* government was formed. Under this approach, the former colonies, now *states*, had a great deal of independent authority. A few years after the conclusion of the war, the current federal government was established. The main impetus for moving away from the confederal government seems to have been economic and military: trade among the states faced a number of barriers and the national government seemed too weak to deal with military threats posed by various European nations and Indian tribes.

Even if the states had no history of independence from one another, the large geographic size of the territories claimed by the United States might have been a barrier to the formation of a unitary nation in 1789, when the present Constitution was put into effect. Communication and the exercise of national authority on a local level would have been difficult. But the Constitution's framers were also concerned with another problem. How could a large population be represented by a single government? To be responsive, and effective, it was thought, elected or appointed representatives must know the people they are representing. But how many people can one individual know? A single government seeking to represent a large population would be confronted with a dilemma. On the one hand, a large number of representatives could be elected. But then the national legislature would have to be very large, perhaps too large to be effective. Alternatively, a smaller number of representatives could be relied upon. This would make the legislature manageable, but it would also tend to detract from the quality of representation because one individual would be responsible for representing a large number of citizens.

In order to accommodate the entrenched belief in state sovereignty and to deal with the representational problem, the framers invented a form of federalism incorporating three central features. First, the states would retain sovereignty in some spheres, and more states would eventually be created from the lands under national control. The Constitution expressly identifies the powers vested in the national government, and the Tenth Amendment, ratified in 1791, specifies: "The powers not delegated to the United States by the Constitution, nor prohibited by it to the States, are reserved to the States respectively, or to the people." Article IV protects the territorial integrity of the states by prohibiting their division or combination without the consent of their own legislatures (and Congress). (But the territory itself may be in dispute. See Box 3–1.) Second, a bicameral Congress was created in which one chamber, the Senate, provides each state with equal representation. The Senate also has the power to approve treaties, which is in part a vestige of the sovereignty of the states. Even today, the Senate can be viewed as a protector of state sovereignty. Third, the national government would have direct power over citizens, rather than having to act upon them through the state governments; accordingly, the citizenry would be represented directly in the House of Representatives. (In yet another vestige of state sovereignty, prior to the ratification of the Seventeenth Amendment in 1913, the Senate was not directly elected by the population; instead, senators were appointed by the state governments.)

This arrangement goes a long way toward resolving the representational dilemma. By vesting a good deal of political authority in small governmental units (the states), it enhances the likelihood that governmental representatives will actually represent the will of the people on important matters. For example, the states have constitutional authority to provide public education, public safety, and roads. They have authority to tax, to zone, to define crimes and punishments, to charter corporations, and to engage in a great many other functions. Nowadays, some of these functions are provided in conjunction with the federal government. They are also constrained by the Fourteenth Amendment's guarantees of due process and equal protection of the laws. But historically, the solution to the representational problem was thought to be allowing local people to control the governance of local matters. Sometimes this idea is discussed in terms of "grassroots" democracy

---

BOX 3–1 One Nation, Indivisible, with Many Borders

[469 US 504]
UNITED STATES
v.
MAINE et al. (Rhode Island and New York Boundary Case)
469 US 504, 83 L Ed 2d 998, 105 S Ct 992
[No. 35 Original]
Argued November 26, 1984. Decided February 19, 1985.

Decision: Long Island Sound and Block Island Sound held to constitute juridical bay under Convention on Territorial Sea and Contiguous Zone.

SUMMARY

The United States brought an action against the states that border the Atlantic Ocean, invoking the original jurisdiction of the United States Supreme Court, in order to determine whether the United States had exclusive rights to the seabed and subsoil underlying the ocean beyond 3 geographical miles from each state's coastline. That action resulted in a determination that the states held interests in the seabeds only to a distance of 3 geographical miles from their respective coastlines. Supplemental proceedings were subsequently instituted to determine the legal coastline of the United States in the area of Block Island Sound and the eastern portion of Long Island Sound. That determination turned on whether Long Island Sound and Block Island Sound constitute a juridical bay under the provisions of the Convention on the Territorial Sea and the Contiguous Zone, since to the extent the Sounds constitute a juridical bay, the waters of the bay are internal waters subject to the jurisdiction of the adjacent states and the line that closes the bay is coastline for purposes of fixing the seaward boundaries of the states. The Special Master appointed by the court concluded that the Sounds in part constitute a juridical bay and that the bay closes at the line drawn from Montauk Point, at the eastern tip of Long Island, to Watch Hill Point on the Rhode Island shore.

On exceptions to the report of the Special Master, the United States Supreme Court overruled the exceptions, adopted the recommendations of the Special Master, and confirmed his report. In an opinion by BLACKMUN, J., expressing the unanimous views of the court, it was held (1) that Long Island Sound and Block Island Sound together constitute a juridical bay, viewing Long Island as an exceptional case of an island which should be treated as an extension of the mainland and as constituting the southern headland of the bay; and (2) that Block Island, which is no closer than 11 miles from what would otherwise be the closing line of the bay, is too removed from the closing line to form multiple mouths and therefore does not affect the closing line.

---

and/or "public choice" theory. The idea that smaller political jurisdictions are better able than larger ones to respond to the preferences of their citizens has evoked great support throughout United States history. It is discussed further toward the end of this chapter. Interestingly, this approach would also provide a special cultural group with a considerable amount of autonomy if it were able to gain political dominance of a state. The Mormons in Utah are the leading example. However, because the national government can act directly on the people and seek to represent them, the chances for separatist movements to develop and be successful in a federal system such as the United States are reduced. This has been especially true since the adoption of the post–Civil War constitutional amendments. The Fourteenth and Fifteenth, in particular, promoted national integration by giving the national government direct responsibility for protecting the civil rights and liberties of individuals against infringement by the states.

ADMINISTRATIVE DECENTRALIZATION

Federalism is a form of *political* decentralization. It divides political authority and sovereignty between the national government and states, provinces, or similar governmental bodies. Hence, political authority is not centralized in the national government but shared by other governmental units. The reasons for this arrangement are overwhelmingly political, but they are also of administrative concern. Here, the managerial perspectives on public administration exert their influence.

Administrative decentralization occurs when administrative responsibility, authority, and discretion are delegated to administrative units having jurisdiction over at least one program or function in a subnational geographic territory. The existence of a field office, or regional office of an administrative agency, is evidence of administrative decentralization. So is a neighborhood school. Administrative decentralization can coincide with federalism—that is, states and provinces can be administrative districts of the national government—but it does not necessarily have to do so. There are a variety of managerial reasons for encouraging administrative decentralization that are largely independent of political concerns.

Traditional American public administrative theory recognizes that organization by "place" may be an appropriate basis for establishing administrative arrangements. This is perhaps particularly true in large nations, especially if their physical characteristics, such as climate, topography, and hydrology, vary widely. Under such circumstances, there is an ever-present likelihood that highly centralized administration, with authority and responsibility vested in an agency's national headquarters, usually in the capital, will fail to adapt to local or regional conditions. Instructions from headquarters may simply fail to fit situations in vastly different geographic settings. For instance, the same prescriptions for combating poverty may not fit rural and urban settings equally well.

Centralized administration can also present the difficulty of becoming too extended and far-flung to ensure responsibility and compliance with national directives by local administrators. Here the concept of the **span of control**—that is, the number of underlings directly reporting to a superordinate—becomes important. It has been recognized that there is a limit to the number of subordinates any given administrative official can effectively supervise. Administrative decentralization is one means of keeping the span of control manageable by organizing on the basis of installations (local administrative units), the heads of which report to field offices, whose heads report to regional offices, whose heads report, in turn, to the agency's national headquarters. By interposing field and regional offices between local administrators and national headquarters, the number of administrators reporting directly to the headquarters can be sharply reduced. Thus, if there were 120 installations reporting, in groups of 10, to 12 field offices, which report, in groups of 2, to 6 regional offices, reporting, in turn, to agency headquarters, the span of control would presumably be functional and the situation in which 120 local administrators reported directly to headquarters would be avoided. At the same time, the regional, field, and installation levels might be able to adapt national guidelines to local conditions and to coordinate the activities of local administrators in the same geographic area.

Decentralization of this type can be by function or by agency, or it can be geographic, by *prefecture*. In the United States, the national system is organized overwhelmingly by agency, meaning that, for the most part, federal agencies have their own regional headquarters that supervise field and installation operations. In France, by contrast, the separate administrative units report to the administrative head of a district, or **prefect.** Such an official would have responsibility for overseeing the operations of several ministries in the district, including, for example, education, health, welfare, and employment. The great advantage of the prefect system is the coordination of administrative operations within a geographic area. Its drawback is that the administrative official in charge of the prefect is not likely to possess sufficient specialization in all areas of administrative operation to foster the highest possible level of efficiency and economy.

The United States federal government does not use the prefect system. It seeks to coordinate the activities of different units, such as the Departments of Education and Housing and Urban Development, within regions through interagency meetings and conferences. However, at the subnational level of government, something approaching the coordination of the prefect system may develop. Here, administrative and political decentralization overlap. Municipal governments, townships, and counties are headed by managers, executives, or other officials or bodies. These officials seek to coordinate and oversee all the administrative activities of that particular unit of government (e.g., the county) within the geographic territory under its jurisdiction. However, because so many functions provided by these units of government overlap, sometimes the administrative arrangements seem to be irrational, fragmented, and uncoordinated. For example, jurisdictional overlaps or disputes among city police, county sheriffs, state police, and sometimes even the FBI are fairly common. A jail in a city may be overcrowded, while space in the county facility is available.

Federalism and administrative decentralization are different in purpose. One promotes political values (representation, union, economic development, and perhaps military strength). The other promotes managerial values of efficiency, economy, administrative effectiveness, and responsiveness to clients and customers. But there is another difference as well. Administrative decentralization does not convey sovereignty to the subnational administrative units, whereas federalism does carry with it the notion that some subnational political units (states or provinces) will be vested with a measure of sovereignty. We will return to these matters shortly.

THE QUEST FOR UNIFORMITY AMONG THE STATES

Federalism and administrative decentralization carry with them the possibility that the nature of individual rights and the enforcement and implementation of administrative programs will vary widely from place to place. This is one of the advantages of these arrangements. But it can also be a drawback. For instance, adapting to local conditions can stand in the way of integration of the nation's economy and further economic development. It can also involve the violation of individual rights and standards of decency to which the political community, as a whole, is committed. In the United States, an example combining these two types of concerns was present prior to the adoption of the federal Civil Rights Act of 1964. In some states, by state law, individuals could be excluded from places of public accommodation, such as motels and restaurants, based on their race. African-Americans, in particular, were also subject to segregation on common carriers (buses, trains) and in public buildings. This was not only offensive to the national commitment of equal protection and decency but, as the Supreme Court reasoned in *Katzenbach v. McClung* (1964),[3] it impeded commerce by making it difficult for blacks to travel.

This is where the legal perspective enters the picture most forcefully. Law, including constitutional law, can be used to protect the most fundamental rights of individuals from infringement by states or administrative units. The idea that federalism can enable local majorities to have a good measure of political control over their lives is sound, but it does not necessarily protect minorities from tyranny by those local majorities. Consequently, it is often necessary that a line be drawn between local control and national protection. Typically, this line will be drawn on the basis of the determination that some rights are so fundamental that they must be given national recognition and protection. However, precisely what those rights will be varies over time and is often difficult to discern.

In the United States, the courts are often called upon to address this question. Historically, it was generally thought that the Bill of Rights (the First, Fourth, Fifth, Sixth, and Eighth Amendments in particular) imposed restrictions on the federal government's treatment of individuals but did not place limitations on the states or their political subdivisions. During the twentieth century, however, constitutional theory has held that the Fourteenth Amendment's guarantee that no state shall deprive any individual of life, liberty, or property without due process of law "incorporates" much of the Bill of

Rights. In other words, whereas at one time an individual's right to freedom of expression or free exercise of religion was protected from *federal* interference by the First Amendment, such rights were not necessarily protected from abridgment by the state governments or their political subdivisions. Protection at the state level would depend on the state constitutions and state judicial decisions. This approach permitted many practices that would be considered anomalous today, including the establishment of religions by the states. Application of the Bill of Rights to the states through the Fourteenth Amendment has expanded the civil rights and liberties of the citizenry immensely. At the same time, however, it has limited the states' ability to adjust their policies in some areas to their own peculiar circumstances. For example, in theory at least, high-crime states and low-crime states must adhere to the same standards of due process, pretrial detention, "speedy trials," and prison conditions.

The judiciary has also dramatically affected federalism by its interpretation of the *commerce clause*. The clause (Article I, section 8, clause 2) authorizes Congress "To regulate Commerce with foreign Nations, and among the several States, and with the Indian Tribes." In the past, many court decisions turned on the question of whether, in seeking to impose uniformity on commercial practices—such as the use of child labor—within the states, Congress had gone beyond its constitutional powers to regulate commerce. In particular, the clause was viewed as an improper basis for regulating commerce for social purposes, such as eliminating undesirable employment practices or conditions, and for reaching activities that only indirectly affected the stream of interstate commerce. Today, however, the vast majority of commercial activity in the nation is considered to be within the scope of Congress's reach. In *Wickard v. Fillburn* (1942),[4] the Supreme Court held that even a crop grown and consumed on a single farm within one state was subject to congressional regulation. The Court reasoned that if a large number of farmers grew a crop, such as wheat, for consumption on their farms, it would have an impact on the national economy even though the crop itself never actually entered the commercial market directly. However, although the clause is broad, it does not give Congress power to regulate morality and social behavior in general. Under the Constitution's Tenth Amendment, such **police power** is reserved to the states.

In *United States v. Lopez* (1995),[5] a slim majority of the Supreme Court held that Congress had exceeded its authority under the commerce clause when it enacted the Gun-Free School Zones Act of 1990, which prohibited knowingly bringing a firearm within 1,000 feet of a public, private, or parochial school. Chief Justice William Rehnquist's opinion for the Court pointed out that if the act were valid ". . . it is difficult to perceive any limitation on federal power, even in areas such as criminal law enforcement or education where States historically have been sovereign. Thus, if we were to accept the [federal] Government's arguments, we are hard-pressed to posit any activity by an individual that Congress is without power to regulate."[6] According to the *Lopez* decision, Congress may use its commerce clause power to regulate (1) the channels of interstate commerce, such as roads; ● persons or things in interstate commerce, and the instrumentalities of interstate commerce (e.g., vehicles, aircraft, and property); and (3) activities having a substantial relation to interstate commerce, that is, an activity that substantially affects interstate commerce. As in *Wickard*, activity that falls into any of these categories can be regulated by Congress even though it takes place wholly within a single state.

The commerce clause also places limits on state and local governments. By judicial construction there is a "negative" or "dormant" commerce clause. It rests on the view that "The Commerce Clause presumes a national market free from local legislation that discriminates in favor of local interests."[7] It prohibits (1) discrimination against interstate commerce, such as regulations requiring that a local resource like timber, milk, or shrimp be processed in-state; or (2) placing excessive burdens on interstate commerce, such as adopting regulations that conflict with those of other jurisdictions. By way of illustration, in *Carbone v. Town of Clarkstown* (1994), a majority of the Supreme Court held that a local "flow control" ordinance discriminated against interstate commerce by requiring that solid waste generated or brought into Clarkstown, N.Y., be processed at a designated facility within the town. The ordinance made it impossible for other facilities to compete for processing the town's garbage and also for recyclers like Carbone to dispose of their nonrecyclable residual solid waste at other (and less expensive) facilities.[8] In a concurring opinion, Justice Sandra Day O'Connor argued that "[t]he increasing number of flow control regimes virtually ensures some inconsistency between jurisdictions, with the effect of eliminating the movement of waste between jurisdictions,"[9] and thereby excessively burdening interstate commerce.

In the wake of judicial interpretations the *commerce clause* and limits on the states through incorporation of the Bill of Rights, the states appear to be left with limited vestiges of sovereignty. The Supreme Court has construed the Tenth Amendment narrowly. In *Garcia v. San Antonio Metropolitan Transit Authority* (1985),[10] it reasoned that "the Framers chose to rely on a Federal system in which special restraints on federal power over the States inhered principally in the workings of the National Government itself, rather than in discrete limitations on the objects of federal authority." In other words, the states' chief protection against federal intrusion into their affairs lies in the political process that affords the states representation in the Senate, rather than in constitutional limitations imposed on the power of the federal government. A decade later, in *U.S. Term Limits v. Thornton*, a sharply divided Court reiterated that under the Tenth Amendment the states retain only those powers they possessed prior to the adoption of the Constitution that it neither transfers to the federal government nor eliminates.[11]

MIXES OF FEDERALISM

Several mixes in the allocation of authority between national governments and those of states or provinces can develop in response to the political interests in federalism, administrative concerns with the impact of decentralization, and a nation's desire to establish uniformity in some areas of public policy and in the definition of rights. David Nice outlines the major models as follows[12]:

1. Nation-centered federalism establishes "the national government as the dominant source in a federal system." It emphasizes the desirability of a national perspective on public policy, the uniform regulation of commerce, and broad national protection of individuals' rights and statuses.
2. State-centered federalism favors state dominance in the political system because "the states are seen as closer to the people and able to adapt to variations in problems or citizen preferences from one part of the country to another."
3. Dual federalism is a system in which "each level of government, national and state, is supreme within its areas of responsibility. According to this model, neither level is dominant, and neither level should interfere in the affairs of the other." For instance, exclusive authority might be vested in the states for education and labor law, whereas foreign affairs might be solely in the domain of the national government.
4. Interdependent models "are based on a sharing of power and responsibility, with the various participants working toward shared goals." These models seek to couple the resources of the national government with the states' representative and administrative capacities as a means of adapting and implementing general policies at the subnational level of government.

During the twentieth century, the United States moved from a system closer to dual federalism to one more aptly characterized as interdependent. Over the past three decades, the character of interdependence has varied from the heavy reliance of President Lyndon B. Johnson's "Great Society" on national initiatives and control to President Ronald Reagan's emphasis on the states' relative independence under the "New Federalism" approach. However, despite shifts in emphasis, the states and the national government are now highly interdependent in a wide range of policy areas and fiscal matters. We will discuss state-national and other intergovernmental relationships after reviewing the major forms found within the United States' 87,000 governments.

AMERICAN GOVERNMENT: THE BUILDING BLOCKS

The vast majority of people in the United States fall under the jurisdiction of several governments. The exact number and mix of functions these governments provide depend upon precisely where one lives. The number of governments per state vary from Hawaii's 21 to Illinois' 6,810. In Hawaii there are only 0.2 governments per 10,000 residents, whereas in North Dakota there are almost 44.[13] It is impossible to do justice to the wide range of variation among the 87,000 governments that exist in the United States. Box 3–2,

BOX 3–2 **All Governments—Employment by Function: 1992 (For October. Covers Both Full-Time and Part-Time Employees. Local Government Amounts Are Estimates.)**

| | | | *Employees (1,000)* | | |
| | | | | *State and Local* | |
Function	*Total*	*Federal (civilian)[1]*	*Total*	*State*	*Local*
National defense[2]	984	984	(X)	(X)	(X)
Postal Service	774	774	(X)	(X)	(X)
Space research and technology	25	25	(X)	(X)	(X)
Education	8,239	14	8,225	2,050	6,174
Highways	565	4	561	261	300
Health and hospitals	1,854	310	1,544	721	823
Public welfare	506	10	496	215	281
Police protection	858	88	770	87	683
Fire protection	344	(X)	344	(X)	344
Sanitation and sewerage	244	(X)	244	3	241
Parks and recreation	345	27	318	42	276
Natural resources	436	232	204	164	40
Financial administration	493	138	355	151	205
Other government administration	399	29	370	52	318
Judicial and legal	374	51	323	114	209
Other	2,303	360	1,943	734	1,209
Total	**18,743**	**3,046**	**15,697**	**4,594**	**11,103**

X Not applicable; [1]includes employees outside the United States; [2]includes international relations.

SOURCE: U.S. Department of Commerce, *Statistical Abstract of the United States* (Washington, D.C.: Government Printing Office, 1995), 322.

displaying the number of federal, state, and local employees allocated to various functions, provides an idea of the activities with which the federal, state, and local governments are most concerned. Box 3–3 shows the size and growth of public employment in the states (including local governments) from 1954 to 1992. It leaves no doubt that much public administrative activity takes place at the subnational levels of government. Although there are great differences among governments at the subnational level, some commonalities can be described.

Municipalities   These are cities, towns, villages, or boroughs, legally defined as public corporations. Their object is to provide governance and public administration to local areas. Cities typically provide a greater range of functions than other municipalities and may have special status under a state's constitution. At a minimum, all municipalities seek to provide for the public safety and some degree of public works. At a maximum, cities may provide not only these functions, but also hospitals, libraries, elaborate zoning and planning, higher education, museums, jails, public parks, recreation, and various licensing and inspection functions.

Municipalities tend to fall into one of three types of governmental structure. The **mayor-council** form of government is found in about half the nation's cities and is especially prevalent in those with 500,000 or more residents. Here, the mayor has primarily executive functions, whereas the council has both executive and legislative ones. In what has been dubbed the "weak-mayor" variant, the heads of the city's departments may be directly elected, thereby limiting the mayor's control over their selection and activity. The council in such a form of government may be directly involved in executive decision making. Under the "strong-mayor" plan, department heads are directly appointed by the mayor, subject to council approval. Here, although the mayor and the council make policy jointly, it is the mayor's legal responsibility to execute it. Most large cities rely on the strong-mayor approach. In practice, of course, each city is likely to have its own hybrid of the strong- and weak-mayor approaches. The mayor-council approach was created to assure a separation of executive and legislative powers and a system of checks and balances. Council members may be elected "at large," that is, citywide, or by wards.

At the other extreme, municipalities with populations of 5,000 or less sometimes rely on the **commission plan** of governance. Here, a number of commissioners, frequently five, are elected at large, generally for a four-year term. One serves as chair of the commission. There is little in the way of a separation of powers; the commission is a deliberative legislative body, yet each commissioner has executive responsibility for the operations of a specific department. The plan is convenient in politically and socially homogeneous jurisdictions. However, where there is marked political conflict, the commission can become deadlocked and administrative operations may not be coordinated with one another.

The **council-manager** plan is the third common form of municipal governance. It is found in about half of all cities in the 10,000–500,000 population range. Historically, the council-manager approach was last to evolve and was a part of the broader effort at administrative reform from the 1880s to the 1920s that included the establishment of merit systems for the selection of civil servants. The council-manager plan reflects the orthodox, managerial approach to public administration in many respects. It assumes that the main problems of cities are administrative, not political. This was often captured in the aphorism that "there is no Republican and no Democratic way to pave a street." It also assumes that although the managers of cities should be responsible to elected officials, administration itself should not be infused with electoral concerns. The council is generally elected at large on a nonpartisan

BOX 3–3 **Bureaucratic Size and Growth in the States, 1954–1992**

State	1954 Number of Employees*	1954 Bureaucratic Load†	1992 Number of Employees	1992 Bureaucratic Load	% Increase in Size	% Increase in Bureaucratic Load
Alabama	77,895	2.5	235,412	5.7	202	128
Alaska	(prior to statehood)		46,027	7.9	—	—
Arizona	28,787	3.8	199,138	5.2	592	37
Arkansas	43,318	2.3	128,584	5.4	197	135
California	438,772	4.1	1,429,841	4.6	226	12
Colorado	51,539	3.9	185,140	5.3	259	36
Connecticut	(not available)		151,167	4.6	—	—
Delaware	11,477	3.6	37,687	5.5	228	53
Florida	109,926	4	664,070	4.9	504	23
Georgia	89,680	2.6	397,053	5.9	343	127
Hawaii	(prior to statehood)		64,539	5.6	—	—
Idaho	21,143	3.6	60,096	5.6	184	55
Illinois	251,288	2.9	567,178	4.9	126	69
Indiana	120,725	3.1	297,585	5.2	146	68
Iowa	90,611	3.5	155,798	5.5	72	57
Kansas	69,235	3.6	157,064	6.2	127	72
Kentucky	66,326	2.3	197,016	5.3	197	130
Louisiana	92,148	3.4	249,344	5.8	171	71
Maine	30,926	3.4	65,148	5.3	111	56
Maryland	69,651	3	239,627	4.9	244	63
Massachusetts	167,521	3.6	277,246	4.6	65	28
Michigan	221,332	3.5	460,471	4.9	108	40
Minnesota	114,543	3.8	239,943	5.4	109	42
Mississippi	57,043	2.6	155,159	5.9	172	127
Missouri	108,851	2.8	247,711	4.8	128	71
Montana	22,248	3.8	54,229	6.6	144	74
Nebraska	51,601	3.9	99,631	6.2	93	59
Nevada	8,213	5.1	66,001	5	704	(2)
New Hampshire	21,059	3.9	51,803	4.7	146	21

basis. It has legislative authority for the city, passing ordinances, developing or sanctioning policy, and approving financial and budgetary proposals. Generally the council consists of five to nine members. It is presided over by a mayor, who may be one of its members. The mayor in this form of government has important ceremonial functions but no significant executive powers. The council hires a manager, who serves at its pleasure. The manager is the chief executive officer of the city and has the authority to appoint and dismiss the heads of administrative departments. The council, in turn, is barred from involvement in administrative matters other than the selection and retention of the manager. City managers are considered professionals and often

BOX 3–3 *Continued*

| | 1954 | | 1992 | | | |
State	Number of Employees*	Bureaucratic Load†	Number of Employees	Bureaucratic Load	% Increase in Size	% Increase in Bureaucratic Load
New Jersey	149,427	3.1	417,409	5.4	179	74
New Mexico	24,853	3.6	102,638	6.5	313	81
New York	540,075	3.6	1,147,540	6.3	112	75
North Carolina	108,903	2.7	368,847	5.4	239	100
North Dakota	24,905	4	37,515	5.9	51	48
Ohio	254,615	3.2	539,719	4.9	112	53
Oklahoma	76,676	3.4	187,811	5.9	145	74
Oregon	56,934	3.7	155,211	5.2	173	41
Pennsylvania	260,188	2.5	510,169	4.3	96	72
Rhode Island	22,836	2.9	47,629	4.7	109	69
South Carolina	58,783	2.8	201,698	5.6	343	100
South Dakota	25,308	3.9	39,172	5.5	55	41
Tennessee	87,188	2.6	253,944	5.1	191	96
Texas	230,232	3	987,993	5.6	329	87
Utah	28,604	4.2	92,955	5.1	225	21
Vermont	13,002	3.4	30,546	5.4	135	59
Virginia	96,109	2.9	344,975	5.4	259	86
Washington	94,193	4	275,419	5.4	192	-35
West Virginia	50,600	2.5	92,232	5.1	82	104
Wisconsin	119,494	3.8	261,595	5.2	119	37
Wyoming	12,411	4.3	36,581	7.9	195	84
Total	4,771,194		13,311,306			

*Combined state and local.

†Bureaucratic load = number of public sector employees per 100 persons in the state population.

(   ) Numbers in parentheses indicate decreases.

SOURCE: Data from Council of State Governments, *The Book of the States, 1954–56, 1994–95* (Lexington, Ky.: Council of State Governments).

hold advanced degrees in public administration. Their jobs may be extremely difficult because it is often impossible for the manager to avoid becoming involved in political disputes—or even the object of them.

Townships These are found primarily in the Midwest and mid-Atlantic states. Originally they were used to identify sections of federal lands. Today, they often constitute civic units as well. They are characteristic in rural areas and provide a minimum of functions, sometimes having responsibility only for roads. Townships rely heavily on the commission form of government.

Counties   These are a comprehensive, general form of government with a wide range of functions. Municipalities, townships, and other forms of government (school districts and special districts) are found within their boundaries. Counties are best considered to be arms of the state government for local administration and governance. Exceptions are in New England, where the states rely on "towns" more than counties; Louisiana, which uses "parishes"; and Alaska, where "boroughs" provide some of the functions supplied by counties elsewhere. Their number varies widely from state to state, as does their size. On average, there are sixty-five counties per state. Some are highly urbanized, such New York County (Manhattan), whereas others are rural. Counties have no sovereignty or inherent authority. They are unincorporated. Their functions vary widely, but with few if any exceptions, they include some law enforcement functions, tax functions, and record keeping. Many counties have important responsibilities for education, recreation, roads, and civic activities. The typical county is governed by a board of elected commissioners, which is also frequently called a board of supervisors. About two-thirds of the counties have boards of three to five members, but some have as many as thirty or more.[14] The board has policy and administrative functions. It oversees a number of appointive officials who carry out executive responsibilities. In addition to the board, voters typically elect a number of other county officials including sheriffs, judicial officers, clerks, treasurers, assessors, and coroners. Some counties have professional managers and/or elected executives. In rural areas, the county may be the main focus of governance. In more urban settings, the coexistence of counties and municipalities may lead to a patchwork of overlapping functions and haphazard relationships. (Box 3–4 shows how the states vary in terms of number and governance of counties.)

School Districts and Other Special Districts   Special districts are "single-purpose" governments. They deal primarily with such areas as water, sewage, recreation, highways, bridges, fire protection, cemeteries, libraries, and utilities. School districts are a special case. They were established to give local communities control over the education of their children. In the past, the independence of school districts was a guarantee of diversity. Today, however, school systems must meet so many state and federal requirements that a good deal of educational uniformity exists. For the most part, school districts are governed by boards. Most of these are elected, but a substantial minority are appointed by municipal or county officials. Other special districts, sometimes called "authorities," are also headed by boards, but here a higher proportion of the members are appointed. Special districts often overlap several municipal and/or county governments, and the board may be composed of elected or appointed representatives of those units of government. Special districts frequently exercise considerable powers of taxation and authority to charge user fees and incur debt. For the most part, however, the average citizen seems unconcerned with their composition and operations—at least as long as the latter are satisfactory. Historically, special districts have been considered a way of taking particular functions, such as cemeteries, water, and libraries, out of the political arena and of making it possible to manage them in a "businesslike" manner. Sometimes, of course, school districts and other special districts like those for fire protection can become embroiled in political controversy.

States   In many respects, the *structure* of state governments tends to parallel that of the federal government. The executive branch in all states is headed by an elected governor. With the exception of Nebraska, all states use a bi-cameral legislature. The upper house is invariably called the *senate*, whereas the lower house may be called an *assembly* or *state house*. The states also provide for independent judiciaries having the power of judicial review. The highest court in most states is called the *state supreme court*. Despite these structural similarities, however, many states differ markedly from the pattern of politics and administrative arrangements found at the national level. They also differ from one another.

One of the striking differences is the nature of state constitutions. Only those of Massachusetts (adopted in 1780) and New Hampshire (adopted in 1784) have had the longevity of the U.S. Constitution, which was adopted in 1789. Most states have had more than one constitution. Louisiana has had eleven. Only those of Connecticut and Vermont are as concise as the federal Constitution. Many are much wordier. Most have also been amended more frequently than the U.S. Constitution. Some, such as those of California and South Carolina, have been changed more than 400 times.[15] These differences reflect the virtue of federalism in enabling each state to adapt its governmental powers and processes to its own economic, political, and social conditions and needs.

They also reflect the ability of organized pressure groups to advance their interests by having provisions written into the state constitutions. State constitutions are far more detailed than the federal Constitution, sometimes resembling ordinary legislation in spelling out provisions for roads, sewer systems, and even zoos.[16] Many of them are easier to amend, which accounts in part for the tendency to treat them as vehicles for the expression of substantive policy as well as statements of the procedures by which the state governments operate. In several states—including large ones such as California, Florida, Massachusetts, and Illinois—constitutional amendments can be initiated directly by the people.[17] All state constitutions provide for checks and balances, suffrage and elections, taxation and appropriations, local government, public education, state institutions, and law enforcement.[18]

The states also vary greatly in their administrative structures. Every governor is considered the head of state administrative operations, but the governor's power to appoint, engage in fiscal management, and supervise administrators varies considerably from one state to another. In several states six or more administrative officials are elected by the voters. Among those most frequently elected are attorneys general, lieutenant governors, treasurers, secretaries of state, auditors, and superintendents of education. Among additional elective state administrators are agricultural commissioners, controllers, and commissioners for insurance, land, labor, highways, railroads, corporations, and charities. University regents and others may also be elected.[19] Generally speaking,

BOX 3–4 **Counties: Number and Governance, 1991**

State	County Designation	Number of Counties	Governing Body
Alabama	County	67	County Commission
Alaska	Borough	23	Borough Assembly and Mayor
Arizona	County	15	Board of Supervisors
Arkansas	County	75	Justices of the Peace
California	County	58	Board of Supervisors
Colorado	County	63	Board of County Commissioners
Connecticut	(unorganized areas)	8	
Delaware	County	3	Levy Court Commission or County Council
Florida	County	67	Board of County Commissioners
Georgia	County	159	Board of County Commissioners
Hawaii	County	4	Council and Mayor
Idaho	County	44	Board of County Commissioners
Illinois	County	102	County Board
Indiana	County	92	County Commissioners and Councils
Iowa	County	99	Board of Supervisors
Kansas	County	105	Board of Commissioners
Kentucky	County	120	Judge Executive and Justices of the Peace or Commissioners
Louisiana	Parish	64	Police Jury Commission
Maine	County	16	Board of Commissioners
Maryland	County	23	Board of Commissioners or Elected-Executive Council
Massachusetts	County	14	Commissioners
Michigan	County	83	Board of Commissioners
Minnesota	County	87	Board of Commissioners
Mississippi	County	82	Board of County Supervisors
Missouri	County	115	County Court
Montana	County	56	Board of County Commissioners

the greater the number of elected administrative officials, the less control the governor has over state public administration. Elected officials may be opposed to the governor's policies and administrative programs. The governor has no official role in selecting those officials and cannot fire them. Their responsibility is to the voters, who may see no problem in electing administrative executives who are opposed to one another. Moreover, elected administrators may tend to develop closer relationships with the legislature than with the governor.

The governor's ability to oversee administrative matters is also complicated by the unwieldy structures of many state governments. In 1978, on average, a governor had some eighty-five state agencies reporting directly to him or her. The number of separate agencies could reach well over a hundred.[20] In recent years, efforts have been undertaken in several states to reform these administrative structures by consolidating such agencies into a few

BOX 3–4 *Continued*

State	County Designation	Number of Counties	Governing Body
Nebraska	County	93	Board of Commissioners or of Supervisors
Nevada	County	17	Board of Commissioners
New Hampshire	County	10	Board of Commissioners or County Delegation
New Jersey	County	21	Board of Freeholders
New Mexico	County	33	County Commissioners
New York	County	62	Board of Supervisors or County Legislatures or Board of Representatives
North Carolina	County	100	Board of County Commissioners
North Dakota	County	53	Board of County Commissioners
Ohio	County	88	Board of County Commissioners
Oklahoma	County	77	Board of County Commissioners
Oregon	County	36	Board of Commissioners or County Courts
Pennsylvania	County	67	Board of County Commissioners
Rhode Island	(unorganized areas)	5	
South Carolina	County	46	County Council
South Dakota	County	66	Board of County Commissioners
Tennessee	County	95	Board of County Commissioners or Council
Texas	County	254	County Judge and County Commissioners
Utah	County	29	Board of County Commissioners or Council
Vermont	County	14	Assistant Judges
Virginia	County	95	Board of Supervisors
Washington	County	39	Board of County Commissioners or Council
West Virginia	County	55	Board of County Commissioners or of Supervisors
Wisconsin	County	72	Board of Supervisors
Wyoming	County	23	Board of Commissioners

SOURCE: Tanis Salant, "County Governments: An Overview," *Intergovernmental Perspective* (Winter 1991): 8.

departments, because from a managerial perspective, the governor's span of control is simply too large to be effective. In part, however, the fragmented administrative structures of the states reflect the competing concerns of public administration. Some independent boards and commissions are designed to exercise judicial functions and to be independent of the rest of the government to a considerable degree. Others provide political representation for the interests of distinct economic, social, or geographic groups. Still others are engaged in executive functions and are most likely to be placed more closely under the governor's control.

Since the 1920s, the job of preparing state budgets increasingly has been moved from the legislature to the governor. Today, the formulation of an **executive budget,** that is, one prepared by the governor or a budget agency in the executive branch, is the focus of much administrative activity. During the 1980s, as the states played a more active role in the provision of services and the application of constraints within their jurisdictions, the state budget emerged as a major vehicle for state planning.

Finally, in discussing the states, it is necessary to note that there are widespread variations in the patterns of their party politics, the professionalization and strength of their legislatures and administrative components, the scope of services and regulations they provide, and their mix of administrative responsibility among the counties, local jurisdictions, and the state governments themselves. When taken together, these differences can make administrative life in one state quite different from administrative life in another. They can also lead to serious complications in trying to draft federal legislation and programs that require state administration of a certain caliber. We will return to this problem after we briefly review the federal government's administrative structure.

The Federal Government   We have already mentioned many of the salient features of the federal government's administrative component in our discussion of the rise of the contemporary American administrative state (Chapter 2). This is not the place for a discourse on the nature of federal administration and politics, but a brief summary will provide the reader with a useful overview. It may be helpful to refer to Box 3–5 as we review the administrative structure of the federal government. Like the states, the federal administrative structure is fragmented. It consists of departments, agencies, commissions, corporations, and a number of miscellaneous units. Departments are generally considered the most important and comprehensive administrative units. They enjoy the highest formal status. Today, there are fourteen departments, although their number has varied over the years. There are marked differences in their sizes and budgets. The Department of Defense (DOD) overshadows all others in size and complexity. On the other end of the scale, the Department of Education and the Commerce Department are relatively small. The structure of these departments also differs considerably. Some approach the pyramidal, hierarchical organizational form generally associated with bureaucracy. Others are conglomerates of separate, somewhat autonomous units and are best construed as "holding companies." The DOD is among the latter, being composed of the Army, Navy, and Air Force, among other units (see Box 3–6). Typically, departments are distinguished from other units, such as agencies, by the comprehensiveness or national importance of their missions.

Independent agencies are administrative units outside the departments with responsibility for more limited areas of public policy. The Environmental Protection Agency, the Small Business Administration, and the National Aeronautics and Space Administration are examples. These agencies are called "independent" because they are not within departments. In practice, however, they may be more tightly controlled by the president than some departments. Independent agencies may be quite large, though the scope of their mission is often limited, focusing on a particular group of people or sector of the economy. Some independent agencies, such as the General Services

BOX 3-5 **The Government of the United States**

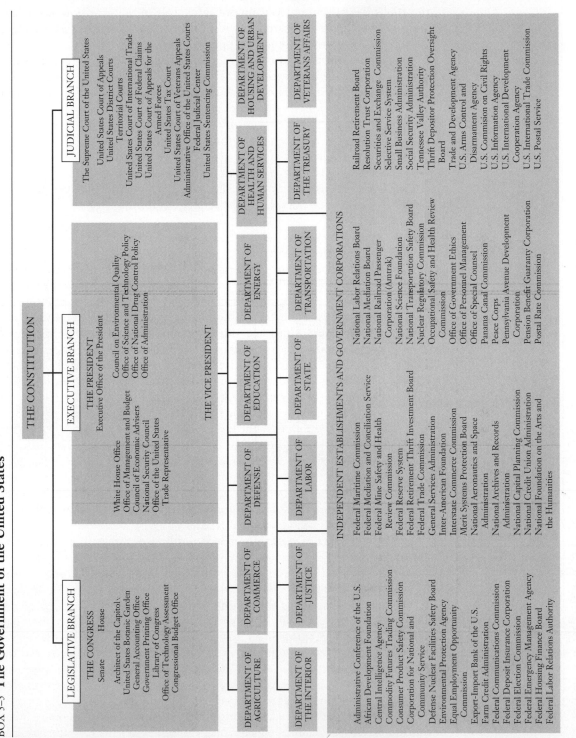

SOURCE: *The United States Government Manual, 1995/96* (Washington, D.C.: Government Printing Office, 1995), 22.

BOX 3-6 **The Department of Defense**

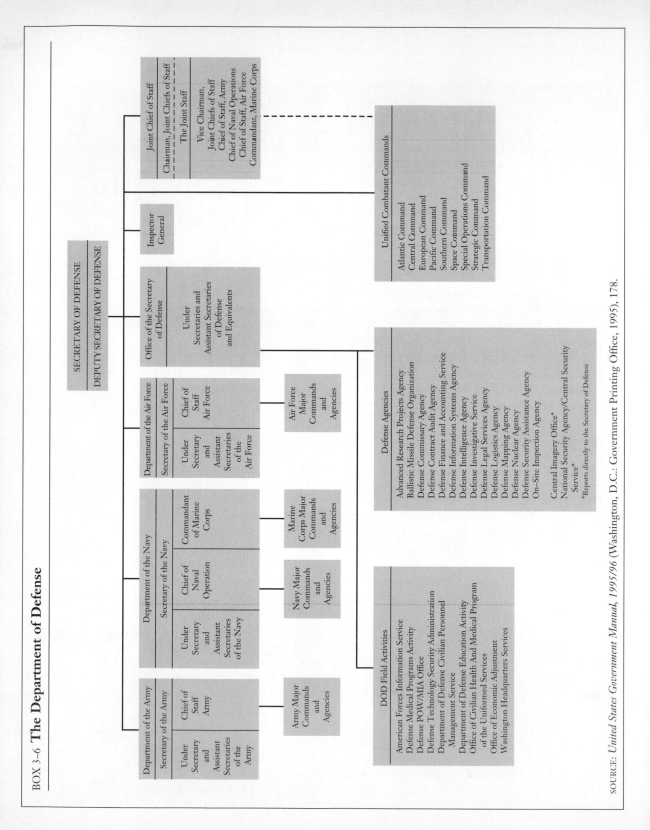

SOURCE: *United States Government Manual, 1995/96* (Washington, D.C.: Government Printing Office, 1995), 178.

Administration and the Office of Personnel Management, engage in over-head administrative functions, including supply, security, and personnel.

Independent regulatory commissions are another kind of unit. These commissions are intended to be autonomous and removed from direct presidential control. Among the better known regulatory commissions are the Federal Communications Commission, the Securities and Exchange Commission, the National Labor Relations Board, and the Federal Trade Commission. Such commissions are headed by a bipartisan group of commissioners appointed by the president with the advice and consent of the Senate. They hold staggered terms and are not removable by the president except for specified kinds of causes. The president may disagree with them in terms of policy, but he cannot replace them for this reason until their terms expire. They are not subject to a number of executive orders or to all of the same Office of Management and Budget controls that apply to other departments and agencies. The regulatory commissions have quasi-legislative and/or quasi-judicial functions; they may make rules for regulation of some sector of the economy and enforce those rules, which often requires judicial-style hearings. The basic idea behind the regulatory commission is that by taking an area out of legislative politics, it is possible to weigh competing perspectives on a matter, such as the rates common carriers can charge or what constitutes an unfair labor or trade practice, and to arrive at decisions that are judicious in their definition of the public interest. (Regulatory administration illuminates so much of public administration that Chapter 9 is devoted to it.)

Federal corporations, such as the Tennessee Valley Authority (TVA) and the Federal Deposit Insurance Corporation (FDIC), differ from other federal units primarily in that they sell a product or service. (The organizational structure of the FDIC is shown in Box 3–7.) The Postal Service corporation sells mail service; the TVA sells electricity; the FDIC sells insurance. Such administrative units can be run according to private sector methods. They are allowed to generate their revenues through sales, and as long as they do not run a deficit, need not rely on budgetary appropriations for their funds. When successful, this gives the corporations a large measure of financial independence from the legislature and budgetary process. By contrast, when unsuccessful, federal corporations may turn to Congress for additional funding. In most other respects, however, the legal status of corporations is similar to that of other agencies. Like all governmental agencies, they are subject to constitutional constraints.

In practice, federal administrative arrangements are somewhat more complicated than presented here. Hybrids can be found among the independent agencies and the regulatory commissions. There are a number of agencies called *boards*, and there are foundations, institutes, and institutions. Interagency committees and advisory committees are plentiful. Some executive branch units are in the Executive Office of the President (EOP), such as the Office of Management and Budget, whereas others having related functions, such as the Office of Personnel Management, are outside the EOP. Many of the reasons for these organizational arrangements are discussed in Chapter 4. Basically, they reflect the competing managerial, political, and le-

BOX 3–7 **The Federal Deposit Insurance Corporation**

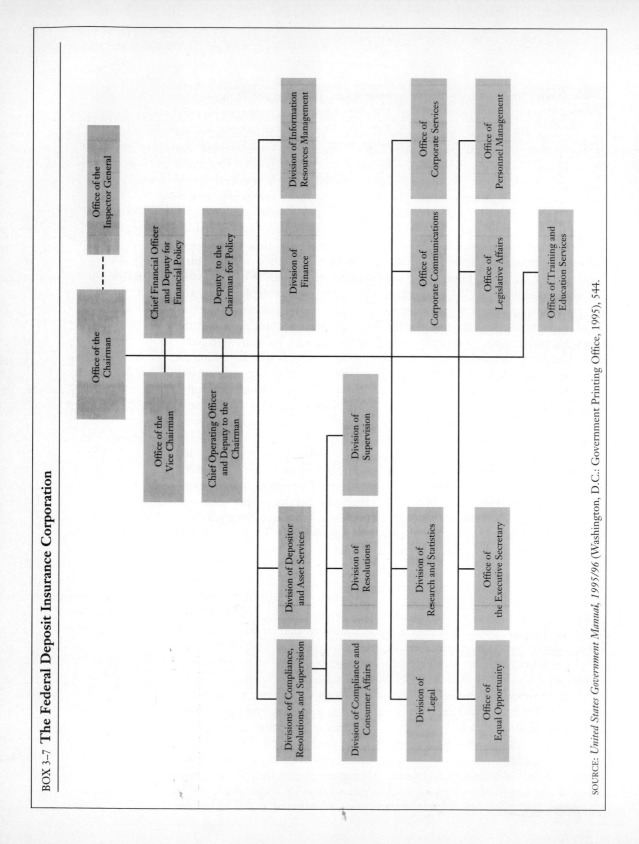

SOURCE: *United States Government Manual, 1995/96* (Washington, D.C.: Government Printing Office, 1995), 544.

galistic perspectives toward public administration. Their net result, however, is further governmental fragmentation and complexity in trying to coordinate governmental activity and policy. Not only does the American governmental and political structure make coordination among the different levels of government difficult, it also makes coordination within governments a considerable task. This can complicate intergovernmental relations greatly.

INTERGOVERNMENTAL RELATIONS

Federal and State Relations

Federalism requires coordination and cooperation of two major types. One is between the national government and state governments; the other is between or among the states. It also permits direct relationships between the national government and political subdivisions within the states. Historically, relationships between the national and state governments have preoccupied American thinking about federalism. The central question has always concerned the extent of state sovereignty in the federal system. What, precisely, are the powers reserved to the states by the Tenth Amendment? As early as the 1790s, Virginia and Kentucky argued that the states possessed the sovereignty to declare acts of the federal government to be void on the grounds that they violated the U.S. Constitution. The Virginia and Kentucky "resolves" were in response to the federal Naturalization, Alien, and Sedition Acts of 1798. They were wrapped up in electoral politics, but the fact that the Virginia resolves were drafted by James Madison, who played a leading role in the drafting and ratification of the U.S. Constitution, and that Kentucky's statement was written by Thomas Jefferson, gave this view of federalism some credibility. By the 1820s and 1830s, John Calhoun of South Carolina had developed a similar notion about the states' rights to nullify federal laws they viewed as unconstitutional. In 1832, South Carolina actually attempted to enforce this approach, but after President Jackson threatened to use military force against the state, a compromise was reached and the state repealed its nullification ordinance. The logical extension of this view of states' rights occurred at the time of the Civil War, when eleven states seceded from the federal union.

For the most part, the Civil War put to rest the theory that each state has an inherent right to define the scope of *federal* powers. Every now and then, however, a state governor may refuse to abide by a federal statute, sometimes involving civil rights, and may even make a dramatic show of the affair. These legal battles are fought out in the courts and for the past several decades the federal judiciary has not generally seen things from the states' point of view. In fact, the federal courts have been so active in applying the U.S. Constitution to the states that a kind of "juridical" or "judicial" federalism has developed. It is not unusual for federal judges to be involved in the drawing of state legislative districts, the operation of public schools, or the reform of state and local prisons and jails.

Another fundamental question in federal-state relationships is equity. To what extent should each state be treated equally by the federal government? Should federal revenues to the states follow a strict formula? Should they be based on politics? Should they take state population, state size, and state need into account? One can ponder the philosophical concerns involved in these questions. As a practical matter, however, politics is frequently the motivating force behind federal allocations to states and their subdivisions. There is considerable variation in (1) the general federal presence in the states in the form of federal civilian and military employment, military bases, and federal allocation of contracts; and (2) the total federal spending per capita within states. Sometimes the politics involved in federal allocations depends heavily upon the memberships on various congressional committees and the relationship between these committees and the federal administrative units with which they deal. For instance, membership on the House Armed Services Committee has long been associated with disproportionately high military spending in one's district.[21]

As the concern with equity suggests, a great deal of contemporary federal-state relationships involve money. The basic pattern of the expansion of federal relationships with state governments has involved federal grants to states as part of the federal government's attempt to achieve some national policy. This approach is not really new; the Morrill Act of 1862 provided federal aid to state land-grant colleges in an effort to further education, especially that involving agricultural techniques. The Federal Aid Road Act of 1916 made federal funds available to the states for highway construction as part of a policy intended to modernize road transportation in the wake of the growing utility of the automobile. What has changed in recent years is the scope of federal grants and the degree of cooperation and coordination that they require of the states. From 1964 to 1980, federal contributions to state and local spending increased from about 14 percent of all state and local spending to about 25 percent; they declined during the 1980s in both absolute and proportional terms, but then began to rise again in the early 1990s.

In recent years, the federal government has relied heavily on three types of grants to further national policies at the state level:

1. *Categorical grants* are provided for specific programs and are subject to strict federal regulations as to how they may be used. Welfare, airports, and highway programs are examples. Sometimes the states are required to participate in funding operations undertaken through such grants. The federal strings attached to such grants may reach matters that the states could legitimately consider to be within their sovereignty, such as speed limits, drinking age, public personnel, and collective bargaining regulations. However, because the states are not compelled to participate in these programs, prevailing constitutional logic has been that their rights as sovereign entities have not been violated. The proportion of all federal grant money that was categorical rose from 73 percent in 1978 to just over 88 percent in 1993.

2. *Block grants* are less tightly circumscribed by federal regulations. They provide federal funding for a general policy area of governmental activity, such as community development, education, health services, and crime control, and leave a good deal of flexibility to the states in deciding how the funds should be used. This means that within the framework of general federal guidelines, each state can adapt the federal policy to its own circumstances.

3. *Revenue sharing* began in 1972 as a process in which the federal government disbursed funds to state and local governments to use, generally, as they saw fit. The major restriction was that the government must not engage in prohibited forms of discrimination. The amount of money transmitted to state and local governments through revenue sharing was predetermined by a complex formula. State governments were eliminated from the program in 1980. Most revenue-sharing funds were spent on equipment, streets, and roads rather than on social services and health programs. In part this was because such funds were so limited; but state and local officials were also apparently reluctant to use revenue-sharing grants in ways that would increase their political vulnerability and reduce their maneuverability in times of federal cutbacks.[22] This was good politics; general revenue sharing was phased out in 1987. General-purpose grants now constitute only 1 percent of all federal grants.

Grants can also be classified according to how the funds are distributed. *Formula grants* are based on a decision rule, such as *x* dollars per public school pupil in daily attendance. The rule is frequently written into the legislation creating the grant, though it could also be established by the administering agency. Members of Congress and their staffs often pay a great deal of attention to the effect any given formula will have on federal spending within their states or districts.

Project grants require jurisdictions seeking funds to submit applications describing how they intend to use the money. The administrative agency makes allocations with reference to these proposals from the total sum made available to the program area by the legislature. Consequently, project grants allow for considerable administrative discretion and promote politicking after the legislature has established the general parameters and scope of funding.

Matching grants require the recipient to contribute some of its own resources to the activity for which the funds are earmarked. Matching does not necessarily require that a state or local jurisdiction put up one dollar for each dollar it receives.

In thinking about grants, it is also important to note that while some are fixed, others are open-ended. In the latter case, the amount allocated will depend upon the number of individuals who are eligible for a program or treated by it or upon other factors such as reimbursible cost overruns.

The grant system is now a deeply entrenched feature of federalism. The Reagan administration sought to reorganize it in order to reduce paperwork, other administrative costs, and the federal budgetary deficit while at the same time encouraging the states to take on more responsibility. In particular, an effort was made to consolidate categorical grants into broad block grants, and general revenue sharing was terminated. However, despite some successes, Reagan's approach met considerable resistance in Congress. As an institution, the legislature demonstrated a powerful orientation toward protecting state, local, and private beneficiaries of existing programs funded by federal grants. Election year 1996 witnessed much rhetoric regarding moving from categorical to block grants, but what will come of it, if anything, remains to be seen.

The grants approach also lies at the heart of third-party government (mentioned in Chapter 1). Many federal objectives—including law enforcement, education, provisions for individuals' welfare, and the fostering of better administrative techniques—are now promoted through grants and dependent upon state and local governmental implementation. However, these subnational governments may, in turn, rely on not-for-profit organizations and privatization to achieve the specific goals. The system combines federalism and administrative decentralization in a way that is managerially, politically, and legally complicated. Third-party government places a premium on maintaining accountability and monitoring implementation. Traditional management has relied on conformance with procedural requirements for these purposes. The new public management (NPM) contends that such controls tie public administration up in red tape. Instead, it favors establishing measures of performance and monitoring them.

Federal money can buy cooperation and coordination, but it is not the only means of achieving these objectives. Cooperation between the states and the national government can be voluntarily established. State governors communicate with the state's representatives in Congress. An annual conference of governors also serves as a vehicle for expressing state concerns to the national government. Mayors engage in similar activities. There are also a number of organizations, such as the Council of State Governments and the National League of Cities, that engage in lobbying efforts to promote states' and cities' general interests. In drafting their regulations for the administration of grant programs, federal agencies may be sensitive to state and local governmental concerns.

However, where cooperation of this nature fails, coordination can also be imposed through congressional exercise of powers under the commerce clause. This can go a long way toward regulating the treatment of any person, product, or substance that bears a substantial relationship to interstate commerce, whether or not state lines are actually crossed.

There are three characteristics of federal-state relationships that bear further mention. One is the extent to which they make thinking about federalism in terms of states versus the national government inappropriate. States and the federal government may be opposed to one another on occasion, but the real focus now is on programs and the role public administrators at different levels of government will play in implementing them. Interdependency has replaced dual federalism. As Morton Grodzins, one of the preeminent analysts of federalism in the 1960s, observed, "In virtually no field does the complete body of law with respect to a given governmental activity have its source in one of these so-called levels of government. In a typical case a mixture of federal, state and local regulation covers an area of regulation or activity."[23] Grodzins punctuated the point with a description of a county health officer in a rural area of a border state. His delineation of this official's functions and responsibilities will give the student of public administration much to ponder:

> The sanitarian [health officer] is appointed by the state under merit standards established by the federal government. His base salary comes jointly from state and federal funds, the county provides him with an office and office amenities and pays a portion of his expenses, and the largest city in the county also contributes to his salary and office by virtue of his appointment as city plumbing inspector. It is impossible from moment to moment to tell under which governmental hat the sanitarian operates. His work of inspecting the purity of food is carried out under federal standards; but he is enforcing state laws when inspecting commodities that have not been in interstate commerce; and somewhat perversely he also acts under state authority when inspecting milk coming into the county from producing areas across the state border. He is a federal officer when impounding impure drugs shipped from a neighboring state; a federal-state officer when distributing typhoid immunization serum; a state officer when enforcing standards of industrial hygiene; a state-local officer when inspecting the city's water supply; and (to complete the circle) a local officer when insisting that the city butchers adopt more hygienic methods of handling their garbage. But he cannot and does not think of himself as acting in these separate capacities. All business in the county that concerns public health and sanitation he considers his business. Paid largely from federal funds, he does not find it strange to attend meetings of the city council to give expert advice on matters ranging from rotten apples to rabies control. He is even deputized as a member of both the city and county police forces.[24]

Grodzin's description of the sanitarian is helpful because it indicates the extent to which any given public administrator may perforce have to be concerned with the integration of the functioning of the various levels of government. It also shows how managerial, political, and legal concerns can bear upon the job of an individual public administrator. The sanitarian is selected according to a managerial approach, the merit system. He or she has to take legalistic concerns and court decisions into account when enforcing the law and cannot be oblivious to politics when attending meetings of the city council. No doubt sanitarians also want higher appropriations for their positions if these will make it possible to do a better job. Consequently, sanitarians are likely to be concerned with budgets—and the politics that surrounds them. Nor is the sanitarian unique. Nonfederal public administrators in education, housing, transportation, corrections, and other fields have similarly complex roles.

A second aspect of federal-state relationships that should be considered is the concept of **entitlements**—a large number of federal programs, administered with state and local personnel, that involve providing benefits to private individuals. Welfare, unemployment insurance, health, education, and public housing are some of the major policy areas in which this practice is found.

A state's participation in these programs may be voluntary, but the private individual's eligibility for the benefits may be established under federal regulations. Thus, once a state is involved in such a program, it may be confronted with a number of people who are "entitled" to benefits. Moreover, their number may grow over the years, adding not just to the expense of funding the benefits but also to the cost of administering the program. Where states provide matching funds, the costs of a given program to the state may escalate rapidly. Yet the state is not free to reduce the number of beneficiaries at will by redefining eligibility. Moreover, under federal court rulings, it may be very difficult for a state to cut off an individual's benefits without affording that person a good measure of due process, sometimes culminating in a judicial-style hearing.[25] Due process also costs money and adds to the fiscal burdens upon the state. As a matter of popular administrative belief, it may even cost more than allowing ineligible people to continue to receive benefits!

There are several serious economic problems that entitlements pose for the states. They make it difficult to cut state budgets in some areas. They can also pass a heavy burden to the states when the federal government engages in reduced funding or program cuts. For example, if the federal government reduces welfare benefits, will the state have to make up the difference, if not as a matter of law, as a matter of political practice and humanity? If the state can also engage in program cuts, on what basis should it decide to reduce benefits or eligibility—and what will the federal courts say about this approach? These are hardly hypothetical issues. The federal contribution as a proportion of total state and local spending declined markedly during the 1980s. This passed a considerable political, administrative, and financial burden to the states. What the individual views as an "entitlement," the state or local administrator may consider a federally imposed "mandate" for which the state bears the cost. This is a feature of federalism that state administrators find especially problematic, as the following description of Medicaid indicates: "The mission of today's Medicaid manager is to control costs without cutting eligibility, benefits, or reimbursement, and despite numerous internal, environmental, and intergovernmental constraints. As a job description, this assignment leads inevitably to frustration. . . . [T]he managers are losing the war: Medicaid costs continue to escalate dramatically, the rising costs thrust enormous burdens on state budgets, and the vision of a decent yet cost-effective program slips further away."[26]

By the mid-1990s, considerable sensitivity to *unfunded* federal mandates had developed. Federal environmental and education legislation in the 1980s imposed billions of dollars of annual costs on state and local governments. Congress gained a clearer understanding of the issue and took legislative and other steps to make sure that the federal government did not lightly thrust extensive costs on these governments—just as most of the states adopted measures intended to protect their local governments from state-level unfunded mandates in the 1980s.[27] To date, however, the efficacy of efforts to reduce unfunded mandates is uncertain.[28]

Third, the huge growth of grant programs and funds since the 1960s created a qualitatively different relationship between the federal government and the nation's local governments, especially its large cities. Many of the "Great Society" programs of the Johnson presidency were oriented toward the urban poor. Cities—even neighborhoods—forged direct financial relationships with the federal government. Since that time, the famous **Dillon's rule,** which holds that local governments possess only those powers expressly allocated to them by the states, has frequently been circumvented, if not nullified, by direct federal funding of local administrative activities. The mayors and administrators of large cities may at times be more oriented toward federal agencies than those in their own state capitals.

Interstate Relations

Interstate relations are another aspect of American federalism that is of importance to public administration. The states not only need to get along with the federal government but, as quasi-sovereign entities, they must find ways of coordinating their activities with one another. They seek ways of cooperating in joint endeavors. When necessary, they must also attempt to resolve disputes in a satisfactory manner. The fact that, with the exception of Alaska and Hawaii, each state shares at least one border with another accentuates the need to develop harmonious and mutually beneficial relationships among the states. The range of problems that can arise as a result of different state policies is enormous. Coordinating road construction, establishing uniform drivers' licensing and drinking-age regulations, agreeing on means of rebating sales taxes collected from out-of-state residents to the state in which they live, agreeing on the types of vehicles (large trucks and tandem trucks) and equipment (studded snow tires) that can be operated on a state's roads, joint law enforcement activities and insect control programs, and many, many more matters are the stuff of everyday interstate relations. More exotic matters concern border disputes, one state's discrimination against residents or former residents of another state with regard to such matters as jobs, welfare benefits, public housing, higher education, the issuance of occupational licenses, and the granting of permits to engage in commercial exploitation of a state's fisheries and other natural resources. Clearly, interstate relations carry with them potential for chaos and disarray. In fact, that is one reason why the national government under the Articles of Confederation was abandoned and replaced by the present constitutional system.

The U.S. Constitution fosters coordination among the states in several areas. The main one is commerce, which was particularly problematic in colonial times and under the Articles of Confederation. Among the powers granted to the federal government are the authority to regulate commerce among the states, with foreign nations, and with Indian tribes. The federal government can also establish legal-tender money, levy tariffs, enact maritime law, grant patents and copyrights, and set standard weights and measures. These powers cut deeply into state sovereignty. Once the federal government takes action in any of these areas, state policies contrary to federal regulations may be preempted and viewed as unconstitutional. Thus, now that the federal government has sought to regulate and penetrate the economic life of the nation to a large extent, a very wide range of state concerns must comply with federal law. These include occupational health, safety, compensation, and collective bargaining matters; banking regulations; use of roads; transportation of products across state lines; and relationships with foreign nations and their political subdivisions, including Canada and Mexico. In addition, as noted earlier, the Constitution's commerce clause has been used as a vehicle for promoting civil rights through legislation prohibiting discrimination in employment, in public accommodations, housing, banking, insurance, and on common carriers.

The Constitution also promotes cooperation among the states. Here the main means is the **full faith and credit clause.** It reads, "Full Faith and Credit shall be given in each State to the public Acts, Records, and judicial Proceedings of every other State," and that "A person charged in any State with Treason, Felony, or other Crime, who shall flee from Justice, and be found in another State, shall on Demand of the executive Authority of the State from which he fled, be delivered up, to be removed to the State having Jurisdiction of the Crime" (Article IV). Under this clause, one state is bound to recognize the legal acts of another, even though their policies may differ. For instance, a marriage that is legally performed in one state must be recognized by another, even though the second state may have different health and age requirements. Similarly, a divorce decree of one state must be recognized as legal in another, although the grounds for divorce vary considerably among the states. The same is true of wills and other civil instruments. The extradition of persons accused or convicted of crimes is also required.

However, the cooperation anticipated through Article IV has not been perfect. When residents of one state go to another as migrants for the purpose of gaining a divorce and then return to their native state, a jurisdictional issue may arise. Even when a divorce granted in one state is recognized by a second state, related child custody and property settlements may be subject to the jurisdiction of the second state. Extradition is usually smooth, but sometimes a state governor is reluctant or unwilling to return an individual to the state from which he or she fled. What is a crime in one state may be an act of heroism and virtue in another, as was true of civil rights protests in the 1960s. The unfair or harsh treatment that one accused of a crime is likely to receive in the state seeking extradition may also be a barrier to his or her return. Thus, while in most instances the full faith and credit clause does promote cooperation, there have been enough exceptions to generate a good deal of litigation and a whole area of study and adjudication called "conflict of laws."

The Fourteenth Amendment's **equal protection clause** is also of importance to interstate relations. It prohibits a state from discriminating against nonresidents and new residents in some contexts. For instance, regulations requiring substantial residency in a state before becoming eligible for state welfare benefits have been challenged successfully under this amendment.[29] Interestingly, in a leading case, a state made an administrative argument that residency requirements facilitated budgetary planning and reduced fraud.[30] The

Supreme Court, however, was less impressed with these concerns than with the free movement of individuals from one state to another and their equal treatment under the law. Nevertheless, in some circumstances, including public employment and higher education, states may treat established residents differently from nonresidents or newcomers. States may also require new residents and nonresidents to take occupational tests prior to being permitted to practice a trade or profession within their jurisdiction. The full faith and credit clause does not require one state to recognize occupational licenses granted by another. Lawyers, for example, may be required to take a bar examination in every state in which they seek to practice. Ultimately, it is for the federal judiciary to decide whether state policies having a discriminatory impact on newcomers or nonresidents are constitutional. Generally speaking, in reaching their conclusions, the courts weigh the state's rationale or interest in propounding regulations of this nature against their infringement on the equal protection and other constitutional interests of individuals.

Another form of cooperation among the states is anticipated by the Constitution. Article I, section 10, allows a state to enter into an "Agreement or Compact with another State," *provided* that Congress gives its consent. The Supreme Court has interpreted congressional consent to be pertinent only when such agreements or compacts increase the political power of the states and encroach upon the powers of the federal government.[31] Interstate compacts have been important means by which two or more states can tackle a common problem, such as pollution, health, the protection of natural resources and wildlife, and dealing with traffic congestion and transportation in a metropolitan area. Compacts may include the national government as a party. They sometimes create governmental "authorities" such as the Port of New York Authority, which was established by New York State and New Jersey in 1921. Authorities of this nature are single-purpose governments, although they can be quite extensive. The Port Authority, for instance, is involved in the operation of airports, trains, buses, bridges, tunnels, and land and sea terminals. Although interstate authorities facilitate coordination among the states involved, they also fragment government responsibility and may make it difficult to coordinate the provision of municipal services.

States can also coordinate many of their policies without entering into formal compacts. For instance, in 1983 the governors of New York, New Jersey, New Hampshire, Connecticut, Massachusetts, Rhode Island, and Pennsylvania sought to coordinate state laws concerning the minimum drinking age.[32] They reasoned that a uniform drinking age would promote highway safety and save lives by reducing the number of people who drive from one state to another in search of a "legal beverage." The possibilities for states simply to agree to coordinate policies are virtually endless. However, different economic and cultural interests in the states often dictate disparate policies. For instance, independent-minded Vermont was notably uninvolved in the northeastern governors' efforts.

Another means of coordination among the states rests in the adoption of uniform laws. The most successful of these has been the Uniform Commercial Code, which covers a number of commercial transactions and is subscribed to by all the states, except Louisiana. Other attempts at uniformity in the face of the diversity anticipated by federalism have fared less well. As noted in Chapter 2, about two-thirds of the states have adopted administrative procedure acts, but these are somewhat competing models.

Where it is envisioned that the states will need an ongoing organization to facilitate coordination, a regional commission may be established. There is an Appalachian Regional Commission for economic development, and a New England Regional Commission for river-basin planning.[33]

Relationships among Local Governments

The overwhelming proportion of the 87,000 governments in the United States are below the state level. A typical large metropolitan area includes several municipalities, school districts, and special districts or public authorities. It may overlap county and state lines (see Box 3–8). Although there are clearly many common interests among adjacent local governments and those in close proximity to one another, there are also some aspects of their relationships that are almost inevitably competitive. Like states, municipalities compete with each other for business investments in offices, manufacturing facilities, shopping malls, and other forms of economic development. They also compete for federal and state grants and other public investments. They compete in the same labor markets for their public employees. Frequently, the actions of one jurisdiction will have problematic effects on its neighbors. For example, it is not uncommon for municipalities or counties to locate landfills at the edges of their boundaries, leaving their neighbors to cope with the pollution, health hazards, and damage to property values that they cause. Local zoning decisions can affect other jurisdictions. A shopping mall in a newer suburb may pose threats to the retailers in downtown areas of central cities and older suburbs. Sporting events, rock concerts, and other mass spectator activities can create traffic jams and congestion across municipal lines. Suburban strip development may impede the flow of traffic into central cities. According to one view, suburbs are able to exploit the specialization in central cities without paying for its social and other costs.[34]

At the same time, though, some of the activities in one jurisdiction are likely to have beneficial spillover effects on others. The same concert or sporting event that ties up traffic may bring patrons to the area's motels, restaurants, bars, and shops. The location of hospitals, universities, and theaters in one town may improve the quality of life and desirability of locating in nearby ones. Coordinating and managing these relationships is a major political and administrative concern.

The traditional managerial perspective on relationships among local governments favors reduction of the number of independent municipalities through consolidation or the imposition of countywide or even regional governance.[35] The managerial perspective is particularly critical of the overlapping and duplicative functions performed by adjacent municipalities and

BOX 3-8 **The Intergovernmental Maze: Counties, Cities, and Towns in the St. Louis Metropolitan Area**

SOURCE: John L. Andriot, *Township Atlas of the United States*, (McLean, Va.: Andriot Associates, 1979), 367.

the high overhead costs they incur. Economies of scale may be lost and co-ordination may be expensive. If regional problems are not treated on a regional basis, then resources may not be expended in the most cost-effective manner. Consolidation has sometimes been achieved by transferring municipal functions to the encompassing county. Annexation of smaller jurisdictions by central cities also reduces the number of independent governments in an area. In Florida, the Miami–Dade County Metropolitan Government has sought to reassign governmental functions in order to reduce costs and increase effectiveness.

The political and NPM perspective on the plethora of local governments is quite different. It views small-scale governments as a means of enhancing political responsiveness and representativeness. Historically, general-purpose local governments were a manifestation of grassroots democracy. The New England town meeting epitomizes the democratic and participatory self-government that can be achieved at the local level. Residents are afforded a meaningful opportunity to express their views in a public forum and to approve or disapprove of proposed governmental activities. Such government may be viewed as an end in itself, but the contemporary public choice and NPM approaches take their logic further.[36] The multiplicity of municipalities in a large urban area may offer diverse combinations of public services. They may emphasize different educational, economic, developmental, crime control, and recreational points of view. If considered analogous to an economic market, individuals (that is, the customers or consumers of public services) might choose to locate in those jurisdictions that suit their needs best. The presumed competition among municipalities for residents might impel them to be responsive to the public's demands for services. Moreover, because the "citizen-consumer" pays taxes, the competition might extend to the provision of such services in the most efficient fashion, thereby meeting the traditional managerial concerns head-on.

The dispute between the traditional administrative-management approach and the political/public choice perspective remains unresolved. Those who support consolidation question the virtue of self-government that causes problems for neighboring jurisdictions. One town's public choice to locate its dump near the water supply of another, whose residents have no say in the matter, hardly appears democratic. How responsive a small government is to its voters depends on a number of factors, including the citizens' interest in the local community, the degree of competition between candidates or parties, and the quantity of resources available. The extent to which individuals locate and *relocate* themselves in accordance with the mixes of services provided by different governments is generally unknown (and perhaps very limited). Therefore the validity of a fundamental premise of the public choice approach remains in doubt. By way of counterpoint, large jurisdictions may not achieve the economies of scale predicted by those favoring consolidation.[37] Given these divergent perspectives and the practical impediments to consolidation, "interlocal" governmental relations are certain to remain an area of challenge to public administrators for some time to come.

Whatever the fate of consolidation, there is strong interest in coordinating public services. From 1954 to the mid-1980s, the federal government promoted the creation of Regional Councils, also called Councils of Government, as a means of coordinating the administrative activities of subnational governments. By 1980 there were over 660 such councils blanketing the country. They were involved in several policy areas, including planning, criminal justice, water quality, housing, and economic development. When President Ronald Reagan's administration reduced federal participation in local governmental affairs, their number dropped to about 530. Most states continue to sponsor coordination through the use of planning and development districts in which local governmental units participate.[38] The NPM's emphasis on responsiveness to customers in the form of "one-stop shopping" for government services places a strong emphasis on coordination and the relaxation of jurisdictional boundaries. It strongly favors the integration of human services so that customers can have their needs met with few visits to agencies. For instance, rather than having to go to different agencies for assistance with housing, nutrition, health, job training, employment, and financial assistance, a human services integration model would enable customers to contact one administrator only who would arrange for provision of the services for which they were eligible. Human services integration and other coordination can be aided immensely by contemporary information technology's capacity to allow agencies to share information and identify overlaps and gaps in their programs.

CONCLUSION

One can see many forces at work in the structuring of public administration in the United States. In fact, the nature of the 87,000 governments and their interrelationships are so complex that it is often difficult for governmental officials and citizens alike to keep track of administrative authority and responsibility. Perhaps the best way of understanding the contemporary American administrative state is to view it as a contest or tension between fragmentation and diversity on the one hand, and coordination and uniformity on the other.

Political, as opposed to administrative, judgment stands largely on the side of fragmentation and diversity. It favors federalism as the solution to the problem of developing a representative government in a large territory. It also favors political decentralization as a means of affording the population a good measure of influence over matters of local governance. But it was also a political judgment to establish a *national* government as a means of coordinating activities among the states and of promoting uniform policies for economic development, military strength, and other purposes. This was accomplished through a constitution that clearly reflects the tensions between fragmentation and coordination. The Constitution protects state sovereignty in some respects and creates a national government that depends on the states in several others, including representation in the Senate. But it also gives the national government considerable power over commerce and has been interpreted to require state protection of many rights that are thought to be too fundamental to vary from jurisdiction to jurisdiction. It must be noted that although constitutional law may promote uniformity in one sense, it frequently fosters diversity in another. Thus, when states are forbidden from abridging someone's free exercise of religion or freedom of speech, individual diversity is protected even though the same constitutional standard is imposed upon all the states.

For the most part, administrative judgment stands on the side of coordination and uniformity. Federal administrators devote a great deal of time, money, effort, and thought to seeking ways of implementing national programs in conjunction and coordination with state and local governments. But public administration in the United States is itself fragmented and decentralized. Coordinating activities among the agencies of one government can be difficult—from the lowest level to the highest. This is not a reflection of poor management; rather, it is a consequence of the mix of political, legal, and managerial approaches that dominate our public administrative theory and practice. Ironically, managerially based efforts to take the administration of many local matters, such as schools, cemeteries, and transportation, out of politics have contributed to further fragmentation and made coordination all the more difficult. This has made some yearn for the days of old, before administrative reforms got hold of governments, when coordination was imposed by political machines and strong political parties, relying heavily on patronage. But must coordination come at the price of "dirty politics and corrupt government"?

Although historical analysis might lead one to answer with a resounding "yes," the student and practitioner of public administration should reject such a trade-off as inapt. The system can work, it *does* work, and it can work well. Of course, it can still be improved. But improvement depends in part on public administrators who can integrate the competing values and perspectives found in public administration and coordinate administrative activities among different levels of government. The system often depends on such integration. Viewed in this context, the "sanitarian" mentioned earlier is an inspiration.

NOTES

1. U.S. Department of Commerce, *Statistical Abstract of the United States* (Washington, D.C.: Government Printing Office, 1995), 297.
2. According to Alfred Malabre, "The Outlook," *The Wall Street Journal*, 5 August 1991, taxpayers must work, on average, until May 8 of each year to meet the combined federal, state, and local tax bill. The date was April 28 during President Reagan's first term.
3. *Katzenbach v. McClung*, 379 U.S. 294 (1964).
4. *Wickard v. Filburn*, 317 U.S. 111 (1942).

5. *United States v. Lopez*, 514 U.S.—; 131 L.Ed. 2d 626 (1995).
6. Ibid., 641.
7. *Carbone v. Town of Clarkstown*, 128 L.Ed. 399, 409 (1994).
8. Ibid.
9. Ibid., 418.
10. *Garcia v. San Antonio Metropolitan Transit Authority*, 469 U.S. 528 (1985).
11. *U.S. Term Limits v. Thornton*, 514 U.S.—; 131 L.Ed. 2d 881 (1995).
12. David C. Nice, *Federalism: The Politics of Intergovernmental Relations* (New York: St. Martin's Press, 1987), 4–9.
13. U.S. Department of Commerce, *Statistical Abstract, 1995*, 297.
14. Daniel R. Grant and H.C. Nixon, *State and Local Government in America*, 3d ed. (Boston: Allyn & Bacon, 1975), 380.
15. Robert Lorch, *State and Local Politics*, 2d ed. (Englewood Cliffs, N.J.: Prentice-Hall, 1986), 15.
16. George Berkley and Douglas Fox, *80,000 Governments* (Boston: Allyn & Bacon, 1978), 40–41. New York's constitution has limited the width of certain ski trails.
17. Lorch, *State and Local Politics*, 14.
18. Grant and Nixon, *State and Local Government in America*, 114.
19. Ibid., table 12-1.
20. Berkley and Fox, *80,000 Governments*, 99.
21. R. Douglas Arnold, *Congress and the Bureaucracy* (New Haven, Conn.: Yale University Press, 1979).
22. Nice, *Federalism*, 92.
23. Morton Grodzins, *The American System* (Chicago: Rand McNally, 1966), 80; quoted in Grant and Nixon, *State and Local Government in America*, 37–38.
24. Morton Grodzins, "The Federal System," in *Goals for Americans*, ed. by the American Assembly (Englewood Cliffs, N.J.: Prentice-Hall, 1960), 265–266; quoted in Grant and Nixon, *State and Local Government in America*, 37–38.
25. See David H. Rosenbloom and Rosemary O'Leary, *Public Administration and Law*, 2d ed. (New York: Marcel Dekker, 1996), chap. 3; *Goldberg v. Kelly*, 397 U.S. 254 (1970); *Mathews v. Eldridge*, 424 U.S. 319 (1976).
26. Michael Sparer and Lawrence Brown, "Between a Rock and a Hard Place: How Public Managers Manage Medicaid," in Frank Thompson, ed., *Revitalizing State and Local Public Service* (San Francisco: Jossey-Bass, 1993), 303.
27. David Walker, *The Rebirth of Federalism* (Chatham, N.J.: Chatham House, 1995), 266.
28. Ibid.
29. *Shapiro v. Thompson*, 394 U.S. 618 (1969).
30. Ibid.
31. *Virginia v. Tennessee*, 148 U.S. 503 (1893).
32. *New York Times*, 6 December 1983.
33. Ann O'M. Bowman and Richard C. Kearney, *The Resurgence of the States* (Englewood Cliffs, N.J.: Prentice-Hall, 1986), 29.
34. Theodore J. Lowi, *The End of Liberalism* (New York: Norton, 1969), 197.
35. See Nice, *Federalism*, chap. 8.
36. See Robert Bish and Vincent Ostrom, *Understanding Urban Government* (Washington, D.C.: American Enterprise Institute, 1973), for a classic discussion.
37. Nice, *Federalism*, 188.
38. Bowman and Kearney, *The Resurgence of the States*, 162; Walker, *The Rebirth of Federalism*, 274–276.

ADDITIONAL READING

PETERSON, PAUL. *The Price of Federalism.* Washington, D.C.: Brookings Institution, 1995.

RIVLIN, ALICE. *Reviving the American Dream.* Washington, D.C.: Brookings Institution, 1992.

WALKER, DAVID. *The Rebirth of Federalism.* Chatham, N.J.: Chatham House, 1995.

ZIMMERMAN, JOSEPH. *Contemporary American Federalism.* New York: Praeger, 1992.

STUDY QUESTIONS

1. Some believe that the United States has too many governments in the sense that governmental authority is too fragmented and that the cost of redundancies and loss of coordination is too high. Would you favor abolishing any levels or kinds of government? Why or why not?

2. What are some of the externalities and spillover effects that public universities cause for the municipalities and counties in which they are located? How might universities and local governments deal with these?

3. There have been periodic calls to realign the functions of government so that the national government would be responsible for, say, defense, foreign affairs, and health; whereas the subnational governments would have complete control over welfare and housing policy. Assuming such realignments were politically feasible, which functions would you place at the state level? Local level? Why?

PART TWO | *Core Functions*

Chapter 4	Organization: Structure and Process
Chapter 5	Public Personnel Administration and Collective Bargaining
Chapter 6	Budgeting
Chapter 7	Decision Making
Chapter 8	Policy Analysis and Implementation Evaluation

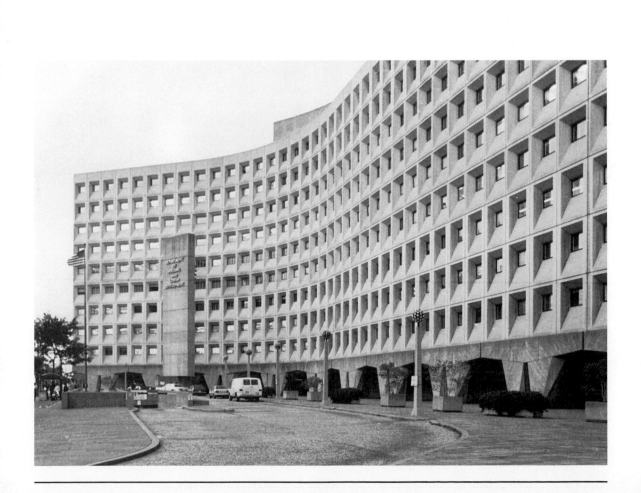

CHAPTER 4 | *Organization: Structure and Process*

Organizations can be designed to achieve certain values and objectives. Because so much of contemporary life involves organizations, much attention has been paid to designing organizations appropriately. In public administration, bureaucratic organization has been very common. Bureaucracy, a form of organization with several structural and procedural attributes, will be discussed in this chapter as will contemporary efforts to improve on it and to design better organizations. Organization always involves relationships among employees, including supervisors. The "scientific management" and "human relations" approaches have defined the classic ways of structuring such relationships. The new public management (NPM) is currently offering new ways of organizing public agencies. At present, there are distinct managerial, political, and legal approaches to organizational structure and process. One possible way of synthesizing these approaches is through a more participatory form of public organization.

Public administration concerns *organized* activity aimed at the provision of services and the application of constraints to individuals and groups. It requires *organization*. But organization can take many different forms and can maximize many diverse values. The *structure* of an organization affects the behavior of the organization as a whole and of the individual members of it. The same is true of the *processes* through which organizations operate. The structure and process of an organization can also have an impact on its clients and customers. By designing organizational structures and processes of one kind or another, different values can be maximized, different needs can be served, and different purposes can be achieved. Therefore, the organization of administrative activity ranks at the forefront of questions with which the student and practitioner of public administration must be concerned. As in other areas of public administration, though, there are few simple answers. Rather, there are competing responses to this basic issue: How should the public agencies be organized?

ORGANIZATION THEORY

Organization coordinates human activity. Armies are a contemporary example that reaches back to antiquity. As human cultures developed from hunter-gatherer societies to the "postindustrial," technocratic ones found in some places today, greater reliance was placed on organizations as a means of achieving social, economic, and political purposes. The twentieth century has been characterized by the development of an "organizational society"[1]—that is, a society in which a great deal of our waking time is spent in organizations, such as schools, universities, workplaces, and places of worship, recreation, and health care. Although organizations have existed for centuries, contemporary organizations represent a qualitative change in the way we go about our lives. The crux of the modern organizational society is suggested in Amitai Etzioni's comprehensive yet succinct definition of organization:

> Organizations are social units (or human groupings) deliberately constructed and reconstructed to seek specific goals. Corporations, armies, schools, hospitals, churches, and prisons are included; tribes, classes, ethnic groups, friendship groups, and families are excluded. Organizations are characterized by: (1) divisions of labor, power, and communication responsibilities, divisions which are not random or traditionally patterned, but deliberately planned to enhance the realization of specific goals; (2) the presence of one or more power centers which control the concerted efforts of the organization and direct them toward its goals; these power centers also must review continuously the organization's performance and re-pattern its structure, where necessary, to increase its efficiency; (3) substitution of personnel, i.e., unsatisfactory persons can be removed and others assigned their tasks. The organization can also recombine its personnel through transfer and promotion.[2]

Inherent in modern organization is the assumption that organizations should be rationally designed to achieve their purposes effectively and efficiently. It is perhaps above all the commitment to rationality that separates contemporary organizational society from earlier periods in human history.

Unfortunately, the task of designing organizations that effectively and efficiently achieve their purposes can be extremely complicated. It is obvious that an "organizational society" may not mesh well with cultural and political values that emphasize individualism and individual rights. "The problem of modern organizations is thus how to construct human groupings that are as rational as possible, and at the same time produce a minimum of undesirable side effects and a maximum of satisfaction."[3] Working or participating in an organization can be frustrating and alienating. Rather than being tools for the rational attainment of goals, organizations can emerge as powerful masters that seek their own survival, aggrandizement, and maximization of power. Organizations can also infringe upon the human rights of individuals to privacy, to freedom of expression and association, to peace, and even to love. They can also stand at odds with individual efforts at further occupational, professional, and psychological self-development.

Efforts to come to grips with the rise of modern organizations have led to the development of a self-conscious body of thought called "organization theory." Given its fragmented character, it might be more appropriate to speak in terms of *theories* of organization, but there are some premises that seem to underlie most of the thinking in this area.[4] Among these premises are the following: (1) the structure of an organization affects its behavior; (2) the structure of an organization affects the behavior of its workers, participants, and perhaps even casual members; (3) organizational processes also affect organizational and individual behavior; (4) organizations can be rationally (or scientifically) designed structurally and procedurally to achieve their goals in an effective and efficient manner; (5) organizations can usefully be conceptualized as systems that respond to and affect their environments and seek to gain information about the efficacy of those responses; and (6) organizations may have cultures that partially define how their members conceptualize organizational activity and the environment.

In general, organizational theory is "generic" in the sense that it does not make distinctions between public and private organizations. All organizations share some characteristics, and virtually all significant ones are regulated by governments in one way or another.[5] Nevertheless, by and large, public sector (or governmental) organizations face legal-constitutional, political, and market conditions that distinguish them from most private organizations. Some theorists concentrate on these distinctions in an effort to develop better knowledge about public organizations.[6] To date, organization theory has made some important strides; but it remains true, as Charles Perrow, a leading theorist, observed, that "[w]e have probably learned more, over several decades of research and theory, about the things that do *not* work (even though some of them obviously *should* have worked), than we have about things that do work."[7] What are some of the lessons we have learned?

COMMONALITIES IN PUBLIC ADMINISTRATIVE ORGANIZATION

There are certain aspects of organization theory that are so commonplace and ingrained that they have become part of the society's culture.[8] They serve as a platform for almost all discussions of how public administration should be organized.

Bureaucracy

Some aspects of the concept of bureaucracy and the attributes of that form of organization were already discussed in Chapter 1. But bureaucracy has been so central to public administration that we must continually return to it. In fact, for some, "modern organization" is virtually synonymous with "bureaucracy." This is because so many organizations make use of structural and procedural characteristics that are associated with bureaucracy. According to the highly influential theory developed by Max Weber, these characteristics, in turn, make bureaucracies behave in predictable ways.

Weber was a German sociologist (1864–1920) who used an "ideal-type" approach to identifying the structure, process, and behavior of bureaucratic organization.[9] The "ideal type" was not intended to be an observed reality. Rather, it is a mental construct that claims to identify what would emerge if a phenomenon (such as bureaucracy) could develop into its most complete form, that is, what it would be like if there were no militating forces to limit its full development. Thus, Weber does not purport to describe reality; but he does identify the essence of bureaucracy. (Examples of federal agencies that meet Weber's criteria are presented in Boxes 4–1 and 4–2.) In abridged form, bureaucracy in Weber's concept consists of the following structural elements:

1. Specialized jurisdictions, offices, and tasks; that is, a division of labor and authority regarding the achievement of the organization's goals.
2. A hierarchy of authority to coordinate the activities of the specialized offices and to integrate their jurisdictional authority. In the most rational bureaucratic design, the organization is headed by a single individual authority.
3. A career structure in which individual employees of the bureaucratic organization move through various specializations and ranks. Movement is based on merit and/or seniority.
4. A bureaucratic structure that tends to be permanent. It remains intact regardless of the flow of members in and out of it. Society becomes dependent on the bureaucracy's functioning to the extent that chaos results if it is destroyed.
5. By implication, bureaucracies are large organizations.

BOX 4–1 **Organization of the Department of the Interior**

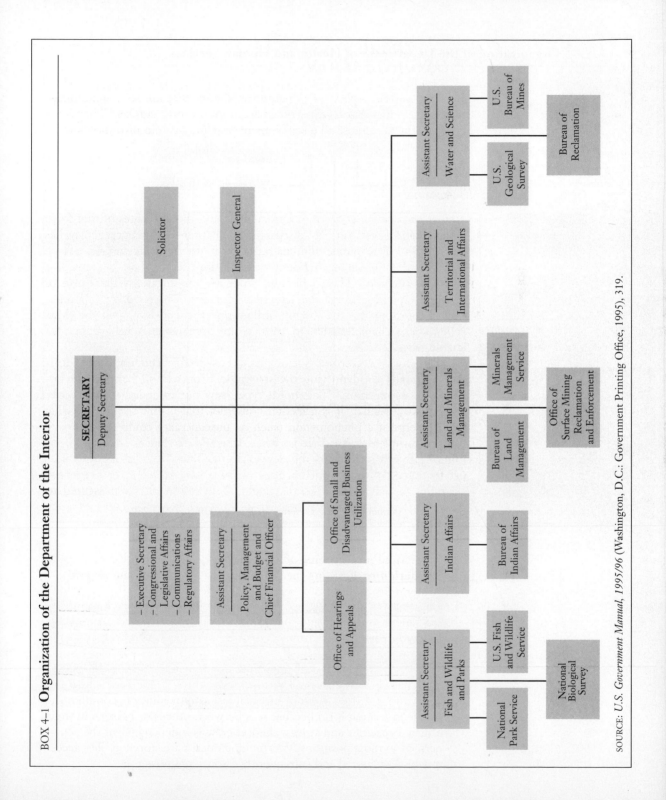

SOURCE: *U.S. Government Manual, 1995/96* (Washington, D.C.: Government Printing Office, 1995), 319.

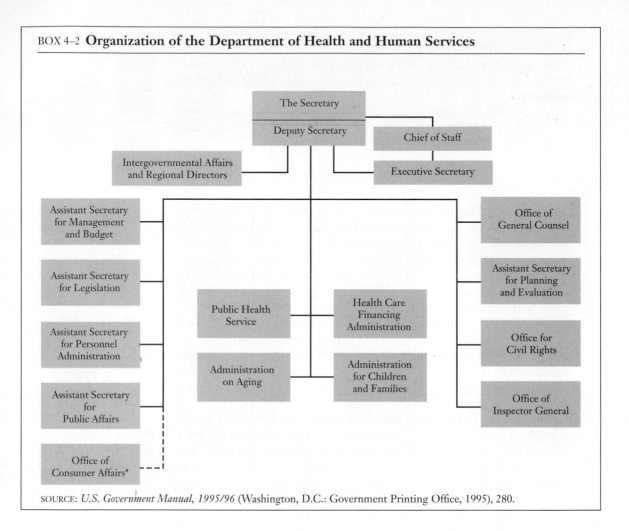

BOX 4–2 **Organization of the Department of Health and Human Services**

SOURCE: *U.S. Government Manual, 1995/96* (Washington, D.C.: Government Printing Office, 1995), 280.

Procedurally, bureaucracy is

1. *Impersonal or dehumanizing.* This was considered by Weber to be bureaucracy's "special virtue" because it eliminates "irrational" emotional elements from the performance of the individual bureaucrats and the organization as a whole.
2. *Formalistic.* Because bureaucracy does not depend on persons but rather on offices (literally, "desks"), virtually everything about its structure and operation is written down in a formal fashion. In addition, communication is in written form because it is between offices or persons in their official capacities and at least theoretically is independent of the actual persons in those positions. Written documents are stored in files, access to which is limited and is frequently a source of power.

3. *Rule-bound.* Bureaucracy operates according to formal rules that are in writing and can be learned. The object of the rules is to specify proper office procedure and to assure regularity in dealing with outsiders. These rules also seek to ensure impersonality and bolster hierarchical authority.
4. *Highly disciplined.* Individual bureaucrats are bound by the bureaucracy's rules and authority structure. They may be disciplined for rule infractions and insubordination.

As a result of these structural and procedural characteristics, bureaucracy is

1. *Highly efficient.* Weber regarded bureaucracy as the most efficient form of organization. It acts with continuity, precision, rationality, expertise, speed, and discipline. Its use of discretion is predictable, because it is structurally and procedurally constrained. Bureaucracy is reliable and reduces the emotional costs of attaining its goals. In Weber's view, bureaucracy compared with other forms of organization as did the machine with nonmechanical modes of production.
2. *Powerful.* Its power stems largely from its rationality, expertise, reliability, and continuity. Weber maintains that the well-developed bureaucracy is virtually uncontrollable by outsiders and that society becomes dependent on it for the provision of services and the application of constraints. Thus, the organizational tool (bureaucracy) tends to emerge as the master of society.
3. *Ever-expanding.* Bureaucratic expansion is prompted not only by efficiency and power, but also by the quantitative and qualitative growth of tasks requiring organized administration in a complex society. However, even as Weber described the advantages of bureaucracy, he admonished against its tendency to engulf society:

It is horrible to think that the world could one day be filled with nothing but those little cogs [bureaucrats], little men clinging to little jobs and striving towards bigger ones. . . . This passion for bureaucracy . . . is enough to drive one to despair. . . . [W]hat can we oppose to this machinery in order to keep a portion of mankind free from this parcelling-out of the soul, from this supreme mastery of the bureaucratic way of life.[10]

Two additional points require emphasis. First, when Weber referred to individual bureaucratic employees as "cogs," he was recognizing the extent to which bureaucracy is dehumanizing; it turns the individual into an appendage to a machinelike organization. The organization is not supposed to adapt to the individual's personal, emotional, psychological, mental, or even physical idiosyncrasies. Rather, the individual is *standardized* to fit the particular organizational slot in which he or she is to be used. The organization revolves around positions and offices, not persons. Second, the power of bureaucratic organization is not derived just from its structural and procedural attributes but also flows from its *rationality*. People comply with bureaucratic orders and decisions because they accept them as legitimate. Their legitimacy is based on the belief that they are rational, reflect trained expertise and not irrational whims, and are regulated by law or official directive. In the ideal-type bureaucracy—although not, of course, in its real-world counterpart—an arbitrary, capricious, or personally discriminatory decision or order is an impossibility.

There has been a great deal of debate over the utility of Weber's concept and theory of bureaucracy. Although current consensus appears to be that Weber provided a brilliant and useful statement, four points of contention remain. First, however bureaucracy might function as an ideal type, we live in a real world in which bureaucratic organizational behavior seems markedly at variance with Weber's ideas. Warren Bennis, a leading contemporary organizational theorist, seems to have captured this point best. He writes that real-world bureaucracy is characterized by

- bosses without (and underlings with) technical competence;

- arbitrary and zany rules;

- an underworld (or informal) organization which subverts or even replaces the formal apparatus;

- confusion and conflict among roles;

- cruel treatment of subordinates based not on rational or legal grounds but upon inhumanity.[11]

The NPM is also critical of bureaucracy's rule-bound and hierarchical qualities. It views bureaucracy as obsessed with procedure, but relatively unconcerned with results. In consequence, the NPM holds that bureaucracy is so tied up in red tape that it cannot respond efficiently to customers.

A second criticism is that Weber failed to understand the extent to which specialized expertise is inherently at odds with formal hierarchical authority. The point here is that the formal superordinate ("boss") becomes actually dependent on subordinates who have greater specialized technical expertise in various areas of the bureaucracy's operation. As Victor Thompson observes:

> Whereas the boss-man [worker] relationship is *formally* unilateral with rights running in one direction from the boss to the man, the advance of personal specialization is converting the relationship *informally* into a unilateral one with ability running from the man to the boss. Authority is centralized, but ability is inherently decentralized because it comes from practice rather than from definition. Whereas the boss retains his full *rights* to make all decisions, he has less and less *ability* to do so because of the advance of science and technology.[12]

This growing gap between ability and authority can be the source of great stress for the "boss," who is responsible for operations over which he or she has far less than full control. The NPM emphasizes employee empowerment precisely because "Management too often is happily unaware of what occurs at the front desk or in the field. In fact, it's the people who work closest to problems who know the most about solving them."[13]

Third, as these two criticisms suggest, Weber may have overstated the extent to which bureaucrats can and do behave rationally. Herbert Simon, whose work in the 1940s and 1950s revolutionized public administrative thinking, reminded us that "human behavior in organizations is best described as 'intendedly rational. . . .'"[14] Complete rationality is frustrated by incomplete knowledge and information as well as by individuals' multiple, unranked preferences. Decision makers in organizations do not generally know what all the consequences of an important decision will be. Nor are they always able to determine which course of action suits their preferences most fully. The concept of "bounded rationality," as Simon's view has come to be called, is now an important aspect of the study of human behavior and decision making in organizations. (Chapter 7 is devoted to decision making.)

Finally, Weber's ideal-type analysis is widely considered of limited utility in designing real-world organizations because it fails to take into account the vast cultural differences among societies. In some national bureaucracies there are strong service ethics and high degrees of formalism and impersonality. Elsewhere, these characteristics are weak and bureaucratic encounters involve a good deal of personalization, pleading, and bargaining. Further, whereas the authority and legitimacy of a bureaucrat in Germany, France, or Austria may be strengthened by the high social status accorded to such functionaries, in other societies, such as the United States, the bureaucrat may be more or less an object of derision. Recognition of cultural variations that bear upon the operation of bureaucracies has prompted analysts to devote considerable attention to comparative public administration. It is hoped that by doing so, it will eventually be possible to analyze the effects of environmental and cultural factors on public bureaucracies.

Still, these criticisms should not be taken as rendering the Weberian analysis useless. All one needs to do is to belong to an organization, or better yet, try to form one, to realize how dependent American society is on the principles of bureaucratic organization. Specialization (often by committee), hierarchy (for coordination, often by a governing board or council of some type), and formalized procedure (Robert's rules) are well-known attributes of contemporary organizations, whether they be social clubs, university departments, or governmental units. Although sometimes contrasted with bureaucracy, successful market-driven firms can also be organized bureaucratically.

Scientific Management

Scientific management is a second aspect of organization theory that has worked its way into American culture. This approach developed, or at least was popularized, through the work of Frederick Taylor,[15] whose life span more or less coincided with Weber's. However, while Weber came to protest the transformation of employees into "cogs," Taylor embraced this transformation as a prerequisite for scientifically finding the most efficient way of accomplishing any given task. By contemporary standards, much of what Taylor had to say appears naive, paternalistic, inaccurate, and sometimes just plain silly. However, Taylorism became a worldwide movement and continues to have an important legacy in the public sector in the United States. Taylor developed four core principles of scientific management:

1. Management should study the mass of traditional knowledge possessed by workers and devise a way to accomplish each task, reducing it to a body of scientific laws of production. This requires time-and-motion studies that determine precisely the one best way of performing a specific work operation. For instance, Taylor developed a "science" of shoveling.
2. Workers should be scientifically selected according to physical, mental, and psychological attributes. If the one best way of shoveling coal is to do it in 21-pound loads, then a worker who has the physical strength and stamina to perform this operation would be selected. Equally important, Taylor stressed seeking workers who would "appreciate" management's help in making them more productive.
3. The worker should be scientifically motivated to do as management instructs. Taylor stressed tying productivity to pay through "piece-rate" pay plans, in which the worker was paid according to how much he or she produced. Taylor also thought the frequency with which pay should be given could be scientifically determined in the interests of maximum motivation. He also recommended developing effective sanctions against workers who failed to do as they were told.
4. Work should be redivided so that management has more responsibility for designing work processes and work flow. This proposal fostered the rise of a "science" of efficiency engineering.

It was characteristic of Taylor's optimism that he assumed that scientific management would yield greater cooperation between workers and management. He believed his system would lead to greater productivity and therefore a higher standard of living for any society in the long run. The greater productivity would yield more profit to go around and therefore would reduce conflict over the distribution of revenues derived from the sale of products or services. Workers would lose some control over their work, but they would increase their standard of living.

In specific terms, Taylor's legacy has been pronounced in professionalized management, industrial engineering, industrial psychology, deskilled jobs, and a group of activities found in contemporary personnel administration. In the public sector, position classification and job design continue to reflect many of the attitudes and ideas of scientific management. More generally, Taylorism strongly reinforced the idea that the individual worker should be treated as an appendage to a machine, should perform only those functions that a machine or animal—today we might add robot—could not perform more cheaply. Workers should not be encouraged to participate in the designing of work processes and work flow, because these were matters for scientific managers. It also contributed to the still prevalent idea that productivity is the primary object of organization and that the "good" organization is the one that efficiently produces what it is intended to. In this view, the bottom line, so to speak, is output; what happens to the worker in the process—boredom, alienation, lack of personal growth, occupational disease—is of secondary concern. Work is to supply products and services, not to develop the full capability of workers.

Of course, when one lays bare the premises of Taylorism, it can sound dreadful. Yet as a society, the United States continues to define the workplace in terms of efficiency and productivity. The prevalent attitude is that good performance should be rewarded and inadequate productivity punished. Moreover, even on such emotionally wrenching issues as plant closings, large-scale downsizing, and mandatory retirement, many prefer to enhance organizational efficiency rather than to reduce human and community costs.

The Human Relations Approach

The dehumanization explicit in Weber's ideal-type bureaucracy and implicit in Taylorism has been considered by some to be dysfunctional even in organizational terms because it runs counter to the needs of the human beings who actually make up the organization. Amitai Etzioni describes the problem posed by highly rational, dehumanizing organizations:

> Generally the less the organization alienates its personnel, the more efficient it is. Satisfied workers usually work harder and better than frustrated ones. Within limits, happiness heightens efficiency in organizations and, conversely, without efficient organizations much of our happiness is unthinkable. Without well-run organizations our standard of living, our level of culture, and our democratic life could not be maintained. Thus, to a degree, *organizational rationality and human happiness go hand in hand.* But a point is reached in every organization where happiness and efficiency cease to support each other. Not all work can be well-paid and gratifying, and not all regulations and orders can be made acceptable. Here we face a true dilemma.[16]

In large part, the object of the **human relations approach** has been to try to alleviate this dilemma by developing ways of making work in organizations more socially and psychologically acceptable to employees while at the same time enhancing or at least maintaining efficiency. Thus, the human relations approach accepts efficiency and productivity as the legitimate values of organization but seeks to maximize these by eliminating the dysfunctions caused by overspecialization, alienating hierarchical arrangements, and general dehumanization.

Ironically, the human relations approach grew out of a rather elaborate but standardly conceptualized set of experiments in the scientific management tradition. Elton Mayo, Fritz Roethlisberger, and others conducted studies at the Hawthorne Works of the Western Electric Company in Chicago from 1927 to 1932.[17] The experiments started from the premise that the physical conditions at work would directly affect productivity. For instance, it was hypothesized that an increase in illumination would lead to greater production per worker. This turned out to be the case, but as the experiment proceeded and lighting was reduced to the original level, it was observed that productivity remained higher than it had been before the study began. From a scientific management perspective this was puzzling indeed. Eventually, the experimenters concluded that to some extent the workers were actually responding to the experiment itself, that is, the attention being devoted to them, rather than to the levels of illumination. This phenomenon was dubbed the "Hawthorne effect." In the context of organization, it stands for the premise that social and psychological factors can play a major role in determining the productivity of workers. This conclusion was a radical departure from the Weberian and Taylorist traditions emphasizing dehumanization because it asserted that human factors were key contributors to organizational efficiency. Put simply, the illumination experiment was taken to mean that if greater attention were paid to the worker as a person, the worker would feel a greater degree of self-esteem and happiness and would consequently be more productive.

As the Hawthorne studies continued, the researchers observed that workers socialize with one another and may form groups or informal organizations. As a result, workers tend to respond to changes in the work environment or formal organization as groups rather than as individuals. The responses could be functional in the sense of promoting greater productivity, or they could be dysfunctional, from the formal organization's perspective, by limiting productivity. A "functional" response would be, for example, that the production group would "cover" for a member who was having an off day and going slower than the norm. A "dysfunctional" response might be a mild, but symbolic, form of physical violence used against individual employees who exceed the group's norm for productivity. Such a collectively enforced limitation may be effectively imposed even though under the piece-rate pay plan it is in any given individual worker's economic interest to be as productive as possible. In short, the workplace may have a culture that affects both overall productivity and individual behavior.

Several very important conclusions were drawn from the Hawthorne experiments. These became the basis for further research and the development of the human relations approach to organization. Among them were that (1) productivity is strongly affected by social and psychological factors, not simply by physical ability and stamina; (2) noneconomic rewards and sanctions are significant determinants of workers' motivation and their level of job satisfaction; (3) the highest degree of specialization is not necessarily the most efficient approach to dividing labor; and (4) workers may react to management, the organization, and work itself as members of groups or informal organizations rather than as individuals. To the extent that these conclusions were accepted and acted on, human relations became an explicit central facet of organizational theory and behavior. It is important to remember, however, that the human relations approach did not assert that the ultimate objective of an organization was to increase the workers' happiness—the end remained efficiency and productivity. In short, the human relations approach conceptually put the human being back into the organization.

As this approach developed, organization theory placed greater emphasis on serving both the economic and noneconomic needs of workers and designing jobs to make them socially and psychologically satisfying. It also began to emphasize worker-management communication and worker participation in decision making concerning the way a product was to be manufactured or a service rendered. Perhaps especially important was the emergence of a new view of the complexity of the workers' motivation. Weber saw workers as cogs who were harnessed to a machine over which they had no control, while Taylor saw them as essentially one-dimensional and responsive only to economic rewards and sanctions. By the late 1930s, however, a new view found its way into print in Chester Barnard's very influential book entitled *The Functions of the Executive*.[18] Barnard was a successful manager of the New Jersey Bell Telephone Company and had a keen understanding of the complexities of human motivation at work. He emphasized the obvious in reminding those imbued with the principles of scientific management that organization depended on the willingness of its members to serve. Such willingness generally had to be induced and could be withdrawn by a participant at any time. Consequently, authority in organizations did not simply flow downward from the top; those on the bottom could also exercise power by refusing to cooperate. In Barnard's view, there was a "zone of indifference" in which workers would follow the directives of management without question. But orders beyond this zone would be questioned and perhaps opposed, subverted, or circumvented.

The zone of indifference is notably *personalized*. In theory, it can vary with each subordinate-superordinate relationship. The human relations approach followed through on this insight by dealing with personal and interpersonal behavior in organizations. A new dimension was added to organization theory, which had previously focused on the organization itself, rather than on the behavior of its members. Attention could now be more profitably turned to such key subjects as leadership and motivation.

Leadership

In *The Functions of the Executive*, Barnard called attention to the role of leadership in organizations. **Leadership** is a term that can be defined in several ways. However, at its core is the concept of consistent ability to influence people, to motivate them to serve a common purpose, and to fulfill the functions necessary for successful group action. Leadership is doing the right thing, whereas management is doing the things right.[19] The organization theory approach to leadership raises at least two broad concerns: What are the qualities of leadership? How is leadership exercised?

An early attempt to define the qualities of leadership focused on the personality traits of individuals who were clearly successful leaders. To an extent, this approach was derived from Max Weber's theorizing about "charismatic" authority.[20] According to Weber, some individuals are endowed with extraordinary qualities that induce others to follow their leadership. Religious leaders who are believed to be in contact with supernatural forces are a classic example. Some political leaders can also be considered "charismatic" in the technical Weberian sense. Many more have a kind of presence or charm that is now often called "charisma." And there is no doubt that many people are willing to follow their lead at least partly for this reason. Yet, when researchers try to pin down precisely the personality traits that contribute to leadership, they are unable to come up with any consistent listing. Some leaders are introverted, shy, bland, and given to procrastination, whereas others are flamboyant, eccentric, and decisive.

Failure to identify a set of personality traits of leaders suggests that leadership may be purely *situational*. In this view, circumstances external to the individual leader account for leadership. In other words, the corporation and the economy make the successful manager, rather than the other way around. Although the situational approach is valuable, it can also be too mechanistic. It would suggest that Ronald Reagan's personality had nothing to do with his historic landslide electoral victory in 1984, or that Michael Dukakis's was irrelevant to his poor showing in 1988. Clearly, the personal qualities of someone in a position of leadership can make a difference even though much of what leaders accomplish may be dictated by situational forces and circumstances.

Recent dissatisfaction with the strict situational approach has led to further efforts to discover something about the personalities of leaders. One psychological approach is to study leaders' level of ego development.[21] Findings thus far suggest that as compared to most social groups that have been studied, managers have a higher awareness of self and inner feelings. They are also more likely to think in terms of contingencies and multiple possibilities, as opposed to dichotomous categories such as "right" and "wrong." Rather than view rules as fixed, they tend to see them as guidelines subject to change and challenge.

Leaving aside the disputed ground of personality traits, are there any qualities and skills that seem to be prerequisites for effective leadership in a wide variety and large number of situations? Among those qualities and skills often mentioned are the following:

1. *Belief in the possibility of success.* Leaders want to change or maintain some aspect of social, political, or economic life. They must believe that there is a significant, though possibly small, likelihood that their efforts will make a difference. Anyone who takes the stance that "there's nothing I can do about it anyway" is not very likely to influence others to work toward a common goal.

2. *Communication skills.* Leaders must communicate with followers. Generally, this requires substantial verbal skill. Followers must have a reasonably clear picture of what is expected of them if they are in fact to work in a coordinated way toward a desired common purpose.

3. *Empathy.* Leaders often have a deep understanding of the psychology, thought processes, aspirations, and fears of their followers. Empathy not only facilitates communication but also enables the leader to find successful ways of influencing people. Empathy, of course, is not sympathy. The leader may remain detached or aloof yet still be able to enter the mental processes of the followers. Perhaps J. Edgar Hoover, former director of the Federal Bureau of Investigation, is the most familiar example of this. Few would have found him "warm." Yet he was extremely effective in building the FBI into a strong federal police agency partly because he understood the outlook of a large number of Americans on crime, communism, and morality. By 1974, the FBI had a central file of some 159 million fingerprints, and the number was increasing by about three thousand per day. These were mostly supplied by state and local agencies and private employers. But because of his ability to dispel Americans' fears of a national police agency while playing on their anxiety concerning communism, Hoover built the FBI into precisely such an agency with very little real opposition.[22]

4. *Energy.* Tales of the long hours put in by leaders are legion. The "workaholic" label probably fits many. To cite only a few examples, Eugene Lewis observes that Hyman Rickover, "father" of the U.S. nuclear Navy, and Robert Moses, who oversaw the building of more roads, bridges, tunnels, and parks than perhaps anyone in recent history, devoted tremendous time and attention to gaining detailed understanding of the projects and technologies that might be appropriate for their organizations.[23]

5. *Sound judgment.* Continuing leadership may depend substantially on the exercise of sound, reasoned judgment. Emotional, arbitrary, or capricious responses to situations are not the hallmark of long-lasting leadership—at least where the followers are free to abandon the leader. History is rife with examples of the downfall of leaders who irrationally engaged in disastrous blunders. One of the problems leaders may face is developing a feeling of infallibility, which will make sound judgment all the more difficult. In organizational terms, it is generally considered important for leaders to maintain an unbiased, disinterested (but not uninterested) posture with regard to the organization's members. This helps the leader keep matters in perspective. One should always consider such questions as How major or minor is an infraction or an individual's incompetence from the perspective of keeping an organization functioning toward the achievement of its goals? How serious a threat is some event or action occurring outside the organization? For instance, should scarce resources be expended to fight off every threat to a public administrative organization's jurisdiction, no matter how minor or remote?

6. *Constancy.* Leaders need to manage the trust placed in them by their followers. They must make it clear where they stand and avoid waivering capriciously, for self-aggrandizement, or opportunistically. Even though followers may disagree with a leader's specific position, they need to know he or she can be counted on to act in reasoned, consistent ways.

7. *Self-management.* Leaders must be aware of their own strengths and weaknesses and act accordingly. Leaders do not have to do everything themselves. There is no reason to expect leaders to master all the specializations found in large, complex organizations. They must remain focused on what they can achieve and contribute best. Leaders who become engulfed in routine tasks that could be done just as well or better by others are squandering their time.[24]

There are a number of other qualities that leaders often possess but which appear to be less essential. Intelligence is one. Certainly the "best and the brightest" are often in a position of leadership. But many leaders are not the most intelligent people found in a society. Nor does it appear crucial that leaders have technical proficiency in the work performed by their organizations, though many of them do. Finally, leadership is sometimes defined in terms of decision making, but some effective leaders have avoided decisions whenever possible.

In view of the generality of contemporary knowledge about leadership, some have sought to learn more by studying the organizational careers of individuals who were exceptionally successful public administrative leaders. For instance, Eugene Lewis's book, *Public Entrepreneurship: Toward a Theory of Bureaucratic Political Power* (1984), considers in depth the "organizational lives" of Hyman Rickover, J. Edgar Hoover, and Robert Moses. These men were eccentric in many respects, but Lewis found some common keys to their leadership.

First, each saw organizations as tools for the achievement of his own goals. These goals were not simply rising to the top but rather accomplishing something substantive through the organization. Hoover created a national police force, Rickover brought the U.S. Navy into the atomic age by demonstrating the desirability and feasibility of submarines driven by nuclear power, and Moses pursued his vision of the public good by building parks and improving transportation in the greater New York City area.

Second, Lewis finds that "the [highly successful] public entrepreneur typically 'owns' all or some of the reality premises of the society in one or more areas of specialized concern."[25] Such entrepreneurs dominate media accounts, legislative hearings, and various meetings pertinent to their area of specialization and interest. In this way, the leader comes to "own" some aspect of public policy. Hoover "owned" statistics pertaining to crime. Rickover "owned" nuclear power in the Navy, Moses "owned" the construction of parks and bridges in metropolitan New York.

Third, successful public administrative leaders grasp the potential impact that effective organizations can have. As Lewis puts it, "The public entrepreneur, somewhere during his career, comes to understand that *the large, complex public organization is the most powerful instrument for social, political, and economic change in the political universe.*"[26] Public organizations can provide a base of political power that protects the leader from opponents and serves as a lever for exercising influence on important external political actors, such as legislators. At the height of their influence, Hoover and Moses were untouchable by their political opponents.

Another important characteristic is that "each entrepreneur conveyed to his listeners the impression that he possessed a knowledgeability and a capacity to carry out monumental tasks that no other element in the political system seemed able to accomplish."[27] Rickover would introduce a new technology to submarine warfare that would make for a "true submarine," that is, one that could remain submerged for very extended periods of time. Hoover would control crime and subversion. Moses would mobilize the resources for huge projects, such as the Triboro Bridge. Robert Caro described the bridge, which connects the Bronx, Manhattan, and Queens, as follows: "Its anchorages, the masses of concrete in which its cables would be embedded, would be as big as any pyramid built by an Egyptian Pharaoh, its roadways wider than the widest roadways of the Caesars of Rome. . . . [It] would require enough concrete to pave a four-lane highway from New York to Philadelphia, enough to reopen Depression-shuttered cement factories from Maine to Mississippi. . . . [F]urnaces would have to be fired up at no fewer than fifty separate Pennsylvania steel mills. . . . [A]n entire forest would have to crash on the Pacific Coast on the opposite side of the American continent."[28]

Finally, public entrepreneurs like Hoover, Rickover, and Moses expand their "ownership" of areas of public policy. They extend the boundaries of their organizations in order to bring more and more under their control. This reduces uncertainty and maximizes autonomy, though it may eventually undercut the democratic processes of representative government. Perhaps Hoover is the best example. He expanded the FBI's role in society from combating narrowly defined federal crimes to working with local police forces throughout the nation to combating the alleged threat of subversion by communists and fellow travellers. The FBI grew from a small, ineffective adjunct of the Department of Justice to a virtually autonomous police agency with a presence throughout the nation. In theory, Hoover was subordinate to the president, the attorney general, and Congress. In practice, even when he was clearly out of touch with the nation's changing attitudes and concerns, he remained largely impervious to outside control. Indeed, Lewis observes that when Hoover died in office in 1972, it "was viewed by friend and foe alike as fortunate. . . ."[29]

Not all leaders in public agencies operate on the scale of Lewis's entrepreneurs. Norma Riccucci studied six federal senior executives who worked within their agencies to make major contributions in promoting human rights, health, environmental safety, and public integrity. She found that they all had the following:

1. *Political skills*, or the "ability to maneuver effectively within their policy environment"
2. *Management and leadership skills*, including the "ability to plan, organize, communicate clearly, motivate staff, and set realistic goals and to be honest, fair, understanding, knowledgeable of agency politics, and expert in their fields"
3. *Technical expertise* in their various fields
4. *Strategies* for achieving their goals

In summarizing their personalities, Riccucci frequently used the following terms: "integrity," "morality," "honest," "trustworthy," "ethical," and "good sense of humor."[30]

Discovering some of the basic qualities associated with leadership does not suggest we should ignore the contributions of the situational approach. The qualities necessary to lead may depend on the situation or precisely what the job is. Some functions require high reliability. Slipups at NASA, in firefighting, on aircraft carriers, and in dealing with nuclear power or waste can be fatal. Making mistakes when writing up parking tickets is merely annoying. Trust and constancy can also be more important in some situations than in others. For instance, one of the premises of federal freedom of information policy is that unless the government is able to protect the privacy of private parties under some specific circumstances, it will not be able to obtain the information it seeks from them.

The situational approach emphasizes the importance of adopting the most effective leadership style for the organization and the job concerned. The root of this approach lies in Chester Barnard's insight that organizations depend on individuals' willingness to serve and the extent of their zone of indifference. Using a related perspective, Amitai Etzioni has developed a useful scheme for organizing our thoughts about the appropriate leadership style in any given organization. He proposes that individual involvement in an organization can be based primarily on (1) a moral commitment to its goals and purposes (**moral involvement**); (2) a calculation that participating in the organization serves some individual need (**calculative involvement**); or (3) a belief that although the individual would rather not be associated with the organization, there is no viable alternative (**alienative involvement**).[31] Etzioni goes on to suggest that the appropriate kind of power used in organizations will depend on the nature of the involvement of most participants. In his view, normative power is most appropriate for organizations based on moral involvement, remunerative power for calculative involvement, and coercive power for alienative involvement. In short, the leadership style of voluntary organizations for the civic good should differ from the leadership style in a public bureau that processes applications for the renewal of drivers' licenses. Both should differ from the style in which a prison superintendent attempts to induce compliance from the prisoners.

Etzioni's perspective suggests that leadership styles can range from highly authoritarian through more democratic to laissez faire. Authoritarian leadership may be necessary when involvement is largely alienative. Here, even if physical coercion is unavailable, the leader can choose to keep organizational participants under tight and punitive supervision. Democratic leadership can be helpful where involvement is calculative because it can enable the leader to be more aware of the participants' personal reasons for willingness to serve in the organization. For instance, some may want status, others financial gain. Laissez-faire leadership, in which coordination and pursuit of group goals are organized almost entirely by the members, is potentially appropriate where involvement is moral. For instance, volunteers in building emergency sandbag dikes to prevent flooding of their hometown need materials and overall coordination, but they are not likely to require much supervision once they know how to fill, distribute, and place the bags.

A more thoroughly developed analysis of "How to Choose a Leadership Pattern" was presented by Robert Tannenbaum and Warren H. Schmidt in the *Harvard Business Review* in 1958. In 1973, they added a "Retrospective Commentary" to their classic article.[32] Like Etzioni, they emphasize the desirability of congruence between "forces" in the manager and those in the subordinates. The original article posited a continuum from a **boss-centered** leadership style to a **subordinate-centered** style. Although drawn more complexly in their article, the basic continuum was as follows, moving progressively from boss-centered to subordinate-centered leadership.

BOSS-CENTERED LEADERSHIP

1. The manager makes a decision and announces it.
2. The manager "sells" the decision to subordinates.
3. The manager presents ideas and invites questions.
4. The manager presents a tentative decision subject to change.
5. The manager presents a problem, obtains suggestions, and makes the decision.
6. The manager defines the restrictions pertinent to a decision and asks subordinates to make the decision as a group.
7. The manager permits subordinates to make decisions within broad limits defined by the manager.

SUBORDINATE-CENTERED LEADERSHIP

As the leadership style changed from highly boss-centered to more subordinate-centered, subordinates were given greater freedom and opportunities for participation in organizational decision making.

This scheme was modified by the authors in 1973, in response to a number of social and work-related changes that had occurred in the 1960s. Especially important were greater opposition to the exercise of hierarchical managerial authority, demands for participation in the workplace, and increasing concern with the quality of work life. In the 1973 version, subordinates were called "nonmanagers" and the labels on the continuum were changed. The boss-centered end was called "manager power and influence," whereas the other end was "nonmanager power and influence." There was also greater recognition that managers were dependent on the willingness of nonmanagers to accept their decisions and that an organization's environment could impose constraints on its decision making. For example, consumer groups and environmentalists might have to be taken into account.

Having posited these leadership styles, Tannenbaum and Schmidt reasoned that the most suitable one in any given context would depend on the managers, the subordinates or nonmanagers, and the organizational situation. For managers, the main concerns would be their personal beliefs in the desirability of participation and their willingness to tolerate risk and uncertainty. For the subordinates, the main forces would be their willingness to participate in decision making, their understanding of and identification with the goals of the organization, and their tolerance for ambiguous direction as opposed to highly specific instruction from hierarchical authorities.

An important conclusion is that the leadership style should be determined by the congruence of forces in the manager and those in the subordinates. A subordinate-centered leadership style would be inappropriate where subordinates did not want to share authority and participate in decision making. Conversely, where the subordinates do want greater freedom and participation, a boss-centered leadership style would be inappropriate. Nor, of course, could a manager who is uneasy when exercising authority or one who is opposed to subordinate participation simply change his or her style to make it congruent with the outlook of the subordinates.

"Forces" in the situation stem from pressures on the organization, the nature of its work tasks, problems, and objectives. For instance, in work that routinely involves severe time pressures or a crisis atmosphere, such as firefighting, it is inappropriate to hold group discussions and reach group decisions while the work is going on. Decisions must be made and followed quickly. In some situations, workers are so widely dispersed and unsupervised that they must have a good deal of autonomy while they are doing their jobs. Police are a good example. The size of organizational units and the nature of technologies used are other situational forces that should be considered.

Whatever the leadership style, leaders generally perform some similar functions for organizations. Sometimes a conceptual distinction between two broad types of leadership is useful. **Expressive leaders** play a fundamental role in goal setting and in gaining adherence to the norms and objectives of an organization. They also represent the organization to the outside world. **Instrumental leadership** involves maintenance of the organization in terms of securing the resources needed for its operation and assuring that they are distributed properly. Expressive leadership is embodied in the definition of leadership as "the capacity and will to rally men and women to a common purpose."[33] Instrumental leadership is better conveyed by the view that "leadership is the ability to provide those functions required for successful group action."[34] One individual can combine both types of leadership, though they are often separated.

Expressive leaders are likely to be engaged in the roles of organizational spokesperson, nurturer of effective interpersonal relations within the organization, and developer of commitment to the organization. In the latter role leaders may also attempt to increase the motivation of the organization's members. Instrumental leaders tend to be more involved in the functions of coordination, motivation through the use of remunerative power, and procurement of resources. Either type of leader can be an innovator or manager of an organization in times of crisis. It should be noted again with emphasis, however, that these roles and functions are not likely to be wholly distinct. A leader does what is necessary for the effective functioning of an organization—and what is necessary at any moment varies very widely from organization to organization and from situation to situation.

Most approaches to administrative leadership tend to assume that the leader is in a hierarchy, often at or near the top. The human relations approach recognized that this is not necessarily true of the leaders of informal organizations. The NPM takes yet another view. It opposes hierarchy and puts considerable emphasis on teams. Teams are formal work groups that may be comprised of employees at all levels—managerial, supervisory, and rank and file. Team leaders are not necessarily the highest-ranking employees. They may be formally designated or simply emerge. If the use of teams becomes characteristic of public administration in the future, they should offer fertile ground for gaining a much better understanding of leadership.

Leadership is only part of an equation. There are those who are led, followers who are willing to serve. Consequently, any discussion of leadership must be complemented by a consideration of motivation.

Motivation

Scientific management theory assumed that workers were motivated by the manipulation of remunerative rewards and sanctions. Heavy emphasis was placed on piecework, under the assumption that if a worker could earn more by producing more, he or she would be motivated to work harder. Similarly, if productivity and pay could be increased by the introduction of highly specialized work tasks, this body of theory assumed the worker would perform them, however boring, mind-deadening, and physically uncomfortable they might be. This approach to motivation was dealt a severe blow by the Hawthorne experiments and the human relations approach. Initially the human relationists had a set of observations about workers' motivation, but they lacked a theory that could explain them.

An important breakthrough occurred in 1943, when Abraham Maslow introduced "A Theory of Human Motivation."[35] Maslow hypothesized that there is a hierarchy of human needs, that humans are satisfaction-seeking animals, and that they are therefore motivated in a never-ending quest for greater satisfaction of their needs. In Maslow's scheme, human beings first seek to satisfy their physiological needs, such as hunger and thirst; then, once these are met, they seek to fulfill safety and shelter needs. Next they focus on social needs and seek a sense of belonging. At the fourth level of needs, they want self-esteem and social status; finally, they seek "self-actualization," or true self-fulfillment (see Box 4–3).

When viewed in the light of the human relations approach, it is not difficult to see some immediate implications of Maslow's theory. First, if the happy worker is the productive worker, then work should satisfy the workers' needs at whatever level they may be. If workers seek social activity, then the organization should provide opportunities for it. If they seek self-esteem or self-actualization, then they will probably need some control over the structuring of their jobs and some opportunity to participate in decision making. At the very least they cannot be ordered around like dumb beasts in the Taylorist tradition. In practical terms, this means that several elements of bureaucratic organization may be at odds with human needs. Certainly hierarchy and specialization militate against self-actualization, self-esteem, and the social needs of those who are denied control over their work processes and social interactions on the job—meaning a lot of employees other than those at the top. The lack of opportunity to complete an entire unit of output, such as a report or an automobile, is also problematic in terms of self-esteem and self-actualization. Formalization and impersonality would seem seriously to undercut the fulfillment of social needs. The entire sense of being but a mere "cog" ought to be sufficient to deflate the self-esteem of even the most arrogant of individuals.

This has an important second implication: It may render bureaucratic organization somewhat out of date. It is possible that as a society develops economically and politically, the plurality of public employees may be seek-

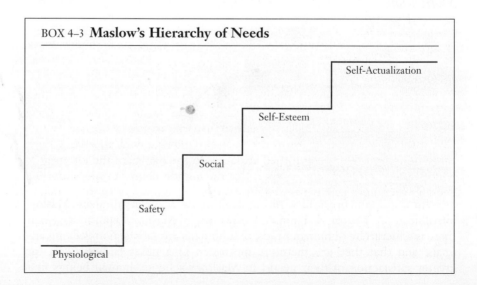

BOX 4–3 **Maslow's Hierarchy of Needs**

Self-Actualization

Self-Esteem

Social

Safety

Physiological

ing to satisfy needs at the top levels of Maslow's hierarchy. They may want meaningful work (status, self-esteem) and influence over the directions their agencies are taking (self-actualization through public policy making).[36] Unless bureaucracies can respond to these needs, their employees will be somewhat dissatisfied and organizational efficiency may consequently suffer. Those taking this general perspective have argued that therefore "democracy is inevitable"[37] in organizations and that traditional structural arrangements of bureaucracy will have to be modified. Perhaps it is not too much to say that according to this view we are in an "administrative revolution"[38] that will democratize our organizational life the way that political revolutions of the past brought much of the Western world from aristocracy to more democratic governments.

Despite the enthusiasm of some for Maslow's theory and its implications, others have remained unconvinced. At least two general criticisms are frequently directed at Maslow's hierarchy. First, although Maslow offered a theory that in principle could be empirically tested, it has been very hard to test it well. Consequently, it tends to remain inadequately tested. Moreover, some people find it counterintuitive. Many of us may be at the same level in our hierarchy of needs but nonetheless motivated by different stimuli. For instance, the *strength* of an individual's needs for self-esteem may vary in ways that do not seem to be explained by the hierarchy. Second, Maslow's categories are so broad that unless further refined they seem to offer little connection between the design of work and motivation in the workplace. This problem has been addressed by Frederick Herzberg and his associates.[39]

Herzberg hypothesized that job satisfaction is affected by two types of factors in the workplace. Hygiene factors include working conditions, supervisory relations, salary, and administrative policies. They are called **hygienes** after medical terminology to connote that they are environmental and contextual factors that can be attained by preventing undesirable conditions (like dirt in drinking water). Hygienes are considered to have the capacity to make workers dissatisfied if they are inadequately met. However, they do not lead to job satisfaction per se. On the other hand, **motivators,** including advancement, responsibility, the job itself, recognition, and achievement, could produce greater job satisfaction.

The implications of the Herzberg model are similar to those of Maslow's hierarchy. Motivation depends more on opportunities for advancement, responsibility, recognition, and achievement than on the type of hygiene factors that were of greater concern to the scientific management approach. Even more important, Herzberg turned attention to the nature of the job itself as a motivator. This led to the prospect that the highest degree of specialization, though seemingly productive, could dampen an employee's motivation. It also suggested that workers' motivation could be enhanced by allowing them to participate in the designing of jobs. Like Maslow's theory, however, Herzberg's approach has not won universal acceptance. Empirical tests of its propositions have led to different conclusions, and a debate continues as to its utility.

Some believe that cultural, social, economic, and psychological variation among a large work force make it unreasonable to assume that all workers can be motivated by fulfilling the same needs. For example, based on the work of David McClelland, there is reason to believe that some people are far more achievement-oriented than others. They will be motivated by the opportunity to achieve, while others, who are more or less at the same level of Maslow's hierarchy, will not.[40] The same could be true with regard to the other motivators identified by Herzberg.

Expectancy theory is an alternative approach that eliminates this problem.[41] It assumes that workers have a variety of goals and that the strength of their preferences for them varies. Moreover, it proposes that their motivation on the job will depend on the extent to which they expect a certain activity to lead to some degree of satisfaction of these goals. For instance, if they want higher pay and they think greater productivity will lead to it, the workers will be more productive. But the same is true if they want recognition or a sense of achievement and believe that these goals can be attained through greater productivity. According to this approach, the key to motivation is affording workers some opportunity to achieve their desired goals and making clear what activities or efforts on the job they can reasonably expect to lead to attainment of these goals.

Based on expectancy theory, organizations should emphasize recruiting personnel whose personal goals can be fulfilled while serving the needs of an organization itself. Additionally, rewards and sanctions must be clearly linked to performance. There is no coherent body of theory about individual personality type and motivation in organizations. However, people do vary widely in their approach to work. Some possibilities are set forth in Box 4–4 on pages 165–167.

Contemporary Approaches to Organization Theory

Today, organization theory is a diverse, interdisciplinary enterprise. If there is any unifying paradigm, it is methodological rather than substantive. Contemporary organization theory seeks to develop and test empirical propositions pertaining to all important aspects of organizational behavior, including structure, change, and psychology. Unlike some earlier approaches, it tries to separate facts from values and to use a modern social scientific method for determining relationships among observable aspects of organizational behavior. To a large extent, it relies on systems theory to aid in the conceptualization of such relationships.

The Systems Approach   The systems approach can be quite elaborate, but at its core is the simple concept that an organization (or other functional entity) constitutes a system that is distinct from its environment.[42] It is a system because its parts are interrelated. The system responds to stimuli from the environment and obtains feedback (information) concerning the impact of its

BOX 4–4 **Organizational Personalities: A Sampling**

According to Anthony Downs:

1. CLIMBERS—a "climber seeks to maximize his own power, income, and prestige, he always desires more of these goods." Climbers seek to increase the power, income, and prestige of their positions in ways that will create the least effective resistance.

2. CONSERVERS—"Conservers seek to maximize their security and convenience. . . . [They] are essentially change avoiders. In this respect, they are the opposite of climbers."

3. ZEALOTS—officials who "act as though pursuit of the public interest means promotion of very specific policy goals . . . regardless of the antagonism they encounter or the particular positions they occupy."

4. ADVOCATES—"are basically optimistic, and normally quite energetic. . . . [T]hey are strongly subject to influence by their superiors, equals, and subordinates. Nevertheless, they are often quite aggressive in pressing for what they believe best suits their organizations."

5. STATESMEN—are loyal to the nation or the society as a whole. They "can persist in maintaining a generalized outlook even when their responsibilities are quite particular. However, they do not like conflict situations and seek to reconcile clashes of particular viewpoints through compromises based upon their broad general loyalties."

According to Robert Presthus:

1. UPWARD-MOBILES—have "the capacity to identify strongly with the organization, permitting a nice synthesis of personal rewards and organizational goals." They make "special efforts to control situations and people." They "stress efficiency, strength, self-control, and dominance. [Their] most functional value is a deep respect for authority."

2. INDIFFERENTS—reject the values of status and prestige. Their "aspirations are based on a realistic appraisal of existing opportunities. Escaping the commitments of the 'true believer' and the anxiety of the neurotic striver, he receives big dividends in privacy, tranquility, and self-realization through his extravocational orientation."

3. AMBIVALENTS—have a fear of authority and an inability to accept the organization's collective goals, "which violate his need for personal autonomy. His 'tender minded' view of human relations disqualifies him for the 'universalistic' decision making required for success on organizational terms. Since his preferences include a desire for creativity and for a work environment that permits spontaneity and experiment, the structured personal relations,

BOX 4–4 *Continued*

stereotyped procedures, and group decision making of big organization prove stifling. . . . If his values did not include prestige and influence, a happier accommodation might be possible. . . ."

According to Leonard Reissman:

1. FUNCTIONAL BUREAU-CRATS—are "oriented towards and [seek] recognition from a given professional group outside of rather than within the bureaucracy." For this group, bureaucracy is just another place to practice their profession.

2. SPECIALIST BUREAU-CRATS—display "a greater awareness of an identification with the bureaucracy." They seek both professional and bureaucratic recognition and therefore can be "overly meticulous about the rules and regulations" of the organization.

3. SERVICE BUREAUCRATS—enter "civil service primarily to realize certain personally held goals which center about rendering service to a certain group." The service bureaucrat's task is using the bureaucratic mechanism to achieve these goals.

4. JOB BUREAUCRATS—are "immersed entirely within the structure" of the bureaucracy. They seek "recognition along departmental rather than professional lines," and strive for the "improvement of the operating efficiency of the bureau. His aspirations consist of achieving material rewards and increased status through promotions. He strongly adheres to the rules and the job constitutes his full center of attention and the end to be served."

According to Michael Maccoby:

1. THE CRAFTSMAN—displays "the work ethic, respect for people, concern for quality and

responses. A diagram of a basic systems model is presented in Box 4–5 on page 168.

Another way of thinking about a system is that it is an organization that converts inputs (stimuli) into outputs. For public agencies the inputs could be demands for the development or improvement of programs (e.g., crime control), while the conversion could be the combination of these demands into a change in public policy, such as more police patrols or community policing, which would be the output. The conversion process concerns how the organization responds to demands for changes in its programs and operations. Inputs can also be in the form of support for the organization and its policies and programs.

Some systems are treated as closed, which means it is assumed that everything is known about their internal functioning and their relationship to the environment. A heating device controlled by a thermostat is an example. The

---

BOX 4–4 *Continued*

---

thrift. . . . [H]is interest is in the process of making something; he enjoys building. . . . Although his virtues are admired by everyone, his self-containment and perfection do not allow him to lead a complex and changing organization."

2. THE JUNGLE FIGHTER— "The jungle fighter's goal is power. He experiences life and work as a jungle (not a game), where it is eat or be eaten, and the winners destroy the losers. . . . There are two subtypes of jungle fighters, lions and foxes. The lions are the conquerors who when successful may build an empire; the foxes make their nests in the corporate hierarchy and move ahead by stealth and politicking."

3. THE COMPANY MAN—is "the well-known organization man, or functionary whose sense of identity is based on being a part of the powerful, productive company. His strongest traits are his concern with the human side of the company, his interest in the feelings of the people around him and his commitment to maintain the organization's integrity."

4. THE GAMESMAN—is a new type. "His main interest is in challenge, competitive activity where he can prove himself a winner. . . . [H]e likes to take risks and to motivate others to push themselves beyond their normal pace. He responds to work and life as a game."

SOURCES: Anthony Downs, *Inside Bureaucracy* (Boston: Little, Brown, 1967), chap. 9; Robert Presthus, *The Organizational Society* (New York: Knopf, 1962), 203, 218, 285–286; Leonard Reissman, "A Study of Role Conceptions in Bureaucracy," *Social Forces* 27 (March 1949): 305–310; Michael Maccoby, *The Gamesman* (New York: Simon & Schuster, 1976), 42–45, copyright © 1976 by Michael Maccoby, reprinted by permission of Simon & Schuster, Inc.

---

system puts out heat predictably with changes in the temperature of the environment. The environment responds to this output, the thermostat provides feedback on the response, and the outputs cease when a certain temperature is reached. Closed-systems theory tends to focus on stability (equilibrium), control mechanisms, and predictable responses. Some relatively simple public administrative operations can be viewed as closed systems. For instance, the operations of a motor vehicle bureau in renewing automobile registrations might be treated in this fashion. The registrant submits the required payment and documentation of insurance and inspection (inputs); the bureau processes these (conversion) and issues the registration (output). Should something in the environment change, such as the sale of the car, the bureau receives notification (feedback) and responds according to its regulations.

Open systems, by contrast, are viewed as too complex to be so predictable. It is recognized that the relationships between the parts of the sys-

BOX 4–5 **A Systems Model of Politics**

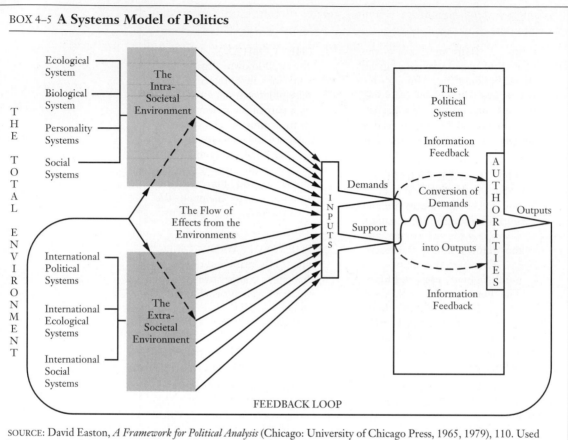

SOURCE: David Easton, *A Framework for Political Analysis* (Chicago: University of Chicago Press, 1965, 1979), 110. Used by permission of the University of Chicago Press and David Easton.

tem and the system and its environment are not fully understood. Both the environment and internal operations of the open system are viewed with an expectation of uncertainty. Many believe that the open-systems concept is more useful for analyzing most public organizations. By way of illustration, many of the operations of the U.S. Department of Agriculture fit this model. Inputs often depend on such diverse and relatively unpredictable matters as the weather, pest control, consumer preferences, the relative strength of the dollar against other currencies, foreign policy, and the trade preferences of other nations. Feedback about the impact of outputs can be obscured by any of these factors as well. Conversion becomes more difficult where so much uncertainty and complexity prevail. Politics and individual preferences, as well as intraorganizational rivalries and other factors, come into play. Outputs can become highly unpredictable. The great benefit of the open-systems model is that it can help order our thoughts about the operations of public agencies or other organizations under such circumstances.

Open-systems theory has focused greater attention on organizational environments. Organizations can be seen as cooperating with and adapting to their environment. They adjust to its pressures, which enhances their ability to persist. For instance, public sector organizations are often required by legislators and political executives to take on new functions. How well they can assimilate and integrate new tasks is likely to have a bearing on the organization's long-term prospects for survival. The U.S. Civil Service Commission (1883–1979) is an excellent example of an organization that failed to adapt to a rapidly changing environment, and, consequently, was disbanded. Between 1965 and 1978, it struggled to combine new equal opportunity and affirmative action functions with traditional personnel administration. It also sought to be responsive to political appointees while protecting the somewhat competing interests of career civil servants. In 1973, these pressures led the commission's chairman, Robert Hampton, to ask, "What is our identity?" "What is our purpose?" And, "Why do we exist?"[43] By 1979, it didn't!

The concept that public organizations either adapt to their environment or perish fits the normative tenet of democratic constitutionalism that public administrators ought to be responsive to elected and politically appointed policy makers, including judges, and, perhaps in some areas, directly to constituencies and clientele groups as well. But organizational theorists such as Charles Perrow[44] and William Scott[45] argue that organizations may sometimes be more oriented toward *controlling* their environment than adapting to it. In Scott's words, "Organizations must ingest those necessary elements in their environment that enable them to survive. . . ."[46] Perrow reminds us that the environment can be conceptualized in strategic terms on the basis of network and ecological models.

Networks sort out the environment by identifying the external organizations with which an organization routinely deals *and* some of the other organizations that interact with those external organizations.[47] For example, organization A may deal with organizations B and C, which, in turn, deal with organizations D, E, and F. Organization A might be a city bus system, whereas B and C might be transportation systems in the surrounding suburbs and counties. B and C might bring A a substantial number of its rush-hour riders. D and E might be the labor unions representing B and C's employees. F might be an organization that supplies B and C with new buses from time to time. Thinking about these relationships as networks makes it evident that A's ridership can be affected by B and C's operations, which depend on D and E's activities to some extent. A has no direct relationship with D and E, but they can disturb its environment. Conceivably, A might be interested in supporting B and C in efforts to control or eliminate D and E. In any event, D and E are in A's network. F, on the other hand, is only very remotely related to A's functioning, because B and C are readily able to find substitutes for the buses it supplies.

The *ecological model* also considers the environment to be of critical importance to organizations. Its focus is change. As Perrow describes it,

The ecological model identifies three stages in a process of social change. First is the occurrence of *variations* in behavior. They may be intended or unintended; it doesn't matter. In organizations, a production crew might gradually vary its techniques, or a shortage of gasoline might lead to a variation in truck-delivery practices. Second, natural *selection* occurs as some variations are eliminated because they are undesirable and others are reinforced because they work. The criterion of effectiveness is survival. Third, there is a *retention* mechanism that allows those "positively selected variations" to be retained or reproduced. Since nothing ever stands still, either for those in the organization or for its environment, over the long run positively selected variations that become stable activities will be subject to further variation.[48]

The systems approach has also enhanced analysis of the internal workings of organizations. It enables us to think in terms of "subsystems" and their relationships with one another as well as to the organization as a whole and the environment. Daniel Katz and Robert Kahn identify some common subsystems as "production subsystems," "supportive subsystems" (procurement, etc.), "maintenance subsystems" (personnel management), "adaptive subsystems" (concerned with organizational change), and "managerial subsystems" (controlling the other subsystems).[49] These subsystems are likely to have different and somewhat competing priorities and ideologies supporting them. The managerial subsystem seeks control, while a production subsystem may seek autonomy. In the public sector, it may be useful to think of programs or policy areas as the production subsystems of organizations. Recognizing subsystems' existence and interaction often yields a more sophisticated understanding of agencies and other organizations.

The Organizational Culture Perspective   The systems approach focuses attention on the organization as something that acts. For the most part, organizational systems theorists believe that there is some rationality to such action. James D. Thompson, whose *Organizations in Action* (1967)[50] has been a leading contributor to the systems perspective, viewed organizational rationality as produced by an appropriate relationship among three types of activities: input, technological, and output.

Any claim that an organization is rational implies that organizations can think, which immediately seems at odds with the commonsensical view that inanimate things lack mental processes. However, Mary Douglas, one of this century's great anthropologists, wrote a book called, *How Institutions Think* (1986).[51] The essence of her claim is that a social institution serves as a "suprapersonal cognitive system"[52] that confers identity, remembers and forgets, classifies, and makes life and death decisions. Further, she argues that "the individual's most elementary cognitive process depends on social institutions."[53] In this formulation, not all social institutions are organizations (momentary instruments are an example), but some, like bureaucracy, are.

Douglas's theory is very complex and controversial. Further analysis and discourse will be required before its potential for effectively enlightening us about the activities of public administrative organizations will be determined. However, the extreme quality of Douglas's argument can serve to allay doubts that, whether or not organizations actually "think," they certainly can have an impact on the cognitive processes and value systems of their members. This is the organizational culture perspective.

Organizational culture stands in contrast to approaches emphasizing the importance of structure and the systems framework. As Steven Ott explains, the organizational cultural school

> assumes that many organizational behaviors and decisions are almost predetermined by the patterns of basic assumptions existing in the organization. Those patterns of assumptions have continued to exist and influence behaviors because they have repeatedly led people to make decisions that usually worked for the organization. With repeated use, the assumptions slowly drop out of peoples' consciousness but continue to influence organizational decisions and behaviors—even when the organization's environment changes. They become the underlying, unquestioned—but virtually forgotten—reasons for "the way we do things here."[54]

Controls on individual member's thinking and behavior consist primarily of beliefs, assumptions, norms, and values that constitute the organization's culture.

The cultural perspective makes several important contributions to thinking about organizations. First, as Douglas's theory suggests, it can help explain how organizations can be said to "do the thinking." Organizational culture both conditions and reflects how individuals in organizations define issues, challenges, and phenomena; sort them out; evaluate; and decide. Thus the organizational culture perspective helps explain the impact of professionalism on the behavior of individuals in organizations.

Second, the organizational culture perspective helps explain why organizations that have similar structures may nevertheless behave very differently. Bureaucratic structure is very common, but individual bureaucracies often behave very differently and the behavior of public administrative bureaucracies in different countries can be strikingly different. Moreover, though structurally similar, sometimes the contents of organizational cultures fit the expectations of the larger society well, and sometimes they are out of sync with it. For instance, there was a public outcry in 1991 after several members of the Los Angeles Police Department were videotaped brutally beating a black motorist. In part this was because radio conversations between police officers and dispatchers revealed that brutality, racism, and other illegal practices were considered normal within the department's culture.

Third, variations among organizations and within the same organization over time can be partly explained by differences or changes in the strength of organizational cultures. Some organizations have very strong cultures that serve to unify and focus the behavior of their members. This was true of the FBI under Hoover and NASA during the Apollo period. In other organizations, culture is a weak force. According to some analysts, NASA's significant number of operational failures during the 1980s, including the explosion of *Challenger* and the death of its crew, were in part due to a shift from an organizational culture that valued sound engineering above all else to one in which the values of effective management took on greater importance.

Fourth, the organizational culture perspective helps explain why organizations once considered rational (in some sense) act in inappropriate ways. For instance, the culture of the U.S. Civil Service Commission emphasized policing the personnel system to prevent partisan political encroachments long after new concerns, including equal opportunity, became of much greater national concern.

The Evolutionary Approach   One final contemporary approach to organization theory should be mentioned because it fundamentally rejects the view that organizational survival is due to rationality and therefore provides a wholly different perspective to consider. In *Time, Chance, and Organizations* (1985), Herbert Kaufman seemingly builds on the ecological approach but reaches the rather different conclusion that "the survival of some organizations for great lengths of time is largely a matter of luck."[55] He argues that randomness rather than rationality may explain organizational survival because, when all is said and done, organizations can change only marginally, whereas environmental changes are volatile. Furthermore, the very flexibility of organizations required for change has disadvantages for their coherence and persistence. Kaufman sees real advantages to the demise of some organizations and their replacement by newer ones, just as one would expect evolution to advance an animal or plant species. He writes, "Instead of striving to *lower* organizational death rates and *extend* organizational longevity, we should, according to the implications of the evolutionary hypothesis, concentrate on *maintaining* birth rates and organizational diversity."[56] Put simply, there is no particular reason to resist change.

Sorting it Out   What are we to make of all this diversity of organization theory? Organizations are highly varied and many are very complex. Therefore, it is not surprising that no one theory or approach explains everything about all organizations. Rather, the various theoretical approaches and frameworks reviewed here provide tools for analyzing organizational activity. Sometimes these tools can be used in complementary fashion; at other times, the use of one may preclude the use of another. But in all cases, one or another of them should help explain why organizations do what they do.

Contemporary organization theory includes both private and public organizations. However, there are some key differences between the public and private sectors. When we focus specifically on public agencies, the distinct perspectives of the managerial, political, and legal approaches to public administration should be considered in some detail.

MANAGERIAL PERSPECTIVES ON PUBLIC ORGANIZATION

The *traditional managerial perspective* in public organization grows largely out of the "classical" approaches of Weber and Taylor. It is sometimes considered an extension of those approaches, and with them is referred to as the public administrative "orthodoxy." It has been said that 1937 was the high noon of this orthodoxy—and that the clock stopped![57] It was in that year that the orthodoxy's principles were more or less codified in a volume called *Papers on the Science of Administration*, which was edited by Luther Gulick and Lyndall Urwick.[58] Gulick's own article, "Notes on the Theory of Organization," has been of particular importance in the managerial tradition.[59]

The orthodox managerial perspective emphasizes efficiency, economy, and effectiveness as the values that should inform the structure and process of public administrative organizations. It views the division of labor (specialization) as the fundamental key to economic rationality and productivity. But, once the work is divided, need it not be coordinated in some fashion? Gulick answers that coordination can be by (1) *organization*, "that is, by interrelating the subdivisions of work by allotting them to men who are placed in a structure of authority, so that the work may be coordinated by orders of superiors to subordinates, reaching from the top to the bottom of the entire enterprise"[60]; and (2) *idea*, "that is, the development of intelligent singleness of purpose in the minds and wills of those who are working together as a group, so that each worker will of his own accord fit his task into the whole with skill and enthusiasm."[61] Gulick thought that an enterprise could not be truly effective without utilizing both these bases of coordination, but he tended to stress organization for its reliability, predictability, and economy.

Gulick repeated many of Weber's observations, but he turned them into prescriptions. He believed that the organization coordinating the specializations should be hierarchical and culminate with "one master."[62] Hierarchical authorities should be in control in fact as well as in theory. Their control should be ensured by limiting their span of control, that is, the number of subordinates who are directly responsible to any single superordinate. Gulick and others in this tradition believed that the appropriate span of control could be determined more or less scientifically. The work of executives was aimed at maintaining coordination and control. It consisted of POSDCORB, an acronym that may well continue to describe the core curriculum of many public administrative master's degree programs today:

Planning: working out in broad outline the things that need to be done and the methods for accomplishing them

Organizing: establishing the formal structure of the enterprise

Staffing: the personnel function

Directing: decision making and communicating orders

COordinating: interrelating the various parts of the work

Reporting: supplying information through recordkeeping, research, inspection

Budgeting: fiscal planning, accounting, and control.

These POSDCORB activities were thought to include all functions of the chief executive and the heads of organizational subdivisions. Importantly, Gulick averred that some of them could be undertaken by *staff* employees, which are employees who are not in the *line* (or chain) of direct authority, but rather act as assistants or advisers to those in such positions. The distinction between line and staff became quite important in the orthodox tradition, which admonished that the two functions should not be mixed, as this blurs the assignment of responsibility.

Another central feature of Gulick's organizational theory was the idea that there was essentially one most efficient way to organize any given governmental function. Thus, it could be organized by *purpose* (e.g., education, health, welfare); *process* (engineering, accounting); *clientele or materiel* (farmers, veterans, the poor, or a natural resource); or by *place* (state, region, city, rural areas). Each of these bases of organization had advantages and disadvantages in terms of the relevant organizational values of efficiency, economy, and effectiveness. A listing of these developed by the author is set out in Box 4–6.

The purpose/process/clientele/place scheme has been very influential in the thinking about government organization. Because it is somewhat abstract, a few examples may help to clarify its utility. Let's assume that every government agency uses lawyers in some capacity. How should these lawyers be selected, remunerated, directed, and so forth? One approach (by purpose) is to place a general counsel's office in every agency. Here lawyers are employed within the agency in which they function; they occupy some subdivision of it, and they are directed by its hierarchy. On the other hand, it would be possible to place all government lawyers in one department and assign them as needed to assist the various agencies and other departments in carrying out their organizational functions. In the latter case, the lawyers would be selected, remunerated, directed, and assigned by one department, such as a Department of Justice or Department of Legal Affairs. What would be the benefits and drawbacks of each approach? The second approach (by process) would tend to promote professionalism among the legal staff and to ensure that the legal staff was fully up-to-date on matters of law and legal technology. But, unlike the first, it might also lead to a situation where the lawyers were unresponsive to the needs of the agencies that they were assigned to assist. They might view the clarification and development of legal principles to be more important than the achievement of the missions of other agencies and thereby place process over purpose. So how would one choose?

Before addressing this question, another example is in order. Suppose we are organizing a poverty program. It would certainly simplify things if one agency could deal with the totality of problems facing poor people, ranging from health and housing to nutrition, family structure, education, job training and so on. Such human services integration or client-centered administration would make governmental service more accessible to the poor and would reduce the paperwork involved in dealing with them. It might be especially important where poor people are deterred from seeking governmen-

BOX 4–6 **Scientific Administration: Advantages and Disadvantages of Different Organizational Bases**

Organization by Purpose (such as education, health, welfare):

Advantages:

- Serves purpose better
- Public prefers it
- Elicits more energy and loyalty from employees

Disadvantages:

- Requires substantial overlaps
- Ignores new technologies
- Loses sight of subordinate parts of work

Organization by Clientele or Materiel (farmers, the poor, veterans):

Advantages:

- Simplifies and allows coordination of contact with consumer
- Eliminates duplication
- Centralizes information

Disadvantages:

- Clientele may take over
- Sacrifices specialization
- May be hard to apply (citizens fall into overlapping categories)

Organization by Process (teaching, law, engineering, accounting):

Advantages:

- Utilizes technical skill maximally

- Utilizes automation maximally
- Permits coordination
- Fosters professionalism, career service

Disadvantages:

- May be difficult to apply
- Process may hinder purpose
- Fosters arrogance, resistance to democratic control

Organization by Place (state, region, rural, urban areas):

Advantages:

- Allows greater coordination
- Adapts total program to area served
- Cuts red tape in dealing with other governmental units (state, local)
- Cuts costs for travel, etc.

Disadvantages:

- Makes it difficult to maintain uniformity
- Encourages short-sighted management geared to local problems
- May make it difficult to specialize
- May be vulnerable to local pressure groups

SOURCE: Compiled by the author, based on L. Gulick and L. Urwick, eds., *Papers on the Science of Administration* (New York: Institute of Public Administration, 1937).

tal assistance by inadequate transportation or all the impersonal red tape involved. Moreover, such an organizational scheme might make it easier to coordinate governmental dealing with the clientele group. But could such an agency provide the best health care or health advice? Could it provide the best available education or family counseling? According to common sense and the Gulick scheme, the answer appears to be probably not. Those who are specialists in the problems of the poor are not likely also to be specialists in health, housing, education, nutrition and other matters. So how does one decide?

To a very considerable extent, the scientific principles approach is only as good as its ability to answer this question on the basis of some body of thought more exacting than intuition, common sense, or judging from experience.

The purpose/process/clientele/place scheme has been severely criticized for not even approaching the level of scientific exactness that it purports to possess. The most devastating attack on the orthodoxy in this context came from Herbert Simon, who dismissed the purpose/process/clientele/place scheme as no more than proverbial.[63] And like proverbs, he argued, its premises come in twos. "Haste makes waste" is balanced out by "He who hesitates is lost." The scheme itself suggests that, for example, organization by process promotes professionalism on the one hand, and unresponsiveness on the other.

Simon went on in *Administrative Behavior* to argue that there could be a science of administrative organization, but that it would have to separate out facts from values with great care. After so doing, it could develop a body of knowledge based on the factual context of administrative and organizational behavior.

In intellectual terms, the orthodox approach was dealt a devastating blow by Simon's critique. It was also impaled by Dwight Waldo's very influential work, *The Administrative State*.[64] Waldo attacked the classical approach on its own terms. He demonstrated that "efficiency" and "economy" could not be treated as values in an operational sense because they did not provide sufficient direction for public administrative action to be useful in practice. Moreover, far from being apolitical, Waldo showed that the traditional approach contained an implicit political theory. It stressed hierarchy and centralization and was at many points at odds with democratic political theory. This cast doubt on the utility of the concept that there can be a strict separation of politics and administration, because, as Waldo argued, any public administrative theory is likely also to be a political theory.

Together, Simon and Waldo destroyed the intellectual underpinnings of the orthodox approach. Their critiques were successful in discrediting the earlier claims that orthodox theory was "scientific." Certainly none would deny that it contained a great deal of common sense; equally, however, few would continue to accept its advocates' claim to scientific, apolitical, and value-free knowledge of public administration. But as valuable as their critiques of the earlier theoretical paradigm were, Simon and Waldo were not successful in replacing it with a new one. Of course, they are not to be faulted for this, since in the fifty-odd years since they wrote their ground-breaking books, no one else has been able to develop a unified general public administrative or organization theory that has gained anywhere near the following that the orthodoxy once had.

Although the NPM shows considerable promise in this regard, it has yet to solve the problem of holding empowered, results-oriented public administrators accountable for the means they employ. It emphasizes building an administrative culture that makes arbitrary or discriminatory treatment of individuals or regulated parties unthinkable. Vice President Al Gore believes that "the federal government is filled with good people trapped in bad systems . . ."[65] who can safely be deregulated. However, U.S. constitutional design rests on other premises, as James Madison long ago explained:

> If men were angels, no government would be necessary. If angels were to govern men, neither external nor internal controls on government would be necessary. In framing a government which is to be administered by men over men, the great difficulty lies in this: you must first enable the government to control the governed; and in the next place oblige it to control itself.[66]

The more Madisonian one's view of human nature, the more assurances one is likely to want from the NPM that government will be comprised of good people doing the right thing.

One of the important consequences of the failure to develop a new theoretical paradigm for public organization theory has been a continuing reliance on the orthodox approach in practice. This obviously creates some serious difficulties for public administration. Practitioners and political leaders who must contend with actual public administrative practice on a day-to-day basis must have some body of thought and set of values to inform their actions. They must carry out public administration and they must have some reasons for doing what they do. They must also be able to explain these reasons in acceptable terms. Frequently, therefore, they fall back on the orthodoxy for its commonsense wisdom.

In fact, public organization theory, as actually practiced by some, is still reflected in the words of the Brownlow Committee's report on Administrative Management (1937) and the federal Reorganization Act of 1939, two of the core documents of the orthodox approach. The Brownlow report asserted that "real efficieny . . . must be built into the structure of government just as it is built into a piece of machinery."[67] The Reorganization Act, which has since been superseded by similar statutes, identified the main purposes of reorganizing the federal administrative structure as: (1) economy, (2) efficiency, (3) consolidation "according to major purposes," (4) reduction of the number of agencies, and (5) "elimination of overlapping and duplication of effort."[68]

Contemporary managerial perspectives on organization emphasize the importance of being results-oriented. The NPM and related approaches reject the orthodox view that structure is the key to cost-effective performance. They argue that successful administration requires clear objectives and flexible processes for achieving them. Structure should be designed to facilitate performance rather than to control employees, information, and resources. Organization should be designed more from the bottom up than the top down. It should flow from the needs of service delivery. Decentralization and the reduction of hierarchy are typically favored. Several results-oriented organizational strategies have been deployed in recent decades. **Operations management** seeks to identify the specific operational responsibilities of government agencies and to design their organizations and work flows to maximize productivity.[69] This approach does not deny or belittle the importance of politics and law in the public sector. But it does concentrate on the obvious need to perform governmental functions productively within the parameters set by politics and law. Among the many functions of government that may be suitable for the operations management approach are such activities as the issuance of drivers' licenses and vehicular registrations; the maintenance of highways, roads, and other infrastructure; sanitation; water purification and supply; flood control; snow removal; and the provision of welfare benefits to eligible individuals.

One of the most useful tools of the operations management approach is the development of flow charts that map out and graphically display the relevant government operation in its entirety. Box 4–7 presents a simple example of how the process of applying for a government benefit might appear on a flowchart. Some operations would be much more complex and require far more elaborate, even mazelike, diagrams. It is often helpful to be able to visualize a government operation in its entirety in order to make it more efficient and productive. For example, the operations management approach can facilitate the elimination of unnecessary procedural steps or the combination of some procedures in order to simplify processes. Operations management

BOX 4–7 **Flowchart for Processing Welfare Applications**

Input: Eligible client referred to welfare office

Processing Steps

1. Client → completes application 2. Application → checked for errors 3. Client → interviewed by intake worker 4. Welfare → payment determined 5. Payment → authorized 6. Check printed and mailed

Output: Client gets check

SOURCE: Adapted from Stephen R. Rosenthal, *Managing Government Operations* (Glenview, Ill.: Scott, Foresman, 1982), 41.

also encourages the gathering of information about each step as a means of planning workloads and allocating the organization's resources more efficiently. Coupled with the analysis of organizational networks, it can also identify potential disturbances in the environment.

Management by objectives, or **MBO,** is a very common results-oriented approach. MBO can be outlined as follows:

1. Setting goals, objectives, and priorities in terms of results to be accomplished in a given time
2. Developing plans for accomplishment of results
3. Allocating resources
4. Involving people in implementation of plans, with emphasis on communications for responsiveness and on broad sharing in [establishing] authoritative goals and objectives
5. Tracking or monitoring of progress toward goals and objectives, with specific intermediate milestones
6. Evaluating results in terms of effectiveness, efficiency, and economy
7. Generating and implementing improvements in objectives and results.[70]

MBO appears to be underappreciated in public administration's academic literature. It was emphasized at the federal level during President Richard Nixon's administration but then fell out of favor—perhaps as a result of guilt by association. However, surveys of cities suggest that its popularity has been increasing in urban administration, with well over half reporting usage in the 1980s. Evidence shows that MBO produces large productivity gains when top management is committed to it.[71]

Total quality management, or **TQM,** recently attracted great attention in the public sector. TQM was initially developed by W. E. Deming.[72] Deming's version emphasizes the need to build quality into an organization's products rather than to weed out defects later on. His approach involves analyzing defect rates and finding ways of reducing them. Other advocates of TQM, such as P. Crosby and J. Jurand, advocate instilling in employees an intolerance for any defects or deviations from the letter of product specification requirements.[73] Although these approaches are sometimes viewed as poles apart, TQM has been so widely used that a working synthesis has developed. Its main elements are:

1. "The customer is the ultimate determiner of quality." No matter how marvelously designed or engineered from an artistic or technical perspective, a product must be adjudged a failure if customers find it unsatisfactory.
2. "Quality should be built into the product early in the production process (upstream) rather than being added on at the end (downstream)."
3. "Preventing variability is the key to producing high quality."

4. "Quality results from people working within systems, not individual efforts." If quality is inadequate, then it is most likely that the systems, not the workers, are at fault. Individualized employee performance standards or objectives are misguided because individuals cannot control the system. In Deming's view, ranking employees and/or using merit pay or annual reviews is wrong.

5. "Quality requires continuous improvement of inputs and processes." Here, TQM is at odds with much of the NPM and NPR's effort to get agencies to focus on outputs. From a TQM perspective, too much emphasis on outputs will lead organizations to cut corners and fail to recognize that improving inputs and processes leads to better quality. Deming even went so far as to make the elimination of MBO part of the overall TQM package.

6. "Quality improvement requires strong worker participation" because the workers are most acutely aware of how inputs and processes affect quality.

7. "Quality requires total organizational commitment." "TQM is an extremely demanding regimen. It requires *all* members of an organization to *constantly* change in order to improve, even after achieving what seems to be a high standard of performance."[74]

TQM is currently in use at all levels of government, in many universities, and in private firms. A Federal Quality Institute (FQI) was created in 1988 to advise agencies on how to adapt TQM to their needs. However, by the mid-1990s FQI was eliminated and several agencies, including the General Accounting Office and the Air Force, were having second thoughts about the utility of their TQM programs. Budget pressures and the NPR's pressure for downsizing, privatizing, and results may have been factors. But as James Swiss contends, the fit between TQM and government is imperfect. TQM was developed for the production of products, not services. It can be adjusted, but customer evaluation is a much broader endeavor. First, few, if any, customers care what the workers who produce their VCRs and toasters look like. The appearance of their social workers, police, waiters, and waitresses is part of the overall service. The process through which a CD gets into a store is of little interest to customers; Social Security's process for getting their checks to them can be of major concern, especially if the checks are late. Variability is less controllable in service delivery than in manufacturing.

Second, defining customers is not always easy for government agencies that do not sell anything. Based on the mission statement of the Department of the Interior printed in Box 4–8, who are the department's customers? They even include future generations. But *no one* in the department will be around to see if four or five generations from now these customers will be delighted with what was done today. There are also multiple customers with competing objectives and perspectives. Without profit as a guide, how are they to be prioritized? Because government is overwhelmingly not market-driven, the market cannot be expected to determine how its scarce resources and services are allocated.

BOX 4–8 **Objectives of the Department of the Interior**

In formulating and administering programs for the management, conservation, and development of natural resources, the Department pursues the following objectives: the encouragement of efficient use; the improvement of the quality of the environment; the assurance of adequate resource development in order to meet the requirements of national security and an expanding national economy; the maintenance of productive capacity for future generations; the promotion of an equitable distribution of benefits from nationally-owned resources; the discouragement of wasteful exploitation; the maximum use of recreational areas; and the orderly incorporation of Indian and Alaska Native people into our national life by creating conditions which will advance their social and economic adjustment.

SOURCE: *United States Government Manual, 1972/73* (Washington, D.C.: Government Printing Office, 1973), 251.

Finally, "Orthodox TQM depends on an extremely strong organizational culture with an almost single-minded commitment to quality. In order to shape that culture, the managers must be continuously involved in improving management. . . ."[75] The turnover among political executives in government may simply be too rapid, abrupt, and jarring for TQM to operate well.

To date, public sector TQM has been more debated than evaluated. The few case studies available suggest it can work, but it can also fail. Studying the New York City Department of Parks and Recreation, Steven Cohen and William Eimicke found success in the face of formidable obstacles:

> The process of TQM implementation has been messy and unorthodox at the NYC parks department. It has not followed the TQM rulebook. Parks teams typically used only a handful of TQM analytic tools. Some of their midlevel managers misunderstood and even sabotaged quality improvement projects. In some cases, managers tried to use TQM as a method to push their pet projects. Nevertheless, despite these problems, the costs of learning how to work in this new way are more than absorbed by the benefits of the first projects.[76]

By contrast, at the Internal Revenue Service, Bonnie Mani found "no statistically significant difference when one compares productivity before and after TQM implementation."[77] However, she concluded that "TQM does redefine and consolidate traditional principles of public administration, and there are visible signs that the philosophy made a difference in IRS's culture."[78] If TQM is old wine in new bottles, she concludes it nevertheless tastes better!

Performance-Based Organizations (PBOs) are a results-orientated organizational format promoted by the National Performance Review (NPR). The idea is to place core governmental "factory" operations into units that resemble private firms. PBOs are highly deregulated, but they are not privatized because they perform functions considered to be inherently governmental. The government corporation model is also considered unsuitable, either because of the PBO's functions or because of its inability to generate sufficient revenues through the sale of a service or product. The Federal Aviation Administration became a flagship model in 1996. Being freed from much regulation by law and the Office of Personnel Management, it was able to reduce 1,069 pages of internal regulations to 41 and drop the number of position descriptions it uses from 155,000 to 2,000.[79] Proponents claim the agency will become much more cost-effective and air safety will increase. The Patent Office is another prospect for conversion to a PBO.

Organizational culture change is a prerequisite for MBO, TQM, and PBOs to work. Traditional attitudes toward employees and organizational attributes must change. Two main approaches have been widely discussed: organizational humanism and organizational development.

Organizational humanism is discussed in *The Human Side of Enterprise*, where Douglas McGregor developed a contrast between two managerial approaches.[80] "Theory X" assumed the average worker was indolent, found work distasteful, lacked ambition, was lacking in creativity, was largely indifferent to organizational needs, and in favor of close and continuous supervision. By contrast, "Theory Y" assumed that people can find work natural and enjoyable, can be creative and exercise self-control, and that "[t]he motivation, the potential for development, the capacity for assuming responsibility, the readiness to direct behavior toward organizational goals are all present in people. Management does not put them there. *It is the responsibility of management to make it possible for people to recognize and develop these human characteristics for themselves.*"[81]

McGregor and other proponents of Theory Y argue that its application increases productivity and satisfies workers at the same time. Rensis Likert describes "the kind of organization created by the most successful managers" in the organizational humanist vein:

> This human system is made up of interlocking work groups with a high degree of group loyalty among members and favorable attitudes and trust between supervisors and subordinates. Sensitivity to others and relatively high levels of skill in personal interaction and the functioning of groups also are present. These skills permit effective participation in decisions on common problems. . . . Responsibility for the organization's success is felt individually by the members and each initiates action, when necessary, to assure that the organization accomplishes its objectives. Communication is efficient and effective. . . . The leadership in the organization has developed what might well be called a highly effective social system for interaction and mutual influence.[82]

Likert argues that an organization along these lines, which he calls "System 4," is a key to financial success in the private sector.

Organization development (OD) is an example of an approach for improving organizations that embraces and builds upon Theory Y assumptions.

It assumes that organizations will be more effective at problem solving and coping with their environments when there is more trust, support, and cooperation among their members. OD involves the use of "change agents," or consultants, to increase one or more of the following: trust, confrontation of organizational problems, openness among employees, personal enthusiasm and satisfaction, group and self-responsibility, and creativity. OD relies on psychological theory to help members of an organization understand and change their attitudes toward themselves, their roles, other employees, and the organization.[83]

Critics of the organizational humanism approach argue that many workers fit the assumptions of Theory X more than those of Theory Y. Additionally, critics such as H. Roy Kaplan and Curt Tausky charge that organizational humanism lacks empirical grounding.[84] Consequently, some view Theory Y as highly ideological. Yet ideologies as well as technological and scientific developments have the potential to change relationships in the workplace. As indicated by MBO and TQM, there is reason to believe that interest is growing in extending employee participation in organizations.

THE POLITICAL APPROACH TO PUBLIC ORGANIZATION

Since the end of World War II, several observers have noted the extent to which politics is central to the organization of public bureaucracies. Today this may sound obvious—but it must be remembered that ever since the 1880s, theorists of public administration in the United States had been claiming that politics should be kept almost totally distinct from administration. The NPR continues to insist that public administration should be businesslike and market-oriented and that its factory operations can be separated from its policy functions. Those who view public organization as a question of politics start off from three premises.

First, it is assumed that government is different from private organization. In other words, the prospects for generic organization theory are limited and consequently distinctions must be made between public organization and private organization. Paul Appleby, in *Big Democracy* (1945), wrote, "In broad terms the governmental function and attitude have at least three complementary aspects that go to differentiate government from all other institutions and activities: breadth of scope, impact, and consideration; public accountability; political character."[85]

Second, whereas orthodox theory is concerned with hierarchical authority in an administrative sense and the NPM with customer-driven organization, the political approach emphasizes the development, maintenance, and location of political power—that is, the authority to make political decisions concerning policies, means of implementation, and general operations of public administrative agencies. According to the political approach, power is a central facet of administrative organization and public agencies can be neither efficient nor effective without cultivating it. Norton Long drew attention to this in a 1949 essay entitled "Power and Administration":

> The lifeblood of administration is power. Its attainment, maintenance, increase, dissipation, and loss are subjects the practitioner and student can ill afford to neglect. . . .
>
> The power resources of an administrator or agency are not disclosed by a legal search of titles and court decisions or by examining appropriations or budgetary allotments. Legal authority and a treasury balance are necessary but politically insufficient bases of administration. Administrative rationality requires a critical evaluation of the whole range of complex and shifting forces on whose support, acquiescence, or temporary impotence the power to act depends. . . .
>
> It is clear that the American system of politics does not generate enough power at any focal point of leadership to provide the conditions for an even partially successful divorce of politics from administration. Subordinates cannot depend on the formal chain of command to deliver enough political power to permit them to do their jobs. Accordingly, they must supplement the resources available through the hierarchy with those they can muster on their own, or accept the consequences in frustration. . . . [A]dministrative rationality demands that objectives be determined and sights set in conformity with a realistic appraisal of power position and potential.[86]

The third premise of the political approach is that representation is a major force behind the organization of public agencies. Long wrote, "the bureaucracy is recognized by all interested groups as a major channel of representation. . . ."[87] Consequently, in practice a great deal of effort is exerted by groups, political officials, and others who want to see a particular set of values represented in the missions and programs of public agencies. This often makes for an untidy situation in which agencies have highly diverse, overlapping, and conflicting goals. Yet, to the extent that representation is actually present, it has been noted that "[e]xecutive branch structure is in fact a microcosm of our society. Inevitably it reflects the values, conflicts, and competing forces to be found in a pluralistic society. The ideal of a neatly symmetrical, frictionless organization structure is a dangerous illusion."[88]

The political approach's interest in representation also leads it to consider the public sector work force in a radically different way than does the managerial approach. The concept of **representative bureaucracy**[89] holds that the social backgrounds and statuses of public administrators can affect their performance on the job. Members of the middle and lower classes, or men and women, may have disparate perspectives based on their experience and socialization. These different outlooks can lead them to define problems and design solutions in dissimilar ways. The concept also maintains that the social composition of government agencies is related to their legitimacy among members of the public. For example, an all-white police force might be considered less legitimate in African-American neighborhoods than would an all-black or racially integrated one.

The concept of representative bureaucracy, which is now ingrained in public personnel administration in the United States, is discussed further in the following chapter. Here, however, it should be noted how starkly the notion that public services can be made into representative organizations through their personnel contrasts with the view, espoused by Weber and Taylor, that workers ought to be molded into impersonal cogs for the sake of efficiency.

In emphasizing these three factors, the political approach to public organization holds that "established organization doctrine [the orthodoxy], with its emphasis on structural mechanics, manifests incomplete understanding of our constitutional system, institutional behavior, and tactical and strategic uses of organization structure as an instrument of politics, position, and power. Orthodox theories are not so much wrong when applied to the central issues of executive branch organization as largely irrelevant."[90] Here again, then, we find that to an extent the political and traditional managerial approaches, starting from different premises, end up talking past one another.

The political approach is not as highly focused as the managerial perspectives. Starting from the premises listed above, it proceeds to develop a number of observations that are not necessarily linked to each other in a coherent fashion. Among these are the following.

Pluralism

The organization of public agencies and governmental executive branches should be pluralistic. In other words, they should be highly representative of the competing political, social, and economic groups in the society as a whole. Agencies should provide representation to these interests and public policy should be made through the political competition among agencies. This approach requires that organizational missions be compound rather than unified or that there be many separate organizations. Overall, the public sector must address a number of different concerns without establishing any formal set of priorities. An older mission statement of the U.S. Department of the Interior may present the classic example (see Box 4–8). Diverse missions of this kind generate broad support for agencies and enable administrators to shift emphasis from one aspect of their program to others in conjunction with the need to maintain and strengthen support among their constituencies and to minimize opposition. Pluralism is also generated by overlapping missions among agencies. Perhaps the best current example is found in federal personnel administration. Each of the following is directly involved, but each has a different focus, as their names imply: the Office of Personnel Management, the Merit Systems Protection Board, the Federal Labor Relations Authority, and the Equal Employment Opportunity Commission.

As Harold Seidman notes, in practice,

> Federal programs are likely to have multiple purposes. Disagreements as to priorities among diverse and sometimes conflicting objectives are a major source of current controversies. Is the major purpose of the food stamp program to dispose of

surplus agricultural commodities or to feed the poor? Is mass transportation a transportation or an urban development program? Are loans for college housing a housing or education function? Should the Federal water pollution control program have as its principal objective health protection, or should it be concerned more broadly with the development of water resources?

Major purposes cannot be ascertained by scientific or economic analysis. Determination of major purpose represents a value judgment, and a transitory one at that.[91]

Autonomy

Pluralism requires that government structure reflect the diverse interests of the society. Representation further demands that there be a high degree of autonomy among the many organizational units in a governmental administrative structure. Autonomy enables different units to focus on providing representation to their constituencies or clienteles. Sometimes autonomy evolves under political pressure and administrative leadership; at other times it is built into law. Constitutionally, independent regulatory commissions (IRCs) are not considered part of the executive branch. Independent agencies, such as the EPA, and even some units within the departments, like the FBI, can also achieve a high degree of autonomy. Organizational autonomy may be politically desirable to emphasize the potential for representation, but it also makes unified action and executive control of public administration difficult.

The Legislative Connection

The political approach to public organization also stresses the connection between legislative committees and administrative agencies. In fact, many consider legislative committees and subcommittees to be the key adjuncts of public agencies. According to this view, organizational hierarchy within the executive branch does not encompass the actual hierarchy of authority, which would have to include at the very least the chairpersons of committees and subcommittees in the legislature and their staffs. To a large extent the organizational structure of the federal executive branch and that of Congress in terms of committees and subcommittees are directly related. The proliferation of executive branch organizational units went hand in hand with the growth of subcommittees. Moreover, agencies and subcommittees develop mutually supportive relationships over time. The Government Performance and Results Act of 1993 specifically formalizes the link between (sub)committee and administrative programs by requiring federal agencies to formulate and prioritize specific program goals in consultation with Congress. A public administrator may very well feel accountable, and psychologically and politically responsible to members of the legislature, as well as to political executives and others in the executive branch.

Decentralization

The orthodox approach to public organization addresses the question of centralization versus decentralization from the perspective of efficiency and economy. Decentralization in the sense of establishing field offices and regional offices is considered useful in making government services available to the citizenry. But decentralization also complicates coordination and control of administrative units. Hence, a balance must be struck at some point. This is often dictated by the span of control, among other considerations. Once again, the political approach asks a different question and reaches a different conclusion.

From the political perspective, decentralization cannot be considered separately from representation. For instance, Herbert Kaufman observes that "while [decentralization] is sometimes defended on grounds of efficiency, it is more frequently justified in terms of effective popular participation in government."[92] In fact, Kaufman believes that during the 1960s, "the most sweeping expression of the unrest over lack of representativeness [was] the growing demand for extreme administrative decentralization, frequently coupled with insistence on local clientele domination of the decentralized organizations. Dramatic manifestations of this movement occurred in the antipoverty program and in education."[93]

The last point is worth exploring. At the federal level, less than 15 percent of all employees are located in the metropolitan Washington, D.C., area. The others are located in agency field and regional offices, domestic or abroad. There is a certain logical order in the location of federal agencies' regional offices in ten major cities, including San Francisco, Denver, Boston, New York, and Atlanta (see Box 4–9). But the location of field offices for various administrative operations often appears haphazard. Within a given region, the separate bureaus of a single department may locate their field offices in different cities. Thus, if an individual wants to deal with one administrative unit in the field he or she may have to go to a different city than if he or she wants to deal with another unit of the same department. Prior to the NPR consolidation and elimination of some of its 1,200 field offices in the 1990s, the Department of Agriculture had as many as twenty or more "regional maps," that is, ways of dividing up the country in terms of the location and jurisdiction of the field offices of their various bureaus.

A major explanation for this approach to organizational decentralization is political. As Kaufman points out, representation may be facilitated by it.[94] Another factor is the relationship between a bureau and a member of the legislature. Field offices are affected by pork barrel politics. Agencies can also locate them in an effort to gain or maintain legislators' support. It may well be helpful to place a field office in the home district of a legislator with whom the bureau wants particularly to cooperate. The gerrymandering of field office jurisdictions may also reflect an effort to develop a harmonious relationship with particular members of the legislature. Here, the bureaus (agency subsystems) seek to adapt to or control their environment in ways that detract from the organization's overall coherence.

BOX 4–9 **Standard Federal Regions**

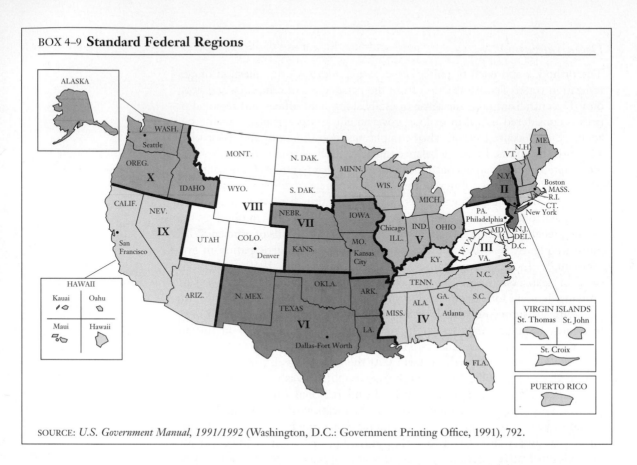

SOURCE: *U.S. Government Manual, 1991/1992* (Washington, D.C.: Government Printing Office, 1991), 792.

A Checklist of Political Questions on Administrative Organization

Harold Seidman has examined the political approach to public organization in great detail in his book, *Politics, Position, and Power: The Dynamics of Federal Organization.*[95] In his conclusion he provides a checklist of the issues that must be addressed in any proposed reorganization. His questions serve as a useful summary of the considerations discussed above. They can be paraphrased or quoted as follows:

1. "What is the nature of the constituency that is being created or acquired, and to what extent will it be able to influence policies and program administration?"
2. How broad is the constituency? Does it represent narrow interests opposed to some aspects of the administrative program?
3. What committees in Congress will have jurisdiction over the administrative program, and what is their attitude likely to be in view of their constituencies?
4. What is the tradition of the department in which a program is to be placed? Will it be supportive, hostile, or indifferent?

5. "What are the constituencies to whom the administering agency responds? Would there be any obvious conflicts of interest?"
6. "Where are the loci of power with respect to program administration: the President, the agency head, the bureaus, congressional committees, professional guilds, interest groups...?"
7. What are the limitations on access to those with decision-making responsibility for the program?
8. "Does the program design foster dominance by a particular professional perspective and will this result in distortion of program goals?"
9. Will the organization of the program be designed so as to facilitate cooperation with other governmental units having overlapped or related responsibilities?
10. "What safeguards are provided to assure that no group or class of people is excluded from participation in the program and an equitable share in program benefits?"
11. Will the form of organization engender status, visibility, and public support to the extent appropriate for the program function?
12. How do the structural and procedural arrangements affect the definition of responsibility and accountability for the program? Do they encourage "buck passing"?[96]

To Seidman's list could be added questions about the supervision of the program within the executive branch. Of particular interest would be whether the political executives in charge of it will require senatorial confirmation, whether they will be appointed directly by the president, or whether they will be appointed by department heads. No doubt additional issues could also be raised. However, these considerations should provide a reasonably comprehensive guide to the political approach to organization.

THE LEGAL APPROACH TO PUBLIC ORGANIZATION

The legal approach to public organization is rarely discussed as a coherent body of principles and premises. Rather, it must more or less be defined from the writings of scholars, decisions of judges, and relevant legislative enactments. Its main thrust is to establish a structure in which fair adjudication or resolution of conflicts can take place. Such a structure must enable opposing sides to be given notice of the issues to be contested; to be afforded an opportunity to present evidence or information supporting their interpretation of rules or laws, and to have an opportunity to explain their behavior and intentions. But most important, perhaps, adversary procedure must afford each side a fair forum in which to challenge the evidence, claims interpretations, and information presented by the other. Traditional adjudication uses adversary procedure, as is best exemplified by courtroom procedure, replete with complex rules of evidence. Alternative dispute resolution (ADR) relies more heavily on settling conflicts through negotiation, mediation, or arbitration.

(These dispute resolution techniques are discussed in the context of labor relations in the next chapter.)

Independence

It has long been asserted by those supportive of the legal approach to public organization that administrative agencies exercising adjudicatory functions must enjoy a good deal of independence from the rest of the government. Some legal scholars thought that any adjudication by administrative agencies was "executive justice" and, consequently, "one of those reversions to justice without law."[97] The idea that agencies could combine legislative functions (rule making), enforcement (execution), and adjudication was particularly disturbing to many. This helps explain why IRCs, which often rely heavily on adjudication, evolved. But at the time, the evolving concept was that administrative adjudication could be vested safely in independent regulatory commissions. At the federal level, the first of these, the Interstate Commerce Commission (ICC), was created in 1887 and authorized to regulate transportation, especially the railroads, in the public interest. Over the years several other independent regulatory commissions, boards, and agencies were created largely under the rationale that "just as we want our judges to be independent of political influence, so we want agencies that exercise judicial functions to be similarly independent. The larger the judicial function, the stronger the reasons for independence."[98] In other words, where agency operations are concerned with adjudication, they should be insulated from partisan and other political pressures. The effort to establish such independence involves several structural arrangements.

The Commission Format

Frequently agencies that exercise quasi-judicial functions are headed by a board of commissioners rather than a single political executive or other hierarchical authority, as would generally be dictated by managerial and political approaches to public organization. As Kenneth C. Davis explains, "just as we want appellate courts to be made up of plural members, to protect against the idiosyncrasies of a single individual, we want agencies that exercise judicial power to be collegial. So the ICC has eleven members, the FCC seven, and the FTC five."[99] Moreover, since the missions of these agencies are defined as regulation in the *public* interest, they should not be controlled by one political party or another. Rather they should be allowed to develop a long-term, nonpartisan perspective. Thus, there are typically limits on the number of commissioners who can belong to the same political party. Such arrangements guarantee minority party members some degree of participation and an opportunity to voice their opinions. If necessary, they may file dissenting opinions. In addition, commissioners who are typically appointed by the chief executive with legislative consent, generally hold their offices during staggered, fixed terms and are protected from removal solely on political grounds. This prevents the president or a governor from replacing all the commissioners at will.

Depending on the context, the commission format may reach deep into the administrative structure of such an agency. Staff may be responsible and accountable to individual commissioners, thereby fragmenting authority. The commission may also become politically divided along partisan or policy lines. An organizational chart of the ICC is presented in Box 4–10; notice that several offices were directly responsible to the chairman rather than the managing director.

Insulation from Ex Parte Influences

It stands to reason that if the commissioners of an agency with judicial functions are to be independent in their decision making, they must be insulated from pressures applied by the legislature and perhaps other groups. Yet it ap-

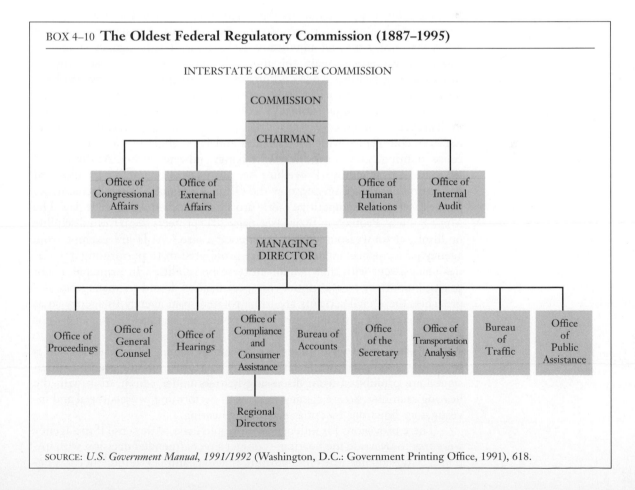

BOX 4–10 **The Oldest Federal Regulatory Commission (1887–1995)**

INTERSTATE COMMERCE COMMISSION

SOURCE: *U.S. Government Manual, 1991/1992* (Washington, D.C.: Government Printing Office, 1991), 618.

pears equally true that the views of legislators and others may be helpful in determining what is in the public interest. The legal approach tries to solve this dilemma by encouraging widespread participation in the *rule-making* procedures of such agencies, while at the same time prohibiting one-sided contacts with agency decision makers when they are engaged in adjudication. Such one-sided contacts are called **ex parte,** and they are considered an unfair breach of the requirement that each side have a fair opportunity to present its case. The legal approach has been so insistent upon this that in at least one case, *D.C. Federation of Civic Associations v. Volpe* (1972),[100] a federal court of appeals ordered a district court to require the secretary of the Department of Transportation to establish a decision-making process that would enable it to act free "from extraneous pressures unrelated to the merits of the question."[101] The point of such procedures was to exclude pressure from a member of Congress!

Independent Hearing Examiners–Administrative Law Judges

Just as the legal approach favors the independence of agency heads who engage in adjudication and their insulation from ex parte communications, it holds that others making adjudiciary decisions within the agency should be similarly autonomous. Again, this approach stands in stark contrast to the orthodox managerial insistence on hierarchy. It also contravenes the emphasis on representation and widespread participation encouraged by the political approach to public organization. Hearing examiners, who are also called administrative law judges (ALJs), preside over administrative hearings involving issues of compliance with agency rules and laws, eligibility for benefits, license granting, some forms of rule making, and rate setting. At the federal level, the Administrative Procedure Act of 1946, as amended, provides that the central personnel agency, now the Office of Personnel Management, select ALJs through competitive merit procedures and establish their pay. The Merit Systems Protection Board (see page 221) protects them from discipline or dismissal for reasons other than "good cause." ALJs are exempt from agency performance appraisals and are prohibited from performing any duties inconsistent with their adjudicatory responsibilities. In principle, if not practice, contrary to the notion of specialization found in managerial approaches, these civil servants are to be rotated from agency to agency so as not to become overly supportive of the policy perspectives of one agency or another.

In addition to these provisions for independence, the ex parte rule is strictly interpreted. Officials in the agency to which a hearing examiner is assigned are prohibited from discussing matters under adjudication with the hearing examiner. So are agency employees performing prosecutorial and investigatory functions except as part of the hearing.

These provisions for independence would make little sense if the agency were free to override the hearing examiner's recommended decision with impunity. Consequently, through custom, practice, and law, a tendency has developed for the administrative law judge's opinion to be upheld unless it appears to "(1) be flatly unjustifiable in light of the facts; (2) be obviously contrary to and disruptive of agency policy objectives; (3) have been reached in a procedurally reckless manner destined to elicit court review; (4) be unnecessarily harsh on a party; and (5) be likely to attract unwanted political reprisals."[102] However, in order to guard against a misguided decision by a single hearing examiner, procedures may provide for an appeal within an agency. This adds another adjudicatory process and structure to the agency's organization.

Staffing for Adjudication

The legal approach toward public administration holds that the adjudicatory activities of public agencies will often follow trial-like procedures. This approach is buttressed by constitutional requirements for procedural due process under certain circumstances. The adjudicatory model contains an implicit structure that goes beyond the existence of independent hearing examiners. It also includes other kinds of organizational positions, including investigatory and prosecutorial units. Investigators have been identified as key functionaries in many regulatory contexts.[103] Because they must exercise a good deal of discretion, their supervision and training become critical considerations for the proper functioning of the agency. This introduces the need for hierarchical positions to oversee their behavior and staff units to keep them fully cognizant of changes in agency policy, law, and technique. Prosecutors also require supportive arrangements, including staff to do research; analyze private parties' requests for rate increases, licenses, and other benefits; and help prepare cases and briefs for adjudication.

ADR

Alternative dispute resolution offers much greater flexibility than traditional adjudication and is strongly supported by the NPM. The Negotiated Rulemaking Act (1990) and the Administrative Dispute Resolution Act (ADRA) (1990) provide new frameworks for dispute resolution by federal agencies. The Negotiated Rulemaking Act allows agencies to develop proposed rules on a consensus basis through negotiation. The main purposes are to facilitate rule making (see Chapter 9) and to reduce the number of lawsuits challenging agency rules. Theoretically, agencies should negotiate as equals with other interested parties. Ultimately, though, they are responsible for the content of rules. Mediation or other means of facilitation may be used. The ADRA requires agencies to have dispute resolution specialists on their staffs and to promote ADR in contract and other legal conflicts.

Both acts look toward a sharing of authority with outsiders, including mediators, and to greater administrative responsiveness. They conflict with orthodox management's emphasis on unity of command and clear lines of authority. They also pose a challenge to organizational cultures that view negotiation as unprofessional and a devaluation of technical expertise.[104] Although the responsiveness they may afford is favored by the political approach, it comes at the price of obscuring accountability.

In sum, there is a legal approach to public organization that differs substantially from the managerial and political approaches. It emphasizes independence rather than hierarchy, procedural fairness and regularity rather than efficiency, and individual rights rather than group representation. In the ADR version it favors sharing authority and responsiveness even at some cost to accountability and reliance on specialized expertise. Although it probably achieves many of its goals, it is not surprising that the legal approach to public organization is frequently attacked by those seeking to promote managerial and political objectives. Once again, therefore, we find the tendency for public administrative practices to confirm Miles's law: "Where one stands depends on where one sits." What are the prospects for a synthesis of the approaches to public organization?

THE FUTURE

Many believe that public organizations of the future will look considerably different from those reflecting the managerial, political, or legal perspectives of today. But it is possible that they will synthesize many of the characteristics of contemporary organizations based on these approaches. Certainly, there are widespread tendencies toward change. But they point in somewhat different directions.

Fundamental Assumptions

At the root of the general claim that public organization will look quite different in the future is the notion that contemporary administrative agencies are rapidly becoming outmoded. This is a central tenet of the NPM. For a variety of reasons, traditional organizations seem unable to adapt to the rapid pace of change in contemporary life. According to this assumption, agencies today are authoritarian, rigid, defensive, unable to utilize effectively their human resources, alienating, and repressive. In short, they simply lack the flexibility to keep up with the constantly changing technological, political, economic, and social environments with which they must interact. Hierarchy, in particular, is unable to tap the full talents and utilize the perspectives of employees in the lower and even the middle ranks. Moreover, it tends to overemphasize the authority and overstate the ability of those at the top in an age when a person's "knowledge and approach can become obsolete before he has even begun the career for which he was trained."[105] In this view, the era is rapidly passing when a "great leader," dominated by a single idea—such as assembly-line production—can effectively run an organization over a decade or so. Similarly, one might observe that the use of relatively static representational devices, such as advisory committees, creates structures of privilege that are too resistant to change to be sufficiently adaptive.[106] Adjudication, too, might be criticized for emphasizing adversary relationships rather than seeking to promote cooperation and problem solving in complex areas of public policy such as the regulation of utility rates. It also tends to emphasize procedure over substance. Change seems inevitable, but there are two emergent models, both with deep roots in American culture—**democratic organization** and market-based organization.

Democratic Organization

"Democracy becomes a functional necessity whenever a social system is competing for survival under conditions of chronic change."[107] Democracy in this view will include:

1. Full and free *communication*, regardless of rank and power.
2. A reliance on *consensus*, rather than the more customary forms of coercion or compromise to manage conflict.
3. The idea that *influence* is based on technical competence and knowledge rather than on the vagaries of personal whims or prerogatives of power.
4. An atmosphere that permits and even encourages emotional *expression* as well as task-oriented acts.
5. A basically *human* bias, one that accepts the inevitability of conflict between the organization and the individual, but which is willing to cope with and mediate this conflict on rational grounds.[108]

Moreover, a scientific attitude of inquiry and experimentation will prevail, loyalty to organizations per se will decline as those who are less committed are likely to be more able to take advantage of change, and structural arrangements will be flexible and task-oriented, rather than based on fixed specializations, rigid jurisdictions, and sharply defined levels of hierarchical authority.

Employee Participation   Participative organizations, according to this look into the future, will encourage the participation of employees at all levels in decisions affecting their work and, perhaps, in the formulation of broad agency policies. The rationale here has been summarized as follows: "Such participation has 'involving,' motivating effects which improve worker performance. Participation also increases the quality of organizational decisions by decentralizing them to those points in the organization where the real expertise and best information are located. Participative doctrine also takes the position that members at the lowest levels of the organization possess resources of creativity and capabilities for making worthwhile contributions to the management of the organization."[109] Some have even concluded that worker self-management, in which workers take responsibility for all the POSDCORB functions traditionally performed by management, is likely to be a feature of participative organizations of the future.[110]

The idea of employee participation is not new. Contemporary "agency theory," which grows out of economic assumptions concerning individuals' proclivity toward "self-regarding" behavior directed at maximizing their utilities (preferences), put the desirability of participation in a new light. Agency theory "assumes that social life is a series of contracts. Conventionally, one member, the 'buyer' of goods or services, is designated the 'principal,' and the other, who provides the goods or services, is the 'agent'. . . . The principal-agent relationship is governed by a contract specifying what the agent should do and what the principal must do in return (e.g., . . . pay a wage and benefits . . .)."[111] In the abstract, each employee of an organization could be considered an agent, free to attempt to write the terms of his or her contract with it. This ignores collective bargaining and some other aspects of personnel law, but it does call attention to the prospect that self-regarding behavior will lead to shirking and other forms of cheating.

One response to such potential behavior is to try to minimize the organizational characteristics that would foster undesirable self-regarding activity. Charles Perrow identifies some of these characteristics as follows:

- *"The measurement of individual effort or contribution is encouraged*. . . . It is a continuing legacy of nineteenth-century individualism, celebrating individual rather than cooperative effort."

- *"A preference for leadership stability and generalized authority dominates. . . ."* as opposed to a practice of alternating "leadership tasks according to the skills of the individuals, thus avoiding stable patterns of dependency in subordinates and self-fulfilling assumptions of expertise in leaders."

- *"Tall hierarchies are favored* . . . based on unequal rewards and notions that coordination must be achieved by giving orders."[112]

Minimizing these characteristics in the public sector would "debureaucratize" organizations and transform the exercise and distribution of authority within them. In other words, greater equality and participation among employees in running an organization could check undesirable self-regarding behavior to an extent.

How would employee participation actually work? Here the advocates of democratic organization tend to be less certain. Presumably, however, in large organizations participation will be among groups of workers or workers' committees or "quality circles." The precise scope and structure of employee participation necessarily remains vague when we engage in speculation about the future. One aspect does seem certain, however: Such participation, if it occurs at all, will go well beyond collective bargaining as presently constituted.

Advocacy Administration   Organizational democracy in the future may include an increased reliance on **advocacy administration,** which involves "the passionate commitment of those with professional skills and official standing to use these assets on behalf of the least powerful and wealthy members of the community."[113] Advocacy can take at least three forms: (1) advocacy from outside the government, which we will discuss in the next section; (2) "advocacy from within a government agency established to act in a manner adversary to other public agencies and programs, as in the Office of Economic Opportunity advocacy law program"[114]; and (3) advocacy by administrative officials on behalf of their clientele or constituency groups.

At the root of the advocacy concept is the belief that the adversary model of adjudication can be generalized to provide effective representation to all elements of the political community, including those who face special difficulties in organizing. Governmental structure will continue to be pluralistic, but in order to provide comprehensive representation, government may have to organize disadvantaged groups or, at least, place spokespersons who can effectively identify and represent their interests within the governmental structure. It may be possible to accomplish the latter by making public services socially representative of the society's composition as a whole. Special counsels, as associated with the federal Merit Systems Protection Board (see Chapter 5), may also be used to advocate the rights of some group of individuals.

Advocacy administration also will require a changed view of hierarchical authority. Advocates' right to advocate, that is, to oppose the policies and programs of administrative hierarchies, must be protected. The notion of "insubordination" has little relevance in this context, as does the managerial approach's desire to eliminate duplication, overlap, and conflictual lines of authority and responsibility. Yet advocacy would differ from adjudication in that the policy decisions would be made by elected bodies and political executives, rather than independent hearing examiners. Evidence would be political as well as factual, and advocacy would not be bound by the rules of trial-like adversary procedure.

Citizen Participation   Citizen participation, a form of advocacy from outside the government that is a longstanding feature of public administration in the United States, may become an even more important factor in the future. Such participation can be through advisory committees, citizen boards, or similar arrangements. For instance, according to Lewis Mainzer, there is a "national network of some 30,000 elective farmer committees" that participate in public administration.[115] Citizen participation can also be directly built into administrative decision making. This approach has been evident in the controversial use of "community action programs" which "offer citizen participation in and control of public administration. Local neighborhood representatives are held to be more truly spokesmen of the disadvantaged citizens, of the spirit of the local community, than the politicians of city hall and city council."[116] Community action approaches may be used to control or influence schools, public housing developments, zoning, police conduct, and other aspects of local, neighborhood administration. In some cases, citizen participation may be facilitated by the governmental provision of professional planners, lawyers, or others to the citizen groups. New York State's Department of Environmental Conservation employs full-time "citizen participation specialists" whose job is to facilitate citizen involvement in environmental policy decision making. Finally, citizen participation can be encouraged through open hearings on matters being considered by administrative agencies, such as changes in utility rates, zoning changes, and the building of roads or housing developments. Such hearings are often sparsely attended, but they afford public administrators an opportunity to hear what some citizens have to say.

Citizen participation is obviously based on the notion that one does not need to be an expert in technical matters of public policy to be able to form a valuable opinion about the desirability of pursuing one course or another. As the "policy consumer," the average citizen is considered an adequate judge of the benefits and problems of public policies. This approach poses a threat to hierarchy, specialization, and the belief that trained expertise should provide the dominant basis for participation in public policy making. In some forms, such as open hearings and community action programs, it also tends to challenge the political perspective's reliance on established groups and formal organizations as the basis for representing the views of the citizenry in public administration. (The public and public administration is the subject of Chapter 10.)

Market-Based Organization

Marketlike public administration is a second model for administrative organizations of the future. It is strongly advocated by the NPM and the NPR. At its core is the belief that marketlike competition leads organizations to be both efficient and responsive to customer preferences. The NPR vision shares some of the elements of democratic organization just discussed. It strongly favors employee empowerment and disfavors hierarchy. Empowerment would enable those who actually deliver services to the public to decide how to do so. The empowered employee is held accountable for his or her performance, that is, for results. Management's main job is not to control employees, but to be entrepreneurial in creating and marketing valued services or products for customers. Organizations will be successful if they satisfy their customers. Customers will drive public agencies to be efficient and responsive.

The market model is based on the same politics-administration dichotomy embraced by the orthodoxy. Like the orthodoxy, it is overwhelmingly managerial and places a very high premium on efficiency, or a variant of it, such as cost-effectiveness. Administration is business, not policy. Ideally, the NPM would institutionalize the dichotomy by privatizing and separating factory operations from political ones, as in the case of PBOs. Presumably, PBOs will be flat, rather than hierarchical, for the sake of flexibility and will afford a great deal of employee participation for the intelligence and efficiency it yields.

The market model does not provide for direct citizen participation in public administration. It serves customers, not citizens.[117] Individuals participate as customers; perhaps groups can do the same (e.g., group fares or discounts). One risk, already present in bureaucratic politics, is that agencies may be responsive to their customers at the expense of the wider public's interests. Farmers, slaughterhouses, food processors, shippers, supermarkets, and restaurants are the customers of agencies engaged in food safety. They tend to resist regulation as unnecessary until a tragedy occurs and the public loses confidence in their products.

Market-based public administration is so new that it is difficult to see how it deals with three key questions. First, how can politics be separated from administration? Orthodox administration insisted that separation was possible and tried to take politics out of personnel and the management of cities, ports, bridges, parks, and other infrastructures. But personnel remained infused with policy issues: Should social diversity be emphasized? Should veterans have preferences? Should collective bargaining be allowed? Should employees be disciplined for off-the-job behavior? Similarly, city managers often have a very difficult time avoiding politics. Cost-effectiveness is only one criterion for distributing services. Who benefits and who pays may be of more interest to residents and their elected representatives. Public authorities for parks, highways, and bridges have sometimes had a great impact on individual neighborhoods, suburbanization, and the quality of life in central cities.

Second, actual markets register customer preferences and thereby allow stratification according to ability and willingness to pay. There are niches and boutiques. People who can afford better services and products are apt to buy them. Can the same principle be applied to public sector programs? Express mail costs more. Should there be express lines at motor vehicle departments or Social Security offices for those who are willing to pay for quicker service? Should neighborhoods that are willing to pay more have better quality water, trash pickup, snow removal, or fire protection? Should public schools be organized according to their ability to attract customers? Should scarce resources like 911 services be sold to subscribers? Inequality is already a fact of life in the United States; would market-based public administration increase it?

Finally, how will market-based administrative organizations be held accountable? The NPM is certainly correct that traditional accountability mechanisms focus on processes rather than results and can strangle public administration in red tape. But accountability for results alone is also problematic. It is a cliché that the Italian Fascists made the trains run on time. Inevitably, the results orientation will have to be blended with and tempered by the values of the political and legal approaches. But how can this be done without *re*regulating the agencies and processes the NPM has struggled so hard to *de*regulate?

Addressing these issues is not to disparage the market-based model. No approach to organizing public administration has yet been able to satisfy our three general perspectives or maximize all our competing goals. But there is both progress and hope. The movements toward democratic organization and market-based public administration embrace both employee participation and responsiveness. These values have already had a major impact on revamping public personnel management, which is central to all public administration. It is the subject of Chapter 5.

NOTES

1. Amitai, Etzioni, *Modern Organizations* (Englewood Cliffs, N.J.: Prentice-Hall, 1964), 1.
2. Ibid., 3.
3. Ibid., 2.
4. A classic volume on organization theory is James G. March, ed., *Handbook of Organizations* (Chicago: Rand McNally, 1965).
5. Barry Bozeman, *All Organizations Are Public* (San Francisco: Jossey-Bass, 1987).
6. Harold Gortner, Julianne Mahler, and Jeanne Nicholson, *Organization Theory: A Public Perspective* (Chicago: Dorsey, 1987).
7. Jay M. Shafritz and Philip Whitbeck, eds., *Classics of Organization Theory* (Oak Park, Ill.: Moore, 1978), 322.
8. Dwight Waldo, "Organization Theory: An Elephantine Problem," *Public Administration Review 21*, no. 4 (1961): 210–225, at 220.
9. Max Weber, *From Max Weber: Essays in Sociology* (New York: Oxford University Press, 1958), trans. and ed. by H. H. Gerth and C. W. Mills, especially chap. 8; Max Weber, *The Theory of Social and Economic Organization* (New York: Free Press, 1947), trans. and ed. by A. M. Henderson and Talcott Parsons, especially chap. 3.
10. Quoted in Reinhard Bendix, *Max Weber: An Intellectual Portrait* (Garden City, N.Y.: Doubleday, 1962), 464.
11. Warren Bennis, "Beyond Bureaucracy," *Transaction* 2 (July/August 1965): 32.
12. Victor Thompson, *Modern Organization* (New York: Knopf, 1961), 47.
13. Al Gore, *From Red Tape to Results: Creating a Government That Works Better & Costs Less: The Report of the National Performance Review* (Washington, D.C.: U.S. Government Printing Office, 1993), 67.
14. Herbert Simon, *Models of Man* (New York: Wiley, 1957), 196.
15. See Frederick Winslow Taylor, "The Principles of Scientific Management," in Shafritz and Whitbeck, *Classics of Organization Theory*, 9–23. For a fuller discussion see Frederick W. Taylor, *Principles of Scientific Management* (New York: Norton, 1911).
16. Etzioni, *Modern Organizations*, 2.
17. For a good review, see George C. Homans, "The Western Electric Researches," in *Readings on Modern Organizations*, ed. Amitai Etzioni (Englewood Cliffs, N.J.: Prentice-Hall, 1969), 99–114.
18. Chester I. Barnard, *The Functions of the Executive* (Cambridge, Mass.: Harvard University Press, 1938).
19. Warren Bennis, *Why Leaders Can't Lead* (San Francisco: Jossey-Bass, 1989), 18.

20. Weber, *From Max Weber*, chap. 9.
21. See Alon Gratch, "The Personality of the Corporate Leader: Testing for Traits That Make a Manager," *New York Times*, 3 February 1985.
22. Eugene Lewis, *Public Entrepreneurship: Toward a Theory of Bureaucratic Political Power* (Bloomington: Indiana University Press, 1984), 109.
23. Ibid.
24. Bennis, *Why Leaders Can't Lead*, 21–22.
25. Lewis, *Public Entrepreneurship*, 238.
26. Ibid.
27. Ibid., 240.
28. Robert A. Caro, *The Power Broker* (New York: Random House, 1975), 386; quoted in ibid., 201.
29. Lewis, *Public Entrepreneurship*, 153.
30. Norma Riccucci, *Unsung Heroes* (Washington, D.C.: Georgetown University Press, 1995), 226–231.
31. Amitai Etzioni, *Complex Organizations* (New York: Free Press, 1961), 8–16.
32. Robert Tannenbaum and Warren H. Schmidt, "How to Choose a Leadership Pattern," *Harvard Business Review* 36 (March/April 1958): 95–101; Tannenbaum and Schmidt, "Retrospective Commentary," *Harvard Business Review* 51 (May/June 1973): 1–10.
33. J. D. Williams, *Public Administration: The People's Business* (Boston: Little, Brown, 1980), 136.
34. Ibid.
35. Abraham Maslow, "A Theory of Human Motivation," *Psychological Review* 50 (July 1943): 370–396.
36. See Cary Hershey, *Protest in the Public Service* (Lexington, Mass.: Lexington Books, 1973), for further theoretical development and examples.
37. Philip E. Slater and Warren Bennis, "Democracy Is Inevitable," *Harvard Business Review* 42 (March/April 1964): 51–59. See also George Berkley, *The Administrative Revolution* (Englewood Cliffs, N.J.: Prentice-Hall, 1971).
38. Berkley, *The Administrative Revolution*.
39. Frederick Herzberg, B. Mausner, and B. Snyderman, *The Motivation to Work* (New York: Wiley, 1959); Frederick Herzberg, *Work and the Nature of Man* (Cleveland: World Publishing, 1966).
40. See David McClelland, *The Achieving Society* (Princeton, N.J.: Van Nostrand, 1961); David McClelland, "That Urge to Achieve," in Walter E. Natemeyer, ed., *Classics of Organizational Behavior* (Oak Park, Ill.: Moore, 1978), 88–94.
41. John P. Campbell et al., *Managerial Behavior, Performance, and Effectiveness* (New York: McGraw-Hill, 1970); V. H. Vroom, *Work and Motivation* (New York: Wiley, 1964).
42. David Easton, *A Framework for Political Analysis* (Englewood Cliffs, N.J.: Prentice-Hall, 1965); James D. Thompson, *Organizations in Action* (New York: McGraw-Hill, 1967); Daniel Katz and Robert L. Kahn, *The Social Psychology of Organizations*, 2d ed. (New York: Wiley, 1978).
43. Robert Hampton, "The Basic Question," *Civil Service Journal* 13 (January–March 1983), 2–5.
44. Charles Perrow, *Complex Organizations*, 3d ed. (New York: Random House, 1986).
45. William Scott, "Organicism: The Moral Anesthetic of Management," *Academy of Management Review* 4, no. 1 (1979): 21–28.

46. Ibid. 23.

47. Perrow, *Complex Organizations*, 192–208.

48. Ibid., 210.

49. Katz and Kahn, *The Social Psychology of Organizations*, 52.

50. James D. Thompson, *Organizations in Action* (New York: McGraw-Hill, 1967).

51. Mary Douglas, *How Institutions Think* (Syracuse, N.Y.: Syracuse University Press, 1986).

52. Ibid., x.

53. Ibid., 45.

54. Steven Ott, *The Organizational Culture Perspective* (Chicago: Dorsey, 1989), 2–3.

55. Herbert Kaufman, *Time, Chance, and Organizations* (Chatham, N.J.: Chatham House, 1985), 67.

56. Ibid., 134.

57. Harold Seidman, *Politics, Position, and Power* (New York: Oxford University Press, 1970), 9.

58. Luther Gulick and Lyndall Urwick, eds., *Papers on the Science of Administration* (New York: Institute of Public Administration, 1937).

59. Ibid., 3–13.

60. Ibid.

61. Ibid.

62. Ibid.

63. Herbert Simon, *Administrative Behavior*, 2d ed. (New York: Free Press, 1957), 20–36 (originally published in 1947).

64. Dwight Waldo, *The Administrative State* (New York: The Ronald Press, 1948); see also Waldo, "Development of the Theory of Democratic Administration," *American Political Science Review* 46 (March 1952): 81–103.

65. Gore, *From Red Tape to Results*, 2.

66. *Federalist Paper No. 51*, in C. Rossiter, ed., *The Federalist Papers* (New York: New American Library, 1961), 322.

67. President's Committee on Administrative Management, *Report of the Committee* (Washington, D.C.: Government Printing Office, 1937), introduction.

68. 53 Stat. 36 (1939).

69. See Stephen R. Rosenthal, *Managing Government Operations* (Glenview, Ill.: Scott, Foresman, 1982).

70. Chester A. Newland, "Policy/Program Objectives and Federal Management: The Search for Government Effectiveness," *Public Administration Review* 36 (January/February 1976): 20–27, at 26.

71. Robert Rodgers and John Hunter, "A Foundation of Good Management in Government: Management by Objectives," *Public Administration Review* 52 (January/February 1992): 27–39.

72. W. Edwards Deming, *Out of the Crisis* (Cambridge, Mass.: MIT Center for Advanced Engineering Study, 1986).

73. P. Crosby, *Quality Is Free* (New York: McGraw-Hill, 1979); J. Jurand, *Jurand on Leadership for Quality* (New York: McGraw-Hill, 1988).

74. James Swiss, "Adapting Total Quality Management (TQM) to Government," *Public Administration Review* 52 (January/February 1992): 356–362.

75. Ibid., 359.

76. Steven Cohen and William Eimicke, "Project-Focused Total Quality Management in the New York City Department of Parks and Recreation," *Public Administration Review* 54 (September/October 1994), 455.

77. Bonnie Mani, "Old Wine in New Bottles Tastes Better," *Public Administration Review* 55 (March/April 1995): 157.
78. Ibid.
79. Editorial: "The New Flight Path Plan for the FAA," *Washington Post*, 31 March 1996, C6.
80. Douglas McGregor, *The Human Side of Enterprise* (New York: McGraw-Hill, 1960); see also Douglas McGregor, *The Professional Manager* (New York: McGraw-Hill, 1967).
81. Douglas McGregor, "The Human Side of Enterprise," in *Readings in Managerial Psychology*, ed. H. J. Leavitt and L. R. Pondy (Chicago: University of Chicago Press, 1973), 748.
82. Rensis Likert, "Human Organizational Measurements: Key to Financial Success," in Natemeyer, *Classics of Organizational Behavior*, 293–297, at 294–295. See also Rensis Likert, *The Human Organization* (New York: McGraw-Hill, 1967).
83. See Wendell French, "Organization Development: Objectives, Assumptions and Strategies," in Natemeyer, *Classics of Organizational Behavior*, 348–362.
84. H. Roy Kaplan and Curt Tausky, "Humanism in Organizations: A Critical Perspective," *Public Administration Review* 37 (March/April 1977): 171–180.
85. Paul Appleby, *Big Democracy* (New York: Knopf, 1945); the quoted passage can be found in Jay Shafritz and Albert Hyde, eds., *Classics of Public Administration* (Oak Park, Ill.: Moore, 1978), 105.
86. Norton Long, "Power and Administration," *Public Administration Review* 9 (Autumn 1949): 257–264. As quoted from Long's essay, "Power and Administration," as it appears in Francis E. Rourke, ed., *Bureaucratic Power in National Politics* (Boston: Little, Brown, 1965), 14–16.
87. Ibid., 17–18.
88. Seidman, *Politics, Position, and Power*, 13.
89. Samuel Krislov and David H. Rosenbloom, *Representative Bureaucracy and the American Political System* (New York: Praeger, 1981).
90. Seidman, *Politics, Position, and Power*, 13.
91. Ibid., 19–20.
92. Herbert Kaufman, "Administrative Decentralization and Political Power," in Shafritz and Hyde, *Classics of Public Administration*, 356. Originally published in *Public Administration Review* 29 (January/February 1969): 3–15.
93. Shafritz and Hyde, *Classics of Public Administration*, 354.
94. Ibid., 353–356.
95. Seidman, *Politics, Position, and Power*.
96. Ibid., 284–285; and Harold Seidman and Robert Gilmour, *Politics, Position, and Power*, 4th ed. (New York: Oxford University Press, 1986), 340.
97. Roscoe Pound, "Justice According to Law," *Columbia Law Review* 14 (1914): 1.
98. Kenneth Culp Davis, *Administrative Law and Government*, 2d ed. (St. Paul: West, 1975), 17.
99. Ibid.
100. 459 F.2d 1231 (1972). For a discussion, see Kenneth F. Warren, *Administrative Law in the American Political System* (St. Paul: West, 1982), 211.
101. As quoted in Warren, *Administrative Law*, 212.
102. Warren, *Administrative Law*, 289.
103. Eugene Bardach and Robert Kagan, *Going by the Book* (Philadelphia: Temple University Press, 1982), especially chaps. 5 and 6. See also Pietro S. Nivola, *The Urban Service Problem* (Lexington, Mass.: Lexington Books, 1979).

104. Nancy Manring, "ADR and Administrative Responsiveness," *Public Administration Review* 54 (March/April 1994): 197–203.

105. Slater and Bennis, "Democracy Is Inevitable," as it appears in Shafritz and Whitbeck, *Classics of Organization Theory*, 306.

106. Krislov and Rosenbloom, *Representative Bureaucracy*, chap. 3; Theodore J. Lowi, *The End of Liberalism* (New York: Norton, 1969); Grant McConnell, *Private Power and American Democracy* (New York: Knopf, 1966).

107. Slater and Bennis, "Democracy Is Inevitable," in Shafritz and Whitbeck, *Classics of Organization Theory*, 305.

108. Ibid., 304.

109. Marvin Meade, "'Participative' Administration—Emerging Reality or Wishful Thinking?" in *The Politics of the Federal Bureaucracy*, 2d ed., ed. Alan Altshuler and Norman Thomas (New York: Harper & Row, 1977), 102–112.

110. See Dick Olufs, "Workers' Self-Management in the Public Service," in *Public Personnel Policy: The Politics of Civil Service*, ed. David H. Rosenbloom (Port Washington, N.Y.: Associated Faculty Press, 1985).

111. Perrow, *Complex Organizations*, 224.

112. Ibid., 233.

113. Lewis C. Mainzer, *Political Bureaucracy* (Glenview, Ill.: Scott, Foresman, 1973), 132.

114. Ibid.

115. Ibid., 136.

116. Ibid., 139.

117. Gore, *From Red Tape to Results*, 6.

ADDITIONAL READING

BAN, CAROLYN. *How Do Public Managers Manage?* San Francisco: Jossey-Bass, 1995.

COHEN, STEVEN, AND WILLIAM EIMICKE. *The New Effective Public Manager.* San Francisco: Jossey-Bass, 1995.

KAUFMAN, HERBERT. *Time, Chance, and Organizations.* Chatham, N.J.: Chatham House, 1985.

OTT, STEVEN. *The Organizational Culture Perspective.* Chicago: Dorsey, 1989.

RAINEY, HAL. *Understanding and Managing Public Organizations.* San Francisco: Jossey-Bass, 1991.

SEIDMAN, HAROLD, AND ROBERT GILMOUR. *Politics, Position, and Power,* 4th ed. New York: Oxford University Press, 1986.

STUDY QUESTIONS

1. Consider the university or college that you attend from an organizational design perspective. What values does its organizational form emphasize? What objectives appear to be promoted by these values and the design? Are there any values or objectives that you think are appropriate to the institution, but suffer as a result of its organizational design? Does the organizational design cause you any problems personally?

2. Can you identify some public administrative organizations that should not be considered "bureaucratic" from a Weberian perspective?

3. Choose any public administrative function with which you are familiar. How could it be organized to *maximize* efficiency, representativeness, and equity?

4. Draw up a list of the potential advantages and disadvantages of organizing public schools to be market-based. On balance, do you personally support or oppose such organization? Why? What does your conclusion suggest about making other types of public organizations market-based?

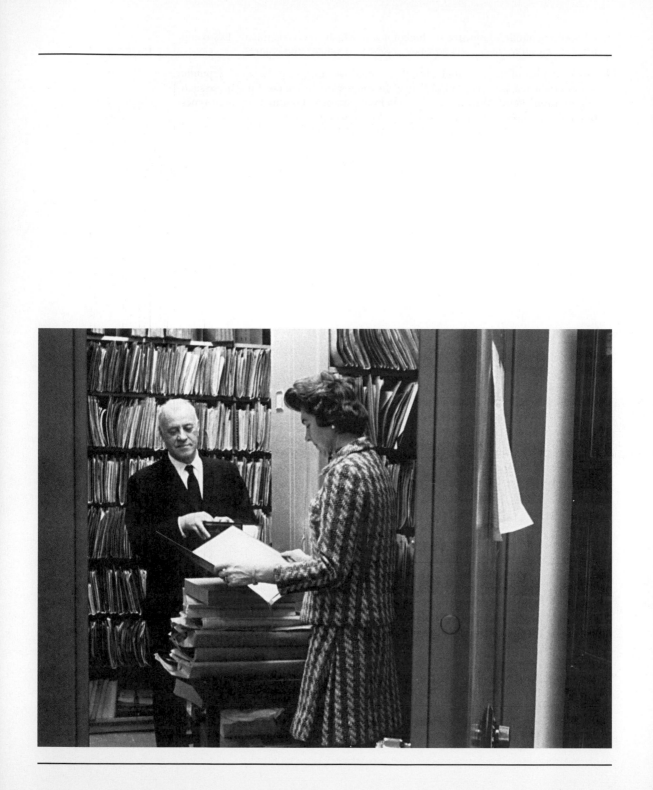

CHAPTER 5 | *Public Personnel Administration and Collective Bargaining*

This chapter discusses the history of public personnel administration in the United States, emphasizing how the three major historical phases of public personnel administration maximized certain values but failed to deal adequately with others and revealing how these failures subsequently led to reforms. The historical phases have been (1) the era of "gentlemen" (1789–1828), (2) the "spoils system" (1829–1882), and (3) the "merit system" (as it has evolved since 1883). The federal civil service reform of 1978 is discussed, as are the new public management (NPM) reforms of the 1990s. The chapter then explores the managerial, political, and legal perspectives toward public personnel administration. The process and politics of public sector collective bargaining are also examined.

There are about 17 million people employed by the 87,000 governments in the United States. If you were in charge of managing them, according to what criteria and under what organizational arrangements would you select, assign, train, discipline, promote, and pay these civil servants? How would you motivate them to provide the highest levels of performance? How would you ensure their loyalty to the nation and their willingness to co-operate with their jurisdictions' political leadership? Would you engage in collective bargaining with them? These are among the central questions of contemporary public personnel management. They raise issues that seem to defy permanent resolution and remain quite perplexing. To a very large extent, the nation's ability to achieve its goals through public administrative action depends upon the performance, honesty, and motivation of public employees. Although we think in terms of institutions and principles, in the final analysis, organizations and governments are not charts and words on pieces of paper; they are made up of people and it is necessary somehow to organize the conditions of their employment. Today, no one seriously disputes the central importance of public personnel administration. Some prefer to call it human resources management—a term that emphasizes the importance of people. As in other areas of public administration, personnel policy can be analyzed from the different perspectives provided by the managerial, political, and legal approaches.

HISTORICAL BACKGROUND

Sometimes public personnel administration seems to be in such a mess that we are tempted to ask how it ever arrived at such a state. In 1993, the National Performance Review (NPR) complained, "talk to a federal manager for 10 minutes: You likely will hear at least one personnel horror story. The system is so complex and rule-bound that most managers cannot even advise an applicant how to get a federal job. . . . The average manager needs a year to fire an incompetent employee, even with solid proof."[1] But such charges were hardly novel; public personnel administration's historical development in the United States has been largely in response to successive calls for reform. In this area of public administration, therefore, it is particularly necessary to understand the past in order to comprehend the present and anticipate the future.[2]

Public Personnel Administration According to "Gentlemen"

It is possible to divide the evolution of public personnel practice in the United States into three broad periods. Each was characterized by a different style of politics, of which public personnel was an integral part. First was the era of "gentlemen," which began with Washington's first administration in 1789 and ended with the inauguration of President Jackson in 1829. President Washington wanted to get the fledgling administrative system off to a sound start. He realized the importance of his administration in setting precedents. For Washington, the primary criterion in making appointments was "fitness of character." Fit characters were those with high standing in the community and personal integrity. They tended to be members of the upper class. Some lacked any apparent technical qualifications of competence for the jobs to which they were appointed, but they did bring a measure of greater prestige to the new government. They were also capable of learning what they needed to know on the job. At the time, public administration was relatively simple and many of its tasks could be effectively achieved by anyone with a modest degree of literacy.

Washington hoped his fit characters would perform honestly and efficiently, but he also sought effectiveness. This brought forth another and somewhat competing criterion for selection. By 1795, when the division between the Hamiltonian and Jeffersonian visions of how active the federal government should be became apparent, Washington realized that politics could be important in the selection and assignment of public personnel. He considered appointing a public administrator who opposed his policies to be a sort of "political suicide."[3] In other words, he sought political loyalty as well as social and administrative fitness.

Washington's precedents were carried forward by his successors, though with a differing emphasis. President John Adams began to stress politics to a greater extent, although he still made appointments from the upper class. In addition, the regime's first political dismissals have been attributed to him. It was Jefferson, however, who first developed a reasonably clear theory about the role politics should play in public personnel administration.

Upon entering office, Jefferson complained that Adams had stocked the federal government's administrative apparatus with members of the opposition Federalist party. He thought that this situation could be remedied primarily in two ways. First, he sought to forbid federal administrators from taking any active part in electioneering. This was the federal government's earliest attempt to develop *political neutrality* in the administrative branch. By taking federal employees out of politics, Jefferson would be neutralizing the Federalist influence that could be waged against his Republican party. But his vision of political neutrality may have gone well beyond that. He argued that electioneering was inconsistent with the spirit of the Constitution and the administrative officials' responsibility to it. Public administrators were seen as exercising a public trust in the public interest rather than a partisan political role.

Like Washington, however, Jefferson recognized that public administrators did have a political role in terms of public policy. Consequently, he sought to appoint Republicans until the balance between them and Federalists in the administrative branch roughly matched the balance between the two parties among the electorate at large. In other words, he sought to make the federal service politically *representative* of the partisanship of the nation as a whole. In practice, however, Jefferson overwhelmingly appointed Republicans throughout his tenure.

Presidents Adams and Jefferson differed more politically than socially. Although Jefferson paid lip service to making some appointments from outside the upper class, in practice he and Adams continued the tendency established by Washington of equating fitness with high social status. Presidents Madison, Monroe, and John Quincy Adams did little to alter this approach. Moreover, with the exception of the second Adams, who was philosophically opposed to making appointments and dismissals based on politics, these presidents inherited a federal service that matched their political outlook, and they found no reason to make many political dismissals. The tenure of federal administrators became secure and several remained in their jobs well into old age. There was even a tendency for civil service positions to be informally "bequeathed" to the incumbent's heirs when death made the ultimate removal. The federal service during this period was well managed, honest, efficient, and effective. Historical consensus holds that it reflected the highest ethical standards in the nation's history.

Public Personnel Administration According to "Spoils"

All this was changed by the inauguration of President Jackson in 1829. There has been historical debate as to whether it was really Jefferson or Jackson who made the first significant patronage dismissals and patronage appointments.[4] However, the fact of the matter is that Jackson institutionalized the spoils system by developing a politically convincing rationale for it. Upon becoming president, Jackson declared that public sentiment was strongly in favor of "reform" of federal personnel administration. Why? What was wrong with public personnel during the era of "gentlemen"? Jackson's views were as follows:

1. The long tenure of federal administrators in office made them unresponsive to the public and the public interest. In Jackson's well-known words, "The duties of all public officers are, or at least admit of being made, so plain and simple that men of intelligence may readily qualify themselves for their performance; and I cannot but believe that more is lost by the long continuance of men in office than is generally to be gained by their experience."[5]

2. The upper-class bias of the federal service was intolerable in a democratic (republican) nation such as the United States. Jackson's constituency was largely from the western and frontier areas and of middle- or lower-class status. They were mostly without formal education and a high proportion were illiterate. It is reputed that Jackson himself was unable to read fluently. Jackson thought such people ought to have an opportunity to participate in government by becoming public administrators. As he put it, "in a free government the demand for moral qualities should be made superior to that of talents."[6] By making appointments from among his constituents, Jackson would be able to reward his loyal supporters and strengthen himself politically. How-

ever, he may also have believed that "rotation" in office constituted "a leading principle of the republican creed" and was good for the political system.[7] To this end, he proposed that most administrators should not hold their positions for more than four years.

3. The long tenure of federal administrators had contributed to a serious problem of superannuation (old age) in the public service. Jackson believed that the elderly gentlemen were simply unable to rise to the tasks at hand and, consequently, the government was not functioning as well as it might. Related to this was the notion that a government job was a kind of property to which the incumbent civil servant had a right. Jackson and his political following found this position to be wholly antithetical to democratic principles.

Jackson's reforms were straightforward. He sought to establish a maximum term of four years in office for federal administrators. Previously, the Tenure of Office Act of 1820 set a four-year term for some federal employees, but it allowed their appointments to be renewed, and few removals were made. Jackson's proposed term would coincide with presidential administrations, thereby allowing the newly elected president to distribute "the spoils of victory"[8] among his supporters without facing the unpleasant necessity of actually dismissing incumbents, whose appointments would simply expire as a matter of law and/or custom. Unlike Jefferson, no pretense of creating partisan balance would be made. The victorious political party would simply feast upon federal administrative jobs.

Jackson's program was severely opposed by the opposition party, the Whigs, until 1840. In that year, sometimes called the year of the great "Whig sellout," the Whigs embraced the spoils system with a vengeance.[9] From then on until the administration of President Andrew Johnson (1865–1869), the spoils system thrived. Among its chief effects were:

1. *A serious decline in administrative ethics, efficiency, and performance.* The spoils period was racked with scandals, petty and large. A plethora of superfluous administrative jobs were created to pay off the party faithful. Incumbents, recognizing their limited tenure, often sought to make the most of their positions through embezzlement, bribery, and extortion.

2. *A thorough intermixing of public administration and partisan politics.* Sometimes administrative appointments had nothing to do except engage in partisan acts and electioneering. Some never showed up at their federal offices, being assigned in practice to party headquarters. One of the more notorious practices was for the parties to levy "political assessments" of roughly 1 to 6 percent on the salaries of federal administrators. This practice, called an indirect robbery of the federal treasury, enabled the finances of the government and the political party in power to merge to an extent.

3. *A high degree of political competition.* This is something of a mystery, because one would assume that the advantages accruing to the party in

power would be sufficient to ensure its victory in future elections. Logically, spoils should have encouraged the development of a one-party state. In practice, however, the partisanship of the president changed in 1841, 1845, 1849, and 1853. In 1857 there was a marked change in the dominant faction within the Democratic party and in 1860 the modern Republican party achieved its first presidential victory with the election of Abraham Lincoln. The twenty years from 1841 to 1861 were a period of great popular participation (at least among the eligible electorate) in politics and very vigorous partisan competition. One explanation is that the party in power could only distribute so many jobs and inevitably made enemies by disappointing some of its supporters; on the contrary, the party out of power could generate a great deal of support by promising a massive amount of patronage should it be elected (only to cause disappointments later). President after president complained of being besieged by office seekers, and inaugurations became gala events attended by as many as a hundred thousand partisans, many of whom were seeking office. It is reported that Lincoln once said, upon being stricken with smallpox, "Tell all the office seekers to come in at once, for now I have something I can give to all of them!"[10]

4. *A reduction in the social class status of federal administrators.* The federal service became more representative of the social class composition of the population as a whole. This was a very important change, ending the possibility of the development of an elite civil service. Some consider it a great administrative strength to have a civil service representative of the nation's social composition.[11] The 1978 Federal Civil Service Reform Act calls for a federal work force that reflects the nation's social diversity.

Public Personnel Administration According to "Merit"

The development of the administrative state spelled the doom of spoils, at least in terms of formal theory and practice, if not in each and every jurisdiction. In fact, patronage has fallen so out of favor under contemporary public personnel and constitutional theory that in 1976, 1980, and again in 1990 the Supreme Court handed down decisions that make such firings unconstitutional in the vast majority of circumstances.[12] (See Box 2–11.)

Commitment to a merit system began to develop at the federal level in the 1860s and 1870s. By 1883, it had been written into law—a law, the Pendleton Act (Civil Service Act), that was not superseded until the enactment of the Civil Service Reform Act of 1978. From the 1880s to the turn of the century, several states and cities followed suit in adopting "merit" as the basis of public personnel administration. The last serious national challenge to the merit system seems to have been in the election of 1896, when Populist candidate William Jennings Bryan echoed President Jackson in declaring that "a permanent office-holding class is not in harmony with our institutions. A fixed term in appointive offices . . . would open the public service to larger numbers of citizens without impairing its efficiency."[13] Bryan's statement provides a clue as to the issues behind the adoption of "merit."

We have been using the term "merit" in quotation marks because in some respects it is a misnomer. The cornerstone of the merit system has been the open, competitive examination as a tool for selecting public servants. There have been important political and administrative reasons for the heavy reliance placed upon such examinations. However, it is crucial to note at the outset that many merit examinations remain inadequately validated, which means that it cannot be demonstrated that they predict much, if anything, about a candidate's on-the-job performance. At the same time, such examinations frequently exhibit a bias or disparate impact against applicants who are members of minority groups, including those of African-American and Hispanic or Latino backgrounds. Some view the merit system as a barrier to equal employment opportunity and primarily as a means of keeping minorities out of the public service. We will have much more to say about this issue shortly. First, though, it is desirable to review briefly the chief causes and arguments for the adoption of the merit system as part of the civil service reform of the 1880s.

The civil service reformers of the 1870s and 1880s have been persistently misunderstood by those concerned with public personnel administration. In part, this is because the reformers themselves made somewhat misleading statements. Misinterpretation is also due to a peculiar situation in which the public personnel profession has come to treat as an end in itself what to the reformers was merely a means. The reformers had major political ambitions and viewed the adoption of the merit system as a means of bringing about political change. In their more candid moments, they were quite frank about this. Although they generally couched their arguments for reform in terms of efficiency and morality, these always remained secondary considerations to the leading reformers. For instance, the reformer Carl Schurz noted that "the question whether the Departments at Washington are managed well or badly is, in proportion to the whole problem, an insignificant question."[14] The "whole problem" was the character of patronage politics, which tended to prevent middle-class political activists, like the reformers themselves, from obtaining elective and appointive positions of political leadership. The spoils politicians tended to be responsive to lower-class and ethnic interests—the urban poor and immigrants were the mainstay of the most powerful political machines. In order to displace such politicians and assume what the reformers considered to be their own place of natural leadership in the society, it would be necessary to destroy the spoils system. In the revealing words of Dorman B. Eaton, another leading reformer, "We have seen a class of politicians become powerful in high places, who have not taken (and who by nature are not qualified to take) any large part in the social and educational life of the people. Politics have tended more and more to become a trade, or separate occupation. High character and capacity have become disassociated from public life in the popular mind."[15] Schurz was even more blunt in claiming that the point of civil service reform was to "rescue our political parties, and in great measure the management of our political affairs, from the control of men whose whole statesmanship consists in the low arts of office mongering, and many of whom would never have risen to power had not the spoils system furnished them with the means and opportunity for organizing gangs of political followers as mercenary as themselves."[16]

Like Jackson's introduction of the spoils system, then, the introduction of civil service reform was premised largely on the desire to attain broad political change. But that does not mean that the reform movement was devoid of administrative objectives. By the 1880s, the spoils system had become a relatively easy target for change.

The spoils system was rapidly becoming viewed as anachronistic—a harmful legacy of simpler preindustrial times. In his inimitable style, Schurz squarely addressed this matter: "There are certain propositions so self-evident and so easily understood that it would appear like discourtesy to argue them before persons of intelligence. Such a one it is, that as the functions of government grow in extent, importance and complexity, the necessity grows of their being administered not only with honesty, but also with trained ability and knowledge."[17] As the government became more heavily engaged in regulatory policy and administration, it seemed inevitable that the spoils system would have to be replaced.

The spoils system was also vulnerable because its corrupt practices interfered with industrialization. In its heyday, spoils turned the nation's custom houses into hotbeds of graft. Vast overstaffing, bribery, and extortion were common. By the late 1870s, the rising industrialists and proponents of industrialization had become opposed to patronage politics because it was harming international commerce. In 1877, an official federal commission studying the impact of spoils on the customs house in New York City concluded that patronage was "unsound in principle, dangerous in practice, demoralizing in its influence on all connected with the customs service, and calculated to encourage and perpetuate the official ignorance, inefficiency and corruption which, perverting the powers of Government to personal and party ends, have burdened the country with debt and taxes, and assisted to prostrate the trade and industry of the nation."[18]

There is a persistent thread running through this opposition to the spoils system. Both the reformers and the industrialists stood to gain by diminishing the impact of the lower-class and immigrant population in politics. The reformers thought the participation of these groups in machine politics tended to reduce the influence of middle-class Anglo-Americans—a category to which many of the reformers belonged.

Woodrow Wilson, often considered the founder of self-conscious American public administration, had this to say about the rising tide of immigrants:

[The] character of the nation . . . is being most deeply affected and modified by the enormous immigration which year after year pours into the country from Europe: our own temperate blood, schooled to self-possession and to the measured conduct of self-government, is receiving a constant infusion and yearly experiencing a partial corruption of foreign blood: our own equable [tranquil] habits have been crossed with the feverish habits of the restless old world. We are unquestionably facing an ever-increasing difficulty of self-command with ever-deteriorating materials, possibly with degenerating fibre.[19]

Wilson's thoughts were quite candid regarding the role of civil service reform in containing the impact of immigrants on the nation's political culture. He noted that "civil service reform is eminently wise and imperatively necessary for good government, but it is not democratic in idea. . . . It substitutes for the average man or the 'man of the people,' the man of the schools. . . ." But he believed reform would serve the nation well because "the only way in which we can preserve our nationality in its integrity and its old-time originative force in the face of growth and imported change is by concentrating it, by putting leaders forward vested with abundant authority in the conception and execution of policy."[20]

A new class of industrialists was especially fearful of the rise of "socialist" labor unions and political parties, which in all likelihood would find both leadership and support among immigrant workers. In addition, the politically perceptive industrialist might have understood that once the political parties were denied "assessments" and could no longer count on patronage as a means of winning votes and inducing political participation, they would inevitably turn to the wealthy sector of society to finance their operations and campaigns. Political historians note that popular participation in politics crested in the 1890s and at the same time the U.S. Senate began to emerge as a "millionaires' club."[21] In fact, the political system is still trying to cope with low electoral turnouts and the role of money in politics. Politically, there is no doubt that the chief battle lines concerning reform were drawn between industrialists and upper middle-class Anglo-Americans on the one hand, and the lower-class, immigrant populations, and spoils politicians on the other. In some ways, this split was part of an even more acute division lasting until the 1910s between the Progressive movement, which was antiurban, antimachine, and xenophobic, and Populist sentiment, which tried to forge a national political party out of agrarian and immigrant interests.

Politics aside, however, the spoils system did have serious administrative drawbacks. In the reformers' view, these could be remedied by adopting the following public personnel program:

1. *Selection of public employees based on open competitive examination.* Open examinations can be taken by anyone with the requisite background qualifications, such as age, literacy, and citizenship. They prevent politicians from selecting a group of the party faithful and administering the examination to them only. Competitive examinations require that appointments be made in the order of examination scores, that is, those who score highest are appointed first. This also prevents politicians from making placements based on politics.

   Open, competitive examinations are a highly effective means of preventing patronage appointments, but they also have an administrative logic. Assuming that the examination scores are an adequate predictor of the level of on-the-job performance, which is not always the case, such examinations promise to select the most competent and efficient applicants for the public service. As the spoils system receded into the political past, this was viewed by public personnel administrators as the chief virtue of the merit system. The examinations are relatively cheap to administer and use as selection devices; it is also widely believed that they produce the best, that is, the most efficient, civil servants.

2. *Depoliticization of the public service.* The reformers believed that the fundamental principle informing the public service should be politically neutral competence. Public employees should function on the basis of their trained ability to accomplish the governmental tasks at hand. Their authority and legitimacy flow from their professional and technical competence rather than their partisan activities. This line of reasoning required the reformers to insist that the vast majority of administrative positions were not political, either in a partisan or policy-making sense. The public service should be organized like a business, according to this view. The Civil Service Act of 1883 contained some provisions aimed at abolishing political assessments and political coercion.

3. *Tenure in office.* The spoils system was based on the premise that the rotation of public servants in and out of office was a desirable practice in a democratic nation. The reformers preferred tenure to be based upon the competence of public employees and not subject to political or partisan considerations. Originally, the reformers thought this could be accomplished by merit selection. Hiring officials would lose the opportunity to engage in political favoritism, which, in the reformers' view, would eliminate the incentive for making dismissals based on political grounds. However, beginning in the 1890s it was viewed as desirable to provide public employees with a measure of legally protected tenure. After some earlier efforts, the Lloyd-La Follette Act of 1912 assured that dismissals from the federal service would only be for such cause as would promote the efficiency of the service. Some procedural protections were included in the act, but by today's standards, they were rather limited.

4. *A civil service commission.* The reformers thought that public personnel administration should be policed by a central personnel agency, such as a civil service commission. A strong, independent agency could protect the public service against incursions by patronage-oriented politicians. The Civil Service Act of 1883 provided for a three-person, bipartisan Civil Service Commission (CSC) appointed by the president with the advice and consent of the Senate. The act gave the commission rule-making and investigative authority.

The reformers achieved lasting success in 1883 with the passage of the Pendleton Act (Civil Service Act), which was largely written by Dorman B. Eaton. Two factors determined the timing of its enactment. First, President Garfield was assassinated by a disappointed office seeker in 1881, and public opinion was quick to blame the spoils system rather than the demented assassin. Second, the Republican party suffered substantial setbacks in the congressional elections of 1882 and was seeking to protect itself against the Democrats' spoils, should that party go on to win the presidency in 1884.[22] There is little doubt that reform-oriented public personnel administration would have been adopted sooner or later in any event. Several cities, including New York, Albany, Buffalo, Syracuse, Chicago, Evanston, and Seattle, introduced merit systems during the 1880s and 1890s. New York was the first state to adopt such a program (1883), but it was another two decades before the next state, Massachusetts, followed suit. Today, some merit provisions exist in the overwhelming number of jurisdictions. (A summary of merit principles is presented in Box 5–1.)

The reform of 1883 established an institutional and conceptual framework for federal personnel administration that lasted until 1978. During that period, several additional personnel concepts were developed and implemented. By the 1920s, federal personnel officers were less obsessed with combatting patronage and more concerned with achieving greater efficiency in the public service. Prior to the 1930s, the CSC was primarily an examining agency. In 1931, it embarked on a program of centralizing personnel functions under its authority. Soon the commission had taken on responsibilities for position classification, efficiency ratings, and retirement administration. As it became a more centralized personnel agency, the commission retained its "policing" outlook, though now this was aimed at other agencies as well as at politicians.

By the late 1930s, the CSC had come to be viewed as an obstacle to effective personnel management because it was so concerned with enforcing restrictive rules and statutes. In 1938, President Franklin D. Roosevelt issued an executive order that decentralized federal personnel management somewhat by requiring each agency to establish a division of personnel supervision and management. The vast expansion of the federal service during the 1940s made even greater decentralization desirable. In 1947, President Truman issued an executive order that placed much more responsibility for personnel management in the individual departments and agencies. Truman's decentralized approach was written into the Classification Act of 1949. Subsequently, agencies became responsible for position classification, evaluation, promotion, and many other personnel functions.

Decentralization of federal personnel administration changed the role of the CSC. Many viewed its continuing concern with "policing" as inappropriate, but the CSC had difficulty in changing its focus from enforcement and inspection to the development of broad policies for the improvement of federal personnel management. Ironically, the commission became involved in aiding the president with the selection of political executives. By the 1970s, many personnel specialists, political executives, and some members of Congress considered it an inappropriate administrative structure for contemporary personnel management. The commission format also lost favor at the state and local levels. Many of these governments moved to place the major personnel functions in a department or division directly responsible to the

BOX 5–1 **Merit System Principles**

Federal personnel management should be implemented consistent with the following merit system principles:

1. Recruitment should be from qualified individuals from appropriate sources in an endeavor to achieve a work force from all segments of society, and selection and advancement should be determined solely on the basis of relative ability, knowledge, and skills, after fair and open competition which assures that all receive equal opportunity.

2. All employees and applicants for employment should receive fair and equitable treatment in all aspects of personnel management without regard to political affiliation, race, color, religion, national origin, sex, marital status, age, or handicapping condition, and with proper regard for their privacy and constitutional rights.

3. Equal pay should be provided for work of equal value, with appropriate consideration of both national and local rates paid by employers in the private sector, and appropriate incentives and recognition should be provided for excellence in performance.

4. All employees should maintain high standards of integrity, conduct, and concern for the public interest.

5. The federal work force should be used efficiently and effectively.

6. Employees should be retained on the basis of the adequacy of their performance, inadequate performance should be corrected, and employees should be separated who cannot or will not improve their performance to meet required standards.

7. Employees should be provided effective education and training in cases in which such education and training would result in better organizational and individual performance.

8. Employees should be:

   A. protected against arbitrary action, personal favoritism, or coercion for partisan political purposes, and
   B. prohibited from using their official authority or influence for the purpose of interfering with or affecting the result of an election or a nomination for election.

9. Employees should be protected against reprisal for the lawful disclosure of information which the employees reasonably believe evidences:

   A. a violation of any law, rule, or regulation, or
   B. mismanagement, a gross waste of funds, an abuse of authority, or a substantial and specific danger to public health or safety.

SOURCE: 5 U.S. Code, Sec. 2301.

chief executive. This approach was followed by the federal government in the Civil Service Reform Act of 1978.

MANAGEMENT, POLITICS, AND LAW IN PUBLIC PERSONNEL ADMINISTRATION

Each of the three approaches to public administration discussed in the first chapter can be found in the historical development of public personnel administration. Managerial principles and premises were most evident in the period of administration by "gentlemen," the reform program of the 1880s and 1890s, and during the 1930s and 1940s. Assignments were made on the basis of fitness and merit; tenure was during good behavior and competent, efficient performance. The public service was viewed as largely nonpolitical and in the service of the nation as a whole. Efficiency, honesty, and morality were highly valued. Although some political removals were made, there was no widespread practice of spoils or rotation in office. Politics was most clearly manifested in the spoils system. Here, it was believed that the public service should be politically and socially representative of the dominant political party first, and technically competent second. Representation and political responsiveness rather than efficiency and economy were the fundamental values behind public personnel practices at this time. Rotation in office was valued as a means of promoting popular participation in government. Legal considerations were most clearly evident in the reform movement, although as a means of promoting managerially oriented personnel administration. The Pendleton Act and subsequent reform-oriented practices place much public personnel management in a law-bound environment. Complaints, like those of the NPR, are often voiced that public personnel administration has become so legalistic that it is too rigid to be effective and that political executives lack the flexibility to handle personnel in a productive way. This is precisely the state of affairs that the reformers sought. As George William Curtis, perhaps the leading reformer, put it, "What we want is to intrench the principle and practice of Washington in the law."[23] Another reformer explained, "We consider that fixed rules, however imperfect, are better than arbitrary power."[24] More recently, the judiciary has placed constitutional restraints upon the handling of public personnel as a means of preventing abuses derived from the arbitrary exercise of power. This approach favors fairness of procedure and equality of treatment, and often turns public personnel management into an adversary, legalistic procedure.

Historically, the chief problem of public personnel administration in the United States has been a tendency to organize it according to one or another of the managerial, political, or legalistic approaches, and an inability to combine the three. Certainly the spoils system went overboard on the political dimension, but reform understated the importance of politics in the public service and especially the desire to have a public service that is representative, in some sense, of the general population. Similarly, contemporary personnel practices are frequently so legalistic and protective of employees' rights that it becomes very difficult for managers to discipline or to motivate their work forces. For the same reason political executives may find it hard to gain adequate action on their policy initiatives. These conflicts are hardly moot. The perceived conflict between traditional managerial personnel administration in the form of the merit system and political considerations in the form of representation (equal employment opportunity/affirmative action) has been one of the most persistent and pressing domestic political issues facing the nation. Similarly, drawing a proper line between the legal rights of employees and the needs of political responsiveness and managerial flexibility has resulted in a great deal of litigation. At the federal level, a major effort was made to resolve these conflicts in the federal civil service reform of 1978. In the mid-1990s, the NPR sought even more radical changes.

Civil Service Reform, 1978

The Civil Service Reform Act of 1978 was hailed by President Carter as the centerpiece of his efforts to reorganize the federal government to make it more manageable, efficient, effective, and politically responsive.[25] His administration was candid in proclaiming that the act had both managerial and political goals. The president himself said that "there is not enough merit in the merit system. There is inadequate motivation because we have too few rewards for excellence and too few penalties for unsatisfactory work."[26] Alan Campbell, chairman of the Civil Service Commission, which was established by the 1883 reform and phased out of existence by the 1978 reform, put forward the political perspective: "Every new administration feels the negative aspects of the bureaucracy's pressure for continuity. New policy makers arrive with mandates for change and find that though they can change structures and appearances, it is very difficult to make dramatic changes in direction."[27] But how could managerial and political goals be achieved simultaneously? And could this be accomplished without wholesale reduction of the legal rights of federal employees?

The reform act was accompanied by massive politicking in Congress. Employee unions, veterans' groups, civil rights and minority interest groups, congressional committees and subcommittees, and officials in the presidential office brought a variety of perspectives to bear on the question of what should be done to improve federal personnel management. Given the diversity of perspectives, the final statute was necessarily a compromise.

The major conceptual achievement of the reform act was the separation of many of the managerial, political, and legal aspects of federal personnel administration from one another. The effort made by the Civil Service Commission to combine these diverse perspectives contributed to its lack of direction and ultimate demise. Under the reform, to a considerable extent, separate functions were housed in separate agencies. Thus, starting with the clearest case first, a Merit Systems Protection Board (MSPB) was created to deal with many of the legalistic concerns of federal personnel management (see Box 5–2). The MSPB included an Office of the Special Counsel, which

BOX 5-2 **The Merit Systems Protection Board**

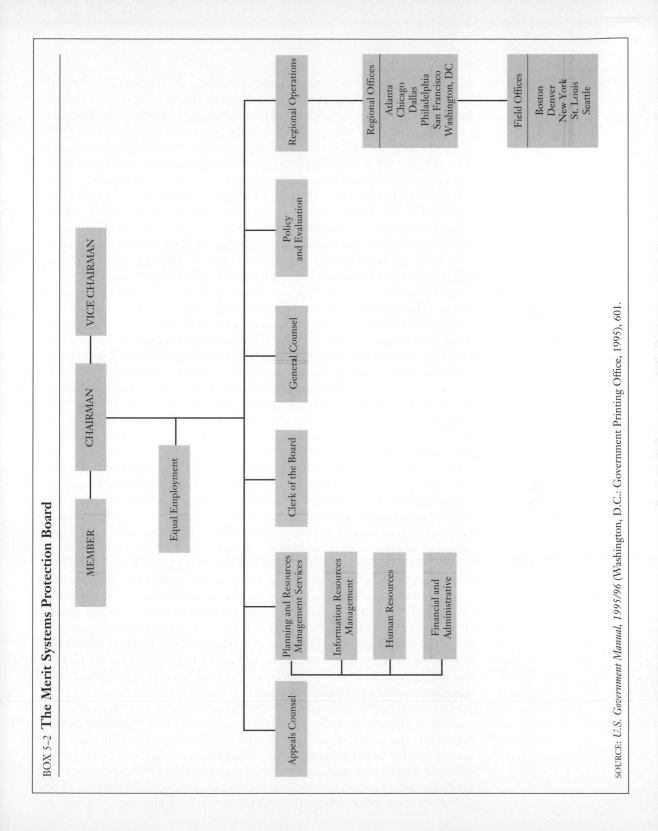

SOURCE: *U.S. Government Manual, 1995/96* (Washington, D.C.: Government Printing Office, 1995), 601.

subsequently became an independent administrative entity. The Special Counsel function is to assure that personnel laws and regulations are followed and that merit system principles and requirements are not violated. It investigates the activities of agencies, federal managers, and officials. The MSPB can levy sanctions against federal employees who violate personnel regulations. The agency also hears appeals of adverse actions, such as demotions or dismissals, against federal employees. It is considered the watchdog of the federal merit system and protector of the legal rights of federal employees. The MSPB has specific authority to protect whistle-blowers, who expose waste, fraud, or abuse, against reprisals. In recent years, the MSPB has done a number of in-depth studies of various subjects of importance to federal personnel management. Among these are surveys of sexual harassment in the federal service and analyses of why employees leave the government.

A second agency created by the reform, the Federal Labor Relations Authority (FLRA), also embodies the legalistic approach to public personnel. It oversees the process of collective bargaining in the federal service (though not in the Postal Service). The FLRA makes a variety of rulings concerning fair and unfair labor relations practices and the aspects of employment that can be collectively bargained. It also has authority to resolve questions concerning the representation of federal employees by labor unions and can play a role in the resolution of disputes between unions and the government. We will have more to say about collective bargaining in the public sector later in this chapter. Here, however, it is desirable to note that collective bargaining combines the legalistic, political, and managerial approaches. The procedures for collective bargaining are highly legalistic and the FLRA, like regulatory commissions generally and especially like the National Labor Relations Board, its counterpart for the private sector, holds adjudicatory hearings and makes rulings having the force of law. However, the actual practice of collective bargaining—that is, the give and take of bargaining sessions, as well as the actual substance of rulings—is often highly political in content. At the same time, though, many aspects of collective bargaining reflect managerial concerns, particularly limiting the scope of bargaining to protect managerial authority.

A more clearly political mission was vested in the Equal Employment Opportunity Commission. The EEOC was created by the Civil Rights Act of 1964, but it did not have authority over federal employment practices at that time. The federal equal employment opportunity (EEO) function was vested in a number of agencies, including the CSC. The decision to give the EEOC this authority for federal EEO was highly political, made at the urging of civil rights and minority groups who believed that the EEO program could not successfully be implemented under a personnel agency that viewed its primary mission in managerial terms. In their view, allowing those who make public personnel rules to enforce antidiscrimination measures was tantamount to allowing "the fox to watch the chickens." They saw a conflict because the merit system and merit examinations emerged as major barriers to the achievement of a high degree of minority employment in the upper levels of federal service. The 1978 reform act seeks a federal service that is socially representative of the nation's work force as a whole. The act defines "underrepresentation" of EEO target groups and outlines procedures for overcoming it. Part of the EEOC's mission is to promote the representation of minorities and women in the federal work force. Although much of the EEO process is legalistic, the ultimate objective of representation is political. From 1971 until 1995 this was pursued primarily through the process of "affirmative action." However, the Supreme Court's ruling in *Adarand Constructors v. Peña* (1995) cast serious doubt on the constitutionality of many affirmative action practices.

The reform act assigned the CSC's managerial functions to an Office of Personnel Management (see Box 5–3). This agency was designed to serve as the president's arm for positive, effective personnel management. It inherited

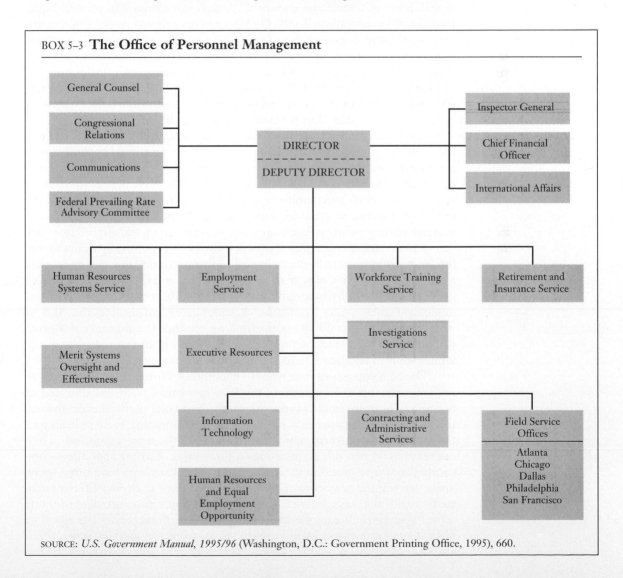

BOX 5–3 **The Office of Personnel Management**

General Counsel

Congressional Relations

Communications

Federal Prevailing Rate Advisory Committee

DIRECTOR
DEPUTY DIRECTOR

Inspector General

Chief Financial Officer

International Affairs

Human Resources Systems Service

Employment Service

Workforce Training Service

Retirement and Insurance Service

Merit Systems Oversight and Effectiveness

Executive Resources

Investigations Service

Information Technology

Contracting and Administrative Services

Field Service Offices

Atlanta
Chicago
Dallas
Philadelphia
San Francisco

Human Resources and Equal Employment Opportunity

SOURCE: *U.S. Government Manual, 1995/96* (Washington, D.C.: Government Printing Office, 1995), 660.

from the CSC such managerial functions as responsibility for testing, training, operating benefits and retirement systems, and general oversight of the personnel operations of federal agencies. In addition to placing the managerially oriented personnel agency closer to the president than was the more independently organized bipartisan CSC, the reform act mandated the use of some new management tools, including a merit pay system and a performance appraisal system, which are discussed below.

The NPR changed OPM's role substantially. About two-thirds of the central personnel rules were eliminated, leaving OPM with much less to enforce. Decentralization allows the departments and agencies to develop their own personnel systems to a very large extent. OPM's training functions were closed down or transferred elsewhere, though it continued to provide high-level executive education. Today, OPM's main operational responsibilities are the federal employees' health and retirement benefits programs. It continues to perform background investigations of candidates for some federal jobs, but there has been much talk of privatizing, reorganizing, or transferring this function. The NPR wants OPM to act as an expert consultant to other agencies and to assist in the design of performance-based organization. At this point, however, OPM's future is very much in doubt.

Another central feature of the reform act bears mention here. The top career managerial positions in the federal service were largely converted into a Senior Executive Service (see Box 5–4). Previously these positions (along with some others) were called the supergrades. The theory behind the SES is largely an effort to combine the political and managerial approaches to public administration. It rests on the belief that (1) there is a body of skill or professionalism called "public management" that can be transferred from organizational setting to organizational setting; (2) it is politically desirable for top federal managers to move among administrative units in order to develop a more comprehensive view of the public interest; and (3) political executives need greater flexibility in assigning and directing these top career officials to implement their policy mandates. A major issue concerning the SES is whether it will inevitably be politicized, or whether the managerial aspects will be able to withstand the pressures of transition from one presidential administration to another. There are about 8,000 positions in the SES.

The SES consists of four types of appointees. **Noncareer** appointments can constitute up to 10 percent of the total number of positions allocated to the SES. These are political appointees who assist the political executives at the top levels of departments and agencies, implementing their policies and programs. **Limited-term** appointments can also be purely political. They can serve nonrenewable terms of up to three years. **Career** appointees constitute the largest group in the SES. These federal servants have often spent many years in the government and may have worked their way up the ranks to the top of the career service. **Limited emergency** appointments who can serve for up to eighteen months, are the fourth category, but to date one that has not been important. In addition to the four types of appointments, there are two types of positions, **career reserved** and **general.** Only career

BOX 5–4 Conditions of Employment for Career SES Executives

Staffing	Compensation, Benefits, and Awards	Performance Appraisal	Accountability
Must compete at least governmentwide for initial career SES appointment and have managerial qualifications approved by a Qualifications Review Board. Serve one-year probationary period.	Six pay rates.	Organizational and personal goals set annually in collaboration with supervisor.	Less than fully successful annual performance appraisal can lead to removal from SES. Entitled to informal hearing at MSPB.
	Base pay rate set by appointing authority.		
	Pay rate may be raised or lowered once a year.	Supervisor rates executive according to established goals.	
Can be reassigned within agency to any SES position for which qualified. No grades in SES.	May be increased any number of rates, but reduced only one rate per year.	Performance Review Board must have a majority of career SES members.	Failure to be recertified results in removal from SES. Entitled to formal hearing at MSPB.
Cannot be involuntarily reassigned within 120 days after appointment of new agency head or noncareer supervisor.	Eligible for a $10,000 Meritorious Rank award and a $20,000 Distinguished Rank award once every five years.	"Fully Successful" rating is basis of eligibility for bonus and rank award.	If removed for performance or failure to be recertified, entitled to GS-15 level position with retention of salary.
Must receive fifteen days' written notice in advance of reassignment; sixty days' written notice if outside commuting area.	Eligible annually for performance bonus of 5 percent to 20 percent of base pay.	Performance evaluation cannot take place within 120 days after beginning of a new presidential administration.	Can reenter SES at later date, but only competitively.
Cannot be involuntarily transferred between agencies; OPM facilitates voluntary mobility.	Total compensation ceiling at Executive Level I, with any excess "rolled over" to next fiscal year.		When eligible, can elect discontinued service retirement if removed from SES for performance, failure to be recertified, RIF, or failure to accept reassignment or transfer of function to another commuting area.
Can accept presidential appointment and retain "fallback" rights to SES position.	Can accumulate unused annual leave, which converts to cash at time of leaving government.		
Can be RIFed* only under competitive procedures, and guaranteed fallback to a GS-15.	Provided with opportunities for executive development, including sabbaticals.		Entitled to protections and appeals similar to those for non-SES members in cases of adverse actions.
Can be reinstated to SES following voluntary separation or RIF if completed probationary period.	Eligible for "last move home" expenses upon retirement if previously geographically reassigned as a career SES appointee within five years of optional retirement or when already eligible for retirement.		(Removal from SES for performance is not an adverse action.)

*RIF—Reduction-in-force; that is, dismissed as part of a cutback or downsizing process.

SOURCE: U.S. Office of Personnel Management, *The Senior Executive Service* (Washington, D.C.: OPM, 1990), 17.

appointees can be assigned to the former; any type of appointee can be placed in the latter.

Finally, the Civil Service Reform Act provided for "personnel research programs and demonstration projects." It allows the OPM to suspend the application of many personnel regulations in order to experiment with new approaches and techniques. Projects can involve up to 5,000 employees (not including any who may be in a control group) and last up to five years. They can be undertaken in most federal agencies, though not in security agencies, government corporations, or the General Accounting Office.

The Civil Service Reform Act of 1978 has been flexible enough to accommodate much of the policy change sought by the NPR. Personnel has been deregulated to a substantial extent. Through incremental changes, almost 50 percent of the federal work force has been placed outside the government's traditional statutory framework for personnel (Title 5 of the U.S. Code). Agencies are now more likely to be covered by statutes written specifically for their personnel needs. They are also apt to have more flexibility than before in deciding how to implement legal requirements. The "one size fits all" approach OPM inherited from the CSC has been eliminated from a broad range of personnel practices. The NPR reported the following changes:

- OPM scrapped the 10,000-page, notoriously complex *Federal Personnel Manual* and abolished the confusing and daunting Standard Form (SF) 171 for applicants.

- OPM developed an electronic bulletin board, called OPM called Mainstreet, for communicating with federal human resource managers throughout the government.

- OPM introduced more "family-friendly" workplace measures, including encouraging employees to use up to five days of their sick leave annually to devote to family care.[28]

We have discussed the historical development of public personnel administration in the United States and the conceptual problems presented by its organization in some detail so that the reader will not fall victim to a pervasive tendency to place "technique over purpose" in the area of public personnel.[29] We now turn to a more techniques-oriented review of the major public personnel functions. This discussion is organized according to our threefold categorization of public administration into managerial, political, and legalistic approaches.

MANAGERIAL PUBLIC PERSONNEL ADMINISTRATION

Both orthodox and new public management (NPM) public personnel administrations seek to maximize the values of efficiency, economy, and administrative effectiveness through the recruitment, selection, placement, pay, training, and general treatment of public employees at work. The underlying assumption behind managerial public personnel administration is that the public service should be apolitical and businesslike. Employees should be selected, placed, promoted, and paid on the basis of their competence to perform governmental work. There should be adequate protection of public employees from political encroachments. Orthodox managerial doctrine envisions the public service as a career in which employees serve the public interest by developing long-term expertise in government operations and programs. It favors career growth and development through training. It also relies on retirement systems that encourage public employees to remain in the government throughout their work lives. By contrast, the NPM does not emphasize public administration as a career. In its view, much government requires essentially the same skills as business. Employees should transfer freely from one sector to the other. Accordingly, public employees should participate in general social security systems and they should be able to take the retirement funds they accrue while in government with them when they leave. Logically, the NPM is more apt than traditional management to consider training a cost or short-term investment rather than a means of upgrading government's human resources. Both approaches believe that employees should be appraised periodically as a means of indicating how their performance could be improved. Finally, career employees should have adequate benefits in their retirement. Each of these functions is valuable and each contains some controversial aspects.

Position Classification

Position classification is one of the most important aspects of traditional public personnel management. In a sense, the entire traditional personnel program rests upon it. Position classification is the system of designing jobs, organizing them into useful managerial and career categories, and establishing their rates of pay. A good position classification system provides a convenient inventory of everything that government workers do. The "position" is the work actually done, and according to rules established as early as 1923, the classification system should be based on the following principles:

1. Positions and not individuals should be classified. In other words, unlike the military, rank is vested in the position itself, not in the individual who happens to occupy that position. Membership in the SES is a major exception to this rule at the federal level.
2. The duties and responsibilities pertaining to a position constitute the outstanding characteristics that distinguish it from or make it similar to other positions. Among the classification factors frequently used are the nature and variety of the work; the nature of supervision received by whoever is occupying the position; the nature of available guidelines for performance of the work (that is, is the work routine or does it require flexible responses to ever-changing situations?); the originality required;

the purpose and nature of person-to-person work relationships; the scope and nature of decision making; the nature and extent of supervision over other employees; and the qualifications required. Sometimes, these considerations are grouped into four categories: the difficulty of duties, supervisory responsibility, nonsupervisory responsibility, and requisite qualifications.

3. The individual characteristics of an employee occupying a position should have no bearing on the classification of the position.

4. Persons holding positions in the same class (level of position and kind of duties and responsibilities) should be considered equally qualified for any other position in that class.

In trying to grasp what is involved in position classification it may prove useful to think in terms of categories of positions, such as executive; administrative, professional, and technological; clerical, office machine operator, and technician; and trade, crafts, and manual labor. Within each of these broad categories would be a number of positions such as receptionist, keyboarder, file clerk, or stenographer. Each of these positions would bear a classification and a rank. The rank would be related to pay. For the sake of example, consider a federal position classified as "Supply Clerk GS-3." There is a position description explaining what a supply clerk at this level does (answers telephone inquiries, posts information from order contracts to order cards, determines replenishment needs through mathematical formulas—and three pages more of description). The supply clerk position is part of a general series of supply positions. The "GS-3" stands for General Schedule, grade 3. A more senior supply clerk might be a GS-4 or higher and would have broader responsibilities. In theory, unless a special security clearance is required, any supply clerk GS-3 in one agency would be suitable for employment in the same class of positions in another agency. To take the matter one step further, each of the grades in the General Schedule would be paid at a different rate. Thus, GS-1s, who are at the bottom of this classification system, on average receive the lowest rates of pay, and GS-15s, who are now in the highest general grade, receive the highest. (Most GS 16 through 18 positions were phased out when the SES was created.)

There is no doubt that position classification is a valuable managerial tool. How else might a very large work force be organized? Classification tells managers and employees what the occupants of positions are supposed to do. It makes it possible to design career ladders for advancement. It facilitates testing applicants for competence. It provides a basis for evaluating the performance of government workers. At the same time, however, position classification can be problematic. Among the most serious complaints about the practice of position classification is that it is dehumanizing for the employee. In essence, the job is designed and classified without regard to the employee who holds it. The organization is viewed as a set of positions (specializations) that are coordinated in some fashion, typically through hierarchy. An employee may be able to contribute more to the organization than the position he or she is in allows. For example, a keyboarder may have the ability and willingness to take shorthand dictation, but that would require classification as a stenographer and higher pay. Hence, allowing a typist to function as a stenographer would be prohibited by position classification principles. The employee can neither go beyond the level of work required in the position nor fall short of it. Working "out of class" is particularly opposed by unions, especially when employees are doing higher-level work without receiving more pay. These problems are particularly evident where classifications are narrow and very specific, as opposed to broadly banded into categories such as clerical or technical.

Position classification practices, which were associated with Frederick Taylor's scientific management (see Chapter 4), have also tended to design jobs in a stultifying fashion (see Box 5–5). They have stressed the need for order and conformity in governmental positions, sometimes at the expense of the interest the job could possibly hold for the incumbent. This has led to boredom and alienation among employees. Nowadays, there is growing concern that job design take the following considerations into account:

1. Job rotation, that is, developing a classification and career system that enables employees to move through several positions. This enables the employee to use several skills and avoid the boredom that comes with the repetitive performance of routine tasks.
2. Job enlargement, or placing more tasks within a position description.
3. Job enrichment, or vesting greater authority, responsibility, and autonomy in positions.

Another problem with position classification is that position descriptions can become rapidly outdated as technology and the work of governmental agencies change. Position classifiers may not be able to keep pace with all the constant changes; but agency managers are not likely to favor limiting the introduction of new technologies and tasks to enable the classifiers to catch up. Then, too, there has been a problem of "grade creep," or a tendency for positions constantly to be reclassified at a higher level. Collective bargaining also presents a problem for position classification. Unions contend that classification levels and pay should be subject to bargaining and that more positions should be created to take account of workers' increased seniority. For example, to return to the case of Supply Clerk GS-3, a union might want to see a classification system that would create a position of Senior Supply Clerk GS-4 (or higher) so that someone who has held the position for, let's say, fifteen years would not be paid at the same rate as a newcomer (even though they do the same work). Finally, as a practical matter, position classification systems are seldom as neat in practice as they are in theory. For instance, the federal government has not only a General Schedule, but also a wage board system for industrial-type jobs, a foreign service classification system, a postal classification system, the SES, a system denoted "GM" for managers and supervisors at the GS 13 through 15 ranks, and an executive-level system for political executives. In state and local sys-

BOX 5–5 **Position Classification Standards**

Series	Grade
GS-305	3

FILE CLERK GS-3

Duties
Works in a file organization which provides service to an office concerned with processing claims.

—Receives all types of incoming mail, segregates and arranges in proper working order associating materials by case number with proper file folder, and assigning proper designation to assure priority of processing.

—Locates appropriate folders in files, identifies both folder and file with name and file number; records charge-out date, destination, and initials charge card; and dispatches folder to the proper operating element.

—Recharges folder file when moved from one operating element to another for control purposes; maintains suspense file of actions to be taken by operating elements at future dates; and initiates search for folders not in file, using charge cards and knowledge of work flow in operating elements.

—Performs a variety of related duties such as sequencing checks, pulling files designated for retirement or transfer, assuring protection of contents of files, expanding or contracting file storage as necessary, and participating in records inventories and record reconciliations.

Factor 1, Knowledge Required by the Position

—Knowledge of functions and work flow within and among operating elements.

—Knowledge of terminal digit (numerical) system and filing procedures.

—Knowledge of subject matter and processing procedures for standardized material.

tems, position classification often falls victim to partisan politics and is subject to a number of abuses.[30]

Contemporary thinking holds that complex classification systems should be simplified. The number of classifications should be reduced and positions should be classified in broad bands. Broad banding enhances flexibility in assigning functions to employees and in moving employees among positions. It also requires less paperwork and effort to classify positions. The NPM strongly favors broad banding at the discretion of individual agencies.

Recruitment, Selection, and Promotion

Recruitment, selection, and promotion are among the core functions of public personnel management. The managerial approach to them dictates that efficiency and economy be the ultimate values in performing these functions. Efficiency stresses the need to obtain the most productive and capable em-

---

BOX 5–5 *Continued*

Series	Grade
GS-305	3

Factor 2, Supervisory Controls

Assigned work is performed independently following established procedures. Supervisor is available to resolve unusual problems. Work is reviewed for accuracy and promptness by systematic spotchecks.

Factor 3, Guidelines

Procedures are well established. Written and oral guides provide specific instructions for processing material. A substantial portion of these instructions may be memorized and there is little interpretation necessary. When instructions do not apply, problems are referred to the supervisor.

Factor 4, Complexity

Performs a variety of related duties including searching, filling requests for files, association of materials, establishing priorities, etc., which require consideration of the differences among cases processed by operating units.

Factor 5, Scope and Effect

The purpose of the work is to provide prompt service in the daily flow of materials to and from operating units. The work affects the general efficiency of the serviced units.

Factor 6, Personal Contacts

There are recurring contacts with personnel in various operating units of the organization.

Factor 7, Purpose of Contacts

Contacts are for the purpose of obtaining and exchanging factual information regarding cases being processed.

Factor 8, Physical Demands

Work requires a great deal of standing, walking, stooping, reaching and pulling typically involved in filing activities.

Factor 9, Work Environment

Work is performed in an office setting.

SOURCE: U.S. Civil Service Commission, *Position Classification Standards* (Washington, D.C.: Civil Service Commission, May 1977), TS-27.

---

ployees; economy demands that this be accomplished as inexpensively as possible. The NPM also embraces these values, but in the United States it adds concern that employees reflect the nation's social diversity.

Recruitment is the process of encouraging individuals to apply for government positions.

The critical elements of a successful traditional management recruitment program aimed at procuring the most efficient, effective employees, consists of (1) governmental efforts to upgrade the image of public employment; (2) efforts to recruit for careers rather than single jobs; (3) efforts to give examinations at convenient times and convenient places; (4) the elimination of pointless background requirements, such as age or non-job-related training requirements; and (5) efforts to reach all segments of the population. Of course, the value of economy dictates that government spending on these functions vary with its actual needs for personnel.

Selection is the process of choosing among applicants. In the United States a very wide variety of approaches is used, but there is a dominant pattern stemming from the nineteenth-century reform period. This is reliance on an open, competitive examination of some kind, which can potentially generate the greatest degree of competition among applicants. Competitive examinations are those in which the hiring of individual test takers is in accordance with their exam scores. In a purely competitive examination the person who achieved the highest score would be hired first, whereas the person who scored the lowest passing grade would be hired last if enough positions were available. In practice, however, most jurisdictions modify this approach by allowing selection from among groups of applicants, such as those obtaining the three or ten highest scores. The latter approaches are called the "rule of three" or "ten" or any other number. The rationale for them is to provide the hiring authority with some discretion in making selections but nevertheless assure that the selection process is open and competitive.

Selection by examination may involve the use of an **eligibles register.** This is simply a list of those who passed an examination, ranked in the order of their scores. Under the "rule of three" approach, for example, if a vacancy occurred, the appropriate eligibles register would be consulted and selection would be from among the top three scorers on the list. If another vacancy occurred, selection would be from among the remaining two highest scorers, plus whoever scored fourth highest (that is, ranked fourth on the eligibles register). If someone is passed over a number of times (typically three) he or she will be deleted from the register, despite his or her score. Computerization makes it possible to create an eligibles register for any particular job from among applicants who have passed a relevant examination. Sometimes this procedure is called a person search, which is a flexible means of generating eligibles registers as they are needed.

Examinations can be **assembled** or **unassembled.** Assembled examinations require that a test of some kind be taken. Unassembled examinations are really nothing more than the submission of résumés or completion of forms that subsequently become the basis of a "rating" or scoring process. Within these two categories, there are a variety of possibilities:

1. *Performance examinations.* These are devices intended to determine whether the applicant can perform the tasks required in the position for which someone is being hired. Keyboarding and equipment operation are functions in which performance examinations are generally used. In such an instance, the examination might be, for example, to determine how many words a minute a person can process accurately.
2. *Written examinations.* These may stress achievement, aptitude, or both. They are typically of the multiple-choice, machine-scored variety. Some jurisdictions purchase them commercially, rather than develop-

ing their own. A major virtue of such examinations is that they are inexpensive to administer.

3. *Oral examinations.* These are often considered more practical for upper-level positions involving discretionary authority or positions for which there are few applicants. Generally, an oral examination is administered by a panel who have an established set of criteria for making a judgment. The candidate may appear before the panel alone or with a group of other applicants.

4. *Assessment centers.* Assessment centers try to duplicate some of the approaches of performance examinations, but for positions in which the tasks are less concrete and evaluated more subjectively. Individuals may be put through a series of activities that simulate some of the critical aspects of the job for which someone is being hired. Such activities may consist of getting along with others, engaging in leadership, or exercising discretion. Ratings are generally made by a panel, with predetermined criteria for assessment.

No matter which kind of examination is used, it is critical that the selection device be *valid.* In other words, the score on the examination must be predictive of the likely level of performance on the job. Yet for many positions this is difficult to achieve and demonstrate. The chief problems in validating examinations are threefold. First, it is difficult to construct an examination that truly reflects on-the-job conditions. This is especially true for positions involving the exercise of interpersonal skills, policy making, and discretion. However, it can also be a problem in performance examinations, because the environment in which an individual works can affect productivity. Sometimes this problem is addressed by distinguishing between **job proficiency,** that is, the actual ability to do the work, and **job performance,** which is the reality of how much work gets done. A simple example is a typist who, although proficient, performs far better in a room alone than in a pool with ten or twenty other typists. Although it may be possible to test for this, it may also be very expensive or impractical to do so. Aspects of the work environment, such as noise, degree of privacy, and the extent of time pressures, that can affect performance are called **situational factors.** Total quality management (TQM), discussed in the previous chapter, is very much oriented toward eliminating situational factors that militate against quality improvement.

A second problem is that there may be very little variation in the scores of those who are actually selected for governmental positions. The dynamics of contemporary selection are such that there are typically many more applicants than position openings. There have been cases of some 15,000 individuals applying for less than 100 jobs. Under such circumstances it is highly likely that those selected will have virtually the same scores on the examinations, and their scores are likely to be very high. When this occurs, it is difficult to validate an examination simply because there is no way of knowing how well someone with a much lower score would have performed. Those with lower scores cannot be hired, of course, because of the rule of three or similar approach. It is important to note that the problem is that the examination cannot be satisfactorily validated, not that it is necessarily invalid. In other words, the exam may be valid, but there is no convincing way of demonstrating this statistically.

Third, to validate an examination, the level of performance by employees who took it must be measured. Again, the object is to show a relationship between examination score and performance level on the job. If the latter cannot be measured well, then validity cannot be demonstrated. Performance appraisal is possible for some jobs, but extremely difficult in any systematic fashion in others. We will have more to say about this momentarily.

Despite these problems, there is a well-developed set of approaches to merit examination validation. The best is the **criterion-related** approach. It seeks to relate examination scores to on-the-job performance in one of two ways. First, it may be **predictive,** that is, it takes the actual scores of those selected and associates them statistically with these employees' on-the-job performance at some later time. Predictive validation is very difficult to establish for the reasons discussed above. **Concurrent validation** is a technique that administers the examination to those already employed and then seeks to determine the statistical relationship between their scores and their performance appraisals. The chief virtue here is that there may be more variation in score among those taking the examination. However, performance remains difficult to measure objectively, and this approach also runs the risk that extraneous factors may contribute to both an employee's score and performance level. For instance, an employee who is well liked personally and consequently has a high degree of self-esteem may obtain both a higher score and higher performance appraisal than one who is isolated in and alienated from the workplace—even though under neutral social conditions both might score or perform equally.

Other types of validation do not technically seek to relate job performance to examination scores. **Content validation** merely seeks to establish whether the contents of the examination match the contents of the job, that is, does the examination reflect the knowledge, skills, abilities, and aptitudes necessary to perform well on the job. This runs into the problem of proficiency versus performance. **Construct validation** seeks to determine whether the examination ascertains the existence of "psychological constructs," such as honesty, reliability, or tact. It does not seek to show how these constructs are related to on-the-job performance. Finally, **face validity** simply addresses the question of whether the examination appears reasonable on its surface. For example, an examination that tests the current events or historical knowledge of applicants for the position of garbage collector or dogcatcher may appear ridiculous and therefore lack face validity. Interestingly, however, the many examinations that have tested precisely for such knowledge in the past were premised on a very different concept of public servant—one who was imbued with civic virtue and knew much about public affairs.

We have dwelt on examinations and validation at some length because they are currently areas of crisis in public personnel administration. First, far too frequently, so-called merit examinations have had a harsh racial or ethnic impact, which has made it all the more difficult for members of some minority groups to gain public employment. The examinations' discriminatory impact stems in part from the inequality of opportunity in society at large, especially in education. Such an impact thus flies in the face of equal opportunity and the political approach's emphasis on representative government. It can be tolerated only if the examinations truly are highly predictive of job performance—and perhaps not even then. Indeed, two of the major federal examinations administered to college graduates for general administrative careers, the Federal Service Entrance Exam and the Professional and Administrative Career Exam (PACE), which replaced it, were abandoned largely because of their negative impact on the employment of African-Americans and Hispanics. Certainly, there can be no legitimate reasons for using an examination that is not predictive of job performance and tends to work against equal employment opportunity. However, as our discussion indicates, it may be impossible to demonstrate that an examination is valid, even if it is.

Second, the examination process has a tendency to become complex and cumbersome. If examinations are given only once or a few times a year, many of those ranking high on the eligibles register may be employed in the government or elsewhere by the time a particular agency tries to make a hire. Those remaining are theoretically qualified, but the hiring authority may have doubts about someone toward the bottom of the eligibles list. Because the examinations are frequently administered and scored by a central personnel agency, there also tends to be a good deal of red tape involved, with accompanying delays. In 1989, a major study aimed at improving the federal service concluded that "the complexity of the hiring process often drives all but the most dedicated away."[31] The NPR seeks to change this by eliminating centralized examinations and letting agencies establish their own selection procedures, which may consist of deciding which applicants to interview on the basis of their résumés.

In 1994, OPM sought to eliminate some of the problems associated with central examinations and registers. The Administrative Careers With America (ACWA) examination, which went into use in 1990 as the successor to PACE, was made optional and its register was closed to new applicants. Agencies switched to "case" examining, which works as follows. Job vacancies are announced through OPM's Federal Employment Information System. Agencies, with OPM's assistance, rate only those who apply for a vacancy. They may use ACWA or other methods to construct a register for the specific vacancy. The new system remains competitive, but it is more efficient and flexible than relying on central registers. Information technology exists for use in rating applicants.

The traditional managerial approach also stresses efficiency and productivity as the basis for *promotion*. According to this approach, promotions are generally made on the basis of written examinations and/or performance appraisals. The promotional examination resembles the merit entrance examination except that it is open only to those employees who qualify for consideration for promotion. Performance appraisals are discussed below.

Promotions remain a controversial aspect of public personnel management. The plain hard fact is that, in hierarchical organizations, there are fewer positions at the top than at the bottom. Therefore, there is a limit on how high up an employee can rise. Most employees will always be lower down in the organization's ranks. Thus, promotions tend to be "zero-sum"; that is, one employee's gain (promotion) is another's lost opportunity. The competition can be fierce and can lead to discord among employees. This is one of the virtues of a written promotional examination. As long as the examination is accepted as legitimate and fair, it settles the issue without any possibility of favoritism or office politics playing a role. Similarly, promotion by seniority, which is a principle often stressed by unions in collective bargaining, tends to minimize discord. However, seniority is not necessarily the best indicator of productivity and consequently the managerial approaches tend to discourage it. Sometimes merit-oriented promotion and seniority are combined by restricting the opportunity for promotion to those who have been on the job for a given number of years. Presumably, in the flexible, flatter (e.g., less hierarchical) organizations favored by the NPM, employees (or teams) can be rewarded for the results they produce without having to be promoted to new positions.

Performance Appraisal

Performance appraisals have gained greater attention since the 1970s, as governments at all levels have been under public pressure to be more efficient, economical, effective, and responsive. The Federal Civil Service Reform Act of 1978 provided for individual performance appraisals. The NPM and the NPR have strong performance orientations, though where TQM is used performance is not viewed as a product of individual ability or effort. Although there is a wide variety of performance appraisal techniques, evaluating employee productivity remains problematic. The main difficulties are that appraisals reflect varying degrees of subjectivity, that it is often impossible to quantify the output of public employees in any meaningful fashion, and that there tends to be very limited variability in the level of appraisal. In the past, 98 percent of all federal employees routinely obtained a "satisfactory" efficiency rating. Today, many performance appraisal techniques stress a combination of self-appraisals, peer ratings, and group or external ratings. Of course, the more tangible the employee's work product, the greater the probability of designing a performance appraisal approach that truly serves to indicate the level of an employee's productivity.

To some extent, public sector performance appraisal is a "process in search of a technique."[32] Typically, appraisals are concerned with the performance factors and employee traits displayed in Box 5–6. However, there are several ways of assessing these characteristics. Appraisals are generally done

BOX 5–6 **Performance Appraisal by Graphic Rating Scale**

Person evaluated _____ Position _____
Location _____

PERFORMANCE FACTORS	Out-standing	Very Good	Satis-factory	Unsatis-factory	Un-known
1. Effectiveness					
2. Use of time and materials					
3. Prompt completion of work					
4. Thoroughness					
5. Initiative					
6. Perseverance					

ETHICAL CONSIDERATIONS					
7. Loyalty to department					
8. Loyalty to peers					
9. Loyalty to subordinates					
10. Sense of ethics					
11. Cooperativeness					
12. Responsibility					
13. Commitment of service					
14. Open-mindedness					

ABILITIES, SKILLS, AND FACULTIES					
15. Technical skills					
16. Communication skills					
17. Judgment					
18. Analytical ability					
19. Ability to organize					
20. Ability to inspire and influence staff					
21. Ability to inspire and influence others than staff					
22. Flexibility and adaptability					
23. Imaginativeness and creativity					
24. Ability to develop subordinates					
25. Breadth of concepts					

Date evaluated _____ Evaluator _____
The above appraisal was reviewed with me on _____

_____
(Signature of Person Evaluated)

Comments _____

by supervisors, peers, the employees themselves, by groups, by external evaluators, or by some combination of these. When appraisal is by supervisors, coworkers, subordinates, and customers, it is called a "360" (degree) evaluation. The techniques strive for objectivity, but where an employee's work is essentially qualitative (e.g., writing reports, supervising others, evaluating grant applications, procuring supplies/weaponry), appraisal will inevitably contain subjective judgments. Among the major techniques are:

1. *Rating scales*, as in Box 5–6, which are easy to administer, relatively inexpensive, clear, and in widespread use. Customer surveys can easily use rating scales to assay individual (and/or organizational) responsiveness, promptness, politeness, and so forth.
2. *Essay reports* focusing on an employee's need for further training and his or her potential and ability to obtain results. This technique is time-consuming.
3. *Checklists* consisting of statements about the employee's performance. The rater checks the most appropriate statements. Some of these may be given greater weight than others in reaching an overall appraisal.
4. *Critical incidents*, an approach requiring the supervisor to keep a log of employees' performance, indicating incidents of both good and poor performance.
5. *Forced choice* requires supervisors to rate employees on the basis of descriptive statements. The statements are constructed so that the supervisor cannot be certain which ones are most indicative of employee performance that the personnel office will deem most desirable. An example is presented in Box 5–7. Forced choice enhances objectivity but results in evaluations that are difficult for supervisors and employees to interpret and use as a means of improving performance.
6. *Ranking* or comparing employees to one another.
7. *Forced distribution* requires the rater to place employees in categories such as top 5 percent, next 10 percent, next 25 percent, and so on.

All of these techniques have pros and cons in terms of objectivity, usefulness, cost, and ease of administration. None is best for all positions and circumstances. The search for better performance appraisal techniques retains a high priority in the managerial approach. The NPR seeks to augment customer satisfaction surveys with quantitative, results-oriented performance measures. It views most, if not all, of the factors in Box 5-6 as inadequate because their relationship to the achievement of results is indirect and unclear.

Pay

The traditional managerial approach also stresses economy and productivity in determining the pay levels of public employees. Pay systems are typically linked to position classification systems, but they tend to be problematic and controversial for a variety of reasons. First, it is currently held that pay sys-

---

BOX 5–7 **Performance Appraisal by the Forced-Choice Technique**

Person Evaluated _____
Position _____
Organization Unit _____
Date _____
Evaluator _____
Instructions: Please place a check on the line to the left of the statement that best describes this employee.

This employee _____ a. is loyal to his or her supervisor _____ b. uses imagination and creativity _____ c. is thorough and dependable _____ d. accepts responsibility willingly

This employee _____ a. completes work promptly and on time _____ b. pays much attention to detail _____ c. works well under pressure _____ d. works well without supervisory guidance

This employee _____ a. always looks presentable _____ b. shows initiative and independence _____ c. works well with others in groups _____ d. produces work of high quality

---

tems should seek to motivate employees to be more productive. To the extent that pay is a motivator, governments should seek to establish a clear link between an employee's performance rating and his or her level of pay. In some jurisdictions, efforts are made to grant increases in the pay of public employees largely on the basis of increased productivity. The major difficulties in this regard seem to be twofold. On the one hand, merit pay or pay for greater productivity is most suitable to positions where the worker's output is tangible and measurable. Benchmarking, revenue production, and other measures can be more readily used in these contexts. Collecting garbage is an example. The total tons collected per employee or team per workday is measurable, as is the geographic area covered by a sanitation crew. Keyboarding and a variety of other governmental jobs also lend themselves to productivity measurement. But jobs involving a qualitative output and the exercise of discretion tend to be unsuitable to meaningful productivity measurement. For instance, how would you measure the productivity of a police officer? By the number of tickets issued, the number of arrests made, the number of domestic disputes settled, the number of endangered lives saved? Clearly, these all say something about the officer's performance, but so does the crime rate on his or her beat and the feeling of security or insecurity that residents there have. One could argue that arrests are a poor indicator of productivity, because they signify that the officer has failed to deter crime. But it would be equally ludicrous to hold a single officer responsible for the crime rate in any particular area. Similarly, how can the productivity of a public employee exercising judicial functions be evaluated? Administrative law judges and hearing examiners make decisions in individual cases. Although we could measure the time it takes them to reach and write opinions, what we are really interested in is the quality of those decisions in terms of justice and the public interest. Within broad limits, we care very little whether one such employee hears more cases per year than another. A promising approach for resolving some of these difficulties is for an employee and his or her supervisor to discuss appropriate performance goals and ways of assessing progress toward them. Various peer review systems also help assess performance.

Pay is also complicated by the desire to make it comparable with pay in the private sector. It is generally held that an employee in the public sector should earn what he or she would earn if doing the same work in the private sector. In the federal government, **comparability** is assessed on the basis of a survey done by the Bureau of Labor Statistics. The survey presents some challenging technical problems, but the main difficulty is that there are not true private equivalents for a large number of public sector jobs. Again, the problem is the qualitative aspect. Many of the features of a typical bureau chief's job can be compared to those of private sector executives—but the public sector job is ultimately different because for the most part it does not sell products or services and it involves qualitative questions about public policy and the public interest.[33] To pay a bureau chief based on the number of employees he or she supervises rather than on the basis of his or her development and implementation of effective public policies in the public interest is to miss the main dimension of the job. Under the Federal Employees Pay Comparability Act of 1990, beginning in fiscal 1994 (October 1, 1993–September 30, 1994), comparability also reflects the fact that employment costs vary from one geographic area to another. The act allows locality payments to maintain the principle of comparability throughout the United States.

"Pay caps" are another complication. Basic pay in the General Schedule system cannot exceed Executive Level V pay. (Executive levels are mostly for presidential appointments to the top positions in departments and agencies. Executive Level I is for the heads of cabinet departments, such as the Department of State. The heads of independent agencies, such as the Federal Emergency Management Agency, are often at Executive Level II. The members of regulatory commissions and minor agencies are often at Executive Levels III and IV; Executive Level V is primarily for political executives who are just above SES.) A table of General Schedule pay for 1996 is presented in Box 5–8. Most GS levels have ten pay steps, which allow for pay increases and differences within grades. At the state and local governmental levels and in some federal agencies, such as the Postal Service, pay is set primarily through collective bargaining (discussed later in this chapter).

Comparability refers to wage and salary rates among different employers. **Comparable worth** concerns the pay rates for different occupations by the same employer. The Equal Pay Act of 1963 prohibits pay differentials based on sex for employees performing similar jobs under similar working conditions for an employer. However, it does not prohibit different rates of pay to men and women if they are not in the same jobs. The concept of comparable

BOX 5-8 General Schedule Base Pay

1996 General Schedule salaries for those not covered by locality pay.

Step	1	2	3	4	5	6	7	8	9	10
GS-1	$12,384	$12,797	$13,208	$13,619	$14,032	$14,274	$14,679	$15,089	$15,107	$15,489
2	13,923	14,255	14,717	15,107	15,274	15,723	16,172	16,621	17,070	17,519
3	15,193	15,699	16,205	16,711	17,217	17,723	18,229	18,735	19,241	19,747
4	17,055	17,624	18,193	18,762	19,331	19,900	20,469	21,038	21,607	22,176
5	19,081	19,717	20,353	20,989	21,625	22,261	22,897	23,533	24,169	24,805
6	21,269	21,978	22,687	23,396	24,105	24,814	25,523	26,232	26,941	27,650
7	23,634	24,422	25,210	25,998	26,786	27,574	28,362	29,150	29,938	30,726
8	26,175	27,048	27,921	28,794	29,667	30,540	31,413	32,286	33,159	34,032
9	28,912	29,876	30,840	31,804	32,768	33,732	34,696	35,660	36,624	37,588
10	31,839	32,900	33,961	35,022	36,083	37,144	38,205	39,266	40,327	41,388
11	34,981	36,147	37,313	38,479	39,645	40,811	41,977	43,143	44,309	45,475
12	41,926	43,324	44,722	46,120	47,518	48,916	50,314	51,712	53,110	54,508
13	49,856	51,518	53,180	54,842	56,504	58,166	59,828	61,490	63,152	64,814
14	58,915	60,879	62,843	64,807	66,771	68,735	70,699	72,663	74,627	76,591
15	69,300	71,610	73,920	76,230	78,540	80,850	83,160	85,470	87,780	90,090

SOURCE: U.S. Office of Personnel Management (Washington, D.C.: Office of Personnel Management, 1996).

worth seeks to extend the principles of comparability and equal pay to situations where men and women are performing dissimilar jobs that nonetheless are work that could be considered of equal value to an employer. The concept of comparable worth is especially important to an employer that has a high degree of occupational segregation, by sex, in its work force. Many public employers are characterized by such segregation because they employ individuals in a broad range of occupations. For instance, in 1981, 32.5 percent of all women in the federal General Schedule worked in occupations that were at least 90 percent female. About 55 percent of all General Schedule employees filled positions in which at least 80 percent of the other employees in the same positions were of the same sex.[34] Although the extent of segregation by gender had moderated by the late 1980s, some occupations continued to be "women's occupations" paid at lower rates than what seemed to be comparable "male occupations." "Comparable" in this sense can be assessed in terms of required level of education, skill, responsibility, and so forth.

The advocates of establishing pay based on comparable worth argue that women are discriminated against because the occupations into which they are segregated are underpaid. In their view, the labor market reflects social discrimination and stereotyping in establishing pay for occupations such as nursing. Los Angeles and the states of Minnesota, New York, New Mexico, Iowa, and South Dakota are among the jurisdictions that have instituted comparable worth. Opponents of comparable worth argue that if women, such as nurses, are dissatisfied with their pay, they should go into other occupations or try to raise their wages through collective bargaining. However, the key to comparable worth may lie less in the desirable trend of opening opportunities for women in what were once considered "male occupations" than in desegregating all occupations. Social factors still play an important role in occupational choice, and that is why Johnny is still not very likely to grow up to be a nurse. The Equal Employment Opportunity Act of 1972 can be used as a basis for seeking to obtain comparable worth through litigation. But it is difficult to win such suits because the challenger must show that pay scales were depressed because of intentional sex discrimination.

Determining levels of public sector pay is complicated much further by politics. In recent years, politicians' electoral campaigns and taxpayers' dissatisfactions with government have often focused on the "bloated, unproductive" public sector. When inflation is rampant or budgets seem to defy balance or cities tread on the verge of bankruptcy, freezing or cutting the pay of public employees has become almost a reflexive response. Such freezes or reductions serve as indicators of the politicians' toughness and seem to offer the taxpayers some relief. Yet it is unclear why public employees should bear the brunt of fighting inflation or be penalized for providing services—such as police and fire protection and education—that are clearly in the public's interest. Whatever the sensibility of the "bash the bureaucrat" syndrome, however, public employees' pay is vulnerable in difficult economic times.

Finally, in considering the pay of public employees, attention must be paid to fringe benefits and pensions, both of which are often substantially greater in the public sector than among comparably salaried employees in the private sector. Recent presidents have favored basing public employees' comparability on "total compensation," which includes fringe benefits.

Cutbacks

From the late 1970s to the present time, the desire to reduce the public sector payroll in an effort to reduce taxes, balance budgets, and stimulate economic growth in the private sector has led to widespread reductions-in-force (RIFs) in the public service. The managerial approaches stress the need to cut the least productive employees and services first and to abandon functions that can be supplied as well or better by the private sector.

Like promotions, cutbacks are controversial and problematic because there are clear winners and losers. At present, the main approaches to cutbacks involve (1) providing some employees with greater protection than others, such as veterans or more senior employees; (2) relying on attrition, that is, the retirement of employees, their voluntary separation from the public sector, or their disability or death, without refilling their positions; (3) offering "buyouts" and "early" retirements as an incentive for employees to leave the public sector voluntarily; and (4) employing "across-the-board" cuts among all levels of employees and all governmental functions. Recently, "job sharing," or splitting one position between two or more part-time employees, has also gained attention. As the managerial approach argues, the main problem with these processes is that they may not lead to cuts where they are most desirable from an organizational standpoint. Indeed, there have been instances where early retirements have led to the separation of highly valued and necessary employees who subsequently had to be replaced, netting the government very little, if any, savings. The NPR's effort to remove almost 300,000 federal employees engaged in control functions such as auditing has met with some frustrations because of the haphazard nature of buyouts and the effects of seniority and veteran preference on RIFs.

Political Neutrality

Running throughout the managerial approaches to public personnel administration is the concept that the civil service should be politically neutral in a partisan sense. Managerially oriented public administration holds that to a very large extent the public sector faces the same kinds of organizational and managerial conditions and problems as the private sector and that partisanship has no legitimate place in the vast majority of public personnel and managerial decisions. The notion that functions such as street paving and sanitation are inherently nonpartisan is illustrative. The functions of the public sector in this view have much to do with the public interest and very little to do with the immediate electoral interests of political parties. To a very large extent, the contemporary concept of political neutrality grew out of the nineteenth-century civil service reform movement and was a reaction to the abuses of the spoils system. However, not only can the mixing of partisanship and personnel be seen to impede efficiency and foster corruption, but it can also symbolize a perversion of the public interest, leading the citizenry to believe that the public service is engaged in the promotion of its own narrow partisan interests.

At the federal level, regulations for political neutrality are embodied in the Hatch Act. The original act, passed in 1939, prohibited employees from taking an active part in political management or in partisan political campaigns. In 1993, the act was revised at the urging of federal employee unions, who considered it too restrictive. Most employees are now allowed to engage in a wide variety of campaign activities including giving speeches, holding offices in political organizations, stuffing envelopes and making telephone calls, and distributing campaign literature. The main remaining restrictions deal with soliciting money for political purposes. The 1993 revision does not apply to the Senior Executive Service, Administrative Law Judges, several law enforcement positions, and agencies with defense, intelligence, or other missions that could be compromised by public displays of partisanship, such as the MSPB and the Federal Election Commission. Many state and local governments also have political neutrality regulations.

The main difficulty with political neutrality regulations is that they do not specify precisely what they prohibit. Some of the restrictions are clear, but it is not always evident when a political statement crosses a forbidden line. For instance, under the original Hatch Act, federal employees were disciplined for such behavior as stating "unsubstantiated facts about the ancestry of a candidate" (calling him an S.O.B.?), failing to "discourage a spouse's political activity," and voicing "disapproval of treatment of veterans while acting as a Legion officer at a closed [American] Legion meeting."[35] Uncertainty may tend to inhibit public employees' freedom of speech more than is necessary to promote the value of partisan neutrality in the public service. It is important to note that although political neutrality regulations place substantial limitations on public employees' political rights, they also protect employees from being coerced by elected officials and political executives to engage in partisan activities.

Despite their interference with the public employee's constitutional rights under the First and Fourteenth Amendments, the Supreme Court has upheld the constitutionality of regulations for political neutrality in no uncertain terms.[36] In its view, legislatures have the power to establish such restrictions because they promote the legitimate objectives of creating and maintaining an efficient and nonpartisan civil service.

THE POLITICAL APPROACH TO PUBLIC PERSONNEL ADMINISTRATION

The political approach to public personnel stresses radically different values than the managerial approaches and leads to emphasis on different techniques and considerations. Perhaps its underlying value is to maximize the responsiveness of the public sector work force to political officials and to the public at large (not as individual customers). The political approach deemphasizes the analogy between public and private employment and stresses the extent to which the public service is *public*. According to this approach, what is most significant about the public sector is that it makes and implements public policy, that it provides public goods and services that cannot or should not be supplied by the private sector, and that it is an integral part of a constitutional system of government.

Responsiveness

The quest for *responsiveness* has taken several forms. Underlying most of them, however, is the idea that public employees should not use their positions to subvert the general political goals being pursued by the elected component of government and the political community as a whole. Concern with responsiveness reflects the view that public administration is not simply a politically neutral, technical, managerial endeavor, but rather has to be considered in terms of the political choices facing the nation.

The most outstanding effort to ensure responsiveness is reliance on the widespread use of political patronage in recruiting, selecting, and promoting public employees. The primary function of patronage was probably to sustain political parties—and the demise of patronage has coincided with the decline of parties in the United States. But there is another logic as well, and one that ensures the responsiveness of public administrators to the public: The people elect political officials who espouse a political program outlined in a party platform and then the elected officials appoint public administrators who are sympathetic to the party's policies. This promotes administrative responsiveness to elected officials and, by extension, to the public. Moreover, in patronage systems, the ability of the elected officials to fire, reassign, or promote public administrators virtually at will comes very close to assuring that the administrators will not act in ways that subvert the programs of the political officials. In other words, patronage can be used to instill accountability. But today, as noted earlier, patronage-based personnel actions are generally unconstitutional abridgments of public employees' freedom of belief and association. Still, the Supreme Court's patronage decisions do not take politics out of the public service completely.

Some of the arrangements of the Federal Civil Service Reform Act of 1978 seek to bring a permissible amount of political responsiveness into the federal personnel system. The Senior Executive Service is composed predominantly of top-ranking career civil servants. By law, 10 percent of allocated positions in the SES can be purely political (patronage) appointees. Members of the SES can be reassigned, voluntarily transferred from agency to agency, given different kinds of work, and reduced in grade with far greater flexibility than most federal career servants. They are subject neither to the position classification system nor the normal adverse action system for demotions based on poor performance. The rationale behind the SES was in very large part to make these high-ranking administrative officials responsive to political executives. In addition, it was thought that moving SES members from bureau to bureau and possibly from agency to agency would enable them to develop a broader concept of the public interest, one that was not overly supportive of the aims of any particular narrow interest group. Aside from affording these administrators new opportunities and challenges, the act made them eligible for large financial bonuses in return for sacrificing some of the security they had previously held. It is interesting to note that the reform act seeks to ensure some continuity in the higher civil service by prohibiting the involuntary reassignment of members of the SES within 120 days of the appointment of a new political executive in a supervisory position over them. The act also requires that 70 percent of all positions in the SES be filled with individuals with not less than five years of current, continuous administrative service.

The effort to assure responsiveness has also led to other kinds of ideological and political screening. At various times in the nation's history, for instance, the loyalty of public employees to the United States has been the subject of investigation. The most elaborate loyalty-security program existed in the late 1940s and early 1950s, a period generally referred to as "McCarthyism" after Senator Joseph McCarthy of Wisconsin. During part of that time, the loyalty of *every* federal employee and applicant was subject to question. Loyalty was defined largely in terms of adhering to an uninformed anticommunism, which was a rather repressive, limited political vision. Loyalty-security hearings probed employees on such things as whether they read the *New York Times* or Tom Paine, whether they believed in racial integration, peace, freedom, and civil liberties, whether they provided religious training for their children, and whether they engaged in or believed in premarital sex. One federal employee was even asked if he sympathized with the underprivileged![37] In retrospect, had not so many lives been damaged by the program and had not the creativity of the federal service suffered so badly, the fetish with loyalty-security would be easily dismissed as aberrant. After all, seeking social equity, engaging in premarital sex, supporting racial integration, supporting the recognition of "red" (mainland) China, and reading high-quality newspapers are usually no longer considered even remote indicators of disloyalty. However, at the time there was a very real fear in Congress and the society at large that federal employees were not responsive to the dominant values of the American political community and that they would use their positions to undermine the goals being sought by elected officials.

The effort to assure the responsiveness of public administrators also forms the basis for much legislative activity vis-à-vis public personnel administration. Legislatures, including the U.S. Congress, frequently have committees that deal with matters pertaining to the civil service and public personnel. Other legislative committees become involved in personnel from time to time in the course of their exercise of oversight of administrative programs. These legislative activities not only concern the general quality and legality of agencies' personnel management, they also serve as a focal point for groups seeking changes in public personnel arrangements. For example, labor unions representing public employees and organizations seeking to promote the equality of various social groups, such as African-Americans and women, frequently appear at legislative hearings dealing with public personnel policy. They may also actively lobby members of the relevant legislative committees as a means of promoting their objectives.

Legislative involvement in public personnel administration sometimes results in programs and policies that are in conflict with the objectives of the managerial approaches. Veteran preference is an outstanding example. The logic of the merit system or that of results-oriented public administration makes no provision for awarding preferential treatment to those who have served in the nation's armed forces. Yet at the federal level and in the overwhelming majority of the states, some veterans are provided with such a benefit. Typically, a number of points are added to a preference recipient's score (usually five or ten). In some cases, recipients of veteran preference are placed at the top of the eligibles register. In either case, veteran preference can have profound effects on the order in which individuals are selected for the civil service. Sometimes veteran preference makes a shambles of ordinary merit hiring practices, and it has had a very adverse effect on the employment of women. Veterans may also be granted preferences in retention during reductions in force.

Another example of legislative involvement in public personnel administration in response to interest groups tending to undermine the logic of the traditional managerial approach occurs in statutes authorizing collective bargaining in the public sector. We will have much more to say about this subject later in this chapter. Here, however, it should be pointed out that labor relations statutes may authorize collective bargaining over such matters as position classification, promotion, and pay—all of which are central to the traditional managerial program for public personnel.

Representativeness

The political approach to public administration stresses the value of *representativeness*. Public bureaucracies are considered to be political, policy-making institutions that exercise public power. One line of thought is that this power can be controlled and channeled in the public interest if the bureaucrats and agencies are representative of the political community at large. Representativeness is related to responsiveness because it is assumed that a representative bureaucracy will have perspectives on questions of public policy similar to those of the majority in the legislature and in the electorate.[38] In terms of public personnel administration, the quest for representativeness historically has centered on the need to select public administrators who are socially and/or politically representative of the nation's general population. The Pendleton Act of 1883 even included a provision for apportioning civil service appointments in the District of Columbia by the appointees' state of residency and according to the relative size of the states' populations. The political approach's emphasis on representation sometimes brings it into conflict with the traditional managerial perspective.

Today, the quest for representativeness in public bureaucracies is manifested to the greatest extent in a concern with equal employment opportunity and affirmative action (EEO/AA). One justification for such programs is that equal opportunity contributes to distributive and social justice; EEO is fair and ought to be practiced for that reason alone. Another justification stresses the supposed connection between the social representativeness of a public bureaucracy and its representativeness in a political and policy sense. Although the links between social background and policy behavior of public administrators have yet to be understood fully, some governmental policymakers have based the effort to establish greater social representation in the federal bureaucracy on the assumption that there is a close connection between the two.[39] Another aspect of the theory of representative bureaucracy stresses that the allegiance of various social groups to the government can be enhanced by including their members in all institutions of public power, including public bureaucracies. Finally, it is sometimes argued that government serves as an example (or model employer) for the society at large and that therefore its behavior has widespread ramifications for private personnel practices and the general treatment of groups. Whatever the intellectual and empirical viability of these approaches, it is clear that the federal government and many states have expressed a policy commitment to a socially representative work force and that EEO/AA has emerged as a central element of public personnel administration.

Equal employment opportunity began to emerge as a major personnel concern in the 1940s, when the first program for nondiscrimination was established in the federal government. The program was introduced against a background of rampant racial discrimination and segregation in the federal service. Although progress was uneven and a true commitment seemed to be lacking, by the 1960s EEO was a central programmatic effort in the personnel field. The Civil Rights Act of 1964 placed the policy of establishing EEO in federal personnel management on the basis of statute. The Equal Employment Opportunity Act of 1972 strengthened this commitment and extended it to state and local governments, many of which were under their own programs earlier. The Federal Civil Service Reform Act of 1978 further strengthened the commitment to EEO by making a socially representative federal work force a policy objective.

The main reason why an EEO program is necessary is that traditional managerially oriented public personnel administration neither produced socially representative bureaucracies nor prevented racial, ethnic, gender, and religious discrimination. The managerial quest for efficiency and a smoothly functioning public administration sometimes served as a rationale for blatant discrimination. When Woodrow Wilson extended the practice of racial segregation in the federal service, he claimed that it would reduce social "friction" that interfered with administrative operations.[40] More important, merit examinations for a wide range of careers, including police, fire, sanitation, and general administration, have all too frequently manifested an adverse disparate impact against African-Americans, Hispanics, and perhaps Native Americans. In fact, many civil rights activists have considered the merit system to be the chief contemporary barrier to equal opportunity and a socially representative public work force.

Women, too, have faced a host of barriers to equal employment opportunity. In the past they were excluded from many positions in law enforcement and from positions requiring travel with male coworkers. The latter exclusion was based on a fear of "moral dangers." Until the 1970s, pregnancy could legally be a basis for discrimination. MSPB studies continue to find high levels of sexual harassment of women in the federal service (see Box 5–9). Even today, women, like minorities, are underrepresented in the SES.

In recent years, equal employment opportunity and representativeness have also begun to encompass those with disabilities. The Americans with Disabilities Act of 1990 is a landmark in this regard. Its major aspects are outlined in Box 5–10. The act's main principle is that employees with disabilities should be accommodated as much as is feasible.

That contemporary merit practices sometimes tend to be at odds with the objectives of EEO is clear, but precisely why remains elusive. Part of the reason is that there is not equal opportunity in United States society to gain the skills, knowledge, abilities, and perhaps aptitudes that the merit system considers predictors of efficient and economical on-the-job performance. Second, the merit system has not in fact prevented discrimination. The rule of three, for example, has sometimes been used to pass over qualified minority, handicapped, and female candidates. Fairness in promotions seems especially to have been lacking for members of these groups. Moreover, frequently they have been victims of the "last hired, first fired"* syndrome in times of reductions in force. Third, to an extent, women and members of minority groups appear to have had less exposure to government recruitment networks. In the past, jobs were not advertised in places where they were likely to learn about them. They also had limited access to word-of-mouth networks disseminating information about public sector jobs. Job counseling and advising too often steered members of these groups into stereotypic "black" or "female" jobs. The latter has been a particularly invidious aspect of racism and sexism in the United States.

Since the 1960s public personnel programs have made a commitment to and efforts at establishing greater EEO. For the most part, this commitment is manifested in personnel activities intended to (1) reach all segments of the population in recruitment efforts; (2) eliminate artificial barriers to equal opportunity, such as height and weight requirements; (3) eliminate racial or ethnic bias from merit examinations; (4) establish upward-mobility training programs for minority and female employees; and (5) eliminate all vestiges of

---

*Also called "last in, first out," or LIFO.

BOX 5–9 **Sexual Harassment in the Federal Government**

Is It Sexual Harassment?*

Type of Uninvited Behavior by a Supervisor	Percentage of Women Who Consider It Harassment		
	1980	1987	1994
Pressure for sexual favors	91	99	99
Deliberate touching, cornering	91	95	98
Suggestive letters, calls, materials	93	90	94
Pressure for dates	77	87	91
Suggestive looks, gestures	72	81	91
Sexual teasing, jokes, remarks	62	72	83

	Percentage of Men Who Consider It Harassment		
	1980	1987	1994
Pressure for sexual favors	84	95	97
Deliberate touching, cornering	83	89	93
Suggestive letters, calls, materials	87	76	87
Pressure for dates	76	81	86
Suggestive looks, gestures	59	68	76
Sexual teasing, jokes, remarks	53	58	73

Type of Uninvited Behavior by a Coworker	Percentage of Women Who Consider It Harassment		
	1980	1987	1994
Pressure for sexual favors	81	98	98
Deliberate touching, cornering	84	92	96
Letters, calls, other materials	87	84	92
Pressure for dates	65	76	85
Suggestive looks, gestures	64	76	88
Sexual teasing, jokes, remarks	54	64	77

	Percentage of Men Who Consider It Harassment		
	1980	1987	1994
Pressure for sexual favors	65	90	93
Deliberate touching, cornering	69	82	89
Letters, calls, other materials	76	67	81
Pressure for dates	59	66	76
Suggestive looks, gestures	47	60	70
Sexual teasing, jokes, remarks	42	47	64

*Based on the percentage of respondents who indicated that they "definitely" or "probably" would consider the identified behavior sexual harassment.

BOX 5–9 *Continued*

Has It Happened to You in the Past Two Years?

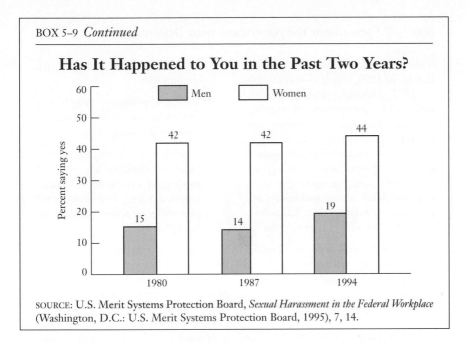

SOURCE: U.S. Merit Systems Protection Board, *Sexual Harassment in the Federal Workplace* (Washington, D.C.: U.S. Merit Systems Protection Board, 1995), 7, 14.

discriminatory thinking and practice from the entire gamut of personnel actions, including promotions, assignments, and position classifications. Although these principles are generally focused most on women and members of minority groups (primarily African-Americans, Hispanics, indigenous North American peoples, Asian-Americans, and Pacific Islanders), they also apply to handicapped persons.

Two broad techniques have emerged to achieve these objectives. One is the EEO Complaint System and related opportunities for litigation before the courts. Contemporary complaint systems seek to provide a quick resolution of problems related to prohibited discrimination. They stress informal resolution and corrective action. However, where neither of these is forthcoming, a complaint system is likely to provide for elaborate adjudicatory hearings at which both sides can present evidence, testify, and seek to rebut the other. To be credible, complaint systems must also offer sufficient remedies, including back pay, promotion, desired training, and other personnel actions. Moreover, discriminatory supervisors must be disciplined.

Although in the abstract, complaint systems often appear eminently fair, in practice they tend to be problematic and to generate anxiety. The most vexing difficulty has been resolving complaints on a timely basis. Supervisors also complain that they are inadequately protected against frivolous or misguided complaints and they cannot do their jobs under the threat of such actions. Complainants, on the other hand, have frequently voiced the view that complaint systems are not truly impartial, but rather tend to favor management.[41]

BOX 5–10 **Facts about the Americans with Disabilities Act**

Title I of the Americans with Disabilities Act of 1990, which took effect July 26, 1992, prohibits private employers, state and local governments, employment agencies, and labor unions from discriminating against qualified individuals with disabilities in job application procedures, hiring, firing, advancement, compensation, job training, and other terms, conditions and privileges of employment. An individual with a disability is a person who

- has a physical or mental impairment that substantially limits one or more major life activities;

- has a record of such an impairment; or

- is regarded as having such an impairment.

A qualified employee or applicant with a disability is an individual who, with or without reasonable accommodation, can perform the essential functions of the job in question. Reasonable accommodation may include, but is not limited to

- making existing facilities used by employees readily accessible to and usable by persons with disabilities;

- job restructuring, modifying work schedules, reassignment to a vacant position;

- acquiring or modifying equipment or devices, adjusting or modifying examinations, training materials, or policies, and providing qualified readers or interpreters.

An employer is required to make an accommodation to the known disability of a qualified applicant or employee if it would not impose an "undue hardship" on the operation of the employer's business. Undue hardship is defined as an action requiring significant difficulty or expense when considered in light of factors such as an employer's size, financial resources and the nature and structure of its operation.

An employer is not required to lower quality or production standards to make an accommodation, nor is an employer obligated to provide personal use items such as glasses or hearing aids.

SOURCE: U.S. Equal Employment Opportunity Commission, EEOC-FS/E-5 (December 1990).

The second technique for achieving EEO has been the use of **affirmative action**.[42] This has been far more controversial and continues to divide American society. Philosophically, affirmative action represents a departure from traditional concepts of equal opportunity. Rather than seeking to assure equal opportunity to compete for civil service positions, affirmative action seeks to assure equality in the outcome of the competition for those positions. It seeks a kind of proportional representation of various social groups in public administrative posts at all levels and in all the nation's governments. The groups toward which affirmative action policies are most directly aimed are African-Americans, Hispanics, Latinos, Native Americans, Asian-Americans, Pacific Islanders, and women. Each has suffered from a great deal of discrimination in public personnel administration. The employment of African-Americans in the postal service was once banned by federal law (1809–1865). Unequal pay and blatant discrimination based on gender was also authorized by federal statute in the past. Proponents of affirmative action generally argue that, at the very least, those who have been discriminated against so thoroughly in the past should be entitled to special, compensatory treatment until effects of past practices have been eliminated. Such preferences may include special recruitment efforts, preferential allocation of training opportunities, and even reevaluation of position classification systems to facilitate the upward mobility of people belonging to those groups.

Part of the controversy over affirmative action is whether the goals established for the employment and promotion of members of the various social groups are really quotas and whether, as such, they conflict with the merit system. Under contemporary guidelines propounded by the Equal Employment Opportunity Commission and OPM, goals should be established to assure that the employment of women and minorities in public personnel systems is proportionate to their numbers in the work force in the area from which these governments recruit their employees. The objective is to establish proportional representation at all levels and in all occupations within public agencies. However, once a goal is established its relationship to the merit system may be unclear.

Merit seeks to select the most qualified applicants, qualification being defined in nonpartisan and ostensibly socially neutral terms. Affirmative action seeks to take social characteristics into account in undertaking public personnel actions and to give at least a temporary preference to the members of some social groups. In practice, the two conflict when candidates for employment or promotion with higher merit system credentials are passed over in favor of individuals with lower merit scores who receive an affirmative action preference. To some this may be seen as sexist, racist, immoral, demeaning, and inefficient; to others the affirmative action preference is merely the removal of an unfair advantage that was previously held by nonminority men. In addition, the merit approach looks primarily at individual qualifications, whereas affirmative action takes a more collectivist approach in addressing the needs of whole social groups. Eventually, the issue may be moot as the merit system is improved to eliminate some of its racial, ethnic, and gender bias and as society makes greater strides toward social equality. However, this underlying tension between the managerial orientations (merit, performance) and the political approach (representativeness) predates the controversy over affirmative action and is likely to outlive it.

Public sector affirmative action also raises serious constitutional questions under the Fourteenth Amendment's Equal Protection Clause. Contemporary equal protection analysis subjects racial and ethnic classifications to strict judicial scrutiny, regardless of whether the intent is to help minorities or not.[43] A heavy burden of persuasion falls on the government involved to show a compelling interest for using the classifications and that they are narrowly tailored to serve that interest. Gender classifications are constitutional if they are substantially related to the achievement of important governmental objectives, which is a somewhat weaker test. (Equal protection analysis is discussed in greater detail in Chapter 11.)

At present, the Supreme Court considers hiring and promotional quotas to be constitutional as a remedy for past proven illegal and/or unconstitutional discrimination.[44] Quotas favoring minorities in layoffs and reductions in force are likely to be illegal and/or unconstitutional because they are not narrowly tailored; they cause nonminority employees to be dismissed according to racial or ethnic criteria.[45] The Court has upheld the legality (but not the constitutionality) of affirmative action that is voluntary (that is, not imposed as a remedy for past proven discrimination) in promotions.[46] Within this general framework and set of tensions, the composition of the federal work force has changed modestly over the past two decades. About 40 percent of all federal employees are (non-Hispanic) white males; about a third are (non-Hispanic) white females. Minorities constitute over a quarter of the federal work force; African-Americans, Hispanics, Native Americans, and women still tend to be disproportionately concentrated in the lower-paying positions.[47]

THE LEGAL APPROACH TO PUBLIC PERSONNEL ADMINISTRATION

The legal approach to public personnel administration places the constitutional relationship between citizen and government above the relationship between public employer and employee. It focuses on and values highly the rights and liberties of individual public employees and applicants for civil service jobs. It particularly stresses the need for fair and equitable procedures in adverse personnel actions or other situations in which an employee or applicant stands to lose or be denied something valuable to him or her. Moreover, the legal approach emphasizes the need for equal protection of the law and consequently opposes racial, ethnic, gender, and some other forms of discrimination. By and large, this approach to public personnel administration stands in contrast to the managerial and political approaches. Its expansive view of employee rights and due process tends to undercut the traditional managerial approach's reliance on hierarchical control and direction of public employees. It may also confound NPM efforts to deregulate public personnel management. Supreme Court decisions have also created constitutional barriers to patronage practices undercutting a basic value asserted by the political approach. The courts have also handed down decisions making loyalty-security programs, such as those of the 1940s and 1950s, difficult to establish within constitutional grounds. At some points, however, the political and legal approaches are in greater agreement, such as in the realm of EEO and equal protection. In reviewing the main thrust of the legal approach as it concerns public personnel, it is important to bear in mind that virtually all the important developments in this area occurred within the past four decades. Consequently, it is only relatively recently that the courts have emerged as a primary participant in the formulation of public personnel policy and practice.

The Constitutional Rights of Public Employees and Applicants

In the early 1950s some federal civil servants were dismissed from their employment on the grounds that a reasonable doubt existed as to their loyalty to the United States. Ostensibly, at least, as noted above, this doubt was created by behavior labeled "un-American," which sometimes included absurdities such as having intelligent friends! Prior to dismissal, an employee might have gone through a hearing before a Loyalty Review Board. The members of the board would be furnished, by the FBI or the Civil Service Commission, with information impugning the loyalty of the employee. The information would come from informants unknown to the board and their statements might be unsworn. The employee was not afforded a right to confrontation and cross-examination of these adverse "witnesses." In one case that reached the Supreme Court, part of the evidence against an employee labeled disloyal was that she had written a letter to the Red Cross protesting the segregation of blood by race. A lower court decision, which was affirmed by an equally divided Supreme Court, held that although justice seemed to have been compromised, "the plain hard fact" was that there was no constitutional prohibition on the dismissal of public employees because of their political beliefs, activities, or affiliations.[48] In other words, public employees had few constitutionally protected civil rights and liberties, and consequently, it was not necessary to develop elaborate procedures to protect them against misguided and damaging dismissals.

The constitutional doctrine prevailing at the time is generally called the **doctrine of privilege.** It held that because public employment was voluntarily accepted by the employee and because no one had a "right" to a government job, the government was free to set virtually any conditions it saw fit with regard to public service. Even though these conditions infringed on the ordinary constitutional rights that employees held as citizens, they were not necessarily unconstitutional because the employee accepted them voluntarily and because, technically, employees always retained their constitutional rights, they just lost their jobs for exercising them. Justice Holmes once captured the essence of the doctrine of privilege in his famous statement that "the petitioner may have a constitutional right to talk politics, but he has no constitutional right to be a policeman."[49] Such reasoning was obviously too simplistic and ill suited to a large-scale administrative state in which millions of people work for governments. In addition, the doctrine applied to others seeking governmental benefits or largess, such as welfare and licenses of various types. By the late 1950s it was becoming increasingly clear to the courts that the doctrine of privilege condoned too many abuses and tended to erode the fundamental constitutional rights of too large a segment of the United States population. Consequently, dramatic constitutional change was in the offing.

By the 1970s the Supreme Court indicated that it had "fully and finally" rejected "the concept that constitutional rights turn upon whether a governmental benefit is characterized as a 'right' or as a 'privilege.'"[50] It also called the distinction between rights and privileges "wooden."[51] Instead, the Court declared that public employees do indeed have constitutional rights and that these cannot be "chilled," abridged, violated, or denied simply because the individual works for the civil service (see Chapter 11). Where there is some infringement on the constitutional rights of public employees today, such as in the area of political neutrality, the government is required to demonstrate that such limitations are directly related to the necessities of the workplace or serve some overriding value, such as good, nonpartisan government.

A comprehensive treatment of the contemporary constitutional rights of public employees as they affect public personnel management would take volumes. Here, we will just identify some of the most outstanding instances of judicial involvement in public personnel. One of these is in the area of procedural due process, which addresses the fairness of the procedures under which a public employee is subjected to an adverse personnel action. Today, public employees are likely to have a *constitutional* (not just statutory or administrative) right to a hearing in adverse actions if (1) the basis of those actions is the exercise of an ordinary constitutional right, such as freedom of association; (2) the action is likely to damage the employee's reputation, such as labeling him or her dishonest or immoral; (3) there is something about the employee (age perhaps) or the job (possibly highly specialized) that would drastically reduce the civil servant's future employability if dismissed; or (4) the employee holds a contractual, tenure, or other "property interest" in the job.[52] The legal approach to public personnel administration places a strong emphasis on adversary procedure. Hearings are generally before impartial examiners and may be so elaborate as to resemble actual courtroom procedure. Employee and employer (supervisor) are pitted against one another at the hearing, yet at the same time, or in the future, they may have to work together. In some respects, elaborate hearings are inappropriate from managerial perspectives. They seriously compromise control and direction through the exercise of hierarchical authority and they exaggerate the adversity of relations between superordinates and subordinates. The extent to which the legal approach now dominates the procedure for dismissals is indicated by the chart in Box 5–11, which displays OPM's outline of the standard traditional federal procedure. The chart indicates that managers need to build up their cases for dismissal, rather than just assert that in their judgment dismissal is warranted. It also indicates that removals can be complicated by EEO antidiscrimination regulations and by grievance procedures negotiated through collective bargaining.

Freedom of expression is another area in which the courts have dramatically changed the nature of public personnel administration. Today public employees have a broad constitutional right to engage in "whistle-blowing"; that is, they are relatively free to speak out about waste, abuse, fraud, corruption, dangers to the public health or safety, or even misguided policy in the public service. Their right to disseminate such information to the public is protected even if their statements are inaccurate (as long as the employee did not display a reckless disregard for truth or falsity). The right to "whistle-blow" recognizes that the public employee's ultimate loyalty should be to the public rather than to a specific agency or manager. Consequently, it places strains on efforts to promote efficiency through loyalty to the organization and strict obedience to agency leadership.[53] Other forms of speech on matters of public concern are also constitutionally protected.

Developments in the area of freedom of association have also been revolutionary. There the courts declared that public employees have a constitutional right to join organizations, including labor unions. This reversed a policy followed by some states that outlawed public sector labor organizations. Moreover, it fostered the development of elaborate collective bargaining in the public sector—a development that radically changes public personnel management, as we will soon consider. Further, the Supreme Court has held that public employees cannot constitutionally be compelled to join organizations, including political parties and labor unions.

The judiciary has handed down a number of decisions that protect the broad constitutional liberties of public employees. Among the most important of these are those dealing with mandatory maternity leaves. The traditional managerially oriented practice required a woman to begin a maternity leave well before the expected date of birth of her child. This made it possible to plan for a replacement employee for her and also was thought to assure that her physical condition would not interfere with her ability to perform her job. However, the Supreme Court found such rationales to be unsatisfactory.[54] It held that unless the maternity leave is geared to the woman's individual medical condition, that is, her ability to do her job, or begins very late in the term of a normal pregnancy, it constitutes an unconstitutional infringement on a woman's liberty to choose whether to have a child.

The courts have also been active in delimiting the constitutional conditions for drug testing in the public service. In *National Treasury Employees Union v. Von Raab* (1989),[55] the Supreme Court found no Fourth Amendment barrier to random testing of customs agents. The decision was broad enough to indicate that such testing of other law enforcement and public safety employees would also be constitutional.

The legal approach has had an important impact on equal employment opportunity. The judiciary has played a significant role in establishing standards for determining what kinds of personnel practices constitute unconstitutional violations of the right to equal protection of the laws. Today, under Supreme Court rulings, a personnel practice having an adverse impact against a specific social group will *not* be unconstitutional unless it is intentionally discriminatory. However, where courts have found discriminatory treatment to be unconstitutional, they have sometimes responded with far-reaching intervention in public personnel administration. They have found several merit examinations to be unacceptable and have imposed such remedies as hiring and promotion based on racial quotas.[56] Importantly, even where an intent to

BOX 5–11 OPM's Outline of the Federal Demotion and Dismissal Process

1. Appeals and Grievances

The employee can generally appeal a removal or reduction in grade to the Merit Systems Protection Board, or if he or she is in the bargaining unit, can grieve the action under the negotiated grievance procedures unless the negotiated procedure excludes these types of actions. The employee has to choose between the two and cannot do both. Here is an outline of the procedures for reductions in grade and removals based on unacceptable performance, taken under Part 432 of Title 5, Code of Federal Regulations, and reassignment or demotion for unsatisfactory performance as a manager or supervisor under Subpart 1 of Part 315.

REDUCTIONS IN GRADE AND REMOVAL BASED ON UNACCEPTABLE PERFORMANCE

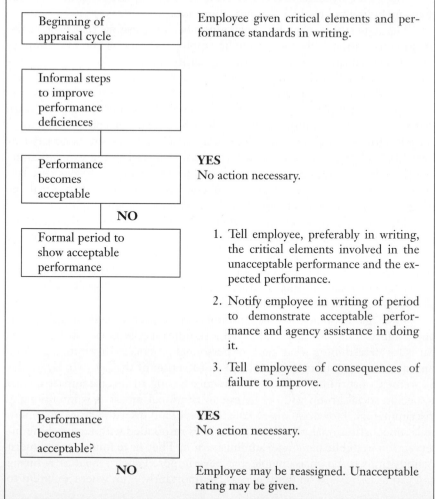

Beginning of appraisal cycle	Employee given critical elements and performance standards in writing.
Informal steps to improve performance deficiences	
Performance becomes acceptable	**YES** No action necessary.
NO	
Formal period to show acceptable performance	1. Tell employee, preferably in writing, the critical elements involved in the unacceptable performance and the expected performance. 2. Notify employee in writing of period to demonstrate acceptable performance and agency assistance in doing it. 3. Tell employees of consequences of failure to improve.
Performance becomes acceptable?	**YES** No action necessary.
NO	Employee may be reassigned. Unacceptable rating may be given.

BOX 5–11 *Continued*

Notice of Proposed action

1. Thirty days' advance written notice of reduction in grade or removal.

2. Specifies only instances of unacceptable performance occurring in the past year and critical element(s) involved.

Employee's answer

1. Reasonable time to answer orally and in writing.

2. Right to representation.

Decision issued

1. Written decision issued within thirty days after date that notice period expires.

2. Decision to reduce in grade or remove concurred in by higher-level official.

3. Decision to take action specifies instances of unacceptable performance.

Decision to take action?

NO
Action terminated.

YES

Action effected

Right to appeal to MSPB

Competitive service or perference eligible employees in the excepted service may appeal to MSPB.

OR

Other possible review routes

1. Negotiated grievance procedure if employee covered under applicable agreement.

2. EEO procedures if formal complaint before appeal filed.

3. Agency administrative grievance by nonpreference eligible excepted service employee.

SOURCE: U.S. Office of Personnel Management, *Taking Action on the Problem Employee* (Washington, D.C.: Government Printing Office, 1984), 10–11.

discriminate cannot be proven, civil rights and EEO *legislation* has formed the basis of such remedies.

The Liability and Immunity of Public Employees

The mere declaration of constitutional or legal rights does not ensure their enforcement. Independent enforcement mechanisms may be necessary where new legal or constitutional rights have been established. This is especially true where these rights stand in contravention of long-standing administrative, political, or social practice. The recently created constitutional barrier to patronage dismissals is a good example. Thus far, the judiciary has tended to promote enforcement of employees' constitutional rights through two types of approaches. One, as discussed earlier, is the requirement of procedural due process in adverse actions. The other can be described briefly but has very far-reaching ramifications.

In the 1970s the Supreme Court expanded the scope of public employees' liability in civil suits for damages for violating an individual's constitutional rights. But the individual whose rights have been violated may be another public servant. At the state and local levels, if a supervisor, public personnel administrator, or other official violates a subordinate's constitutional rights, the latter may file a civil suit seeking damages.[57] The same is true of applicants whose constitutional rights have been violated. The suit may be against the official as an individual and may seek punitive damages, that is, more money than the actual amount of damage caused by the unconstitutional action. For instance, a supervisor who fires a subordinate for joining a union or other association may be vulnerable to such a suit. So may an official whose actions are unconstitutionally discriminatory. The standard by which such liability is determined today is whether it was reasonable (in the reviewing court's judgment) for the official to be aware that his or her actions were in violation of the Constitution.[58] Where the official should have reasonably known that the actions were unconstitutional, he or she may be liable, regardless of intent. The point of liability is not only to compensate individuals for wrongs done to them, but, as the Supreme Court has declared, also to deter public officials from violating individuals' constitutional rights. Consequently, it becomes an important enforcement mechanism that strongly encourages public officials scrupulously to avoid abridging the constitutional rights of others.

In *Bush v. Lucas* (1983), the Supreme Court held that federal employees cannot sue supervisors for damages for breach of their First Amendment rights because Congress had established an elaborate alternative protective scheme, including appeals to the MSPB.[59] This decision recognizes another remedy; it does not increase or reduce the scope of federal employees' constitutional rights.

In passing, it should be noted that municipalities may also be found liable in suits where their policies result in the violation of constitutional rights. Here, the standard is not whether the municipality reasonably should have known, in some sense, that its policies were unconstitutional. Rather, the sole issue is whether its policies did in fact lead to an unconstitutional abridgment of individual rights.[60] Because public employees now have a wide array of First, Fourth, Fifth, and Fourteenth Amendment rights, civil suits are quite common.

COLLECTIVE BARGAINING

It is evident that the managerial, political, and legal approaches to public personnel administration stress different values and frequently conflict with one another. This has the tendency to fragment personnel practice, making it somewhat incoherent. For instance, merit, EEO, and veteran preference co-exist on uneasy terms, as do traditional hierarchical managerial authority, the NPM's effort to deregulate personnel practices, and constitutional procedural due process. According to contemporary constitutional interpretation, political patronage and the rights of public employees clash even more directly. These tensions and conflicts raise the question running throughout much public administration of whether it is possible to synthesize or combine the three approaches in some fashion. At the moment, in terms of public personnel administration, the answer is to some extent, but not completely. For the most part, progress toward this end has been made through the rise of a new model of public personnel administration—one that stresses **codetermination** of policy through the process of collective bargaining.

Until the 1960s, collective bargaining in the public sector was frequently considered antithetical to constitutional democracy in the United States. It was thought absurd that organized public employees could bargain with the government as a coequal, or that matters of public policy would be determined in any forum other than the legislature, elected executive, or courts. In particular, strikes were feared because they represented a breakdown of the public order and could lead to chaos. Many states viewed collective bargaining as a threat to sovereignty, and the federal government had no general policy or practice for collective bargaining by its employees.

All of this changed with remarkable rapidity. In large part, the rise of collective bargaining has been related to the growth of public employment and the political pressures exerted by unions. Many unions viewed the public sector as a promising recruiting ground in the face of declining private sector union membership. Today public sector collective bargaining is found in the federal government and almost all states. Yet to a very large extent it remains a patchwork of practices. There is no national law on the subject, and state laws and practices vary widely in their coverage and content. Nonetheless, a common pattern has emerged. Public personnel policy is now largely determined through a framework of collective bargaining procedures that incorporate substantial parts of the managerial, political, and legal approaches to personnel administration.

The basic pattern consists of the following: employees in the same occupations (teachers, police, firefighters, clerks, etc.) or performing similar kinds of work (general administrative work, for instance) organize into

bargaining units. Through an election or submission of union membership cards to the employer, a majority of the employees in the unit can designate a single union to bargain on behalf of all the employees in the unit. This is called **exclusive recognition** (of the union). Precisely what can be bargained over is called the **scope of bargaining.** This may be relatively comprehensive and include wages, hours, fringe benefits, position classification, promotion procedures, training, discipline, grievances, holidays, sick leave, seniority preferences, overtime assignments, and other working conditions. Conversely, it may be narrow and confined largely to matters of discipline and the issuance of safety clothing, coffee breaks, and parking spaces. It is useful to think of the scope of bargaining in terms of items over which bargaining is mandatory, items over which it is permitted, and items over which it is prohibited. Where labor and management cannot reach agreement on matters that are subject to mandatory bargaining, an impasse results. Resolution of the impasse can take many forms, including mediation, fact finding, and arbitration. Once there is agreement among the parties or an arbitration award is handed down, a contract is signed and goes into effect. Some states have permissive policies toward public employee strikes for resolving impasses (see Box 5–12). Again, depending on the scope of bargaining, this may amount to codetermination by labor and management of the conditions of employment.

The collective bargaining approach outlined above readily takes advantage of managerial, political, and legal perspectives. It is no accident that the first federal executive order on the subject declared that labor-management relations could foster both efficiency and democracy.[61] From a traditional managerial perspective, the emergent collective bargaining model promotes the following. First, it clearly defines the rights of management and makes these nonbargainable. Examples would be the right to direct employees and determine the budget of an agency. Second, it facilitates communication between management and employees, which provides supervisors and other officials with valuable information as to how efficiency and economy can be improved. A closely related benefit is that it facilitates the participation of employees in determining the conditions under which they work. Within limits, such participation may create greater job satisfaction, loyalty to the organization, and, therefore, efficiency. Finally, the employee grievance system (discussed below) negotiated through collective bargaining serves to alert management to serious problems and unfit supervisors. Yet collective bargaining is not primarily a management tool and it clearly presents challenges to managers who cling to traditional practices and doctrines of hierarchical authority.

The political approach is also evident in the collective bargaining model. On the one hand, the value of representation is fundamental to public sector collective bargaining. Part of the purpose of organized labor relations is to provide civil servants with a voice in determining the nature of working conditions in government employment. Apart from actual bargaining sessions, public employees are to be represented by unions in many personnel matters and unions are frequently consulted on changes in public policy that may affect their jobs.

At the same time, however, the political approach demands that public sector collective bargaining practices serve the public interest and do not undermine the responsiveness of government to the electorate. Consequently, certain limitations have been placed on public sector labor relations that make the collective bargaining process quite different from private sector practices. Most notably in this context are serious restrictions on the scope of bargaining and the prohibition of strikes. Many jurisdictions have enacted a strong management rights clause that severely limits the items over which collective bargaining can take place. Frequently, agency missions, budgets, public policies, technologies, recruitment, selection, and sometimes the basis for disciplinary proceedings are outside the scope of bargaining. Within the ambit of these limitations lie some very fundamental conditions of work. For instance, in some jurisdictions teachers cannot bargain over the number of pupils per class or the school calendar; similarly, police may not be able to bargain over deployment (one- or two-person patrols), weapons, and defensive gear. Some employees, including most nonpostal workers in the federal government, are prohibited from bargaining over wages and hours. These restrictions are a legacy of the concept of sovereignty, that is, the idea that government is the supreme representative of the citizenry and cannot be compelled to capitulate to or share its authority with private organizations. The main point of a limited scope of bargaining is to ensure that matters of public policy are determined by representative governmental institutions rather than through a special process that entitles a group of individuals (public employees) to assert its will.

Some prohibitions on the right to strike are found in all the states and in the federal government. Although not always effective, these restrictions raise the cost of strikes to employees and unions and probably serve as a deterrent to them. Many view the strike as fundamental to any serious collective bargaining process. However, by and large the political approach to public administration has ruled it out not only because it could lead to chaos or anarchy, but also because it tends to provide organized public employees with a means of undercutting the responsiveness of government to the citizenry. For example, teachers and parents have an interest in school calendars and curriculum. Providing teachers with the right to bargain over these matters and use the strike in an effort to compel the government (school board) to accept their will gives the teachers leverage over public policy that is not available to parents. The parents can neither collectively bargain nor strike. They can vote for school board members and lobby, but so can teachers. According to the political approach, if government is to be responsive to the public interest, then public policy cannot be the outcome of labor negotiations and strikes. The public interest cannot be held hostage by striking public employees or bargained over in negotiating sessions.

It is problematic whether these restrictions on the public sector collective bargaining model reduce its coherence and limit its effectiveness. It is clear that the model cannot work well or be meaningful if the scope of bargaining is too narrow to serve as a vehicle for employees to affect their working conditions. It may also be true that management will not take public

BOX 5–12 **State Permissive Strike Policies: A Sampling**

Alaska	All public employees except teachers	Right to strike for semiessential and nonessential workers. Police, firefighters, and hospital employees may not strike. Limited strike right for public utilities, sanitation, snow removal, and schools, after exhaustion of mediation. Other workers may strike upon majority vote.
California	All public employees	Under a 1985 California State Supreme Court ruling, strikes are legal "unless or until it is clearly demonstrated that such a strike creates a substantial and imminent threat to the health or safety of the public."*
Hawaii	All public employees	Strike permitted after exhaustion of impasse-resolution procedures and sixty days after issue of fact-finding report. Ten days' notice by union is required. Strikes endangering public health and safety are illegal, as determined by PERB (Public Employment Relations Board) and courts.
Minnesota	All public employees	Strikes prohibited except where employer refuses request for binding arbitration or refuses to submit to arbitration or to an arbitration award. Teachers have right to strike following expiration of contract, sixty days of mediation, and ten days' notice. Nonteaching local employees and state employees may strike after expiration of contract, forty-five days of mediation, and ten days' notice.
Montana	All public employees	Strikes permitted. Nurses must give thirty days' notice; no other nurses' strike may occur within 150 miles.

BOX 5–12 *Continued*

Ohio

Public employees in jurisdictions of 5,000 or more, except police, firefighters, and related employees

Ten days' notice of intent to strike must be supplied to state Employment Relations Board. Employer can seek court order against strikes presenting a clear and present danger to the health and safety of the public. The order automatically expires after sixty days.

Oregon

All public employees except police, firefighters, and correctional institutional guards

Strikes permitted unless it creates a clear and present danger of threat to the public health, safety, or welfare. Mediation, fact-finding, and thirty-day cooling-off period must be exhausted; ten days' notice must be given.

Pennsylvania

All public employees except prison guards and court employees

Strike permitted after exhaustion of impasse-resolution procedures, unless strike presents clear and present danger to public health, safety, or welfare.

Vermont

All local public employees except guards and court employees

Strikes permitted thirty days after fact-finding report where parties have not agreed to arbitration and there is no danger to public health, safety, or welfare. Teacher strike may be prohibited by courts if it endangers a sound program of education.

Wisconsin

Local public employees

Strike permitted if both parties withdraw their final offer, and ten days' notice is given by union. Strike is illegal if it poses imminent threat to public health, safety, or welfare.

County Sanitation District No. 2 v. Los Angeles County Employees Association, L.A. 31850, May 13, 1985.

SOURCE: Richard C. Kearney, *Labor Relations in the Public Sector* (New York: Marcel Dekker, 1984), 220–221. *IPMA News*, October 1983, 7–8 (for Ohio). *Public Administration Times*, 1 June 1985, 1, 4 (for California). Idaho and Illinois also allow public employees to strike under some circumstances.

employees seriously in bargaining sessions unless the employees have a weapon such as the strike. The absence of the right to strike requires some other means of resolving impasses. This brings us to the legal approach.

Overwhelmingly, the public sector collective bargaining model is moving in the direction of arbitration as a means of resolving impasses. **Arbitration** can be over *interests* such as wages and hours or over *grievances* involving the mistreatment of an employee or other violation of a contract. It can take many forms. The most forceful interest arbitration is compulsory and binding. This compels the parties to enter into arbitration when an impasse occurs and requires them to accept the arbitrators' award. Arbitration is a judicial-style process. The individual arbitrator or panel hears the views and proposals of both sides in what amounts to an adversary proceeding. The facts are then weighed, principles according to which a judgment will be made are considered, and a decision is handed down. In **final offer arbitration** the arbitrator is limited to choosing from the contract proposal made by each side. This format puts pressure on management and labor to make reasonable offers, lest the arbitrator select the other's proposal. In *whole package* final offer arbitration, the arbitrator is limited to selecting one offer in its entirety. *Item-by-item* final offer arbitration allows the arbitrator to select from among the two sides' proposals. For instance, the arbitrator may choose management's wage proposal and labor's proposal for protection against layoffs.

Grievance arbitration often involves discipline and work assignments. It can be quite similar to adverse action hearings. It is very common and places challenges and constraints upon public managers, who now find their flexibility in dealing with employees to be severely limited. (Box 5–13 presents some examples of grievance arbitration decisions in the federal service.)

Because collective bargaining favors negotiation and agreement by the parties themselves, arbitration is generally viewed as a last resort for resolving impasses. Less intrusive approaches include mediation, fact-finding, and med-arb (mediation-arbitration). Mediators work with the parties to reduce the distance between their proposals. They generate "supposals": suppose management does this, will you do that? They also keep the negotiators focused on the issues, rather than allowing personalities and the desire to win for the sake of winning get in the way of settlement. Fact finders are used when the parties disagree over an empirical matter such as increases in the cost of living since the last contract was signed and matters of pay comparability.

Interest and grievance arbitration make much of the collective bargaining model look like a quasi-judicial process. It appears that by regulating strikes the public sector model has taken conflict off the streets and away from the collective bargaining table and placed its resolution in the hands of arbitrators who act like judges.

Comprehensive programs for collective bargaining provide for Public Employment Relations Boards (PERB) or equivalent agencies, such as the Federal Labor Relations Authority. These agencies adjudicate or oversee the adjudication of unfair labor practice charges, disputes over the authorized scope of bargaining, the appropriateness of the bargaining units that em-

---

BOX 5–13 **Grievance Arbitration Decisions in the Federal Service: Some Examples**

10004 Did the agency have just cause for demoting the grievant for reporting to work while intoxicated?

Yes, but grievant must be paid the differential rate for all work performed in the higher classification. Demotion for the offense was within the range of discipline penalties. When management reduces the employee's classification, the arbitrator reasoned, it must assign duties within the confines of the new (lower) classification, and cannot require the employee to perform duties within the higher classification at the lower rate of pay.

10007 Was the change of grievant's work location a violation of the agreement?

Yes. Grievant should have been provided a work area which would diminish her embarrassment caused by the profanity and physical exposure of patients, and possible health hazards. Although management has a right to assign work to employees, the working conditions of the job must be considered in the assignment.

10015 Were the changes in the basic workweek of the aggrieved employees instituted by the agency in violation of the agreement?

Yes. Management was required to pay each grievant the difference between the overtime rate and amount actually paid at the straight time rate for each Saturday and Sunday actually worked. The Shipyard management was not faced with an emergency when the decision to change the workweek was made. Further, management failed to consult properly with the union.

10023 Did management have just cause for imposing a three-day suspension on the grievant for his use of profane language?

No. The disciplinary action was striken from the grievant's record and the grievant was made whole for three days lost pay. Although grievant did use profane language, he did not do so with knowledge that his broadcast lines were open and that he was transmitting. Further, due to lax enforcement by management of regulations against use of profanity, the arbitrator concluded that it was reasonable for the grievant to believe that such violations were tolerated by management.

SOURCES: U.S. Civil Service Commission, *Digest of Labor Arbitration Awards in the Federal Service* (Washington, D.C.: Civil Service Commission, March 1978).

---

ployees seek to organize, and other matters. PERBs may also have rule-making authority regarding labor relations.

The judiciary's concern with constitutional rights and values has led it to hand down a number of decisions that have had a major impact on public sector collective bargaining. One, already mentioned, is that public employees have the right to join unions, though there is still no constitutional right actually to engage in collective bargaining. Another is that the "union shop," that is, an arrangement whereby all employees in a collective bargaining unit must join the exclusively recognized union, is an unconstitutional abridgment of public employees' right to freedom of association.[62] However, an "agency education, health, mental health, social services, and transportation indicated that about 78 percent of such organizations contracted out for some services, functions, or goods.[67] Privatization remains controversial.[68] For obvious reasons public sector employees and their unions oppose it. It can obscure accountability. Whether (and when) it promotes significant cost savings for comparable service is frequently disputed. However, privatization does enable governments to avoid many of the costs of their own personnel systems. When a function is contracted out, the government does not have to recruit, test, select, promote, discipline, provide direct benefits, bargain, or otherwise deal with those workers who perform it. From a personnel standpoint, contracting out simplifies in the extreme. And the temptation to do so is often great, even when the potential cost savings may be negligible or marginally negative. Of course, every government will define some functions as "core" and, therefore, not subject to privatization.

Recently, greater attention has been paid to the prospects of using decentralization and deregulation within the public sector as a means of reducing the appeal of privatization and making government more competitive. Encouraging government employees to compete on a cost basis for functions that might otherwise be contracted out should bring greater efficiency to the public sector. Part of that efficiency may come by building greater flexibility into public personnel systems and developing more harmonious labor relations. In 1996, the federal Office of Management and Budget substantially revised its policy on privatization, for the first time since 1983, with regard to employee involvement in decisions on whether to contract out a function or produce it in-house.[69]

Thus, decentralization/deregulation and privatization can be used in tandem or in competition with each other. Core functions that cannot be privatized can still benefit from personnel reforms. Government may also benefit by reconfiguring personnel practices to enable public employees to compete favorably with private organizations for the provision of other functions. To the extent that change will emphasize QWL, public employees, the government, and the public at large may all be better off.

But it is impossible to know how all the pressures on contemporary public personnel will direct future developments. Nevertheless it is safe to say that change—perhaps rapid and constant—is clearly inevitable.

NOTES

1. Al Gore, *From Red Tape to Results: Creating a Government That Works Better & Costs Less* (Washington, D.C.: Government Printing Office, 1993), 22.
2. There are several excellent histories of the federal service that emphasize personnel administration. See Frederick Mosher, *Democracy and the Public Service*, 2d ed. (New York: Oxford University Press, 1982); Paul P. Van Riper, *History of the United States Civil Service* (Evanston, Ill.: Row, Peterson, 1958); Leonard D. White's four-volume series, *The Federalists, The Jeffersonians, The Jacksonians*, and *The Republican Era* (New York: Free Press, 1965), paperback editions; and Stephen

Skowronek, *Building a New American State* (Cambridge, England: Cambridge University Press, 1982).

3. David H. Rosenbloom, *Federal Service and the Constitution* (Ithaca, N.Y.: Cornell University Press, 1971), 36.

4. See ibid., 38–41 and chap. 2, for a discussion of Jefferson's appointment policy and that of Jackson.

5. Quoted in ibid., 49.

6. Ibid., 56.

7. Ibid., 49.

8. See Jay M. Shafritz et al., *Personnel Management in Government* (New York: Marcel Dekker, 1978), 16.

9. Rosenbloom, *Federal Service and the Constitution*, 55.

10. Shafritz et al., *Personnel Management in Government*, 33.

11. Van Riper, *History of the United States Civil Service*, chap. 17, 558–559.

12. *Elrod v. Burns*, 427 U.S. 347 (1976); *Branti v. Finkel*, 445 U.S. 506 (1980); *Rutan v. Republican Party of Illinois*, 497 U.S. 62 (1990).

13. Quoted in Rosenbloom, *Federal Service and the Constitution*, 70–71, note 1.

14. Quoted in ibid., 71. Many of the civil service reformers' statements were published in books and pamphlets that are now difficult to obtain. The referencing here is to a source that discusses their ideas in a historical context.

15. Quoted in ibid., 73.

16. Ibid.

17. Ibid., 71.

18. Ibid., 67.

19. Quoted in John A. Rohr, *To Run a Constitution* (Lawrence: University Press of Kansas, 1986), 72.

20. Ibid., 231.

21. Matthew Josephson, *The Politicos* (New York: Harcourt, Brace & World, n.d.), 438.

22. Ari Hoogenboom, *Outlawing the Spoils* (Urbana: University of Illinois Press, 1961).

23. Rosenbloom, *Federal Service and the Constitution*, 80.

24. Ibid.

25. *New York Times*, 3 March 1978. See also David H. Rosenbloom, ed., "Public Administration Forum: Civil Service Reform, 1978: Some Issues," *Midwest Review of Public Administration* 13 (September 1979): 171–188.

26. *New York Times*, 3 March 1978.

27. Alan K. Campbell, "Civil Service Reform: A New Commitment," *Public Administration Review* 38 (March/April 1978): 102.

28. Gore, *Creating a Government That Works Better & Costs Less: Status Report, September, 1994* (Washington, D.C.: Government Printing Office, 1994), 98–99.

29. Wallace Sayre, "The Triumph of Techniques over Purpose," *Public Administration Review* 8 (Spring 1948): 134.

30. See Jay M. Shafritz et al., *Personnel Management in Government*, 2d ed. (New York: Marcel Dekker, 1981), chap. 4.

31. Gore, *From Red Tape to Results*, 22.

32. Charlie B. Tyer, "Employee Performance Appraisal: Process in Search of a Technique," in *Public Personnel Administration*, ed. Steven Hays and Richard Kearney (Englewood Cliffs, N.J.: Prentice-Hall, 1983), 118–136. The discussion in this paragraph is based on Tyer's essay.

33. See, among others, Paul Appleby, *Policy and Administration* (University, Ala.: University of Alabama Press, 1949).

34. See Joy Grune and Nancy Reder, "Addendum—Pay Equity," *Public Personnel Management* 13 (Spring 1984): 70–80, for a discussion of occupational segregation by sex.

35. *National Association of Letter Carriers v. Civil Service Commission*, 346 F. Supp. 578 (1972), at 581.

36. *Civil Service Commission v. National Association of Letter Carriers*, 413 U.S. 548 (1973).

37. See Rosenbloom, *Federal Service and the Constitution*, chap. 6.

38. See Samuel Krislov and David H. Rosenbloom, *Representative Bureaucracy and the American Political System* (New York: Praeger, 1981), for a comprehensive discussion.

39. See U.S. Commission on Civil Rights, *The Federal Civil Rights Enforcement Effort—1974*, vol. 5 (Washington, D.C.: Commission on Civil Rights, 1975), 6.

40. Arthur Link, *Wilson: The New Freedom* (Princeton, N.J.: Princeton University Press, 1965), 251.

41. See David H. Rosenbloom, *Federal Equal Employment Opportunity* (New York: Praeger, 1977), 126–138. See also Robert Vaughn, *The Spoiled System* (New York: Charterhouse, 1975); and M. Weldon Brewer, *Behind the Promises* (Washington, D.C.: Public Interest Research Group, 1972).

42. See Rosenbloom, *Federal Equal Employment Opportunity*, chap. 5, for a discussion.

43. *Adarand Constructors v. Peña*, 115 S. Ct. 2097 (1995).

44. *United States v. Paradise*, 480 U.S. 189 (1987).

45. *Wygant v. Jackson*, 476 U.S. 267 (1986).

46. *Johnson v. Transportation Agency*, 480 U.S. 624 (1987).

47. U.S. Office of Personnel Management, *Federal Staffing Digest*, vol. 3 (August 1991): 1; Barbara Saffir and Stephen Barr, "A Snapshot of Women and Minorities in Federal Jobs," *Washington Post*, 3 January 1994, A17.

48. *Bailey v. Richardson*, 182 F2d 46, 59 (1950); 341 U.S. 918 (1951).

49. *McAuliffe v. New Bedford*, 155 Mass. 216, 220 (1892).

50. *Sugarman v. Dougall*, 413 U.S. 634, 644 (1972).

51. *Board of Regents v. Roth*, 408 U.S. 564, 571 (1972).

52. Ibid. See also *Cleveland Board of Education v. Loudermill*, 470 U.S. 532 (1985).

53. See Robert Vaughn, "Statutory Protection of Whistleblowers in the Federal Executive Branch," *University of Illinois Law Review*, no. 3, (1982): 615–667; and "Public Employees and the Right to Disobey," *Hastings Law Journal* 29 (November 1977): 261–295. Although the legal right to whistle-blow is well established, whistle-blowers often face their employer's wrath for appearing to be disloyal to their organizations. Reprisals against whistle-blowers, though illegal, are common and difficult to prevent.

54. *Cleveland Board of Education v. LaFleur*, 414 U.S. 632 (1974); argued and decided with *Cohen v. Chesterfield County School Board*.

55. *National Treasury Employees Union v. Von Raab*, 489 U.S. 656 (1989).

56. See David H. Rosenbloom and Carole C. Obuchowski, "Public Personnel Examinations and the Constitution," *Public Administration Review* 37 (January/February 1977): 9–18; *United States v. Paradise*, 480 U.S. 189 (1987).

57. This is true at present for state and local public employees under 42 U.S. Code section 1983. It does not apply to federal employees whose right of freedom of speech has been abridged; it may not apply in instances of violation of other constitutional rights of federal employees. See *Bush v. Lucas*, 462 U.S. 367 (1983).

58. *Harlow v. Fitzgerald*, 457 U.S. 800 (1982).

59. 462 U.S. 367.

60. See *Owen v. City of Independence*, 445 U.S. 622 (1980).

61. Executive Order 10988 *Federal Register* vol. 27, 17 January 1962; 551.

62. *Abood v. Detroit Board of Education*, 430 U.S. 209 (1977).

63. *Chicago Teachers Union v. Hudson*, 475 U.S. 292 (1986).

64. *City of Madison, Joint School District No. 8 v. Wisconsin Employment Relations Commission*, 429 U.S. 167 (1976).

65. *Bishop v. Wood*, 426 U.S. 341, 349–50, (1976).

66. National Partnership Council, *Partnership Handbook* (Washington, D.C.: Government Printing Office, 1994), 3.

67. Council of State Governments, *Book of the States, 1994–1995* (Lexington, Ky.: Council of State Governments, 1995), 411.

68. See generally, Donald Kettl, *Government by Proxy: (Mis?)Managing Government Programs* (Washington, D.C.: CQ Press, 1988); and John Donahue, *The Privatization Decision* (New York: Basic Books, 1989). For a specific dispute, see John Pulley, "Privatization Efforts Could Prove Costlier," *Federal Times*, 29 April 1996, 9.

69. Christy Harris, "Workers Get More Say in Contracting Out," *Federal Times*, 29 April 1996, 5.

ADDITIONAL READING

BAN, CAROLYN, AND NORMA RICCUCCI, EDS. *Public Personnel Management*, 2d ed. New York: Longman, 1997.

HAYS, STEVEN, AND RICHARD KEARNEY, EDS. *Public Personnel Administration: Problems and Prospects*, 3d ed. Englewood Cliffs, N.J.: Prentice-Hall, 1995.

INGRAHAM, PATRICIA. *The Foundation of Merit*. Baltimore: Johns Hopkins University Press, 1995.

SHAFRITZ, JAY M., NORMA RICCUCCI, DAVID H. ROSENBLOOM, AND ALBERT HYDE. *Personnel Management in Government*, 4th ed. New York: Marcel Dekker, 1992.

VAN RIPER, PAUL P. *History of the United States Civil Service*. Evanston, Ill.: Row, Peterson, 1958.

STUDY QUESTIONS

1. Many observers believe that contemporary public personnel systems are too complicated to be either efficient or fair. Based on the chapter and your own experiences, if you could recommend one change to a state legislative or U.S. congressional committee dealing with personnel, what would it be? Why?

2. The issue of whether public employees should be allowed to strike has been a concern of public personnel administration. Do you think all strikes by public employees should be prohibited? Why or why not? If you favor a right to strike, should any limitations be placed on it? What would these be, if any? Why?

3. Having read the chapter on personnel, what aspects of the contemporary nature of public personnel management would attract you to the public sector? Which, if any, would you find objectionable?

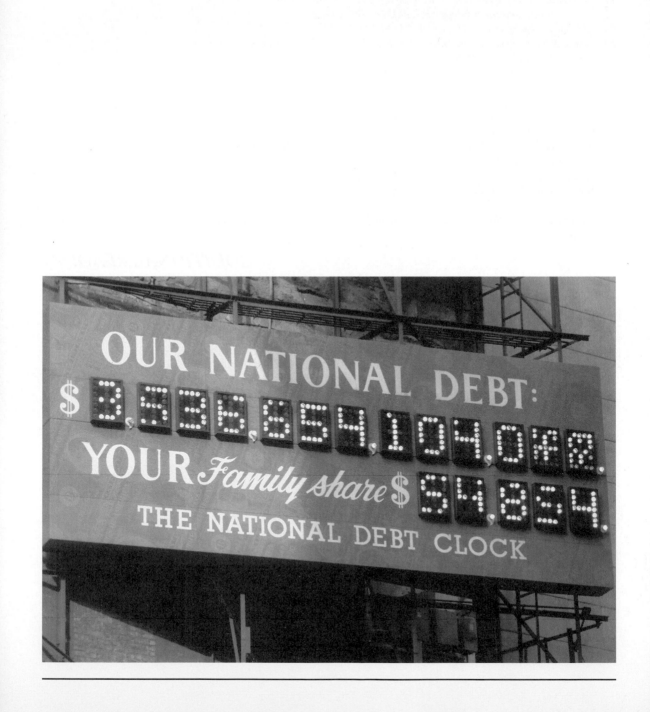

CHAPTER 6 | *Budgeting*

Governmental budgets are currently an area of general concern and controversy. As governmental activity has consumed a greater proportion of society's resources, considerable attention has been paid to taxation and other sources of government revenues. The federal budget not only funds governmental activities but also has been used as a tool to help regulate the economy's business cycles. Budget processes are exceedingly complex. This chapter presents theories about how budgets should be formulated and executed, analyzing the strengths and weaknesses of the various approaches. As do other aspects of public administration, budgets involve managerial, political, and legal concerns, which in this case may come into sharp, almost unresolvable, conflict.

Budgeting is a public administrative activity of preeminent importance. Along with personnel, organization, and decision making, it is at the core of public administration. And, like those other subjects, it is generally surrounded by controversy and calls for reform. It appears that in view of the competing perspectives on public administration, no single budgetary process can satisfy everyone. Moreover, budgeting is so complex in its political and economic ramifications that in some respects it defies control and even understanding. But, of course, that is part of what makes public administration challenging and interesting.

In essence, a governmental budget is a statement of revenues and expenditures. It indicates how much money a government proposes to raise and spend. Equally important, it provides a record of past expenditures. But this definition is a bit too simple. The budget is also intimately related to taxation. Will revenues be generated through taxes? If so, what kinds? Sales taxes, income taxes, corporate taxes, value-added taxes, property taxes, excise taxes, luxury taxes? What will the mix be? Will funds also be raised through borrowing? If so, how? On the expenditure side, budgets indicate how governmental activity will be conceptualized. Will expenditures be categorized by "objects," such as equipment, supplies, and salaries of government employees? Will they be categorized by function, such as health or defense? By program, such as equal employment? Other critical questions are: What will the actual amounts of allocation be? How will these decisions be made? What considerations will be brought to bear upon them? These are the chief concerns of the budgetary process, and it is easy to see from them that budgeting can be quite perplexing. Although we cannot provide all the answers in this chapter (indeed, no one can do so even in volumes), we can at least help the reader understand the theoretical and practical considerations that are pertinent to the formulation of budgets and the selection of various budgetary strategies or techniques. We will start by mapping out some general considerations and then proceed to a discussion of managerial, political, and legal approaches to budget making.

THE SIZE AND GROWTH OF BUDGETS

Governmental spending is an indicator of the extent of governmental intervention in the life of society. But like the administrative state generally, its scope is difficult to comprehend. How does one make a budget of some $1.5 trillion, as in the federal government, seem concrete? Some seek to do so by indicating that such a budget averages the spending of over $40,000 per second every second of the year. Others tell us the weight and length of this trillion-plus in $1 bills. Still others suggest that the best indicator of the size of the budget is the proportion of all spending in the society that is governmental. This latter measure generally looks at government expenditures as a percent of the gross domestic product (GDP), which can be defined as the monetary value of all goods and services produced in the nation in a given year. Today, the combined spending of all governments in the United States is about one-third of the GDP. (See Box 6–1.) In 1929, by contrast, it was only about 10 percent. The federal government's budget alone accounts for about 22 percent of the GDP. Its receipts are about one-fifth of the GDP. Such figures convey the fact that governments now raise and spend a great deal of money and that the scope of governmental activity has been increasing; but such huge amounts of money necessarily remain difficult to grasp.

Some greater clarity could be achieved by looking at how the money is spent. But here we run into a fundamental problem. Should we report on expenditures in terms of such things as the number of pencils, pens, and paper clips bought by governments? The miles of highway built? Or the broad categories of governmental activity, such as transportation? Shall we include "tax expenditures," which, as explained in Box 6–2, are governmental spending only in the sense that they are funds not collected in the first place because of special provisions in the tax code? It is evident that any number of categorizations of spending are possible, and this has been a subject of considerable controversy over the years. We will return to this problem later in the chapter. For now, however, it may prove helpful to mention the relative proportion of federal, state, and local budgetary expenditures that go to broad, general functions. Despite a good deal of overlap, governments in the United

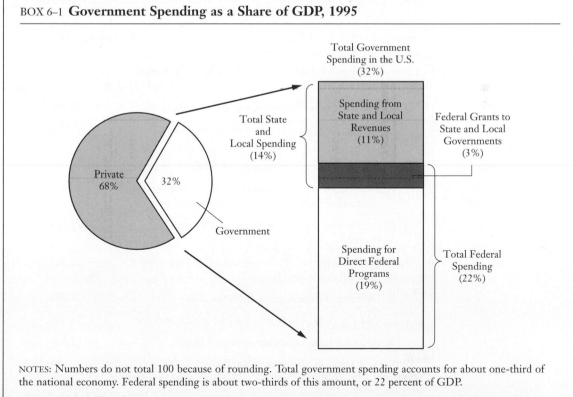

BOX 6–1 **Government Spending as a Share of GDP, 1995**

Total Government Spending in the U.S. (32%)

Total State and Local Spending (14%)

Private 68%

32%

Government

Spending from State and Local Revenues (11%)

Federal Grants to State and Local Governments (3%)

Spending for Direct Federal Programs (19%)

Total Federal Spending (22%)

NOTES: Numbers do not total 100 because of rounding. Total government spending accounts for about one-third of the national economy. Federal spending is about two-thirds of this amount, or 22 percent of GDP.

SOURCE: U.S. Office of Management and Budget, *A Citizen's Guide to the Federal Budget, Fiscal Year 1997* (Washington, D.C.: Government Printing Office, 1996), 2.

BOX 6–2 The Top Ten Tax Expenditures, 1998 Estimates

Tax expenditures are features of the individual and corporation income tax laws that provide special benefits or incentives in comparison with what would be permitted under the general provisions of the Internal Revenue Code. They arise from special exclusions, exemptions, or deductions from gross income or from special credits, preferential tax rates, or deferrals of tax liability.

Tax expenditures are so designated because they are one means by which the federal government carries out public policy objectives; in many cases they can be considered as alternatives to direct expenditures. For example, investment in capital equipment is encouraged by the investment tax credit;

a program of direct capital grants could also achieve this objective. Similarly, state and local governments benefit from both direct grants and the ability to borrow funds at tax-exempt rates.

Because tax expenditures can be viewed as alternatives to direct federal spending programs, it is desirable that estimates of tax expenditure items be comparable to outlay programs. Thus, tax expenditures are shown as outlay equivalents, that is, the amount of budget outlays required to provide the same level of after-tax benefits by substituting a direct spending program for the tax expenditure. The accompanying table displays estimates of tax expenditures classified by function.

Item	Amount (millions of dollars)
1. Employer contributions for medical insurance and care	78,815
2. Owner-occupied mortgage interest deduction	60,490
3. Exclusion of pension contributions—employer plans	59,950
4. Step-up basis of capital gains at death	30,710
5. Deductibility of nonbusiness state and local taxes other than owner-occupied homes	30,425
6. Accelerated depreciation, equipment and machinery	23,215
7. Deductibility of charitable contributions other than education and health	22,325
8. Deferral of capital gains on home sales	18,725
9. Old Age Survivors Insurance for retired workers	18,110
10. Property taxes on owner-occupied homes	17,515

SOURCE: U.S. Office of Management and Budget, *Budget of the United States Government, Fiscal Year 1996: Analytical Perspectives* (Washington, D.C.: Government Printing Office, 1995), 39–42.

States are somewhat specialized. The federal government allocates a large proportion of its budget to defense, income security, and health programs (Social Security and Medicare in particular); the states spend a higher proportion on highways and education; and local governments spend the greatest proportion of their funds on education and utilities.[1] If we looked at the outlay of funds in different terms, we would find that the proportion budgets allocated to the salaries of public employees is highest at the local level and lowest at the federal level, with the states falling somewhere in between. Box 6–3 presents a broad categorization of the proportion of federal revenues coming from different sources and expenditures going to different functions. Box 6–4 shows similar information for the states.

These figures and comparisons provide some idea of the size of governmental budgets in the United States, but they do not tell us about the causes of growth of governmental expenditure. In general, it is believed that governmental spending grows as a result of the same factors that give rise to the administrative state (see Chapter 2). As the society and economy become more complex, government intervenes in an effort to protect and promote the public interest. Antisocial behavior and harmful economic practices are regulated; governmental services are provided to enable individuals to contribute to continued economic development. Yet it is an inescapable fact that budgets tend to be wrapped up in electoral politics as well. Funds are sometimes allocated to help incumbents with reelection or, less commonly, to unseat them. For instance, so-called pork barrel projects are undertaken to bring funds, jobs, and capital improvements to a legislator's district.[2] It is also politically easier to allocate more funds rather than less to functions supported by powerful interest groups or important constituencies and voting blocs. As in the area of personnel, cutbacks and decline are painful, whereas growth can be used to resolve or smooth over conflicts. As we will see, it is especially for these political reasons that some politicians and analysts believed that the federal budget process had gotten out of control and that severe reforms are necessary if the political community is to cure its tendency toward deficit spending.

Sources of Revenues

Governments have to obtain the money they spend from somewhere. They cannot simply print as much as they want and expect it to retain its value. They can borrow funds from private parties, but unless loaning the government money is compulsory, competitive interest will have to be paid. Borrowing causes debt, which must eventually be repaid. The options of printing money and unlimited borrowing notwithstanding, funds must be generated through other means. Taxation ranks foremost among these. A wide variety of taxes has been developed over the years, though Americans are probably most familiar with three types.

Individual and Corporate Income Taxes   Taxes levied on the income individuals earn from wages, salaries, and some forms of investment are called

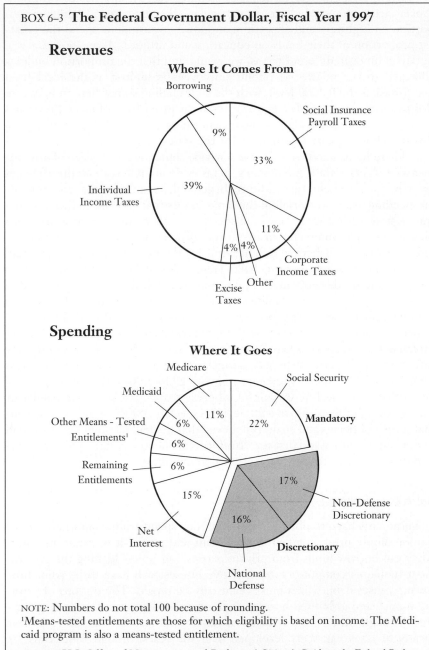

BOX 6–3 **The Federal Government Dollar, Fiscal Year 1997**

Revenues

Where It Comes From

- Borrowing 9%
- Social Insurance Payroll Taxes 33%
- Individual Income Taxes 39%
- Corporate Income Taxes 11%
- Excise Taxes 4%
- Other 4%

Spending

Where It Goes

- Medicare 11%
- Medicaid 6%
- Social Security 22% **Mandatory**
- Other Means - Tested Entitlements[1] 6%
- Remaining Entitlements 6%
- Net Interest 15%
- Non-Defense Discretionary 17%
- National Defense 16% **Discretionary**

NOTE: Numbers do not total 100 because of rounding.

[1]Means-tested entitlements are those for which eligibility is based on income. The Medicaid program is also a means-tested entitlement.

SOURCE: U.S. Office of Management and Budget, *A Citizen's Guide to the Federal Budget, Fiscal Year 1997* (Washington, D.C.: Government Printing Office, 1996), 7, 10.

BOX 6–4 **State Taxes and Expenditures**

PERCENT DISTRIBUTION OF STATE TAX COLLECTIONS
BY MAJOR TAX CATEGORY

Year	*Sales & Gross Receipts Taxes*	*Income Taxes*	*License Taxes*	*Other Taxes*
1980	49.4	36.8	6.3	7.5
1985	48.8	37.8	6.3	7.1
1990	49.0	39.2	6.3	5.5
1992	49.5	38.4	6.6	5.5

GENERAL EXPENDITURE OF STATE AND LOCAL GOVERNMENTS, 1992

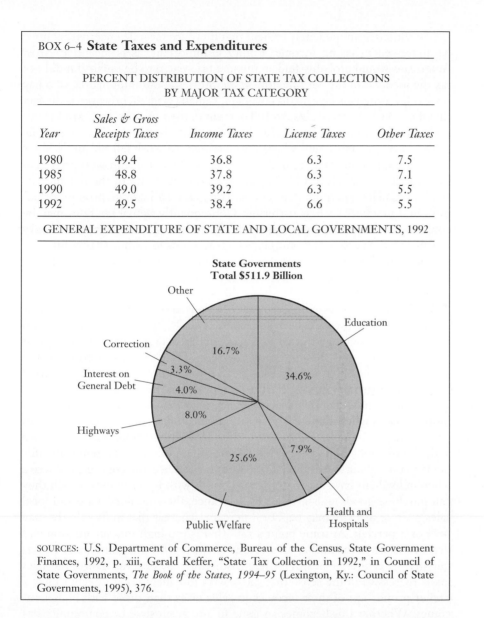

**State Governments
Total $511.9 Billion**

Other — 16.7%
Correction — 3.3%
Interest on General Debt — 4.0%
Highways — 8.0%
Public Welfare — 25.6%
Health and Hospitals — 7.9%
Education — 34.6%

SOURCES: U.S. Department of Commerce, Bureau of the Census, State Government Finances, 1992, p. xiii, Gerald Keffer, "State Tax Collection in 1992," in Council of State Governments, *The Book of the States, 1994–95* (Lexington, Ky.: Council of State Governments, 1995), 376.

income taxes. Such taxes can be progressive, that is, they tax people with greater incomes at a higher rate than those with lesser incomes. They may also be flat rate, taxing everyone at the same percentage of income regardless of the amount of income any given individual earns. For example, in a progressive system, someone making $100,000 per year might be taxed at 50 percent, whereas someone making $5,000 might be taxed at 5 percent. In a flat-rate system both would pay the same percentage, such as 20 percent. An income tax can also be regressive if it taxes people with lesser incomes at a higher rate than those with greater incomes.

It should be immediately evident that there are several concerns that must be addressed in taxing income. Equity is important, as is incentive. Most Americans would probably find an income tax system to be unfair if it did not tax the incomes of the very wealthy *at all.* Stories about millionaires who pay no taxes routinely receive media coverage. Equally evident, however, is the fact that if people were taxed close to 100 percent of their income, they would have no economic incentive to work. But between these extremes, what is equitable in the setting of rates, and where do incentives to work fall off intolerably? These are questions that are inherently debatable, but the answers arrived at by a society at any given time do set limits on the utility of the income tax. High rates place a premium on reducing one's *taxable* income through deductions and practices such as bartering. Consequently, actual tax rates may be considerably lower than nominal ones. The federal government places heavy reliance on the personal income tax, which accounts for about 39 percent of its revenues. It also levies a corporate income tax, accounting for about 11 percent of its revenues. Almost all the states also use income taxes.

Sales Taxes   Taxes levied on the sale of goods and services in states and/or local jurisdictions are called **sales taxes.** Currently, in states using them, sales tax rates typically range from 3 to 8 percent. Sales taxes can generate a great deal of revenue, and they are easy to collect. They are also flexible in the sense that the jurisdiction in question can exempt certain items, such as food purchased at grocery stores. Such exemptions can reflect the values of any given community. For instance, Connecticut has exempted clothing and footwear costing less than $50 from sales taxes. On the other hand, sales taxes have some potential drawbacks. First, they are highly visible, because they are added to the bill for almost everything one buys. This makes it politically difficult to raise their level. Second, the sales tax can become counterproductive when individuals have alternative jurisdictions with lower rates in which they can purchase goods and services. For instance, the combined state and local sales tax rate in a city may be 7 or 8 percent, whereas that in its suburbs may be 4 or 5 percent. At some point a rate that is too high in a jurisdiction will drive consumers to another area or out of the market altogether, and consequently the economic health of the jurisdiction may decline. Third, the sales tax is regressive in the sense that those with low incomes are likely to pay a higher proportion of their incomes in sales taxes than those with higher incomes. Whether this becomes an issue in any given state or community depends on the prevailing view of what equity requires.

Real Property Taxes   Taxes on real estate of various kinds are called **property taxes**—the mainstay of local governmental revenues. But, as in the case of sales taxes, there is considerable variation among local governments in the extent to which they rely on property taxes. In some states, such as those in New England, almost all local governmental revenues may come from property taxes. Elsewhere, it is typical for local governments to raise only about half or less of their revenues in this fashion (Alabama, Louisiana). Again, there may be competition among jurisdictions with regard to property tax rates. Where the rates in one city or town are high compared with neighboring jurisdictions, some people may locate in those jurisdictions to seek lower rates. This can lead to a stagnant or declining tax base in the place with higher rates and could eventually be a factor in a serious financial crisis. Of course, local jurisdictions with high property tax rates may provide better services, including education, public safety, and sanitation. Among the major problems with the property tax is the tendency for it to be inequitably administered over time. The tax assessments on similar dwellings may vary considerably, especially if one has been bought and sold more frequently during periods of high inflation. Sometimes, too, the property tax acts as a deterrent to improving one's house. The addition of rooms, porches, swimming pools, and so on, can lead to a higher tax assessment. It is also possible that when property values and tax assessments rise, families or individuals with stable incomes will find the increasing tax burden too great. Property taxes are also regressive, as richer people tend to spend a lower proportion of their wealth on housing than do poorer people. In addition, as the value of real property—such as farmland near urban and suburban areas—increases, so too may the tax on it, even though the incomes of those living on or farming the land remain relatively constant.

Additional Taxes and Sources of Revenue   There is also a variety of other sources of governmental revenues, including *excise taxes, motor fuel taxes, business taxes, inheritance taxes, capital gains taxes, license fees, user fees, lotteries, sale of utilities,* such as water or electricity, and the *operation of liquor stores.* Governments can also borrow money through the sale of bonds and other forms of loans. The sources of federal revenues are displayed in Box 6–3; those of local governments and states are in Box 6–4.

It is evident that in considering raising governmental revenues several general concerns must be taken into account. An inequitable taxing arrangement can promote a popular tax revolt, as was witnessed in California through Proposition 13 (1978), in Massachusetts through Proposition 2½ (1980), and elsewhere. Equity is related to political feasibility, which is another consideration. Some forms of taxation are simply too unpopular with the general public or with powerful constituencies to be applied or raised beyond certain levels. For example, it has been urged by some sober voices that the federal government should place a heavy tax on the sale of gasoline—perhaps as much as a dollar a gallon. This would raise the cost and presumably encourage conservation, as well as raise funds that could be used for the development of other energy sources and cheaper means of transportation. However, under normal conditions, the political feasibility of such a high tax is low.

The administrative feasibility of different forms of taxation must also be considered. Can a particular tax be administered, or will it be evaded on a widespread basis? For instance, property taxes that base assessments on aspects of the interiors of houses may be difficult to apply. To do so, assessors would have to gain entrance to dwellings and be able to snoop around in them. Aside from questions of individual privacy and taxpayer resentment of administrative intrusion, such a system could take a great deal of time to administer on an equitable basis. It would be much easier to base assessments on the exteriors of houses, their last sales price, or their assumed market value. Similarly, in societies where cash registers are not generally used, applying the sales tax can be difficult. Income taxes can be problematical in some service areas of the economy, where payment of fees in cash may be the norm. Taxing tips has been a long-standing problem. Administrative feasibility is also concerned with the efficiency with which revenues can be raised. For instance, it is generally more efficient to collect taxes through withholding than by billing individuals once or twice a year. One of the arguments in favor of a flat income tax is that it is simple to file and inexpensive to administer.

Governments must also consider the elasticity of a means of raising revenue. As previously noted, some forms of taxation can be counterproductive; that is, raising the tax or user fee may actually provide less revenue, because it will encourage individuals to move from one jurisdiction to another, shop elsewhere, or avoid publicly provided services such as transportation that are considered too costly. Eventually, of course, all tax and revenue-raising devices can reach their limits of efficacy by draining too much from the private sector and reducing private initiative to work. Although we are sometimes accustomed to believe that governments can raise as much money as they want, in truth there are substantial limitations on the ability of the public sector to finance itself. These limits must be taken into account in developing governmental budgets if political and economic crises are to be avoided. This brings us to a consideration of some fundamental concerns involved in public sector budgeting.

Countercyclical Governmental Fiscal Policy

For the most part, state and local governments cannot run substantial budgetary deficits for any length of time. Many are constitutionally or legally required to have balanced operating budgets. They can fund developmental projects through capital budgets, which do permit long-term debt. But they do not typically treat these budgets as a tool for encouraging or discouraging short-term economic growth. By contrast, however, at times the federal government has planned for deficits as a means of managing the nation's economy. This is another development that coincides with the expansion of the contemporary administrative state. Prior to the 1930s, the balanced budget was sacrosanct. A federal budget that *planned* to spend more than it anticipated in revenues would have been taken as a sign that the government was profligate and out of control. The government's credit, or at least so it was thought, would falter and an economic panic might ensue. Such deficits as did occur were unplanned. By the mid-1930s, however, another approach began to emerge. This is commonly called the **Keynesian approach** after the British economist who developed it, Lord John Maynard Keynes.[3] In its simplest form, Keynesian economics hold that once the government's role in the economic life of a capitalist society becomes substantial, government spending can be used to counteract the normal boom-and-bust tendencies of the business cycle. In other words, if governmental spending is a considerable proportion of a nation's GDP, then government should have substantial leverage over the business cycle fluctuations in that nation. Deficit spending—that is, spending more than is raised in revenues—can be used to stimulate the economy out of recession or depression. A government surplus—that is, raising more revenues than are to be spent—can be used as a means of regulating economic growth and limiting inflation.

To the extent that a government subscribes to the Keynesian approach, it is evident that budgeting has great ramifications for the economy. It is no longer simply a consideration of deciding what kinds of activities government should engage in, what they will cost, and how revenues may be raised to finance them. Rather, the budgetary process must also take into account the government's role in trying to keep the economy on an even keel. This being the case, governmental spending and revenue raising must be related to the economy generally as opposed to the funding of governmental programs alone. In the United States, this role for government was placed on a legal footing by the Employment Act of 1946, which created a policy that the federal government should promote full employment to the extent "practicable" in the society. This statute is often considered a landmark in the political and economic development of the United States because it signified the weakening of an ideology of laissez-faire capitalism and called for governmental intervention in the economy.

Despite the Employment Act, however, Keynesian economics remains in dispute. The main problem may be less in the theory itself than in practice; it is difficult to apply. First, it is hard to analyze the economy and coordinate the analysis with a lengthy budget-making process. It now takes eighteen months or longer to formulate a federal budget for one year. The fiscal assumptions upon which a budget is built may fail to match a fast-changing economy. Second, the politics of the budgetary process make it difficult to generate surpluses—required by the Keynesian countercyclical approach when needed to curtail economic growth. The electoral interests of members of Congress often dictate federal spending on projects in their districts in election years and it is particularly painful for many legislators to have to campaign in a district with high levels of unemployment.[4] But the absence of political discipline can be costly. Deficit spending tends to be inflationary, which can create pressures for interest rates to rise. Higher rates, in turn, dampen borrowing for business investments and can slow down economic growth. Slower growth is likely to have a negative impact on the government's ability to raise revenues through income taxes. Consequently, in such a scenario, reducing the deficit or balancing the budget becomes even more difficult. Countercyclical fiscal policy requires delicate economic balancing that has often been upset by the real world of electoral politics.

Largely as a result of these difficulties, the Keynesian approach in the United States has laid the groundwork for the development of huge budgetary deficits. Box 6–5 presents a history of federal surpluses and deficits since 1940. It shows that deficits increased sharply in the 1980s, but that by the mid-1990s they were beginning to decline and were projected to be eliminated sometime after the year 2000. There have been deficit budgets in all but eight years since 1931. The federal debt now stands at about $5 trillion. Economists and political scientists are uncertain of the impact of a national debt of this size.[5] It amounts to over 50 percent of the annual GDP and costs the government about $195 billion a year in net interest payments. About 70 percent of this sum is owed to the public, the rest is money the government owes its own trust funds. The debt is also related to interest rates, which affect the value of the dollar against other currencies and international trade. Still, from a comparative perspective it may not be as burdensome or damaging as the national debts of some other countries. For instance, in 1989, Italy's national debt was a whopping 99.2 percent of its gross national product (a measure that is similar to GDP).[6]

Whatever the actual problems posed by deficit spending and the national debt, however, many believe that the government should be required to balance the budget on an annual basis. To the extent that the business cycle re-

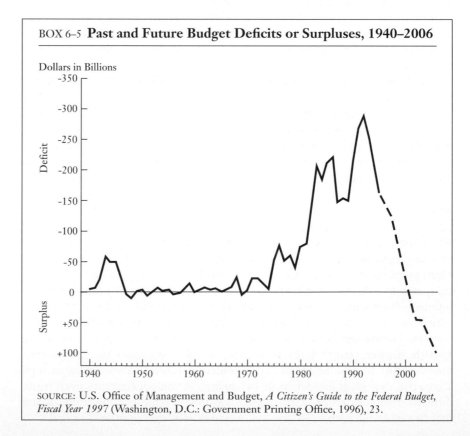

BOX 6–5 **Past and Future Budget Deficits or Surpluses, 1940–2006**

SOURCE: U.S. Office of Management and Budget, *A Citizen's Guide to the Federal Budget, Fiscal Year 1997* (Washington, D.C.: Government Printing Office, 1996), 23.

quires regulation, they argue that other tools, such as adjusting interest rates, should be used. In fact, some members of Congress introduced a constitutional amendment for this purpose. The Republicans' 1994 "Contract with America" called for such an amendment, but it was never approved by Congress. Nevertheless, the **balanced budget amendment** represents a real concern over whether governmental spending is simply out of control. The deficit problem has been a focal point of much political concern to the federal government.

Supply-Side Economics

The election of Ronald Reagan to the presidency in 1980 brought controversial **supply-side economics** to the federal government. This approach argues for a reduced government role in the economy—less regulation, lower taxes, and limited, if any, countercyclical spending. The basic concept is that governmental intervention in the economy is less efficient than free-market competition in allocating goods and services, directing investments, and generating economic growth. High taxation, in particular, is viewed as unhealthy because it removes money from the private sector, which supply-siders view as the productive sector, and places it in the hands of government, which allegedly uses it in an economically unproductive fashion. In this view, private investment in a new brewery is inherently more economically productive than government investment in a collective good, such as a public university system.

In economic terms, the supply-side approach either failed or was not adequately tested, depending on one's point of view. Beyond a doubt, the Reagan administration ran up the largest federal deficits in the nation's history. The federal debt more than doubled during the Reagan years, as government spending continued to grow. Unemployment reached a low of 5.4 percent (as compared with 5.5 percent under President Carter), and inflation was kept at low levels. But the economy grew at a rate of 2.6 percent, the same as it had during the last half of the 1970s. In summing up supply-siders' general disappointment, William Niskanen, a former member of the Council of Economic Advisers under Reagan, said, "We have a bigger government, with higher spending. We've slowed regulation down, but we haven't reversed it. In other words, there was no Reagan revolution."[7]

One should also remember that growth in the GDP is not synonymous with a rise in the quality of life. As an indicator, the GDP measures antisocial as well as prosocial economic activity. For instance, as auto theft and household burglaries increase, so does expenditure on insurance and antitheft devices—which contributes to growth in the GDP.

The supply-side movement has mobilized political pressure to prevent or reduce growth in the size of the government and governmental work forces. Governmental programs involving regulation and redistribution are particularly under attack. In fact, some believe that the supply-side mentality threatens to "dismantle" America.[8] (One might look at the savings and loan debacle in this context). In addition, many local governments are exploring the economics and politics of "privatizing" services such as sanitation (garbage collection), prison construction and administration, and even fire protection. Whether private companies will be able to supply such services efficiently, equitably, and satisfactorily in the long run remains unclear. However, public administrators at all levels of government are now paying much greater attention to the possibilities of privatization. In fact, although no one appears to know the exact figure, it is often alleged that at least one-third of the work of federal agencies is now contracted out to private research and policy analysis firms. Although not imbued with supply-side economics, "New Democrats" such as Clinton and Gore, are also committed to balancing budgets and reducing governmental growth. The National Performance Review (NPR) has been the administration's leader in this effort.

THE FEDERAL BUDGETARY PROCESS

The development of the contemporary federal budgetary process has its roots back in 1921 when the Bureau of the Budget was created as a unit within the Treasury Department. Prior to that time, the budget was a somewhat haphazard and largely congressional function. There was little coordination in the process, and no rigorous effort was made to connect revenues to expenditures in the budget itself. In 1939, as part of the development of the modern presidency, the Bureau of the Budget was placed in the newly created Executive Office of the President. This reorganization solidified the president's roles as administrator in chief and manager of the economy through countercyclical fiscal policy. It also emphasized the president's responsibility for developing a comprehensive budget for transmittal to Congress. In 1970, the Bureau of the Budget's functions were expanded to include greater responsibility for the way federal agencies were managed, and it was accordingly renamed the Office of Management and Budget (OMB). Throughout this time, the federal government has adhered to an annual budget. However, in 1974 it was decided to begin the fiscal year on October 1, rather than July 1. (The fiscal year [FY] is numbered according to the year in which it ends, i.e., FY 1998 ends on September 30, 1998.) In 1974, Congress created the Congressional Budget Office (CBO) to provide it with an independent source of information about the economy and the assumptions involved in the president's budgetary proposal. In a sense, the CBO was intended to balance the influence of OMB. This demonstrated the tendency to try to control one agency with another, giving testimony to the continuing relevance of the separation of powers and the application of checks and balances.

One of the problems with the budget process after the 1974 reforms was the development of "multiple budgets."[9] The president had one, but so did Congress. Disagreement between the two sometimes led to the failure to enact a budget by the beginning of the fiscal year. Instead, "continuing resolutions" (or CRs) were passed to maintain government funding. In FY 1996, failure to enact a budget or CRs led to two partial government shutdowns. Supplemental appropriations, future obligations, and projected expenditures are also practices that threaten the concept of a unified annual budget.

The hallmark of the federal budgetary process is complexity. (Box 6–6 presents a glossary of budgetary terms.) There are several things going on at once. The budget for one year is being executed; the budget for the next may be under legislative consideration; the budget for the year after the one being considered by Congress is simultaneously being developed in the executive branch; and, in many instances, agencies are engaged in a consideration of the likely costs of their programs five years into the future. But these activities only begin to tap the surface of the budgetary activity that is going on. The Council of Economic Advisers, some officials in OMB, some of the president's aides on fiscal policy, and parts of the Treasury and Labor Departments are trying to develop information and projections that will accurately describe the performance of the economy during the fiscal year for which the budget is being developed. This is necessary if revenues are to be estimated accurately and spending is to be matched to them, as the current emphasis on balancing the budget requires. At the same time, the CBO may be evaluating the economic assumptions developed in the executive branch for the budget two years hence and also evaluating aspects of the budget proposal for the next fiscal year.

As a result of concern with the federal debt, the budgetary process has undergone change so frequently in recent years that describing it is like trying to hit a rapidly zig-zagging target. The current approach, which is framed by the Budget Enforcement Act of 1990, contains a host of technical provisions, complex procedures, and deadlines for enacting the budget. But some of the deadlines are almost certain to be missed on occasion, and the procedures and techniques underlying budgetary calculations are subject to change. The entire system broke down in 1995, when Congress and the president could not agree on a complete budget until April 1996—about halfway through the fiscal year. Consequently, it is probably best to outline the budgetary process in broad, general, and conceptual terms.

Stages in the Budgetary Process

The federal budgetary process can be divided into five stages, which more or less match state approaches as well: (1) formulation of individual agencies' budgets; (2) preparation of the executive budget by the central budget agency (OMB), in consultation with the president and/or his advisers; (3) presentation of the budget to the legislature by the chief executive; (4) legislative action on the proposed budget and enactment of legislation appropriating funds; (5) execution of the budget by the executive branch. There is much about these stages that is highly technical, but they can be

BOX 6–6 **Glossary of Budgetary Terms**

AUTHORIZING LEGISLATION—Legislation enacted by the Congress to set up or continue the operation of a Federal program or agency. Authorizing legislation is normally a prerequisite for subsequent appropriations, but does not usually provide budget authority (see below).

BUDGET—A plan of proposed receipts and spending for the coming fiscal year.

BUDGET AUTHORITY (BA)—Authority provided by law to enter into obligations that will result in immediate or future outlays. It may be classified by the period of availability, by the timing of congressional action, or by the manner of determining the amount available. The basic forms of budget authority are:

Appropriations—Authority that permits Federal agencies to incur obligations and to make payments.

Authority to borrow—Authority that permits Federal agencies to incur obligations and to borrow money to make payments.

Contract authority—Authority that permits Federal agencies to enter into contracts or incur other obligations in advance of an appropriation.

BUDGET RECEIPTS—Income, net of refunds, collected from the public by the Federal Government through the exercise of its governmental or sovereign powers. Budget receipts also include gifts and contributions. Excluded are amounts received from business-type transactions (such as sales, interest, or loan repayments) and payments between Government accounts. (See offsetting receipts.)

BUDGET SURPLUS OR DEFICIT—Differences between budget receipts and outlays.

CONCURRENT RESOLUTION ON THE BUDGET—A resolution passed by both Houses of Congress, but not requiring the signature of the president, setting outlay and receipt targets for the Congress.

CONTINUING RESOLUTION—Legislation enacted by the Congress to provide budget authority for specific ongoing activities when a regular appropriation for those activities has not been enacted by the beginning of the fiscal year.

CREDIT BUDGET—A plan of proposed direct loan obligations and guaranteed loan commitments. Budget authority and outlays associated with the credit budget are included in the budget totals.

CROSSWALK—Transforming the spending limits in the twenty-one functional categories of the Concurrent Budget Resolution into spending ceilings for individual congressional committees.

CURRENT SERVICES ESTIMATES—Estimates of receipts, outlays and budget authority for coming fiscal years that assume no policy changes from the year in progress. The estimates include the effects of anticipated changes in economic conditions (such as unemployment or inflation), beneficiary levels, pay increases, and changes required under existing law.

DEFERRAL—Executive branch action that temporarily delays the obligation of budget authority. Deferrals may be overturned at any time by an act of the Congress.

FEDERAL FUNDS—Amounts collected and used by the Federal Government for the general purposes of the Government. There are four types

BOX 6–6 *Continued*

of Federal fund accounts: the general fund, special funds, public enterprise revolving funds, and intra governmental funds. The major Federal fund is the general fund, which is derived from general taxes and borrowing. The other forms of Federal funds involve earmarked collections, such as those generated by and used to finance a continuing cycle of business-type operations.

FISCAL YEAR—The Federal Government's yearly accounting period, which begins on October 1 and ends on the following September 30. The fiscal year is designated by the calendar year in which it ends; e.g., fiscal year 1986 begins on October 1, 1985, and ends on September 30, 1986. (From 1844 to 1976 the fiscal year began on July 1 and ended on the following June 30.)

IMPOUNDMENT—Any action or inaction by an officer or employee of the Federal Government that precludes the obligation or expenditure of budget authority provided by the Congress (see deferral and rescission).

OBLIGATIONS—Amounts of orders placed, contracts awarded, services received, or similar legally binding commitments made by Federal agencies during a given period that will require outlays during the same or some future period.

OFF-BUDGET FEDERAL ENTITIES—Federal entities or programs that are excluded from the budget under current law. Social Security has been a major off-budget program.

OFFSETTING RECEIPTS—Collections deposited in receipt accounts that are offset against budget authority and outlays rather than being counted as budget receipts. These collections are derived from Government accounts (intragovernmental transactions) or from the public (proprietary receipts) through activities that are of a business-type or market-oriented nature.

OUTLAYS—Payments, normally in the form of checks issued or cash disbursed, net of refunds, reimbursements, and offsetting collections. Outlays include interest accrued on the public debt.

RECONCILIATION—A reconciliation directive is a provision in the concurrent resolution on the budget that calls on various committees of the Congress to recommend legislative changes that reduce outlays or increase receipts by specified amounts. A reconciliation bill contains these changes.

RESCISSION—A legislative action canceling budget authority previously provided by the Congress.

SEQUESTRATION—The Gramm-Rudman process of requiring specific automatic spending cuts if Congress and the president exceed the act's maximum deficit amounts.

SUPPLEMENTAL APPROPRIATION—An appropriation enacted subsequent to a regular annual appropriation act. Supplemental appropriation acts provide additional budget authority for programs or activities (including new programs authorized after the date of the original appropriation act) for which the need for funds is too urgent to be postponed until the next regular appropriation.

TAX EXPENDITURES—Provisions of the Federal income tax laws that allow a special exclusion, exemption, or deduction from gross income or provide a special credit, preferential rate

---

BOX 6–6 *Continued*

---

of tax, or deferral of tax liability. Tax expenditures frequently have results similar to spending programs, loan guarantees, or regulations.

TRUST FUNDS—Amounts collected and used by the Federal Government for carrying out specific purposes and programs according to a statute or trust agreement and speci-

fied by law as being trust fund money, such as the social security and unemployment trust funds. Trust funds are not available for the general purposes of the Government. Trust fund receipts that are not needed immediately are generally invested in Government securities and earn interest for the trust fund.

SOURCES: Office of Management and Budget, *United States Budget in Brief, Fiscal Year 1986* (Washington, D.C.: Office of Management and Budget, 1985), 80–81; and Stanley Collender, *The Guide to the Federal Budget: Fiscal 1988* (Washington, D.C.: Urban Institute Press, 1987), 164 (for "sequestration").

---

described in broad terms as follows. Box 6–7 diagrams much of the federal budget process.

Agency Budgets   In July of each year, the OMB calls upon the agencies to submit their budget proposals by September. In practice, agencies may begin preparing their budgets much earlier. Those responsible for formulating each agency's budget requests typically ask bureau chiefs and other agency officials to supply dollar figures and the policy and administrative assumptions behind them. For instance, a bureau chief may assume that a large increase in funding will be necessary if the size of its clientele, such as senior citizens, veterans, or individuals who are HIV positive, is rapidly growing. The agency's budget office analyzes and coordinates these responses in formulating a tentative budget in response to OMB's directives. The budget should reflect the OMB's instructions and policy guidelines, which reflect the president's assumptions as to priorities within the spending caps established by the Budget Enforcement Act or other legislation.

Preparing the Executive Budget   After receiving the agencies' initial budget proposals, the OMB thoroughly analyzes them. Generally, the OMB seeks to cut spending requests, but it can also recommend increases. In the process, the OMB holds hearings with the agencies' budget officers. It may ask them to defend their policy assumptions and to submit additional information. The OMB submits a tentative executive budget to the president and then finalizes it in accordance with his recommendations. The director of OMB, who is usually viewed as the president's chief budget officer, generally wields great influence in the formulation of the final executive budget proposal. During the process of formulating the budget, the director and other OMB adminis-

BOX 6–7 **Enacting the Federal Budget**

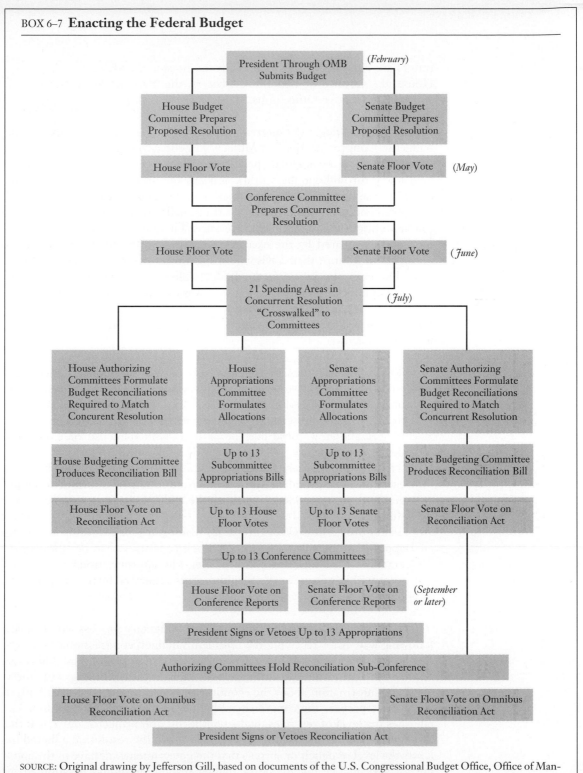

President Through OMB Submits Budget *(February)*

House Budget Committee Prepares Proposed Resolution

Senate Budget Committee Prepares Proposed Resolution

House Floor Vote

Senate Floor Vote *(May)*

Conference Committee Prepares Concurrent Resolution

House Floor Vote

Senate Floor Vote *(June)*

21 Spending Areas in Concurrent Resolution "Crosswalked" to Committees *(July)*

House Authorizing Committees Formulate Budget Reconciliations Required to Match Concurrent Resolution

House Appropriations Committee Formulates Allocations

Senate Appropriations Committee Formulates Allocations

Senate Authorizing Committees Formulate Budget Reconciliations Required to Match Concurrent Resolution

House Budgeting Committee Produces Reconciliation Bill

Up to 13 Subcommittee Appropriations Bills

Up to 13 Subcommittee Appropriations Bills

Senate Budgeting Committee Produces Reconciliation Bill

House Floor Vote on Reconciliation Act

Up to 13 House Floor Votes

Up to 13 Senate Floor Votes

Senate Floor Vote on Reconciliation Act

Up to 13 Conference Committees

House Floor Vote on Conference Reports

Senate Floor Vote on Conference Reports *(September or later)*

President Signs or Vetoes Up to 13 Appropriations

Authorizing Committees Hold Reconciliation Sub-Conference

House Floor Vote on Omnibus Reconciliation Act

Senate Floor Vote on Omnibus Reconciliation Act

President Signs or Vetoes Reconciliation Act

SOURCE: Original drawing by Jefferson Gill, based on documents of the U.S. Congressional Budget Office, Office of Management and Budget, and Congress.

trators are likely to be in contact with the president's advisers at the White House, the Council of Economic Advisers, the National Security Council, and other Executive Office units.

Presenting the Budget to Congress   The president is required to present the budget to Congress by the first Monday in February. Because the budget is a statement of governmental priorities, affects everyone in the nation (and many throughout the world), and has important implications for the economy, the budget message is sometimes a major political event. It should be remembered, though, that constitutionally speaking, only Congress can appropriate money from the Treasury. Therefore, despite its influence, the budget prepared by the executive and transmitted to the legislature is really nothing more than advisory—it has no legal force or standing of its own. For example, in 1995, the budget Clinton presented to the newly elected Republican-dominated Congress was clearly dead on arrival.

Congressional Action   The budgetary process in Congress involves three main sets of actors:

- The *CBO* examines the assumptions of the president's budget and works out alternative projections of revenues and expenditures. It also provides an analysis of the budget's likely impact on the economy. It may engage in a discussion of the priorities inherent in the president's budget and how these may be at odds with its sense of Congress's desires.
- The *House and Senate Committees on the Budget* work with the CBO in examining the president's proposal. These committees formulate a budget resolution intended to establish the budget's maximum spending authority.
- The *Appropriations Committees in the House and Senate* develop and bring appropriations bills to the floor of each legislative chamber for consideration by the legislature as a whole. The appropriations committees work within a framework of requirements generated by the budget committees.

In its broadest terms, the congressional budgetary process works in the following way. After receiving the president's budget, congressional committees develop spending and revenue plans for the coming fiscal year. These are transmitted to the budget committee in each house. Working with these plans and information about the economy provided by the CBO, the budget committees prepare the congressional budget resolution. The resolution establishes the level of revenues, budget authority, and projected outlays. If the assumptions behind the resolution are correct and the resolution adhered to, it sets the level of deficit or surplus that the government will have in the coming fiscal year. The congressional budget resolution should be adopted by Congress by April 15, but it is usually later.

After the resolution establishes the parameters of the budget, the appropriations committees work with the various congressional committees in formulating the thirteen annual appropriations bills. In practice, the House Appropriations Committee takes the leading role in this aspect of the process. However, because both houses must pass identical appropriations bills, activity in the Senate is equally important. In June, the House Appropriations Committee should report its version of the spending bills to the whole House, which is supposed to pass final versions by the end of the month. All appropriations legislation should be passed by both houses by October 1. Box 6–8 estimates the fruits of all these efforts—outlays by agencies.

The Continuing Saga of the Budget: Execution

As lengthy and complex as adopting the federal budget may be, its enactment is only the beginning. It must also be executed. Execution is the aspect of budgeting that most affects the performance of government and the economy, and in that sense it is the most critical phase of the budget process. Yet execution is subject to all kinds of pitfalls. First, suppose that for one reason or another the budget's projection of revenues falls short. Perhaps the economy has performed worse than anticipated and consequently revenues from income taxes have fallen off because of higher than anticipated unemployment and slower than anticipated growth in personal and corporate income. Consequently, if the government spends at the levels authorized by the budget, it may run a deficit that is considered too large and/or too inflationary. Under such circumstances, a number of steps are possible.

Sequesters   If either the budget authority or outlay caps are breached, discretionary funds may be sequestered to bring spending into line with the caps. Sequesters are imposed by the OMB, except in the case of supplemental appropriations passed by Congress after June 30. In that case, the cap in the program category for the coming fiscal year is reduced by the amount appropriated over the cap for the current fiscal year.

Whereas discretionary spending requires that Congress enact a law, mandatory spending will occur unless Congress does so. Mandatory spending is considered "uncontrollable" because it represents the financial impact of programs and commitments already established. For instance, "entitlements," such as payments under Medicare or to veterans, are available to all eligible individuals who apply. As the number of such individuals increases, or if the payments are linked to inflation, the costs of entitlements will increase. Permanent appropriations to pay interest on the national debt are another example of mandatory, or uncontrollable, spending. Such spending is also subject to sequesters, but under a different process.

The Budget Enforcement Act introduced the concept of "pay-as-you-go" (PAYGO). This requires that mandatory spending and taxation legislation not increase the deficit. Conceptually, the idea is that increases in some mandatory spending must be offset by decreases in other spending or by tax

BOX 6–8 **Projected Federal Outlays by Agency (in billions of dollars)**

Agency	1994 Actual	Estimate					
		1995	1996	1997	1998	1999	2000
Legislative Branch	2.6	2.8	3.0	3.0	3.0	3.0	3.1
The Judiciary	2.7	3.1	3.3	3.4	3.4	3.5	3.6
Executive Office of the President	0.2	0.2	0.2	0.2	0.2	0.2	0.2
Funds Appropriated to the President	10.5	10.9	10.8	10.8	10.7	10.7	11.1
Agriculture	60.8	62.3	62.3	62.7	61.3	62.5	63.4
Commerce	2.9	3.6	4.1	4.4	4.6	4.7	7.1
Defense—Military	268.6	260.3	250.0	246.1	244.2	249.6	257.9
Defense—Civil	30.4	31.2	31.9	32.6	33.6	35.4	36.3
Education	24.7	32.9	30.7	29.3	28.5	28.6	28.4
Energy	17.8	16.1	15.8	15.5	14.5	14.2	13.9
Health and Human Services	278.9	301.4	331.4	357.5	384.6	412.4	444.2
Housing and Urban Development	25.8	26.9	26.3	29.6	30.1	30.6	29.3
Interior	6.9	7.3	7.3	7.2	7.1	6.9	6.7
Justice	10.0	11.8	13.5	15.5	16.7	17.5	18.3
Labor	37.0	31.9	35.9	37.5	37.8	38.3	39.1
State	5.7	6.3	5.5	5.5	5.4	5.3	5.2
Transportation	37.2	38.0	37.3	36.8	36.5	36.6	35.5
Treasury	307.6	351.8	386.1	406.1	425.5	447.0	466.5
Veterans Affairs	37.4	38.2	38.0	39.5	39.7	39.8	41.6
Environmental Protection Agency	5.9	6.3	6.6	7.0	7.2	7.1	6.9
General Services Administration	0.3	1.1	0.6	0.6	0.7	0.8	0.7
National Aeronautics and Space Administration	13.7	14.2	14.1	14.0	13.7	13.5	13.3
Office of Personnel Management	38.6	40.3	42.8	44.8	47.5	50.0	52.2
Small Business Administration	0.8	0.7	0.4	0.5	0.1	0.2	0.5
Social Security Administration	345.8	363.4	381.7	404.6	426.5	449.1	475.2
On-budget	(31.9)	(32.1)	(32.4)	(38.7)	(41.5)	(44.4)	(50.3)
Off-budget	(313.9)	(331.3)	(349.4)	(365.9)	(384.9)	(404.7)	(424.9)
Other independent agencies	11.5	8.6	14.3	18.2	17.5	13.5	10.6
On-budget	(10.4)	(7.9)	(13.7)	(17.8)	(18.0)	(14.5)	(12.0)
Off-budget	(1.1)	(0.7)	(0.6)	(0.4)	(−0.4)	(−1.0)	(−1.4)

BOX 6–8 *Continued*

Agency	1994 Actual	Estimate					
		1995	1996	1997	1998	1999	2000
Allowances	—	—	−0.4	−0.5	−0.8	−0.9	−1.0
Undistributed offsetting receipts	−123.5	−132.9	−141.5	−147.8	−154.7	−157.9	−164.3
On-budget	(−87.9)	(−92.8)	(−96.6)	(−98.1)	(−99.8)	(−97.3)	(−97.5)
Off-budget	(−35.6)	(−40.0)	(−45.0)	(−49.7)	(−54.9)	(−60.6)	(−66.8)
Total	**1,460.9**	**1,538.9**	**1,612.1**	**1,684.7**	**1,745.2**	**1,822.2**	**1,905.3**
On-budget	(1,181.5)	(1,246.9)	(1,307.1)	(1,368.1)	(1,415.6)	(1,479.1)	(1,548.6)
Off-budget	(279.4)	(292.0)	(305.0)	(316.6)	(329.6)	(343.1)	(356.7)

SOURCE: U.S. Office of Management and Budget, *The Budget for Fiscal Year 1996* (Washington, D.C.: Government Printing Office, 1996), 216.

increases. Tax cuts would have to be offset by spending cuts. Each program does not have to satisfy PAYGO, but the total must or a sequester will be imposed. For instance, the massive personnel cuts called for by the NPR in 1993 were considered an offset for the cost of new anticrime legislation. Even if sequestration is unnecessary, the president may want to reduce or revise spending during the current fiscal year through a variety of techniques.

Hiring Freezes   The president can refuse to allow vacant federal positions to be filled through **hiring freezes.** This probably does not amount to much of a savings relative to the entire budget. However, it is a symbolic act that may be politically desirable. It is also true that agencies may not be able to spend the funds appropriated to them if their programs are drastically understaffed.

Impoundments   An **impoundment** occurs when the president refuses to allow an executive agency to spend the funds that have been allotted to it. Impoundments can take two forms. **Rescissions** are terminations of funds for an agency or program. **Deferrals** are delays in the spending of appropriated funds. They can be undertaken for policy or administrative reasons. If Congress does not vote to rescind the funds within forty-five days (of continuous legislative session, rather than calendar), the president is obligated to release the funds. The constitutionality of impoundments has long been in doubt. The first impoundment occurred during Thomas Jefferson's presidency, but the exercise of impoundments seems not to have reached crisis proportions until recent times. In the early 1970s, President Nixon impounded some $12 billion earmarked for highway, health, education, and environmental projects. This provoked a number of lawsuits, most of which were lost by the president. It also encouraged the 1974 Budget and Impoundment Control Act. Under this legislation, the president was authorized to impound funds, but subject to congressional approval. However, the provision for deferrals relied on a type of "one-house veto" that was declared unconstitutional in *Immigration and Naturalization Service v. Chadha* (1983).[10] Subsequently, several members of Congress and some cities brought suit against deferrals on the basis that Congress would not have granted deferral authority to the president had it known that it would not be able to exercise a legislative veto over his actions.[11] Under current legal interpretation, deferrals cannot be made for policy reasons, but only for efficiency, savings, dealing with contingencies, or other reasons specified by statute.

As a result of this litigation, the president's executive power under Article II of the Constitution cannot be said to include impoundments. Legislation passed in 1996 granting the president a "line-item veto" may enhance the president's ability to cut spending up front, rather than later on through impoundments. However, it also threatens constitutional integrity by shifting much of a legislative function—budget making—to the executive and by providing for congressional overrides of presidential item vetos. Even if constitutional, however, the line-item veto's efficacy in reducing spending remains uncertain. Over forty state governors have some form of such a veto power. Experience is mixed, and because the states are required to plan for balanced budgets, perhaps not very instructive. In some cases, certainly, governors are able to threaten a line-item veto of a legislator's pet program as part of the bargaining that normally goes on in politics.

A second set of problems associated with the execution of budgets occurs at the agency level. Agencies need flexibility in administering their programs. They need to be able to respond to changes in the environments of their programs, to new demand levels, and to unexpected success in accomplishing their purposes. After all, one of the chief reasons for the creation of administrative authority is to enable government to react more rapidly and flexibly than is generally plausible through coordinated congressional and presidential action. So what happens when an agency has funds earmarked for one program that it feels should be spent elsewhere in view of new circumstances? Remember, the agency may have formulated its initial budget request two or more years earlier. Two devices are commonly used to shift funds around within agencies. One is called **transfers.** Money can be transferred from one purpose to another if Congress has authorized this process in advance. Transfers are particularly common in the field of foreign affairs, where depending on regime changes abroad, government agencies may want to spend more or less on aid and military assistance. Closely akin to the transfer is **reprogramming.** Under this process an agency is not authorized in advance to switch funds from one program to another but rather must consult first with the relevant committees in Congress to obtain permission to do so. Despite all the attention paid to funding agencies at the stage of formulating the budget, relatively little is paid to these devices, which can result in the movement of billions of dollars from one purpose to another.

One additional process at the agency level bears mention. It is commonly assumed that if an agency fails to spend its entire appropriation it must return the leftover portion to the Treasury. However, some agencies are authorized to retain the money and apply it to next year's budget. Again, the sums accumulated in the "pipeline" of "no year" money can be substantial, reaching several hundred million dollars for the government as a whole.

When one puts all these elements together, it is evident that the budget as enacted may be at some variance from the budget as executed. Very substantial sums can be involved in supplemental appropriations, deferrals, rescissions, transfers, reprogramming, and in the "pipeline." These procedures are often used to promote political ends, as apart from administrative economies. They open the prospect for continuing controversy over funding even after appropriations have been authorized. But this is only one of several problems associated with the federal budgetary process.

Constant Problem Areas

Among the major problems with the federal budget process that we have not yet emphasized are the following.

The Length of the Budget Cycle   The entire budget cycle from its start in agencies to the finish of the fiscal year takes about thirty months. This has several problematic consequences. It often means that the assumptions about the economy and the needs of any given program that were present at the start of the cycle are inappropriate later on. This is one reason that flexibility in execution is so desirable. The interdependence of the United States and foreign economies, the rapidly changing character of international relations, and even the unpredictability of the weather's impact on agriculture and energy consumption all make even one-year predictions somewhat unreliable.

The length of the budget cycle has an impact on presidential transitions. A newly elected president, who may have run against the incumbent, spends January 20 to September 30 under the budget established by his predecessor and already being executed by the agencies. The presidential budget proposal that would go through the next fiscal year (that is, from October 1 of the year of presidential inauguration to September 30 of the next calendar year) has already been worked on in the executive branch for some nine months or so. The new president is in a position to modify this budget somewhat, but a radical refashioning is difficult, though possible, as the Reagan administration demonstrated in 1981. A new president elected in 2000, taking office in January 2001, will not be able to work with a budget wholly of his or her own proposing until October 1, 2002—almost a full two years after the electoral campaign that may have provided a mandate for change. It is no wonder presidents often find administrative matters so exasperating. A positive feature of the length of the budget cycle, however, is that it makes for administrative continuity. It is sometimes proposed that the government move away from the annual budget to a two-year budget, but although this might reduce the amount of effort per year that goes into formulating a budget, it would not alleviate the political problems associated with the long time frame.

Playing the Budget Game   Sometimes budgeting takes on the aura of a game, with the various agency players trying to increase their shares and elected officials trying, at least ostensibly, to keep taxes down and promote administrative economy. A number of agency strategies are common. One is to threaten to cut the most popular or politically desirable functions first. Thus a school district will frequently threaten to cease providing transportation to students if the voters do not approve higher taxes. So, too, do federal agencies threaten to cut out popular services unless their full funding requests are met. The National Park Service once even threatened to close the Washington Monument in such a game! (Such a closure—along with many others—did occur in FY 1996, when at considerable expense to the taxpayers, the government was partly shut down for lack of a budget! A chronology of the shutdown is presented in Box 6–9.) Agencies also pad their requests in the expectation that they will subsequently be reduced. This promotes a kind of budgetary ritual that involves a lot of noise, activity, handwringing, newspaper headlines, and virtually no significant change. Agencies can play the "camel's nose" game and seek to obtain seed money—limited

---

BOX 6–9 **No Government Today!**

From November 14 to November 19, 1995, and then again from December 16, 1995, to January 6, 1996, the federal government was partly shut down. There was no natural disaster, no subversion, no attack by a foreign foe. Rather, the constitutional separation of powers was hard at work: Congress and the president were unable to come to terms on a budget. Here's what happened:

November 13: President Clinton vetoed a bill that would have provided funds for continuing government operations because it included cuts in educational and environmental programs and an increase in Medicare premiums.

November 14: No agreement is reached, and about 800,000 federal workers throughout the nation are dismissed until further notice. National monuments, museums, and the National Zoological Park close. About 340 White House staffers are barred from work,

and about 90 remain on duty. "Essential" federal employees, including air-traffic controllers and safety personnel, continue to work, as do military personnel and about two-thirds of the Department of Defense's civilian employees. (The term "essential" causes a stir among pundits and public employees. Is the partially closed Office of Government Ethics essential? Eventually other terms are adopted.)

November 15: The shutdown spreads to government contractors who are told to stop working on agency projects. Treasury loses an estimated $15 to $25 million because of the Securities and Exchange Commission's inability to charge a fee. The Secretary of the Treasury says he will use billions of dollars from government retirement accounts to keep the government from defaulting on its debt payments.

November 16: The Grand Canyon is closed; steps are taken to close the nafunds for a one-year program—with the expectation that, like a camel, once they get their nose under the budgetary "tent," more is sure to follow. Finally, **repackaging** is a common ruse used to seek increased funding. Under this approach, an existing program is explained in terms that seem to fit with a president's new priorities. Although it is difficult to become irate about these games, they are inherently dishonest and can hardly raise the levels of public debate and voter information about the way the government operates.[12] Games may be complicated by deep disagreements between the executive and legislative branches.

Raising the Ceiling   The federal government has never fully accepted the idea that long-term deficits are legitimate. There is something psychologically pleasing about the notion of a balanced budget. Consequently, it has been thought that there should be a statutory limitation on the size of the federal government's accumulated deficit (the federal debt). But Congress and the president have found it impossible or undesirable to live within the confines of these debt ceilings, so with routine frequency they simply vote to

---

BOX 6–9 *Continued*

---

tion's largest national parks. Congress, also without appropriations, keeps its staff hard at work.

November 17: No progress.

November 18: Concern grows that the shutdown will prove very costly and, if continued, will jeopardize the Department of Veterans Affairs' hospitals, federal prisons, and benefit payments to the public.

November 19: The president and Congress agree to balance the budget by 2002. Legislation is passed putting federal employees back to work. Plans are made to fund the government until December 15 in the hope of enacting a budget for fiscal 1996 by then.

December 16, 1995–January 6, 1996: Redux on a smaller scale. About 284,000

federal employees furloughed. The public seems fed up, and Congress gets most of the heat. Government is reopened, but there is still no agreement to fund it through the remainder of the fiscal year.

April 25, 1996: After the two shutdowns and thirteen stopgap funding measures, the nation has a budget. The president appears victorious in preventing deep cuts in the administration's favored programs. The congressional Republicans, so seemingly invincible after their spectacular victories in the 1994 elections, appear to be in disarray.

The total cost of the two shutdowns was estimated at $1.4 billion, leaving many to wonder whether this is any way to run a government already strapped for cash.

SOURCES: Christy Harris, "Clinton, Congress Finalize 1996 Budget," *Federal Times,* 6 May 1996, 3; "Shutdown Chronology," *Washington Post,* 20 November 1995, A19. Author's interviews and observations.

raise the ceiling and increase the debt. When Congress failed to raise the ceiling in FY 1996, the secretary of the treasury kept the government from defaulting by borrowing from various funds. This prompted calls for his impeachment among some seemingly irate congresspersons. In the end, though, whatever leverage the ceiling may have given, the legislature was lost when public opinion turned against the Republican-led Congress. Eventually, the ceiling was lifted in return for a presidential promise to achieve a balanced budget within seven years.

Uncontrollable Spending   Perhaps all these problems point in the direction of what seems to be the most serious problem with federal budgeting at the present time: To a very large extent, perhaps involving as much as 75 percent of the budget, federal spending is uncontrolled in the sense that funds are committed in advance for the foreseeable future. Such commitments take three main forms. First, there is payment of the federal debt, generated by the borrowing that accompanies deficit spending. Payment cannot legally or constitutionally be avoided and real as opposed to technical default by the federal government would surely spell disaster for the nation. Interest payments on the debt alone account for about 15 percent of budget expenditures. A second kind of uncontrollable spending involves entitlements (see Chapter 3). Entitlements arise out of governmental commitments to groups of citizens. Social Security, various welfare, Medicare, Medicaid, and veterans' benefits are examples. The expense of entitlements tends to rise over time as the number of people in the eligible group expands. For instance, as the proportion of the population that is elderly expands, so too expands the number of individuals entitled to Medicare and Social Security benefits. In addition, there is a tendency to raise the level of the benefits. Cost of living adjustments (COLAs) may be granted to beneficiaries to compensate for inflation. Especially as the size of the entitled group expands, pressure is put on members of Congress and the president to increase the amounts of payment to them. Finally, uncontrollable spending is derived from contractual obligations entered into by the government. Often these are multiyear and involve cost overruns and adjustments for inflation that become quite substantial. However, it should be borne in mind that despite the label "uncontrollable," all of these costs can be reduced over time. As part of a general reaction to the "uncontrollable" problem, federal agencies now make five-year projections of the cost of their programs.

A BUDGET THEORY, OR THEORIES ABOUT BUDGETING?

For the most part, the difficulties we have been discussing are problems of practice. The mixing of political, economic, administrative, and legal concerns in the area of public budgeting makes it difficult to develop a budgetary process that adequately satisfies all government needs. Although we have been focusing on the federal level, the same would be true for the states. The main differences are that states do not engage in countercyclical spending, though they may reduce taxes to stimulate economic growth, and that they are under greater pressure to avoid annual deficits. Interestingly, in the 1980s, many states had surpluses that stood in stark contrast to the federal government's huge deficit. As noted earlier, states make a distinction between capital budgets, which is money used for the building of projects, and operating budgets, which are the costs of running the governmental enterprise. Consequently, their surpluses are sometimes partly the result of accounting techniques. Another difference is that the state legislatures tend to play a smaller role in budgeting than does Congress. They are generally deferential to the governor. Several states also differ from the federal government in that they use a biennial rather than an annual budget.[13]

One might look to the states as laboratories in which different approaches to budgeting might be undertaken. There is enough variation among them to provide a fruitful field of investigation. The ways in which they raise revenues differ widely, as do their spending patterns. Some states rely heavily on income taxes and fund huge educational programs or welfare programs, whereas others rely on sales taxes and provide a much reduced program of public services. The behavior of local governments also varies substantially with respect to raising and spending revenues. However, despite all these "laboratories" and variations, it is still true that the United States has not worked out a dominant theory of public budgeting that can answer what has long been considered the most basic question on the expenditure side: "On what basis shall it be decided to allocate x dollars to activity A instead of activity B?"[14] We can study the variety of budgetary processes, sources of revenue, and allocation of expenditures ad nauseum without finding an answer to this question. As usual, however, part of the reason for this is that different perspectives generate different answers. Those who view budgeting as a managerial endeavor stress one set of values, those who see it as political emphasize another, and those imbued with legalistic concerns still others. Therefore, there are theories of budgeting rather than a single budget theory. And, as in other areas of public administration, there is a vigorous contest among these theories for influence and dominance.

The Managerial Approach to Public Budgeting

The orthodox managerial perspective on public administration seeks to develop an approach to budgeting that promotes the values of efficiency, economy, and managerial effectiveness. It seeks to use budgeting to cut out waste, encourage the highest level of productivity, and strengthen managerial control over the operation of government. The new public management shares some of these goals but puts greater emphasis on performance and responsiveness to customers. It favors financing agencies through user fees where feasible, and making programs compete for them. In this view, market forces are the best way of promoting efficiency and customer satisfaction.

The first major step in the development of the traditional managerial approach to budgeting occurred in 1914, when the New York Bureau of Municipal Research called for the development of a performance budget. Later, in 1949, the influential First Hoover Commission called for the use of performance budgeting in the federal government. To understand the importance of the performance budget one must remember that it was predated by lump-sum appropriations and the **line-item** budget. Lump-sum budgets simply gave agencies funds to expend more or less as they saw fit, with very little political control over how the funds were actually used or misused. The lump-sum approach was chaotic and left the activities of public administrators pretty much beyond the scrutiny of elected officials. The line-item budget was adopted to rectify this situation. It requires that appropriations be linked to objects of expenditure. (Box 6–10 provides an example of categorizing outlays by objects of expenditure.) Although these objects could be defined in different ways, the tendency was to place every significant expenditure on a separate line in the agency's budget. For instance, the salaries of each employee might be listed separately, as might the cost of pencils, paper, pens, and so forth. The chief executive or legislature could then go down the list of agency requests for appropriations and cross out, reduce, or, as is less likely, augment the agency's funding request for any of the items. This obviously provides a great deal of control of *how* money is spent, but it tells elected officials very little about what is supposed to be accomplished by the agency. In other words, what are all those pencils for?

BOX 6–10 **Federal Outlays by Leading Objects of Expenditure**

Salaries	$134,520,000,000
Pensions	60,300,000,000
Electric, gas, and sanitary	2,715,249,000
Rent	2,500,000,000
Passenger air charter	490,394,000
Office furniture	271,643,000
30-mm or smaller guns	198,295,000
Stationery and forms	103,504,000
Lodging at hotels and motels	38,080,000
Tobacco products	34,407,000
Brooms, brushes, mops, and sponges	14,026,000
Building demolition	11,383,000
Luggage	7,209,000
Personal toiletries	4,136,000
Bottles and jars	416,000

SOURCE: Barbara Saffir, "Sizing Up Uncle Sam," *Washington Post*, 28 May 1995, C3.

What is it that the agency does? And how much does it cost? Enter the **performance budget.**

The Performance Budget   This type of budget seeks to answer these questions without losing control over expenditures. At a minimum, it involves the following:

1. "The *formulation* and adoption of a plan of activities and programs for a stated time period." In other words, what is the agency intending to do, why, how much of it, and when?
2. *Funding*, that is, relating program costs to resources, or determining what kind of agency performance can be obtained within the confines of the resources available.
3. *Execution*, or the achievement of the authorized plan, within the time frame, and resources allocated to it.[15]

Performance budgeting contains at least the seeds of all modern managerially oriented public budgeting strategies. It fits in well with specialized organizational designs, as the subunits of agencies could be considered the "activities" for which funding is targeted. For example, in a public hospital, "food service," "ward service," "x-rays," "surgery," and "housekeeping" might be considered activities and they might also form separate administrative organizational units. Performance budgeting promotes the managerial goal of allowing evaluation of administrative performance because it often requires that "performance reports" accompany budget requests. Consequently, performance budgeting has a concrete meaning to public managers: activities and organizational units tend to coincide; performance is measured and evaluated (in some fashion); and budgetary requests and appropriations are connected to performance levels.

The use of performance budgeting has made considerable headway in American government at all levels. However, even though most states use it in some aspects, only a few could be considered to adhere rigorously to the performance concept. Among the common complaints about performance budgeting are that (1) it does not afford the legislature the same level of participation and control as does the line-item budget and (2) it is not refined enough to deal with the complexity of administrative operations. Enter the **program budget.**

The Program Budget   Program budgeting is often considered interchangeable with performance budgeting, but there is a significant difference, at least in theory. Whereas performance budgeting concentrates on activities and tends not to overlap organizational units, program budgeting looks at the purpose (not activities) of governmental administration and seeks to relate funding to the achievement of these purposes. Program budgeting may tend to overlap administrative organizational units, but it does not necessarily do so. It is also prospective in the sense of seeking to adopt policies based on the prospects for the achievement of their goals at given levels of cost. In other words, it incorporates a cost-effectiveness approach, while exploring various administrative approaches to obtaining any given level of benefit at the lowest cost.

Returning to our example of performance budgeting in a hospital may help clarify the difference between these two systems of budgeting. Listing costs by activities does not provide us with an idea of what the purpose of a hospital is. It tells us what it does, but not what its ultimate goal is. Program budgeting, on the other hand, would identify the goals of the hospital and seek to relate funding to these. For instance, "housekeeping" might be redefined in terms of providing "sanitation," and an appropriate level of sanitation might be defined. Next, different ways of obtaining that sanitary level might be mapped out, along with their projected costs. Then the approach providing the desired level at the lowest cost would presumably be selected and funded. Such an exercise can involve interesting choices. For instance, if the hospital is concerned with sanitation in surgery rooms and if it must pay employees who sanitize the rooms a night-rate differential (higher wage rate), then, all other things being equal, the hospital might elect to schedule as much surgery as possible during the times (mornings and afternoons) when the rooms can be cleaned at a lower cost. Similarly, the performance budgeting activity of taking x-rays could be redefined in program budget terms as part of a wider objective of "diagnosing." The success of the operation of the x-ray department at this point would be related to the utility of using x-rays to diagnose medical problems and the cost of x-rays would be compared to the cost of other diagnostic techniques. This would have obvious implications for the purchase and use of different types of x-ray equipment and for the decision as to who should operate it, technicians, medical doctors, or teams of both.

Perhaps policing provides a more familiar example of the distinction between the performance budget and the program budget. "Patrolling" under the performance budget could become "crime control" under a program budget. Then different types of crimes could be targeted for reduction, and police officers and other resources could be assigned accordingly.

These examples should help clarify the difference between performance budgeting and program budgeting, but they are not intended to suggest that program budgeting is not without very substantial problems. These were made quite evident by the introduction of a particular kind of program budgeting into the federal government in the 1960s. The federal experience with the Planning Programming Budgeting System (PPBS) provides so many lessons that it should be considered in some detail.

PPBS was once hailed as a revolutionary approach to budgetary and administrative decision making with almost messianic qualities.[16] It promised to solve many of our budgetary problems, many of our administrative ones, and even our political conflicts over how governmental funds should be spent. It was used by Secretary of Defense Robert McNamara in the early 1960s in an effort that was popularized as getting more "bang for the buck." In 1965

President Johnson made it mandatory for most federal agencies. By 1971 it was discontinued as a requirement for all agencies. The essence of PPBS was to do the following:

1. Analyze program goals in operational terms. For example, instead of saying the goal of a program is to promote highway safety, the goal would be presented as averting x number of deaths through traffic accidents, averting y number of serious injuries, averting z number of lesser injuries, and reducing property damage by w percent.
2. Analyze the total costs of programs over one and several years.
3. Analyze alternative ways of achieving the goals. This would be done from a cost-effective approach. In the example above, how much does it cost to avert a death through the use of seat belts versus the cost per death averted through better driver training?
4. Develop a systematic way of considering the costs and benefits of all governmental programs in a comparative fashion. In other words, what is the cost of a death averted through driver training versus the cost through public health activities or the cost through promotion of world peace? What are the total benefits of each approach?

At first glance, this sounds eminently reasonable. What does it cost the government to do what it seeks to do? How could it do it for less? Certainly these are important questions. However, PPBS was hard to apply and, even where applied, did not always determine how funds should be appropriated. Why did PPBS not work out in practice?

First, the goals of governmental programs may be unclear and lacking in any operational content. For example, how does one operationally define "promoting world peace" or creating the "new world order" called for by President Bush in 1991? To some, these goals mean avoiding the death of members of the U.S. armed forces in combat. To others, they mean promoting U.S. control of foreign nations through the use of military force. Even more complicated is the situation where a program, such as food stamps, is put together by a coalition of diverse and economically antagonistic interests. Under such conditions an operational definition of the objectives of the program would threaten to destroy the coalition and the program along with it. While PPBS cannot work without operational goals, in some policy areas the U.S. political system may not be able to work well *with* them, because they exacerbate conflict and make it difficult to build majority coalitions. This may turn out to be a serious problem for the Government Performance and Results Act of 1993 as well because it requires agencies to formulate specific goals. (This act is discussed further on page 311.)

Second, cost-benefit analysis can be exceedingly difficult even where goals are clear. This is especially true in governments where there are so many program overlaps. In addition, some costs and benefits cannot be quantified. Yet, at least in government, these may be of great political importance. For example, what is the benefit derived from a public park? From a strong civil rights policy? From intervening in the Middle East or the Balkans to promote peace? How does one assess the costs and benefits of any specific course of activity on the reputation of the president and his ability to exercise the functions of that office effectively?

Third, projecting the costs and benefits of different administrative means of obtaining objectives can be highly speculative or even impossible. In short, often not enough is known about how government can achieve its goals to enable us to predict the consequences of one particular strategy versus another.

Finally, even where the analysis was undertaken with sufficient rigor, while the PPBS approach could inform political decision makers, it could not necessarily resolve the key issues in choosing policy alternatives. Returning to our macabre example of deaths averted, we can illustrate this point by drawing upon the work of Elizabeth Drew.[17]

In an article called "HEW Grapples with PPBS," Drew found that the Department of Health, Education, and Welfare (HEW) had programs intended to avert deaths caused by disease and through traffic accidents. The cost of averting a death by promoting the use of seat belts was $87; the cost of averting a death by attacking cancer of the cervix was $3,470. In cost-benefit terms (assuming each death averted to be of equal benefit), the greatest benefit for the least cost would have had HEW allocate its resources to programs in the following order:

> Seat belt use
> Automotive restraint devices
> Avoiding pedestrian injury
> Motorcyclist helmets
> Arthritis
> Reducing driver drinking
> Syphilis
> Cancer of the cervix
> Lung cancer
> Breast cancer
> Tuberculosis
> Driver licensing
> Cancer of the head and neck
> Colorectal cancer

Now suppose you have limited resources to give HEW for these worthy objectives (as taxpayers and legislatures do). Are you willing to allocate funds to motorcyclist helmets over cancer of the cervix or breast cancer? What would the National Organization for Women say about a decision to follow the logic of cost-benefit analysis in this case? What would motorcyclists say about being required to wear helmets? What would philosophers say about the choice available to those who die in motorcycle accidents for failure to wear a helmet? What would they say about the "choice" available in getting cancer of the breast or cervix? Should these differences affect one's budget allocations?

The point here is not that PPBS cannot be useful in providing an indication of the costs and benefits of various programs. However, it should be evident that it cannot answer the classic question, "On what basis shall it be decided to allocate x dollars to activity A instead of activity B?" In fact, although conceived as a managerial system of budgeting, PPBS tends to illustrate the fundamentally political nature of budgeting. If one could actually use PPBS to resolve the matter of policy choice, then the political priorities of the nation would be clear and several political problems would be solved.

PPBS died in the federal bureaucracy largely for the reasons just discussed—and also because it was very difficult to apply where programs overlapped several agencies, as is so often the case in the federal bureaucracy.[18] But that does not mean it is not appropriate for some kinds of budgetary decisions. It is used in some state and local governments, apparently with satisfactory results, for some functions. Still, its failure at the federal level sparked interest in other managerial approaches to budgeting. Perhaps most important among these has been **zero-base budgeting (ZBB).**

Zero-Base Budgeting   ZBB is intended to give budgetary decision makers a choice among different funding levels for different programs and activities. It starts from the intellectual premise that the budgeting process should be used to review the political desirability and administrative effectiveness of governmental programs. The concept of zero base is that existing programs and activities should not automatically be funded, but rather should have to justify their continuation as part of the yearly budget cycle. In theory, each program and activity is vulnerable to zero funding in each new fiscal year.

The main elements of ZBB are as follows:

1. The identification of *decision units*. These are the lowest-level organizational or programmatic units for which budgets are prepared.[19] Each decision unit must have a manager who is identified as responsible for the operation of that administrative entity as a whole.
2. The formulation of *decision packages*. These are derived from a comprehensive yearly review of each decision unit's purposes and functions. This review considers such questions as what would happen if the decision unit were not funded at all, what would happen with 50 percent funding, 75 percent, and so on, how can its operations be improved, and can a greater benefit-cost ratio be developed? Once the review is completed, the decision unit's operations are divided up according to the perceived importance of its activities. Those activities of top priority are in the first decision package, those of secondary importance in a second decision package, and so on. The operations, costs, and benefits of these packages are presented in a comprehensive fashion to budgetary decision makers.
3. The ranking of decision packages by top-level managers. This establishes organizationwide priorities and seeks to coordinate the agency's choice of level of activity with the amount of funding that is likely to be

forthcoming. The key to ranking decision packages is not simply choosing from among different activities, but also deciding on different levels of activity within any given package.

Like other budget processes, ZBB is complex and difficult to understand in the abstract. Consequently, an example is in order. Peter Pyhrr, the developer of the ZBB concept, provided the following illustration.[20] For "residential refuse collection" in a city, the decision unit is the administrative operations responsible for collecting and transporting all residential solid waste for disposal. The decision package would evaluate different ways of performing this function and different levels of activity. Different means would include such approaches as the following:

1. Requiring residential users of the service to purchase plastic bags and place their garbage in them
2. Using neighborhood dumpsters
3. Collecting from garbage cans rather than plastic bags
4. Using "barrel" trucks rather than conventional trucks with the capacity to crush (compact) the garbage
5. Contracting out to private firms for refuse collection

The cost of each of these means would be assessed, and this assessment would go a long way in dictating the choice as to which would be used.

Different levels of activity would then be considered. For instance, these might involve pickup once a week, or twice a week for garbage and different levels of activity for brush collection. When the decision packages were ranked, the most desired means would be linked with the most desired level of activity. In this fashion it might turn out that pickups twice a week could be afforded when dumpsters were used, but that otherwise pickups would have to be limited to once a week.

As in the case of virtually all known budgetary strategies, ZBB has some limitations. The analysis can become too complex or cumbersome to be useful. The identification of decision units runs into the problem of specifying objectives in clear operational terms. Assessing costs can be difficult or impossible. In addition, as the garbage example above suggests, shifting the cost of a function may pose difficult problems for analysis. Requiring residents to purchase plastic bags pushes some of the costs from the city onto the private citizens. Anytime this occurs there is likely to be an equity issue. Is the cost of plastic garbage bags substantial enough to pose an economic hardship for the city's poorest residents? Additionally, because plastic is a petrochemical, is there a significant cost to the nation imposed by requiring the use of scarce energy resources (petroleum) in this fashion? Is one way of collecting garbage environmentally sounder than another? Of course, the city manager or council may view some of these issues as national problems subject to congressional attention. But if dumpsters posed a health problem for residents, it could not be ignored at the local level. When we try to apply ZBB at the federal level, such shifting costs from one program to another may be a more substantial problem.

Despite these problems, several jurisdictions have had success with ZBB or some adaptation to it. However, it seems to have been misapplied in the federal government during the Carter administration. The main difficulties were that (1) perhaps out of political and organizational necessity, decision units were identified to coincide with agencies and bureaus rather than programs and activities and (2) the ZBB approach was applied governmentwide rather than selectively. Pyhrr called Carter's approach "absolute folly."[21] Others detected a note of shrewdness: ZBB became little more than an overlay on traditional budgeting processes; consequently, it was easy to apply, engendered little controversy, and enabled Carter to take credit for a major reform!

PPBS and ZBB are leading examples of the managerial approach to budgeting. Although they do improve the budgeting process and generate much information that is pertinent to budgetary choices, neither has been fully satisfactory thus far in reducing the budgetary process to a purely managerial endeavor. In truth, they are probably not intended to do so entirely; but they do tend to downgrade the political nature of budgets and the political choices inherent in budgetary decisions.[22]

The federal Government Performance and Results Act of 1993 (GPRA) is the latest federal effort to strengthen the links between performance and budgeting. GPRA was a congressional initiative, though it enjoys strong support from the NPR for its results orientation. It requires agencies to formulate five-year **strategic plans** in conjunction with OMB and Congress (that is, committees and subcommittees). The plans should include performance goals that are related to the achievement of specific, and preferably measurable, outcomes. The plans, goals, and measures will help Congress and OMB assess the efficacy of programs and appropriations for them. GPRA does not require governmentwide performance budgeting, but several agencies will be selected by OMB to participate in pilot programs aimed at connecting budget decisions to performance.

Like the other budget approaches, GPRA will yield useful information about government programs to budget makers. If programs are not performing well and there is no reason to believe greater funding will improve them, they are sure to be targets for restructuring or termination. Programs that are working well may not require additional funding. In other cases, adjusting funding levels may improve performance or cost-effectiveness. All this makes sense in managerial terms. However, because GPRA requires agencies to set goals in consultation with Congress, it may also become a vehicle for greater legislative micromanagment of the executive branch. This brings us to the politics of public budgets.

The Political Approach to Public Budgeting

The political approach to public budgeting emphasizes several concerns: representation, consensus and coalition building, and the locus of power in allocating funds. Incrementalism has been the favored political approach to public budgeting in the United States. This approach tends to treat last year's appropriation to an agency or program as a base that should be diminished only under unusual and highly controversial circumstances. The base being more or less untouchable, the real discussion is over the increment that will be allocated to an agency or program during the next fiscal year. Moreover, incrementalism shies away from comprehensive analysis, the specifications of clear goals, and program evaluation. This approach is politically comfortable for several reasons but, at the federal level and in some states, it may no longer be able to withstand the pressures to reduce deficits and the national debt. Even in times of budget cutting, though, incrementalism is apt to be used in reverse, that is decrementalism.[23] A decremental approach would cut agency budgets and programs by a limited percentage each year until expenditures and revenues came into balance or deficits were reduced to politically tolerable levels.

Incrementalism makes it possible to provide widespread representation to groups and interests in the society. Any socially and economically diverse society, including the United States, is made up of antagonistic interests. Incrementalism allows these sectors to be represented in government even though they are at cross-purposes. This is true because it does not demand a comprehensive statement of the objectives of governmental activity and because it does not rigorously question the base appropriation to existing agencies and functions. Consequently, it is possible to have governmental programs that conflict with one another without giving serious consideration to the issue of whether the failure to make fundamental choices among them is in some sense irrational. For instance, the federal government has subsidized tobacco growers and at the same time tried to discourage smoking by the public.[24] The growers are represented in the Department of Agriculture. Public health interests are represented in the Department of Health and Human Services. Each can be funded in the budget process, and until deficits were considered a major problem, neither was very concerned about having its level of appropriation reduced from that of the past fiscal year. In this case, incrementalism worked as a kind of compensatory device for the tobacco growers, who stood to lose a great deal when it was concluded by the U.S. Surgeon General that "smoking is dangerous to your health." The representation of diverse interests and their funding allows public policy to be made through compromise: few, if any, interests that achieve formal representation in the administrative structure are threatened with immediate loss. Rather, change occurs over the long run as declining support for an interest is reflected in decreasing budgetary increments.

Another factor favoring incrementalism is that it allows the building of consensus and coalitions by providing funding to diverse interests. Coalitions make it possible for political parties to exist and for politicians to be elected. Consensus is fostered where conflict is muted. And conflict can be avoided where the objectives of government are stated in terms that can be virtually universally accepted. Again, "nutrition," "defense," "health," "justice," and "peace" are examples. Almost everyone in the society might agree that these are desirable governmental objectives in the abstract. However, the reaction may be quite different when they are translated into specific programs with specific objectives—to subsidize farmers, avert deaths in one way or another, deploy nuclear weapons and build bases, require school desegregation through busing, represent the interest of the fetus in court, and destabilize foreign regimes through covert activities. A primary difficulty with PPBS and ZBB is that they exacerbate conflict, break down consensus, and make it difficult for the political system to work well at the national level. Incrementalism, on the other hand, allows funding for a variety of activities that when left unanalyzed and ill-defined enable different groups and citizens to define and conceptualize them in their own favorable terms.

Similarly, incrementalism enables parties and politicians to build broad coalitions by providing governmental funding to diverse and competing interests. The classic example of such a coalition was put together by Franklin D. Roosevelt. He was able to gain widespread support of southerners, unions, urbanites, and members of minority groups. This "New Deal Coalition" remained the backbone of the Democratic party well into the 1960s.[25] It was routine for Democrat to oppose Democrat on civil rights issues, but the basic coalition held together at least until the election of 1968. Of course, the typical legislator does not have to develop such a grand coalition. He or she has to be more concerned with voters in a specific district. One way of building a coalition there is to engage in "pork barrel" allocations, getting as much public funding into the district as possible. This promotes the economic health of the community and is likely to provide more jobs. "Pork barreling" can be done without regard to ideology. For example, even communities in which there is strong support for reducing military appropriations generally are likely to want military bases in their own states kept open. Incrementalism fits this approach to coalition building because it does not threaten existing governmental facilities and spending, but rather promises more and more. If a legislator's district is large and diversified enough, as in the case of senators from states such as California and New York, the incremental approach can also be used to support conflicting interests within the electoral constituency. It is not unusual for rural-urban conflicts to be diminished in this fashion in an effort to build statewide support. Simultaneous subsidies for mass urban transportation and spending for rural highway development are common examples.

Congressional support for the incremental approach also stems from the fact that incrementalism tends to place the locus of power for budgetary decisions in the legislature. Although GPRA may prove to be a major exception, most managerial approaches strengthen the executive's role in the budgetary process. Some of them, such as PPBS, have had a marked centralizing bias within the executive branch.[26] They have militated against administrative decentralization and administrative responsiveness to the legislature. Under such circumstances, the "budget bureau" displaces the legislative appropriations committees as the key organizational participant in the budgetary process. This also tends to place power over budgetary decisions in the hands of unelected administrators as opposed to elected legislators. If one views budgets as political statements, then incrementalism has the benefit of placing the locus of power in the hands of the citizenry's elected representatives. Presumably, legislators can be held accountable to their constituencies and presumably they will therefore be responsive to them at least in the areas where the electorate has identifiable and salient interests. In addition to potentially enhancing the representative qualities of government in this fashion, incrementalism helps to maintain the viability of checks and balances by maintaining the historic legislative role of the power of the purse intact.

The nature and advantage of incrementalism have been summarized by Aaron Wildavsky and Arthur Hammond in a passage that is worth quoting at length:

> Whatever else they may be, budgets are manifestly political documents. They engage the intense concern of administrators, politicians, leaders of interest groups and citizens interested in the "who gets what and how much" of governmental allocations. Participants in budgeting use its political components as aids to calculation. They drastically simplify their task by concentrating on the relatively small portion of the budget that is politically feasible to change. The previous year's budget, the largest part of which is composed of continuing programs and prior commitments, is usually taken as a base needing little justification beyond that offered in the past. Attention is normally focused on a small number of incremental changes, increases and decreases, calling for significant departures from the established historical base of the agency concerned. Parts of the total budget are given to various administrative agencies, appropriations subcommittees, Budget Bureau divisions, and other interested parties for special attention. This fragmentation is increased because all budgetary items are not evaluated together, but are dealt with in sequence by the various participants, so that only a small number of items need to be considered by any participant at any one time.[27]

However, although this approach maximizes important political values, it has limitations. Budgets are political documents, but they are also economic documents and managerial documents. Incrementalism makes it difficult to avoid waste and promote administrative efficiency. The natural tendency is to spend more and avoid cuts. At the same time, raising taxes is so politically unpopular that the tendency is for the budget to be unbalanced and for deficits to grow. This promotes inflationary pressures, which may have to be countered by raising interest rates. The latter may hamper economic growth and affect international trade by increasing the dollar against other currencies. But even if taxes were raised to match the ever-continuing incremental increases in spending, it might cause problems for the economy. Eventually government might collect and reallocate a great deal of money from the private sector, which might seriously sap the economy's vitality and even the viability of capitalism as traditionally present in the United States.

By avoiding a clear identification of governmental objectives and priorities, incrementalism also makes public administration difficult. How do you manage an agency whose goals are unclear and contradictory? What does efficiency and economy mean in this context? More than one top-level administrator has found these questions frustrating in the extreme.

These problems of incrementalism are so profound that drastic measures are being considered to limit its negative impact on the economy. As mentioned earlier, one such measure that has gained some credence in recent years has been a balanced budget amendment. Although there are several variants, the basic idea is to force the federal government to balance the budget on an annual basis, unless a clear emergency were present and an extraordinary majority of the Congress agreed to let it be unbalanced. Of course, to some extent, balancing the budget is a matter of accounting practices. The federal government would show a far lesser deficit if it used a capital budget. Programs such as Social Security can also be put "off budget" by converting them into trust funds (see the glossary in Box 6–6). Consequently, a constitutional amendment might fail to accomplish its purpose, while at the same time expanding the political power of a minority of each congressional chamber.

Sunset provisions are another approach to keeping incrementalism in check. Sunset legislation provides for the termination of programs at some future date, often five years, unless they are reauthorized by statute at that time. This means that the programs will go out of existence if no legislative action is taken and, consequently, the burden is placed on those administrators and political actors who favor their continuance to justify the need for such programs. The sunset concept is incorporated in zero-base budgeting, because there is a presumption that each agency should justify all the budgetary allocations to it (not just the increment) on an annual basis. Sunset provisions are very common in the states. Thus far, experience with sunset provisions has been mixed. It seems to work least well in programmatic areas where there are narrow and strongly organized interest groups, such as occupational licensing administration. Where there are broad and well-articulated conflicting interests involved, sunset provisions can promote better accountability and evaluation of the performance of agencies and programs. (Sunset provisions are discussed further in Chapter 8.)

The Legal Influence on Budgeting

Today, the courts also have an important influence on budgets. The legal approach to public administration seeks to protect constitutional integrity and rights of individuals, assure equal protection under the law, and promote procedural fairness and equity. In some instances, seeking to promote or maximize these values can lead to sizable and identifiable costs for the political community. This is especially true where the judiciary finds that wide-ranging institutional reforms are necessary in order to protect individuals' rights. Such cases often involve prison reform, the reform of public mental health institutions, and school desegregation involving major changes in the operation of entire public educational systems.[28] Some courts have been involved in statewide reforms in each of these areas. As mentioned in Chapter 1, in the early 1980s, about half of Boston's budgetary appropriations were "presided over" by federal and state judges.[29] In one case, *Missouri v. Jenkins* (1990, 1995), a federal district court effectively imposed a local property tax to pay for a school desegregation plan involving lavish spending on magnet school facilities until the Supreme Court eventually said its remedy was inappropriate.[30]

There are two key aspects of judicially fostered reforms of this nature. First, generally speaking, the courts do not actually *require* a legislature to spend money on a function such as incarceration or public mental health care. Rather, the judicial logic is essentially stated to the legislature as follows: "You don't have to run prisons, mental health facilities, or public schools, but if you choose to do so, then you must not violate the constitutional rights of prisoners, patients, and students in the process."[31] Thus, the legislature is given a way out—it does not have to maintain the function or appropriate money to bring it up to constitutional standards. But the choice is often a hollow one. States may curtail some public mental health care or educational programs, but they are highly unlikely to stop imprisoning or institutionalizing dangerous persons or to terminate a public role in education. Nevertheless, by framing the issue in this fashion, the courts generally avoid the necessity of forcing the states to budget funds for any specific function.

Second, the judiciary is cognizant of the costs of its decrees, but overall, it does not consider limited resources to be a legitimate excuse for failing to protect someone's constitutional rights. As one court put it, "Inadequate resources can never be adequate justification for the state's depriving any person of his constitutional rights."[32]

In the abstract this approach may not present any particular issues in terms of budgeting. However, in concrete terms genuine allocational problems do arise. For instance, one court decreed that the state's mental health facilities would have to have at least one shower or tub for each fifteen patients, at least one toilet for each eight patients, no single room with less than 100 square feet of floor space, and a temperature range between 68 and 83 degrees Fahrenheit.[33] In addition, it ordered that more staff be hired. These reforms cost money; where will it come from? This is a question that the judges do not have to address directly. They do not know if the funds will come from housing programs for the elderly, nutrition programs for malnourished elementary school pupils, or the taxpayers in general. By seeking to define the rights of some groups in isolation from all the competing potential claims on the public treasury, the courts do not have to balance the constitutional rights of some against the economic needs of others. In short, the courts do not consider the possible trade-off of more floor space for the insane leading to less for the elderly. This fits the judiciary's historic role in protecting members of the political community who are inadequately protected or represented by the other branches of government. But it also fragments the budgetary process even further, because in a practical sense the judges are allocating money for some groups of people without assessing their claims relative to those of other groups. The judiciary is generally inclined to rely on a contractarian, as opposed to utilitarian, basis for fundamental rights. The legislature, in turn, may victimize other politically weak groups who remain without meaningful judicial protection. This would occur, for example, if a state raised the temperature in its mental health facilities with money that previously would have gone into public housing for the elderly or poor. No doubt an administrator in charge of such a housing program would find it frustrating to see appropriations earmarked for that function shifted to upgrading conditions in the public mental hospitals.

Yet the judicial influence on budgeting does not have to be so dramatic. There are countless public administrative activities and programs that tend to spend more money in one neighborhood than another. Schools, streets, lighting, sanitation, building inspection, police, and fire protection are some of the leading examples. Would unequal allocations be unconstitutional in violation of equal protection where neighborhoods evidenced a great deal of residential segregation by race or ethnicity, by age, or by wealth? The answers to these questions depend on interpretation of the federal or state constitution, the precise nature of the functions, the administrative intent in providing them on an unequal basis, and the nature of the social divisions among the neighborhoods. In some cases involving schools and public works, however, courts have found that the equal protection rights of the residents were violated by unequal spending. In such instances, judicial decisions force a reallocation of funds that can have a substantial impact on the budgets of local governments or even states.[34] Judicial decisions regarding local governmental liability and public personnel practices have also had very significant price tags.

CONCLUSION: THE SEARCH FOR A SYNTHESIS

It is evident that the managerial, political, and judicial approaches all identify important concerns in the area of public budgeting. It is also apparent that the approaches are at odds with one another at a number of points. What are the prospects for synthesis? At present, one would have to respond, "Not good!" The judicial influence does not seem to lend itself readily to integration with executive and legislative budgetary processes. Managerial and incremental budgeting can be combined to an extent, but performance and program budgeting appear to be at odds with the incremental approach. GPRA can potentially provide a bridge, but it may also enhance congressional micromanagement of the executive. Still, progress can be made if we avoid across-the-board approaches in developing budgetary strategies. Clearly managerial orientations are appropriate for some governmental functions, but not for others. Many of the functions of local governments are particularly subject to improvement through PPBS and ZBB approaches—and these strategies have been more successful at that level than in the federal government. On the other hand, incremental approaches are useful when it is politically difficult to establish clear objectives and priorities without denying some groups representation and weakening consensus and political coalitions. One approach to synthesis therefore is to "fudge" the issue somewhat.

This appears to have been what happened with the federal experience with ZBB. Where ZBB's assumptions did fit the nature of programs and agencies, ZBB was used in a sensible fashion. However, where this managerial approach simply did not fit, whole agencies might be defined as decision units; objectives might be defined in vague, unoperational terms; and analysis might be perfunctory. This enabled such agencies to recast the incremental approach into the language and form of ZBB. Another possibility is to admit openly that there cannot be a single budgetary process and to treat agencies and programs differently. GPRA provides some flexibility by recognizing that some agency programs do not have measurable objectives.

The continuing federal budgetary crisis may lead to other reforms and the development of new budgetary techniques. Whatever course is chosen in the future, however, one thing is certain—budgeting will remain an area of controversy for public administrators, elected officials, political executives, interest groups, commercial interests, and the public at large. The way in which budgetary questions are framed has a great deal to do with the outcome of contests for public dollars. Both the budget *process* and *allocations* are of critical political, economic, and organizational importance in the modern administrative state.

NOTES

1. Robert Lorch, *State and Local Politics*, 2d ed. (Englewood Cliffs, N.J.: Prentice-Hall, 1986), 302–303.
2. See Morris P. Fiorina, *Congress: Keystone of the Washington Establishment* (New Haven, Conn.: Yale University Press, 1977); Edward R. Tufte, "Determinants of the Outcomes of Midterm Congressional Elections," *American Political Science Review* 69 (1975): 812–826.
3. John Maynard Keynes, *The General Theory of Employment, Interest, and Money* (New York: Harcourt, Brace, and World, 1935).
4. See Tufte, "Determinants of the Outcomes."
5. A useful place to start on this issue is Charles Schultze, *The Politics and Economics of Public Spending* (Washington, D.C.: Brookings, 1968). See also Robert Heilbroner and Peter Bernstein, *The Debt and the Deficit* (New York: Norton, 1989).
6. Heilbroner and Bernstein, *The Debt*, 44.
7. Peter Kilborn, "Where the Reagan Revolution Went Awry," *New York Times*, 8 November 1987. The facts reported in the paragraph are from this source.
8. Susan Tolchin and Martin Tolchin, *Dismantling America: The Rush to Deregulate* (Boston: Houghton Mifflin, 1983).
9. Jonathan Fuerbringer and Nathaniel Nash, "Seven Ways to Reinvent the Budget Process," *New York Times*, 27 September 1987, quoting Louis Fisher.
10. *Immigration and Naturalization Service v. Chadha*, 462 U.S. 919 (1983).
11. *City of New Haven v. United States*, 809 F.2d 900 (1987).
12. For a comprehensive discussion, see Aaron Wildavsky, *The Politics of the Budgetary Process*, 4th ed. (Boston: Little, Brown, 1984).
13. Lorch, *State and Local Politics*, chap. 11.

14. V. O. Key, Jr., "The Lack of a Budgetary Theory," *American Political Science Review* 34 (December 1940): 1137–1140.
15. Catheryn Seckler-Hudson, "Performance Budgeting in Government," in Albert Hyde and Jay M. Shafritz, eds., *Government Budgeting* (Oak Park, Ill.: Moore, 1978), 80–93, esp. 81. See also Robert D. Lee, "Developments in State Budgeting: Trends of Two Decades," *Public Administration Review* 51 (May/June 1991): 254–262.
16. Hyde and Shafritz, *Government Budgeting*, includes several works on this subject. See section III.
17. Elizabeth Drew, "HEW Grapples with PPBS," *The Public Interest* 8 (Summer 1967): 9–27.
18. Allen Schick, "A Death in the Bureaucracy: The Demise of Federal PPB," *Public Administration Review* 33 (March/April 1973): 146–156.
19. See Graeme M. Taylor, "Introduction to Zero-Base Budgeting," in Hyde and Shafritz, *Government Budgeting*, 271–284, esp. 273; and Peter A. Pyhrr, *Zero-Base Budgeting* (New York: Wiley, 1973).
20. Peter A. Pyhrr, "Zero-Base Approach to Government Budgeting," *Public Administration Review* 37 (January/February 1977): 1–8.
21. *Houston Post*, 8 April 1977. See also Robert Anthony, "Zero-Base Budgeting Is a Fraud," *Wall Street Journal*, 27 April 1977.
22. Aaron Wildavsky, "The Political Economy of Efficiency: Cost-Benefit Analysis, Systems Analysis, and Program Budgeting," *Public Administration Review* 26 (December 1966): 292–310.
23. Aaron Wildavsky, *The New Politics of the Budgetary Process* (Glenview, Ill.: Scott, Foresman, 1988).
24. A. Lee Fritschler, *Smoking and Politics*, 4th ed. (Englewood Cliffs, N.J.: Prentice-Hall, 1989).
25. For some of the dynamics, see Samuel Lubell, *The Future of American Politics* (Garden City, N.Y.: Doubleday Anchor, 1955).
26. Wildavsky, "The Political Economy of Efficiency," 26.
27. Aaron Wildavsky and Arthur Hammond, "Comprehensive versus Incremental Budgeting in the Department of Agriculture," in Hyde and Shafritz, *Governmental Budgeting*, 236–251 at 237.
28. David H. Rosenbloom and Rosemary O'Leary, *Public Administration and Law*, 2d ed. (New York: Marcel Dekker, 1997); and Donald Horowitz, *The Courts and Social Policy* (Washington, D.C.: Brookings, 1977).
29. Robert Turner, "Governing from the Bench," *The Boston Globe Magazine*, 8 November 1981, 13.
30. *Missouri v. Jenkins*, 495 U.S. 33 (1990); 132 L. Ed. 2d 63 (1995). See Rosemary O'Leary and Charles Wise, "Public Managers, Judges, and Legislators: Redefining the 'New Partnership,'" *Public Administration Review* 51 (July/August 1991): 316–327.
31. In one case, a Virginia county was required to maintain a public school system because in abandoning it, the county was seeking to prevent racial integration; *Griffin v. County School Board of Prince Edward County*, 377 U.S. 218 (1964). See also Richard Lehne, *The Quest for Justice* (New York: Longman, 1978).
32. *Hamilton v. Love*, 328 F. Supp. 1182, 1194 (1971).
33. *Wyatt v. Stickney*, 325 F. Supp. 781 (1971), et seq. See also "The *Wyatt* Case: Implementation of a Judicial Decree Ordering Institutional Change," *Yale Law Journal* 84 (1975): 1338–1379.

34. *Hawkins v. Town of Shaw*, 437 F.2d 1286 (1971); *San Antonio Independent School District v. Rodriguez*, 411 U.S. 1 (1973); Lehne, *The Quest for Justice*; Horowitz, *The Courts and Social Policy*, chap. 4.

ADDITIONAL READING

FISHER, LOUIS. *Presidential Spending Power*. Princeton, N.J.: Princeton University Press, 1975.

HEILBRONER, ROBERT, AND PETER BERNSTEIN. *The Debt and the Deficit*. New York: Norton, 1989.

MILLER, GERALD. *Government Financial Management Theory*. New York: Marcel Dekker, 1991.

SCHICK, ALLEN. *The Federal Budget*. Washington, D.C.: Brookings Institution, 1995.

WILDAVSKY, AARON. *The New Politics of the Budgetary Process*. Glenview, Ill.: Scott, Foresman, 1988.

STUDY QUESTIONS

1. Some advocate a constitutional amendment that would require the federal government to balance its budget on an annual basis. What would be the chief advantages and disadvantages of such an amendment? Do you favor it? Should such an amendment have a clause allowing an unbalanced budget in times of emergency?

2. What kinds of changes in U.S. government and politics would make program budgeting easier to apply? Would you favor such changes?

3. Think of a recent political campaign that involved the issue of government spending. Evaluate the candidates' remarks and positions on matters of spending, taxation, and budgeting. Whose position would you support, and why?

4. What are the fundamental differences between the budgetary process in the federal government and in the state where you reside? What are some of the major consequences of these differences?

CHAPTER 7 | *Decision Making*

This chapter reviews varied approaches to decision making, which many view as the essence of higher-level public administration and street-level effectiveness. The traditional managerial approach to decision making relies on bureaucratic organization to promote rationality. It favors rational-comprehensive decision making that specifies objectives and identifies the most satisfactory means of achieving them. Many believe that this approach does not fit the U.S. political system well. The new public management (NPM) favors decentralized decision making based on market criteria and employee discretion. The political approach favors a kind of pluralistic give and take in decision making. This permits coalition building but generally leads to incremental decisions that modify past policies only relatively slightly. The legal approach favors an adjudicatory model to assess the reasonableness of decisions. An approach called "mixed scanning" is a partial synthesis of these approaches. No matter what approach is taken, however, there are important pitfalls to be avoided when making administrative decisions; a list of common ones is considered toward the end of the chapter. Finally, a major issue for the future is raised: How profoundly will the use of computers affect both our thinking about administrative decision making and the actual deciding?

Public administration involves the formulation and implementation of public policies intended to provide services and/or impose regulations upon individuals, groups, and organizations in the political community. Consequently, a large part of the job of some public administrators requires that they make decisions defining the objectives of public policies and choose appropriate means for achieving them. In essence, administrative decision making is simply the choice from among competing alternatives of the ends and means that an administrative program or organization will pursue and employ. But how should public administrators go about the business of deciding among these alternatives? How, in practice, do they actually decide? How can administrative decision making be improved? What are the inherent limitations on administrative decision making? These are important administrative questions that should be considered by students and practitioners of public administration. This chapter will address them by considering the managerial, political, and legal approaches to administrative decision making and by considering a technique that can serve as a partial synthesis.

THE TRADITIONAL MANAGERIAL APPROACH TO DECISION MAKING

The traditional managerial approach to public administration stresses the need for rationality in decision making. It also seeks to enable public administrators to make rational decisions in the most efficient, economical, and effective manner. One way to introduce rationality into the decision-making process is to design a system that helps the public administrator choose from among competing alternatives by (1) reducing the number of alternatives that need to be considered, (2) reducing the number of values that must be assessed in making a choice from among the alternatives, (3) assuring that the administrator knows how to make a rational choice, and (4) providing the administrator with sufficient information to select from among the alternatives. In very large part, such an organizational design will be bureaucratic.

Specialization

Specialization is the preeminent means of reducing the number of alternatives that a public administrator can consider when making a decision. Jurisdictional specialization among public agencies confines the authority of public administrators to relatively well-defined areas of public policy. For instance, the public administrator in the Department of Agriculture does not have to be concerned with issues of national security under the jurisdiction of the Department of Defense. Nor do public administrators in different agencies need to determine the social value of the various programs they administer as compared to those implemented by other agencies. Specialization within agencies has a similar effect. Some public administrators will formulate policies and rules, whereas others will enforce them. Even though the two acts are obviously and intimately connected (or at least should be), the individual engaged in enforcement may be in a position to make some choices over means, but is generally not in a position to consider the objective of the rule or policy itself. For example, a public personnel administrator engaged in the enforcement of an equal employment opportunity program may be able to make decisions regarding the appropriateness of an agency's efforts to hire and promote women and members of minority groups. If resources are scarce, such an administrator may also have to decide which agencies and what grade levels should be most closely monitored. A wide variety of additional decisions may also have to be made by such an official. However, being charged with enforcement, the public administrator in question will not have jurisdictional authority to determine that affirmative action is an inappropriate means of pursuing equal opportunity, or more drastically, that equal opportunity is not an objective with which public personnel administrators should be concerned. Of course, many cases are much more mundane, as when a public manager in charge of any particular unit is concerned solely with the internal operating efficiency and effectiveness of that unit. Specialization breaks up the functions of public agencies into manageable units; therefore, the questions, issues, problems, and alternatives facing any given individual public administrator will be limited accordingly.

Specialization also limits the values that a public administrator must take into account in making choices from among competing alternatives. Public administrators must be concerned with promoting the public interest as it relates to their authority. They are not free to choose from among policy alternatives in an unfettered fashion. For instance, the Department of the Interior is charged with promoting conservation of the nation's natural resources. It is not authorized to decide that conservation is a senseless public policy and that the agency should concentrate its efforts on ensuring exploitation and consumption. Sometimes the political heads of agencies do try to depart radically from an agency's historical values, but this almost always causes turmoil in the administrative structure and is seldom fully successful. Thus, for the public administrator, the question in decision making is, "Within the set of values embodied in my official authority, what should and can be done?"

Answers may be narrowed by an agency's culture generally and by "premise controls." Specifically, specialization can affect the cognitive premises and thought patterns of individuals. Being socialized into and working in an agency, a skilled trade, or a profession often has an impact on the way people define situations. The decision maker "voluntarily restricts the range of stimuli that will be attended to ('Those sorts of things are irrelevant,' or 'What has that got to do with the matter?') and the range of alternatives that would be considered ('It would never occur to me to do that')."[1] The importance of premise controls varies not only with the nature of specialization but also with the character and level of work. Charles Perrow explains:

> Premise controls are most important when work is nonroutine . . . and this is one
> reason scientists and other professionals have such latitude in organizations. Their

premises are well set in their training institutions and professional associations. Premise controls are also most important near the top of the organization because managerial work there is less routine, [and] the consequences of decisions are hard to assess immediately. . . . But . . . premise controls exist at all levels, created and reinforced by schools, the mass media, and cultural institutions in general.[2]

Hierarchy

The hierarchical nature of bureaucratic organizations also narrows the range of choices available to decision makers. Hierarchy defines the authority of public administrators. Typically, those with less authority have more limited choices confronting them. Some public administrators make virtually no important decisions, but rather handle a large number of repetitive, routine cases. They simply determine whether the case at hand fits one category or another—and they do so without exercising any significant discretion. An example would be an employee in a motor vehicle department who administers an eye test. Criteria for passing are established elsewhere in the organization, and the employee at the testing station simply observes whether a particular individual has met those criteria.

However, even as one goes up the organizational ranks to positions with substantial authority over specific programs, hierarchy continues to limit the responsibility of officials and thus helps define the values with which they must be concerned. This is not to say that midlevel public administrators have no difficult choices to make. But it is only when one reaches the very top levels of an organizational structure that it is typically necessary to consider choices from among a wide variety of competing and conflicting values. Street-level administration, which is discussed on pages 336–338, is an important exception.

To some extent, as this discussion suggests, specialization and hierarchy tend to overlap one another in the sense of limiting authority. But the distinction is within the kind of authority being limited: Specialization limits jurisdictional authority, whereas hierarchy limits managerial authority. The difference is somewhat subtle but it can be conveyed in the distinction between the following two statements: "I'm not responsible for what they do in that operation" (specialization) and "I don't make the rules" (hierarchy). In sum, hierarchy enables those with superior authority to define and limit the value choices available to subordinates. Although this process has informal aspects, in bureaucratic organizations it is often maintained through formal requirements.

Formalization

Formalization is particularly important in facilitating decision making through reducing alternatives available by specifying precisely the factors and information to be taken into account in exercising choice. As the term "formalization" suggests, standardized forms may be used to solicit the information that is deemed by the public agency to be relevant to its decision making. Certain

information is included; other information is excluded. The exclusion, in particular, tends to simplify decision making because it limits what must be considered. However, exclusions may prevent individuals from presenting mitigating
information. For example, at one time, several states had long residency
requirements for those seeking welfare benefits. These were intended to prevent individuals from moving into the states in order to receive benefits that
were higher than those available elsewhere. But the application processes did
not ascertain the individual's intent or reasons for migrating to the state, which
could well have involved family matters such as moving in with one's parents or
other relatives. Rather, the regulations and formal process assumed that newcomers were drawn by higher benefits and attributed this motive to all of them.
Eventually such residency requirements were declared unconstitutional,[3] but
they remain a vivid illustration of how formalization is used to ensure that if the
organization does not anticipate its relevance, some information will be ignored by it. In a case like the one just described, formalization is used to attain
the goals of impersonality and procedural equality (see Chapter 1).

Formalization may also include a more direct statement of values. It
can indicate to a decision maker the relative weight to be assigned to different
factors when there is a potential conflict among them. A clear statement of this
kind can be found in the old U.S. Civil Service Commission's early set of instructions on affirmative action: "Agency action plans and instructions involving goals and timetables must state that all actions to achieve goals must be in
full compliance with merit system requirements."[4] This clearly placed the
value of merit above that of social representation in federal personnel administration. For those making decisions on the implementation of affirmative action, the CSC's statement of values acted as a constraint that substantially reduced the alternative courses of action permissible.

Merit

The traditional managerial approach to public administration also affects the
decision-making process by seeking to assure that public administrators have
the technical ability to make the most rational choices. It also seeks to guarantee that they will use this ability free of partisan political considerations.
The quest for technical expertise and nonpartisanship is embodied in the
merit system. Competent employees are defined as those who are able to understand the jobs they are hired to do, who can process the information before them, and who can grasp such concepts as specialization and hierarchy.
They are further expected to perform their functions efficiently. Their actions are to be governed by the agency's hierarchy, rules, and values, as well
as by the rule of law. They are not supposed to take their personal political
beliefs or affiliations into account when implementing the will of the legislature or of their superordinates.

The constraints of the traditional managerial approach on decision making are frequently reinforced by the development of organizational cultures
that characterize the agency. These develop as agencies begin to express a con-

sistent set of values, as they recruit individuals for their highest career positions who reflect these values, and as the values become expressed through procedural mechanisms and formalization. According to Harold Seidman, a long-time analyst of federal administration: "Each agency has its own culture and internal set of loyalties and values which are likely to guide its actions and influence its policies." Therefore, "institutional responses are highly predictable. . . ."[5]

In the ways described above, the traditional managerial approach promotes an organizational design that has a very important impact on public administrative decision making. The approach necessarily accepts the reality of "bounded rationality" (see Chapter 4), because not all the consequences of a complex decision are likely to be known in advance. However, it attempts to enhance rationality through specialization, hierarchy, formalization, and technical competence.

The effort to structure decision making for rationality sometimes takes the form of "grid regulations" ("grid regs"). Grid regs display the intent of written rules in tabular form. Box 7–1 presents an example of the grid regs developed for the Social Security Disability Insurance (SSDI) program. The agency's rules make SSDI available when there is no job in the national economy that the impaired individual can perform on a sustained basis. The regulations in Box 7–1 categorize work as "light" (Rule 202) and "medium" (Rule 203). Age, education, and previous work experience are taken as the determinants of disability. Rule 202.01 states that an impaired worker of advanced age (55 and over), who has limited education and is unskilled should be considered disabled. By contrast, Rule 202.03 places an individual of the same age and education but with transferable skills in the category of "not disabled."

Grid regs clearly reduce the discretion of individual administrators and hearing examiners in determining the status of the individuals whose cases are before them. They clarify policy and promote uniform treatment. They prevent decision makers from taking factors that the rules consider extraneous into account. At the same time though, the regulations make it difficult or impossible for hearing examiners to assess the personal situation of each claimant. Consequently, an individual closely approaching advanced age (50 to 54) will sometimes be treated differently from one who is 55, even though for all other intents and purposes there is no significant physical or mental difference between them. Thus, the rationality of grid regs very much depends upon the appropriateness of the categories that they incorporate.[6]

The traditional managerial approach to decision making can generate a number of techniques. MBO (discussed in Chapter 4) is an example. But most generally, the traditional managerial approach favors what is known as the rational-comprehensive model of decision making.[7]

The Rational-Comprehensive Model

Determining Objectives In simplified form, the rational-comprehensive model consists of the following steps. In making decisions, the public administrator must first determine the objectives of public policy. These objectives should be identified in operational terms, in ways that can be observed and, better still, measured. Again, equal employment opportunity (EEO) as applied to the public sector provides a good example. If the objective is defined as equal opportunity in public employment, then the objective will necessarily remain vague and difficult to implement. Equal opportunity may be undefinable. (Is it simply nondiscrimination, or equalizing opportunity by equalizing education, nutrition, housing, etc., or is it actually compensating for the disadvantages placed upon groups by the society?) Nor can EEO be seen or measured directly, though some surrogate indicators can be developed. If, on the other hand, equal opportunity is defined as the social representation of groups in the public sector work force, there will be an objective that can be readily observed and measured. Social representation is simply far more tangible than opportunity. However, as discussed above, the public administrator does not have a free hand in establishing objectives. He or she is constrained by authority, specialization, hierarchy, law, and political factors. If the legislature is completely clear about what it wants, it will severely reduce the alternatives available to the public administrator trying to interpret its will.

Considering the Means   Once the objectives of public policy are established, various means for accomplishing them must be considered. If the requisite comprehensiveness is to be achieved, virtually all the potential means that can be identified must be scrutinized. This may require heavy reliance on theory, because it is highly unlikely that all the potential means have at one time or another been tested and evaluated in actual practice. According to the rational-comprehensive model, in considering the potential means to the objectives, the public administrator is required to try to project *all* the consequences of each of the means on all the various areas of governmental concern.

Continuing with the equal employment opportunity (EEO) example, several means could be identified. Assuming that the objective is defined in terms of social representation, as is actually the case, then trying to recruit and later promote members from all segments of the population and eliminating barriers that some groups may face in competing for employment may be viewed as appropriate means. Similarly, protections might be afforded members of underrepresented groups in reductions in force. In addition, various special training programs to promote their upward mobility in the civil service could be developed. Other potential means include governmental programs, similar to those used by the military, to fund students' college and graduate educations in return for the students' commitment to join the civil service for a specified number of years. The elimination of veteran preference would still be a means of promoting the employment of women. The objective of social representation could also be achieved by firing nonminorities (white males) to make room for African-Americans, Hispanics, women, and other EEO target groups. Another possibility would be eliminating compet-

BOX 7–1 **Social Security Disability Insurance "Grid Regs"**

RESIDUAL FUNCTIONAL CAPACITY: MAXIMUM SUSTAINED WORK CAPABILITY LIMITED TO LIGHT AND MEDIUM WORK AS A RESULT OF SEVERE MEDICALLY DETERMINABLE IMPAIRMENT(S)

Rule	Age*	Education	Previous Work Experience	Decision
		LIGHT WORK		
202.01	Advanced age	Limited or less	Unskilled or none	Disabled
202.02	do†	do	Skilled or semiskilled—skills not transferable	do
202.03	do	do	Skilled or semiskilled—skills transferable	Not disabled
202.04	do	High school graduate or more—does not provide for direct entry into skilled work	Unskilled or none	Disabled
202.05	Advanced age	High school graduate or more—provides for direct entry into skilled work	Unskilled or none	Not disabled
202.06	do	High school graduate or more—does not provide for direct entry into skilled work	Skilled or semiskilled—skills not transferable	Disabled
202.07	do	do	Skilled or semiskilled—skills transferable	Not disabled
202.08	do	High school graduate or more—provides for direct entry into skilled work	Skilled or semiskilled—skills not transferable	do
202.09	Closely approaching advanced age	Illiterate or unable to communicate in English	Unskilled or none	Disabled
202.10	do	Limited or less—at least literate and able to communicate in English	do	Not disabled
202.11	do	Limited or less	Skilled or semiskilled—skills not transferable	do
202.12	do	do	Skilled or semiskilled—skills transferable	do
202.13	do	High school graduate or more	Unskilled or none	do
202.14	do	do	Skilled or semiskilled—skills not transferable	do
202.15	do	do	Skilled or semiskilled—skills transferable	do
202.16	Younger individual	Illiterate or unable to communicate in English	Unskilled or none	do
202.17	do	Limited or less—at least literate and able to communicate in English	do	do
202.18	do	Limited or less	Skilled or semiskilled—skills not transferable	do
202.19	do	do	Skilled or semiskilled—skills transferable	do

BOX 7–1 *Continued*

RESIDUAL FUNCTIONAL CAPACITY: MAXIMUM SUSTAINED WORK CAPABILITY LIMITED TO LIGHT AND MEDIUM WORK AS A RESULT OF SEVERE MEDICALLY DETERMINABLE IMPAIRMENT(S)

Rule	Age*	Education	Previous Work Experience	Decision
202.20	do	High school graduate or more	Unskilled or none	do
202.21	do	do	Skilled or semiskilled—skills not transferable	do
202.22	do	do	Skilled or semiskilled—skills transferable	do

MEDIUM WORK				
203.01	Closely approaching retirement age	Marginal or none	Unskilled or none	Disabled
203.02	do	Limited or less	None	do
203.03	do	Limited	Unskilled	Not disabled
203.04	do	Limited or less	Skilled or semiskilled—skills not transferable	do
203.05	do	do	Skilled or semiskilled—skills transferable	do
203.06	do	High school graduate or more	Unskilled or none	do
203.07	do	High school graduate or more—does not provide for direct entry into skilled work	Skilled or semiskilled—skills not transferable	do
203.08	do	do	Skilled or semiskilled—skills transferable	do
203.09	do	High school graduate or more—provides for direct entry into skilled work	Skilled or semiskilled—skills not transferable	do
203.10	Advanced age	Limited or less	None	Disabled
203.11	do	do	Unskilled	Not disabled
203.12	do	do	Skilled or semiskilled—skills not transferable	do
203.13	do	do	Skilled or semiskilled—skills transferable	do
203.14	do	High school graduate or more	Unskilled or none	do
203.15	do	High school graduate or more—does not provide for direct entry into skilled work	Skilled or semiskilled—skills not transferable	do
203.16	do	do	Skilled or semiskilled—skills transferable	do
203.17	do	High school graduate or more—provides for direct entry into skilled work	Skilled or semiskilled—skills not transferable	do

BOX 7–1 *Continued*

RESIDUAL FUNCTIONAL CAPACITY: MAXIMUM SUSTAINED WORK CAPABILITY LIMITED TO LIGHT AND MEDIUM WORK AS A RESULT OF SEVERE MEDICALLY DETERMINABLE IMPAIRMENT(S)

Rule	Age*	Education	Previous Work Experience	Decision
203.18	Closely approaching advanced age	Limited or less	Unskilled or none	do
203.19	do	do	Skilled or semiskilled—skills not transferable	do
203.20	do	do	Skilled or semiskilled—skills transferable	do
203.21	do	High school graduate or more	Unskilled or none	do
203.22	do	High school graduate or more—does not provide for direct entry into skilled work	Skilled or semiskilled—skills not transferable	do
203.23	do	do	Skilled or semiskilled—skills transferable	do
203.24	do	High school graduate or more—provides for direct entry into skilled work	Skilled or semiskilled—skills not transferable	do
203.25	Younger individual	Limited or less	Unskilled or none	do
203.26	do	do	Skilled or semiskilled—skills not transferable	do
203.27	do	do	Skilled or semiskilled—skills transferable	do
203.28	do	High school graduate or more	Unskilled or none	do
203.29	do	High school graduate or more—does not provide for direct entry into skilled work	Skilled or semiskilled—skills not transferable	do
203.30	do	do	Skilled or semiskilled—skills transferable	do
203.31	do	High school graduate or more—provides for direct entry into skilled work	Skilled or semiskilled—skills not transferable	do

*Advanced age = 55 and over; closely approaching advanced age = 50–54; younger individual = 18–49.
†do = ditto.

SOURCE: U.S. Department of Health and Human Services, Social Security Administration; regulations in *U.S. Federal Register*; vol. 43, 55369–53370, 28 November 1978.

itive merit examinations and the "rule of three" (see Chapter 5) in favor of pass examinations that would yield a more diverse pool of eligibles. One could go on and on identifying potential means in this context, and that is precisely what the rational-comprehensive model seeks to assure.

Choosing the Best Alternative   Once all the potential means for achieving an end are identified, it is necessary to choose among them. According to the traditional managerial approach, this choice should be made so as to maximize efficiency, economy, and effectiveness. Where these three values are not in full harmony with one another, an appropriate balance is to be struck among them. Although the latter may prove difficult, there is no doubt that these values can serve as helpful guides. For instance, in terms of EEO, they would probably rule out establishing programs to pay for the higher education of women and members of minority groups in return for a commitment on their part to work for a relatively short period. Affording large-scale training to minorities and women might also prove very expensive. Aside from potential political and legal problems, firing white males could lead to widespread demoralization and inefficiency. On the other hand, relying solely on broad recruitment efforts might prove ineffective in bringing about change. To choose the most desirable means under such circumstances, a program might be developed using training, aggressive recruitment of women and members of minority groups, and the modification of veteran preference and various personnel devices to relax the disparate effects of competitive examinations and the rule of three. The result, at least in theory, is a comprehensive program designed to operate within the confines of what is acceptable in terms of efficiency, economy, and effectiveness. Whether such a program can be immediately applied in practice, given political and legal constraints, however, is another matter.

Critique of the Rational-Comprehensive Model

The rational-comprehensive model, derived from the traditional managerial perspective on public administration, has some important benefits. It is comprehensive and provides a good deal of direction in the choice of potential means to identified policy objectives. It encourages the public administrator to think a problem through and to apply his or her technical expertise in identifying the best solution. If we look upon public administrative decision making as a problem-solving endeavor, then the rational-comprehensive model is often very useful. Nevertheless, in practice this model is not always suitable to the actual nature of governmental decision making. As discussed earlier in other contexts, efficiency, economy, and even effectiveness are not necessarily dominant values in government. First, the objectives of governmental policies are not always clear. For instance, the Department of the Interior is charged with making sure that there is an "equitable" distribution of the benefits from nationally owned land and resources. But what does that mean? What is equitable in this context? What kind of technical expertise does the public administrator possess to define "equitable" in meaningful and politically acceptable terms? Second, many agencies are charged with doing one thing or another "in the public interest." Although it is probably necessary for the political community to believe that there *is* a public interest, it may be impossible to identify what the public interest requires in operational terms. This is because as soon as we become specific, we tend to generate conflict. For instance, veterans may agree that equal employment opportunity is in the public interest, but they are likely to disagree that, therefore, the public interest requires the elimination of preferences for their own group. In pluralistic politics, consensus is built by developing inclusive coalitions that tend to offer something to many significant political groups, without being very specific concerning the aims of a policy and the priorities within it. Looking at EEO in the federal government, we can see the effect of this tendency. The program was established with a clear focus on black employment; subsequently, women and Hispanics were included within its ambit; today, it includes not only these groups but also Native Americans, Pacific Islanders, Asian-Americans, veterans, and the handicapped. In some localities, homosexuals have sought to be included within equal opportunity and civil rights programs. This approach builds broad coalitions supporting the public administrators' programs, but it makes it difficult to say precisely what a program's goals are in operational terms or to establish priorities. Thus, veteran preference has an adverse impact on the employment interests of women. Nor are the employment interests of African-Americans and Hispanics identical. Gains for one group are not necessarily associated with greater employment opportunity for the other.[8] Latinos, Mexican-Americans, Cuban-Americans, and Puerto Ricans, often lumped together for statistical purposes in EEO reports, may each have very different employment interests.

An additional problem with the rational-comprehensive model is that it assumes that public administrators have the time to approach problems in a dispassionate way, to identify comprehensively all the potential means of achieving identified objectives, and to assess all these means in terms of efficiency, economy, and effectiveness. Although circumstances in which the public administrator is truly proactive in this fashion may exist, many practitioners of public administration would find such a scenario quite alien to their work environment. To a very large extent, public administration in the United States is not proactive, but rather reactive. It requires that public administrators react relatively quickly to problems, deadlines, or crises. Many hardly have enough time to identify even one potential means toward an end, much less to try to identify all potential means and then determine which is best in terms of efficiency, economy, and effectiveness.

Another difficulty with the rational-comprehensive approach is that the very specialization of which it makes such strong use may also become a liability. We are all familiar with the image of the government's right hand not knowing what the left one is doing. This is because the hands operate in different spheres, under different time constraints, and with different objectives in mind. But modern government, of course, has more than two hands; it has almost countless tentacles. The public administrator operating one of these is bound, on occasion, to be at odds with the actions of another. This is how the State Department came to back one side in the 1971 India-Pakistan war while the Department of Defense backed the other![9] Or how one agency seeks to preserve wilderness and wetland areas while another fights to develop them. Returning to our familiar EEO example, an EEO office might oppose programs for comprehensive labor relations, because these would make priorities in reductions-in-force a subject for collective bargaining, in which the interests of minority workers might not be well protected.

To some extent, specialization also makes it difficult to assess the full costs of any particular governmental course of action. An agency making decisions in a complex policy area is likely to create new problems for other agencies. For instance, when the Department of Defense seeks to deploy a new advanced weapons system or NASA undertakes a new program of space exploration, it will inevitably have consequences for other governmental programs, including those concerned with exploiting and stockpiling strategic resources and programs dealing with scientific education. The Department of Energy's production of nuclear weapons has created environmental problems that affect other federal and nonfederal agencies. In terms of the rational-comprehensive model, the problem is that these shifted costs are difficult to assess because they tend to get lost in the system of specialized jurisdictions. The problem is compounded by the fact that, as the administrative state grows, less and less is truly external to governmental concerns, so even costs that are shifted from government to society tend eventually to become a public policy concern.

A final criticism of the rational-comprehensive model is that because it relies on theory and abstract expertise, it can produce decisions that are inappropriate in terms of practice. This allegedly is one reason why centralized planning has not worked out as well as anticipated in a variety of political communities.[10] It also partly explains why various budgeting techniques, such as PPBS and ZBB, have not worked out as well as anticipated in the United States (see Chapter 6).

THE NEW PUBLIC MANAGEMENT AND DECISION MAKING

Market Criteria

The NPM strongly favors basing public administrative decisions on market criteria. National Performance Review (NPR) includes a section on "using market mechanisms to solve problems"; it favors entrepreneurial organizations, considers customer satisfaction of key importance, and seeks to set up performance-based organizations to mirror private corporations in performing government's "factory" operations.[11]

Markets are generally considered to create two types of efficiencies. First, they allocate goods and services efficiently in terms of matching production to customer demand. Organizations dependent on market transactions for their revenues or incomes are impelled by economic incentives to offer what customers want. In free, nonmonopoly markets, firms that fail to do so will suffer economically and eventually will fail. This stands in contrast to traditional bureaucracies or other nonmarket operations using hierarchy to determine which goods and services will be offered. To return to an earlier example, agencies are more likely to satisfy their training needs if they can select programs in an open market as opposed to being required to rely on what is prescribed and offered by a central personnel agency. The clunky consumer products manufactured by government organizations in the former Soviet Union are emblematic of the problem of matching centralized decision making to consumer preferences.

Second, markets foster technical efficiency, sometimes called X efficiency. Technical efficiency is typically calculated in terms of the inputs used to produce outputs. The less input per output, the greater the efficiency. All things being equal, organizations that are more technically efficient have an advantage in competitive markets. The proposition that organizations in competitive markets will necessarily be more technically efficient than nonmarket administrative operations is less widely accepted than the belief that they will have greater allocational efficiency. However, it is an article of faith in the NPM. And, undeniably, "bureaucracy" is used in most quarters to denote technical as well as allocational inefficiency.

In the NPM's view, therefore, requiring administrative units to respond to market pressures forces their decision making to be more concerned with customer satisfaction and technical efficiency. It also holds that empowering frontline employees to respond to customers' needs and to solve production and other problems will enhance both types of efficiency. Further, entrepreneurial organizations, which the NPM assumes will be nonhierarchical, develop goods and services that customers demand. They are proactive in serving the public and creating value. In sum, markets are better than rules—especially centralized controls—in producing public service efficiently.

There is a huge literature on the market theory that underlies the NPM.[12] But there is too little experience with market mechanisms in the U.S. public sector to provide a strong empirical basis for many of the reforms recommended by the NPR, and supporters of reinventing government more generally. Time will tell whether their reforms are implemented and, if so, how well they work. More is known about the decision making of empowered frontline public employees in nonmarket settings.

Employee Empowerment

Street-level administrators have long been "empowered" in the sense that the NPR uses the term. These are public employees who interact directly with segments of the public in a variety of service and regulatory capacities.[13] They include police, social workers, parole officers, teachers, and housing and health inspectors, among others. They can be considered empowered because:

1. They exercise a great deal of discretion in frequent face-to-face encounters with clients, customers, and those whom they regulate.
2. They have considerable independence within their organizations and do not work under direct visual or close proximate supervision.
3. Frequently, limited resources require that they provide services or enforce the law selectively.
4. In the aggregate, their decisions constitute the policy outputs of the agencies for which they work.

Police are probably the best example. They have tremendous discretion in determining when and how to act upon individuals. In many places, without broad discretion they probably could not survive. They often work alone or in pairs, without immediate hierarchical supervision. Selective enforcement and nonenforcement of the law is a necessity. They cannot possibly ticket every jaywalker, speeder, litterer, or person whose dog is unleashed. To a very large extent, their actions determine what the police force does. Does it treat people fairly and reasonably? Does it mediate, ignore, or squelch domestic disputes? Does it make the acceptable speed limit 5 or 10 miles higher than the posted limit? Does it discriminate against members of minority groups and treat them harshly?

Although street-level administrators have a great deal of discretion, they are not wholly unconstrained or without official guidance.[14] They rely on law, agency guidelines, and the expertise and training required for their jobs. In many situations, they also use intuition to assess the actions of those with whom they are interacting. Court cases reveal that sometimes police officers cannot explain how they correctly determined that someone was transporting illegal drugs; they just knew it.[15] Research indicates that street-level administrators' personal values and those of their fellow employees have a great impact on their decision making.[16] Personal values may act as a filter through which law, guidelines, principles derived from training, and intuition are either embraced and acted upon or resisted. Failure to enforce the rules always raises issues where the rule of law is highly valued. However, American society seems willing to tolerate nonenforcement when it is reasonable and involves everyday behavior of minor consequence. Problematic patterns of practice arise when the law is applied more harshly to some groups than others. For instance, it is well-documented that African-Americans, Hispanics, "hippie types," and Asians are disproportionately stopped by law enforcement personnel along the southern border, on highways, and in airports.[17] Blacks with out-of-state license plates are particularly likely to be stopped by state and local police.[18]

Concern that street-level administrators may abuse their discretionary authority has led to efforts to constrain them with rules. This diminishes the very flexibility that is sometimes necessary for successful street-level administration. Compliance with the rules can become an end in itself, rather than a means to a public policy goal. A popular stereotype is the housing or Occupational Health and Safety Administration (OSHA) inspector who writes up tens of minor violations of minimal (or no) importance instead of helping solve real problems.

The NPR rejects the rule-bound approach. It favors letting street-level administrators rely on "common sense" to a greater extent by reducing the number of regulatory rules (so there is less to enforce) and by freeing street-level administrators from many of the agency controls and reporting requirements they have traditionally faced.[19] Accountability, in this view, should be for results, rather than for strict adherence to a set of procedures of dubious efficacy. The empowered public administrator will have greater discretion, but will be held more accountable for policy outcomes. Based on what is known about street-level administrators, the success of the NPR model will depend on recruitment and socialization that ensures decision making that is fair minded and technically, politically, and legally correct.

THE POLITICAL APPROACH TO DECISION MAKING: THE INCREMENTAL MODEL

Critics of the rational-comprehensive model of decision making argue that it is unrealistic, that its values do not necessarily match those of the polity, that it does not fit the nature of contemporary administrative operations, and that it requires administrators to exercise a degree of rationality and comprehensive expertise that is beyond their ability.[20] These critics suggest that another process is more suitable to the public sector in the United States—a process that has been dubbed the **incremental model**.[21] It is important to note that discussions of this model develop a dual argument. First, that the incremental approach is in fact the approach most characteristic of public administrative operations in the United States, and second, that it is the model that *should* be relied on to the greatest extent. Its proponents claim that it fits the nature of United States politics and political institutions well and that it is a model that public administrators can actually apply. As will become evident, the incremental model is highly compatible with the political approach to public administration.

It is generally maintained that the incremental model recognizes the vagueness of many of the stated objectives of public policy. Such vagueness is considered endemic in a pluralistic political community and often seems to be the price of building a consensus strong enough to operate administrative programs at all. Politics, in this view, often requires that the objectives of public policy not be expressed in operational terms. Here is the difference between EEO and affirmative action (AA), for example. It is easier to build a consensus in favor of EEO, because in the abstract anyone can support the principle of equality of opportunity. However, when it is operationalized in terms of the use of goals and timetables for the purposes of hiring members of specific social groups, support for the program may decline drastically. Affirmative action identifies some groups as beneficiaries and others as those who will potentially bear a heavy burden. Consequently, some who can support EEO in the abstract are inevitably turned into opponents of an AA program. A similar phenomenon occurs in terms of agency missions to serve "the public interest" or assure "equity," and so forth. As long as these terms remain ill-defined in an operational sense, a broad coalition can support the programs designed to administer them. (This point is illustrated by the case study of benzene in the workplace, presented on pages 348–352.)

If the price of defining an objective is loss of political support and the demise of an administrative program, public administrators will be reluctant to express their missions or objectives in comprehensive and operational terms. Rather, they will prefer to move slowly, step by step toward a somewhat improved state of affairs, even though this may require some backtracking and constant modification of policies and means of implementing them. In other words, such an approach will be incremental and will be considered by many to be in step with the style of U.S. politics.

The incremental model of decision making follows from the political approach to public administration. It stresses the need for public administrators to be responsive to the political community, to be politically representative of the groups that comprise it, and to be accountable to elected officials. Together, these values dictate that administrative decision making should involve public participation; that public administration should be based on the development of political coalitions and political consensus; and that it should allow nonexpert, political officials not only to give direction to public administrators, but also to exert pressure on them to decide in favor of one policy application or another.

The incremental model specifies the following general process for administrative decision making.

Redefining the Ends   Means and ends are not treated as distinct from one another. The model recognizes that policy objectives may be too unclear to serve as ends in any operational sense. Consequently, the ends of government policy are often defined by the means available to an agency for moving in some general policy direction. In the affirmative action example, for instance, this would require that, if used at all, hiring or promotional goals and timetables would be in addition to merit examinations, veteran preference, the rule of three, and so forth. It would be recognized that it is politically impracticable to reform the personnel system in one fell swoop but that eventually greater equal opportunity or social representation could be achieved by developing limited programs toward those ends. If the means to achieve full social representation of all ethnic and racial groups in the society are not available without such major reform, the end of social representation itself may be redefined. Thus, it may become the proportional representation of minorities and women of working age. This too might be unattainable, and the end might be further redefined as proportional representation of these groups in the work force. Such an objective might be further scaled down to be the proportional representation of such people in the work force in the occupations in which government personnel engage. A still further modification might be that any given agency's staff should be proportionally representative of minority groups and women in the work force in the occupations *and* in the geographic area in which the agency recruits its personnel. In such a scenario, the means available eventually determine what the end of public policy will be—at least until it is possible to employ other means or build a consensus for other ends.

Arriving at a Consensus   The test of a good decision is agreement or consensus in favor of the policy and method of implementation it develops. Means and ends are treated as packages that are more or less acceptable to relevant communities of interest. The package that is most acceptable—that has the greatest consensus behind it—is typically considered the "best" approach. In this sense, representativeness and responsiveness trump efficiency, economy, and effectiveness as the values to be sought in choosing means. The traditional managerial values are not treated as inconsequential by the incremental model, but they are not weighed as preeminent. A program that does *less* and costs *more* may be more acceptable in the incremental model than one that is more economical and efficient. There are several additional points implied by this view.

1. Because the test of a good policy is the level of political support it generates, decisions are not actually tested against their impact in producing a change in a given area of social, economic, or political life. Rather, the test is the maintenance of political support, often expressed through increases in budgetary allocations. Consequently, even a program that is overwhelmingly *symbolic* and has no discernible impact on society other than generating support can be considered successful. Perhaps the U.S. Commission on Civil Rights could be considered an agency with predominantly symbolic functions.

2. Because the test of a good policy is not its impact on some target in the society but rather the support it generates, to oppose a program it is generally necessary to demonstrate what would be better. In other words, it is not enough to say that the program doesn't work; one has to indicate what *will* work. The latter, of course, is likely to be difficult and may very well be politically infeasible because it threatens the coalition in support of the existing program.

3. This procedure for judging administrative decisions tends to be an obstacle to policy evaluation and to make performance appraisal difficult. Here again, the disjuncture between the political and managerial approaches to public administration is evident. (Policy evaluation is discussed in the next chapter.)

Making a Satisfactory Decision   In the process of incremental decision making, analysis tends to be more limited than in the rational-comprehensive approach. Administrative decision makers taking the incremental approach will consider a few means-ends packages and select one that is *satisfactory*. Little or no effort is made to reach an optimum decision that maximizes the pertinent values. Decisions are guided by past practice and tend not to rely heavily on theory. However, a substantial degree of comprehensiveness may be built into the incremental decision-making model by encouraging the participation of relevant interest groups, other agencies, members of the legislature, and concerned individuals in the process of deciding on a policy. To some extent this approach is found in the federal Administrative Procedure Act of 1946 and many similar state statutes. Under such legislation, when an agency is considering adopting a new policy through informal rule making, it generally must publish its proposed rule changes and an explanation of them in a public forum. It may explain the rationale behind its proposals in considerable detail. Interested parties are given a chance to respond in writing or through hearings, and the agency is supposed to take these responses into account before issuing its final rules. Often advisory committees are created or authorized to participate in agency policy making. More elaborate rule making, called "formal" rule making or "rule making on the record," provides a quasi-judicial forum in which many informed interested parties can present their perspectives to administrative law judges or other presiding officials.

By providing such pluralistic representation, a degree of comprehensiveness is developed in an agency's consideration of what can and should be done. Here is an area where the political approach's emphasis on pluralistic administrative organizational structure reinforces its approach toward decision making. Overlapping agency missions require the participation of several administrative units in making major decisions, and these units are likely to express differing perspectives. Compromises will be developed in the interests of maintaining cooperation and support. In general, radical departures from past practices and policies will be limited.

A Critique of the Incremental Model

It is obvious that the incremental approach has some major advantages in terms of representation and responsiveness. But its limitations are perhaps equally clear. First, it is inherently conservative to the extent that it may become extremely difficult for government to effectively penetrate the society in the ways it generally intends. Pluralism tends to be self-reinforcing. Every interest seeks its own governmental spokesperson (bureau or agency). The more administrative units involved, the more difficult coordination becomes. Consequently, more and more interagency committees are created. Policy judged by consensus will place a heavy emphasis on building and maintaining political support. As a result, conflict resolution and conflict avoidance will be stressed. Lawyers will work out acceptable lines of turf for the overlapping programs of different agencies or bureaus. Budgeters will seek to assure that relative levels of funding remain constant. "Hyperpluralism" or gridlock can even lead beyond conservatism to immobilism as the description, in Box 7–2, of the Food and Drug Administration's experience with Red Dye #3 indicates.

A second difficulty with the incremental model is that because it relies on the successive taking of small steps in modifying policy, it is possible eventually to end up with very undesirable and totally unforeseen consequences. One well-documented, outstanding example of this was the "Bay of Pigs" invasion of 1961. A military force of anticommunist Cuban exiles was formed and trained in the United States and some Central American countries. The force was created as a somewhat remote contingency that could be used in an effort to overthrow the regime of Fidel Castro. Step by step, the force was enlarged and strengthened. Eventually, President Kennedy was confronted with the question of what to do with it. He did not want to turn it loose in the United States, nor were other countries willing to accept it. There seemed only one alternative, which was to let it invade Cuba. It did so, with the help of the United States, and was destroyed by the Cuban governmental forces. In writing about this sorry episode, Theodore Sorensen said:

> This plan was now or never, for three reasons: first, because the brigade was fully trained, restive to fight and difficult to hold off; second . . . because his only choice was to send them back to Cuba or bring them back to this country, where they would broadcast their resentment; and third, because Russian arms would soon build up Castro's army. . . .[22]

A related limitation of the incremental model is that it can produce *circularity* in policy making. Taking step after step without a clear objective or a comprehensive plan can lead administrators to repeat past processes and organizational arrangements even though at an earlier time these were modified because of their perceived defects. For instance, the federal government's EEO program was shifted into its central personnel agency twice and out of it twice. Each second shift was accompanied by a well-worn rationale.[23] In other words, the incremental approach is particularly susceptible to failure to maintain an "organizational memory." The rational-comprehensive model's effort to identify all possible means is likely to lead to a consideration of previous efforts (if any). Adjudication, which is discussed in the next section, also enhances organizational memory. It often involves an exhaustive search for past decisions that may be relevant to a present one.

Finally, the incremental model of decision making does not fit fundamental decisions intended to redirect the society or commit it to some large-scale venture. Despite its limitations in practice, comprehensive planning seems more appropriate in such cases. It is partly for this reason that societies seeking rapid economic development have tended to avoid incrementalism. However, because incrementalism virtually requires a pluralistic political system and fragmented administrative organization in order to be comprehensive, rejecting incrementalism can reduce a political community's emphasis on developing and maintaining representative political institutions. Of course, much depends on the degree of heterogeneity in the society. To some

BOX 7–2 **The Perils of Incrementalism—Immobilism at the FDA (1960–1996)**

On February 1, 1985, the Food and Drug Administration (FDA) postponed a decision to ban Red Dye #3 for the twenty-sixth time in twenty-five years. The dye is used in a variety of beverages, vitamins, cereals, dessert foods, and maraschino cherries. Based on animal studies authorized in 1977 and completed between 1981 and 1983, the FDA determined that Red Dye #3 is a carcinogen (at least in laboratory animals). Based on the Delaney Amendment (1960) to the Food, Drug and Cosmetic Act, any substance whose ingestion is believed to cause cancer in animals or humans must be banned for human consumption. The amendment is unequivocal; it does not require a risk assessment. But the FDA does not have final authority to ban products such as Red Dye #3. That authority is shared with the secretary of the Department of Health and Human Services, in which the FDA is located, and with the Office of Management and Budget, which has authority to oversee the issuance of regulatory rules by some agencies. The stakes are high, and so is the level of interest-group activity. The Public Citizen Health Research Group and other consumer advocates have lobbied and sued to have the dye banned. Several trade groups, including the National Food Processors Association, the Certified Color Manufacturers Association, and the Cosmetic, Toiletry and Fragrance Association, have actively lobbied over the years for modification of the Delaney Amendment. At least eight senators and thirty members of the House of Representatives lined up on the sides of the trade groups. Many of these legislators represent states or districts where the proposed ban would have an unfavorable and substantial economic effect. The pressure on the FDA was so intense that, at one point, it completely reversed itself within a two-day period (April 11–12, 1984).

The dispute continued throughout the 1980s, with supporters of the dye claiming to represent the American people, who "like their cherries red," and opponents, such as Congressman Ted Weiss (D-NY), voicing continuing frustration that as late as the summer of 1989, the product was still being sold: "FDA scientists have concluded that Red Dye No. 3 causes cancer. The ostensible grounds for further study [advanced by the advocates of the dye] . . . have already been studied and dismissed . . . by a panel of expert governmental scientists. . . . Under the law, the FDA has no option but to follow through with its stated intentions to terminate the provisional listing of Red Dye No. 3. . . . It is high time that it did so." Maybe, but then again, the FDA has much to do and it obviously hasn't viewed the dye as an "imminent risk" to the public. The outcome—at least for now—is as close as your supermarket's shelves. But if you buy chocolate covered cherries, don't forget to look in the chocolate, too.

SOURCES: Marian Burros, "The Saga of a Food Regulation: After 25 Years, Still No Decision," *New York Times*, 13 February 1985; Brooke Masters, "They're Still Dyeing to Keep Maraschinos Red," *Washington Post National Weekly Edition*, 24–30 June 1989, 32.

extent, however, the debate over rational-comprehensive planning versus incrementalism is also a controversy over the nature of political systems.

THE LEGAL APPROACH TO DECISION MAKING

The legal approach to public administrative decision making relies on adjudicatory procedure in an effort to assure (1) that individuals, groups, corporations, or other parties are not denied their rights or otherwise treated contrary to law; and (2) that decision making is reasoned and based on sound information. Adjudication is a special form of incrementalism, one bounded by an elaborate, formalized procedure and rules intended to identify (1) the facts of a situation, (2) the interests of opposing parties, and (3) the balance between these interests that best fits legal requirements and/or best serves the public interest.[24] It is assumed that by going through adjudicatory procedure in a large number of instances dealing with essentially the same area of public policy, it will be possible eventually to build a body of principles that defines the public interest.

It is useful to think of adjudication as falling into two broad categories, prospective and retrospective. **Prospective adjudication** frequently involves requests by regulated utilities, transportation companies, radio and television broadcasters, and so forth for the right to modify some aspects of their service, such as their rates, routes, or programming. It may also concern requests for licenses to operate a business or provide a service in a regulated sector of the economy. Formal rule making under the Administrative Procedure Act (APA) is prospective and uses an adjudicatory format. Prospective adjudication also occurs when one applies for a variety of social welfare benefits. It frequently requires that the private party file a request for some kind of change and supply information and a rationale for its request. Typically, the public agency undertakes an analysis of the request. Assuming there is some controversy involved, such as whether the applicant is eligible or granting the request is in the public interest, a hearing before an impartial administrative law judge or hearing examiner may be held. During the hearing the party requesting the change will be afforded the opportunity to present more information relevant to the request. The staff of the regulatory agency may present countervailing information pertaining to its view of what the public interest requires, as outlined in the relevant statutes. Both sides may be able to present witnesses and confront and cross-examine witnesses on the other side. Third parties may be invited to submit statements either orally or in writing. The hearing examiner may play an active role in trying to clarify the issues, information, and opinions before the agency. This stage of adjudication will end when the hearing examiner issues a decision. Generally, the decision will be reviewed at a higher level in the agency, often by a "commission" of some kind. It may be ratified, rejected, or amended at this stage. The whole process will be legalistic in the sense of being bound by established rules of procedure (that is, the order of the proceeding, who can appear as a witness, the form cross-examination takes, and the nature of the information that can be presented at the hearing). Administrative adjudication makes use of adversary procedure, but it is generally more flexible than courtroom procedure, especially in terms of rules of evidence and the more active role frequently played by the hearing examiner.

A second type of administrative adjudication is **retrospective.** Here, an alleged wrongdoing comes to the attention of an administrative agency. This may occur through the filing of a complaint against an individual, corporation, or other party. Such a complaint may allege unfair competition, deceptive advertising, an unfair labor or personnel practice, or other form of behavior that violates law or agency regulations. Sometimes the agency becomes aware of the alleged wrongdoing through its own preliminary investigations, monitoring of reports, audits, and similar means.

Once a wrongdoing is alleged, the agency is likely to undertake an elaborate investigation to determine what actually occurred. If agency officials in a "prosecutorial" role believe that the situation warrants further action, notice is given to the party charged with the wrongdoing. That party is then afforded a formal opportunity to respond, either orally or in writing. In many cases, this response will be in the form of a hearing presided over by an administrative law judge or independent hearing examiner. Again, the hearing will resemble a judicial trial, although it is likely to be more flexible. The party charged with the wrongdoing may have a right to be represented by counsel, to present witnesses, and to confront and cross-examine adverse witnesses. Adversary procedure is used to establish the truth of what occurred and varying interpretations of the rules governing the action. The hearing examiner will issue a decision, which will probably be subject to review at some later stage within the agency or by another governmental body.

Adjudication is an important means of making administrative decisions in several policy areas, especially regulation, personnel administration, and the granting or termination of social welfare benefits. Its best advantage is considered to be that it enables administrative bodies to act in a judicial fashion that is detached from political pressures. This encourages them to develop an independent view of the public interest that is informed by their expertise, to make decisions in an incremental fashion supporting that view, and to develop a body of law or precedent that helps identify the public interest on a continuing basis. Adjudication is especially useful where the legislature cannot agree or establish a comprehensive policy, where there is a need to make adjustments on a continual basis, as in the setting of rates for public utilities, and where flexibility is desired. It is also a useful process where decisions must turn on idiosyncratic factors, such as the intent, financial status, or physical condition of a party, or the extent to which a party was acting in good faith or reasonably. Adjudication is especially suitable where the enforcement of a rule, law, or policy requires the weighing of several criteria in the context of a specific situation.

Adjudication is particularly useful in assuring that decisions are made on the basis of adequate information and are reasonable. Rules of evidence screen out information that is considered unreliable. Confrontation and cross-examination test the validity of the information upon which the adjudicative decision is made. The APA authorizes judicial review of agency decisions that are allegedly arbitrary, capricious, or an abuse of discretion. It requires that formal rule making be supported by substantial evidence. The Fourth Amendment, which is very important in street-level administration, prohibits "unreasonable" searches and seizures. At the very least, it requires that administrators be able to articulate a reasonable basis for their actions involving searches or seizures. For instance, intuition alone is an insufficient basis for a police officer to stop a motorist to check on his or her license or the vehicle's registration.[25] Public administrators' liability for violations of individuals' constitutional rights depends on whether they reasonably should have known better. (The role of the Constitution in American public administration is the subject of Chapter 11.)

A good example of the utility of adjudication occurs in the area of public employees' complaints of prohibited discrimination. It would be very difficult to identify, in the abstract, every personnel situation in which such an employee might be discriminated against. Prohibited discrimination ranges from dismissals, to scheduling of work hours and coffee breaks, to assessment of the performance of an employee and evaluation of his or her attitude. Such assessments of attitude, especially, can be incredibly subtle. Social stereotyping can cause "initiative" in one person to be labeled "aggressiveness" or "abrasiveness" in another who belongs to a different social group. Moreover, because discrimination is subjective and rarely openly stated nowadays, it is necessary to probe the behavior and motivation of a supervisor who has allegedly engaged in such a prohibited practice. This may require reviewing his or her past record in dealing with minorities, women, or men as a group. Adjudication is a useful vehicle for allowing one side to present a case and the other to defend his or her actions. An impartial weighing of the information (evidence) in a wide variety of cases can lead to the development of a body of principles identifying prohibited discrimination and helping to determine when it occurs. Presumably, such a body of principles will take into account the interests of individuals in being treated fairly as well as the public interest in enabling supervisors to manage their employees. It is difficult to imagine how equal employment opportunity policy could be enforced without at least some reliance on adjudication. The same is true for a variety of other areas of public policy.

By the same token, adjudication also has serious limitations. Adjudication is a peculiar form of incrementalism. It shares the major pitfall of that approach to decision making. It is possible to make a series of incremental decisions in a policy area without being fully cognizant of the resultant state of affairs toward which those decisions are ineluctably leading. One might find examples of this problem in several areas of adjudicative decision making. A case of intimate concern to public administrators involves the rights of public employees. Through a series of judicial decisions and administrative hearings, the constitutional and legal protections afforded public employees in adverse actions evolved from being minimal prior to the 1950s to being extremely comprehensive by the early 1970s. Decisions involving substantive rights, equal protection, and procedural due process built upon one another to the point where it appeared to many that the public service was becoming unmanageable. Sanctions could not be levied effectively against public employees whose performance or behavior was inadequate in some respect. For instance, by 1987, a constable in Harris County, Texas, found he could not constitutionally fire a probationary employee who, upon hearing of an assassination attempt on President Reagan, exclaimed, "Shoot, if they go for him again, I hope they get him." It is difficult to imagine that a court looking at a totally clean slate would have reached the conclusion that the First Amendment protects a probationary employee in a law enforcement office who makes such a statement at work. But to a majority of the Supreme Court, that result seemed to be compelled by past decisions, even though many—including four dissenting justices—would find that the decision "boggles the mind."[26]

Adjudication has other limitations as well. It is time-consuming. It can lack uniformity, as when different hearing examiners reach different conclusions in similar cases. The content of the decisional **case law** (that is, the legal principles that can be derived by analyzing decisions in previous cases) is not readily accessible to the public or to interested outside parties. It may even be obscure to the public administrators who are governed by it. The adjudication of federal equal employment opportunity complaints and labor-related issues are examples of the latter problem. In neither area is the content of the case law highly publicized or particularly clear in its principles, yet supervisors and employees are supposed to abide by the content of the rulings.[27] Adjudication also limits outside participation. Individuals and organizations can file the equivalent of "friend of the court" briefs under some circumstances, but there is no provision for the general, open participation of the public or interest groups in such proceedings. In addition, adjudicatory decisions can be tied to an eclectic set of facts that may tend to distort the principles underlying decisions. Hard cases make bad law precisely because there are at least two opposing and seemingly equally valid sets of principles upon which they can be decided. In such instances, decisions may turn more than usual on the way the cases are presented to the hearing examiner or judge, upon the personal sense of justice or view of the public interest held by such officials, or even upon their biases.

A final criticism of adjudication is that it places public administrators and individuals or organizations in an antagonistic, adversary position where such a relationship is inappropriate to the public policy ostensibly being promoted. Examples include the public service supervisor and public employee, teacher and pupil, and social welfare caseworker and welfare recipient. In each of these instances, cooperative and supportive relationships are generally considered more appropriate than hostile ones. Yet when such parties enter adjudication, their relationship becomes adversarial. Moreover, adversary procedure encourages each side to present the strongest, most forceful case. This often results in exaggerated allegations that place the opposing party in the worst possible light. Behavior and motives are portrayed in black-and-white terms. This leads each party to distrust the other even more, and the conflict is exacerbated. Eventually, one will "win" and the other will "lose." A great deal of anxiety and emotional stress occurs. In the meantime and even afterward, the parties may have to continue working together in a relationship that can hardly be functional. For instance, in an EEO complaint a supervisor will be accused by an employee of engaging in prohibited discrimination. Adjudication is likely to involve allegations that the supervisor is "racist," "sexist," "ethnically chauvinistic," or the like. Thus, the supervisor is portrayed as "immoral" and essentially unfit for his or her job. The supervisor, on the other hand, is likely to claim that the action of which the employee complained was taken because the employee is somehow inadequate in terms of capability, judgment, and/or character. If carried to its logical extreme, adjudication of this sort can develop an air of absurdity: an allegedly inadequate employee versus an unfit supervisor, all within the confines of a merit system in which annual performance appraisals are used.

THE CASE OF BENZENE IN THE WORKPLACE

We have been discussing the managerial, political, and legal approaches to public administrative decision making as though they are easily separable or come in distinct packages. In practice, public administrators are forced to combine these approaches in their day-to-day decision making. This may lead to "public management by groping along," as Robert Behn suggests.[28] But sometimes, perhaps frequently, the decision-making approaches converge in one area of public administration in a way that clearly highlights their advantages and disadvantages. The effort by the federal Occupational Safety and Health Administration (OSHA) to reduce the hazards of benzene in the workplace provides an excellent illustration.

The Occupational Safety and Health Act of 1970 states that the secretary of labor

> in promulgating standards dealing with toxic materials or harmful physical agents . . . shall set the standard which most adequately assures, to the extent feasible, on the basis of the best available evidence, that no employee will suffer material impairment of health or functional capacity even if such employee has regular exposure to the hazard dealt with by such standard for the period of his working life.

Benzene is a rapidly evaporating, aromatic liquid produced by the petroleum and petrochemical industries for use in manufacturing motor fuels, solvents, detergents, pesticides, and other organic chemicals. It is known to be associated with leukemia, a cancer attacking white blood cells. No safe level of benzene, which is measured in its airborne state in parts per million (ppm), is known.

Following what he understood to be the legislative mandate, the secretary of labor issued standards reducing the allowable levels of benzene from 10 ppm to 1 ppm in the rubber, petroleum refining, and petrochemical industries. The costs to the industries were projected to range from $1,390 to $82,000 per worker (in physical plant changes and first-year costs). The secretary was sued by the American Petroleum Institute partly on the grounds that he exceeded his statutory authority, because the reduction from 10 ppm to 1 ppm was not feasible. The case reached the Supreme Court level under the title *Industrial Union Department, AFL-CIO v. American Petroleum Institute* (1980).[29] Part of the issue was what "feasible" meant in the context of the statute.

To answer this question, one might turn to the legislative record and attempt to discern the intent of Congress. Supreme Court Justice Rehnquist did this and concluded:

> I believe that the legislative history demonstrates that the feasibility requirement . . . is a legislative mirage, appearing to some Members [of Congress] but not to others, and assuming any form desired by the beholder. . . .
>
> In sum, the legislative history contains nothing to indicate that the language "to the extent feasible" does anything other than render what had been a clear, if somewhat unrealistic, standard largely, if not entirely, precatory. There is certainly nothing to indicate that these words . . . are limited to technological and economic feasibility. [Concurring opinion.]

The words "to the extent feasible" may not mean anything specific in the context of the statute, as Rehnquist argues, but the mirage they conjured up was crucial to Congress's decision making. They were offered as a substitute for the original language of the OSHA bill as a means of forming a coalition in support of greater regulation of workplace health and safety. The words may have had different meaning to different members of Congress, but they reduced opposition to the bill and generated greater support for it.

This is an example of incremental decision making. It is accepted that eliminating toxic substances from the workplace is a desirable policy objective. Such a policy is viewed as a step forward in improving American life. But it is a small and tentative step because the statute does not identify the substances deemed toxic and the standards for determining the feasibility of eliminating them. Were it to do so, it would face so much political controversy and opposition that it might be entirely impossible to move in the desired policy direction of creating safe workplaces. For example, identifying benzene as a toxic substance in the bill itself would have provoked opposition from the petroleum, rubber, and petrochemical industries, as well as their lobby organization, the American Petroleum Institute. Because benzene is used in pesticides, agricultural groups might also have become involved, and so on. But benzene would not be the only toxic substance identified in the bill, and consequently opposition from other industries and economic sectors would have been forthcoming. Members of Congress whose districts included the industries that would clearly be adversely affected might well oppose the bill. Politically, the way around this problem is to do just what Congress did; that is, to form a broad coalition in favor of a desired policy objective by avoiding taking any specific regulatory steps. The bill was neither comprehensive in its identification of toxic substances, nor particularly rational in its language. But it was passed and it did establish a process for making America's workplaces safer.

A more rational-comprehensive approach was left to OSHA and the secretary of labor. OSHA developed the following standard: "Whenever a carcinogen is involved, OSHA will presume that no safe level of exposure exists in the absence of clear proof establishing such a level and will accordingly set the exposure limit at the lowest level feasible." Feasibility here was defined in terms of the technologies available for eliminating the toxic substance, the devices available for measuring its presence, and the costs likely to be incurred. In the case of benzene, technology and measurement dictated 1 ppm. OSHA did consider the costs to the industries, but it "did not quantify the benefits to each category of worker in terms of decreased exposure to benzene. . . ." It reasoned that because the costs were bearable by the industries, the new standard was feasible. From a market perspective, the American Petroleum Institute considered the costs too high for many American companies to bear under the pressure of global competition. OSHA's assumption was that 1 ppm of benzene was the lowest level feasible and therefore the one that was safest. This assumption was a key issue in the subsequent adjudication in the federal courts.

Industrial Union Department, AFL-CIO v. American Petroleum Institute divided the Supreme Court so much that although it was able to reach a judgment, it was unable to formulate a single opinion to which a majority of the justices could subscribe. This is called decision by plurality, rather than majority opinion. Four justices, Stevens, Stewart, Powell, and Chief Justice Burger, expressed the view that the secretary's rule of 1 ppm was not supported by appropriate findings. At a minimum, they reasoned that before promulgating any standard, the secretary was required to "make a finding that the workplaces dealt with in the standard are not safe in the sense that significant risks are present and can be eliminated or lessened by a change in practices."

Chief Justice Burger issued his own concurring opinion in which he warned against the pitfalls of rational-comprehensive decision making in the regulatory area: "When the administrative record reveals only scant or minimal risk of material health impairment, responsible administration calls for avoidance of extravagant, comprehensive regulation. Perfect safety is a chimera; regulation must not strangle human activity in the search for the impossible."

Justice Powell also concurred separately. Although he agreed with the plurality of the Court that OSHA failed to meet its statutory obligations, he emphasized that he did not think "the statute requires the quantification of risk in every case. . . . [N]either the statute nor the legislative history suggests that OSHA's hands are tied when reasonable quantification cannot be accomplished by any known methods."

Justice Rehnquist was the fifth justice to concur in the Court's judgment that the secretary's regulation was invalid. However, his opinion was based on a completely different line of reasoning. He considered the Occupational Safety and Health Act to be unconstitutional for at least three reasons: (1) It violated the separation of powers by delegating legislative policy-making authority to the executive branch; (2) it did so without "any guidance" to the secretary of labor; and (3) "the standard of 'feasibility' renders meaningful judicial review impossible."

Justice Marshall dissented in an opinion joined by Justices Brennan, White, and Blackmun. He argued that adjudication was an inappropriate model for determining whether the secretary had acted properly. If his rule was not in keeping with Congress's intent, Marshall suggested that Congress was free to rewrite the statute to correct the defective interpretation. But adjudicatory decision making could not adequately resolve the matter. In Marshall's words, which underscore the limitations of adjudication,

> three factors . . . in my view, make judicial review of occupational safety and health standards under the substantial evidence test* particularly difficult. First, the issues often reach a high level of technical complexity. In such circumstances the courts are required to immerse themselves in matters to which they are unaccustomed by training or experience. Second, the factual issues with which the Secretary must deal are frequently not subject to any definitive resolution. . . . Causal connections and theoretical extrapolations may be uncertain. Third, when the question involves determination of the acceptable level of risk, the ultimate decision must necessarily be based on considerations of policy as well as empirically verifiable facts. Factual determinations can at most define the risk in some statistical way; the judgment whether that risk is tolerable cannot be based solely on a resolution of the facts.

This case study of decision making concerning benzene in the workplace juxtaposes the rational-comprehensive approach, incrementalism, market considerations, and adjudication, which is a particular variant of incrementalism, as noted earlier. It suggests that the legislature and the courts face serious institutional limitations in decision making. Public administrators are also constrained by institutional barriers, but sometimes their tasks are further complicated by the likelihood that their implementation of vague legislative mandates will be overturned by the courts. The case shows how the managerial, political, and legal styles of decision making can be opposed to one another—how what is acceptable reasoning under one is unacceptable under another. One strategy for improving decision making is to try to over-

---

*When reviewing administrative decisions, the courts are usually called upon to employ one of two standards: substantial evidence or preponderance of evidence. The former is evidence that reasonably supports a conclusion. The latter requires that the conclusion be more likely than not. Both standards are weaker than the requirement in criminal cases that the defendant be guilty beyond a reasonable doubt. The standard of "clear and convincing" proof or evidence may require more than a preponderance of evidence, but less than the criminal standard.

come the shortcomings of each approach by introducing the corrective technique discussed in the next section.

SYNTHESIZING DECISION-MAKING APPROACHES

Each of the decision-making approaches reviewed here has advantages and disadvantages. None is fully suitable for all areas of public administration. Therefore, as in other aspects of public administration, it becomes necessary to try to develop a synthesis through which the advantages of each of the managerial, political, and legal approaches can be maximized while their limitations are minimized. To date, the most comprehensive approach to accomplishing this in the context of decision making has been the **mixed-scanning approach.**[30]

Mixed scanning attempts to combine incrementalism, including adjudication, with the rational-comprehensive approach. It can accommodate market-based decision making as well. This approach to decision making was developed by Amitai Etzioni, who illustrates it as follows:

> Assume we are about to set up a worldwide weather observation system using weather satellites. The rationalistic approach would seek an exhaustive survey of weather conditions by using cameras capable of detailed observations and by scheduling reviews of the entire sky as often as possible. This would yield an avalanche of details, costly to analyze and likely to overwhelm our action capacities (i.e., "seeding" cloud formations that could develop into hurricanes or bring rain to arid areas). Incrementalism would focus on those areas in which similar patterns developed in the recent past and, perhaps, on a few nearby regions; it would thus ignore all formations which might deserve attention if they arose in unexpected areas.
>
> A mixed-scanning strategy would include elements of both approaches by employing two cameras: a broad angle camera that would cover all parts of the sky but not in great detail, and a second one which would zero in on those areas revealed by the first camera to require a more in-depth examination. While mixed-scanning might miss areas in which only a detailed camera could reveal trouble, it is less likely than incrementalism to miss obvious trouble spots in unfamiliar areas.[31]

Mixed scanning requires decision makers to differentiate between fundamental decisions pertaining to long-range goals and more limited decisions that are made within the context of those goals. This distinction between fundamental and limited decisions is akin to the distinction made by the managerial approaches between politics and administration. However, Etzioni recognizes that public administrators may make fundamental and limited kinds of decisions and simply argues that they ought to be clear about what it is they are doing. Moreover, he believes that by clarifying the relationship among types of decision making, the shortcomings of each can be substantially reduced.

Several examples of the utility of mixed scanning can be found in federal administration in the United States. The Executive Office of the President, in particular, contains a number of units that are essentially charged with taking a long-range view of a particular policy area and evaluating policy options. The Council of Economic Advisers is responsible for analyzing the national economy and its various segments, advising the president on economic developments, evaluating governmental programs, and recommending policies for economic growth and stability. Basically, it keeps track of markets and alerts the president to failures, threats of failure, or problems. The National Security Council has somewhat more complex operating responsibilities, but its main function is to advise the president with respect to the integration of domestic, foreign, and military policies relating to the security of the United States. Presidential commissions in various policy areas, including Social Security, Central America, and nutrition, are also used as mixed-scanning devices. In addition, various administrative operations can include a mixed-scanning function, as when agencies make five-year budget projections that try to develop a realistic appraisal of where they should be headed. Any of these devices can serve as checks on administrative "drift" through incrementalism and on the overly complicated and unrealistic qualities of the pure rational-comprehensive decision-making model.

Mixed scanning often involves organizations charged with taking a long-range view of policies, programs, and environmental changes. Another way of achieving the benefits of mixed scanning is to engage in periodic exercises in strategic planning. Strategic planning is a deliberate attempt to force important organizational and/or policy changes in response to any number of foreseeable environmental shifts, such as changing demographics or technologies. For instance, universities could have foreseen that demographic projections for the early 1990s indicated that there would be a declining number of people in the U.S. population of traditional college age and could have planned appropriate responses.

Strategic planning involves several steps: developing a strategy for doing the planning; surveying trends, forces, clients, competitors, and networks in the organization's environment; surveying internal resources, capabilities, and strategies; identifying alternative ways of adapting mandates and values to projected changes; developing a step-by-step approach for adjusting to the future; and describing the organization's "vision of success" to its members and other relevant groups.

There are several hurdles to successful strategic planning, but like institutionalized mixed scanning it can help correct the limitations of the rational-comprehensive, short-term market-based, and muddling-through approaches. At a minimum, success generally requires a strong sponsor and constant effort to keep the planning exercise on track, time, and realism.[32]

What to Avoid

Whichever administrative decision-making approach is employed, there are several pitfalls that should be avoided. As a public administrator, it is all too easy to make mistakes. There are many sources of pressure; time, interest groups, members of the legislature and their staffs, the media, chief executives and their staffs, personal advancement, and personal goals are among the more common. Specialization may limit the public administrator's view and definition of reality, and administrative jargon may obscure matters. Furthermore, group decision making carries within it a tendency toward conformity, the stifling of dissent, and constant reinforcement of the agency's traditional view of matters. It is also difficult to know precisely when to decide and when to await further development before adopting new policies and new procedures.

Among some of the more commonly identified obstacles to sound administrative decisions are the following:

1. *Lack of clarity of goals.* As the incremental decision-making model suggests, sometimes the political price of having an administrative program at all is the absence of clear goals. Public administrators also display a tendency to confuse ends and means: the agency's continued existence and growth may become the true end, and its programs merely a means for justifying that end, rather than vice versa. The development of administrative ideologies touting the importance of the agency and its programs is often a sign of this ends-mean inversion. Where such ideologies are taken at face value by decision makers, misplaced priorities are likely to become a problem.

2. *Confusion of the public interest with that of a clientele group or constituency.* The nature of bureaucratic politics in the United States places emphasis on the formation of alliances among bureaucratic agencies, legislative (sub) committees, and interest groups. Such relationships can easily distort a public administrator's view of the public interest. There is also a tendency to confuse the reaction of interested parties (that is, constituencies) with the view of the public more generally. This has commonly been apparent in the decision-making process of regulatory agencies.

3. *Rigid conservatism in the sense of strict adherence to rules, procedures, and past practices.* For various reasons discussed in Chapter 4, bureaucratic organization—especially hierarchy—can cause public administrators to feel personally insecure. Under such circumstances, rigidity is often a favored course of action. It is less likely that one will be disciplined or affected adversely when "going by the book" than when taking risks to further one's vision of the public interest.

4. *Specialization causing public administrators to oversimplify reality.* It is likely that any social or economic problem is the result of several factors and will have several effects. Specialization may confine the vision of any group of public administrators to one or a few of these causes and effects and, hence, an appreciation of the whole problem is lost. For example, a former head of the U.S. Equal Employment Opportunity Commission, who was engaged in designing a better EEO *complaint* system, once told the principal author that "*all* racial and sexual

discrimination in the federal service was interpersonal." Yet the evidence is overwhelming that much discrimination, probably most, was built into the system of examinations, position classification, and job design.

5. *"Overquantification" causing public administrators to deemphasize qualitative factors in making decisions.* As the NPM complains, pressures for accountability, political neutrality, and job security, as well as an emphasis on objective technical expertise, make public administrators reluctant to exercise "subjective" judgment. Consequently, they seek quantitative indicators of qualitative performance. Sometimes these indicators are satisfactory, but at other times they lead administrators to decide in favor of what will look best in terms of quantity. For instance, a hearing examiner dealing with adverse action complaints or EEO cases may decide cases rapidly, because that can be quantified, rather than seek to provide the highest degree of justice in each one. When emphasis on quantitative compliance detracts from qualitative performance—as it could in the above example—the relationship between the two is *pathological*, because it does not further the agency's mission.

6. *Reluctance to engage in policy and program evaluation.* It is axiomatic that decision makers need information about the impacts of their decisions to make improvements. However, largely for political reasons, administrative agencies may be reluctant to gather information and engage in analysis that makes their past decisions and program implementation look seriously inadequate. Such analysis also facilitates the ability of outsiders to review and understand an agency's operations. Consequently, there is sometimes a tendency to engage in only the most perfunctory and superficial kind of policy and program evaluation. Agencies also contract private firms to engage in evaluative studies, occasionally with the tacit understanding that a strongly critical review will make the agency unlikely to use that firm in the future. Administrative culture tends to be intolerant of internal and external criticism. Thus public administrators often fall into a highly defensive posture when confronted with challenges to their internal hierarchies, past decisions, and present procedures.

Computers and Information Systems

New technological developments in the use of information are occurring at a very rapid pace. Computers and management-information systems were considered exotic just a few years ago. Now they are common. Like other decision-making tools, computers assist in the process of gathering and organizing information. In the view of some, such as Herbert Simon, the advent of the computer and attendant information systems has the potential to revolutionize public administration.[33] These developments enable public administrators to cope with the complexity of the programs and policies they implement. Computerization makes the rational-comprehensive model more usable by enabling the public administrator to compare and project the likely consequences and costs of alternative means of implementing public policies. Eventually, computers may be able to "think" in nontrivial ways that are relevant to rational administrative decision making.

Computerization can also facilitate employee empowerment. "Informating" the workplace in the late twentieth century is as dramatic a change as was automating it earlier. In the past, managerial authority was justified and bolstered in part by control of information. Computerization emphasizes the dissemination and sharing of information. Shoshana Zuboff, a leading analyst of "informated" work, finds that:

> As the new technology integrates information across time and space, managers and workers each overcome their narrow functional perspectives and create new roles that are better suited to enhancing value-adding activities in a data-rich environment. As the quality of skills at each organizational level becomes similar, hierarchical distinctions begin to blur. Authority comes to depend more upon an appropriate fit between knowledge and responsibility than upon the ranking rules of the traditional organizational pyramid.[34]

The computer enhances individual employees' problem solving and reduces the relevance of traditional managerial control functions.

Computers can also be beneficial to the incremental and adjudicatory models. Incrementalism is deeply concerned with making decisions that gain political support among relevant communities and constituencies. Computers can assist in this effort by making it possible to analyze rapidly information gained by public opinion polls, community surveys, and from voting results. They can also aid in the analysis of the limited means-ends packages under consideration. They can help provide a better "organizational memory" to incremental decision makers. Computerized legal information systems have already demonstrated their ability to bring previous decisions and principles to the attention of lawyers, who, in turn, may raise them in presenting their cases before judges and administrative law judges.

No matter which decisional approach is taken, computers and information systems can clarify thinking. They cannot resolve value conflicts among the managerial, political, and legal perspectives, but they can help us to foresee the consequences of choices made within the framework of these perspectives. As in the case of many new technologies, computers also carry some risks. They can be used to reduce individuals' privacy.[35] They sometimes promote excessive impersonality and reliance upon inappropriate quantifiable indicators of qualitative performance.

As in other areas of public administration, when considering decision making, the student and practitioner should avoid the once common tendency to believe that there is always "one best way" and that technological and organizational processes can automatically resolve policy conflicts over competing values. Certainly, the different managerial, political, and legal approaches are all more useful in some circumstances than in others. The problem is to improve them and to determine when each should be used alone or combined with one or another.

NOTES

1. Charles Perrow, *Complex Organizations*, 3d ed. (New York: Random House, 1986), 129.
2. Ibid., 130.
3. *Shapiro v. Thompson*, 394 U.S. 618 (1969).
4. See David H. Rosenbloom, *Federal Equal Employment Opportunity* (New York: Praeger, 1977), 113; Robert Hampton, Chairman, U.S. Civil Service Commission, "Memorandum for Heads of Departments and Agencies," 11 May 1971.
5. Harold Seidman, *Politics, Position, and Power* (New York: Oxford University Press, 1970), 18.
6. The Supreme Court upheld the legality of grid-regs in *Heckler v. Campbell*, 461 U.S. 458 (1983).
7. See Charles Lindblom, "The Science of 'Muddling Through,'" *Public Administration Review* 19 (Spring 1959): 79–88; Herbert Simon, *Administrative Behavior* (New York: Free Press, 1965 [originally copyrighted in 1945]); Alan Altshuler and Norman Thomas, eds., *The Politics of the Federal Bureaucracy*, 2d ed. (New York: Harper & Row, 1977), chap. 3.
8. See *Personnel Administrator v. Feeney*, 422 U.S. 256 (1976); and David H. Rosenbloom and Peter Grabosky, "Racial and Ethnic Competition for Federal Service Positions," *Midwest Review of Public Administration*, 11 (December 1977): 281–290.
9. Peter Wolf and Rochelle Jones, "Bureaucratic Defense in Depth," in Ronald Pynn, ed., *Watergate and the American Political Process* (New York: Praeger, 1975), esp. 216–217.
10. For an interesting discussion from the perspectives of individual administrators, see David Granick, "The Red Executive," in *Organizations and Human Behavior*, ed. Gerald Bell (Englewood Cliffs, N.J.: Prentice-Hall, 1967), 218–230. See also Joseph LaPalombara, ed., *Bureaucracy and Political Development* (Princeton, N.J.: Princeton University Press, 1963).
11. Al Gore, *From Red Tape to Results: Creating a Government That Works Better & Costs Less* (Washington, D.C.: Government Printing Office, 1993), chap. 2; and Al Gore, *Common Sense Government Works Better & Costs Less* (Washington, D.C.: Government Printing Office, 1995).
12. A good overview of the salient questions can be found in Charles Lindblom, *Politics and Markets* (New York: Basic Books, 1977). Among the more influential critiques of market theory are Deborah Stone, *Policy Paradox and Political Reason* (New York: HarperCollins, 1988); and Amitai Etzioni, *The Moral Dimension* (New York: Free Press, 1988).
13. Michael Lipsky, *Street-Level Bureaucracy* (New York: Russell Sage, 1980).
14. See David Rosenbloom and Rosemary O'Leary, *Public Administration and Law*, 2d ed. (New York: Marcel Dekker, 1997), chap. 6.
15. *New Mexico v. Bloom*, 561 P.2d 925; *Delaware v. Prouse*, 440 U.S. 648 (1979).
16. See Rosenbloom and O'Leary, *Public Administration and Law*, chap. 6, for a review of the literature.

17. S. Duke and A. Gross, "Casualties of War," *Reason* 25 (February 1994): 20–27.

18. Ibid.

19. Gore, *Common Sense Government.*

20. See Stone, *Policy Paradox and Political Reason.*

21. Lindblom, "The Science of 'Muddling Through'"; Amitai Etzioni, "Mixed-Scanning: A 'Third' Approach to Decision-Making," *Public Administration Review* 27 (December 1967): 385–392, and reprinted in Altshuler and Thomas, *The Politics of the Federal Bureaucracy* pp. 139–146; and Etzioni, "Mixed Scanning Revisited," *Public Administration Review* 46 (January/February 1986): 8–14.

22. Theodore Sorenson, *Kennedy* (New York: Harper & Row, 1965), 296.

23. See Rosenbloom, *Federal Equal Employment Opportunity,* chaps. 3 and 4.

24. Kenneth Warren, *Administrative Law in the American Political System* (St. Paul, West, 1988), chap. 7.

25. *Delaware v. Prouse,* 440 U.S. 648 (1979).

26. *Rankin v. McPherson,* 483 U.S. 378 (1987).

27. See Patricia Ingraham and David Rosenbloom, eds., *The Promise and Paradox of Civil Service Reform* (Pittsburgh: University of Pittsburgh Press, 1992), chaps. 7 and 11.

28. Robert Behn, "Management by Groping Along," *The Journal of Policy Analysis and Management* 7 (Fall 1988): 643–663.

29. 448 U.S. 607 (1980).

30. Etzioni, "Mixed-Scanning."

31. Ibid., reprinted in Altshuler and Thomas, *The Politics of the Federal Bureaucracy,* 143.

32. See John Bryson and William Roering, "Initiation of Strategic Planning by Governments," *Public Administration Review* 48 (November/December 1988): 99–104.

33. Herbert Simon, "Applying Information Technology to Organization Design," *Public Administration Review* 33 (May/June 1973), esp. 276.

34. Shoshana Zuboff, *In the Age of the Smart Machine* (New York: Basic Books, 1988), 6.

35. See Alan F. Westin, *Privacy and Freedom* (New York: Atheneum, 1967).

ADDITIONAL READING

LINDBLOM, CHARLES. "The Science of 'Muddling Through,'" *Public Administration Review* 19 (Spring 1959): 79–88.

MARCH, JAMES. *Decisions and Organizations.* Oxford: Blackwell, 1989.

MURRAY, MICHAEL. *Decisions: A Comparative Critique.* Marshfield, Mass.: Pittman, 1986.

SIMON, HERBERT. *Administrative Behavior,* 3d ed. New York: Free Press, 1976.

WILSON, DAVID. *Top Decisions.* San Francisco: Jossey-Bass, 1986.

STUDY QUESTIONS

1. How are decisions made at the college or university that you attend? What values are maximized by this approach? In your opinion, what are its advantages and disadvantages?

2. How do you make decisions when

   a. You think about your career plans?

b. You are involved in a social activity?

c. You are called upon to resolve some disagreement between friends, coworkers, fellow students, or relatives?

Does your decision-making process differ in varied contexts? If so, how?

3. "Interactive TV" enables the viewer to send electronic signals instantaneously to the broadcaster. These signals can indicate agreement or disagreement with statements or propositions made on the TV program. Elaborate interactive systems would also enable the viewers to indicate the general level of intensity of their preferences.

Some believe that interactive TV is a way of improving government decision making by allowing the public to register its preferences on matters of public policy. Do you think interactive TV would have any utility in improving public administrative decision making? Why or why not?

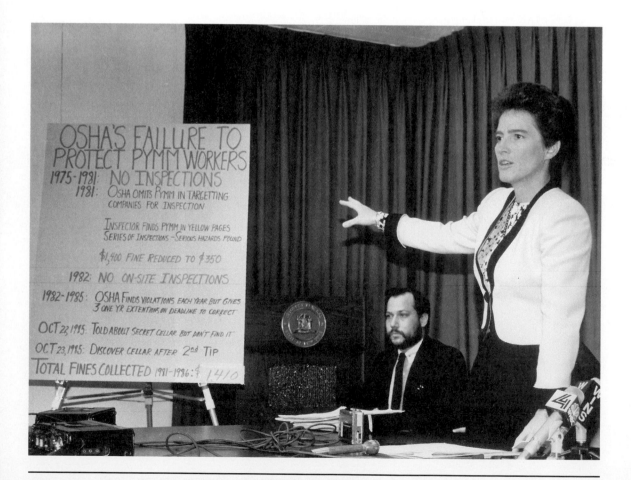

CHAPTER 8 | *Policy Analysis and Implementation Evaluation*

Public administration's penetration of the economy and society has fostered concern with how well public policies work and how their implementation could be improved. This chapter focuses on two ways of judging policies, namely, policy analysis and implementation evaluation. Policy analysis considers the extent to which a policy achieves its objectives. It also assesses how the process through which the policy is implemented contributes to the achievement of such objectives. Implementation evaluation focuses on whether implementation maximizes appropriate values. The traditional managerial, political, and legal perspectives tend to agree that implementation can be problematic if it allows too much discretionary authority to individual administrators. However, the new public management favors broad discretion. Each of these perspectives may be more suitable for evaluating policy in a particular area of public administration, such as overhead administrative functions, sociotherapy, or regulation.

Public administration is an activist part of government. It is a means by which government seeks to intervene in aspects of the economy, society, and polity. For example, public administration has been used to try to prevent imbalances in economic markets, protect consumers, prevent harm to the environment, and provide financial, medical, psychological, and other assistance to individuals who appear to be otherwise unable to care adequately for themselves in these respects. It also seeks to protect the legal rights of the citizenry vis-à-vis private groups and subordinate governmental jurisdictions. When called upon to be the arm of governmental intervention in these spheres of life, public administrators are required to *implement* policy. The question of how successfully public policy is being implemented inevitably arises. And, if the answer is, "Not successfully enough!" then is the problem with the implementation, the policy, or both? In essence, seeking answers to such questions is *policy analysis and implementation evaluation.*

THE GROWING CONCERN WITH POLICY ANALYSIS

Although these questions seem normal enough, it has only been in recent years that public administrators began to pay serious attention to systematic policy analysis. In part this is because of a shift in the nature of administrative intervention in the 1960s that made public administration more salient in the workplace, in neighborhoods, in families, and in the society generally. President Lyndon Johnson's "Great Society" program, for instance, rested very much upon the premise that public administration could intervene successfully in a wide range of aspects of life to promote greater equality of opportunity among the citizenry. However, perspectives on implementation tend to follow what is known as "Miles's law"—"Where one stands depends on where one sits." What one person considers to be a *service* provided by public administration, another may consider to be a *constraint*. Whereas an employee may view public administrative intervention to protect him or her from toxic substances in the workplace as a valuable governmental service, the employer may view it as an untoward administrative interference in legitimate business considerations. As public administration provides more services to people, it also engages in more extensive regulatory activities.

By the 1970s, it was evident that many individuals and groups thought that the administrative state had gone too far in regulating their activities. Many also thought it had the additional consequence of sapping individual initiative and sense of responsibility for making one's own decisions and taking care of oneself. Some policies for broad social change, conceived in hope in the 1960s, appeared to fail. Perhaps even worse, they seemed to linger on well after their inadequacies were widely understood. In truth, many of the policies being implemented by public administrators were established by legislatures, but nonetheless opposition often focused on "the bureaucrats."

Seat belts provide an example of the kind of web of administrative implementation that many view as counterproductive and individually debilitating governmental intervention in the society. Originally, seat belts were an option one could choose to have installed in one's car. The federal government was dissatisfied with leaving this option up to the individual, because so many people opted not to buy seat belts. It then made seat belts mandatory equipment in new cars—with the cost being borne by the buyer. Even though new car buyers were required to have seat belts in their cars, they might still decide not to use them. Again the government's effort to protect motorists seemed frustrated. Next, new cars were required to be equipped with devices, such as buzzers, flashing lights, and ignition interlocks to prod people to use seat belts. No doubt, these policies had some success. More people were probably using seat belts and more serious injuries and deaths were probably averted. Nevertheless, many people still refused to use their seat belts—and many simply disconnected all those prodding devices. Daunted, but not yet ready to surrender, the federal government sought to require either that automatic seat belts be installed or that automobile manufacturers install air bag safety systems to cushion motorists in the event of a collision. Subsequently, the National Highway Traffic Safety Administration sought to rescind these regulations. Its action resulted in litigation that reached the Supreme Court.[1] All this cost money: Administrators had to be paid, automobile manufacturers had to engage in developing seat belts, air bags, and prodding devices, consumers had to buy the belts and devices, lawyers had to be paid when litigation ensued, and groups for and against these measures employed lobbyists to try to make their points with Congress and the National Highway Traffic Safety Administration. It also seemed to bother a lot of people who did not want to be required to or compel others to buy seat belts or air bags. The whole scene led many to ask, "Why not just leave it up to the individual whether he or she wants to use seat belts?" or "Why not just legally require all drivers and passengers to fasten their belts and fine those who don't?" There may be good answers to these questions, and finding them is much of what policy analysis is about.

Public administrative intervention in the economy, society, and polity makes policy analysis more salient. The more the administrative state intervenes in our lives, the more we want to know about the effects it is having. However, an additional development of far-reaching consequence for public administration coincided with increasing attention to the problems of the administrative state. This was the rapid development of analytic techniques, especially in the social sciences, that could be used to assess the impacts of administrative interventions and to ascertain the costs and benefits associated with public administrative implementation of policies. In one sense, the basic question is at least as old as Woodrow Wilson's call in the 1880s for a new study of administration that could "discover, first, what government can properly and successfully do. . . ."[2] The development of new analytic approaches, statistical techniques, and social scientific methodologies gave impetus to the development of "public policy analysis" as an area of study and applied research. Some broad aspects of these methodologies are outlined further on in this chapter.

By way of introduction, it should also be mentioned that in a practical sense policy analysis was strengthened by a number of related administrative developments. Among these were a congressional requirement that, in many policy areas, a percentage of a program's budget be set aside for program evaluation; the enactment of the Freedom of Information Act of 1966, which facilitated greater public access to the information that makes policy analysis feasible; the development of program budgeting; and the growing tendency to place "sunset" clauses in enabling legislation. The latter provide that programs will be self-terminating after a period of time, often five years, unless the administering agency can convince the legislature that the program is effective and still desirable or necessary. Policy analysis can help in this regard by showing whether a program is having the intended impact in a cost-effective manner and with a favorable benefit-cost ratio. By the 1980s, policy analysis had become central to much federal rule making as well.

In sum, a variety of political and technical developments coalesced in the 1970s to focus greater attention on policy analysis as a part of public administration. In fact, policy analysis may now be considered a true part of the core of contemporary public administration.

APPROACHES TO ANALYZING PUBLIC POLICY

It is sometimes useful to distinguish between two aspects of public policy. One is called **policy output,** the other **policy impact.**[3] These are obviously linked, but they can be separated for analytical reasons to avoid confusion. The formulation of public policy involves establishing the objectives to be attained and at least sketchily outlining the general means to be used in seeking to achieve these. For instance, to return to a familiar example, if a legislature decides that equal employment opportunity is a desirable objective, it may enact a statute intended to regulate the behavior of employers so as to facilitate the achievement of this aim. The statute may also vest responsibility for implementing or enforcing its provisions in an administrative agency, such as an equal employment opportunity commission. Presumably, if the legislature is serious in its intentions, it will allocate sufficient budgetary and personnel resources to the administering agency and also grant it the legal powers to accomplish its mission. The formulation of public policy is often highly politicized and may involve hotly contested elections, votes in the legislature, and extensive lobbying activities. The outgrowth of policy formulation is the policy output—that is, an official statement of governmental intent, delineation of powers and methods, and allocation of resources. Policy outputs can involve tangible and/or symbolic activity. Statutes, congressional resolutions, presidential proclamations, and the allocation of staff and funds are all policy outputs.

Today, it is widely accepted that public administrators also make policy outputs, such as rules and strategic plans. In fact, the federal Government Performance and Results Act of 1993 (GPRA) requires federal agencies to formulate strategic plans with more specific program objectives than those typically found in authorizing legislation passed by Congress. Such objectives should be measurable and their implementation should be feasible. The creation of policy outputs by administrative agencies violates a major tenet of the traditional managerial approach—that administration must be separate from politics. It is acceptable to the National Performance Review (NPR) because the strategic plans are formulated in consultation with the Office of Management and Budget and congressional (sub)committees. Therefore, the administrative role falls broadly within the NPR's focus on "*how* government should work, not on *what* it should do."[4]

Policy Outputs   Policy outputs are extremely important in politics and administration. They are statements of the goals of the polity and are prerequisites to the attainment of these through administrative action. However, from the perspective of policy analysis, it is crucial not to confuse policy outputs with policy impacts. The outputs themselves do not tell us very much about actual performance or the achievement of stated objectives. The outputs are essentially *activities*. It is hoped that they are positively related to the effective achievement of a policy objective. But today, only a naive political observer would assume simply because a statute is enacted, an administrative agency empowered, or funds spent that a governmental purpose is actually achieved. Too much has been learned about the limits of governmental action to assume that the output necessarily has the intended impact.

Policy Impacts   Policy impacts by contrast are concerned with performance: What effect is the policy output having on the intended target? Is the objective being achieved? If not, why not? If so, is achievement related to administration? At what cost? With what side effects? These are the types of questions that are most pertinent when we engage in policy analysis with regard to the activities of public administrative agencies. Unfortunately, the answers we seek are sometimes very elusive. This is due partly to the limitations of analytic techniques, partly to problems of measurement, partly to lack of information, and partly to the complexity of so many governmental programs.

Impact Analysis

Before the impact of a policy can be ascertained, it is necessary to identify the content of that policy in operational terms. In other words, the policy must have some specific content that lends itself to observation. Many policies do just that. For instance, a policy of reducing taxes to stimulate economic growth is something that can be analyzed. But many policies are too vague in their objectives or too resistant to measurement to be systematically observed. Policies to promote some aspects of the public interest, where there are competing visions of what the public interest is, are an example. Such policies may be extremely important—after all, they are the stuff of which politics is made and over which wars and revolutions are fought—but their content may simply not be suitable for the policy analysis techniques and methods currently available to us. Still other policies fall somewhere in between these two categories. In principle their impact can be evaluated; in practice it becomes difficult to separate out the impact of the policy itself from other factors. In one well-documented example, an analysis of the policy of strict enforcement of speeding laws by Connecticut seemed at first to show that the policy did substantially reduce traffic fatalities.[5] On further consideration, however, it turned out that there were several other factors aside from the strict enforcement that were confounding the analysis. For instance, strict enforcement was only part of a larger safety campaign involving better driver training, safer cars, use of seat belts; even the weather was a factor. This type of problem is not inconsequential, for very often specific policy outputs are part of a larger concern with a general political, economic, or social problem.

Assuming that the objectives of the policy outputs are suitable for it, an **impact analysis** may be undertaken. Impact analysis can be defined as being "concerned with examining the extent to which a policy causes change in the intended direction."[6] The basic idea behind impact analysis is causality. Does the policy cause change? Or is the change, if any, or some of it, independent of the policy?

Answering such questions can often be very complex in the context of public administration. This is not the place to review the subject in depth, but the student should be alerted to some of the major hurdles to policy analysis involving public administrative activity.

Limited Opportunities for Experimentation   One way to try to assess the impact of a policy is to apply it to one group but not to another composed of similar individuals. This is called an **experimental design** and has many variants. In the public sector, however, opportunities for experimentation are frequently limited by political, moral, and/or legal concerns. For example, suppose you are in the public health service and you want to analyze the impact of treating people for syphilis. Can you treat some while creating a control group by withholding treatment from others in similar condition even though ample resources are available to treat everyone? In essence, this was done over a period of four decades by the U.S. Public Health Service in Tuskegee, Alabama, and it was not a happy story (see Box 8–1).[7] What about constructing experiments to provide welfare, nutrition, medical assistance, police protection, education, or voting rights to some but not others in an effort to assess the impact of policies? Although some creative approaches to experimentation are politically, morally, and legally feasible in these areas, many technically appropriate approaches are ruled out.

The well-known "New Jersey negative income tax experiment" is an example of both the utility and difficulties of experimentation. It was conducted from 1968 to 1972 in several cities. The negative income tax is a governmental payment to individuals having little or no income. It is designed so that the payment is reduced as an individual or family receives other income,

---

BOX 8–1 Experimental Research Design: The Case of "Bad Blood"

From 1932 to 1972, the United States Public Health Service (PHS) conducted a study on the effects of *untreated* syphilis on African-American men in the area around Tuskegee, Alabama. The "Tuskegee Study" involved 399 men with syphilis; 201 others were used as controls. The Public Health Service's primary interest was in learning about the impact of the disease on blacks in its final stages. They found that untreated syphilis can cause skin tumors and ulcers, mutilating bone destruction, heart damage, paralysis, insanity, and blindness. Apparently, the dominant view of the PHS was that, "There was nothing in the experiment that was unethical or unscientific." Once the experiment became highly publicized in 1972, much of the nation was not so sure.

According to James H. Jones, "Journalists tended to accept the argument that the denial of penicillin [to the untreated group] during the 1940s was the crucial ethical issue." Earlier forms of treatment were ineffective, painful, and in some respects as bad as the disease.

However, the men may have benefited greatly from penicillin, and withholding it from them condemned the untreated men to a painful life with a very debilitating disease. But some observers thought a moral problem was inherent in the experiment from the outset. The *St. Louis Post–Dispatch* argued, "The fact is that in an effort to determine from autopsies what effects syphilis has on the body, the government from the moment the experiment began withheld the best available treatment for a particularly cruel disease. The immorality of the experiment was inherent in its premise." Jones's book, *Bad Blood*, makes it clear that the study was also inherently racist.

Eventually, a lawsuit was filed on behalf of the untreated men and their heirs. The case was settled out of court, with the government agreeing to pay $37,500 to each of the "living syphilitics," $15,000 to the heirs of each of the "deceased syphilitics," $16,000 to each living member of the control group, and $5,000 to the heirs of each of the "deceased controls."

SOURCE: James H. Jones, *Bad Blood: The Tuskegee Syphilis Experiment* (New York: Free Press, 1981), 8, 9, 217.

---

presumably from employment. However, within the range of income that defines eligibility for the negative tax, the reduction in the payment is always *less* than the amount of the other income the individual or family receives. For instance, if the basic payment is $3,000 to a family with no income, a family that earns $1,000 would receive less than the $3,000 payment but more than a payment of $2,000, thus assuring that it would be better off economically as a result of its earnings. The scheme is intended to create an incentive to earn income. It is viewed as potentially preferable to conventional welfare programs because it encourages recipients to find employment. The family earning $1,000 might be eligible for a negative income tax payment of $2,500, which would leave it with $3,500 instead of the $3,000 it would have received if it had no outside income at all.

A central question pertaining to the negative income tax is at what point the reduction of payments (the reduction rate) becomes a disincentive to seek or engage in paid work. Clearly, if one could receive $3,000 by not working at all and only $3,100 after earning $1,000 in an unpleasant job (because of a reduction rate of 90 percent), one might decide not to work. As a matter of public policy design, the "best" reduction rate would reduce total governmental negative income tax payments to the extent feasible while maintaining a satisfactory incentive for recipients to work. Experimentation would seem to be an excellent way of establishing what the best rate would be.

The New Jersey experiment was sponsored by the federal Office of Economic Opportunity and comprised 1,300 families. Half of these were in the experimental group and half in a control group that received no payments. Those in the control group were interviewed periodically, as were those in the experimental group. Several combinations of payment levels and reduction rates were tried among those in the experimental group. At first, the overall conclusion seemed to be that the negative income tax could be designed in a way that did not create a significant disincentive to work. However, upon subsequent analysis, it was found that six months after the experiment began, New Jersey *independently* changed its welfare policies by offering generous benefits to eligible families, including those in both the experimental and control groups. Once these new benefits were taken into account, analysis suggested that rather than establish an incentive to work, the negative income tax would inherently present a disincentive. This finding was precisely the opposite of what supporters of the negative income tax policy had initially expected.[8]

The New Jersey negative income tax experiment demonstrated the possibilities of using experimental design. It enabled policy makers to test an idea without having to implement it on a statewide or nationwide basis. After the experiment was conducted and analyzed, support for the negative income tax waned and the concept was more or less abandoned. The experiment was expensive to carry out, but in the end it may have saved a great deal by forestalling the implementation of a misguided policy. At the same time, however, the episode demonstrated how difficult experimentation can be. New Jersey's decision to change its welfare laws while the Office of Economic Opportunity was sponsoring the experiment illustrates how unplanned events and external conditions can interfere with the logic of an experimental design. Here, the experimenter's painstaking care in establishing basic payment levels was rendered almost entirely irrelevant by New Jersey's action. Moreover, the initial conclusion derived from the experiment was subsequently reversed when the full import of the unplanned change was understood.

Assuming Causality in Nonexperimental Analyses   The limited opportunities for experimentation in the public sector force policy analysts to rely upon other approaches. Some of these can be convincing at best but misleading at worst. A nonexperimental approach simply assumes a connection between the availability or level of a program and a condition in the target population.

For instance, one can analyze the nutrition of children who receive school lunches through governmental programs. One might find that their nutrition is adequate; but one should not assume on that basis that this is due to the availability of the lunches alone. Perhaps other information could be brought to bear on the situation in an effort to ascertain causality. For instance, are the lunches the *only* food consumed by some of the students? What do the others eat? Still, without a control group, one cannot be sure what the students would do for nutrition in the absence of the lunch program.

A similar problem arises in what is called a **preprogram-postprogram analysis.** Here, the condition of the target population prior to the implementation of the program is compared with the condition afterward. Comparison can be in terms of any number of criteria that seem relevant. For instance, if one wants to assess the impact of affirmative action on patterns of federal employment, one could look at the employment of a group, such as African-Americans, prior to the use of affirmative action. Salary, grade, and occupation could be some of the aspects of employment considered. The patterns observed could be compared with patterns after the implementation of affirmative action. One might find changes or the absence of change. And one might be tempted to attribute this to the use of affirmative action. Without further information, however, that could be a serious mistake. A wide variety of factors—including job-market conditions and demographic and general attitudinal change—could have contributed to changing employment patterns independently of the use of affirmative action. Moreover, even if there were no changes, does this mean that the program does not work in terms of maintaining and preventing deterioration of the present level of equality of opportunity? Without more to go on, this question cannot be answered within the framework of the nonexperimental research design.

One way of improving on preprogram-postprogram comparisons is to establish the rate of change before the introduction of a new policy such as affirmative action. By projecting this rate of change into the postprogram period, we can obtain a rough idea of what would have been expected had the new policy not been adopted. Then the projections could be compared with the observed reality. Of course, this approach remains vulnerable to variations in confounding conditions. But in the absence of these, focusing on the rate of change may often provide a better basis for assessing the impact of an alteration in policy.

Quasi-Experimental Research Designs   The opportunity for truly experimental research designs is often limited in public administration. Nonexperimental designs are not likely to be very satisfactory, especially in complicated policy areas where the political and administrative salience of solid policy analysis is often greatest. Sometimes it is possible to bridge this gap somewhat by developing a **quasi-experimental design.** Such designs often try to determine the impact of policies by contrasting performance between groups exposed to the policy and those not exposed while statistically controlling for confounding conditions. Federalism, which allows for such great variation among governmental policies, often facilitates such comparisons. For example, one state may enforce mandatory seat belt laws whereas neighboring states do not. Subsequently, one could compare motorist fatalities or serious injuries in these states. If the state enforcing the use of seat belts had fewer fatalities or serious injuries it would *suggest* that the policy was responsible. That is the general idea of quasi-experimental designs. However, elaborate precautions have to be taken in such research to assure that the conclusion is valid. For instance, in the foregoing example, it would probably be advisable to compare fatalities or serious injuries per mile driven on the states' roads, because one state may have a much greater number of drivers than the other. The topography of the state, the number of miles of roads in urban and rural areas, the nature of licensing procedures, the demographic character of drivers, such as average age, percent over 70 or under 20, and several other factors would probably have to be taken into account before being relatively sure that the seat belt policy was having the intended effect.

Interpreting Results   Taking so much into account obviously makes for a difficult analysis that may be very time-consuming and expensive. Moreover, the results of such a study may be equivocal. It is unlikely that analysis will lead to such conclusions as, "Spending x dollars to compel drivers to use seat belts saves y lives per year." In fact, one of the great problems of policy analysis is that so many studies are unable to ascertain what kind of effect, if any, a policy is having. It is important that the public administrator not draw the wrong lesson from this. Simply because the impact of a policy cannot be satisfactorily ascertained through our available methods of policy analysis does not mean that the policy is not working. It may be working, and even working well, even though we are unable to demonstrate, in an analytically satisfactory way, that it is doing so. By contrast, even where policy analysis suggests that a policy is working well, the public administrator should always bear in mind that there may be some factor that was not taken into account in the analysis that explains the seeming success. For instance, reorganizing and redeploying a police force may coincide with a reduction in crime rates. However, such a reduction could stem from a number of other factors, including economic, demographic, and social changes.

Moreover, although policy impacts may be observable in the short run, strong policy analysis must also consider the long run. It must be concerned with the target group in the future, the policy's impact on nontarget groups ("spillover" effects), and the options created or foreclosed by the policy. For instance, a welfare policy aimed at providing aid to poor children may successfully accomplish that while simultaneously and unintentionally encouraging teenage pregnancy in poor families. It may also create a disincentive to remain employed among members of the "working poor," a nontarget group. If such a policy encourages a higher birth rate among the poor, eventually public policy addressing the health and educational needs of poor children is likely to cost more. Because resources are scarce, funds to do so will limit their availability for other purposes. Additionally, policy analysis should also be sensitive to the symbolic importance of governmental actions. Even if a policy has no discernible impact, it may be an important political indicator of a government's interest in dealing with a problem.

In practice one of the important issues in discussions of the results of policy analysis is who has the burden of proof. Must public administrators demonstrate that their programs are having the intended effect, or is the burden on others to show that the programs do not work? Sometimes, shifting the burden of proof in such discussions is tantamount to determining the outcome of the debate or dispute. For instance, whoever has the burden of proof in demonstrating that civil service examinations predict on-the-job performance in white-collar occupations is likely to lose. This is not necessarily because the exams do not actually predict performance, but rather because it is so difficult to *prove* that they do. Common sense may often be the best guide in these matters, but sometimes when political interests are at stake, common sense, as the saying goes, is uncommon.

Process Analysis and Implementation Studies

Ascertaining the impacts of public policies is often difficult or impossible. However, policy analysis should not be confined to considering impacts; it can also be used to assess the *process* through which a policy is being implemented. **Process analysis** concerns the way in which a particular policy or program is implemented.[9] Its importance can be succinctly stated: "The content of a particular public policy and its impact on those affected may be substantially modified, elaborated, or even negated during its implementation. Obviously, it is futile to be concerned with the impact of a particular policy if it has not been implemented."[10]

Surprisingly, however, policy analysis often neglects process analysis. In part this may be because it calls for a different type of approach than impact analysis. Whereas the latter tends to deal with aggregate data, such as crime rates or traffic fatalities, process analysis requires that the analyst become intimately aware of the administrative process through which the policy is implemented. For instance, if the policy is mandatory use of seat belts, one would have to look at the process of getting people to buckle up. Do public relations approaches work? Do police officers issue tickets for nonuse? Are penalties applied? If so, are they substantial? Just as the enforcement of other traffic laws may vary widely, so might that be the case with a mandatory seat belt law. In that event, it would not simply be the policy but the enforcement also that one would expect to have an impact on the area of behavior (driving).

In recent years, much process analysis has taken the form of "implementation" studies. These have identified some key factors affecting the execution of policies. One is the number of points at which different administrators must make decisions concerning implementation. In general, the more decision points there are, the less likely it is that the policy will be implemented as those who formulated it intended. Serious underfunding of programs is another barrier to successful implementation. Sometimes the goals or objectives of policies are so unclear that different agencies and public administrators adopt disparate approaches to defining and implementing them. For instance, during the early years of affirmative action in the federal personnel system, some agencies adopted goals and timetables that, if implemented, would have left their work forces *less* socially representative of the nation's working population. One agency even sought to increase occupational segregation by sex by establishing a 100 percent hiring goal for women in clerical positions. This may have provided more jobs for women, but it was a peculiar—though plausible—interpretation of the policy of using affirmative action to achieve equal employment opportunity.[11]

Implementation studies have focused attention on the design of public policies. **Policy design** should maximize the likelihood that implementation will be successful (as defined by the policy makers). In a discussion of "The Deadly Sins in Public Administration," Peter Drucker, a leading expert on management, identifies the following conditions as fatal to effective implementation: (1) lack of clear, preferably measurable, goals; (2) several objectives addressed at once, with no clear priorities; (3) assumption that personnel and funds will solve complex problems; (4) policies or programs tried out on a grand scale; (5) failure to learn from feedback; and (6) inability to abandon policies or programs when they become unnecessary or fail to achieve the desired results.[12]

Implementation studies suggest that a process analysis may be the place to begin policy analysis. If the implementation is such that there is no logical reason to expect a policy to have much or any impact, then there is no need to go further. Nevertheless, process analysis is sometimes neglected because it may require access to public administrators and the ability to monitor aspects of their behavior over substantial periods of time. But such access can be perceived by administrators as a potential source of conflict, for in the area of process analysis, evaluation of administrative behavior is seldom far beneath the surface.

IMPLEMENTATION EVALUATION

Implementation evaluation depends on policy analysis, but it is a different enterprise. In terms of public administration, the question is whether the implementation of the policy is appropriate, rather than whether it has the intended impact at all. Policy analysis may enable us to agree that a policy produces outcomes. In part that is because we tend to share a certain analytical paradigm that we agree can make such things knowable. However, in public administration, as we have seen throughout this book, such a consensus on normative questions is often missing. Just as what we are likely to view as "good" public administration depends on our perspective, what we consider properly executed policy will often depend on whether we adopt a managerial, political, or legal perspective.

MANAGERIAL PERSPECTIVES ON IMPLEMENTATION

Assuming that a policy has some traceable impact in the intended direction on its target, how can we determine if its execution is "optimal," or whether it is "satisfactory" or "not good enough"? The traditional managerial and new public management (NPM) perspectives present distinctive sets of answers to this question.

Traditional Management

The traditional managerial perspective values effectiveness, efficiency, and economy in implementation. It places much less importance on such other concerns as customer satisfaction, public participation, and procedural due process.

Effectiveness   In this context effectiveness will focus on the process of implementation. Among the major questions likely to be asked are: Is the administering agency effectively (that is, rationally) organized? Is the behavior of the public administrators involved *predictable?* Are patterns of authority and responsibility clear? Is feedback within the agency sufficient? Is communication adequate? Are enough resources being devoted to the policy? In short, does the organization of the effort to implement the policy follow the notions of effective management with regard to structure, personnel, budgeting, decision making, and so on? From this perspective, some policies are more suitable for implementation than others. Those that are relatively unsuitable will not be considered to be policies that work well, even though they may achieve their intended objectives. They will not be considered "good" policies because their administrative costs will be judged excessive and they will be thought to be too resistant to "good" (effective) management.

From this perspective there are many policies that simply will not work well. Policies that require "street-level" interactions between administrators who are, at the time, unsupervised and clients or other individuals will inevitably have an unpredictable quality about them. For example, no matter how explicit the formal rules seem to be, one housing inspector, police officer, member of the border patrol, teacher, or other street-level administrator may treat very similar situations, cases, or individuals differently from another administrator.[13] The exercise of discretion is simply unavoidable in many of these interactions. Actions may turn on individual administrators' judgments of the motives of the people with whom they come into contact, or with assessments of their behavior. What is "suspicious" behavior to one police officer may not appear so to another.

The unpredictability of these kinds of interactions presents a problem from the managerial perspective. Administrators may be acting in ways that deviate from the organization's formal guidelines. Consequently, the organization itself may be deviating somewhat from its intended role within the framework of the public policy being implemented. Teachers may be babysitting or controlling students rather than educating them. Police may be punishing suspects by using excessive force rather than simply arresting them and leaving punishment to the courts and prisons. Housing inspectors may be making judgments that have the tendency to allow some areas of a city to deteriorate far more rapidly than others. Moreover, because the individual street-level administrator is so difficult to supervise—and in fact is often the main source of information about his or her activities—the management of the organization may not even be aware of how discretion is being used or abused.

The traditional managerial approach, in turn, will try to develop indicators of performance that constrain the street-level bureaucrat more to the formal guidelines and expectations of the organization. Where these indicators are indeed indicative of what it is the street-level administrator is supposed to be doing, this will be a helpful response. However, in many cases solid indicators cannot be developed. Sometimes, in fact, quantitative indicators of qualitative performance can be counterproductive, as when teachers pass students on to the next grade even though they have not shown satisfactory learning. (In other words, a teacher whose pupils fail to learn is likely to be judged a poor teacher. Consequently, he or she may exaggerate the students' achievements.)

Policies requiring or involving hearings of some sort to determine eligibility for a government program are also likely to be considered less effective from the traditional managerial perspective. Again, the problem is largely one of predictability. Hearings lead to idiosyncratic assessments by examiners or administrative law judges and to unplanned allocations of resources. Their outcomes may be unpredictable and inconsistent.

Policies may also be judged as undesirable from a managerial perspective because their goals are too amorphous. The traditional managerial emphasis on effectiveness favors policies with clear, identifiable goals so that formal organizational arrangements and guidelines can be formulated toward their achievement. In addition, the clearer the goal, the more likely it is that meaningful indicators of performance with regard to its achievement can be developed. From a traditional managerial perspective it is difficult to have an effective implementation process unless there are clear objectives and indicators of performance.

The traditional managerial approach favors techniques for evaluating implementation that allow investigations to remain under the control of an agency's hierarchy. Three common techniques of this kind are the following:

1. *Site visits* by teams of high-ranking administrators and other experts in the agency's employ to assess operations at various installations. As Thomas Dye notes, "These teams can pick up impressionistic data about how programs are being run, whether programs are following specific guidelines, whether they have competent staffs, and sometimes whether or not 'clients' (target groups) are pleased with the services."[14]
2. *Process measures*, such as the number of claims processed, pupils matriculated, or arrests made, are often a useful gauge of activity on a year-to-year or month-to-month basis.

3. *Comparison with professional standards* is useful in some areas where such standards have been established independently by engineers, educators, health professionals, or others. For example, civil service examinations may be evaluated for "construct validity" (see Chapter 5) through comparison to standards set by professional organizations of psychologists or personnel specialists.

Cost-effectiveness combines concern with efficiency, economy, and effectiveness. Its central question is, given that a policy achieves a certain level of success, could another means achieve the same or a higher level at the same or less cost? For instance, if the policy is to have clean streets, will it be cost-effective to use mechanical street sweepers to replace human labor? Would adopting and enforcing antilitter laws be more cost-effective? The traditional managerial perspective is likely to favor the approach that achieves the most output per unit of cost (input).

The traditional managerial evaluation of public policy from the perspective of cost-effectiveness can become quite complicated. The best policy may be considered the one that is most cost-effective, but cost-effectiveness can depend on the level of application of the policy. This is the matter of **marginal costs,** which is embodied in the simple-sounding question "How much will it cost to treat one more case?" Generally speaking, the marginal cost of treating the first case is very high and then decreases until we approach a point where treating each additional case theoretically becomes more expensive than treating the one immediately preceding it. To place the principle in more concrete terms, suppose the public policy is to immunize all children in the United States between the ages of 2 and 5 against a variety of diseases. Suppose further that the policy is premised on the use of public administration to directly administer inoculations (perhaps to those children not provided with them by private doctors). In order to accomplish the public goal an administrative capacity would have to be established. A public health service of some type would be set up. It would occupy physical space, employ medical practitioners as well as administrative staff to manage it in terms of such functions as personnel, budgeting, and organizational design; it would also have clerical staff to assist management and in record keeping. In addition, staff for security and transportation might be necessary. These arrangements cost money: for salaries and supplies of the frontline service providers (the medical practitioners); for the physical plant; for administrative overhead. If such a system were put in place to treat only two or three cases, the cost per case would be very high. However, the cost per case would probably come down dramatically if thousands or perhaps millions of children were inoculated by the system. Here, economies of scale would result from the ability of the same medical practitioners to inoculate more children for the same salary, from the ability of relatively fewer managers (per case treated) to oversee the operation, and from relatively fewer clerical and other staff. No matter how well the system was designed, however, there would be some children who were difficult to inoculate. Perhaps they live in remote areas, drift around from place to place, have parents who are opposed to inoculation for one reason or another. Tracking down such cases for inoculation is probably possible, but the costs of doing so would obviously be much greater than the cost for the majority of children who are brought into a public health center by a parent for inoculation. In other words, achieving 100 percent compliance would probably be *disproportionately* more expensive than achieving only 80 percent compliance. Theoretically, depending on the precise circumstances, gaining compliance from the last 10 or 20 percent might cost as much as or more than treating all the rest of the cases.

This is a common phenomenon in cost-effectiveness analysis and can be applied to a wide range of examples. How much will it cost to pick up the last ton of garbage that is scattered around in the form of litter in an urban area? How much will it cost to educate the slowest student to an eighth-grade reading level, as compared to the average student? How much more will it cost to achieve 100 percent seat belt usage as opposed to 50 or 80 percent?

The traditional managerial approach *tends* to evaluate policy implementation as not working well, in terms of cost-effectiveness, if its marginal costs or average marginal costs are *rising*. If they are decreasing, the managerial perspective may support the treatment of still more cases; if they are level, this perspective may look for additional ways to reduce them (by cutting administrative overhead, for example). However, if no means of saving are evident at the point that marginal costs begin to rise, the managerial perspective will tend to conclude that the policy is being applied to too many cases, that it is too comprehensive, and that another approach should be developed. For example, public health service inoculations can be augmented by activities of the public schools in identifying those who have not been treated or by treating them directly. Garbage collection can be augmented by antilitter laws and deposits on beverage containers. Alternatively, the traditional managerial perspective may simply conclude that the policy itself is too comprehensive in its objectives and cannot be soundly implemented as a consequence. In a sense, the question here is, "How much is enough?" And the managerial answer is often, "As much as will reduce marginal costs to their lowest plausible level." An exception is cases in which universal or highly comprehensive treatment is necessary to make the policy work at all, as might be true in eradicating diseases such as smallpox.

The traditional managerial approach raises a number of questions from political and legal perspectives. The criterion of cost-effectiveness may need to be augmented by cost-benefit analysis. Whereas the cost-effectiveness approach assumes that the value of each unit or case treated is constant, cost-benefit analysis requires assessment of potential differences among these units or cases. It also assumes that greater or lesser application of a policy may have disproportionate benefits. For instance, where do those children not inoculated live? Are they in geographically remote areas? Members of insular religious sects? In crowded urban slums? What effect does not treating them have on the benefits derived from inoculating others? Additionally, those adopting a legalistic approach will augment concerns with cost-effectiveness with constitutional values. For example, what level of compulsion can be used to force those opposed to inoculation to have their children treated? Suppose the basis of resistance is "squeamishness," or suppose it is firmly held religious convictions. Does the application of the policy involve disparate treatment by race or gender? These are the kinds of issues that the analysis of cost-effectiveness in policy implementation does not satisfactorily address.

In short, when applying a cost-effectiveness approach, it is always necessary to remember that the cases or units for treatment must be identical. This was the problem we observed in relation to budgeting in Chapter 6. The cost of averting a death by promoting the use of seat belts or motorcycle helmets is less than by treating or curing cancer of the cervix. From a managerial perspective the "case" is the death averted, and aside from costs, it does not matter much how it is averted (by buckling up or treating cancer). From political and legal perspectives, however, it may matter a great deal *whose* death is being averted. In other words, politics and law focus more on the *distribution* of burdens and benefits, and somewhat less on the cost of distributing them, than does the traditional managerial approach.

Economy is also central to the traditional managerial perspective, which will consider a policy to be executed well when its administrative costs and loss through mistakes, fraud, or waste are minimal. For the most part, this aspect of the traditional managerial approach to evaluating implementation is not controversial. It tends to focus on a process analysis, though it is also concerned with impact in the sense that ineligible people should not be treated by the policy and that the policy should not be constructed in such a way as to facilitate fraud by its beneficiaries. Sometimes, however, this perspective does raise interesting questions from political and legal standpoints.

Passing Costs on to Clients   One classic way of reducing administrative costs is to pass them on to the recipients of services. Often, this is very simple and may involve no more than making would-be recipients apply for a benefit, rather than using the administrative apparatus to go out and find them. For the most part, this pattern is followed in welfare and Social Security programs. Those believing that they are eligible for benefits must apply for them at an administrative office. Sometimes the passing on of costs is more subtle and sometimes it can be quite serious in its consequences (see Box 8–2).

Making the potentially eligible apply for the benefit may deter some people. But even greater deterrence may be accomplished by forcing applicants to wait in line for long periods of time under unpleasant conditions. For instance, a site visit by the author to a large urban welfare bureau revealed that applicants had to stand in a long line that snaked around a dingy, poorly ventilated, hot, and crowded corridor. Many applicants were holding babies or toddlers. It could take several hours to move from the end of the line to the proper administrative official. Seating was virtually nonexistent and closing time was scrupulously guarded, thereby forcing some who may have waited considerable time to return again. Certainly, such conditions deter some individuals from applying for benefits even though they may be eligible to receive them.

BOX 8–2 **Passing Costs on to Others**

Walter Little, Appellant

v.

Gloria Streater

452 U.S. 1, 68 L Ed 2d 627, 101 S Ct 2202

[No.79-6799]

Argued January 13, 1981. Decided June 1, 1981.

Decision: Connecticut's application of its statute charging costs of blood grouping tests in paternity suit to requesting party, to deny indigent putative father such tests, held violative of due process.

SUMMARY

An unmarried woman gave birth to a child, and, as a requirement of the Connecticut Department of Social Services stemming from the child's receipt of public assistance, identified the putative father. The Department then provided an attorney for the mother, who commenced a paternity suit against the putative father in a Connecticut state court. The putative father moved the trial court to order blood grouping tests on the mother and the child pursuant to a Connecticut statute. The statute provided, in part, that the costs of such blood tests shall be chargeable against the party making the motion. Although the putative father asserted that he was indigent and asked that the state be ordered to pay for the tests, the trial court granted the motion only insofar as to order the blood tests, but denied the request that the state pay for the tests. Consequently, no blood grouping tests

were performed because the putative father could not afford their cost. After hearing testimony, the trial court found that the putative father was the child's father, and ordered him to pay child support. The Appellate Session of the Connecticut Superior Court affirmed the trial court's judgment in an unreported per curiam opinion. It held that the statute does not violate the due process and equal protection rights of an indigent putative father, and found no error in the trial court's denial of the putative father's motion that the cost of blood grouping tests be paid by the state. The putative father's petition for certification was denied by the Connecticut Supreme Court (180 Conn 756, 414 A2d 199).

On appeal, the United States Supreme Court reversed and remanded. In an opinion by BURGER, CH. J., expressing the unanimous view of the court, it was held that the application of the statute to deny the putative father blood grouping tests because of his lack of resources, where the statue requires that the costs of such tests be chargeable against the party requesting them, violated the due process guarantee of the Fourteenth Amendment.

Precisely how many is impossible to say. However, it is believed that about one-third of the population eligible for some administrative services fail to utilize them for one reason or another, including unpleasant administrative conditions.[15] In theory, perhaps, those deterred most are those whose eligibility is most questionable. In practice, however, this may not be the case.

Another means of passing on costs is to rule people ineligible for benefits, such as Social Security disability, pending decision of an individual's appeal in an administrative hearing.[16] If the individual subsequently wins, retroactive benefits may not necessarily be awarded. In any event, many individuals elect not to pursue the opportunity for a hearing, even though they may be eligible.

Residency requirements are another potential way of passing costs on to would-be clients. For instance, until the Supreme Court ruled such an approach unconstitutional in violation of equal protection and the right to travel in *Shapiro v. Thompson* (1969),[17] several states had residency requirements for welfare benefits. Connecticut, for example, had a one-year requirement, which it argued would accomplish a number of laudable administrative objectives. It would facilitate planning the welfare budget; it would reduce the number of individuals fraudulently receiving payments from two or more states; it would encourage individuals to seek work (rather than welfare) upon arrival in the state; and it would ensure that recipients of the benefits were bona fide residents of the state. Although the residency requirement may have made sense from a traditional managerial perspective, the Supreme Court considered the cost passed on to the individual to be a sacrifice of an essential right and liberty.

Passing Costs on to Employees   Employees can also be made to bear some of the costs of implementing an administrative program. For example, employees may have to supply their own uniforms, their own transportation for official purposes, or their own continued training through refresher courses and the like as a condition for continued employment. More controversially, employees may bear the costs of occupational disease and exposure to harmful substances in the workplace. In recent years, for example, public employee unions have been protesting against the continued presence of asbestos in public buildings.

Controlling Misuse   The reduction of costs may be quite controversial when it involves an effort by public administrators to assure that clients do not misuse funds allocated to them. For instance, if one wanted to assure that food stamps were used to procure a nutritious diet, the food items for which they could be used would be substantially limited. This would raise political pressures from agricultural interest groups hoping to have their products defined as acceptably nutritious under the program. It would also raise cries that the government is unduly paternalistic in telling people what to eat. What might the Potato Chip and Snack Food Association, a Washington-based trade association, have to say about such a plan? Similarly, efforts to assure that welfare funds to families with dependent children are actually used for the children's benefit can raise difficult issues. Can a case worker insist on entering a dwelling on pain of cutting off the funds?[18] Is advance notice necessary? Are unannounced "midnight raids" allowed?[19] Can a case worker insist that the child's bed be made? That the child have a bed? At what point does the recipient of an administrative benefit have a constitutional right to privacy that cannot be abridged because she or he receives the benefit?

Overlooking Latent Functions   In a classic essay on political corruption, Robert Merton pointed out that the political machine, though corrupt, did have some *latent functions* that were quite beneficial, especially to immigrants seeking employment and favors in exchange for votes.[20] Sometimes the term "welfare bureaucracy" is used as the antithesis of an administrative system that reduces operating costs. Here the bureaucrats themselves are considered to be on "welfare" as a result of administrative overstaffing. Yet if the object is to provide employment, as in the case of public works programs, then overstaffing may not be dysfunctional from a policy standpoint. Moreover, if overstaffing of administrative units is viewed as a way of assimilating social groups and enhancing their opportunities to enter the mainstream of American political, economic, and social life, then the fact that administrative costs may appear excessive may be somewhat beside the point. The latent function, such as assimilation and upward mobility, may be well worth the price from a political standpoint.

The New Public Management

The NPM favors implementation by "steering" rather than "rowing."[21] It favors discretion over rules, and measures success in terms of customer satisfaction and performance.

Alternative Service Delivery   A major premise of the NPM and the NPR are that, wherever possible, government should arrange for the provision of public services rather than deliver them directly itself. In short, it should concentrate on steering, not rowing. This approach, which is derived from business practices, enables government to focus on its core responsibilities and, often, to reduce its costs. For example, the primary function of a university, state or private, is to educate. But it also has a payroll and provides a broad range of services, such as food service. In many cases, these can be delivered more cost-effectively by firms specializing in them and providing them on a regional, national, or even international basis. When a university relies on Marriott, ARA, or a similar firm for food service, it also drastically reduces the amount of time the central administration has to devote to making sure that the students can eat on campus. Presumably, then, the administration can devote more time to educational matters.

The rowing, which is sometimes called "third-party government," can be arranged in several ways, as explained by E. S. Savas in *Privatization: The Key to Better Government*[22]:

1. Contracting with private parties or other governments. Contracts are used for a very wide range of activity: public works, transportation, safety, health and human services, prisons, recreation, and support

functions. Trash collection, street repair and cleaning, building inspection, fire and police communication, landscaping, building and vehicle maintenance, and payroll are among the functions most commonly contracted out by local governments.

2. Franchising is also very common. It provides private firms with a monopoly right to provide services for the government. Taxi and bus transportation are common examples, as are concessions at public parks and zoos. Franchises can be awarded to more than one company, but they limit competition by nonfranchisees. Consequently, they are valuable and may be a significant source of revenue when governments sell them.

3. Grants are used by governments to subsidize third parties that produce desired services. Examples include health services, museums, and performing arts. If tax expenditures (see Chapter 6) are included, then a very wide range of private production is subsidized by grants.

4. Vouchers are used to subsidize consumers rather than producers. Food stamps are probably the leading example, but vouchers are also used for medical services and low-income housing. Some tax expenditures, such as the home mortgage interest deduction, act as vouchers as well.

5. Voluntary services often augment the governmental provision of public goods. Recreation, ambulance service, fire protection, and neighborhood patrols are examples. Government may cooperate with the private groups providing the services by including them in planning and other relevant activities.

6. Self-service relies on private individuals to produce desired conditions, such as low fire and crime rates. Savas claims that "The family as a self-service unit is the original and most efficient department of housing, health, education, welfare, and human services, and it provides a wide range of vital services to its members."[23] The term "coproduction" is often used to denote cases where self-service is combined with governmental action. A simple example is alerting firefighters to where children may be sleeping by putting "tot finder" stickers in appropriate windows.

7. Markets are often juxtaposed to government in the production of goods and services. However, government can regulate markets to foster desired social and economic conditions. For example, equal employment opportunity law seeks to promote economic and social equality, while reducing the acceptability and incidence of discrimination generally. Laws dealing with child labor, minimum wages and hours, and labor relations are also broadly aimed at protecting widely shared social values.

Savas points out that these arrangements can be used in multiple, hybrid, and partial forms. For instance, a city may rely on several approaches for providing ambulance service; tax exemptions for not-for-profit organizations help subsidize their voluntary activities; and services can be partitioned, as in the case of public education where an array of voluntary PTA/PTO activity augments instruction.

Discretion   The NPM also favors less rule-bound and more discretionary public administration. It welcomes the deregulation of public employees as empowerment to find commonsense responses to situations not fully anticipated even by voluminous sets of rules. The NPR prods agencies to negotiate partnerships with other government agencies and businesses. Negotiation can be used to obtain acceptable outcomes and avert lawsuits. In one example, the Army Corps of Engineers used the partnership approach ". . . to accelerate hazardous and toxic waste cleanup projects, resolve conflicts over the operation of multi-purpose dams, handle wetland permits, acquire real estate, even handle internal labor disputes."[24] It reduced its legal caseload by 70 percent and saved millions of dollars in the process. In another example, the Occupational Safety and Health Administration was able to suspend strict enforcement to work with 200 of Maine's most injury-ridden firms. Productivity is reportedly up, and injuries down.[25] In Miami, the U.S. Customs Service formed a partnership with shippers. "Customs employees taught the shippers how to help with enforcement, and the shippers helped Customs to identify high-risk shipments."[26] Subsequently, many shipments cleared the port much quicker and enforcement rates were reported to be at an all-time high.

As the above examples suggest, the NPR differs dramatically from the traditional managerial perspective by not being concerned with uniformity and not fearing that employees will abuse their discretion. By definition, the outcomes of negotiated partnerships will depend on the bargaining positions and skills of the parties involved. Some public employees will be better at it than others and, accordingly, some outcomes will be more in the public interest than others. The NPR's claim is that overall, or on balance, discretionary government will work better and cost less, despite some inevitable mistakes. Similarly, the NPR reflects the belief that in results-oriented public administration, discretion will not breed corruption.

Monitoring and Measuring Performance

It is axiomatic that if government relies on third parties and empowered employees to achieve public purposes it will have to monitor their performance. A variety of contract monitoring approaches have been used.[27] The first step is to develop a strategy for monitoring before the contract is written, negotiated, and signed. Where feasible, specific observable and measurable performance requirements should be included in the contract. For instance, a contract may specify the maximum amount of time a third party has to fill potholes after being notified of them. It may require the contractor to periodically submit its work records to an agency for inspection. Citizen and customer surveys are also useful in some cases, though to develop and implement meaningful ones may be expensive. There is also some risk that if such surveys become as ubiquitous in public administration as in ser-vice rating cards in fast-food restaurants, customers will lose interest in them. Scheduled and surprise inspections can be useful. It is best for gov-ernment to provide for these in the contract itself in order to reduce po-tential legal problems under the Constitution's prohibition of unreasonable searches and seizures (see Chapter 11). Agency complaint and whistle-blower "hot lines" are also useful means of obtaining information on a third party's performance.

Performance measuring is relevant both to third parties and empowered public employees. The NPR's most general measure of performance is cus-tomer service. President Clinton's Executive Order 12862 (see Box 8–3) re-quires federal agencies to set customer service standards and to measure re-sults against them. Agencies must also benchmark their standards against business practices, use customer surveys, and set up systems for dealing with customer complaints. Box 8–4 presents several examples of federal customer service standards.

The NPM is somewhat divided over whether other performance mea-sures should focus on outputs, outcomes, or both. Assessing outputs provides no measure of a program's effectiveness in terms of achieving its goals. But concentrating on outputs, which are typically the product of multiple actors and programs, fails to assess the contribution of each administrative unit to the government's overall performance. The NPR is explicit in favoring a results-oriented approach that measures outcomes, not internal processes. Holding empowered employees accountable demands nothing less. The Ore-gon Benchmarks program also measures outcomes. New Zealand and Great Britain favor output measurement, whereas Canada and Australia are looking at outcomes as well as outputs. GPRA also seeks the dual approach.[28]

The U.S. Office of Management and Budget defines an outcome as "an assessment of the results of a program compared to its intended purpose."[29] An output measure is "a tabulation, calculation, or recording of activity or effort that can be expressed in a quantitative or qualitative measure."[30] Several ex-amples for different kinds of administrative concerns are presented in Box 8–5.

Performance measurement is eminently logical. But it is not new and has had limited success in the past. Measuring outputs alone can drive agen-cies to concentrate on processes without knowing their relationships to out-comes. But, agreeing on what program outcomes should be is sometimes po-litically difficult. The legislative coalitions that enact and support programs often depend on vagueness; they are jeopardized by specific, prioritized goals. Consequently, defining goals is easier in some governments, agencies, and programs than in others. The Oregon Benchmarks program is an ex-ample that is working at the state level. Early experience with GPRA pilot projects in the federal government showed that about 20 percent of the pro-grams involved could clearly define their goals, about 20 percent could not usefully do so, and the rest were somewhere in-between.[31] As in so many other areas of public administration, managerial questions often have polit-ical answers.   *Text continued on page 389.*

BOX 8–3 **Executive Order 12862—Setting Customer Service Standards**

September 11, 1993

Putting people first means ensuring that the Federal Government provides the highest quality service possible to the American people. Public officials must embark upon a revolution within the Federal Government to change the way it does business. This will require continual reform of the executive branch's management practices and operations to provide service to the public that matches or exceeds the best service available in the private sector.

Now, therefore, to establish and implement customer service standards to guide the operations of the executive branch, and by the authority vested in me as President by the Constitution and the laws of the United States, it is hereby ordered:

Section 1. Customer Service Standards. In order to carry out the principles of the National Performance Review, the Federal Government must be customer-driven. The standard of quality for service provided to the public shall be: Customer service equal to the best in business. For the purposes of this order, "customer" shall mean an individual or entity who is directly served by a department or agency. "Best in business" shall mean the highest quality of service delivered to customers by private organizations providing a comparable or analogous service.

All executive departments and agencies (hereinafter referred to collectively as "agency" or "agencies") that provide significant services directly to the public shall provide those services in a manner that seeks to meet the customer service standard established herein and shall take the following actions:

(a) identify the customers who are, or should be, served by the agency;
(b) survey customers to determine the kind and quality of services they want and their level of satisfaction with existing services;
(c) post service standards and measure results against them;
(d) benchmark customer service performance against the best in business;
(e) survey front-line employees on barriers to, and ideas for, matching the best in business;
(f) provide customers with choices in both the sources of service and the means of delivery;
(g) make information, services, and complaint systems easily accessible; and
(h) provide means to address customer complaints.

Section 2. Report on Customer Service Surveys. By March 8, 1994, each agency subject to this order shall report on its customer surveys to the President. As information about customer satisfaction becomes available, each agency shall use that information in judging the performance of agency management and in making resource allocations.

Section 3. Customer Service Plans. By September 8, 1994, each agency subject to this order shall publish a customer service plan that can be readily understood by its customers. The plan shall include customer service standards and describe future plans for customer surveys. It also shall identify the private and public sector standards that the agency used to benchmark its performance against the best in business. In connection with the plan, each agency is encouraged to provide training resources for programs needed by employees who directly serve customers and by managers making use of customer survey information to promote the principles and objectives contained herein.

Section 4. Independent Agencies. Independent agencies are requested to adhere to the order.

Section 5. Judicial Review. This order is for the internal management of the executive branch and does not create any right or benefit, substantive or procedural, enforceable by a party against the United States, its agencies or instrumentalities, its officers or employees, or any other person.

The White House
September 11, 1993

William J. Clinton

BOX 8–4 **Sample Customer Service Standards**

OPM'S FEDERAL EMPLOYMENT INFORMATION SYSTEM

OPM has established the following service standards for job seekers using the Federal Employment Information System:

- We will provide you with courteous and timely service.

- We will update our nationwide job listings every business day.

- We will have Employment Information Specialists available to answer your questions.

- We will provide 24 hours a day, seven days a week access to nationwide job information and application request services through a variety of electronic media.

- We will respond to your requests for applications and/or routine information within one business day.

- We will use your suggestions and complaints to improve our service continually. We will always remember we work for you, the American public.

DEPARTMENT OF STATE

The Department of State issues passports for U.S. citizens and provides information and guidance to U.S. travelers. The State Department offers these services for international travelers:

- You will receive timely and accurate information on travel safety and conditions in foreign countries 24 hours a day, seven days a week.

- You will receive your passport within 25 days after receipt of your application. Service will be provided in a courteous manner and, whenever possible, we will try to meet your travel needs.

- You will receive timely and courteous responses to requests for American citizen services, and services will be provided by knowledgeable and professional personnel.

- Service to persons seeking visas to legally visit or reside in the United States will be provided by knowledgeable, professional, and courteous personnel.

OCCUPATIONAL SAFETY AND HEALTH ADMINISTRATION

OSHA is making these commitments to business:

- Focus OSHA inspections on the most serious hazards.

- Be respectful and professional during inspections.

- Help them identify and control workplace hazards.

U.S. POSTAL SERVICE

- Your First Class Mail will be delivered anywhere in the United States within three days.

- Your local First Class Mail will be delivered overnight.

- You will receive service at post office counters within five minutes.

- You can get postal information 24 hours a day by calling a local number.

SOURCE: Al Gore, *Putting Customers First: Standards for Serving the American People* (Washington, D.C.: Government Printing Office, 1994), 18, 25, 52, 54.

BOX 8–5 **OMBs—Examples of Various Types of Performance Measures**

Workload
(not otherwise
categorized):

    Output   Annually *inspect* 3,200 grain elevators.

    Outcome   Through *periodic* grain elevator *inspection*, reduce the incidence of grain dust explosions resulting in catastrophic loss or fatalities to zero.

Production:

    Output   *Manufacture and deliver* 35,000 rounds of armor-piercing 120-mm projectile shells in FY 1997.

    Outcome   *Produce sufficient* 120-mm armor-piercing *projectiles* to achieve a 60-day combat-use supply level by 1999 for all Army and Marine Corps tank battalions.

Transactions:

    Output   *Process* 3.75 million payment *vouchers* in FY 1995.

    Outcome   *Ensure* that 99.25 percent of *payment vouchers are paid* within 30 days of receipt.

Records:

    Output   *Update* earnings *records* for 45 million employee contributors to the Social Security Trust Fund.

    Outcome   *Ensure* that all earnings *records are posted and current* within 60 days of the end of the previous quarter.

Utilization rates:

    Output   *Operate* all tactical fighter aircraft simulator training *facilities at not less than 85 percent of rated capacity.*

    Outcome   *Ensure* that all active duty tactical fighter aircraft *pilots* are fully qualified having *received a minimum of 32 hours of simulator training* and flown 400 hours in the previous 12 months.

Frequency rates:

    Output   Issue 90-day national temperature and precipitation forecasts *every six weeks.*

    Outcome   Provide users of meteorological forecasts with *advance information sufficiently updated to be useful* for agricultural, utility, and transportation planning.

Timeliness:

  Response times:

      Output   Adjudicative *decision* on all claim disallowances will be *made within 120 days* of appeal hearings.

      Outcome   *Provide* every claimant with *timely* dispositive *determination* on claims filed.

  Adherence to
  schedule:

      Output   *Operate* 95 percent of all passenger trains *within 10 minutes of scheduled arrival times.*

BOX 8–5 *Continued*

Outcome	*Provide* rail *passengers* with reliable and *predictable* train *service.*

Out-of-service conditions:

Output	All Corps of Engineer *locks* on river basin *x* shall be *operational during at least 22 of every consecutive 24 hours.*
Outcome	*Ensure no significant delays* in traffic transiting through river basin *x.*

Defect rates:

Output	*Not more than 1.25 percent* of 120-mm armor-piercing projectiles shall be *rejected as defective.*
Outcome	*No armor-piercing ammunition projectiles* fired in combat *shall fail to explode* on impact.

Mean failure rates:

Output	*Premature* space shuttle main engine *shutdown shall not occur more than once in every 200 flight cycles.*
Outcome	Space shuttle shall be maintained and operated so that *99.95 percent of all flights safely reach orbit.*

Accuracy:

Output	*The position of 300,000 navigation buoys shall be checked monthly.*
Outcome	*All navigational buoys shall be maintained within 5 meters of the charted position.*

Inventory fill:

Output	*Store* a minimum of 3.5 million barrels of *petroleum* stock.
Outcome	Petroleum *stocks* shall be maintained at a level sufficient to *provide a 60-day supply* at normal daily drawdown.

Complaints:

Output	Not more than *2.5 percent* of individuals seeking information *will subsequently re-request the same information because the initial response was unsatisfactory.*
Outcome	*99 percent* of all requests for information *will be satisfactorily handled with the initial response.*

Customer satisfaction levels (Output and outcome measures may often be indistinguishable):

Output	*In 1998,* at least *75 percent* of individuals receiving a service *will rate the service delivery as good to excellent.*
Outcome	At least *90 percent* of recipients will *rate the service delivery* as good to excellent.

BOX 8–5 *Continued*

Efficiency:

Output	Annual transaction costs/production costs/delivery of service costs projected on a per unit basis. *Produce 35,000 rounds of armor-piercing ammunition at a cost of $17.75 per round.*
Outcome	(Not commonly measured as an outcome.)

Milestone and activity schedules:

Output	*Complete 85 percent of required flight-worthiness testing* for Z-2000 bomber *by July 30, 1999.*
Outcome	The Z-2000 *bomber* will be flight-certified and *operational by December 1, 2000.*

Design specifications:

Output	Imaging *cameras* on Generation X observational satellite will have *resolution of 0.1 arc second.*
Outcome	Generation X observational satellite will successfully map 100 percent terrain of six Jovian moons to a resolution of 100 meters.

Status of conditions:

Output	In 1995, *repair and maintain 1,400 pavement miles* of Federally-owned highways to a *rating of "good."*
Outcome	By 2000, *35 percent of all Federally-owned highway pavement miles* shall be *rated* as being in *good condition.*

Percentage coverage:

Output	Provide *doses of vaccine to 27,000 pre-school children* living on tribal reservations.
Outcome	*100 percent* of children living on tribal reservations will be *fully immunized* before beginning school.

Effectiveness:

Output	*Not more than 7,000 in-patients* in military hospitals will be readmitted, postdischarge, for further treatment of the same diagnosed illness at the time of initial admission.
Outcome	*Initial treatment* will be therapeutically *successful for 85 percent* of all hospital admissions.

NOTES: For the purpose of these examples: Some of the outcome measures are much more narrowly defined than would otherwise be appropriate or expected. Some of the outcome measures are not inherently measurable, and would require use of supplementary performance indicators to set specific performance targets and determine whether these were achieved. Some measures include several aspects of performance; italics are used to feature the particular characteristic of that example. Many of the examples of output measures are process or attribute measures.

SOURCE: U.S. Office of Management and Budget, "Primer on Performance Measurement," 23 September 1994, 4-7 to 4-9.

THE POLITICAL PERSPECTIVE ON IMPLEMENTATION

As we have been suggesting, a political perspective on whether a policy is being successfully implemented may differ from a managerial perspective. Again, assuming that the policy has been determined to have some impact, evaluating its execution will depend on how well it fits the values inherent in the political approach. For even if a policy achieves its objectives, the means it uses and values it embodies may be evaluated as either satisfactory or unsatisfactory.

Representation

The political approach tends to view a policy as appropriately executed, within the parameters of the policy actually having a discernible impact on the target, if it affords representation to those individuals and interests most affected by it. Perhaps the use of the value of representation to judge the working of public policy through administrative implementation can best be conveyed by considering it from two perspectives that are common in public administration.

Participation in Decisions about Implementation   Several administrative programs in the United States have emphasized the idea that those most directly affected by the program be granted a voice in deciding how it will be implemented. One well-known instance involved the Taylor Grazing Act of 1934.[32] The policy propounded by the act was to issue permits for the grazing of livestock on the federally owned lands in the West in an effort to prevent denudation (with its consequent dust storms) through overgrazing. The act stated that the regulation of grazing should be made "in cooperation with local associations of stockmen."[33] Eventually this concept was implemented through the election of advisers from among the local stockmen in the various grazing districts. During the first fourteen months, the advisers' recommendations were followed in roughly 98 percent of the decisions involving the allocation of 14,000 permits.[34]

Although the Taylor Grazing Act presented a somewhat extreme case of individual participation in administrative implementation, it is by no means unique. Similar ideas have long prevailed in other agricultural programs and public school education. The Federal Advisory Committee Act of 1972, as noted in Chapter 1, seeks to assure representation of interests through the participation of advisory committees in administrative decision making. During the 1960s, the poverty program sought to make use of local participation through the election of some members of community action agencies. The Model Cities Program of that same decade sought the representation of local communities in urban renewal and revitalization decisions. The poverty program went somewhat beyond other approaches by encouraging the participation of representatives of the local population directly in the implementation of policy.[35]

From the perspective of the political approach, a policy that fosters an administrative system that does not allow participation of those most affected by the program may be judged a policy that is undesirable because it does not provide a measure of self-regulation.

Representation of Demographic Constituency Interests   The political perspective is also concerned that public administrative implementation be deemed to be substantively in the interest of demographic groups in legislative constituencies. For instance, an immunization program that fails to include rural children or severely economically disadvantaged children in urban areas may very well be judged inadequate from a political perspective. This is true even though a cost-effectiveness approach might show that it is dysfunctional in terms of administrative efficiency to try to reach those groups. Similarly, an approach to picking up garbage that leaves some neighborhoods, with identifiable economic or social characteristics, relatively neglected is likely to be challenged from a political perspective. Passing on costs to an identifiable constituency may also be opposed. There are many regulatory and service activities of public administrators that may potentially affect demographic groups differentially. It has even been argued by the attorney general of New York State that allowing a rise in the cost of telephone calls from pay phones would have a particularly adverse impact on poor people, who may have no other access to phones.

Responsiveness

The political perspective's value of responsiveness is related to considerations of representation. However, it sometimes goes beyond the representation of relatively specific interests to a sense of being in step with what the community as a whole seems to want. For instance, in the early 1980s, a grassroots movement against drunken driving developed in several states. Mothers' and students' groups against drunken driving sprang up. Some laws were rewritten in response to the public's pressure. Police began enforcing driving under the influence (DUI) laws more stringently and vigorously. In some states, New York for one, police roadblocks, at which all drivers are stopped as potentially DUI, became common. This redeployment of police, and the inconvenience it creates, is criticized by some. However, it is probably responsive to the concerns of the majority of citizens who care about the matter.

Sometimes the issue of responsiveness acts as a check on administrative logic that, although internally sound, is simply not in touch with reality. In other words, it can be invoked to counteract the "tunnel vision" that sometimes develops as a result of administrative specialization. For instance, an official directive from the now defunct U.S. Department of Health, Education, and Welfare once sought to prohibit "mother-daughter" and "father-son" events at public schools on the grounds that they were manifestations of prohibited sex-role stereotyping and gender-based discrimination. Whatever one thinks of HEW's logic, the public just wouldn't stand for the rule and it was promptly rescinded. The minting of the Susan B. Anthony dollar coin in the 1970s was another example. Administrators in Washington, D.C., were convinced that the coin would be useful. Apparently, serious consideration was given to its size, shape, and design. But as far as the public was concerned, there was no need for the Anthony dollar and they would not use it. (See Box 8–6 for an illustration of responsiveness.)

Decentralization of administrative operations is another aspect of responsiveness that can lead the political and traditional managerial perspectives to diverge on what constitutes proper implementation. It may often be cheaper for administrative agencies not to maintain a large number of field offices or satellite facilities. Instead, individuals wanting something from the administrative agency or compelled to interact with it may be required to travel to its headquarters or less conveniently located field offices. In the state of Vermont, for example, at one time at least, to register a new car brought in from outside the state, one had to travel to the capital, Montpelier, which might be a substantial distance away. There were no local offices in towns to deal with this administrative operation. From a political perspective, such an arrangement is not responsive to the needs of individuals who live in areas remote from the administrative offices. If these remote areas coincide with legislative districts, there is every likelihood that pressure will be placed on elected representatives to require the administrative agencies to maintain

---

BOX 8–6 **Public Comment in Public Administration: What's the Beef?**

In December 1981, the National Cattlemen's Association asked the U.S. Department of Agriculture (USDA) to change its standards for the grading of beef. The cattlemen thought that the public was interested in leaner beef. The USDA proposed new standards for the Prime and Choice grades by requiring less fat in the form of marbling. The department held hearings on the proposed new standards in Des Moines, Dallas, Atlanta, Washington, and Salt Lake City. According to a USDA spokesperson, they received "4,000 comments from various segments of the public, and almost 80 percent were against the changes. The strong common denominator was, rightly or wrongly, the perception that the new regulations would cause consumer confusion and destroy consumer confidence, neither of which would ultimately help the meat industry. And since we are concerned with industry profitability, the new proposals did not seem like a good idea." Consequently, the old standards were retained in response to the public's will as expressed through opportunities for public comment on the USDA's proposed policy change. This is just one illustration of the importance of the public's right to receive notice of administrative agencies' proposed regulations to have the opportunity to respond to them.

SOURCE: Mimi Sheraton, "Department of Agriculture Withdraws Proposed Changes in Grading of Beef," *New York Times*, 21 September 1982.

more convenient field offices in order to be more *responsive* to the needs of the legislators' constituencies. This is one reason why states with large geographic areas and low population densities tend to have more public administrators per capita than do other states.[36]

Accountability

Accountability is a final value that should be considered in addressing the political perspective's evaluation of the implementation of public policy. That perspective demands that public administration be held accountable to elected officials, particularly legislators. Accountability is addressed in greater detail in Chapter 12. Here, however, it is desirable to indicate how the execution of some policies can pose a challenge to it.

Sunshine   It was once said by Supreme Court Justice Louis Brandeis that sunlight is the best disinfectant. Since the late 1960s, federal policy and that of several states has emphasized the desirability of promoting "freedom of information" about the operation of administrative agencies. Some laws require that certain types of meetings and hearings within agencies be open to the public and the press. Although these **sunshine laws** hardly provide any citizen with a right to each and every bit of administrative information, they do serve to *open* the administrative process to public and legislative scrutiny to a very substantial extent. From this perspective, an administrative program that operates in secret may be judged not to be working "well," even though it achieves its objectives at a reasonable level and cost. Covert CIA operations have been opposed on this basis. In fact, Supreme Court Justice Douglas once said that if the public was not told how the CIA spent its money, "a secret bureaucracy is allowed to run our affairs."[37] Some of the administrative arrangements associated with the Executive Office of the President, especially during the Watergate period, the Iran-Contra affair, and much of the Clinton presidency, were criticized on this basis as well. To make the problem more concrete, suppose you were passed or failed on a driver's licensing examination on the basis of unknown criteria? Or were held back in school, with no inkling why that administrative decision was made?

Sunset   Sunset provisions, as noted earlier, are another manifestation of the desire to hold public administrators accountable. From the managerial perspectives, all the reporting and justifying that are involved when agencies operate under a sunset provision (and desire to be continued) can be serious diversions from or barriers to customer satisfaction, monitoring third parties, and/or efficient, economical, and effective operations. Yet from the political perspective, administrative programs that do not labor under such conditions may not be considered policies that work well. For the policy to work well, a review by the legislature at some fixed time is sometimes deemed essential.

General Legislative Oversight   Legislatures in the United States use a committee and subcommittee system partly to exercise "oversight" of administrative operations. They may also create administrative agencies of their own, such as the federal General Accounting Office and offices such as Inspector General, to aid in oversight. In general, a policy that eludes effective oversight, perhaps because it overlaps too many committee jurisdictions, may be judged a policy whose implementation is inherently risky. Even if its objectives are achieved, a policy that is resistant to oversight may be evaluated as a poor means of using public power to intervene in the economy or society because such a policy would be largely beyond the control of elective officials.

Casework   Legislative casework, discussed in Chapter 2, can be a means of promoting the accountability of public administrators to elective officials. Consequently, from a political perspective, a means of policy execution that prohibits the administrators from responding to casework inquiries could be judged undesirable. Of course, sometimes resistance to legislative involvement in administrative routines is understandable because it is desirable to insulate public administration from political pressures. For instance, the IRS may not want to divulge what triggers a tax audit. Other times, though, casework, like process analysis, suggests how implementation can be improved.

THE LEGAL PERSPECTIVE ON IMPLEMENTATION

The legal approach to public administration also asks a distinctive set of questions in evaluating the implementation of public policies. Its focus tends to be on constitutional integrity, equal protection, fairness (procedural due process), and protection of the rights of those individuals who come into contact with public administrative operations. Consequently, because the questions asked by the legal perspective differ from those asked by either of the other perspectives, the answers it reaches may also be different. Here, it is obviously impossible to consider in detail all the fine points that the legal perspective would take in evaluating policy, but some of the more central aspects can be briefly reviewed. Chapter 11 devotes more space to public administration and democratic constitutionalism.

Constitutional Integrity

Sometimes public policies are in conflict with constitutional provisions for the separation of powers and federalism. For instance, during the 1980s the Supreme Court found that the federal government's policy for deporting illegal aliens incorporated an unconstitutional "one-house legislative veto." In the complicated case of *Immigration and Naturalization Service v. Chadha* (1983),[38] the Court held that allowing the House of Representatives to overrule (that is, to exercise a legislative veto over) the attorney general's decision to suspend an order to deport an individual violated two aspects of constitutional integrity. First, it infringed upon the "presentment clauses," which require Congress to present legislative actions such as bills, orders, and resolutions to the president for approval or veto. Because "legislative vetoes" are not presented to the president, and therefore cannot be overridden by a presidential veto, they violate the integrity of constitutional process. Second, the one-house veto defeats the Constitution's provision for a bicameral (two-house) Congress. In the Court's view, bicameralism could not be dismissed as a mere formality or redundancy because the Senate provides representation by state, whereas the House does so by population within the states, and each chamber can serve as a check on the other.

The Court was cognizant that the legislative veto is a convenient shortcut, but it emphasized its commitment to constitutional integrity: "There is no support in the Constitution or decisions of this Court for the proposition that the cumbersomeness and delays often encountered in complying with explicit constitutional standards may be avoided, either by the Congress or by the President. . . ."

The *Chadha* decision was not an aberration. Constitutional procedure and the separation of powers have been invoked in other cases involving contemporary policies.[39] So have a variety of federalism issues. In *Seminole Tribe of Florida v. Florida* (1996),[40] the Supreme Court held that Congress cannot use its powers under the Commerce Clause to undermine the states' Eleventh Amendment protection against being sued in federal court by their own citizens for alleged violations of federal laws.* In *U.S. Term Limits v. Thornton* (1995),[41] the Court narrowly held that the states could not constitutionally impose term limits on their members of Congress. In part, the prevailing argument rested on the belief that allowing term limits would enable the states to change the characteristics of the national government's legislature, thereby substantially altering the federal government's relationship to the people.

Equal Protection

As we have seen, distributional issues often arise in the administrative implementation of public policy. Who shall receive a benefit and where? Who shall be subject to a regulation and will there be discernible patterns of enforcement? The traditional managerial approach to public administration tends to address such issues from a cost-effectiveness or economizing approach. The NPM centers on customers. The political perspective is concerned with the representation of identifiable groups or constituencies and responsiveness to these groups. The legal approach adds yet another dimension.

It focuses more on whether individuals or groups are afforded equal protection of the law.[42] In other words, does the policy place members of some social groups at a disadvantage? If so, is the policy rationally formu-

---

*Citizens may continue to sue a state in which they reside in federal court for violations of federal civil rights laws and the U.S. Constitution.

lated and implemented to achieve a legitimate, important, or compelling governmental purpose? Does the policy intentionally discriminate against groups that have historically been subject to discrimination and disadvantage in the United States?[43] Answers to questions such as these will determine whether the legal perspective will view a policy and/or its execution as appropriate or inappropriate.

In practice, two kinds of problematic cases arise. One is where public policy allocates resources differentially to different racial or ethnic groups or to men and women. Here the issue is likely to be whether such a policy, even if otherwise rationally related to a legitimate governmental purpose, has an unconstitutional or illegal discriminatory intention. For instance, in one case, the town of Shaw, Mississippi, managed to pave streets, put in sewers, streetlights, and other improvements in the white section of town, but not in the black neighborhood.[44] Its actions were found to be unconstitutional by the federal courts. In another case, the school system in San Antonio, Texas, allocated far greater funds per student to a school attended primarily by "Anglos" as opposed to one with a large number of Hispanic students. The city argued that the classification, or basis for distribution of funds, was based on wealth, not ethnicity, and that it rationally served a legitimate purpose. The U.S. Supreme Court agreed.[45]

A second type of problem is the use of social characteristics, such as race, as proxies for some other attribute. One example, though decided under the Fourth Amendment rather than equal protection, concerned the U.S. Border Patrol. The function was to stop motor vehicles near the Mexican border to check on the citizenship or visa status of their occupants. The policy was to stop primarily (if not solely) those people who "looked Mexican." This practice obviously created a proxy—"looking Mexican"—for a condition, namely, being an "undocumented alien." The Supreme Court found the policy to be unconstitutional.[46] Consequently, stopping cars solely on the basis of the ethnic appearance of their occupants is unconstitutional. But from a traditional managerial perspective of trying to make the most efficient, effective, and economical use of scarce personnel and other resources, would it make sense for the Border Patrol to expend time and effort stopping those who "looked 'Anglo'" or even Scandinavian? Here is an area where different approaches to policy evaluation stand in stark contrast. See Chapter 11 for further discussion of the Constitution in the context of public administration.

Procedural Due Process and Protection of Individual Rights

The legal perspective toward public administration also favors providing those dependent upon administrative services or subject to administrative regulation with procedural protections against an adverse action. Thus, whereas the traditional managerial perspective might support immediately cutting off a benefit to a client who is suspected of fraud, and the NPM favors great discretion in dealing with customers, the legal perspective might favor continuing the benefit until the individual is given the opportunity to answer the allegations that he or she had engaged in fraudulent behavior.[47]

The legal approach also takes an expansive position on the importance of individual rights and liberties. Consequently, it may view administrative implementation as not working well if it tends to infringe on these rights. An example already mentioned is the imposition of residency requirements for eligibility for welfare benefits. Other intriguing instances have been such requirements as being available for work on Saturday, despite one's religious beliefs to the contrary, for unemployment insurance,[48] exclusion from extracurricular high-school activities for being married,[49] and a variety of conditions in prisons and public mental health facilities.

Estoppel

The legal approach aligns itself with the traditional managerial approach and stands in stark contrast to the NPM in the increasingly important area of estoppel. In legal jargon, "to estop" means to prevent. The law of estoppel determines when agencies are bound by the advice or information that their personnel give to customers. For instance, a Social Security claims agent or an IRS employee, whose job is to advise customers, may provide incorrect information. Should the agencies be held responsible for their employees' errors? Put differently, should an applicant who is eligible for benefits be deprived of them because a claims agent inappropriately dissuaded her or him from filing a written claim? (See Box 8–7.) Should a taxpayer have to pay a penalty fee for relying on incorrect advice from the tax agency? The traditional managerial perspective does not favor allowing lower-level employees to bind an agency because it would violate the principle of hierarchy. It could also create disarray in administrative systems for determining eligibility for benefits or tax breaks. In addition, some regulations, including Social Security rules and the tax code, are so complicated that errors are inevitable—especially by lower-level customer service personnel who do not have advanced legal training. In the aggregate, such errors could prove very costly to an agency. By contrast, the NPM's emphasis on customer service and employee empowerment logically requires that no customer be left worse off because of an agency representative's mistake. The political approach has no fixed view on such matters, but would handle them through legislative "casework."

As the law now stands, customers are at a serious disadvantage when relying on incorrect official advice or information. They have to show not only that they were made worse off by the agency's poor guidance, but also that they did not act out of ignorance. The latter requirement effectively holds every applicant or taxpayer personally responsible for knowing the laws and published regulations that govern his or her interactions with public agencies. This is true even where the rules are arcane and inaccessible to almost anyone without technical training (see Box 8–7). Of course, agencies are able to release benefits and waive penalties even when

BOX 8–7 **Bearing the Cost of an Administrator's Error**

Richard Schweiker, Secretary
of Health and Human Services
v.
Ann Hansen
450 U.S. 785, April 6, 1981

Ann Hansen met for about fifteen minutes with Don Connelly, a field representative of the Social Security Administration, and inquired as to her eligibility for "mother's insurance benefits." Connelly erroneously told her that she was not eligible and did not recommend that she file a written application or advise her of the advantages of doing so, even though the administration's thirteen-volume Claims Manual instructed field representatives to advise applicants of the advantages of filing written applications and to recommend to applicants who are uncertain about their eligibility that they file written applications. About a year later, Hansen learned that she was in fact eligible, filed a written application, and began receiving benefits. Pursuant to the regulations, she was entitled to receive benefits for up to twelve months preceding her application and she did receive retroactive benefits for that period. She contended that she should also receive retroactive benefits for the twelve months preceding her initial interview with Connelly, since he gave her erroneous information and failed to alert her to the desirability of filing a written application.

The U.S. Supreme Court held that Connelly's error did not prevent the Secretary of Health and Human Services from denying Hansen retroactive benefits for the twelve months

prior to her interview with Connelly. The Court reasoned that the Social Security Administration could not be bound by the errors of its lower-level functionaries, since

the Claims Manual is not a regulation. It has no legal force, and it does not bind the SSA. Rather, it is a 13-volume handbook for internal use by thousands of SSA employees, including the hundreds of employees who receive untold numbers of oral inquiries like [Hansen's] each year. If Connelly's minor breach of such a manual suffices to [prevent Schweiker from withholding the retroactive benefits sought], then the Government is put "at risk that every alleged failure by an agent to follow instructions to the last detail in one of a thousand cases will deprive it of the benefit of the written application requirement which experience has taught to be essential to the honest and effective administration of the Social Security Laws" [citation omitted].

But as Justice Marshall argued, in dissent, "the fault for [Hansen's] failure to file a timely application for benefits that she was entitled to must rest squarely with the Government. . . ."

Their fault, her loss. Very poor customer service. How would you have ruled?

they are not estopped from withholding or applying them. Presumably, an agency administered according to NPM principles would place service to the customer above other values and would rarely penalize someone for following its instructions.

UTILIZING ANALYSIS AND EVALUATION

Policy analysis and implementation evaluation are intended to be useful to politicians and public administrators. At the very least, they should contribute to knowledge about the effects and design of public policies. Ideally, analysis and evaluation would also lead to direct improvements in policy implementation in the short run. But there are barriers to the effective use of such research. First, as Aaron Wildavsky observed, administrative organizations may not be set up to digest evaluation. He wrote:

> Evaluation and organization may be contradictory terms. Organizational structure implies stability while the process of evaluation suggests change. Organization generates commitment while evaluation inculcates skepticism. Evaluation speaks to the relationship between action and objectives while organization relates its activities to programs and clientele.[50]

Second, even if administrative organizations were amenable to analysis and evaluation research, they would still face problems in interpreting such studies. Many evaluations are, quite simply, inconclusive. Some studies are unable to ascertain any significant impact of public policy. Others show very limited effects. The failure to discern impacts may lie in any of the following or some combination thereof: (1) the policy itself, (2) implementation, (3) the evaluation design and methodology, or (4) errors in carrying out the research.

When analysis and evaluation fail to find a policy impact, supporters of the program may argue that *more* funding and authority are needed to make the policy work. Opponents, by contrast, may assert that the policy is misconceived or that implementation is unworkable. Both can speculate about the likelihood of the policy working better in the long run. In essence, the political debates concerning public policies are frequently left largely unresolved by evaluation studies.[51]

Arnold Meltzner has identified "The Seven Deadly Sins of Policy Analysis," all of which detract from utilization.[52] He suggests that there is enough experience with policy analysis to identify the "sins," but not necessarily enough to avoid them. The sins are: (1) "being in a rut," or unable to recognize that circumstances have changed significantly in ways that make former analytical perspectives inappropriate; (2) being too distant, either geographically or conceptually, to have a firm grip on the reality of how a policy is operating; (3) lacking timeliness; (4) offering superficial analysis that misses the roots of problems; (5) providing topical advice, or policy analysis that stems from a crisis and is reactive, that tends to crowd out other policy analysis on less visible or pressing concerns; (6) offering capricious advice, or advice that advocates change for its own sake; and (7) giving apolitical advice that ignores political constraints or opportunities.

Perhaps the utilization of policy analysis and evaluation will become more systematic in the future if (1) the quality of evaluation research improves; (2) evaluation research becomes more institutionalized in agencies such as the federal Office of Management and Budget, General Accounting Office, and Congressional Budget Office; (3) evaluation research can be integrated with policy making in the legislative and executive branches; and (4) evaluation studies include specific plans for utilization.[53]

CONCLUSION: THE COMPLEXITY OF POLICY DESIGN

The diverse managerial, political, and legal perspectives on implementation can make policy design a very complex endeavor. There is little agreement concerning the basic criteria on which implementation should be judged. Cost-effectiveness, customer satisfaction, political accountability, procedural due process, and other relevant values often conflict with one another—both in the abstract and in day-to-day administrative practice. The traditional managerial, political, and legal approaches all favor strictly limiting administrative discretion, especially at the street level. By contrast, the NPM favors broad employee empowerment. No overall synthesis is possible, but one or another of the perspectives might be more suitable to different types of policy.

Overhead Policy   Overhead policies are those concerned with keeping public administrative operations running on a day-to-day basis. They do not include levels of budgeting, the allocation of personnel, or the nature of missions. They *do* include disbursing and accounting for money, personnel functions such as compensating and retiring employees, and the maintenance and interior design of the physical plant of agencies. For the most part, traditional managerial concerns are most appropriate in judging the overhead policies. There is little doubt that efficiency, effectiveness, and economy have been valued here ever since the managerial perspective was first developed.

Sociotherapeutic Policies   These policies—such as the war on poverty and the Model Cities Program—seek to treat an undesirable condition that has become associated with a particular group. The group could have various attributes: it could be economic, urban, elderly, or rural, for example. To a very large extent, sociotherapeutic policy coincides with the idea "welfare" in the label "welfare state." Traditionally, such policies seemed to favor the political perspective in their administrative arrangements. The participation of their beneficiaries and responsiveness to their needs were considered of great importance in their relative success. In the absence of participation and representativeness, these policies become paternalistic; they become regulatory in the sense of controlling individuals' behavior without affording them a voice in the process. Today, the NPM's insistence on customer satisfaction and employee empowerment offers great promise in redesigning sociotherapeutic policy because it emphasizes the individualized or customized treatment of beneficiaries.

Regulatory Policy   Regulation through administrative action comes in many guises. However, some programs are clearly "regulatory" in a very classical sense. These are programs that are engaged in such functions as rate setting for public utilities and common carriers; in zoning; in assuring purity or healthfulness of substances such as food, water, and air; and in promoting "fair" economic competition and eliminating deceptive marketing practices. Regulatory policies generally rely heavily on a legal perspective. Because the rights of private parties are being determined through public administrative action, it has been considered highly desirable to assure the private parties protection against untoward infringements on those rights. In practice, this often means that an adjudicative hearing format is used. Due process is stressed, as is the impartiality of the hearing examiner. There are some good reasons why the legal perspective seems most appropriate to regulatory policy. Traditional managerial perspectives could easily lead to the squelching of the rights of private parties and to harming their legitimate interests. The NPM's partnership approach can clearly lead to inconsistent and less than optimal outcomes. The political approach's emphasis on responsiveness to the general public could easily facilitate a kind of "tyranny of the majority" against the interests and rights of the private parties. The legal perspective, by contrast, seeks to balance the public and private interests in each instance, affording adequate protection to both.

Perhaps this does not take us far enough. After all, public policy does not come neatly packaged with clear labels, and there are many other types of policy, including those that emphasize foreign affairs, national security, macroeconomic policy, economic redistribution, energy, and distribution of the nation's resources. It is not possible in this volume to assess which of the perspectives, if any, would be generally most suitable in any of these areas. Quite possibly, different aspects of each of these policy types would most properly be organized according to one or another of the perspectives. Perhaps one perspective could even dominate a whole policy area. Still, without answering or even addressing these speculations, we hope that our suggestions for analyzing these problems will be helpful. Awareness of what different perspectives demand should help us evaluate policy more comprehensively and eventually may lead us to formulate better means of implementation.

NOTES

1. *Motor Vehicle Manufacturers Association v. State Farm*, 463 U.S. 29 (1983).
2. Woodrow Wilson, "The Study of Administration," *Political Science Quarterly* 56 (December 1941): 481.

3. See David Nachmias, *Public Policy Evaluation* (New York: St. Martin's, 1979), chap. 1. Much of the discussion in the first part of this chapter is based on this source.

4. Al Gore, *From Red Tape to Results: Creating a Government That Works Better & Costs Less* (Washington, D.C.: Government Printing Office, 1993), ii.

5. Nachmias, *Public Policy Evaluation*, 57–61.

6. Ibid., 5.

7. James H. Jones, *Bad Blood* (New York: Free Press, 1981).

8. David Kershaw, " A Negative Income Tax Experiment," in *The Practice of Policy Evaluation*, ed. David Nachmias (New York: St. Martin's, 1980), 27–41; Thomas R. Dye, *Understanding Public Policy*, 6th ed. (Englewood Cliffs, N.J.: Prentice-Hall, 1987), 368–369.

9. Nachmias, *Public Policy Evaluation*, 5.

10. Ibid.

11. David H. Rosenbloom, *Federal Equal Employment Opportunity* (New York: Praeger, 1977), chap. 5.

12. Peter Drucker, "The Deadly Sins in Public Administration," in *Current Issues in Public Administration*, 2d ed., ed. Frederick Lane (New York: St. Martin's, 1982), 421–426.

13. Michael Lipsky, *Street Level Bureaucracy* (New York: Russell Sage, 1980); Pietro S. Nivola, *The Urban Service Problem* (Lexington, Mass.: Lexington Books, 1979); Eugene Bardach and Robert A. Kagan, *Going by the Book: The Problems of Regulatory Unreasonableness* (Philadelphia: Temple University Press, 1982).

14. Dye, *Understanding Public Policy*, 356. The remainder of this paragraph draws heavily from this source.

15. Daniel Katz et al., *Bureaucratic Encounters* (Ann Arbor: University of Michigan, Institute for Social Research, 1975).

16. *Mathews v. Eldridge*, 424 U.S. 319 (1976).

17. *Shapiro v. Thompson*, 394 U.S. 618 (1969).

18. *Wyman v. James*, 400 U.S. 309 (1971).

19. *Parrish v. Civil Service Commission*, 425 P.2d 223 (1967).

20. Robert Merton, *Social Theory and Social Structure* (Glencoe, Ill.: Free Press, 1957), 71–81.

21. David Osborne and Ted Gaebler, *Reinventing Government* (Reading, Mass.: Addison-Wesley, 1992), chap. 1.

22. E. S. Savas, *Privatization: The Key to Better Government* (Chatham, N.J.: Chatham House, 1987), esp. chap. 4, on which much of the following discussion in this section is based.

23. Ibid., 81.

24. Al Gore, *Common Sense Government Works Better & Costs Less* (Washington, D.C.: Government Printing Office, 1995), 81.

25. Ibid., 25–27.

26. National Performance Review, *Reinvention Roundtable* 2 (April 1995): 3.

27. See Savas, *Privatization*, 270–272.

28. Donald Kettl, "Performance Measurement, Benchmarking, and Reengineering," testimony before the Subcommittee on Government Management, Information, and Technology, Committee on Government Reform and Oversight, U.S. House of Representatives, 20 June 1995, 5; U.S. Office of Management and Budget, "Primer on Performance Measurement," 23 September 1994, 4-2.

29. U.S. Office of Management and Budget, "Primer on Performance Measurement," 4-1.

30. Ibid.

31. U.S. Office of Management and Budget, "Assessment of FY 1994 GPRA Pilot Project Performance Plans: Memorandum for Alice Rivlin, John Koskinen, from Walter Groszyk," 10 August 1994, 1, and Attachment A.

32. See Grant McConnell, *Private Power and American Democracy* (New York: Knopf, 1966), chap. 7; Phillip O. Foss, *Politics and Grass* (Seattle: University of Washington Press, 1960); Wesley Calef, *Private Grazing and Public Lands* (Chicago: University of Chicago Press, 1960).

33. McConnell, *Private Power and American Democracy*, 203.

34. Ibid., 204–205.

35. See Daniel P. Moynihan, *Maximum Feasible Misunderstanding* (New York: Free Press, 1970).

36. David H. Rosenbloom and Frank Bryan, "The Size of Public Bureaucracies," *State and Local Government Review* 13 (September 1981): 115–123.

37. *U.S. v. Richardson,* 418 U.S. 166, 201 (1974).

38. *Immigration and Naturalization Service v. Chadha,* 462 U.S. 919 (1983).

39. *Bowsher v. Synar,* 478 U.S. 714 (1986); *Buckley v. Valeo,* 424 U.S. 1 (1976).

40. *Seminole Tribe of Florida v. Florida,* 116 S.Ct. 1114 (1996).

41. *U.S. Term Limits v. Thornton,* 115 S.Ct. 1842 (1995).

42. See *Zobel v. Williams,* 457 U.S. 55 (1983), for a concise statement.

43. *Washington v. Davis,* 426 U.S. 229 (1976).

44. See *Hawkins v. Town of Shaw,* 437 F2d 1286 (1971).

45. *San Antonio School District v. Rodriguez,* 411 U.S. 1 (1973).

46. *U.S. v. Brignoni-Ponce,* 422 U.S. 873 (1975).

47. *Goldberg v. Kelly,* 397 U.S. 254 (1970).

48. *Sherbert v. Verner,* 374 U.S. 398 (1963).

49. *Cochrane v. Board of Education,* 103 NW 2d 569 (1960); *Starkey v. Board of Education,* 381 P.2d 718 (1963).

50. Aaron Wildavsky, "The Self-Evaluating Organization," in Nachmias, *The Practice of Policy Evaluation,* 441–460, quoted passage from 443.

51. Deborah Stone, *Policy Paradox and Political Reason* (New York: HarperCollins, 1988).

52. Arnold Meltzner, "The Seven Deadly Sins of Policy Analysis," in *Current Issues in Public Administration,* 4th ed., ed. Frederick Lane (New York: St. Martin's, 1990), 429–439.

53. David Nachmias and Gary Henry, "The Utilization of Evaluation Research: Problems and Prospects," in Nachmias, *The Practice of Policy Evaluation,* 461–476, esp. 473–475.

ADDITIONAL READING

BUCHHOLZ, ROGENE. *Public Policy Issues for Management.* Englewood Cliffs, N.J.: Prentice-Hall, 1988.

DYE, THOMAS. *Understanding Public Policy,* 8th ed. Englewood Cliffs, N.J.: Prentice-Hall, 1995.

GOGGIN, MALCOLM, ANN O'M. BOWMAN, JAMES LESTER, AND LAURENCE O'TOOLE, JR. *Implementation Theory and Practice.* Glenview, Ill.: Scott, Foresman/Little, Brown, 1990.

JENKINS-SMITH, HANK. *Democratic Politics and Policy Analysis*. Pacific Grove, Calif.: Brooks/Cole, 1990.

STONE, DEBORAH. *Policy Paradox and Political Reason*. New York: HarperCollins, 1988.

STUDY QUESTIONS

1. Can you think of a policy that is attaining its objectives, but through a kind of implementation to which you are opposed? Consider the use of police roadblocks to combat DUI and random urinalysis drug testing of public employees.

2. During the early and mid-1980s, many states raised their drinking ages to 21, in response to federal prompting and as a means of promoting traffic safety. How would you go about analyzing the impact of this policy? What kind of approach would you take and what kinds of information would you seek and use? Suppose your analysis discerned no policy impact; how do you think different political groups would react?

The Convergence of Management, Politics, and Law in the Public Sector:

An Illustration

Chapter 9 | Regulatory Administration: An Illustration of Management, Politics, and Law in the Public Sector

In recent years, regulation has emerged as an area of distinctive concern in public administration. Because regulatory administration encapsulates much of the challenge that contemporary public administration poses for the United States political system, it can be used to illustrate the convergence and clashing of different perspectives. It represents a very direct use of governmental authority to penetrate spheres of life that were once left primarily to the workings of private social and economic forces. For instance, regulatory agencies are engaged in rate setting for utilities and some forms of transportation; they seek to ensure that products sold on the open market are not injurious to the health and safety of consumers; they have the authority to prohibit the use of industrial, mining, and agricultural processes that are deemed damaging to the environment; and they are involved in seeking to protect workers from discrimination and unhealthy or unsafe conditions in employment. Moreover, in general, regulatory administration tends to vest a great deal of authority in the hands of agencies that are by design considerably independent of elected officials. These agencies also tend to combine legislative, executive, and judicial authority. They make rules that constrain the conduct of individuals, corporations, and other organizations; they implement or enforce these rules; and they often adjudicate the application of the rules should a challenge to them arise. Much regulatory administration makes use of judicial processes. It has been an area of administration in which judicial review has been of exceptionally great importance. As the scope of regulatory administration has grown, greater attention has been paid to its economic, political, and social costs and benefits—and many have come to believe that the costs are too high and that regulatory reform or deregulation is often desirable. In this chapter we will consider the development and growth of regulatory administration, the problems it presents, and managerial, political, and legal approaches toward seeking to improve the quality of governmental regulatory activities. Although the discussion focuses on federal regulatory agencies, the reader should bear two things in mind: first, that regulatory administration is illustrative of many of the broader problems and challenges confronting public administration today; and second, that a great deal of what takes place on the federal level is matched by the operation of state regulatory agencies. The latter are especially important in regulating utilities, occupational licensing, consumer affairs, day care and nursing home facilities, and health centers.

THE DEVELOPMENT AND GROWTH OF REGULATORY ADMINISTRATION

Today, much of American economic and social life is the direct subject of administrative regulation by the federal government. It is debatable when federal regulatory activity began in earnest. Some might date it from the 1850s, when the federal government created a Steamboat Inspection Service; others from 1883, when the Civil Service Commission was created to regulate federal personnel administrative practices; still others from 1887 when the Interstate Commerce Commission was created to regulate railroad service. However, it is hardly debatable that until the recent trend toward reform and deregulation began in the 1970s and continued more forcefully through the 1980s, regulation had developed a very broad sweep. (Box 9-1 provides a list of several federal regulatory agencies that are commonly referred to by their initials.) The table in Box 9–2 lists the main regulatory agencies that existed up to the late 1980s, their subject matter, the date of their creation, and their location within the government's administrative structure. The table conveys a good deal of information to which we will be referring throughout this chapter. It should be noted, though, that some of these regulatory activities have fallen by the wayside in the movement toward deregulation. Especially notable in this context has been the demise of the CAB and the ICC and deregulation of some aspects of banking, truck, bus, and rail transportation, and the natural gas and oil industries. Perhaps the most immediate question raised by the table is, "Why so much regulation?"

The general origin of federal regulatory activities is associated with the growing economic, technological, and social complexity of life during the past century or so. The increasing division of labor and greater specialization make us all highly dependent upon one another but less able to assess the

---

BOX 9-1 **Alphabet Agencies**

During the early part of the New Deal (1933–1937), a large number of new federal agencies were created. They were commonly referred to by their initials, such as NLRB, thereby giving rise to the term "alphabet agencies." But for the uninitiated, sometimes alphabet agencies need some unscrambling. The following is a key to the abbreviations used frequently throughout this chapter.

CAB Civil Aeronautics Board

CPSC Consumer Product Safety Commission

EEOC Equal Employment Opportunity Commission

EPA Environmental Protection Agency

FAA Federal Aviation Administration

FCC Federal Communications Commission

FDA Food and Drug Administration

FMC Federal Maritime Commission

FTC Federal Trade Commission

ICC Interstate Commerce Commission

NHTSA National Highway Transportation Safety Administration

NLRB National Labor Relations Board

NRC Nuclear Regulatory Commission

OMB Office of Management and Budget

OSHA Occupational Safety and Health Administration

BOX 9–2 Some Regulatory Agencies of the Federal Government

Agency*	Present Organization	Year of Origin	Responsibility†
Comptroller of the Currency	Dept. of Treasury	1863	National banks
Fish and Wildlife Service	Dept. of Interior	1871	Preservation of fish and wildlife
Interstate Commerce Commission (ICC)	Abolished	1887	Prices, entry in rail, trucking, buses, and inland and coastal waterways
Forest Service	Dept. of Agriculture	1905	Management of resource use
Employment Standards Administration	Dept. of Labor	1913	Wages, hours, and discrimination in employment
Federal Reserve System	Independent	1913	Interest rates, national banks, and banking
Federal Trade Commission (FTC)	Independent	1914	Consumer information, advertising, business practices
Coast Guard	Dept. of Transportation	1915	Ship safety, environmental protection
International Trade Commission	Independent	1916	International "dumping," industry relief
Food Safety and Quality Service	Dept. of Agriculture	1916	Food inspection, grading, and standardization
Federal Energy Regulatory Commission (formerly, Federal Power Commission [FPC]) (FERC)	Dept. of Energy	1930	Prices for natural gas, interstate electricity, oil by pipeline
Food and Drug Administration (FDA)	Dept. of Health and Human Services	1931	Food and drug safety
Federal Home Loan Bank Board	Succeeded by the Federal Housing and Finance Board (1989)	1932	Interest rates and entry into savings-and-loan industry
Commodity Credit Corporation (CCC)	Dept. of Agriculture	1933	Farm commodity pricing
Federal Deposit Insurance Corp. (FDIC)	Independent	1933	Insurance of bank deposits
Federal Communications Commission (FCC)	Independent	1934	Entry into broadcasting, aspects of telecommunications
Securities and Exchange Commission (SEC)	Independent	1934	Information and trading conditions of securities
National Labor Relations Board (NLRB)	Independent	1935	Labor contracts and collective bargaining
Civil Aeronautics Board (CAB)	Abolished	1938	Prices, entry into airline industry
Bureau of Land Management	Dept. of Interior	1946	Management of public lands
Federal Aviation Administration (FAA)	Dept. of Transportation	1948	Airline, airport safety
Animal and Plant Health Inspection Service	Dept. of Agriculture	1953	Food inspection
Federal Maritime Commission	Independent	1961	Shipping

BOX 9-2 *Continued*

Agency*	Present Organization	Year of Origin	Responsibility†
Agricultural Stabilization and Conservation Service (reorganized into Consolidated Farm Service Agency, 1994)	Dept. of Agriculture	1961	Farm acreage allotments
Equal Employment Opportunity Commission (EEOC)	Independent	1964	Ending prohibited employment discrimination
Federal Highway Administration (FHA)	Dept. of Transportation	1966	Truck and bus safety
National Oceanic and Atmospheric Administration (NOAA)	Dept. of Commerce	1970	Management of marine resources and protection of marine mammals
Federal Railroad Administration	Dept. of Transportation	1970	Rail safety
National Highway Traffic Safety Administration (NHTSA)	Dept. of Transportation	1970	Motor vehicle safety and fuel economy
Environmental Protection Agency (EPA)	Independent	1970	Environmental protection of air, water, and land
Postal Rate Commission	Independent	1970	Recommends prices of U.S. Postal Service; reviews post office closure decisions
Occupational Safety and Health Administration (OSHA)	Dept. of Labor	1970	Worker safety
National Credit Union Administration	Independent	1970	Credit unions
Federal Election Commission	Independent	1971	Federal elections
Farm Credit Administration	Independent	1971	Agricultural credit and banks
Agricultural Marketing Service	Dept. of Agriculture	1972	Standardization, grading, inspection
Consumer Product Safety Commission (CPSC)	Independent	1972	Safety of consumer products
Bureau of Alcohol, Tobacco and Firearms	Dept. of Treasury	1972	Firearms, explosives, alcohol, tobacco, commercial arson
Mine Safety and Health Administration	Dept. of Labor	1973	Miner safety
Economic Regulatory Administration	Dept. of Energy	1974	Petroleum pricing and allocation, coal conservation, temperature limits for buildings, energy standards for new buildings
Commodity Futures Trading Commission	Independent	1975	Information and trading conditions of commodity futures
Nuclear Regulatory Commission (NRC)	Independent	1975	Licensing and regulation concerning nuclear reactors

BOX 9–2 *Continued*

Agency*	Present Organization	Year of Origin	Responsibility†
Federal Grain Inspection Service	Dept. of Agriculture	1976	Grain inspection
Office of Surface Mining Reclamation and Enforcement	Dept. of Interior	1977	Environmental effects of surface mining
Office of Government Ethics	Independent	1978	Ethics in the federal executive branch
Federal Labor Relations Authority	Independent	1979	Federal labor relations
Merit Systems Protection Board (MSPB)	Independent	1979	Federal personnel administration
Defense Nuclear Facilities Safety Board	Independent	1988	Dept. of Energy nuclear facilities

*Some agencies listed have been phased out or subsumed by others in the movement toward deregulation.
†Some agencies have nondomestic regulatory or nonregulatory functions as well.

SOURCE: Derived from Lawrence J. White, *Reforming Regulation* (Englewood Cliffs, N.J.: Prentice-Hall, 1981), Tables 3–1, 3–2; updated according to the *United States Government Manual, 1995/96* (Washington, D.C.: Government Printing Office, 1995).

predictability and reliability of each other's behavior. For example, we are dependent upon farmers, food handlers, and processors whom we do not know personally. Since they are anonymous, traditional channels (families, religious organizations, and communities) for exercising control over their behavior and assessing their reliability are unavailable to us. Of course, we can still exercise some personal judgments about the safety of foods, drugs, products, and modes of transportation. Such private organizations as Consumers Union and Underwriters' Laboratories might also help to inform us of dangerous or hazardous products. Liability law affords protection too. It gives producers an incentive to produce safe products and enables us as consumers to obtain compensation if we are injured by those products that are determined to be unsafe. Yet we may want more certainty, especially when the consumption of products or the use of services can lead to disasters. We may also favor regulation when we are informed by private sources of how undesirable some industrial processes are, even though they may pose no immediate danger. For instance, the publication of Upton Sinclair's *The Jungle* (1905), which described the filthy conditions in the meatpacking industry, was a catalyst in the framing of the Pure Food and Drug Act of 1906. The book turned President Theodore Roosevelt into an advocate of the regulation of some aspects of the food and drug industries.[1] To some extent the issue was not that the meat depicted in *The Jungle* was dangerous to one's health after being cooked, but rather that it was so filthy as to be repulsive—that is, even if it wouldn't hurt them, after knowing how it was handled people did not want to eat it. But danger is often real. In 1938, drug regulations were expanded to require testing of new drugs *prior* to marketing after some 107 people were killed by sulfanilamide, a new form of sulfa drug that had been initially hailed as very promising. Similarly, just as once the safety of steamboats was of great concern to passengers who were not in a position to make a sound evaluation, today few of us are able to evaluate the safety of different types of commercial airplanes or of railroad trestles and trackbeds. Consequently, we may turn to the government to assure the safety of these transportation services.

Regulatory administration to assure the safety of products, services, processes, and technologies is currently handled by the FDA, FAA, CPSC, NHTSA, NRC, and a variety of other agencies. It is largely based on science and engineering and tends to rely on inspections and testing for enforcement. A special variant of this type of regulation involves occupational licensing, mostly at the state level, in a number of fields to assure the public that practitioners are competent.

But regulation is not just aimed at assuring safety. We are also economically interdependent and consequently may want some economic practices to be made predictable, reliable, and perhaps stable through regulation. Rate setting is one example. In the 1880s, farmers in some areas were dependent upon railroads to transport their produce to markets. Some railroads sought to take advantage of their monopolies on various routes by charging rates that bore little relationship to the actual cost of transporting the farmers' shipments. If allowed to continue indefinitely, this would most likely have depressed the agricultural sector of the economy, at least in some geographic areas, and/or have driven prices for food in urban areas way up. It was also viewed as fundamentally unfair. In 1887, the ICC was set up to avoid these consequences by regulating railroads in the public interest.

Regulation of this type is intended to create a surrogate for the market. It concentrates on setting prices (or rates) and/or controlling entry into a field of economic activity. It has been most common in transportation (rail, bus, trucking, shipping, and air), the field of public utilities, and some aspects of the FCC's regulation of radio and television broadcasting. In recent years, deregulation of some of these areas has been substantial. Surrogate-market regulation is characterized by economic analysis of costs, rates of return, and distribution of services. Sometimes it is used to subsidize an industry, as when past ICC regulations enabled truckers to compete with railroads on long hauls, even though their real costs were higher. More commonly, surrogate-market regulation creates **cross subsidies** through which one set of customers (such as long-distance callers) pays prices that are intended to subsidize another (users of local telephone service).

Regulation is also used to assure the proper functioning of markets. Antitrust and fair-trade regulations are preeminent examples. The Sherman Antitrust Act of 1890 was intended, in part, to assure that markets did not become noncompetitive through monopolization. The Federal Trade Commission and Clayton Acts of 1914 were concerned with competition, but became the basis of regulatory activity also intended to curb trade practices that distorted market forces, such as false advertising and price fixing.

The list of regulatory activities does not stop there. In recent decades there has also been great concern with environmental regulation. Like Upton Sinclair's *The Jungle*, Rachel Carson's *Silent Spring* (1962) helped crystallize demands for regulation by increasing public awareness of the long-term dangers confronting the environment through chemical pollution and various agricultural, mining, and building practices. Some of these dangers have already materialized, such as "air inversions" and dangerous levels of smog that can be factors in individuals' deaths. Others, such as acid rain, global warming, and the depletion of the earth's ozone layer, threaten to wreak havoc on the ecology of vast geographic areas.

Greater regulation of shipping practices has been a direct result of a number of spectacular oil spills by supertankers and a growing realization that the ecology of the oceans is vulnerable to pollution.[2] One reason why regulation of the environment appears sensible and desirable to many is that the forces of the marketplace do not always seem to work as an adequate check on the short-term practices of a broad range of economic concerns. For instance, in the short term, it may be cheaper for utilities and manufacturers in the Midwest to pass off sulfur dioxide pollution as an externality rather than change their processes or install "scrubbers" to reduce it. An externality is an aspect of a product or its production that is not accounted for in the economic transaction between buyer and seller. In this case, it is a part of production that returns in the form of acid rain and is paid for by the Northeast and parts of Canada.

Environmental regulation relies on engineering, a host of sciences, and economic analysis. It makes use of "environmental impact statements," or analyses of the likely ecological effects of economic development, production processes, and product uses. Inspections and monitoring are also used as enforcement techniques. Today, environmental regulation frequently involves health concerns, as in the case of the disposal and cleanup of hazardous wastes.

Employment is another area of comprehensive regulatory activity. Because it consists of human effort, labor differs from other commodities or factors of production that are bought and sold in markets. Some economic and production practices have such undesirable and major social consequences that they are prohibited through regulation. Child labor and unsafe "sweatshops" are classic cases. Collective bargaining practices, including union organizing, are regulated by the NLRB. The EEOC was created to prevent employment and union practices that illegally discriminate against individuals on the basis of race, color, religion, national origin (ethnicity), or sex. Discrimination based on age or a handicapping condition is also under its current jurisdiction. Congress has considered discrimination along these lines to be *unfair* and also an impediment to interstate commerce and harmful to the nation's economy. Occupational safety and health regulation has grown immensely since OSHA was established in 1970. In part, this has been a response to the growing awareness that the individual worker might be unable to make a sound judgment as to the safety of some substances, such as benzene or asbestos, found in the modern workplace. More specialized regulatory activities exist in some occupations, such as mining.

The regulation of employment practices is so broad and prone to overlap other forms of regulation that it necessarily involves a variety of techniques. The NLRB and the EEOC rely heavily on adjudicatory processes. Accordingly, their operations are largely informed by legal analysis. OSHA, by contrast, relies far more on rule making and inspections. Much of its activity is based on health sciences and engineering.

Although these are the main types of regulatory administration in the United States, they do not encompass all of it. There is also the Federal Election Commission, which regulates some aspects of election campaigns for federal office. Several federal and state agencies are engaged in regulatory activity to protect individuals' civil rights in voting, in places of public accommodation, on common carriers, and in educational facilities. Some federal regulations pertain to state and local jurisdictions, as in civil rights and some aspects of employment and environmental regulatory administration. This creates a kind of "regulatory federalism," in which subnational governments are regulated. Finally, it should be noted that a great deal of federal regulatory activity is augmented by state and local agencies, especially in the fields of health, safety, employment, the environment, and fair-trade practices.

The scope and complexity of regulatory administration make it difficult to generalize about regulatory policy. Some analysts use categories such as "old style" or "economic" regulation (surrogate market, market functioning, and/or single industry) as distinct from "new style" or "social" regulation (health, safety, environment, employment, across industries).[3] Such simplifications are convenient for some purposes, but they must be used with caution: Some environmental and health regulation is older than some forms of economic regulation, and it is not altogether clear why unfair-practice regulation, including discrimination, in employment should be considered "social" rather than "economic." Some analysts link regulatory activity to "market failures," such as monopolization and the creation of undesirable externalities. To the extent that this approach suggests that governmental regulation is justified only when markets fail, it states a policy position, rather than a proof, that is contestable in the political system. The Constitution's interstate commerce clause allows federal regulation in the general welfare, not solely in the event of market failure. Markets do not necessarily produce the social outcomes favored by political majorities. They are also limited in their capacity to take the interests of future generations into account, but political leaders may sometimes be concerned precisely about the nation's future. Conservation policies and the systems of national and state forests are examples of political decisions not to cede the allocation of scarce resources to the here-and-now workings of the market.

Perhaps regulatory administration is best understood as part of a web of controls—economic, social, and legal—over activity that is considered antisocial or otherwise undesirable. Therefore, an important question is, given all the mechanisms for exercising such controls, how is the choice for different types of regulatory administration made?

Political Patterns

Regulatory administration is established as a political response to a problem, real or imagined, in the economy, society, or ecology. It will have costs and produce benefits that may be distributed in a variety of ways. Hence, inevitably there is a "politics of regulation."[4] In considering the origins of regulatory administration, James Q. Wilson has been able to identify several types of political conditions that are associated with the creation of specific regulatory agencies and statutes.

Majoritarian Politics   When the costs and benefits of a governmental policy or activity are widely distributed, we see **majoritarian politics** occurring. "All or most of society expects to gain; all or most of society expects to pay."[5] Wilson believes that the passage of the Sherman Antitrust Act (1890) and the Federal Trade Commission Act (1914) are examples. Neither was aimed at a specific industry; both promised to eliminate unfair, harmful, or unscrupulous economic practices without specifying what these were. Neither was strongly supported nor strongly opposed by business.

Interest Group Politics   When both costs and benefits are narrowly concentrated, **interest group politics** results. "A . . . regulation will often benefit a relatively small group at the expense of another comparable small group.

Each side has a strong incentive to organize and exercise political influence. The public does not believe it will be much affected one way or another; though it may sympathize more with one side than the other. . . ."[6] Perhaps the best single example in the regulatory realm is the Shipping Act of 1916, which since 1961 has been administered by the Federal Maritime Commission. The competition was between those who shipped goods by sea and the shipping companies. Although the public interest was involved in a general sense, the public itself and others not directly or immediately affected were relatively uninvolved in the issues posed. The National Labor Relations Act of 1935 (Wagner Act), which created the NLRB, was another example. It pitted organized labor against industry.

Client Politics   At those times "when the benefits of a prospective policy are concentrated but the costs are widely distributed,"[7] **client politics** prevails. Here, some relatively small and easily organized group stands to benefit, while the costs are "distributed at a low per capita rate over a large number of people." Consequently, there may be little incentive to organize forceful opposition. Wilson finds that the creation of the CAB and many public utility commissions at the state level more or less fits this pattern. He suggests that occupational licensing boards probably do also. However, he notes that sometimes opposition may develop to what would otherwise be a case of "client politics" when public interest groups become involved. Wilson also notes that despite the widespread distribution of relatively low costs, many business or other groups may become involved in discussion of the policy when it is first proposed.

The "client politics" model makes clear that despite the popular view that private enterprise thoroughly opposes government regulation, there is much reason to believe that some industries have sought to be regulated. George Stigler, a Nobel Prize winner in economics, promoted an influential theory about this. In his view, "regulation is acquired by the industry and is designed and operated primarily for its benefit."[8] This is especially true where the industry sees the opportunity of using governmental power to keep new entrants (would-be competitors) out. To accomplish its ends, the industry may seek to "capture" the regulatory agency, often a commission. Such a strategy was first propounded by Attorney General Richard Olney in the early 1890s, with regard to the probable future of the ICC. He wrote: "The Commission . . . is, or can be made, of great use to the railroads. It satisfies the popular clamor for a government supervision of railroads, at the same time that the supervision is almost entirely nominal. Further, the older such a commission gets to be, the more inclined it will be found to take the business and railroad view of things. . . ."[9]

The capture theory was rigorously developed by Marver Bernstein, who hypothesized that regulatory agencies go through predictable "life cycles."[10] At birth they avidly regulate the industries under their jurisdiction on behalf of consumers, rate payers, or the public interest more generally. The second stage is reached when the agency has either eliminated the worst abuses it was created to correct, or, alternatively, becomes frustrated with its inability to do so and the lack of public concern with its activities. At this point, agencies begin to compromise more with the regulated industries and begin to view the industries themselves as an important part of their constituency. In the final stage, the regulatory agency becomes protective of the status quo and often a de facto "captive" of the industry. In the latter case, the industry gains informal but real political control over the appointment of regulatory commissioners and uses the commission's public power for private gain.[11] Such a pattern is frequently descriptive of client politics, but is not necessarily confined to it.

Entrepreneurial Politics   When "a policy may be proposed that will confer general (though perhaps small) benefits at a cost to be borne chiefly by a small segment of society,"[12] we encounter **entrepreneurial politics.** Wilson points to antipollution and auto-safety bills as examples. What is peculiar about this type of politics is the inability of the small segment upon whom the burden falls to block the regulatory policy at issue. Wilson attributes this primarily to the work of people he calls **entrepreneurs,** such as Ralph Nader, whose work was instrumental in the passage of the Auto Safety Act of 1966. An earlier example was Dr. Harvey Wiley, who helped mobilize support for the Food and Drug Act of 1906. This type of policy entrepreneur effectively represents groups that are not directly involved in legislative policy making.

In sum, Wilson concludes that the politics of regulatory policy "follows different patterns, mobilizes different actors, and has different consequences depending, among other things, on the perceived distribution of costs and benefits of the proposed policy."[13]

Wilson's scheme is very useful in gaining an understanding of regulatory policy. Although his categories do not coincide perfectly with the types of regulation discussed above (or any other typology, for that matter), some *tendencies* are evident. Client politics describes much surrogate-market regulation; entrepreneurial politics, much health and safety regulation; majoritarian politics, as noted, is associated with the regulation of the market's functioning; interest group politics is descriptive of much but not all employment regulation. Wilson's discussion encompasses the politics and some of the economic bases of regulation. It is necessary to consider social factors, as well, in order to have a more complete picture of the growth of regulatory administration.

Social Factors

Sometimes the contemporary administrative state is referred to as the "welfare state," and it is alleged that government has placed a safety net underneath everyone in the population to protect those who are unable to care for themselves. Whereas some argue that the safety net is already too broad, others maintain that it needs to be enlarged to encompass some individuals and circumstances for whom or which there is currently inadequate protection. Whatever one's stance on the desirability of the "safety net," it does seem evident that as a society the United States has developed two characteristics in this regard that bear heavily upon regulatory administration and public administration in general.

First, this society has frequently sought to augment personal responsibility with government regulation. The variety of state mandatory seat belt laws provides an outstanding example. The federal government has long required that new cars sold in the United States be equipped with seat belts. There are now very few cars on the roads without them. So the belts are there for anyone to fasten. It is a simple matter of personal responsibility, requiring but a few seconds and little effort to accomplish. However, for one reason or another, the states reasoned that it was *their* responsibility to make sure that everyone buckles up. In many places it is now a regulation to be enforced by the police and courts—not something left up to the individual. The same tendency to use regulation to override (and actually diminish) personal responsibility can be found in consumer affairs. Here, state agencies and the FTC seek to protect the consumer from being deceived or cheated. Laudable though this may be, in the past that was primarily the consumer's personal responsibility. Similarly, some of the OSHA regulations tend to treat workers as though they were incapable of judging how to use equipment safely and move about in the workplace. Whereas, in the past, a cheated consumer or an injured worker might have had recourse after the fact at common law, regulation today is by administrative agencies and seeks to prevent harm in the first place.

Second, it has been observed that, "wholly aside from objective changes in risk, cultural changes in the past two decades [1960s–1970s] have increased our *intolerance of risk*, resulting in greater expectations of security from physical hazards, illness, environmental degradation, and even from being cheated in the marketplace."[14] Greater affluence, sensitivity to power relationships and exploitation, and the growing concern with the quality of life seem to have coincided with the rise of opportunities for entrepreneurial politics, as described by Wilson. Public interest groups and political entrepreneurs both in and out of government have taken it upon themselves to represent and mobilize support for what they perceive to be the public's interest in reducing risks. In retrospect, many readers may find it amazing that prior to 1938 there was no general requirement that drugs be tested before being sold to the public in large quantities.

The growing intolerance of risk and diminished reliance on personal responsibility are factors in the shifting focus of much regulation from surrogate market to environmental and health and safety (both generally and in employment).

THE STRUCTURE AND PROCESS OF REGULATORY ADMINISTRATION

Regulatory administration can also take several organizational forms. In the past, the commission format was most common. This approach to administrative organization was discussed briefly in Chapter 3. Its most distinctive feature is that it is headed by a number of commissioners who form a bipartisan group and typically hold fixed and staggered terms of office. The purpose of this arrangement is to insulate the workings of the regulatory commission from electoral politics. It provides a degree of stability and continuity in the commissions and protects them from rapid changes in leadership when the partisanship of the presidency or majority in Congress changes. Political detachment of this type has been deemed desirable, as it is thought that the commissions' missions are to regulate sectors of the economy or aspects of commerce in the public interest in the long run. They are not intended to engage in rapid ideological shifts in striking balances among the competing interests they must consider. Rather, they are intended to develop a clear vision of the public interest by making highly specific rules, and adjudicating cases that may arise under them. In this fashion, it is thought, they can determine what the public interest is in any given context.

When the ICC, the prototypical federal regulatory commission, was set up in 1887, Congress clearly believed that the policy area of railroad rate regulation ought to be taken out of partisan politics and that the commission was capable of ascertaining the public interest with little direct guidance from the legislature. Eventually, Congress established some commissions with very broad missions and virtually no genuine guidance as to what policies should be adopted. The FCC is perhaps the extreme in this regard. Its mission is to regulate the use of the nation's airwaves for broadcasts in the "public convenience, interest, or necessity." Such a broad mission leaves the commission a great deal of freedom to make policy. It also bespeaks of the legislature's unwillingness or inability to be more active in formulating policy in the regulated area. Coupled with their structural independence, this gives some regulatory agencies a substantial degree of autonomy.[15]

In recent years, it has become more common for regulatory agencies to be placed within executive branch departments. For instance, as Box 9–2 indicates, this is true of OSHA, NHTSA, and some others. Agencies such as the EPA are placed within the executive branch, but not housed in another department. Agencies of this type are not headed by a commission, but rather by a director, who is appointed by the president, with the advice and consent of the Senate, and serves at his pleasure. These structural arrangements are intended to give the president greater influence or control over the policy-making and enforcement activities of the regulatory agencies. However, some relatively new agencies, including the EEOC, the MSPB (Merit Systems Protection Board), and the Defense Nuclear Facilities Safety Board, do retain the traditional commission form.

Regulatory administrators use several processes. As noted earlier, they make *rules*. For example, the FDA has made a number of rules regarding the labeling of drugs and foods. It requires that drug advertising include a statement of side effects, contraindications, and appropriate precautions and warnings. It has also issued rules for "standards of identity" of products such as fish sticks, ice cream, and hot dogs. In one celebrated case, it took two years or so to determine whether a new type of potato chip could be fairly called "potato chip." Some of these rules make rather odd reading: Frozen fried fish sticks are defined as "clean, wholesome, rectangular-shaped unglazed masses of cohering pieces not ground of fish flesh coated with breading and partially cooked. . . . Frozen fried fish sticks weigh up to and including 1½ ounces; are at least three-eighths of an inch thick and their largest dimension is at least three times the next largest dimension."[16] Such a rule has its purpose—to prevent misleading the consumer and to serve specific economic interests. In 1987, for instance, the National Milk Producers Federation and the Committee for Fair Pizza Labeling fought a minor political battle over whether pizza made without cheese should be required to carry a prominent label to the effect that it contains "cheese substitute."[17]

In fact, there is no doubt some rationale behind all the regulatory rules placed in the massive *Federal Register* in any given year. Thus, when OSHA decided to drop some nine hundred rules considered to be "nitpicking," it received some serious objections. Although it is easy to poke fun at some of the regulatory agencies' rules, it must be remembered that they also deal with matters of true gravity, such as auto safety, airline safety, food poisoning, dangerous products, deadly pollution, and radioactive contamination of the environment.

Many regulatory agencies are also engaged in adjudication. Here an agency such as the FTC may charge a business with deceptive advertising practices, or one like the NLRB may be called upon to decide whether an employer or a union has engaged in an unfair labor practice. By and large, *adjudicatory procedure* is regulated by administrative law and constitutional concerns. We will address these topics further on in this chapter. However, there is a good deal of administrative flexibility as to how cases should be selected. This is a matter of *adjudicatory policy.*

In general, adjudicatory policy can be considered either reactive or proactive. Reactive strategies depend upon complaints being filed with the regulatory agency by private parties or other governmental agencies. Agency employees respond to these complaints in several ways: some are dismissed as frivolous; some are routed to more appropriate agencies; some are acted upon in an effort to obtain some form of restitution for the complainant; some lead the agency to take action against the party who has allegedly committed a breach of proper conduct. Additional steps may include investigating, bringing formal charges and holding formal hearings within the agency, to litigating in the courts. Complaints tend to concern matters of "conduct," that is, they involve allegations by an individual that some business enterprise has engaged in an unfair or illegal practice. For example, such complaints may be made by consumers against merchants or repair services, by employees alleging discrimination on the part of their employers, or by unions or employers (including public employers) alleging unfair labor practices. Sometimes such cases are also filed by businesses that believe their competitors are engaging in prohibited practices. By their nature, **conduct cases** pertain to relatively concrete practices and to specific sets of events.

Proactive cases are those developed by a regulatory agency through an investigation or study of some kind. Based on its observations about the practices of a business or group of private parties, the agency may conclude that some violation of law or its rules has occurred. Proactive cases initiated by field investigations often resemble conduct cases. The inspectors may find violations and issue citations, which can become the subject of adjudication. Housing inspectors, OSHA inspectors, and health service inspectors are examples. Many proactive cases, however, are of a different nature. These are called **structural cases,** and they do not arise from specific events, but rather are the result of patterns and broad practices that are deemed by the agency to be prohibited. For example, whereas a health inspector in a restaurant will stick a thermometer into the chili to see if it is too cold, a structural case is more likely to consider whether a chain of restaurants is mislabeling its products or engaging in unfair or anticompetitive practices. Rather than ask, "What temperature is the beef?" or even "Where's the beef?" the structural case will tend to ask, "What is the economic relationship of the seller of the beef to its franchisees and to the producers?"

But structural cases are often far more complicated than this. They deal with the structure of competition in whole industries, such as petroleum products, or patterns and practices of discrimination against members of minority groups or women by a large employer or even within an entire industry. Structural cases are often informed by theory. For example, to learn whether prohibited monopolization has occurred in an industry, a regulatory agency will need to know how firms behave and how pricing operates. Assessing such matters may depend upon a theoretical understanding of the differences between the behavior of firms in competitive markets as opposed to monopoly markets. Similarly, because monopolization per se is not against the public interest, it may be necessary to determine whether the concentration of market power has produced inefficiency or will do so in the future.

Although structural cases have the potential to regulate forcefully what the agency considers to be prohibited practices, they also have some important drawbacks. First, they are very difficult and time-consuming to adjudicate and litigate. The parties charged with the prohibited behavior often have great opportunity to delay these cases and drag them on for years. Second, they often involve new legal theories or new interpretations of existing theory. Consequently, administrative law judges and judges in the courtroom may require a great deal of convincing that the agency's interpretation is correct. Third, they tend to create a personnel problem because agency lawyers often want experience in adjudication and litigation as opposed to the lengthy preparation of cases. Conduct cases offer a far greater opportunity for this experience. Finally, structural cases can engulf very considerable amounts of an agency's resources.[18]

At this point, a word should be said about inspectors, who are functionally agents of rule enforcement that can lead to adjudication. Many regulatory agencies depend on inspectors to implement their policies. Inspectors hold a very complex job. They are street-level bureaucrats who have a great deal of discretion, cannot be fully supervised or held accountable by the administrative hierarchy, and are highly visible and even intimidating to the businesses they inspect. They have the ability to make the regulatory process work well or very badly. Where inspectors provoke hostility on the part of the inspected and when they seek to enforce every rule in a highly technical way, regulation is not likely to work well. Private parties may be evasive; they may seek to require that the inspector obtain a warrant before entering the premises; they will try to fool or mislead the inspector. Where the inspector wins the confidence of those being inspected, the latter may strike a much more cooperative posture and try to take advantage of the inspector's expertise in eliminating dangerous, unhealthful, or other prohibited practices in the workplace. Because the object of regulatory policy in the first place is to evoke responsible social and economic behavior, cooperation and voluntary compliance by private parties with the spirit of regulation can certainly serve an agency's purposes.

Just as the effective police officer seeks to promote the safety of persons and property, rather than to write numerous tickets for minor traffic, noise, and other violations, the effective inspector seeks to promote substantial and voluntary compliance with the spirit of agency regulations and the specific letter of those requirements that protect against immediate dangers or seriously antisocial behavior. Consequently, the effective inspector must be technically competent, honest, tough-minded, and willing to exercise authority while also being empathetic and able to get along well with people. This combination of characteristics, needless to add, is not easy to find. Eugene Bardach and Robert Kagan describe the generalized interaction between a "good inspector" and the regulated businessperson:

> The inspector has three major things he can trade for greater efforts toward responsible social behavior. First, at a bare minimum, he can give the regulated businessman a fair hearing; he can treat him with respect and take his arguments and problems seriously. When he must insist on strict compliance, he gives reasons. In other words, he exhibits *responsiveness*. Second, the inspector can selectively negate, modify, or delay the enforcement of regulations when their literal application to a particular violation would be unreasonable or of secondary importance. In short, he can give *forbearance*. Third, he can provide *information* to the regulated enterprise that reduces the difficulty or cost of compliance, or at least makes the required compliance measures seem understandable and justifiable.[19]

One of the advantages to regulatory agencies of having "good inspectors" is that it may make their missions far more manageable. Voluntary compliance is crucial to the missions of agencies such as OSHA and EEOC, whose jurisdictions cover thousands upon thousands of workplaces.

Regulatory agencies also rely upon *testing* to implement their objectives. This is especially pronounced in the areas of health and safety, but it also pertains to some aspects of consumer affairs generally. Testing may be done by the regulatory agency itself or may be required of the private parties that produce and market a product. The FDA, for instance, relies heavily on testing, but primarily by evaluating the tests done by drug companies and others. The

EPA, by contrast, directly engages in monitoring and testing itself. Testing can be either premarket or postmarket. Drugs, food additives, and other substances for human consumption are likely to be tested in advance of being marketed because of their potential danger. Additional postmarket tests may be undertaken, especially if a suspicion develops that the product is not safe under certain conditions or if some reevaluation of the premarket tests suggests that they were faulty in some way. Product recalls are often the result of postmarket testing. In either case, the testing may be quite elaborate and costly to the producer and the agency. For example, a new drug application at the FDA may contain as many as two hundred volumes.[20]

PROBLEMS IN REGULATORY ADMINISTRATION

It is plausible that no aspect of public administration has been subject to as much criticism as regulation. It is inherently intrusive and consequently annoying to some, who are constrained by it or burdened heavily by its costs. In the 1970s and 1980s, criticism of regulatory administration reached its modern zenith. The network of regulations on businesses had grown dense and complex. Many rules seemed unnecessary, and some appeared pointless or even counterproductive. Compliance costs were high—far too high for the benefits (if any) in the eyes of many. Enforcement was also expensive and often involved litigation, which prompted the courts to play a greater role in public administration. Court decisions added to the fragmentation of control over administration and to the difficulties of coordinating regulatory policy. For much of the period, the nation's economy was in a slump, which was partly attributed to too much regulation. Deregulation and regulatory reform gained political favor, whereas advocating further regulation, especially at the federal level, was perceived as a major political liability. The attack on regulatory policy was also part of a growing dissatisfaction with public administration in general. Accordingly, many of the problems critics found in regulatory administration were considered generic to all administration. Calls for less regulation *and* smaller government went together. Eventually the reformist mood with regard to regulation fueled new public management (NPM) efforts to reinvent public administration more fully. The following were the main concerns voiced about regulatory administration.

Regulation Is Expensive

Nobody knows what the cost of regulation to society may be. However, it is certain that simply adding up the budgets of regulatory agencies at all levels of government would not begin to tell the story. Compliance can be expensive and raise costs. More generally, regulation affects productivity, innovation, and competitiveness. In a series of articles about the state of regulation in the 1970s, prior to relatively extensive deregulation by the federal government, the *Wall Street Journal* provided some examples. It reported that "transportation economists…estimate that price-fixing and waste allowed under the Civil Aeronautics Board, Federal Maritime Commission and Interstate Commerce Commission regulations cost consumers between $8 billion and $16 billion."[21] One example of waste it reported was that "at any given time 40 percent of the trucks on the road are running empty because of government regulations that prevent them from carrying cargo on return trips after making deliveries."[22] This regulation, since abandoned, allegedly cost food retailers alone some $250 million a year. Moreover, at the time, airfares were estimated to be 35 to 50 percent higher than would be the case if the CAB did not try to protect the least efficient carriers. One estimate concluded that meeting OSHA's regulations in iron and steel foundries accounted for more than 30 percent of all capital investment during the 1970s and that regulations could lead to massive declines in productivity per worker.[23] Even these massive costs did not seem to explain the full impact of regulation on the economy.

Regulation Dampens Economic Performance

It has long been thought that regulation has serious negative impacts on the productivity, growth, and innovation of the economy. In this context, regulation has been criticized for doing and not doing at once. Where it regulates competition by restricting entrance to an industry or by setting rates or fares, regulatory administration has been attacked for protecting weak companies or industries at the expense of consumers and others who use their products. The ICC and the CAB, as noted earlier, were criticized from this perspective. Public utility commissions are frequently criticized on this basis as well. Many maintain that surrogate-market regulation inevitably leads to the "capture" of the public regulatory agency by the private enterprises ostensibly being regulated. On the other hand, the FTC has been accused by some of being antibusiness, resulting ultimately in harm to the consumer; the Department of Justice's Antitrust Division has been criticized on the grounds that it vacillates between too vigorous and too lackadaisical enforcement, both of which fail to promote or protect economic competition.[24]

In terms of performance, the FCC has been viewed by some as holding back the nation's progress in communications, and the FDA has kept some useful and safe drugs off the market too long and has inhibited the development of new drugs by the pharmaceutical industry. In 1980, one analyst even claimed that the FDA's regulations would have kept penicillin and aspirin off the market if they had just been developed.[25]

Regulation Produces Delay and Extravagant Red Tape

Another criticism of regulatory administration is that it is too slow. Some examples are legendary; for instance, it took the FDA a decade to develop standards of identity for peanut butter.[26] For thirty-three of its first forty years, the FCC was trying to resolve a dispute between radio stations DOB in

Albuquerque and WABC in New York.[27] In some cases major responsibility for the delays can be attributed to the private parties involved, rather than to the agency, but, nonetheless, delay on the part of regulatory agencies can be frustrating. This is especially likely to be the case when an individual or firm requires a license or permission to perform a service, market a product, or open a place of business.

Red tape is endemic to administrative life and regulatory administration is certainly no exception. Sometimes the agencies create their own red tape. For instance, they write long inspection manuals in obtuse administrative terminology ("bureaucratese"), and require their employees, often inspectors, to fill out lengthy forms pertaining to their official activities. The Department of Transportation's Motor Carrier Safety handbook ran more than four hundred pages, and the Department of Agriculture's instructions on the post mortem inspection of beef carcasses contained fifteen single-spaced pages of instructions for the inspector.[28] Herbert Kaufman conveyed the frustrations and costs of red tape in concrete terms:

> A "Mom and Pop" store with a gross annual income of less than $30,000 had to file tax forms fifty-two times a year. A firm with fewer than fifty employees had to prepare seventy-five or eighty submissions a year for various agencies. A small securities broker-dealer sent thirty-eight submissions to seven different agencies in one year. A plant employing seventy-five people had two of them working half time solely to draw up compulsory plans and reports; a company with a hundred employees made seventy filings or payments each year to the Internal Revenue Service alone; a small radio station assigned two employees full time for four months to supply all the information specified by the Federal Communications Commission for license renewal, and another reported that its application for renewal weighed forty-five pounds. The chairman of the board of a large pharmaceutical firm claimed that his company prepared 27,000 government forms or reports a year at a cost of $5 million. ("We spend," he added, "more man-hours filling out government forms or reports than we do on research for cancer and heart disease combined.")[29]

Incompetence

Although there have been many exceptions and change has occurred over the years, the regulatory commissions, in particular, have frequently been staffed at the top with political appointees of less than impressive qualification. As the *Wall Street Journal* expressed it, "Indeed, the Washington regulatory landscape is strewn with old friends of Presidents, unprepared for their assignments and largely uninterested in the industries they regulate. While some take the work seriously, many others simply slide by, attending hearings, flying around the country speaking to industry groups, and doing little to resolve the complex issues their agencies face."[30] One joke making the rounds back in the 1960s was that if Willard Deason, a close personal friend of President Lyndon Johnson, had given the president a pair of horses, rather than the famous pair of LBJ beagles, he would have been given a seat on the Supreme Court rather than on the ICC. Incompetence was usually dispersed among the regulatory commissions in a way that was not disastrous to any single one. In 1980, however, it was argued that a substantial part of the inadequacy of the Federal Maritime Commission resulted from the allegation that "the top people just aren't qualified people."[31] During the mid-1970s, the CPSC was so mismanaged that only 43 percent of its staff thought that the agency was doing a good job.[32] As late as 1989, the federal government's equal employment opportunity complaint system, overseen by the EEOC, was called "a system of failure" that featured "a siren song luring innocents to the EEOC labyrinth of regulations."[33] On average, it took one and a half years to resolve complaints, though in some agencies the average was closer to three years. Among all federal agencies, it was the EEOC itself that had the highest percentage of workers charging discrimination, some 2.3 percent of its work force. Despite years of effort to improve regulation, investigation of a deadly ValuJet crash in 1996 revealed serious lapses in the FAA's monitoring of the airline's compliance with safety requirements. Only after 110 people were killed did the FAA fully investigate ValuJet and prompt it to shut down completely to revamp its maintenance and safety systems.[34]

In judging the competence of regulatory agencies, it must be borne in mind that sometimes the agencies' missions and statutes are so confusing that it would be difficult for even the most accomplished of appointees to develop sound policies.

Corruption

Regulatory commissions have long been criticized for developing cozy relationships with those they are charged with regulating. A former high-ranking Justice Department official remarked that there are "incredible love affairs going on between the regulators and the regulated."[35] A federal judge, J. Skelly Wright, once asked publicly whether the CAB was not too oriented toward the interests of the industry it was designed to regulate.[36] There are several valid reasons for such "coziness." Some aspects of regulation require frequent contact with representatives of the industry. It is said, for example, that the FDA could not possibly do its job of drug evaluation without frequent personal contacts with the manufacturers. Exchanging information in writing simply would not work. Similarly, it can be useful for members of agencies such as the FCC, ICC, and FMC to be attuned to how the industries they regulate view the present and probable future state of affairs. This may require frequent contact with the regulated, but how else could a regulatory commissioner be expected to make sound policy? A second reason for the "love affair" is that regulatory commissioners are frequently drawn from the industry being regulated or law firms that work on its behalf. This too can be justified on the grounds that regulation requires regulators who are knowledgeable about the industries being regulated. Who is likely to know more than one drawn from such an industry? Sometimes, however, the contacts between the regulated and the regulators give the appearance of impropriety. More problematic, scandals involving regulatory administration sometimes reveal favoritism in the enforcement of the law. For instance, during the early 1980s, some of the EPA's "superfund" money, which was earmarked for the cleanup of toxic waste sites, was disbursed on the basis of partisan motives. Congressional hearings indicated that "funding for the Stringtown site in California was delayed to avoid helping the Senate election campaign of Democrat Jerry Brown. Two sites in New Jersey were funded to help the campaign of Republican Millicent Fenwick."[37] Eventually, the EPA's director, Anne Gorsuch Burford, was forced to resign, as were some additional twenty high-ranking officials. Moreover, the investigations left no doubt that the EPA had defined the promotion of business interests, rather than the public interest, as its chief concern.

The Ever-Increasing Inclusiveness of Regulation

Another criticism of regulatory administration is that there has been a tendency to write overinclusive rules and then to expand them even further. The problem of overinclusiveness is that it is generally difficult to write a set of comprehensive rules in advance that can be applied *strictly and reasonably* in a very wide variety of circumstances. For instance, consider New York City's effort to regulate some 15,000 restaurants. These establishments serve an amazing variety of foods in an astonishing range of settings. Some are among the fanciest in the world; others are run-down take-out shops. Yet all fall under the same rules: Failure to pass inspection is automatic if cold food is more than 45 degrees Fahrenheit or if hot food is less than 140 degrees.[38] It is implausible that a food 1 degree too hot or cold that has just been prepared to order in an otherwise hygienic establishment is dangerous; we have all consumed such food with no ill effects in our own kitchens. Not to be outdone, Bergan County, New Jersey, applied regulations for running concessions on public property to a one-man shoeshine stand that had been operating in the County Courthouse for twenty-seven years. The regulations required the shoeshine man to submit a competitive bid for the operation, use a cash register, post charges and fees, wear a smock (dark brown or burgundy, knee-length, front pocket, three-quarter sleeves), and carry a million dollar liability policy! The county was unimpressed by the shoeshine man's protest that "For 27 years not even a woman has gotten a run in her stocking here" and that "No shoeshine man has a cash register."[39] At the federal level, the Oil Protection Act of 1990 applied equally to spills of toxic oils, such as petroleum, and those of nontoxic edible oils—something that aroused the ire of the American Fats and Oils Association, the Institute of Shortening and Edible Oils, the National Fish Meal and Oil Association, the National Renderers Association, the U.S. Canola Association, and other proponents of the Edible Oil Regulatory Reform Act of 1995.[40] Once rules are written there are strong pressures on inspectors to enforce them rigorously, *even if unreasonably.* Failure to enforce rules can be viewed as corrupt—coziness with the regulated. Moreover, if an inspector mistakenly assumes that a rule violation is inconsequential to the safety of workers or the public, and a tragedy occurs, the inspector will face many liabilities—moral, legal, and professional. When one considers not just the 15,000 restaurants in New York but all workplaces under OSHA's jurisdiction, or all those personnel systems under the EEOC's, for example, the problem of overinclusiveness becomes self-evident.

What is less evident is the reason why regulatory agencies tended to add more and more regulations to their lists without deleting those that became obsolete. This has been referred to as the **regulatory rachet.**[41] An example would be fire codes where, as new technologies such as sprinkler systems and fire-retardant construction materials are required, no effort is made to determine whether older approaches such as fire doors are still necessary. Regulatory officials have treated regulation as "additive" because there is often little or no incentive to abandon older rules, despite their inefficacy. Reasons for this lack of incentive include the following: (1) dropping a rule can be interpreted as a sign of backtracking or capitulating to the regulated; (2) deleting rules does not directly contribute to the agency's regulatory objectives; (3) there is sometimes a risk that in some remote instance a rule that is abandoned will make an important difference; and even (4) deleting rules is considered boring work.[42] Nevertheless, as is suggested in the section on Deregulation and Regulatory Reform, the rachet effect can be weakened when sufficient political pressure is applied to agencies to abolish and simplify rules.

The Regulatory Process Is Out of Control

To a considerable extent, by the late 1970s and early 1980s, these criticisms amounted to the indictment that the regulatory process gets beyond control. Originally, regulatory commissions were structured to be insulated from direct political or partisan control by the elected components of government. Like public administration generally, regulation was supposed to be nonpartisan and devoted to the public interest. Eventually, however, at the federal level the commissions were considered to be a true fourth branch of government, neither directly under presidential nor congressional control, but exercising executive, legislative, and judicial roles. The statutes under which some of them operate provide little direction. To ask an agency to regulate the use of the nation's airwaves in the "public convenience, interest, or necessity" is to provide it with very little guidance indeed. To charge another with regulating unfair and uncompetitive economic practices is not providing much more. Similarly, the FMC operates under a statute that is probably so broad as to justify virtually *any* decision it reaches on matters under its jurisdiction. Moreover, some of the regulatory agencies are charged with enormous tasks and not afforded nearly enough personnel or budgetary resources. The EEOC is an excellent example, though the missions of OSHA, CPSC, and the EPA are also thoroughly daunting.

Determining Success

Finally, there is no agreed upon standard as to levels of success in regulation. Economists prefer to measure success in terms of benefits and costs, but cost-benefit analysis is not always technically feasible or widely accepted as appropriate. Determining what would happen in the absence of regulation is often inherently difficult or even impossible, as is assessing the degree of risk involved in doing things one way or another. One may expect that a landlord strapped for cash might defer elevator maintenance, but who would expect a major airline to skimp on maintenance to the point of flying unsafe planes? Moreover, the costs of regulation are sometimes economic whereas the benefits are social. For example, how can we determine what it is worth to us collectively to have peace of mind for our safety when we use an elevator, take an airplane, or bite into a hamburger? The FDA may inhibit the development and marketing of new drugs, but it also has done a great deal to assure that the drugs actually available to us are not dangerous. We may be able to ascertain the costs of the EEOC's enforcement of antidiscrimination regulations, but how can we measure the benefits gained in the form of fairer treatment for minorities and women? OSHA regulations are expensive, but they do save lives and prevent injuries. At some point we may agree that they are *too* expensive. At some other point the society might favor spending more. But how can we arrive at an acceptable cost-benefit ratio in between?

Regulation, like many other aspects of public administration, confronts the society with some very difficult moral problems. If we agree to safety and antipollution regulation that adds $500 per car, perhaps it is because as a population we are asking the government to require us to do what we believe is good for us and society. If this is true, then we are recognizing that we will not do it as individuals, suggesting that we believe that for any single individual, in the absence of cooperation by others, the costs would be too great for the benefits obtained. This is the basic "collective action" problem. Some benefits to the society require widespread participation or cooperation of individuals whose personal economic incentive is not to join a group effort. (Why be the only one in the country whose car does not contribute to pollution? Why not be the only one whose car does pollute? What tangible difference will it make?) But if the benefits depend on near-universal cooperation or compliance, then how will we evaluate the regulatory problem? Clearly, cost-benefit analysis will not be wholly adequate, especially when assessed in per capita terms (e.g., the cost per vehicle equipped with antipollution devices). Nor do the aggregate costs alone tell us much more than that regulation is expensive.

Concern with the level of compliance raises a related problem. It is obvious that the marginal cost of enforcing regulations may often rise as administrators approach obtaining universal (total) compliance. This is true, for example, where regulation involves inspections of a large number of sites, some of which are very small (as in restaurant inspection) and, possibly, remote as well. The marginal benefits, whether calculable or not, of obtaining greater compliance are likely to decline when the few recalcitrant rule evaders are small establishments with limited capacity to do serious harm. A point might be reached where the marginal costs of more enforcement begin to exceed the marginal benefits. But this would not necessarily be a compelling argument for curtailing enforcement efforts. Legal principles, such as equal application of the law, and social concepts of fairness and risk elimination might well lead to the conclusion that an effort should be made to enforce the regulations in *all* the cases to which they apply.

Consequently, in discussions of regulation, an economically oriented approach such as cost-benefit analysis is often augmented by psychological, social, legal, and political perspectives. Government officials, interest groups, and substantial numbers of political activists generally argue that regulation should reduce individual anxiety and risk concerning the safety of foods, drugs, cars, jobs, motels, hotels, office buildings, elevators, new technologies, and so forth. They also believe that it is partly the job of regulatory administration to protect individuals' lives even when those individuals are reluctant to do so themselves, as in the case of mandatory seat belt laws. This is partly because other people are socially dependent on or socially connected to these individuals and consequently, it is argued, serious injuries or deaths will adversely affect the society as a whole. For example, if the use of seat belts can save the lives of parents, should they be optional in view of the social costs of orphanhood? From a political angle, many favor regulation for the safety of groups in the population who might otherwise be especially vulnerable. The regulation of child labor and nursing homes falls into this category. In this sense, regulation is a microcosm of all public administration. The question it addresses concerns the kind of society we want government to help establish and maintain.

DEREGULATION AND REGULATORY REFORM

The problems involved in regulatory administration prompted a broad movement toward deregulation and regulatory reform that began in the 1970s and continues to the present time. Deregulation is generally supported by one or more of four basic arguments (other than that the cost of regulation is too high). One is that free markets can provide more benefits to the society than regulated ones. This view applies primarily to surrogate-market regulation and some aspects of market-functioning and employment regulation. Deregulation of the airlines and trucking industries are leading contemporary examples, though their success is a matter of dispute.[43]

A second argument raised by those in favor of deregulation is that liability law can be used to assure safety in many aspects of life. For example, the potential of suits against automobile manufacturers can provide them with a great incentive to design safe cars. The same logic would apply to the drugs produced by pharmaceutical companies. Proponents of this approach generally believe that once the incentive is strong enough, the private sector can be innovative and responsible in designing safe products and in developing safe and healthful work processes. And they can do so without having to deal with the unproductive consequences of overinclusive regulatory rules and red tape. However, even if one accepts this view, there may be a dispute as to whether liability laws need to be rewritten in some areas to provide strong enough incentives to market only safe products. After all, if the number of predictable serious injuries is known to be small, redesigning a product may be more expensive than defending (and even losing) a limited number of liability suits.

Another argument advanced against government regulation is that there is great potential for the private sector to engage in self-regulation. For example, many firms and unions do employ safety inspectors and take an active interest in establishing and maintaining healthful and safe conditions in the workplace. In some cases, public law may require enterprises to engage in self-regulation, as in the hazardous waste disposal business, trucking (at least in California), and the manufacture of intravenous solutions by pharmaceutical firms.[44]

Finally, proponents of deregulation sometimes argue that if business enterprises were required to disclose information relevant to the safety, healthfulness, and security of their products, services, or other offerings, then the public could act as its own inspectors. For example, tobacco companies print the tar and nicotine content of their cigarettes. Some states require used-car dealers to reveal known defects in the cars they sell, as did federal regulations for a time. Credit agreements indicate the yearly interest rate, and stock and banking offerings are subject to a number of mandatory disclosure regulations.

The movement toward deregulation in the 1970s and 1980s was augmented by a more complex effort at reforming regulatory administration. Federal reforms generally sought greater coordination, centralized review, and more thoroughgoing assessment of the impact of regulations, as well as a reduction in the production of new regulations.[45] For the most part, the reforms were aimed at augmenting the rule-making provisions contained in the Administrative Procedure Act of 1946 (APA). As noted in Chapter 2, the APA provides for two types of legislative (or substantive) rule making: informal and formal. Informal requires that proposed rules be published in the *Federal Register* for comment, that the agencies maintain a record of comments received, and that they explain the basis of their final rules. Formal is much more procedurally oriented and complicated. It involves quasi-judicial hearings, a showing that the proposed rule is supported by substantial evidence in the record of proceedings as a whole, cross-examination, and a legal prohibition on one-sided (ex parte) communications with the agency decision maker. From the point of view of the reformers, the main shortcomings of the APA are that it does not require rules to meet a substantive policy test, such as the benefits outweigh the costs, and that agencies coordinate their rule making with one another. Under the APA, it is perfectly possible for agencies to work at cross-purposes and issue conflicting rules.

Beginning with President Nixon and continuing through Clinton, presidents have used executive orders to require agencies to address specific values in their rule making, such as costs and benefits, and to submit proposed regulations to the Office of Management and Budget or some other unit for review before initiating APA rule-making proceedings. With a few exceptions, independent regulatory commissions were exempt from the various executive orders because, as a matter of constitutional law, they are not considered part of the executive branch.[46] The most controversial measures were President Reagan's Executive Orders 12291 (1981) and 12498 (1985). The first required agencies to submit cost-benefit analyses of their regulatory objectives to OMB's Office of Information and Regulatory Affairs (OIRA) and to pursue regulatory means that were least costly to society. The second provided that the agencies were to submit draft regulatory programs to OMB for each fiscal year. In practice, the orders enabled OMB to play a substantial policy role in structuring the content of some agency rule making to make it compatible with the administration's objectives.

President Clinton revoked Reagan's executive orders, but nevertheless substantially adhered to the general direction of earlier reforms. His Executive Order 12866 (1993) lists the following twelve principles to guide agency regulatory action:

1. Identify the problems addressed.
2. Assess the contributions, if any, of existing regulations to those problems.
3. Identify alternatives to regulations.
4. Consider risks.
5. Assess cost-effectiveness.
6. Weigh costs and benefits.
7. Base decisions on the best obtainable information.
8. Assess alternatives among regulatory possibilities.
9. Seek the views of state, local, and tribal governments.
10. Avoid inconsistency.
11. Impose the least burden on society.
12. Write regulations in simple, understandable language.

Clinton's order maintains centralized OMB review of much agency rule-making activity, but requires OIRA to operate more openly than in the past and charges the vice president with resolving disputes between it and individual agencies. As part of his overall effort to deregulate the government itself, which is central to the National Performance Review (NPR), Clinton's Executive Order 12661 (1993) calls for the elimination over a three-year period of at least 50 percent of internal administrative regulations not required by law.

The regulatory reforms of the past two decades or so now enjoy broad congressional, judicial, and bipartisan support. Consequently, it appears likely that change in the near-term future will continue to emphasize coordination, simplification, and cost-consciousness. The future of deregulation is less certain. The collapse of much of the savings and loan industry in the 1980s and the 1996 ValuJet episode challenge some of the fundamental premises on which deregulation is based. At present, federal policy regarding deregulation is more tempered than it was a decade ago, and the adoption of new regulatory measures is not out of the question.[47] Within this general framework of regulatory reform and caution regarding deregulation, the various perspectives on public administration offer different visions of what to emphasize in regulatory administration.

PERSPECTIVES TOWARD REGULATORY ADMINISTRATION

The Traditional Managerial Perspective

As in other areas, the traditional managerial perspective toward regulatory administration emphasizes the values of effectiveness, efficiency, and economy. In terms of regulation, effectiveness has often been considered the avoidance of a major failure that is viewed by the public as a crisis or scandal. As James Q. Wilson observes, for agencies such as EPA, OSHA, and the FDA, "a major scandal would be a dramatic loss of life or catastrophic injury among people nominally protected by the decisions of the agency."[48] The Nuclear Regulatory Commission was scandalized by the Three Mile Island catastrophe in 1979. The FAA was severely criticized after the 1979 crash of a DC-10 airplane in Chicago that killed 250 passengers and crew members and again in 1996 after the ValuJet crash. For the FDIC, failure would come in the form of a run on insured banks. The SEC's performance was brought into question in the late 1980s and early 1990s in the wake of a number of major scandals involving leading Wall Street firms and figures.

But how can regulatory administration be managed to avoid scandals and crises while also remaining efficient and economical?

First, the effort to be effective in the sense of avoiding crisis and scandal will dictate a conservative approach to rule enforcement and decision making. There will be a very strong tendency toward strict—even rigid—enforcement of the rules. This is because any exercise of discretion or departure from the rules that results in scandal or crisis will be severely criticized by the legislature, the media, and other political actors. It may trigger legal liabilities. An agency's failure to enforce its own rules that results in tragedy may even bring about a thorough administrative reorganization of its functions. Conversely, even if a crisis develops, when an agency has followed its own rules and when those rules are pursuant to legislation and have been previously tested in the courts, the agency may claim that it has done all it could within its power in the face of an unforeseeable future. It may even turn the crisis into a request for greater authority so that it can handle such events in the future. The FDA, for example, was given greater authority over the marketing of drugs as a result of the sulfanilamide scandal in the 1930s and the thalidomide scandal in the early 1960s, even though the latter, which resulted in the birth of children with misshapen limbs (phocomelia, or "seal limbs"), was mostly confined to Europe and Canada. If nothing else, strictly following the rules tends to absolve an agency of any taint of corruption or inconsistency.

Second, as noted earlier, there will be a strong tendency to avoid delet-ing rules, even though it may appear that they are outmoded. Just as rules tend to be overinclusive, rescinding those that seem unnecessary may mis-takenly overlook a single facility, work process, or economic relationship where the rule would make a difference. Should a scandal or crisis result be-cause of the agency's dropping of the rule, the agency would be subject to massive criticism. When the FDA contemplated redirecting its emphasis vis-à-vis regulation of the food industry from poor sanitation to chemical and mi-crobiological health hazards, it was severely criticized by *Consumer Reports* ar-ticles on the grounds that it had "casually dismissed" the problem of "filth" (see Box 9–3).[49]

Third, the development of new rules and application of new policies will be slow. Major departures from past approaches, such as widespread and im-mediate deregulation, are likely to be avoided because the results may be un-predictable. The cases of airline deregulation and banking illustrate this ten-dency. The CAB, which had resisted deregulation until 1975, waited until af-ter 1977 before approving, on a step-by-step basis, measures that would enhance price competition. The CAB was mindful of the dislocations that might occur if the industry were subjected to immediate and thoroughgoing increases in competition.[50] By contrast, banking was quickly deregulated in the 1980s and by the 1990s much of the savings and loan industry had col-lapsed, and banking as a whole was in serious economic straits.

The major difficulty with cautious approaches from a managerial stand-point is that they can undercut efficiency and economy. Strict enforcement of additive rules and conservatism in responding to rapidly changing conditions and technologies can lead to the expenditure of an agency's human and eco-nomic resources on aspects of regulation that make no real difference in terms of safety, environmental quality, economic competition, and so forth. Enforcement of the rules for their own sake is the essence of a bureaucratic approach, in the worst sense of the term. The key to successful regulation is viewed by many as flexibility based on the sound exercise of discretion. Bardach and Kagan, for example, have considered at length how regulatory administration in several areas, including safety, health, employment, and some aspects of trade practices, can be successfully managed. Among their suggestions are the following:

1. Careful training of inspectors, so that their judgment is more reliable.
2. Specialization of inspectors, so that their knowledge of what they are inspecting is thoroughgoing.
3. Controlling the discretion of inspectors through such approaches as ro-tating the inspectors from site to site, reinspection by others, supervi-sory monitoring of their use of time and their issuance of citations to violators. Supervisors may also find it desirable to meet with inspectors on a regular basis to discuss hard cases and work problems in general.
4. The efficient deployment of inspectors and other personnel so that they are concentrated where the real problems are.

BOX 9–3 **The Food and Drug Administration's "Rat Hair" List**

Pursuant to Title 21, *Code of Federal Regulations*, Part 110.110, the Food and Drug Administration established maximum levels of natural or unavoidable defects in food for human use that present no health hazard. The significance of the defects is aesthetic, and the levels are set in recognition that it is economically impractical to harvest or process raw products that are totally free of the defects listed.

The mixing or blending of food with a defect at or above the action level is not permitted. Food at or above the defect level is regarded as adulterated and subject to enforcement action under the Food, Drug, and Cosmetic Act. The list is updated from time to time through notices in the *Federal Register*. The following are among the foods listed. What did you eat today? Will you eat it tomorrow?

Product	Action Level*	Defect Source
Apple butter	4 rodent hairs/100 grams	Postharvest, processing
Asparagus	10% spears or pieces with 6 beetle eggs and/or sacs; 40 thrips/100 grams; insects (whole or equivalent) 3 mm or longer aggregate to 7 mm/100 grams	Preharvest infestation
Berries (frozen raspberries, blackberries, etc.)	4 insect larvae/500 grams; 10 insects/500 grams	Preharvest infestation
Chocolate and chocolate liquor	60 insect fragments/100 grams; 1 rodent hair/100 grams	Postharvest, processing
Cocoa beans	10 mg mammalian excreta/pound	Postharvest, processing
Cocoa powder	75 insect fragments/50 grams; 2 rodent hairs/50 grams or 4 rodent hairs/any subsample	Postharvest, processing
Coffee beans	10% insect infested or damaged; 1 live insect	Preharvest and post-harvest, processing
Condimental seeds (excludes fennel and sesame seeds)	3 mg mammalian excreta/pound	Postharvest, processing
Corn, sweet canned	2 or more 3 mm long corn ear worm or borer larvae	Preharvest infestation
Oregano:		
Ground	1250 insect fragments/10 grams	Preharvest and post-harvest, processing
	5 rodent hairs/10 grams	Postharvest, processing
Crushed	300 insect fragments/10 grams; 2 rodent hairs/10 grams	Preharvest and post-harvest, processing
Peanut butter	30 insect fragments/100 grams;	Preharvest and post-harvest, processing
	1 rodent hair/100 grams	Postharvest, processing
Pizza sauce	30 fly eggs/100 grams; 15 fly eggs and 1 maggot/100 grams; 2 maggots/100 grams	Preharvest and post-harvest, processing
Tomato juice	10 fly eggs/100 grams, or 5 fly eggs and 1 maggot/100 grams; 2 maggots/100 grams	Preharvest and post-harvest, processing
Tomato puree	20 fly eggs/100 grams, or 10 fly eggs and 1 maggot/100 grams; or 2 maggots/100 grams	Preharvest and post-harvest, processing
Tomatoes, canned	10 fly eggs/500 grams or 5 fly eggs and 1 maggot/500 grams; 2 maggots/500 grams	Preharvest and post-harvest, processing

*Numbers are averages and/or averages per subsamples.

SOURCE: Department of Health and Human Services, Food and Drug Administration, Washington, D.C. 20204 (May 1995).

5. Attempting to resolve violations or complaints of prohibited practices informally, rather than through formal adjudication.
6. Exploring the possibilities for "piggybacking" the functions of different agencies in order to reduce the need for duplication of efforts in inspections, investigations, information gathering, and processing complaints.
7. Shifting some of the burden for complaints to complainants by requiring them to supply more of the information that will be needed for informal resolution or adjudication.
8. Encouraging self-enforcement and self-regulation by educating enterprises as to their obligations and the rationale for the regulations imposed on them.[51]

Management in the regulatory sphere will require a balancing of different concerns in different contexts. It will also require a realization that the approaches to regulatory administration informed by the political and legal perspectives may stress additional and competing values.

The New Public Management Approach to Regulation

The new public management's (NPM) general approach toward regulation stands in very stark contrast to the traditional managerial model. It assumes that ". . . a classic enforcement mentality, built upon the fundamental assumption that a ruthless and efficient investigation and enforcement capability will produce compliance through the mechanism of deterrence" is seriously misguided.[52] It must be replaced by a culture that:

1. Views segments of the public less as a regulated community than as partners who will engage in collaborative risk assessment and cooperative risk abatement
2. Emphasizes customer service for regulatees, which includes setting up single points of contact and one-stop service for them
3. Focuses on impacts and effectiveness rather than outputs and efficiency by setting targets for compliance
4. Defines the unit of work as problems or risks instead of incidents or violations
5. Casts off the myth of universal enforcement in favor of dealing with what is feasible, most important, and presents the greatest risks
6. Uses a range of tactics to resolve problems, including education, strengthening regulatees' commitment and sense of responsibility, working with other government agencies at all levels, and negotiation
7. Strategically selects enforcement targets to strengthen compliance, prompt the building of partnerships, and obtain judicial backing for enforcement efforts
8. Retains the capacity to deal effectively with the worst offenders so that it never appears possible to get away with serious violations[53]

Perhaps the most striking aspect of NPM regulatory enforcement is its willingness to trust regulatees and become partners with them. The NPR tells the following story:

> Following [traditional OSHA] rules, [Bill] Freeman's inspectors would move into a company, spend three months on-site, another three months preparing reports, and then anywhere from six months to two years in court. And when all was said and done, they'd find themselves telling the company to do the same things they'd told them years before. . . .
>
> Fed up with getting nowhere, Freeman went to the 200 companies that had the highest injury rates in the state [of Maine] and offered them a deal: you and your workers draw up a safety program that meets the law's objectives, and we'll stop playing "Gotcha!" No more months-long "wall-to-wall" inspections, no more "ignorance is no excuse" enforcement, no more by-the-book fines. We'll stop being cops. We'll be partners instead—you, your workers, and OSHA. And any time you need help, we'll be there.
>
> Industry's response was immediate and positive. All but two of the 200 signed up. Employer/worker safety teams in the participating firms are identifying—and fixing—*14 times* more hazards than OSHA's inspectors ever could have found, including hazards for which the agency didn't even have regulations. . . .
>
> The new program is working so well that in two years, the group's injury rates dropped 35 percent.[54]

The NPR also reported a productivity increase of 25 percent in one firm. The experiment, labeled "Maine 200" has become a template for enforcement by the Customs Service and other agencies.

Another key feature of NPM regulatory enforcement is the substitution of discretion for rules. The focus is on results, and compliance with rules is considered of secondary or lesser importance. The NPR happily reported that, under heavy pressure from President Clinton, thirty-five agencies reversed the regulatory ratchet by eliminating 16,000 pages of outdated or unnecessary rules and by rewriting about 40 percent of their remaining rules to "conform to a new regulatory spirit of trust and cooperation."[55]

There is little doubt that the NPM model seeks to correct the worst features of the traditional managerial perspective on regulatory enforcement. However, it raises new questions and bears careful watching. The results reported in the Maine 200 experiment and similar arrangements may be "Hawthorne effects" that reflect the positive impact of communication rather than the new enforcement model's direct impact (see Chapter 4). The partnership model may not be inclusive enough to recognize all aspects of the public interest. For instance, critics charge that the Customs Service's focus on partnerships has led it to weaken its efforts at interdicting illegal drugs.[56] Viewing discretionary law enforcement as a positive good may weaken commitment to the rule of law in a society already plagued by high crime rates and lawlessness. Discretionary enforcement also makes it more difficult to hold public administrators accountable, and it expands the potential for corruption (see Chapter 12). Any enforcement model based on trust must also recognize the possibility that some partners are not trustworthy. The FAA's credulousness with regard to ValuJet's claims that its low fares did not reflect inadequate spending on safety may have cost the lives of the 110 persons aboard the ill-fated flight 592. Much regulatory administration is aimed at preventing deception, which is often a real danger to the public where the safety of food, drugs, products, and technologies are involved. Finally, the NPM model does conflict at some points with values that are central to the political and legal perspectives on regulation.

The Political Approach to Regulatory Administration

In the past, it was common for "political hacks" to be appointed to regulatory commissions. Their chief ethos appears to have been to seek reappointment by avoiding enemies rather than by making friends.[57] In practice, this dictated not upsetting the status quo. In consequence, many agencies did seem to be in the last phase of the traditional "life cycle," that of being captured by the industries ostensibly being regulated. Where this was the case, many of the politicos were assured cushy jobs in the industry after they stepped off the regulatory commissions.

Today, however, the situation seems quite different. The movement toward deregulation and regulatory reform, as well as the scrutiny of regulatory activities by public interest groups and legislators have transformed the political approach toward regulatory administration. Two key values have emerged.

One is greater attention to the full range of constituencies of a regulatory program, or expanded representation. In the past, after the life cycle went through its first phase, the constituency of the regulatory agency was often considered to be those groups being regulated. For the ICC, the constituencies were railroads and truckers; for the CAB, the constituency was the airlines; under the Taylor Grazing Act it was the ranchers using public lands; for the FMC, it was the shippers; under the Atomic Energy Act (1946), it was clearly the nuclear power industry; and so on. Today, however, the public, or segments of it, may often be viewed as an important constituency of the regulatory agency. Sometimes the public is presumed to be represented by public interest groups and spokespersons, such as Common Cause and Ralph Nader. In other cases, the agencies simply pay more attention to their mandates to serve the public interest. Thus, the FCC, long faulted for promoting anticompetitive practices in the broadcast industry and being oblivious to the quality of radio and TV programming, has more recently come under pressure to use its influence to improve "kid-vid" (children's TV programming). In other areas, segments of the public, such as the National Association of Retired Persons, have become politically mobilized to make sure that regulatory administration relevant to their interests, such as nursing homes, does in fact serve their needs rather than primarily the desires of the regulated industries. Consumers' groups have also mobilized in this way to gain greater protection of their interests. An important corollary of paying greater attention to the public is the establishment of procedural mechanisms for public participation in administrative decision making. This has been especially pronounced in the regulation at the state level.

William Gormley found the emphasis on representation so new and far-reaching that he called it a "revolution." In his words,

> The most striking finding to emerge from this review of the literature is that public representation in state regulation can promote substantive representation. Citizens' groups have effectively participated in coastal zone management hearings and water quality planning hearings. Ombudsmen have successfully resolved complaints by nursing home patients for whom the regulatory process has been disappointing. Proxy advocates have effectively championed consumer interests in rate relief and more liberal disconnecting policies.
>
> These successes are all the more remarkable because they have involved different settings, strategies, and goals. In environmental regulation, citizens' groups have converted community support and political pressure into formidable weapons. In nursing home regulation, ombudsmen have used technical expertise and jawboning to secure service responsiveness. In utility regulation, proxy advocates have utilized technical expertise, a knowledge of administrative law, and adversarial strategies to promote policy responsiveness.[58]

The second emergent value in the political approach toward regulatory administration is the importance placed on forward-looking assessments of the probable impact of rules or actions on interests that government seeks to protect. Such impact assessments go beyond benefit-cost analyses and have been used to protect the environment, the American family, federalism, and other concerns. Perhaps the best single example is the National Environmental Policy Act of 1969 (NEPA). The act cuts across a wide range of federal administrative activities, including regulation. The purposes are to promote a "productive and enjoyable harmony between man and his environment," to "eliminate damage to the environment and biosphere and stimulate the health and welfare of man," and to "enrich the understanding of the ecological systems and natural resources important to the nation." It requires that administrative agencies develop "environmental impact" statements. These must discuss any proposed action having a substantial impact on the environment. They describe possible adverse environmental effects, alternatives, long-term consequences, and irreversible and irretrievable commitments. The impact statements are to be made available to federal, state, and local agencies dealing with environmental matters, to the president, to the Federal Council on Environmental Quality, and, generally, to the public. Some of these statements can be highly elaborate and expensive, such as the Department of the Interior's report on the trans-Alaska pipeline, which filled nine volumes and cost $25 million to prepare.[59] Although such a vast amount of information can be forbidding, many political actors, such as legislators, their staff, and public interest groups, frequently do devote enough attention to environmental impact statements to assure a greater degree of administrative accountability. The judiciary has also been active in reviewing procedures under NEPA. Where agencies' procedures include public hearings, the impact statements may become the basis for informed public participation in regulatory administration. In addition, the federal judiciary has been friendly to suits by individuals seeking to compel agencies to fulfill their obligations under the act.[60]

The forward-looking impact assessment model used by NEPA has been adopted in a wide range of federal statutes and executive orders. For instance, the Regulatory Flexibility Act of 1980 requires agencies to assess the impact of regulatory measures on small businesses and to minimize those that are adverse. The Paperwork Reduction Act of 1980 calls on agencies to estimate the paperwork "burden hours" their reporting requirements and forms will impose on private parties. Under various executive orders, agencies have been required to assess the impact of proposed regulations on inflation, American families, federalism, and environmental justice.

At the state and local levels, environmental impact statements have fostered a good deal of citizen participation. Much of this takes the form of the NIMBY (not-in-my-backyard) syndrome in which participation is aimed at preventing undesirable public activities from being located in one's neighborhood, town, county, state, or region. Nevertheless, even NIMBY is a form of grassroots participation.

The Legal Approach to Regulatory Administration

Regulatory administration in the United States has been highly legalistic in its approach, processes, and organization. The legalistic quality of regulatory administration is understandable, because regulation affects the rights of individuals, groups such as labor unions, and business enterprises. It also concerns the use and disposition of their property, including intangible property such as trademarks. Additionally, regulatory rules constrain the policies and operations of other administrative agencies and subnational political jurisdictions. Like the managerial and political approaches, the legalistic perspective places a distinct emphasis on certain values.

Adversary Procedure   At the stage of deciding how regulatory rules should be enforced, the legalistic approach tends to favor cases that place the agency or one party against another in an **adversary proceeding.** This follows from the view that regulation involves the definition of rights and obligations pursuant to statutes or agency rules. However, it has two important consequences that distinguish it from other approaches to regulatory administration.

First, the legal approach depends upon the *building of cases* for adjudication. This is true even though many conflicts are settled by consent prior to going to formal hearings or court. Building a record entails uncovering violations. This places the agency in an adversarial role vis-à-vis the individuals, groups, or firms it is investigating. Whereas the managerial and political approaches often tend to view regulatory administration as oriented toward solving problems, the adversarial approach of the legalistic perspective tends to view it as developing, documenting, and winning cases. Moreover, in the adversarial mode, the agency, or part of it, becomes an *advocate* for a perspective. Consequently, it may emphasize the information that supports its case and downplay information or reasoning to the contrary. From the point of view of those being regulated, this can be extremely frustrating. They are generally seeking to run an economic enterprise profitably and within the law, rather than seeking to build a record of winning cases.

Second, the legal approach tends to favor relatively simple conduct cases where one party or the agency alleges that another has violated the law. It tends to shy away from the complicated structural cases that rest on theory and often depend upon novel interpretations of the law. Conduct cases fit the adjudicatory process better; simple conduct cases enable the agency to develop a strong record of winning. In the FTC, for example, there has been a competition between economists and lawyers based largely on the differing perspectives toward structural and conduct cases.

Neutrality and the Administrative Law Judge   At the level of adjudication, the legalistic approach relies on the adversary proceeding before an impartial administrative law judge, similar functionary, or court. In practice, the neutrality of the administrative law judge stands in stark contrast to the traditional managerial emphasis on control through hierarchy, the NPM's effort to form partnerships, and the political perspective's stress on accountability.

Due Process Protection   The rights of the private party being charged with a violation or being sued will be protected through a set of formal procedural requirements. Such parties will often have constitutional protections at the stage in which the agency is gathering information and building its case. For instance, searches, wiretaps, bugging, and the surveillance of mail will be controlled by constitutional standards, although with the proper safeguards against abuse, they may be allowable. If the agency decides to press the case, the regulated parties must be given adequate notice of the charges against them, and of the agency's proposed action. Normally, the parties will be given an opportunity to respond, either in writing or orally. If the matter is serious enough, a hearing is likely to be afforded at some point; the regulated party may also have a right to take the case to court for judicial review of the agency's behavior and decision making. At either the administrative hearing stage or in court, the party will have the right to be represented by counsel, though the agency does not necessarily have to provide counsel for the party. Many of these rights are spelled out in the Administrative Procedure Act of 1946, as amended. At the state level, similar provisions generally apply.

Reasonableness   At the level of determination of the outcome of the case, the legalistic approach will stress fairness not only of procedure, but also in terms of the result. This often involves a judicial assessment of the reasonableness of the agency's action. Until recent years, the judiciary seemed far more concerned with whether a matter was under an agency's jurisdiction and whether proper procedures were followed than in the quality of the agency's decision in terms of its substantive content. Nowadays, however, in an effort to protect the rights and property of individual parties and to check abuses of administrative discretion, the judiciary is more inclined to question the logic of the agency's decision. For example, in *FTC v. Sperry and Hutchinson* (1972), a case involving whether the redemption of S&H Green Stamps was being controlled in an unfair or deceptive fashion, the Supreme Court found that the agency had not done its adjudicatory job properly.[61] The Court found that "the Commission has not rendered an opinion which, by the route suggested, links its findings and its conclusions." Thus the Court held that the case should be sent back to the commission for further consideration. An even more dramatic example of judicial review along these lines occurred in *Motor Vehicle Manufacturers Association v. State Farm Mutual Automobile Insurance Co.* (1983), in which the Supreme Court found that the National Highway Traffic Safety Administration "failed to present an adequate basis and explanation" for rescinding its earlier rule requiring the installation of passive-restraining seat belts on all new cars by 1984 or air bags by a later date.[62] Here the agency, which had the discretion to make the rules in the first place, could not withdraw them in the absence of a well-reasoned and publicly articulated explanation that was considered reasonable by the Court. In *Citizens to Preserve Overton Park v. Volpe* (1971), the Supreme Court authorized federal district courts to take what became known as a "hard look" at the facts and logic on which administrative decisions are made.[63] In the benzene case, discussed in Chapter 7, the Court found that the agency involved, OSHA, had failed to provide scientific support for its regulatory rule.

The courts have adopted this new line of thought to assure that as regulation reaches deeper into society, the personal and property rights of private parties are not undermined. At least one case demonstrates this emphasis with remarkable clarity. *Abbott Laboratories v. Gardner, Secretary of the Department of Health, Education, and Welfare* (1967) involved the intriguing question of whether the Commissioner of Food and Drug could, pursuant to a somewhat ambiguously worded statute, require that drug companies print the generic name for drugs, also having trade names, every time the trade name appeared on a label or in an advertisement.[64] In a surprising step, the Supreme Court agreed that the judiciary should determine whether the commissioner had the authority to issue the regulation before it was actually put into effect or applied to any drug company that might violate it. As the Supreme Court saw it, unless prior review of this kind was granted (within the bounds of the statute that governs such review, the Declaratory Judgment Act), the drug companies would lose regardless of whether they complied or not. If they did comply, the regulation would be treated as lawful and the companies could harm their business interests by printing the generic name. Doing so would require changing their labels, advertisements, and the promotion of their products. It might also encourage far greater price competition. Failure to comply would run the risk of prosecution. In the latter event, even if a company successfully argued that the FDA lacked authority to issue the rule, its public image could be seriously damaged in an area where the public's trust is an important factor in a firm's economic viability.

Property rights have been the focus of recent cases dealing with "regulatory takings." The Constitution's protection of private property rights in the Fifth and Fourteenth Amendments prohibits depriving individuals of their property without due process or just compensation. In *First English Evangelical Lutheran Church of Glendale v. County of Los Angeles* (1987)[65] and *Nollan v. California Coastal Commission* (1987),[66] the Supreme Court held that zoning or environmental regulations may so severely limit the use of private property that they effectively take it from the owners. In *Dolan v. City of Tigard* (1994), which is discussed in Chapter 11 on democratic constitutionalism, the Court placed a significant burden of persuasion on governments when they issue building permits containing conditions that interfere with property rights.[67]

Although the overall direction of judicial review of administrative action since the 1960s has been to take a harder look at the reasonableness of agencies' rules and adjudicative decisions, there are also some relatively clear limits on how much judges can require. In *Vermont Yankee Nuclear Power Corporation v. Natural Resources Defense Council* (1978),[68] the Supreme Court held that the courts should not force agencies to engage in rule-making procedures that are more elaborate than the minimum requirements of the Administrative Procedure Act. In *Chevron v. Natural Resources Defense Council* (1984),[69] the Court held that the judiciary should accept reasonable interpretations of statutes by agencies rather than substitute other plausible (and presumably equally reasonable) ways of reading them. Both of these decisions place agencies in firmer control of the procedures they use and the development of the statutes they enforce. Finally, in *Heckler v. Cheney* (1985),[70] the Court held that, at least under some circumstances, the judiciary should not review agencies' discretionary decisions not to enforce statutes. The *Heckler* case may turn out to be of major consequence because the NPM favors very broad discretion in enforcement.

In sum, the legal approach to regulation emphasizes adversary relationships, the legal obligations and rights of the parties, procedural fairness, and reasonableness in terms of the substantive content of regulatory administrative decisions. Of course, these values and concerns are merely sketched out here; many volumes can be and have been written on the administrative law of regulation.

SYNTHESIS

There are many conflicts and tensions among the managerial, political, and legalistic approaches toward regulatory administration. The managerial approaches' desire for effectiveness, that is, focusing on the impact that regulation has on the regulated parties, is frequently at odds with the political approach's current emphasis on making regulation responsive to organized, broad constituencies. Economy and impact assessment are certainly at odds, at least in the short run, over the requirement that environmental impact statements be developed and publicized. Cost-benefit analysis can be very expensive. Efficiency is frequently at odds with adjudication and procedural due process, which require that agencies "build cases" and adjudicate them fairly (and also at some expense). Adjudication is also in conflict with the traditional managerial perspective's desire to control administrative operations tightly; administrative law judges are not subject to direct hierarchical control by an agency's managers. The NPM favors discretionary enforcement and opposes legal procedure and judicial review. The political perspective's effort to protect broad constituencies, such as consumers, can be in tension with the legalistic approach's emphasis on the protection of the private parties' property and business interests. This was shown in the *Abbott Labs* case by the dissent of Justice Clark, who wrote, "Rather than crying over the plight that the laboratories have brought on themselves [by charging ten to twelve times too much for trade name drugs] the Court should think more of the poor ailing folks who suffer under the practice."

All these values are in competition in a very wide range of aspects of regulatory administration. Can they be synthesized through the development of a perspective that would enable at least some important priorities to be established?

One way of thinking about such a synthesis is first to identify the broad objectives of regulation and then to consider which of the perspectives is most suitable to it. In the past, there has been a tendency to view *all* regulatory administration from the point of governmental penetration of the economy and society. Consequently, some observers thought that *deregulating* surrogate markets while *strengthening* antitrust enforcement was contradictory, even though the objective of each policy initiative is to promote competition. Similarly, deregulation of surrogate markets is not necessarily inconsistent with greater health, safety, employment, or environmental regulation.[71] In the future, finer distinctions should be drawn. For the sake of illustration, the following approach is suggested.

The Public Interest Where the regulatory administration involved concerns a very broad public interest, the political approach seems most suitable. Environmental regulation is a clear case. As NEPA recognizes, what happens to the environment will affect everyone in the nation now or in future generations. That is the justification for the environmental impact statement, even though it is costly and can reduce short-term economic development. If we are all directly and more or less equally involved, then accountability becomes paramount. Otherwise the public loses control of its fate and democracy is very seriously compromised. Robert Dahl, a leading political scientist, has argued cogently that for the same reasons, the public must also be involved in decisions about nuclear weapons.[72] At times it will be difficult to determine when the public interest is so broad that regulatory administration should stress participation and forward-looking impact assessments over other goals. Yet the place to start is by considering each regulatory program individually on its merits from this perspective, rather than trying to prejudge everything at once on the basis of theory.

Balancing the Interests of Private Parties against Each Other   Where regulation aims to strike a proper balance between two private concerns, such as monopoly producers and consumers or businesses and organized labor, the legal approach is most suitable. For example, the regulation of utility and other rates fits into this area. Rate setting was a standard judicial function even before regulatory and public utility commissions were created. The objective is to allow utilities or other regulated enterprises to earn a "fair" rate of return on their investments. Utilities tend to have monopoly status and therefore could gouge the public; conversely, if turned completely over to the political approach's emphasis on representing constituencies, regulatory administration in this area could result in unreasonable harm to the profitability of such enterprises. It could also lead to one group of rate payers absorbing the costs, perhaps unwittingly and unwillingly, of providing service to others. Adjudication of such matters enables a balancing among the competing interests with an acceptable compromise as the result. The adjudication of numerous and repetitive violations of fair trade practices and routine health and safety regulations also seems to protect private parties against intrusive administration while enabling regulation to proceed vigorously. Assessing the fairness of various labor practices has also been largely accomplished through adjudication. In all likelihood, most antitrust activity would fall into the category of balancing rights against one another. However, cases might be so broad as to make the political approach more salient.

Where the legal approach is most appropriate, its efficacy can be enhanced by using alternative dispute resolution (ADR). As noted in Chapter 4, two federal statutes passed in 1990, the Administrative Dispute Resolution Act (ADRA) and the Negotiated Rulemaking Act (NRMA), try to obtain the benefits of adjudication without having to go through laborious adjudicative processes. The ADRA authorizes agencies to substitute ADR for adjudication under the APA. It requires each agency to appoint a senior official to serve as a dispute resolution specialist. The act authorizes minitrials and arbitration in addition to dispute resolution techniques, such as mediation, that strive for voluntary agreement between the parties involved. NRMA aims at avoiding tedious and expensive litigation by having representatives of all the interested parties negotiate regulatory rules (a process sometimes called "reg-neg"). ADR is broadly supported by all but the traditional managerial perspective. The NPM favors it because, by substituting negotiation for command and control enforcement, ADR is closer to the partnership model. From the political perspective ADR is beneficial because it is potentially more inclusive of and responsive to a broad variety of interests that may not gain consideration in formal adjudication. The legal approach will support ADR insofar as the procedures used and outcomes are fair and rational. Along with the other perspectives, the traditional managerial approach appreciates the potential efficiency and economy of ADR. However, it tends to oppose any procedure that compromises administrative authority to determine outcomes or that yields administrative decisions on any basis other than administrative expertise.

Protection against Disaster   Where regulatory administration is aimed at protecting against disastrous events and accidents, as in the regulation of drugs and air transportation safety, a mix of the managerial perspectives may be most suitable. Here the point is prevention; inspections, voluntary compliance, and cooperation are desirable. Whereas all the legal approach demands is minimal compliance with law, the managerial orientation seeks cooperation with the purposes of the regulatory administration. For instance, the FDA punishes violations, but it also tries to get the drug companies to engage in sound premarket testing. Airlines engage in safety maintenance, but few would suggest they should merely comply with a checklist of FAA required procedures. Rather, they carefully consider any additional safety procedures that appear reasonable to them. In a similar way, as the Maine 200 experiment suggests, OSHA is likely to be far more effective in preventing accidents in the workplace when its inspectors avoid a legalistic approach to violations and seek to help firms eliminate genuine safety risks. Until some measure of deregulation set in, banking was another area largely treated from the managerial perspective toward regulatory administration. The purpose was largely to prevent a collapse of a major bank or the banking system as a whole because that would bring economic disaster to the nation or a specific group of people.

Of course, it is necessary to stress once again that in the regulatory world, as in public administration in general, cases do not really come in such neat packages all the time. Many cases will be mixed and more difficult than those presented here. Knowing how best to respond to them is part of the art of public administration.

NOTES

1. Paul J. Quirk, "Food and Drug Administration," in *The Politics of Regulation*, ed. James Q. Wilson (New York: Basic Books, 1980), 191–235, at 194.
2. See Wesley Marx, *The Frail Ocean* (New York: Ballantine, 1967).
3. Lawrence J. White, *Reforming Regulation* (Englewood Cliffs, N.J.: Prentice-Hall, 1981), chap. 3; and Barry Friedman, *Regulation in the Reagan-Bush Era* (Pittsburgh: University of Pittsburgh Press, 1995), chap. 1.
4. Wilson, *The Politics of Regulation*.
5. James Q. Wilson, "The Politics of Regulation," in Wilson, *The Politics of Regulation*, 357–394, at 376.
6. Ibid., 368.
7. Ibid., 369.
8. Quoted in ibid., 358; originally, George J. Stigler, "The Theory of Economic Regulation," *Bell Journal of Economics and Management Science* 2 (Spring 1971): 3. The same basic theory was presented earlier by Grant McConnell, *Private Power and American Democracy* (New York: Knopf, 1966).
9. Quoted in McConnell, *Private Power and American Democracy*, 284.
10. Marver Bernstein, *Regulating Business by Independent Regulatory Commission* (Princeton, N.J.: Princeton University Press, 1955).

11. See McConnell, *Private Power and American Democracy*, chap. 8.

12. Wilson, "The Politics of Regulation," 370.

13. Ibid., 371–372.

14. Eugene Bardach and Robert A. Kagan, *Going by the Book: The Problems of Regulatory Unreasonableness* (Philadelphia: Temple University Press, 1982), 12.

15. See McConnell, *Private Power and American Democracy*.

16. Quoted in Bardach and Kagan, *Going by the Book*, 260 (50 CFR 261.1).

17. Clyde Farnsworth, "Line-Item Pepperoni? Fiscally Sound Anchovies?" *New York Times*, 29 June 1987.

18. Robert A. Katzmann, "Federal Trade Commission," in Wilson, *The Politics of Regulation*, 152–187, at 157.

19. Bardach and Kagan, *Going by the Book*, 130–131.

20. Quirk, "Food and Drug Administration," 207.

21. *Wall Street Journal*, 9 October 1974.

22. Ibid.

23. Bardach and Kagan, *Going by the Book*, 26.

24. Suzanne Weaver, "Antitrust Division of the Department of Justice," in Wilson, *The Politics of Regulation*, 123–151, at 125; and Walter Adams and James Brock, "Why Flying Is Unpleasant," *New York Times*, 6 August 1987.

25. Quirk, "Food and Drug Administration," 203. In 1983, an "orphan drug" law was passed by the federal government. It allows drug companies to market drugs to small numbers of people with unusual medical problems, without first requiring that rigorous and expensive premarket tests be undertaken.

26. Herbert Kaufman, *Red Tape* (Washington, D.C.: Brookings Institution, 1977), 20.

27. *Wall Street Journal*, 15 October 1974.

28. Bardach and Kagan, *Going by the Book*, 36.

29. Kaufman, *Red Tape*, 7–8.

30. *Wall Street Journal*, 25 October 1974.

31. Edward Mansfield, "Federal Maritime Commission," in Wilson, *The Politics of Regulation*, 42–74, at 62.

32. Kenneth J. Meier, *Regulation* (New York: St. Martin's Press, 1985), 104.

33. Marianne Lavelle, "A System of Failure," *National Law Journal*, 24 April 1989: 1, 33–36.

34. The ValuJet crash received a great deal of media attention. The gist of the critique of the FAA is presented in a *Washington Post* editorial, "Tale Spin at the FAA," 19 June 1996, A18.

35. *Wall Street Journal*, 1 November 1974.

36. Ibid., 25.

37. Meier, *Regulation*, 165.

38. *New York Times*, 15 July 1984.

39. Robert Hanley, "Bergen County Fights Nonregulation Shoeshines," *New York Times*, 17 September 1993, B1, B6.

40. Cindy Skrzycki, "The Regulators: Salad Days on the Hill: Food Processors Give Their Oil for a Rule Distinction," *Washington Post*, 13 October 1995, D1-2.

41. Bardach and Kagan, *Going by the Book*, chap. 7.

42. Ibid., 195–196.

43. Paul Stephen Dempsey, "Deregulation and Reregulation: Policy, Politics, and Economics," in *Handbook of Regulation and Administrative Law*, ed. David Rosenbloom and Richard Schwartz (New York: Marcel Dekker, 1994), 175–206.

44. Bardach and Kagan, *Going by the Book*, 224–225.

45. See Friedman, *Regulation in the Reagan-Bush Era* for a detailed discussion.

46. Ibid.; and Angel Manuel Moreno, "Presidential Coordination of the Independent Regulatory Process," *The Administrative Law Journal of the American University* 8 (Fall 1994): 461–516.

47. Examples include the Telecommunications Act of 1996, which requires a considerable amount of initial rule making and other regulation by the Federal Communications Commission and the Lead-Based Paint Hazard Reduction Act of 1992, under which the EPA and Department of Housing and Urban Development issued a comprehensive rule on March 6, 1996. See Marianne Lavelle, "Telecom Bill: More Oversight," *National Law Journal*, 19 February 1996: A14; and Randall Abate, "Regulations' Aim: Get the Lead Out," *National Law Journal*, 24 June 1996: B15.

48. Wilson, "The Politics of Regulation," 375.

49. Bardach and Kagan, *Going by the Book*, 204–205.

50. Bradley Behrman, "Civil Aeronautics Board," in Wilson, *The Politics of Regulation*, 75–120, at 104–120.

51. Bardach and Kagan, *Going by the Book*, chap. 6.

52. Malcolm Sparrow, *Imposing Duties* (Westport, Conn.: Praeger, 1994), ix.

53. Ibid., xxiii–xxvi.

54. Al Gore, *Common Sense Government Works Better & Costs Less* (Washington, D.C.: Government Printing Office, no date [1995]), 25–26.

55. National Performance Review, *Reinvention Roundtable* 2 (Summer 1995): 1, 11.

56. "In Brief," *Washington Post*, 5 February 1996, A19, reported that Senator Dianne Feinstein was highly critical of the Customs Service effort to turn itself from "an enforcement agency into a [trade] facilitation agency." In a 1996 operational plan inspired by the NPR, Commissioner George Weise "listed drug interdiction fourth among seven goals, below 'processing more passengers, cargo and revenues.'"

57. Wilson, "The Politics of Regulation," 378.

58. William Gormley, "The Representation Revolution," *Administration & Society* 18 (August 1986): 179–196, 190.

59. Kenneth C. Davis, *Administrative Law and Government*, 2d ed. (St. Paul: West, 1975), 336.

60. Ibid., chap 21; *Students Challenging Regulatory Agency Procedures v. U.S.*, 412 U.S. 669 (1973).

61. *FTC v. Sperry and Hutchinson*, 405 U.S. 233, 248 (1972).

62. *Motor Vehicle Manufacturers Association v. State Farm*, 463 U.S. 29 (1983).

63. *Citizens to Preserve Overton Park v. Volpe*, 401 U.S. 402 (1971).

64. *Abbott Laboratories v. Gardner*, 387 U.S. 136 (1967).

65. *First Evangelical Lutheran Church of Glendale v. County of Los Angeles*, 482 U.S. 304 (1987).

66. *Nollan v. California Coastal Commission*, 483 U.S. 825 (1987).

67. *Dolan v. City of Tigard*, 114 S.Ct. 2309 (1994).

68. *Vermont Yankee Nuclear Power Corporation v. Natural Resources Defense Council*, 435 U.S. 519 (1978).

69. *Chevron v. Natural Resources Defense Council*, 467 U.S. 837 (1984).

70. *Heckler v. Cheney*, 470 U.S. 821 (1985).

71. See Larry Gerston, Cynthia Fraleigh, and Robert Schwab, *The Deregulated Society* (Pacific Grove, Calif.: Brooks/Cole, 1988), 45, for an opposing point of view.

72. Robert A. Dahl, "Controlling Nuclear Weapons: Democracy vs. Guardianship," Abrams Lecture Series, Syracuse University, March 1984.

ADDITIONAL READING

BARDACH, EUGENE, AND ROBERT KAGAN. *Going by the Book: The Problems of Regulatory Unreasonableness.* Philadelphia: Temple University Press, 1982.

BRYNER, GARY. *Bureaucratic Discretion: Law and Policy in Federal Regulatory Agencies.* New York: Pergamon Press, 1987.

EISNER, MARC. *Regulatory Politics in Transition.* Baltimore: Johns Hopkins University Press, 1993.

FRIEDMAN, BARRY. *Regulation in the Reagan-Bush Era.* Pittsburgh: University of Pittsburgh Press, 1995.

GERSTON, LARRY, CYNTHIA FRALEIGH, AND ROBERT SCHWAB. *The Deregulated Society.* Pacific Grove, Calif.: Brooks/Cole, 1988.

KERWIN, CORNEILUS. *Rulemaking.* Washington, D.C.: CQ Press, 1994.

ROSENBLOOM, DAVID, AND RICHARD SCHWARTZ, EDS. *Handbook of Administrative Law and Regulation.* New York: Marcel Dekker, 1994.

WILSON, JAMES Q., ED. *The Politics of Regulation.* New York: Basic Books, 1980.

STUDY QUESTIONS

1. Deregulation is currently an important political issue. Do you think the United States is "overregulated" in some areas of economic or social life? "Underregulated" in any? What criteria can you develop to help you decide?

2. Some economists are pretty adamant about regulation being treated from a cost-benefit perspective. Assuming it is technically possible to do a solid cost-benefit analysis, do you think such an approach is appropriate in all areas of policy? Where and where not? Why?

3. To what kinds of regulatory administration is your college or university subject? Assess their costs, benefits, and appropriateness (from your own perspective).

PART FOUR

Public Administration and the Public

Chapter 10 | Public Administration and the Public
Chapter 11 | Public Administration and Democratic Constitutionalism
Chapter 12 | Accountability and Ethics
Chapter 13 | The Future

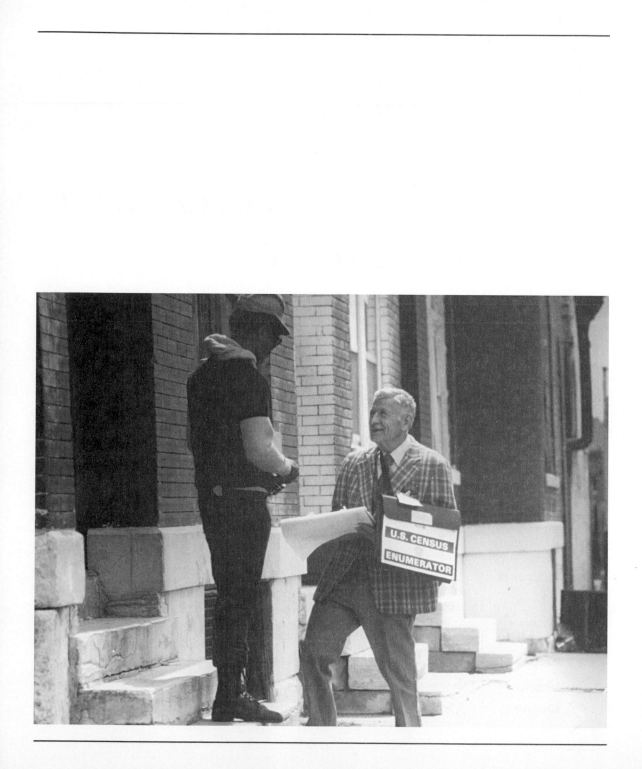

CHAPTER 10 | *Public Administration and the Public*

The public interacts with public administration in several roles: as client, customer, regulatee, participant, and litigant as well as in street-level encounters. Public administration penetrates the economy and society. The public's evaluation of public administration, which is explored in this chapter, is complex. As citizens, people find government wasteful, untrustworthy, and unresponsive. As clients and customers, they find it satisfactory; as regulatees, they are less favorable. The managerial, political, and legal perspectives offer different views of the public. Participation is emphasized by the political perspective and offers some possibilities for strengthening the "public" in public administration. The new public management, by contrast, views the public almost solely as customers. The perspectives can be synthesized to a certain extent by applying them to different areas of public administration, such as service or therapy.

The development and growth of the contemporary administrative state has myriad ramifications for the public at large. Certainly, the public has bene-fited greatly from public administration. Public administrators are concerned with the provision of "public goods," such things as defense of the political community, roads, and public recreational and cultural facilities. They are also actively involved in providing justice, safety, economic security, health, education, and other benefits to the public at large, or segments of it. But the provision of these benefits has not been without important social, political, and economic costs. Too often in the past, public administration texts failed to address the place of the "public" in the public administrative state. Today, by contrast the new public management (NPM) puts relationships with the public at the forefront of public administrative practice.

THE PUBLIC'S INTERACTION WITH PUBLIC ADMINISTRATION

Every person in the United States is affected by some public administrative actions all the time. For example, whether we are awake or asleep, in an ur-ban metropolis or on a remote mountain peak, protecting each of our lives is in some sense the responsibility of public administrators in the Department of Defense. We are all generally affected by the activities of the Environ-mental Protection Agency, the Food and Drug Administration, and the U.S. Department of Agriculture's inspection and crop-related programs. If we lis-ten to the radio or watch TV, the FCC is involved; wherever we are, some police department has formal responsibility for our safety and conduct. The list could go on and on. It would be an interesting exercise to keep track of how many of one's daily activities are in some way affected by a public ad-ministrative agency. But such a review of the extent to which public adminis-trators affect our well-being and have an impact on the structure of our daily lives does not begin to tell the full story of the relationship between the pub-lic and public administrators.

The public interacts directly with public administrators in several con-texts. For the sake of analysis, these can be placed into five main overlapping categories.

Clients and Customers* The public interacts with public administrators as *clients*. The range of possibilities in this context is quite extensive. One study, for example, found that over half (57.5 percent) of a sample of the general population had at least one direct recent contact with an administrative

---

*The dictionary definition of "client" includes "customer." Clients are usually thought of as receiving professional or craft services, whereas customers are shoppers. The NPM used the term customer to emphasize its view that government agencies should operate like market-driven businesses and stores.

agency dealing with one of the following areas: employment, job training, workmen's compensation, unemployment compensation, public assistance, hospital/medical care, or retirement benefits.[1] If public education, postal service, and other functions such as contact with agencies dealing with consumer fraud and the like were added to the list, the percentage of the public acting as clients and customers would escalate considerably. The essence of the client or customer role is that the individual seeks to obtain a benefit or service from an administrative agency. In many cases, the individual client will meet face-to-face with a public administrator.

Regulatees   The public interacts with public administrators as *regulatees*. For instance, four of the more common situations in which members of the public meet public administrators in the role of being regulated are vehicular licenses, traffic violations, income taxes, and police matters.[2] The full extent of interactions in these four categories is unknown, but it certainly does not fully indicate all the possible situations in which the citizen is a regulatee of an administrative agency. As pointed out in the first chapter, often service and constraint are combined. Thus, the client or customer may also be a regulatee, as in the case of individuals seeking public housing, public assistance, and even public education. Moreover, well over 1 million members of society are housed in public mental health facilities and prisons. Such people are not merely *regulated* or *constrained*; they are *controlled* and/or *restrained*. Additionally, many people are subject to legal constraints in the role of employee or employer, especially in terms of regulation of occupational health and safety, equal opportunity, and labor relations.

Participants   The public interacts with public administrators as *participants* in public administration. Many public administrative programs, especially in the realm of agriculture and education, provide for direct public participation. Public utility commissions, housing agencies, and other public agencies often hold public hearings as well. Members of the public respond to agencies' proposals to adopt rule changes. Overall, it appears that the level of public utilization of these opportunities to participate is low (as it is in politics generally), but nonetheless the opportunity is there. In fact, in some cases groups are so effective in using participation to make public administrators responsive to them that they are considered to be an agency's "constituency."

Litigants   The public interacts with public administrators as *litigants*. A limited segment of the population seeks to *litigate* claims or complaints against public administrators. Litigation in this context may mean nothing more than a direct response to an agency's notice that it proposes to do something that will harm the individual, such as cutting off public assistance benefits. It may involve an appeal through administrative hierarchies, a hearing before an administrative law judge, or a suit in a state or federal court. Although the proportion of the public that engages in litigation is small, their cases are often numerous enough to place substantial burdens on agencies' and courts' ability to hear them. For instance, the Social Security Administration adjudicates about 250,000 cases a year. The New York State Department of Social Services held 77,000 hearings in one year (1989).[3] Moreover, the ramifications of a few court decisions on public administration can be very extensive. Thus, Supreme Court decisions requiring procedural due process in many administrative actions have forced welfare agencies, in particular, to change their processes and modify their structures extensively.[4]

Street-Level Encounters   The public interacts with public administrators through *street-level encounters*. Street-level encounters, which were discussed in Chapter 8, are often a feature of the individual role of regulatee. However, sometimes they do not involve regulation per se, but rather an effort by the street-level bureaucrat to determine whether constraints should be applied or whether assistance should be rendered. Police are perhaps the best example. Their role involves both the application of constraints and the provision of assistance. Street-level interaction with them can be touched off in any number of ways, including simply asking them for directions, injuring oneself in an accident of some kind, or engaging in suspicious or prohibited conduct.

In sum, there is little doubt that the public is deeply affected by public administration and is frequently involved in direct interactions with public administrators. These are developments that are part and parcel of the evolution of the contemporary administrative state, developments that cannot help but have important impacts on the public's social, political, and economic environments.

THE INDIVIDUAL IN THE ADMINISTRATIVE STATE

The Individual in Society

Public administration thoroughly permeates American society. Many matters that were once left to families, communities, and religious organizations are now the subject of administrative activity. Examples would be education, child abuse prevention, provision for one's economic security and health in old age, welfare benefits (formerly charity), and housing. Matters of marriage and family are also affected by public administration in terms of welfare, social security, and taxation generally. Even though there is currently a tendency for government to rely on private and not-for-profit organizations to carry out some of its functions, historically, to a considerable extent, administrative services have replaced privately provided social services and administrative controls have replaced more traditional social controls exercised by families, communities, and religious organizations.

Equally important, public administration tends to be bureaucratically organized despite the NPM's successes in changing this to some extent. Bureaucracy, in particular, is often in tension with traditional social values. Consequently, individuals may have to be socialized to interact well with bureau-cracy, and in the process their own values may be modified. In this sense, many have concluded that the public is very strongly affected by public administration.

Following Max Weber, Ralph Hummel has explained that bureaucracy is at odds with society because it relies on "rationally organized action," rather than "social action."[5] Rationally organized action in this context means action that "is a logical means to a clearly defined end" and "is performed in such a manner that its means-ends logic is visible.[6] Hummel explains the differences between this kind of action and social action in practical terms:

> Social action is normally initiated by a human being who has certain intentions or purposes. The action is intended to convey such goals or purposes and is addressed to a social partner whose understanding of the action is a key part of the purpose. Social action, then, consists of a human initiator, the action itself, and a human re-cipient, or co-actor.
>
> Bureaucratic action is reduced to the action itself. It does not have a human originator in the sense of expressing the private will or intentions of a human be-ing; it originates—and this is a key characteristic of bureaucracy as a system—in an office whether or not a specific human being fills the role of officeholder. (In au-tomated bureaucracies, the action may originate in a computer.) Next there is the operation or function itself. What makes it an operation or function, however, is not primarily related to the logical end point which was the original purpose of the action. What makes it an operation or function is determined by whether or not the action meets the values and standards of higher offices charged with control.[7]

Hummel's last point about rationally organized action is very important. It gets at the "one-directional" aspects of bureaucracy and public administration organized according to traditional managerial principles. Commands flow downward through the hierarchy; information flows upward. The client or regulatee supplies information, but cannot give commands. This means the client or regulatee cannot sensibly ask the bureaucrat to modify his or her ad-ministrative behavior and routines. These can only be modified by direction from above in the bureaucracy. In essence, rationally organized action at the level of the client or regulatee tends to be a problem-*processing* activity, rather than problem-*solving* activity. This is something the NPM would change by empowering front-line employees to develop and implement solutions. Prob-lem solving (and NPM administration) virtually demands two-way commu-nication. The difference is as follows: "Let's discuss it" implies social action; "*We* (the agency) will need the following information from you (the client or regulatee)" suggests rationally organized action.

Hummel carries this line of thought at least two steps further. On the level of the individual who works in a bureaucratic setting, he notes that emotional feelings of affection are transformed. In his view, which is intended to portray the impact of bureaucratization at its outermost limits, the individual in bu-reaucratic life is taught (1) not to attach "affect" (positive emotional feelings) directly to persons; (2) to attach affect to their own administrative functions;

and (3) to attach affect to the exercise of power or authority. Note how far this diverges from ordinary social values. Society, in the normal sense of the term, cannot exist where people feel no affect toward one another, where they care primarily about the performance of their own functions, and when they exercise their own power to the exclusion of empathizing with other people or identifying with groups and individuals outside their workplace. In such a "society," there would be no sympathy, trust, love, or other emotional feelings between people. This may sound far-fetched, but, given the impersonality that characterizes bureaucracy, how much sympathy, trust, love, hate, and so forth does one expect from a public administrator, even if one is a colleague?

Hummel also maintains that as bureaucracy permeates society, it creates a tension between its own values and those of society at large. Inevitably, the values of *both* are modified in the process, but those of bureaucracy tend to make greater headway. Ask yourself what you think bureaucracy values most, and then what you personally think is of most importance in life. Hummel's list is shown in Box 10–1.[8] In sum, he finds "the *cultural* conflict between bureaucracy and society is between systems needs and human needs."[9]

One does not have to agree with Hummel entirely to get the picture: public administration, bureaucratically organized, tends to be in tension or conflict with society in terms of styles of action, emotional feelings, and overriding concerns. The differences between societal and bureaucratic values, in shorthand form, are social interaction versus administrative action; feeling versus doing; and belief, randomness, and emotionalism versus specialized expertise, systemization, and impersonality. These ideas are abstract. Perhaps by thinking about some of your own experiences with bureaucratically organized administrative agencies, they will become more concrete. They will also become clearer by considering how the tension between public administration and society affects the individual in the role of client of such administrative agencies.

BOX 10–1 **Bureaucracy versus Society**

Bureaucracy	Society
Precision	Justice
Stability	Freedom
Discipline	Violence
Reliability	Oppression
Caculability of results	Happiness
Formal rationality	Gratification
Formalistic impersonality	Poverty
Formal equality of treatment	Illness
	Death
	Victory
	Love and hate
	Salvation and damnation

The juxtaposition between social action, with its values, and rationally organized action, with its own values, is often clearest when the individual is in the role of client. Clients approach the public administrator with an understanding of the society's culture. But the culture of bureaucracy can require behavior with which they are unfamiliar or ill at ease. As Victor Thompson once pointed out, "The bureaucratic culture makes certain demands upon the clients as well as upon organization employees. There are many people in our society who have not been able to adjust to these demands. To them bureaucracy is a curse. They see no good in it whatsoever, but view the demands of modern organization as 'red tape.'"[10] Such people do not possess "the aptitudes and attitudes needed to obtain reasoned consideration" of their cases by public administrators.[11] Their "low powers of abstraction" and "need to personalize the world" seem to be the most important barriers to their ability to deal effectively with public administrators.[12] Functional illiteracy is also a problem for some clients. Inability to function well in bureaucratic language ("bureaucratese") is a problem for many more. In fact, the entire client–public administrator interaction may be distasteful and threatening to many. As Alvin Gouldner explained, clients are likely to be critical of bureaucracy when they believe it challenges their egos. This commonly occurs in two ways:

(1) A claim which he [the client] believes legitimate is not taken "at face value." He must either supply proof or allow it to be investigated. He is, as one remarked, "treated as a criminal"—he may feel his worth is questioned, his status is impugned. (2) Not only are his claims and assertions challenged, but other details of his "private life" are investigated. The individual enters the situation on "official," "technical," or "public" business, and feels that he ends up by being investigated as a person.[13]

The client role can be difficult for anyone. However, lower-class populations have been identified in particular as having acute difficulty in dealing with public bureaucracies. In part, this is because the agencies they deal with often provide a mixture of service and constraint, as in welfare and public housing programs. Moreover, members of the lower class may typically be heavily dependent on public agencies and consequently feel at their "mercy." In addition, problems of literacy and the juxtaposition between social culture and administrative culture may be most severe for members of the lower class, who may not have been socialized to understand the workings of administrative agencies. In fact, the kind of socialization they receive may be dysfunctional when it comes to presenting their cases and claims, for it appears to emphasize the acceptance of hierarchical authority. As a result, some have even argued that "bureaucratic systems are the key medium through which the middle class maintains its advantaged position vis-à-vis the lower class."[14] Public educational systems and some aspects of social welfare administration are examples. (See Boxes 10–2 and 10–3.)

The norms of the administrative culture tend to permeate mainstream culture in the United States to a very large extent. For example, it has been noted that public school education is typically hierarchically organized and

BOX 10–2 **The Client at a Bureaucratically Organized Welfare Office**

The following is a description by a welfare advocate of a typical client's meeting with a social worker in a bureaucratized welfare agency. Note how many of Hummel's and Gouldner's points apply:

> [I]n the interview booth, they have children's little plastic chairs for clients to sit in and an adult chair for the worker. And so the client, like their chin is on the table and the worker is like hovering over them shouting. And you know, you take a seat in one of those children's chairs and all of the sudden you're clearly not on the same level as the person who's interrogating you. . . .
>
> I don't know how many times I went in with somebody and the worker felt that they had to explain to me how the person had screwed up, and then turn around, you know the way people talk to folks about them as if they're deaf say, "Isn't that true. Didn't I talk to you about this? Didn't I tell you you had to turn your form in and if you didn't this would happen? Isn't that true?" Like they're totally humiliated. . . . [I]t was so effective that very rarely did the client . . . not say, "Yes, it's true." Even if they hadn't, it was better to say "Yes" than to argue that point. They were totally intimidated. And then we had to work on trying to build self-esteem, like trying to model how to respond to this person who is being totally inhumane and degrading and feeling above all as a person receiving the benefits that had no choice; that if you really had a choice, you'd have nothing to do with this place ever again. But guess what folks, you have to come back here tomorrow, and this is how you are treated. You have no choice.

SOURCE: Lucie White, *"Goldberg v. Kelly* on the Paradox of Lawyering for the Poor," *Brooklyn Law Review* 56 (1990): 861–887.

that "the process of obtaining passes, excuses, and permission slips to be granted entrances or exit serves as a useful apprenticeship for dealing with the bureaucracies later in life."[15] Herbert Wilcox found that by the fourth grade children are able to understand something about hierarchical relationships and can read organization charts. By high school, many students are able to perform as well as college students and city managers on a test designed to ascertain understanding of organizational relationships. Based on these findings, Wilcox concludes that "[t]he principles of organization do constitute a cultural trait of high school students. . . . The most important period of acculturation in relation to the trait is prior to age eleven and possibly age nine."[16]

To the extent that administrative values, especially hierarchy and impersonality, replace traditional social values, they can pose a serious problem for the individual in the society. This is not simply that using public agencies effectively may be difficult; there is also the risk that each individual will deal impersonally with others and will feel isolated and relatively unable to

---

BOX 10–3 **New York City's Chief of Human Resources Seeks Welfare**

In 1992, Barbara Sabol, the head of New York City's Human Resources Administration, tried an experiment. Armed with an officially created false identity and disguised in a wig or scarf, sweatshirt, jeans, and glasses, Sabol spent about twenty-three days applying for welfare benefits. She received food stamps, home relief benefits, and a mandatory work assignment. The experience was an eye opener. Her personal documents were lost, she was repeatedly sent to the wrong places and given the wrong forms, she waited in long lines and sat in run-down waiting rooms with broken furniture, defunct telephones, and an abundance of cockroaches. When an interview for which she had waited forty-five minutes finally began, she made the mistake of inquiring about the delay—only to be sent back to wait for another forty-five minutes!

Using the lingo of public administration, Sabol said she felt "depersonalized." Explaining further, she told reporters, "I ceased to be." "I go to this window. They do not ask me my name. They say, 'What is your Zip Code?'" Upon hearing the Zip, the intake worker told the chief, "Baby, you're in the wrong place." In what place should she be? That basic question could stump the system. One "frustrated worker" condescendingly exclaimed, "Listen to me! Look at me! You can't get this unless you have a number. They wouldn't have sent you to me if you didn't have a number." After giving up the charade, Sabol planned no disciplinary actions, but pledged to make the system more user-friendly.

SOURCE: Based on Alison Mitchell, "Posing as Welfare Recipient, Agency Head Finds Indignity," *New York Times*, 5 February 1993, A1, B2.

---

achieve control over his or her environment. Sometimes this feeling is referred to as **anomie.** There are many aspects of American society that have become increasingly impersonal, as the traditional roles of family, community, and religious organizations have been partly superseded by public administration. For instance, day care, after-school care, and care of the elderly are increasingly an organizational as opposed to a family function, deterring and even reporting crime is increasingly a police function as opposed to a community one, and today charity is largely managed by impersonal public or private secular organizations. Even procreation can now be impersonal by "surrogacy" and sperm banks. Contemporary calls for administrative decentralization and devolution to state and local governments reflect the widespread concern that the public is relatively powerless in dealing with large-scale, intrusive federal administration.

The Individual in the Political System

The individual's role in the political system also undergoes major transformations with the rise of the administrative state. First, the electorate's impact on government is attenuated by the difficulties that the officials they elect have in controlling administrative agencies and holding them accountable. Frederick Mosher succinctly summarized the problem three decades ago:

> The accretion of specialization and of technological and social complexity seems to be an irreversible trend, one that leads to increasing dependence upon the protected, appointive public service, thrice removed from direct democracy. Herein lies the central and underlying problem. . . . [H]ow can a public service so constituted be made to operate in a manner compatible with democracy? How can we be assured that a highly differentiated body of public employees will act in the interest of all the people, will be an instrument of all the people?[17]

Today, the delivery of so many government services by "third parties," through privatization and devolution, removes the electorate even further from exercising direct control over public administration.

The ideal of popular sovereignty is compromised by the tendency of the public to become subjects of the bureaucratically organized administrative state. In a classic treatise on *Democracy in the Administrative State* (1969), Emmette Redford claimed that "the first characteristic" of citizens in the administrative state is that ". . .they are dormant regarding most of the decisions being made with respect to them. Their participation cannot in any manner equal their subjection."[18] More recently, the National Performance Review (NPR) made the same point as follows:

> [The traditional administrative state] . . . put the government's customers—which is to say, all of us—at the bottom of the priority list. The first priority was the rules; the second was those who checked whether the rules were being followed (such as auditors and inspectors general); the third was those who made the rules in the first place (such as Congress and interest groups). Customers came in last, if at all. It was a sort of "iron triangle"—special interests told Congress what "the people" wanted; Congress passed laws, and then told the agencies what to do about them.
>
> Citizens, understandably, do not like being low in the pecking order—or worse, being ignored altogether. And honest people . . . don't like being treated like potential criminals.[19]

Even the growing body of research that shows Congress, political executives, and the courts can steer administrative agencies does not resolve Mosher's question. The link between the public and the elected is itself too ambiguous to ensure a high degree of political representation or responsiveness on most policy issues. Voter participation in presidential elections has hovered at just over 50 percent for decades. On average, it is even lower in congressional elections. According to Walter Dean Burnham, a leading political scientist who has studied "the turnout problem" in depth, nonvoting is associated with "indifference to or dislike of politics" and to campaigns based on personalities and images that make it difficult for would-be voters to determine which candidate will best serve their interests.[20] Overall, Burnham estimates that "about 38 percent of American citizens are 'core' or regular voters for major national and state offices; another 17 percent or so are marginals who come to the polls only when stimulated by the dramas of presidential campaign politics; another 45 percent are more or less habitual nonvoters."[21] It is in some ways very telling that the NPR looks toward making agencies responsive to customers, rather than elections, as the primary means of overcoming the public's lack of control over public administration.

As the passage from the NPR quoted on page 462 suggests, democracy and bureaucratically organized public administration clash both in terms of structure and values. Box 10–4 lists the main requirements of each. It indicates that when one moves from being a democratic citizen to a bureaucratic subject, one is crossing into a very different culture and system of rule.

It is not possible to definitively link today's limited participation in politics with the development of large-scale public administration. There is some sense that the country is being run by bureaucrats and a long-term decline in the public's faith in government coincides with a period during which the scope and general salience of regulatory administration increased (see Chapter 9). The information in Box 10–5 substantially reveals the scope of this trend. It indicates that between 1958 and the early 1990s, the public's perception was that government became more wasteful, more oriented toward a few big interests, less trustworthy to do what was right, and less responsive to the ordinary citizenry. Additionally, throughout much of this period, a majority agreed with the statement that "sometimes politics and government seem so complicated that a person like me can't really understand what is going on."

At present, public ignorance about government is abject, which must be partly due to lack of interest. For instance, the average American is more likely to be able to name the Three Stooges than three justices on the Supreme Court (59 percent to 17 percent)![22] Only 6 percent could correctly name the Chief Justice. About a quarter of those polled knew the term of office to which senators are elected.[23]

Some of the public's disaffection is focused on the federal government in particular. In 1992, the public thought Uncle Sam wasted 48 cents out of

---

BOX 10–4 Democracy versus Public Administration

Democracy Requires:	*Public Administration Favors:*
Equality	Hierarchy
Rotation in office	Seniority
Freedom	Command
Pluralism	Unity
Citizen participation	Participation based on expertise
Openness	Secrecy
Community	Impersonality
Legitimacy based on election	Legitimacy based on expertise

BOX 10–5 **The Public's Confidence in Government, 1958–1991**

	Percent of the Public Agreeing				
Statement	*1958*	*1970*	*1974*	*1980*	*1991*
The government wastes a lot of money.	43	69	74	78	75
Government is run for the benefit of a few big interests.	24	50	66	70	70
You cannot trust government to do right most of the time.	23	44	62	73	70
People like me don't have any say about what the government does.	31	36	40	39	34*
Public officials don't care much what people like me think.	25†	47	50	52	59

*In 1989.
†In 1960.

SOURCES: Seymour Martin Lipset and William Schneider, *The Confidence Gap: Business, Labor, and Government in the Public Mind* (New York: Free Press, 1983), figs. 1–1, 1–2; Dan Balz and Richard Morin, "A Tide of Pessimism and Political Powerlessness Rises," *Washington Post*, 3 November 1991; University of Akron Survey Research Center, 5 May 1989.

every dollar.[24] When asked whether the government in Washington can be trusted to do the right thing, between 75 and 80 percent of the public say only some or none of the time.[25] In 1991, only 7 percent of the public expressed "a lot" of confidence in the federal government's ability to solve problems, whereas 23 percent had "none at all." The rest had "some" (31 percent) or "just a little" (38 percent).[26] In late 1995, 52 percent of the public believed that the federal government threatened their financial well-being, whereas 44 percent disagreed with this conclusion.[27]

Although overall support for government is limited, there has been a trend toward favoring giving more power to the states. In 1981, 56 percent of the public wanted to do so; by 1995, the figure was up to 64 percent. Correspondingly, over the same period the percent who wanted to give more power to the federal government declined from 28 percent to 26 percent.[28] Today, the public favors a much larger role for the state and local governments than for the federal government in such key policy areas as welfare, public education, and law enforcement.[29] In sum, the public seems particularly apprehensive about big government in Washington, which is apparently widely viewed as remote, unreliable, and not subject to the public's control.

The Individual in the Economy

The contemporary administrative state also changes the character of the individual's place in the economic system. As public administration penetrates the society and economy to a greater extent, government inevitably gains greater control over the nation's economic resources. (In Chapter 6, we noted that government spending constitutes about one-third of the GDP.) Charles Reich explains this development in straightforward terms:

> One of the most important developments in the United States during the past decade [1950s] has been the emergence of government as a major source of wealth. Government is a gigantic syphon. It draws revenue and power, and pours forth wealth: money, benefits, services, contracts, franchises, and licenses. Government has always had this function. But while in early times it was minor, today's distribution of largess is on a vast, imperial scale.
>
> The valuables dispensed by government take many forms, but they all share one characteristic. They are steadily taking the place of traditional forms of wealth—forms which are held as private property. Social insurance substitutes for savings; a government contract replaces a businessman's customers and goodwill. The wealth of more and more Americans depends upon a relationship to government. Increasingly, Americans live on government largess. . . . [30]

Public administrative control or direction over a large share of the nation's economic resources has important consequences for the individual. First, it makes the individual dependent upon government for his or her economic well-being. If government controls access to resources, occupations, markets, franchises, technologies, and the right to operate such enterprises as utilities, broadcasting, and until recently, air, truck, and rail transportation, then individuals cannot function in a wide variety of economic areas except upon the conditions established by government. In addition, when government takes on responsibility for individuals' economic security in terms of seeking to guarantee full employment, minimal inflation, fair labor standards (wages and hours), healthful and safe working conditions, pensions, adequate housing, health insurance, and so forth, it is inevitable that government becomes the focus of efforts to enhance one's economic status and well-being. Thus, political effort is directed toward obtaining economic benefits or advancement through the adoption of specific public policies. "Loopholes" in the tax code and tax expenditures are prime examples. As Reich points out, this development is not new in kind, but rather in scope.

A second consequence of the accumulation of wealth in the hands of the administrative state is that the government gains greater leverage and control over the individual's life. This is a feature of the contemporary role of government to which political and economic conservatives have long been vehemently opposed. In Reich's words, "When government—national, state, or local—hands out something of value, whether a relief check or a television license, government's power grows forthwith; it automatically gains such power as is necessary and proper to supervise its largess. It obtains new rights to investigate, to regulate, and to punish."[31] This development tends to erode the protections private property once afforded the individual against the exercise of governmental power. Nobel Prize winner, Milton Friedman, is among those economists who have noted the changing economic situation of the individual in the United States and who have protested the encroachments on traditional economic and political freedoms that it entails. In his words:

> Economic freedom is also an indispensable means toward the achievement of political freedom. . . .
>
> The citizen of the United States who is compelled by law to devote something like 10 percent of his income to the purchase of a particular kind of retirement contract, administered by the government, is being deprived of a corresponding part of his personal freedom. How strongly this deprivation may be felt and its closeness to the deprivation of religious freedom, which all would regard as "civil" or "political" rather than "economic," were dramatized by an episode involving a group of farmers of the Amish sect. On grounds of principle, this group regarded compulsory federal old age programs as an infringement of their personal individual freedom and refused to pay taxes or accept benefits. As a result, some of their livestock were sold by auction in order to satisfy claims for social security levies. . . .
>
> A citizen of the United States who under the laws of various states is not free to follow the occupation of his own choosing unless he can get a license for it, is likewise being deprived of an essential part of his freedom. So is the man who would like to exchange some of his goods with, say, a Swiss for a watch but is prevented from doing so by a quota. So is the Californian man who was thrown into jail for selling Alka Seltzer at a price below that set by the manufacturer under so-called "fair-trade" laws. So also is the farmer who cannot grow the amount of wheat he wants.[32]

As Friedman suggests, not all of the freedom lost in conjunction with the government's larger role in the economy can be categorized as "economic freedom." The extent to which matters of personal lifestyles, individual values, and political views can be subject to regulation by government through its control of economic activity can be truly astounding. Reich points to governmental efforts to use "largess" to regulate "moral character." Among his examples are the following: "The District of Columbia denied a married man in his forties a permit to operate a taxi partly because when he was a young man in his twenties, he and a woman had been discovered about to have sexual intercourse in his car. Men with criminal records have been denied licenses to work as longshoremen and chenangoes and prevented from holding union office for the same reason. A license to operate a rooming house may be refused for lack of good character. Sonny Liston [one-time heavyweight champion] was barred from receiving a license to box in New York because of his 'bad character.' Louisiana attempted to deny aid to dependent children if their mothers were of bad character."[33] As noted in Chapter 5, individuals were dismissed from or denied federal employment at one time based on their answers to such questions as "Does your wife have liberal viewpoints?" and "Do you support racial integration?"[34] Incidentally, at one time or another loyalty tests were applied to those seeking fishing licenses, unemployment compensation, driver's licenses, and governmental approval to engage in wrestling and piano selling.[35]

The increasing dependence of the individual on government for his or her economic well-being and the greater governmental power over individuals that is a by-product of this dependence are developments of fundamental importance to the polity. They have occurred in direct association with the rise of the administrative state. As noted in Chapter 2, the increasing penetration of the economy by government has been a major cause of the growth of public administration. Additionally, though, the existence of public administrative authority and capacity has made further governmental penetration feasible. Friedrich Hayek, in a well-known book, viewed the transformation of the United States economy in this regard as overly invasive of individual freedom and as an embarkation on "the road to serfdom."[36] If unchecked, it has been argued, virtually all important individual preferences will be replaced by governmental preferences and all economic and social questions will be transformed into political ones.[37] According to this view, economic dependence on the administrative state can produce totalitarianism because government becomes all powerful when it subsumes the roles traditionally played by families, religious organizations, private groups, communities, and private economic firms.

This argument is an extreme formulation of the transformation that has been taking place in conjunction with the rise of the administrative state in the United States. However extreme, it does pinpoint certain tendencies we can clearly recognize. For example, would you be surprised today to find a member of the public whose prenatal welfare was aided by government funds and care, who was born in a public hospital at public expense, who was raised in public housing with the assistance of public welfare funds, whose diet was subsidized through the food stamp program, whose education was in public school, whose income was earned in the public sector or augmented by public benefits, whose health care was subsidized by the government, and who will be the recipient of governmental benefits in old age?

Although some oppose the contemporary governmental role in the economy on the grounds that it makes the public too dependent on government, much support for the modern welfare state is based on the belief that increased governmental power can be exercised humanely with proper regard for individual freedoms, value preferences, and liberties. In this view, government penetration of the economy is a very suitable means of protecting individuals from abuse by the economic power of other individuals and private firms. Governmental encroachment on traditional economic freedoms may be considered less troublesome than the lack of protection individuals had from boom-and-bust business cycles prior to governmental efforts to mitigate them. As in so many aspects of public administration, the overall picture is hardly so simple as the partisans of one or another particular viewpoint would have us believe.

THE PUBLIC'S EVALUATION OF PUBLIC ADMINISTRATION

The public's evaluation of public administration is complex, and in some respects, puzzling. The data in Box 10–5, discussed previously, clearly indicate that the public has very negative attitudes toward government.

Nevertheless, surveys consistently find that substantial majorities would choose government spending for social programs over tax cuts. For instance, in early 1996, 69.5 percent of the public favored smaller tax cuts and more government spending on health, education, and other social programs.[38] Perhaps surprisingly, support for larger tax cuts and less spending was limited to 22 percent. Broad majorities favor making the federal government work better, as opposed to cutting it back substantially. In a 1995 poll, half the respondents thought the federal government "mainly needs fine tuning to make it more flexible, accountable, and user-friendly," whereas 44 percent thought it "needs to undergo the same kind of dramatic restructuring and downsizing that is taking place in the private sector."[39] In summarizing data like these, Seymour Lipset and William Schneider concluded that "The public supports improving the existing bureaucracy over creating new bureaucracy. And it prefers free enterprise and competition over bureaucracy altogether. But it will accept a bureaucratic solution if that is the only one offered."[40]

Within this overall framework of public opinion, there is considerable variation among groups. For instance, African-Americans are more supportive of social programs than is the public at large. Women are more likely than men to think that government cannot be trusted, the economy is in decline, and federal government is a threat to their financial well-being.[41] People who are better informed about government are more likely to believe that their voice in public affairs matters—though even among the better informed, 31 percent strongly agree that public officials do not care much about what they think.[42] As is explored in the next two sections, the public's view of public administration also varies with the nature of their interactions with it.

Clients and Customers Are Satisfied

There have been a very large number of surveys of individuals' evaluations of their interactions as clients with public administrators. The results have been summarized and analyzed by Charles Goodsell in a book called *The Case for Bureaucracy:*

> Citizens perceive their concrete experiences with bureaucracy in a generally favorable light. Usually the preponderant majority of persons asked describes their recollections or immediate experiences in highly approving terms. Most positive evaluation response rates are at least at the two-thirds level, and many reach beyond 75 percent. Disapproval levels are almost always in the distinct minority, and most fall well below one-third. The vast majority of clients of bureaucracy reports itself as satisfied with the encounter and transaction therein. In most instances bureaucratic personnel are described as helpful, efficient, fair, considerate, and courteous. They are, furthermore, usually perceived as trying to assist, ready to listen, and even willing to adapt the rules and look out for client interest. Also, the actual performance output of bureaucracy is usually praised. The picture presented by citizens in their assessments of bureaucracy appears, in sum, as an almost complete contradiction of the hate image depicted in popular media and academic writing.[43]

What accounts for this disparity between abstract views of bureaucracy and concrete interaction remains something of a puzzle.

One can point to three common explanations, though no doubt others can be developed as well. First, some have argued that the surveys of client/customer evaluations of public administrative encounters are inherently unreliable. Among the pitfalls such surveys allegedly face are that (1) public expectations of bureaucracy are so low that any positive treatment is viewed favorably, (2) respondents to the surveys feel under social (or even political) pressure to answer favorably, and (3) the questions tend to be worded so as to evoke positive responses.[44] There is some truth to these criticisms, but how much is a matter of dispute that defies resolution in the literature of public administration.[45]

Second, Goodsell offers a commonsense approach to understanding why concrete interactions with public bureaucracy as clients tends to be viewed favorably at the same time that bureaucracy in general is viewed negatively:

> Perhaps bureaucracy should be thought of as not so much a terrible beast as a fairly good used car, quite old but well maintained and functioning not all but most of the time. It is those mornings when the car does not start—perhaps once or twice every winter?—that we recognize the machine's fallibility and then malign it furiously. For a fundamental feature of bureaucracy is that it continually performs millions of tiny acts of individual service, such as approving applications, delivering the mail, and answering complaints. Because this ongoing mass of routine achievement is not in itself noteworthy or even capable of intellectual grasp, it operates silently, almost out of sight. The occasional breakdowns, the unusual scandals, the individual instances where a true injustice is done, are what come to our attention and color our overall judgment. The water glass of bureaucracy is quite full, and we have difficulty realizing it.[46]

This explanation of the discrepancy between the public's general evaluation of bureaucracy and its specific evaluations of individual encounters in the role of client or customer is supported by some comprehensive empirical analysis. In what remains the most complete research on the matter, Daniel Katz and associates propose in *Bureaucratic Encounters* that "closer examination . . . reveals that general evaluation is related to specific experience if the experience was negative, but not if it was positive. A negative experience with an agency lowers one's general evaluation of government, but a positive experience does not raise it."[47] In Goodsell's terms, those who experience the car's failure to start curse it forever; those for whom it does start seem to feel lucky and to consider themselves exceptions to a pervasive rule. In other words, despite their own good fortune with bureaucracy, a large share of the public may nevertheless believe that it usually does not work so well.

A third possible explanation is that "general evaluations of bureaucracy may tap the ideological level, and specific evaluations of experiences may tap the pragmatic level" of an individual's thinking about public administration.[48] It is easy to see how this could work. We may be very satisfied with the courteous, prompt, and fair treatment we receive at the Motor Vehicle Department or the post office and still think, as a matter of public policy, these departments and public bureaucracies generally are too expensive for the society to support and too distracting for elected officials to control while performing their policy-making and representational functions as well. Moreover, we could believe that the services we use personally are worthwhile, but those that pertain to other people are undesirable: Those who benefit from the FAA's regulation of airline safety and those who benefit from public welfare programs may be two very separate groups of people. In other words, in pragmatic terms we may like what *we* get from public administration, whereas we begrudge what it gives to others. We like our subsidies but hate our taxes. As a result, legislators find that it is politically easier to spend than to cut back on expenditures or raise more revenues. This is part of the tendency toward deficit spending. But rather than attack the deficit head-on through reducing popular spending or raising taxes, politicians are prone to suggest that budgets can be balanced by tough management that eliminates administrative waste and fraud. Hence, the "bash-and-bureaucrat" syndrome, used with some success by Jimmy Carter and Ronald Reagan, among others.

Each of these explanations for the disparity between the public's general and specific evaluation of public bureaucracy is plausible. Presumably each explains *something* about the disparity and consequently each provides a basis for trying to improve the public's understanding of and interaction with public administration and to improve public administrators' thinking and dealing with the public. Before we develop this theme, however, it is desirable to turn to another kind of public interaction with public administration—that involving direct regulation.

Regulation Is Opposed

Although the constraints and services implemented by public administrative agencies are often mixed, individuals sometimes find themselves in the situation of being directly regulated by a bureaucratic agency. In such an instance, the individual is likely to be summoned to the agency, to have some anxiety at the potential of having his or her interests injured and being subject to constraints on his or her conduct, and, in general, will find the whole episode distasteful. There are important distinctions between seeking a benefit from a public agency and being called to an agency to face penalties of some kind. In the latter case, of course, the transaction is not voluntary on the part of the individual. The agency is very much in control. The individual is treated not as a client or customer but rather as a miscreant of some kind who presumably has done something that is perceived as illegitimate. Subtle burdens may be shifted to the individual that, when considered in total, may be frustrating and make the individual highly critical of the administrative encounter. For example, the administrative officials may be less polite than when dealing with clients; because the individual is compelled to be present, lines and waiting time may be longer; additionally, more probing questions may be asked of the individual and less credence may be given to his or her explanation of some event. To the extent that individuals find themselves in the role of regulatee, therefore, the public's evaluation of public administration may be highly critical.

Katz and associates explored the public's reaction to **constraint agencies** in some depth. Among these were agencies dealing with drivers' licenses, traffic violations, taxation, police matters, and miscellaneous other regulatory activities. The public's general evaluation of these agencies is much more negative than its views of agencies when interacting with them in the role of client or customer.[49] For instance, Katz and associates found that individuals were considerably less likely to believe that they had received fair treatment in their encounters with constraint agencies than in their dealings with service agencies.[50]

These findings indicate that another plausible explanation emerges for the gap between the public's general negative evaluation of public bureaucracy and individuals' satisfaction with their own specific encounters with public agencies as clients or customers. It is quite possible that when asked to evaluate public bureaucracy in the abstract, the public tends to focus more on its distasteful interactions with constraint agencies than on its other encounters with public administrators. In other words, unlike Goodsell's explanation that it is the random breakdowns in an otherwise smoothly functioning public bureaucracy that stick in people's minds, this explanation suggests that *routine* subjection to regulation by public administrators is an important source of discontent with public bureaucracy generally. To the extent that this is true, improving attitudes toward public bureaucracy may require more genuine administrative change and less public relations than Goodsell's explanation suggests.

A Look at Local Government Services

The public's evaluation of local government services has been studied extensively. Using a method called Percent to Maximum (PTM), Thomas Miller and Michelle Miller analyzed 261 citizen surveys administered in forty states during the 1980s.[51] The results cover a total population of over 200,000 Americans and included more than 3,000 questions. PTM converts ratings using different categories and numbers of options into a common scale. For example, it can be used to array three-point scales (good, fair, poor), as well as five-point scales (very good, good, fair, poor, very poor) on a single scale ranging from 0 to 100. A 100 on the scale indicates very good, 75 is good, 50 is neither good nor bad, 25 is bad, and 0 is very bad. As Box 10–6 indicates, Miller and Miller found that, overall, local government services are rated positively. The public thinks well of the twenty-one services studied. Fire protection, library, and trash services were rated above 75.

BOX 10–6 **Average Ratings of Local Government Services Evaluated by Sixty or More Jurisdictions, 1980s**

Service	Average Adjusted PTM	Number of Jurisdictions
Fire	81.1	168
Library	79.3	104
Trash	78.0	142
Water/sewer	73.5	119
Parks	72.3	65
Police	71.8	182
To seniors	69.5	63
Schools	69.4	92
Sewer	69.1	72
Parks/recreation	68.5	83
Open space/recreation	68.0	89
Snow removal	67.0	73
Street lighting	66.9	60
Street cleaning	66.6	67
General maintenance	66.1	79
Health services	64.1	70
Code enforcement	62.3	62
Bus/transit	61.9	71
Animal control	60.3	63
Street repair	58.5	126
Planning/zoning	57.5	75

SOURCE: Thomas Miller and Michelle Miller, "Standards of Excellence: U.S. Residents' Evaluations of Local Government Services," *Public Administration Review* 51 (November/December 1991): 508.

Planning/zoning and street repair were rated lowest, but still somewhat positively. Miller and Miller found that the ratings were very stable from one community to another. Consequently, a PTM score of 70 would be unusually positive for street repair, poor for a library, and slightly below average for police.

Theodore Poister and Gary Henry used the PTM scale to report the public's evaluation of the quality of public and private services in Georgia.[52] Their results are displayed in Box 10–7. Overall, they reinforce Miller and Miller's main findings, but also contain some surprises. The private sector stacks up less well than the conventional view would suggest. For instance, fast-food restaurants rank lower than the U.S. Postal Service and there is no difference between private doctors' offices and public health clinics. Poister and Henry found that respondents who had used a service during the past six months tended to rate it 10 points higher, on average, than the general public did. However, the overall pat-

BOX 10–7 **Citizen Ratings of Public and Private Service Quality in Georgia, 1992**

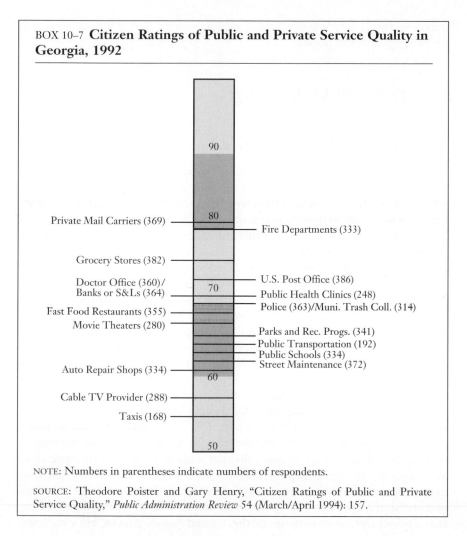

Private Mail Carriers (369)

Fire Departments (333)

Grocery Stores (382)

Doctor Office (360)/
Banks or S&Ls (364)

U.S. Post Office (386)

Public Health Clinics (248)

Police (363)/Muni. Trash Coll. (314)

Fast Food Restaurants (355)

Movie Theaters (280)

Parks and Rec. Progs. (341)

Public Transportation (192)

Public Schools (334)

Street Maintenance (372)

Auto Repair Shops (334)

Cable TV Provider (288)

Taxis (168)

NOTE: Numbers in parentheses indicate numbers of respondents.

SOURCE: Theodore Poister and Gary Henry, "Citizen Ratings of Public and Private Service Quality," *Public Administration Review* 54 (March/April 1994): 157.

tern of responses was not substantially altered: public and private sector ratings were interspersed along the PTM.

Summing up the research on the public's evaluations of public administration is difficult. Not all functions have been studied carefully. As Katz and associates' research suggests, people may evaluate such functions as welfare, public housing, and incarceration much differently than fire protection and libraries. Nevertheless, it is clear that the public thinks more highly of many government services than popular rhetoric would suggest. But as Miller and Miller ask, "Is a 'Good' evaluation for police good enough? Can more be expected from a street repair service that gets only 'Fair' evaluations?"[53] All else being equal, almost everyone would want public administration to enjoy even higher ratings. But all else is rarely equal in the public sector. There are competing values, visions, and different strategies for dealing with the public.

PUBLIC ADMINISTRATIVE PERSPECTIVES ON THE PUBLIC

The Traditional Managerial Approach to the Public

From a traditional managerial perspective, interaction with the public should maximize the values of efficiency, economy, and effectiveness. The overwhelming tendency of this perspective, as we noted in Chapter 1 and elsewhere, is therefore to depersonalize the client or regulatee by turning him or her into a "case." But sometimes this engenders resistance that can frustrate the attainment of these values. In such instances, the traditional managerial approach may seek to take special steps to educate the public in a variety of ways so that its members can deal more effectively with a particular administrative agency. For example, the IRS runs a taxpayers' information service to help individuals fill out their tax returns. Agencies also engage in public relations not only to generate greater political support for their activities but also to help clients, regulatees, and others to understand what they do. Educational efforts can be important, as it has been thought that one reason for the public's generally negative view of public administration is that "the policy makers are remote and their basic goals are not understood."[54]

Another managerial approach for dealing with the public is to institute **ombudsman** arrangements of some sort. In a traditional sense, ombudsmen are independent agents of the legislature who are empowered to investigate specific complaints by individuals alleging maladministration of some kind. Such agents can criticize, publicize and make recommendations, but they cannot reverse the administrative action at issue. Ombudsmen of this kind originated in Sweden in 1808 and can be found in other Scandinavian countries and several other nations. In the United States, Alaska, Hawaii, Iowa, and Nebraska have used ombudsmen at the state level. Several cities also employ them. The IRS, Environmental Protection Agency, and Department of Commerce are among the federal agencies that use ombudsmen in some programs. In the United States, ombudsmen do not fit the traditional concept completely because they are often attached to the administrative agency or executive branch, rather than the legislature. Moreover, in the United States, individual members of state legislatures and Congress are inclined to function as ombudsmen for their constituents, although here the function is referred to as constituency service or casework. In any event, the ombudsman concept is useful from a managerial perspective because it acts as a genuine check on the poor administrative and public relations practices by subordinate public administrators. Even rudeness on the part of the latter can be the basis of an individual's complaint to an ombudsman. The ombudsman is useful in dealing with complaints that would otherwise be channeled through an agency's own hierarchy. Ombudsmen also help educate the public concerning agencies' missions and procedures.

The traditional managerial approach also dictates doing whatever is cost-effective to improve the quality of the public's interaction with public administrators. This may involve using higher levels of technology, such as computers, to process such things as tax returns and drivers' licenses. Or it may involve such mundane procedures as positioning waiting lines so as to be as pleasant as possible. For example, whereas in the New York State Department of Motor Vehicles offices it was once necessary to wait on one line for an eye test and then another to pay for a driver's license, now the whole transaction can take place at one window.

Finally, those pursuing the traditional managerial approach should be wary of its tendency to shift the burdens of cost and time to individual members of the public. For instance, long lines and convoluted steps in an administrative encounter, such as being shunted from clerk to clerk, are sure to be bothersome to a sizable share of the public. So is placing the burden on individuals for supplying information that the government already has in some other office, or requiring individuals to supply multiple copies of pertinent documents as is sometimes done by consumer protection agencies. Public administration can be improved from the clients' perspective through **human services integration.** This approach enables individuals seeking or requiring several services, such as food stamps, public health care, and public housing, to apply to one office only. Such "one-stop shopping" for benefits is easier for clients, enables them to gain a better understanding of what programs are available and how they are related to one another, and may also efficiently reduce paperwork. Appeals processes should also be as simplified as possible, while still being fair. Appeals can provide managers with very useful feedback regarding the accuracy of initial decisions, the clarity of eligibility or other criteria, and gaps in the coverage provided by programs. In general, where investigations are necessary to determine eligibility for benefits of some kind, it is best to use the least intrusive methods. Interactions involving constraints present a complicated problem in this regard, because it sometimes may be less expensive, more efficient, and more effective to *violate* individuals' constitutional and legal rights. Consequently, public managers of policing functions must take special care to avoid any violations of this kind.

Dealing with the public is an area where the managerial values of economy and effectiveness may frequently be at odds with one another. Although it is often cheapest to follow the impersonal approach by treating individuals as cases, this approach may be inappropriate to the function being served. This is particularly true in therapeutic functions, such as mental health care and social work. "Corrections" of prisoners may also be frustrated by too much reliance on impersonality or cost-cutting. It is more expensive to treat each individual on a personal, individual basis in these areas. Yet, by now the record is clear that failure to do so makes it nearly impossible for the administrative function to be performed effectively. In the area of mental health the courts have sometimes required that each patient or resident of a state facility be provided with some amount of individual treatment.[55]

In view of the tension between social values and those embodied in the traditional managerial approach to public administration, there is no doubt that public administrators should be concerned with the public in all facets of their work. Historically, public administrative theory and practice paid inadequate attention to some aspects of dealing with the public. One result has been marked *underutilization* of services provided by public administrative agencies.[56] This, in itself, would tend to make the administrative state less satisfactory in intervening in the society and economy to promote the public interest.

The New Public Management Approach to the Public

The NPM views the public primarily as customers. The term customer is used to denote almost all encounters with public agencies. It includes service and regulatory relationships as well as public employment. Welfare recipients are customers of social service agencies; taxpayers are customers of the IRS; applicants for federal jobs are customers of the Office of Personnel Management and/or other agencies. As customers, the public is to be served in a businesslike manner. The emphasis is on effectiveness, efficiency, and cost reduction.

The NPR notes that the term "customer" raises some concern:

> The National Performance Review has received letters and phone calls from a few taxpayers who objected to being referred to as the government's customers. These people correctly pointed out that they are the government's owners or, at the very least, stockholders. But it is possible to be an owner and a customer too. For example, if you own stock in Ford Motors, your relationship to the company is something like a taxpayer's to the government: you own a piece of it. A Ford stockholder can enter another relationship with the company by buying a Taurus and becoming a valued customer. When taxpayers call the Social Security Administration or stop by the post office, they are customers too. . . .
>
> Applying the customer service concept to government has clear management advantages. . . . It focuses attention on the results the customers want. It highlights the expenditures that yield those results and, by contrast, eliminates the expenditures that don't contribute to good service. . . .
>
> The customers are the people who use the national parks, forests, and waterways; people who are eligible for social security and veterans benefits, people whose lives are diminished by unemployment, illiteracy, crime, pollution, and problems of our major cities. The customer service approach refocuses government on the people. It puts people first.[57]

The NPR places customers in the following categories: beneficiaries; business; the general public; law enforcement; natural resource management; the research and academic community; states, localities, and other partners; travelers, tourists, and outdoor enthusiasts; the U.S. government and federal employees; and veterans.

The NPM's devotion to customer service and satisfaction raises some unsettled issues. Because members of the public are not truly the customers of a wide range of agencies, what they want cannot necessarily be determined by what they purchase. In terms of finding out *how* the public wants government to serve them when it is not market-driven, the NPM relies on surveys to gain feedback from customers. It also imputes preferences to its customers by emulating the best practices in the private sector through benchmarking. According to the NPR, based on surveys, at the broadest level Americans "want a more efficient government, but they are desperate for a more *effective* government."[58] Consequently, they want government to stop doing things it cannot do well or that are unnecessary. They do not want to cut costs at the price of effectiveness. At the level of individual agencies, surveys indicate that the public wants faster and more convenient treatment, as well as specific channels for voicing complaints. The NPR strongly supports human services integration, or "one-stop shopping," for its combination of convenience and reduction of redundancy. Benchmarking has led to some clear improvements, including the Social Security Administrations' "800" telephone service being considered the best in the business.

In the NPR version of the NPM, *what* government should do is also an issue of customer demand. This is clearest where agencies, such as the Postal Service, operate largely like firms in a market. Such agencies should invest in services for which there is strong customer demand and disinvest in or eliminate altogether those without customer support. Where public administration is not marketlike, the NPR relies on surveys to determine what services it should provide. Based on surveys, the NPR concludes that Americans want the federal government to control immigration, help the needy, improve education, reduce crime, protect the environment, and improve jobs and the economy. If investment is to follow customer demand, then the government should focus on these areas.

These approaches to ascertaining customer preferences downplay the utility of traditional political channels for determining what the public wants. In consequence, at least two problems potentially arise. First, the customers of specific agencies are often a limited segment of the population. Responding to them may be at odds with what a majority of the voters would prefer. For instance, the customers of social welfare agencies may have preferences for eligibility and requirements that differ from those of the electorate at large. Similarly, those subject to regulation may want less red tape, more flexibility, and greater responsiveness to their needs. The NPM is willing to give it to them as long as the results are satisfactory. But when it comes to safety and some environmental matters, the public may not be satisfied with holding the regulated accountable after the fact.

Second, political systems like that of the United States have built-in barriers to making public policy by simple majority preferences. For example, providing each state with two senators gives an equal voice to Wyoming and California, even though the latter is roughly sixty-six times bigger in population. Requirements for supermajorities for treaties and other matters also strengthen the voice of those who are in the minority on political issues.

Another set of issues that arises when the public is viewed as customers is which customers to satisfy when not all customers have identical or harmonious interests. In the free market, firms would presumably seek to satisfy customers based on long- and/or short-term profitability. For most public agencies, this option does not exist. Even if they were to substitute survey responses for profits, they are likely to operate under a norm or legal requirement of providing service equally to all customers. The Postal Service is not free to charge its customers the true price of delivering first-class mail—sending it across the street or across the continent costs the same. Consequently, those who primarily send local mail are subsidizing those whose mail goes mostly long distance. Working under a norm of universal service, public school systems cannot write off the customers they find it most costly to serve. The National Labor Relations Board would lose its legitimacy if it were not perceived as reasonably neutral in dealing with the conflicts between its major customers, business and labor. Politics and law, not customer preferences, are usually used to resolve conflicts among the users of government services.

Finally, though not an insuperable problem, identifying customers can be a thorny one. The NPR points out that ". . . the very first step was to figure out who the customer is. Since the customer is the one you try to satisfy, it was natural for many government workers to think that the customer must be the boss, or headquarters, or Congress. . . . But, while they are all important—even crucial—to our success, they are not the customers."[59] Still, who are the customers of the criminal justice system? Lawyers, jurors, the victims, or perpetrators of crimes? Who are the customers of prisons, the inmates or the taxpayers who buy space to confine them? Are the Federal Aviation Administration's customers the flying public, people in neighborhoods near airports, the airlines, pilots, controllers, companies that build passenger airplanes, or airline maintenance firms? As noted above, because different groups served by agencies have disparate interests, answering "all of the above" is not always useful.

These problems are real, but they do not mean that considering the public to be customers is inappropriate or unfeasible. In fact, it can reinvigorate and strengthen agencies' commitment to service. At present, more than 100 federal agencies have set standards for serving customers (and, as is discussed in Chapter 12, agencies can be held accountable for meeting these standards).

The Political Approach to the Public

The political approach to public administration emphasizes the values of representation, responsiveness, and accountability to the public. This often dictates that the public be afforded means for *participating* in public administration. Public participation of some kind is viewed as contributing to the ability of public administrators to understand and respond to the public's concerns. It also requires that the administrators explain their actions, policies, and so forth, to the public and is seen as a means of more completely incorporating the citizenry into the governing of the administrative state. Specifically, it is argued that

1. A lack of citizen participation in modern governance reduces the capacity of the political system to be representative and responsive.
2. Nonparticipation also erodes the quality of citizenship in democratic nations by reducing the citizen's sense of moral and political obligation to take part in governance.
3. Nonparticipation promotes ignorance about the way government functions; participation, on the other hand, promotes understanding.
4. The absence of meaningful channels for citizen participation in government leads to alienation on the part of the public. Without participation, the public feels no sense of "ownership" or responsibility for governmental actions. On the contrary, the citizenry believes that it is acted upon (that is, subject) rather than being an actor in government. Participation also reduces alienation by providing the public with a greater sense of control over its environment.
5. Participation promotes a sense of political community and political integration. It helps individuals see the relationship between what they personally want from government and what others, with conflicting viewpoints, are seeking. Ideally, participation enables everyone to understand and respect each others' political perspectives. Rather than promoting conflict and competition, participation is viewed as promoting cooperation.
6. Participation promotes the sense that government is legitimate and fosters compliance with its decisions. It is important to remember in this context that bureaucracy has been viewed as a means of inducing citizen compliance with "rational-legal" regulatory functions.[60] Its expertise, specialization, and impersonality have been considered particularly important in this regard. However, as noted above, impersonality, in particular, may not be well suited to some administrative functions involving service and therapy. In these areas, individuals are thought to be more apt to comply with administrative decisions, procedures, and directives if they are allowed to participate in their formulation and implementation.

There is a large body of literature and thought behind each of these propositions concerning the desirability of citizen participation in public administration.[61] Each proposition remains debatable, but for the most part, the political approach to public administration is committed to finding means of expanding citizen participation in order to improve civic-mindedness and administration.

Direct Participation   Although there has been a tendency among some to dismiss the political approach's interest in participation as idealistic, it should be noted with emphasis that there are some outstanding examples of long-term citizen participation in public administration. Public school governance is one example. It has strongly emphasized the need for local control and accordingly there has been great diversity in teacher qualifications, curriculum, extracurricular activities, class size, school calendar, extent of collective bargaining, and grouping of pupils in schools by age. Citizen participation has also been an important aspect of agricultural administration for many decades. More recently, New York State's citizen-participation specialists have been effective in facilitating public participation in dealing with environmental problems such as toxic waste sites and water pollution.[62] Participation through organized interest groups is also prevalent, as noted in Chapter 2, and has been institutionalized at the federal level by the Advisory Committee Act of 1972.

These examples of workable citizen participation in public administration notwithstanding, there have also been some remarkable failures. Both the Economic Opportunity Act of 1964 and the Model Cities Act of 1966 sought to incorporate citizen participation in federal programs dealing with the needs of the poor, especially the urban poor. The Economic Opportunity Act was the basis for the poverty program. It sought to incorporate citizen participation through representation on the governing boards of community action programs. These boards also included public officials and representatives of private social service agencies. The representatives of the poor were to be elected by the poor themselves. Participatory community action agencies (CAAs) were also relied on by the Model Cities Program. In both cases, the drive for citizen participation was frustrated. For one reason or another, the poor simply did not participate. As Daniel Patrick Moynihan observed, "The turnouts [in elections to CAAs] in effect declared that the poor weren't interested: in Philadelphia 2.7 per cent; Los Angeles 0.7 per cent; Boston 2.4 per cent; Cleveland 4.2 per cent; Kansas City, Mo. 5.0 per cent. Smaller communities sometimes got larger turnouts, but never anything nearly approaching that of a listless off-year election."[63]

Moynihan claimed that these low turnouts were reflective of the fact that participation is a middle-class value of little interest to the lower class. The poor, in his view, needed money, jobs, housing, and many other things much more than they needed "identity," "a sense of community," and "control over their destiny." Others have argued that representation of the poor was even further compromised by the tendency of their elected representatives to be coopted and to have sometimes docilely allowed the middle-class representatives on community action agencies to direct funds toward the real clientele—not the poor but the city's businesses.[64]

Client-Centered Administration   On balance, therefore, it is reasonable to conclude that participation can work in some programs and among some groups of the citizenry, as in the case of public school governance, farmers, and a considerable range of advisory committees representing economic and social interests. On the other hand, it clearly does not work among all programs and groups, as experience with Poverty and Model Cities Programs indicates. Advocates of greater citizen participation in public administration have argued that, consequently, administrative agencies dealing with clients who for one reason or another are unable to represent themselves effectively should be **client-centered.**[65] Being client-centered is like being customer-oriented except that the "customers" are unable to play their role well. Prime candidates for becoming client-centered include agencies dealing with children, the mentally ill or disabled, illiterates, and, in some cases, the chronically poor.

Client-centered agencies would be advocates for their clientele. They would also promote human services integration where specialization frustrates the ability of clients, such as the poor, to receive all the assistance they need. Combining housing benefits, health programs, and nutritional programs would provide an illustration. Where programs dealing with these areas are placed in different agencies and not integrated even though they are directed toward many of the same clients, the client is apt to face redundancies in filling out forms, to encounter public administrators in three agencies rather than just one, and possibly to face different eligibility standards that frustrate gaining assistance. Equally important, because no one agency has full responsibility for the client, each is likely to be responsive to other interests which may be in conflict with what the client is seeking. Housing agencies may be more responsive to construction, banking, and business interests; health agencies to medical and pharmaceutical interests; and nutritional programs may be placed in agricultural agencies, as is true of the federal food stamp program. Yet it would be hard to argue that health and nutrition are not related, or that housing is not relevant to programs seeking to promote client's health and nutrition. If all these programs were placed in the same agency, the argument goes, it could not help but see the client as the center of things and the other interests as peripheral. The case of "Bad Blood," discussed in Chapter 8, in which the Public Health Service failed to treat people for syphilis in order to aid medical knowledge rather than the health of the patients, is a dramatic example of what can go wrong when agencies are not client-centered. A more mundane benefit of client-centered organization is that it helps eliminate catch-22's and may make service delivery easier.

Coproduction   In some ways, **coproduction** is the opposite of client-centered public administration. Client-centered administration seeks to create organizational structures and programmatic arrangements that focus on the client's interest, because the client is believed to be unable to assert these directly. Coproduction assumes that the public can understand its interests and cooperate with public administrators in performing functions. Coproduction is "the joint provision of public services by public agencies and service consumers."[66] Everyday examples are residents carrying garbage out to the curb for collection and participants voluntarily organizing recreation programs using public facilities. Other possibilities include community-based crime prevention groups; a statewide "green-up" (that is, clean up litter) day, as has long existed in Vermont; and groups such as "friends" of the library, parks, or symphony. Even placing a "totfinder" on a window to help firefighters identify the bedrooms of young children is an act of coproduction of public administration.

The simplicity of some aspects of coproduction should not obscure the political importance of this approach to public administration. It puts forward a different model of administrative service delivery. By being a joint venture, the citizen is a participant, not merely a consumer, customer, or subject. Citizens are jointly responsible for productivity and the quality of services. Consequently, they may learn about how a public administrative function is organized and operated. A citizen-based crime prevention organization cannot fail to learn more about the problems faced by the police and how they cope with them. Moreover, some believe that coproduction can help "to build in citizens a *loyalty* to place, neighbors, and their community."[67] This loyalty results from "face-to-face contact and an investment of energy in the improvement of neighborhoods and communities."[68]

Public Interest Groups   Public interest groups are another vehicle for increasing the participation of citizenry in public administration, albeit somewhat amorphously.[69] In Chapter 2, we noted that public interest groups seek collective goods that do not selectively and materially benefit their membership. While recognizing that the distinction between this type of group and a traditional interest group may at times be blurred, there is a difference in emphasis. Public interest groups seem concerned with "representing the people against the special interests."[70] Common Cause, Consumers Union, the League of Women Voters, and a variety of groups associated with Ralph Nader are examples. These groups often interact with public administrators in an effort to promote the groups' views of the public's interest. They have made considerable use of the opportunity, afforded by the Administrative Procedure Act of 1946, to participate in administrative rule making by submitting information, views, and/or testifying before agencies. They have also made use of the National Environmental Policy Act of 1969 in this regard. Such groups provide an important counterbalance to traditional interest groups in the realm of bureaucratic politics. The average citizen has neither time nor inclination to monitor what agencies are doing, to challenge their proposed rules, or to present his or her perspective to agencies. But the public interest group does, and through constant attention to agency proposals in the *Federal Register* and equivalent volumes in the states, these groups can have an important cumulative impact. In fact, the main issue is less whether they have an impact than whether they actually represent their members in any meaningful sense. There is no way of ascertaining this. Insofar as is known, to the extent that such groups represent the public, it is broad middle-class interests upon which they focus.

The Legal Approach to the Public

The legal approach to the interaction of the public with public administration seeks to assure that individuals' constitutional and statutory rights are protected. This concern has been reflected in a number of changes in constitutional doctrine and administrative law practices over the years, especially since the New Deal. Together, these changes have led to the judicialization of many public administrative practices and greater judicial review of public administrators by the courts. Administrative hearings before administrative law judges or similar functionaries are now a standard feature of public administration in the United States. In most instances, the individual member of the public is entitled to be represented by counsel, provided at his or her own expense, at such a hearing. A very considerable body of constitutional rights for clients, regulatees, and litigants now exists. Street-level encounters are also regulated by constitutional law. The opportunities and rights of individuals to participate in public administrative activities are defined by statute, but once established by law they cannot usually be denied to a specific individual without due process of law. The individual's ability to bring actual litigation has been enhanced by a number of developments, including the enactment of the National Environmental Policy Act and the development of judicial doctrines that make it easier to have "standing"* to litigate an injury to an interest caused by some aspect of public administration.[71] Moreover, in recent years, many federal judges have shown a far greater inclination to exercise oversight of public administrative activities dealing with the public. Judicial involvement in public schools, zoning, mental health care, prison management, and public housing are examples. Concomitantly, the judiciary has greatly expanded the liability of public administrators who violate individuals' constitutional or statutory rights.

In sum, the legal approach has sought to create a network of rights to protect the public against arbitrary, capricious, invidious, or discriminatory administrative action. It has further sought to assure that the treatment of the individual by an administrative agency is fair and that individuals have access to litigation should they be injured by administrative action. (The law of estoppel is an important exception, as discussed in Chapter 8.) Moreover, the judiciary has given public administrators an incentive to protect individuals' rights strictly. If they fail to do so, they may be personally liable for monetary damages in a civil suit initiated by the individual whose rights were violated. We will address some of these developments in greater detail in the next chapter.

SYNTHESIS: PUTTING THE PUBLIC BACK IN PUBLIC ADMINISTRATION

The growing concern with "the public" is one of the most important recent developments in American public administrative theory and practice. In the past, public administration paid lip service to the concept of the "public" and

---

*Standing is the ability to show sufficient stake (e.g., personal injury) to bring suit in a justiciable controversy.

the existence of a public. The notion that somehow the public must be the focus of public administration seemed too threatening and too irrelevant to expert, politically neutral public administration. Many dismissed the concept of a public as too ambiguous, too romanticized a notion, too politically oriented, and too much an aggregation to be of serious use at all.[72] In an effort to make the concept of the public more concrete, the traditional managerial approach tended to focus on the public as clients or regulatees, who were processed as cases. Today, the NPM views the public more as customers. The political approach tended to aggregate individuals into social and economic interest groups. This was an effort to promote the values of representativeness, responsiveness, and administrative accountability through greater opportunities for citizen participation in public administration. Thus, the citizenry was considered in terms of such categories as "farmers," "the poor," and so forth. The Federal Advisory Committee Act of 1972 affords the opportunity for participation through organized interest groups to a wide range of groups of people with whom federal bureaucratic agencies are involved. The legal approach views the public as a collection of individuals who possess certain constitutional and statutory rights that must be protected against administrative encroachment. It regards the protection of these rights as obviously in the public interest.

For the most part, these perspectives are so broad that a synthesis is possible. However, the conflicts among their values and approaches for achieving these values should not be underestimated. In the past, the traditional managerial perspective considered citizen participation to be inefficient and ineffective because it brought amateurs into public administration, which was seen as the domain of professionals and experts. Citizen participation was also viewed as too expensive. Those imbued with the managerial perspective would admit, though, that the citizenry could legitimately act as "authoritative critic" of administrative actions, to use Woodrow Wilson's term.[73] Certainly, the "citizen-subject" or "citizen-consumer" of administrative action could develop a legitimate and informed opinion about it. The trouble was that the citizenry seemed unclear in its evaluation of public administration. In the abstract the public was critical, in the area of services it was generally positive, in the area of constraint, negative.

The traditional managerial approach was also at odds with the legalistic one. The main conflict here has been "judicialization" of public administration, which has the tendency to fragment administrative authority and to be time-consuming. No doubt those committed to the managerial view that administrative legitimacy flows from technical expertise were also opposed to the increasing scope of judicial review and oversight of administrative action.

Finally, there is plenty of potential for the political and legal approaches to clash over the very basic question of "Who is eligible to participate?" Very many categorizations of people for participation in public administration run the risk of violating the constitutional requirements of equal protection (discussed in the following chapter).

Despite these conflicts among the perspectives, matters pertaining to the public and public administration have tended to sort themselves out by *function*. While recognizing that the categories are broad and imperfect, the following patterns have emerged.

Service   The traditional managerial perspective toward the public has been relied on where the function is service of a nontherapeutic nature, such as retirement benefits, unemployment compensation, and workers' compensation. For the most part, these services involve routine handling of numerous individuals who fall into similar categories (e.g., reach the age of retirement). Treating them as "cases" is efficient and apparently does not seriously offend the clients, as is suggested by the public's evaluation of such activities. Nevertheless, the NPM would change the focus from cases to customers and emphasize better service.

Therapy   Therapeutic service and regulation for the purpose of providing therapy, as in public mental health facilities and prisons, tend to require a more client-centered and/or participatory approach. Prisons and residential mental health facilities come close to being totally client-centered in the sense that all the ostensible needs of the client (or regulatee, in this context) are met there. Welfare and some health programs also tend to be client-centered to a considerable extent. Therapy requires individualized attention. This is obviously true in medical and psychological terms, but it is also pertinent in a social sense. It is not an accident that social workers deal with their clients on an individual basis and in a face-to-face context. Social work may involve visits by the public administrator to the home of the client, and a plan of therapeutic action may be developed for each client, based on his or her needs. A basic notion here, though perhaps a somewhat paternalistic one, is that those subject to therapy are unable independently to assert their own interests. Regarding the poor as customers may overlook the possibility that some people are poor because, for one reason or another and sometimes beyond their control, they are unable to function well in markets. Where sociotherapy is organized bureaucratically, as Ms. Sabol (Box 10–3) found, it is unlikely to meet the client's needs.

Regulation   Regulation not involving therapy tends to be organized along the lines of the traditional managerial perspective but is also strongly influenced by legalistic considerations of rights and procedures. Examples would be regulation by police, tax agencies, and motor vehicle departments. Agencies engaged in these functions treat individuals as cases and seek to process them as efficiently and economically as possible. However, because some very fundamental rights are involved, the legalistic perspective has been asserted to a considerable degree as a means of protecting individuals. Customer service standards also help to assure fair, prompt, and less burdensome encounters.

Litigation and Street-Level Encounters   These kinds of interaction between the public and public administrators are largely informed by the values of the legalistic approach. The rights of the individual are specified in some detail and certain procedures are required to assure that these rights are respected. This has gone so far that it may now be considered unconstitutional for the police to approach an individual walking on the street and ask who he or she is and what he or she is doing—unless there is at least a reasonable suspicion that the person has actually done or is about to do something illegal.[74] The courts have been particularly active in defining the constitutional limits on "stop and frisk" operations by police. Litigation, of course, is the full realization of the legalistic perspective. As in the case of regulation, in general, customer service standards can play a significant role in improving these encounters.

Participation   Individuals also participate in public administration. This role is dictated almost entirely by the political perspective, and the values associated with it overlay some of the practices found in the realm of service delivery and therapy. Participation is prevalent in federal agricultural policy. It is important in some environmental and public works policies. The regulation of economic concerns and activities, though not of individuals, also tends to emphasize participation by organized interest groups, as we saw in the previous chapter. But participation is so fundamental a political process for obtaining representativeness, responsiveness, and accountability that it has worked its way into many aspects of public administration. For instance, co-production is a means of participation in service delivery. Client-centered administrative operations are viewed as a means of representing and responding to the interests of individuals who otherwise might not be able to assert their interests well. Mental health patients are a clear example. At a broader level of economic regulation and subsidization, client-centered agencies become "clientele" agencies, such as the U.S. Departments of Agriculture, Commerce, and Labor. Here the political approach is followed in imputing the same sets of interests to all members of a categorical group, such as organized labor, which is seen as the political constituency of the agency. Public school governance is another manifestation of society's overriding concern with the values of the political approach to public administration.

Of course, the association of these approaches and values with different administrative functions in different degrees does create tensions for day-to-day public administration. Yet as long as the society seeks conflicting goals—greater administrative efficiency, customer satisfaction, public participation, strict protection of an individual's constitutional and legal rights—the balance already reached in terms of the public's interaction with public administration seems reasonably sound. No doubt adjustments can be made, but once again, no fundamental changes are likely unless conflicts among the values and goals of public administration can be fully resolved. There is, however, one aspect of the public and public administration that virtually all analysts agree on—the public would benefit from a better understanding of public administration, and public administration would benefit from a public that knew more about its functions, concepts, values, and processes. Let us conclude this chapter by returning, once again, to Woodrow Wilson, who began the self-conscious study of public administration in the United States.

> The problem is to make public opinion efficient without suffering it to be meddlesome. Directly exercised, in the oversight of the daily details and in the choice of the daily means of government, public criticism is of course a clumsy nuisance, a rustic handling of delicate machinery. But as superintending the greater forces of formative policy alike in politics and administration, public criticism is altogether safe and beneficient, altogether indispensable. Let administrative study find the best means for giving public criticism this control and for shutting it out from all other interference.[75]

NOTES

1. Daniel Katz et al., *Bureaucratic Encounters* (Ann Arbor: University of Michigan, Institute for Social Research, 1975), table 2.1.
2. Ibid., 101–116.
3. See Cesar Parales, "The Fair Hearing Process," *Brooklyn Law Review* 56 (1990):889–898.
4. Ibid.
5. Ralph P. Hummel, *The Bureaucratic Experience* (New York: St. Martin's, 1977), 20.
6. Ibid., 27.
7. Ibid., 29.
8. Ibid., 57.
9. Ibid., 56.
10. Victor Thompson, *Modern Organization* (New York: Knopf, 1961), 170.
11. Reinhard Bendix, *Nation Building and Citizenship* (New York: John Wiley, 1964), 129.
12. Thompson, *Modern Organization*, 172–173.
13. Alvin Gouldner, "Red Tape as a Social Problem," in *Reader in Bureaucracy*, ed. R. K. Merton et al. (Glencoe Ill.: Free Press, 1952), 413.
14. Gideon Sjoberg et al., "Bureaucracy and the Lower Class," in *Bureaucratic Power in National Politics*, 3d ed., ed. F. Rourke (Boston: Little, Brown, 1978), 40.
15. Katz, et al., *Bureaucratic Encounters*, 193.
16. Herbert G. Wilcox, "The Cultural Trait of Hierarchy in Middle Class Children," *Public Administrative Review* 28 (May/June, 1968): 222–235, at 231.
17. Frederick Mosher, *Democracy and the Public Service* (New York: Oxford University Press, 1968), 3–4.
18. Emmette S. Redford, *Democracy in the Administrative State* (New York: Oxford University Press, 1969), 66.
19. Al Gore, *Common Sense Government Works Better & Costs Less* (Washington, D.C.: Government Printing Office, no date [1995]), 19.
20. Walter Dean Burnham, "The Turnout Problem," in Pietro Nivola and David Rosenbloom, eds., *Classic Readings in American Politics* (New York: St. Martin's, 1990), 125–155, especially 144, 150.
21. Ibid., 125.
22. Richard Morin, "Unconventional Wisdom," *Washington Post*, 8 October 1995, C5.

23. Richard Morin, "Reality Check: The Politics of Mistrust," *Washington Post*, 29 January 1996, A1, A6.
24. Al Gore, *From Red Tape to Results: Creating a Government That Works Better & Costs Less* (Washington, D.C.: Government Printing Office, 1993), 1. In 1991, the figure was 49 cents on the dollar; Dan Balz and Richard Morin, "A Tide of Pessimism and Political Powerlessness Rises," *Washington Post*, 3 November 1991.
25. Gore, *From Red Tape to Results*, 1; Steven Pearlstein, "Reality Check: The Politics of Mistrust," *Washington Post*, 30 January 1996, A1, A5.
26. Balz and Morin, "A Tide of Pessimism."
27. Pearlstein, "Reality Check: The Politics of Mistrust," A5.
28. Alliance for Redesigning Government/National Academy of Public Administration, *The Public Innovator*, no. 28, 11 May 1995, 2.
29. Ibid., 4.
30. Charles Reich, "The New Property," *Yale Law Journal* 73 (1964): 733.
31. Ibid., 746.
32. Milton Friedman, *Capitalism and Freedom* (Chicago: University of Chicago Press, 1962), 8–9.
33. Reich, "The New Property," 747.
34. See David H. Rosenbloom, *Federal Service and the Constitution* (Ithaca, N.Y.: Cornell University Press, 1971), chap. 6.
35. Ralph S. Brown, Jr., *Loyalty and Security* (New Haven, Conn.: Yale University Press, 1958), vii, 18, 377.
36. Friedrich A. Hayek, *The Road to Serfdom* (Chicago: University of Chicago Press, 1944).
37. Ibid.
38. Michael Fletcher, "Blacks Value Government, Poll Shows," *Washington Post*, 4 March 1996, A13.
39. Gore, *Common Sense Government*, 13–14.
40. Seymour M. Lipset and William Schneider, *The Confidence Gap: Business, Labor, and Government in the Public Mind* (New York: Free Press, 1983).
41. Pearlstein, "Reality Check: The Politics of Mistrust," A5.
42. Morin, "Reality Check: The Politics of Mistrust," A6.
43. Charles T. Goodsell, *The Case for Bureaucracy* (Chatham, N.J.: Chatham House, 1983), 29.
44. Ibid., 31.
45. Ibid., chap. 2.
46. Ibid., 37.
47. Katz et al., *Bureaucratic Encounters*, 186.
48. Ibid., 187.
49. Ibid., 116.
50. Ibid.
51. Thomas Miller and Michelle Miller, "Standards of Excellence: U.S. Residents' Evaluations of Local Government Services," *Public Administration Review* 51 (November/December 1991): 503–513.
52. Theodore Poister and Gary Henry, "Citizen Ratings of Public and Private Service Quality," *Public Administration Review* 54 (March/April 1994): 155–160.
53. Miller and Miller, "Standards of Excellence," 504.
54. Katz et al., *Bureaucratic Encounters*, 188.
55. *Wyatt v. Stickney*, 325 F. Supp. 781; 334 F. Supp. 1341 (1971); 344 F. Supp. 373; 344 F. Supp. 387 (1972); *Youngberg v. Romeo*, 451 U.S. 982 (1982).

56. Katz et al., *Bureaucratic Encounters*, chap. 2.

57. Bill Clinton and Al Gore, *Putting Customers First: Standards for Serving the American People* (Washington, D.C.: Government Printing Office, 1994), 5–7.

58. Gore, *Common Sense Government*, 14.

59. Clinton and Gore, *Putting Customers First*, 6.

60. Max Weber, *From Max Weber: Essays in Sociology*, trans. and ed. H. H. Gerth and C. W. Mills (New York: Oxford University Press, 1958), chap. 8.

61. See Samuel Krislov and David H. Rosenbloom, *Representative Bureaucracy and the American Political System* (New York: Praeger, 1981), chap. 5, for a brief review.

62. Richard Schwartz, "Public Participation and Democratic Decisionmaking: Clean Water for the Empire State?" Paper delivered at the Annual Meeting of the Society for the Study of Social Problems, Chicago, 14 August 1987.

63. Daniel P. Moynihan, *Maximum Feasible Misunderstanding* (New York: Free Press, 1970), 137.

64. William Morrow, *Public Administration* (New York: Random House, 1975), 198.

65. This term gained currency in the movement for a "new public administration." See Frank Marini, ed., *Toward a New Public Administration: The Minnowbrook Perspective* (Scranton, Pa.: Chandler, 1971).

66. Charles Levine, "Citizenship and Service Delivery: The Promise of Coproduction," *Public Administration Review* 44 (Special Issue, March 1984): 181.

67. Ibid., 185.

68. Ibid.

69. See Krislov and Rosenbloom, *Representative Bureaucracy*, 170–175.

70. Ibid., 172.

71. David H. Rosenbloom and Rosemary O'Leary, *Public Administration and Law*, 2d ed. (New York: Marcel Dekker, 1997), chaps. 2, 3, and 8.

72. David Mathews, "The Public in Practice and Theory," *Public Administration Review* 44 (Special Issue, March 1984): 120–125.

73. Woodrow Wilson, "The Study of Administration," *Political Science Quarterly* 56 (December 1941): 498 (originally published in 1887).

74. *Kolender v. Lawson*, 461 U.S. 352 (1983).

75. Wilson, "The Study of Administration," 499.

ADDITIONAL READING

Frederickson, H. George, and Ralph Clark Chandler, eds. "Citizenship and Public Administration," *Public Administration Review* 44 (Special Issue, March 1984): 97–204.

Goodsell, Charles. *The Case of Bureaucracy*, 3d ed. Chatham, N.J.: Chatham House, 1994.

Gore, Al. *Common Sense Government Works Better & Costs Less*. Washington, D.C.: Government Printing Office, no date [1995].

STUDY QUESTIONS

1. Consider a recent interaction you had with some aspect of public administration. How would you describe your role? What approach did the agency or official take toward you in that role? How satisfactory or unsatisfactory was the experience?

2. Do you find yourself to be like the public generally in expressing both criticism and praise of public administration? If so, how would you explain your evaluations of it? If not, what is your personal evaluation of public administration? How did you come by that evaluation?

3. How realistic do you think greater citizen participation in public administration is? Do you favor or oppose it? Why?

4. The National Performance Review indicates that many people are uneasy with the idea that the American people are customers of government. How appropriate do you find the term "customers"? Why?

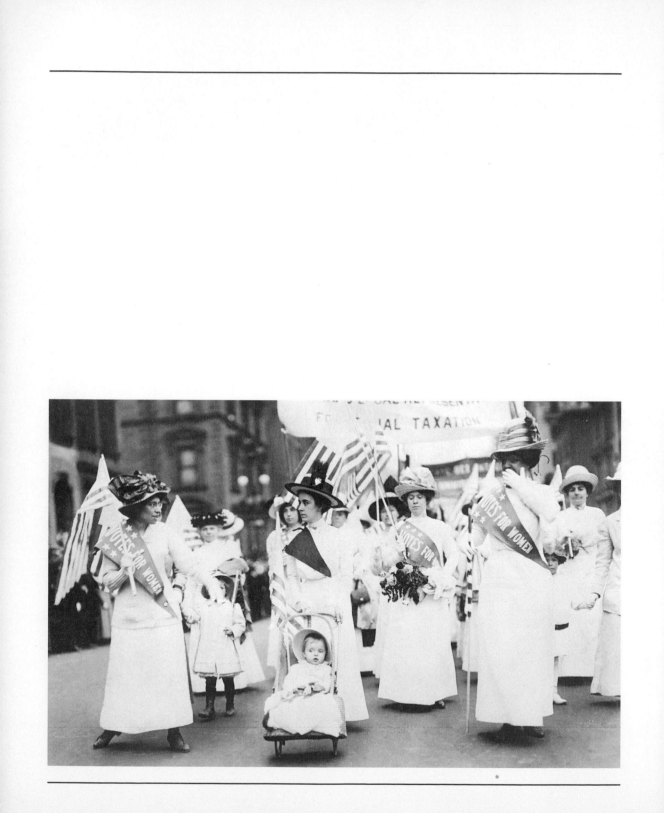

CHAPTER 11

Public Administration and Democratic Constitutionalism

This chapter explains why public administrators must understand constitutional values and discusses the nature of those values. Among the constitutional values considered are the separation of powers, legitimacy, diversity, liberty and freedom, property rights, procedural due process, equal protection, individuality and privacy, and equity. This chapter does not attempt to teach constitutional law per se but rather to explain the nature of these fundamental values in the context of public administration. It sets forth the general structure of several constitutional rights. The concept of state action, which has important implications for privatization and governmental efforts to operate corporate-style agencies, is also analyzed.

Our discussion of public administration's development, core functions, and processes makes it evident that there are times when the values of managerially and politically oriented public administration may be in pronounced conflict with the values and principles of democratic constitutionalism. There have been many instances in which public administrative action, taken in good faith and seeking to maximize values inherent in the traditional managerial and political approaches, has been declared unconstitutional by the courts. The new public management (NPM) is too new to have been subject to significant constitutional tests in court. However, the concept of state action, which is discussed later in the chapter, is particularly relevant to its interest in privatization, public-private partnerships, and corporatelike, performance-based organizations. So deep does the tension between constitutional arrangements and contemporary public administration run, that on one occasion the Chief Justice of the United States observed that, from the perspectives of the modern administrative state, "The choices we discern as having been made in the Constitutional Convention impose burdens on governmental processes that often seem clumsy, inefficient, even unworkable. . . ."[1] Looking at the same problem of the tension between public administration and democratic constitutionalism from the perspective of public administration, Dwight Waldo, one of this century's leading administrative theorists, contended that "It *cannot be solved*—acceptably, workably—given our constitutional system, our constitutional history, and our democratic ideology. All we can hope for is piecemeal solutions, temporary agreements."[2] The objective of this chapter is to provide the beginnings of such a piecemeal solution by imparting an understanding of the nature of the conflicts and tensions between public administration and democratic constitutionalism. A comprehensive appreciation of these conflicts and tensions is an absolute prerequisite to determining how to take public administrative action that both is constitutional and maximizes appropriate managerial and political values. Our approach to this subject will emphasize the fundamental principles and values of the Constitution rather than immediate interpretations of its specific clauses or the historical development of its doctrines. In the process, we will outline the general structure of substantive, procedural, Fourth Amendment privacy, and equal protection rights under contemporary constitutional law.

WHY PUBLIC ADMINISTRATORS MUST UNDERSTAND THE CONSTITUTION

Until recent years, it would have been rare to find a chapter in a text on public administration devoted to a discussion of "democratic constitutionalism." It was frequently taken as a given that Woodrow Wilson was correct when he observed that for the most part the concerns of public administration were far removed from the concerns of framing and amending the Constitution. He saw the two endeavors as so separate that he claimed it was getting to be harder to run (that is, administer) a constitution than to frame one.[3] Today, however, judicial involvement in public administration is so pronounced and the legal approach so strong that the need for public administrators to understand the Constitution is almost self-evident. There are four aspects of the relationship between public administration and the Constitution that should be emphasized in this regard.

First, as Woodrow Wilson indicated, the principles on which to base a sound public administration in the United States "must be principles which have democratic policy very much at heart."[4] But public administration cannot be based on these principles unless it understands them and appreciates their worth. It is difficult to contest seriously the view that the ultimate object for public administration in the United States is a combination of the values of the managerial and political approaches that is fully compatible with constitutional principles and values. This is something that all public administrators should be working toward.

Second, many, perhaps most, public administrators take an oath to support the Constitution. Cynics may dismiss this as a pro forma requirement, utterly devoid of any significant content. However, they may be dismissing this requirement too easily. Upholding the Constitution might be considered more important than routine administrative functions because it is connected to the moral principle that a public office is a "public trust." Moreover, the polity is unlikely to judge administrative action that violates the Constitution as desirable (see Box 11–1). A breach of the oath can constitute perjury, which may be punishable by criminal or other penalties.

Third, as discussed earlier in Chapters 1 and 5, many public administrators are now personally liable in civil suits for damages when they violate the constitutional rights of individuals or groups. Their action violating such rights may also subject them to punitive damages. These damages may be assessed at the amount a jury considers adequate to punish the public administrator and to deter others from taking similar action.[5] In the process of redefining the liability of public administrators at all levels of government, the Supreme Court has arrived at the general standard that the public administrator can be personally sued for damages if he or she knew or reasonably should have known that his or her action would be in violation of others' constitutional rights. Reasonable knowledge of the constitutional rights of the people upon whom public administrators act has become a key aspect of the public administrator's job and competence in the eyes of the judiciary. If for no other reason, public administrators need to understand the Constitution in order to protect their pocketbooks from civil suits for damages.

Fourth, and more generally, there has been a new interest in "constitutional literacy" in the public service. Constance Horner, former director of the Office of Personnel Management, promoted the idea as follows:

We may often disagree about what our shared commitment to constitutional values requires—what liberty or equality or justice demands in any given instance. But discourse about those principles should be the unique, common language of the

57 Cal.Rptr. 623
Benny Max PARRISH Plantiff
and Appellant,
v.
The CIVIL SERVICE COMMISSION OF the
COUNTY OF ALAMEDA, etc., et al.,
Defendants and Respondents.
S.F. 22429.
Supreme Court of California,
En Banc
March 27, 1967.

Mandamus proceeding to compel reinstatement of county social worker after his discharge for insubordination. The Superior Court, Alameda County, Wayne P. Burke, J., entered judgment denying petition, and petitioner appealed. The Supreme Court, Tobriner, J., held that where county failed to secure legally effective consent to search homes of welfare recipients, through early morning mass raids to determine welfare eligibility, and, even if effective consent had been obtained, county could not constitutionally condition continued receipt of welfare benefits upon giving such consent, such raids, in which county directed social worker to take part, transgressed constitutional limitations, and thus social worker, in light of his knowledge as to scope and methods of projected raids, possessed adequate grounds for declining to participate and could not properly be found guilty of insubordination warranting his discharge.

Reversed and cause remanded with directions.

McComb, J., dissented.

Opinion, Cal.App., 51 Cal.Rptr. 589, vacated.

John R. HARLEY
v.
SCHUYLKILL COUNTY et al.
Civ. A. No. 78-861
United States District Court,
E. D. Pennsylvania.
Aug. 23, 1979.

Discharged prison guard filed civil rights suit against county and warden, alleging that his discharge was wrongful in that it was a deprivation of his liberty interest without according him due process, constituted a violation of his First Amendment rights, was based on his refusal to perform an unconstitutional act, and constituted a violation of rights secured under the Pennsylvania Constitution. On a defense motion to dismiss, the District Court, Huyett, J., held that: (1) the right to refuse to perform an unconstitutional act is a right "secured by the Constitution" within the meaning of the Civil Rights Act of 1871; accordingly, in the instant case, prison guard had the right to refrain from performing an act, ordered by the warden, which would have deprived prisoner of his constitutional rights, and (2) a county is liable for acts of its employees which violate Article 1, Section 1 of the Pennsylvania Constitution, where those employees are acting within the scope of their official duties.

Motion denied.

Federal executive. Literacy in these concepts and ideas—constitutional literacy—can help unify and vivify the Federal executive corps. From many professions, it can make one vocation.[6]

Put somewhat differently, public administrators are charged with promoting the public interest. In our system, that requires a commitment to doing so within the framework of the Constitution, which is the supreme law of the land.

Unfortunately, understanding the Constitution is easier said than done. We alluded to this problem in Chapter 1. As far as the public administrator is concerned, the Constitution must be considered a set of values and principles that far exceeds the specific holdings found in past judicial decisions. The case law provides only part of the understanding that is necessary, because the Constitution is largely a document of the imagination. Its current requirements go well beyond its specific language. Rather, those requirements are derived from legal, philosophical, moral, and political considerations as to how the Constitution should be applied in a variety of contemporary circumstances very much unforeseen by the Founders. For example, some of the principles we will consider in this chapter are the notions of "chilling effect," "least restrictive alternative," and the "three-tier structure" of equal protection. Each of these principles is absolutely critical to an understanding of the Constitution today, but none can actually be found in the words of that document. In addition, some very fundamental constitutional rights, such as the right to personal privacy and the right to travel among the states, are derived from the principles and values of the Constitution, rather than specifically enumerated within it.

The broad and unspecific quality of the Constitution can be quite frustrating to those who seek to understand it and model their administrative conduct accordingly. Sometimes it is best to think of the Constitution as a body of values and principles that are inherent in the nation's political culture, social ethos, and history. These values and principles are not articulated all at once. Rather, the courts declare what they are when the proper occasions arise. Such an occasion is one that presents the circumstances in a framework that is suitable for adjudication and develops the constitutional issues with adequate clarity. In most cases where there is a real and protracted dispute over what the Constitution requires, the Supreme Court will be the final judicial arbiter. Its members will follow their consciences and philosophical and political views in interpreting what the words, principles, values, and previous constitutional decisions require in any particular set of circumstances.[7]

At the same time, of course, the justices and judges are not free to "rewrite" or even reinterpret the Constitution at will. There are checks on the courts and the questions they address are framed by the litigation before them, just as the answers they provide are partly framed by past precedents and previous considerations of the nature of constitutional values and principles. Few judges and constitutional scholars truly believe that the Constitution should (or could) be interpreted solely from the perspectives of the Framers' "original intent"—especially because the Fourteenth Amendment (1868) radically extended the Constitution's constraints to state and local governments. But, by the same token, few believe that the "original intent" is irrelevant to present interpretations.

Constitutional law derived in this way has certainly had its oddities over the years. Sometimes one decision is overturned by another within a period of but a few years.[8] Sometimes the incremental declaration of constitutional requirements leads to peculiarities. For instance, in 1922, the Supreme Court ruled that professional baseball was beyond the scope of the commerce clause because it was a matter of personal effort rather than commercial production. It reiterated this view in 1953, though certainly by then judicial interpretation had broadened the commerce clause enough to reach professional sports. Subsequently, the Court held that the federal government could regulate boxing (1955) and football (1957). However, in 1972, it adhered to its earlier rulings regarding baseball, saying that if Congress wanted federal antitrust laws to apply to the national pastime, it would have to say so specifically![9]

Despite its abstract qualities and quirks, the great virtue of the United States' system of constitutional law is that it enables the polity to adapt the fundamental values and principles of an eighteenth-century document to continually changing political, economic, social, international, and environmental circumstances. Moreover, it helps the society maintain a good deal of political consensus on those fundamental principles and values. As a result, rather than trying to govern itself through the "dead hand of the past," the United States has a written, but also a "living," constitution. And, without a doubt, public administration is now a part of it.

We now turn to a discussion of those fundamental principles and values that are most salient to public administrators.

ADMINISTRATIVE STRUCTURE AND CONSTITUTIONAL STRUCTURE

Both public administrative and constitutional doctrine advocate the separation of functions among different structural units, such as agencies, bureaus, or branches of government. However, there are crucial differences. When following the managerial approaches, public administrative agencies place different functions in different units for the sake of specialization and the efficiency, economy, effectiveness, and customer service that is derived from the division of labor. When the political approach dictates the organization of agencies, it is likely that the separation of functions goes by policy area or clientele group and is intended to enhance administrative representativeness and political responsiveness.

The Constitution, on the other hand, seeks to separate powers—legislative, executive, and judicial—for the sake of creating checks and balances that safeguard against authoritarian or tyrannical government. As James

Madison explained in the *Federalist Papers*, the combination of legislative, executive, and judicial power in the same hands could be considered the very essence of tyranny. He also explained that the system of checks and balances was intended to provide "great security against a gradual concentration of the several powers in the same department [i.e., branch of government] . . .[by] giving to those who administer each department the necessary constitutional means and personal motives to resist encroachment of the others."[10] Hence, the different terms of office and modes of election or appointment of members of each house of Congress, the president, and the judiciary. But, as Chief Justice Burger pointed out, it is precisely this system that sometimes makes the federal government seem cumbersome and even unworkable in the contemporary administrative age.

In an effort to try to overcome the slow and cumbersome quality of government according to the separation of powers and checks and balances, since the 1930s the United States has increasingly vested combinations of legislative, executive, and judicial functions in individual administrative agencies. In other words, there has been a tendency to *collapse* the functions of the three constitutional branches into the federal bureaucracy. Regulatory commissions are the clearest example of agencies that engage in legislative functions (rule making), executive activities (implementation and enforcement), and judicial roles (adjudication). Although many criticize bureaucracy for its slow and lumbering qualities, historically, public administration has been viewed as more flexible than government strictly according to the constitutional separation of powers as originally designed. For instance, agency rule making and rescision of rules is far simpler, and generally much quicker, than Congress's legislating. Unlike the House and Senate, individual agencies are unified and coordinated by hierarchy to a very large extent. Agency adjudication is usually faster and more flexible than litigation before the judiciary.

The "collapsing" of the separation of powers into the administrative branch has both administrative and constitutional consequences. Among the most important is that public administrators can be held responsible to each of the three constitutional branches. Aside from serving the public, many federal administrators serve three masters, not one: Congress, the president, and the federal judiciary. Because public administrators exercise functions originally assigned to each of the three constitutional branches, it is to be expected that each of those branches will be concerned about the way those functions are performed. As Madison noted, each of these sets of actors has a different term of office, a different constitutional role, and different interests. Sometimes this has the effect of complicating public administration to the point of exasperation.

One concrete example of this problem was presented in the case of *American Federation of Government Employees v. Phillips* (1973).[11] Phillips was acting director of the Office of Economic Opportunity (OEO). Upon hearing the president's budgetary message, which indicated that the president intended to eliminate OEO and would not seek any additional funding for it, Phillips began to cut back on spending the appropriations previously granted for the then current fiscal year. (Remember, the budgetary message is for the next fiscal year, and does not directly affect the current one.) In Phillips's view, it seemed wasteful and administratively inappropriate to spend money for a program that was likely to come to a screeching halt at the end of the fiscal year. Some of the funds had been earmarked for projects and perhaps equipment that were intended to be of long-run utility. Sinking more funds into start-up projects with no future would be pointless. However, Phillips's cutbacks were opposed by the American Federation of Government Employees, a labor union, because they would eliminate the jobs of some of its members. Intended beneficiaries of some of the previously planned projects also opposed the cutbacks. But Phillips considered himself to be responsible to the president and to be engaging in sound, economizing, public administration.

Phillips's view was deemed inappropriate by a circuit court of appeals. It reasoned that Phillips should not have defined his responsibilities so narrowly. First, he had a legal obligation to spend funds already allotted by Congress. His responsibility was to the law and legislature in this regard. Second, because the president's budgetary message was only a *message*, having no binding quality on Congress, Phillips was wrong to take direction from it. After all, Congress could allocate funds to OEO even though the president was opposed. The separation of powers and checks and balances gives the legislature a critical role in budgeting—that of passing bills authorizing the spending of federal funds. Congress has different constituencies from the president, and it might have a different political outlook on the desirability of OEO. The constitutional world of public administration was far more complicated than Phillips thought.

On the one hand, it is easy to see Phillips's mistake. On the other, was he really wrong in not wanting to spend money for projects that were likely to be abandoned and were unlikely to do much good unless continued for a long period of time? One lesson here is that "democracy is not cheap."[12] The costs of the separation of powers may seem irrational in terms of managerially oriented public administration, but from a constitutional perspective they are thought to be fully justified.

The separation of powers complicates public administration by frequently making it responsible to more than one branch of government and by pulling it in different directions at once, as in *Phillips*. These tendencies often make it difficult for agencies to maximize the values of either the managerial or political approaches to public administration. The unity of structure and control sought by the traditional managerial approach is easily frustrated by the effects of the separation of powers. The representativeness and responsiveness sought by the political approach become muddled when more than one constitutional actor, each having different motives and interests, becomes involved in public administration. The effect may be frustrating from virtually all perspectives.

The irony of constitutional structure is that by placing several masters over public administration, in practice, it may provide public administrators with none. (Recall *Morrison v. Olson*, Box 1–1, in which a Department of

Justice employee with prosecutorial functions was appointed by a court and, by statute, could not be fired by the president or the attorney general except for specific—and very limited—causes.) The efforts of the constitutional branches of government to control the administrative branch are sometimes frustrated by the Constitution itself. But the very same Constitution and system of separation of powers and checks and balances can also frustrate administrative action that is informed by sound administrative values and theories.

There are different conclusions to draw from this irony. One is that public administrators should try to play one constitutional branch off against another in a quest for independence and autonomy. Another is that because the Constitution itself does not establish a fully adequate system of practical control by the constitutional branches over public administrators, administrators' obligations to the Constitution must be augmented by a more direct responsibility to uphold its fundamental values and principles. This is precisely what Article VI of the Constitution requires: "The Senators and Representatives before mentioned, and the Members of the several State Legislatures, and all executive and judicial Officers, both of the United States and several States, shall be bound by Oath or Affirmation, to support this Constitution. . . ." The need to understand constitutional principles and values is evident.

CONSTITUTIONAL VALUES

Legitimacy

There is a stark contrast between the bases of legitimacy on which democratic constitutionalism rests and those values in the managerial and political approaches that are seen as legitimizing public administrative activity. Legitimacy in this context can be thought of as the population's belief that public administrators have a right to help make and implement public policy and to exercise political authority and discretion. Legitimacy is extremely important because it strongly fosters voluntary compliance or obedience to administrative directives and decisions. In its absence, political communities rely more on authoritarian or highly coercive processes, often involving the use of physical force or even terror by the government against the population.

According to the traditional managerial approach, the legitimacy of public administrators' authority is derived from their politically neutral technical competence, their specialized expertise, and the rationality and law-bound quality of their processes. Following Max Weber, sometimes this is referred to as legitimacy based on the rational/legal quality of administrative operations.[13] The NPM holds that performance—especially customer satisfaction—will legitimize public administrative action. The political approach seeks to base administrative legitimacy on the representativeness, responsiveness, and accountability of public administrators and agencies. The Constitution has a somewhat different emphasis. It promotes the principle that governmental legitimacy, including that involving the exercise of administrative power, rests upon the consent of the governed. The Framers provided that the Constitution itself would have to be ratified by special conventions in the states, rather than by the state legislatures. This would assure that the Constitution rest on popular consent, rather than on the consent of state governments. The Constitution also guarantees that each state will have a republican form of government. But consent, in this context, is not merely the agreement of a majority. An extraordinary majority may be required, as in the case of amending the Constitution or approval of treaties by the Senate. Moreover, constitutional principles and values seek to protect the fundamental rights of minorities from encroachment by majorities. In this sense, consent of the governed is intended to include even those groups or individuals that find themselves at odds with the majority of citizens. Their consent, too, is to be valued.

At this juncture, the differences between constitutional theory, on the one hand, and the managerial and political perspectives, on the other, are profound and reach to the very core of the concepts upon which the political system is based. Constitutional theory views the government as an outgrowth of a *contract* formed by "We the People." The contract, which is the Constitution, fixes limits on governmental power, as in the First Amendment's prohibition on "an establishment of religion." The managerial and political perspectives are less contractarian than utilitarian in their fundamental premises. They tend to favor the legitimization of governmental action on the basis of the greatest good for the greatest number, or on a similar formulation of that principle which is often incorporated into their conceptions of the public interest. In practice, they tend to view legitimacy as based on performance rather than on adherence to the contractual terms of the Constitution alone. For both managerial perspectives, such performance is efficient, economical, and effective government. The NPM adds responsiveness to customers. For the political approach, performance is viewed in terms of the representativeness, political responsiveness, and accountability of government to organized constituencies and/or to a majority of the people.

West Virginia State Board of Education v. Barnette (1943)[14] serves as an example of these fundamental differences regarding legitimacy. The case involved a public school system's requirement that all students salute and pledge allegiance to the flag. The political and administrative rationale for the regulation was that it would promote feelings of loyalty toward the United States and a feeling of political community among students. The regulation was enforced with a two-pronged strategy. Students who refused to salute and say the pledge were expelled. If they were not placed in suitable private schools, their parents could face criminal charges for the truancy of their school-age children. This was obviously a heavy-handed strategy, but it could be considered effective and efficient. Given the potential penalties, it was likely that the pupils would at least say the pledge and possibly develop the proper feelings of patriotism. Politically, the measure was probably quite popular. It was wartime, patriotism and loyalty were considered desirable if not essential sentiments, and a majority of the state's population no doubt strongly supported the promotion of such feelings in the schools. Moreover, refusal to salute the flag and say the pledge could be taken as a sign of disrespect for the nation, the majority of citizens who supported it, and the armed forces who were risking their lives and sustaining heavy casualties to protect its liberty and independence. However, one group of citizens was opposed to the salute and pledge. These were the Jehovah's Witnesses, who believed that engaging in the salute and pledge showed disrespect for their God and therefore violated their religion. Despite a decision just three years earlier to the contrary, the Supreme Court held that the compulsory flag salute and pledge violated the rights of a minority not only in terms of their religious freedom, but also because it tended to compel their support (consent) for the political system. In Justice Jackson's eloquent words, "If there is any fixed star in our constitutional constellation, it is that no official, high or petty, can prescribe what shall be orthodox in politics, nationalism, religion, or other matters of opinion or force citizens to confess by word or act their faith therein. If there are any circumstances which permit an exception, they do not now occur to us." The compulsory salute and pledge were unconstitutional because they compelled consent, something wholly antithetical to the Constitution's approach to governmental legitimacy.

Diversity among the Citizenry

One of the most outstanding conflicts between traditional managerially oriented public administration and constitutional values concerns the desirability of uniformity as opposed to diversity. The traditional managerial perspective strongly supports uniformity in a broad range of administrative contexts. It relies on impersonality among public employees to assure that individual diversity in interpreting regulations and implementing programs is eliminated to the extent practicable. Max Weber saw this as the special virtue of bureaucracy and, accordingly, viewed bureaucrats as "cogs."[15] In related fashion, clients are turned into "cases," which can often be treated impersonally, and therefore, with relative uniformity. These aspects of the traditional managerial approach were discussed in greater detail in Chapter 1. By contrast, the Constitution values diversity to a great extent. In some ways, the entire design of the constitutional scheme rests on the desire to maintain and promote diversity. Thus, in *Federalist Paper No. 10*, James Madison argued that a large, extended republican form of government would necessarily include so much social and economic diversity as to preclude the development of a majority faction, that is, majority political group that was united by a common interest that was adverse to the good of the nation as a whole. In fact, he considered fostering diversity to be the first object of government. Additionally, the Constitution incorporates diversity in the sense of federalism, bicameralism, separation of powers, different modes of election and appointment for the constitutional branches, and different terms of office. This is partly intended to assure that the government will not be subject to complete overturn at the hands of a majority united only for a brief time by a common interest or passion.

The political approach to public administration tends to fall in between those two poles on the continuum from uniformity to diversity. It favors diversity to a considerable extent, but has a tendency to try to eliminate groups thought to be politically marginal because of their limited power and deviation from the nation's political, economic, and social mainstream. It also attempts to silence individuals whose opinions are considered dangerous to the political system. For example, the Communist party and its members have been subjected to a number of regulations and restrictions in public employment, labor union affairs, and other aspects of life, the application of which has never even been considered with regard to the Democratic or Republican parties or their members. On the other hand, the political approach seeks diversity in public administration as a means of providing representation and responsiveness to politically "acceptable" groups, such as farmers, union members, social groups, and trade associations. The NPM also rejects the traditional managerial perspective's "one size fits all" approach. It values individualized customer service, but does not appear to have a strong commitment to diversity per se.

Many Supreme Court decisions emphasize the constitutional value of diversity. For instance, in *Barnette* discussed earlier, the Supreme Court pointed out that although the promotion of national unity is permissible, "individual freedom of mind" should be given preference to "officially disciplined uniformity" because history shows that "[t]hose who begin coercive elimination of dissent soon find themselves exterminating dissenters. Compulsory unification of opinion achieves only the unanimity of the graveyard." *Keyishian v. Board of Regents* (1967) presents another example.[16] There, a complicated New York State scheme for excluding persons with subversive ideas from its educational system was under challenge. The U.S. Supreme Court held that the regulations were too imprecise to withstand constitutional scrutiny because they excluded individuals who were not subversive as well as those who were. In the course of its ruling, the Court pointed out that

> our Nation is deeply committed to safeguarding academic freedom, which is of transcendent value to all of us and not merely to the teachers concerned. That freedom is therefore a special concern of the First Amendment, which does not tolerate laws that cast a pall of orthodoxy over the classroom. . . . The classroom is peculiarly the "marketplace of ideas." The Nation's future depends upon leaders trained through wide exposure to that robust exchange of ideas which discovers truth "out of a multitude of tongues, [rather] than through any kind of authoritative selection."

According to this articulation of constitutional values and principles, diversity is absolutely critical to the nation's future. (See Box 11–2 for another test of constitutional values, this one involving freedom of religion.)

Freedom and Liberty

Constitutional values obviously place a very great emphasis on individual freedom and liberty. According to one view of constitutional theory, perhaps

---

BOX 11–2 Putting Constitutional Values in Public Administration: Public School and the Santería Faith

---

The Santería faith is a centuries-old African religion that originated with the Yoruba tribe of Nigeria and was brought to the Caribbean by slaves. About 50,000 people in southern Florida practice the religion, which involves initiation rights lasting three to four weeks. Initiation as a priestess takes place when the high priest determines it is time; it does not depend on age. A schoolgirl, whose age was given as eight or nine, missed a month of public school to undergo initiation rites. The Dade County (Florida) School Board has a policy that five or more unexcused absences in a semester precludes granting a student credit for classes. The school board first questioned whether the Santería faith could be considered a religion and then whether the pupil could be given initiation during the summer when classes were not in session. It received a legal opinion from an attorney to the effect that, "in this instance, the compulsory attendance laws must give way to the freedom of religion laws. We have concluded that an absence of up to a month is a religious necessity when a person is being initiated into the priesthood of the Santería." The board decided to excuse the absence and allow the girl to make up the schoolwork she missed. As another school board attorney put it, "You can't change Christmas to the weekend just because it doesn't fall on Sunday."

SOURCE: "School Case Backs an Ancient Ritual," *New York Times*, 9 December 1984.

---

the dominant view, individual freedom and liberty are antecedent to the Constitution. Because freedom and liberty existed before the creation of the constitutional government in 1789, they are provided both specific and general protections against governmental encroachment in the Bill of Rights. The Ninth Amendment in particular makes this point: "The enumeration in the Constitution, of certain rights, shall not be construed to deny or disparage others retained by the people." Rights to freedom and liberty therefore do not come from the Constitution, they are merely recognized by it as aspects of life that lie outside the legitimate realm of the exercise of governmental power. Such fundamental rights, following the Declaration of Independence, are often considered **natural rights:** "We hold these truths to be self-evident, that all men are created equal, that they are endowed by their Creator with certain unalienable Rights, that among these are Life, Liberty and the pursuit of Happiness." This is not to say they are "absolute"; they can be abridged or infringed when the government has an overriding, compelling need to do so. But the burden will fall upon the government to show that it does, in fact, have such a need and that the means chosen are the least damaging to the exercise of protected rights.

This approach is frequently at odds with public administration in either the traditional managerial or political perspectives. Public administration, as we have seen, provides both services and constraints. It is often involved in direct or indirect regulation and consequently enforces limits on the freedom and liberty of individuals. Such constraints, of course, are considered in the public interest as they are generally intended to promote the public's security, safety, health, welfare, and/or the political and economic viability of the nation. The conflict between constitutional values and principles on the one side and public administration on the other, therefore, is typically over means, not ends. This is likely to be true of NPM administration as well because it is not oriented toward individual rights or due process, which it views as overly regulatory.

There are many dramatic examples of this conflict over appropriate means. The *Keyishian* decision, reviewed above, is one. The Supreme Court had little quarrel with the state's overall objective of barring subversive teachers from the public educational system. The issue was over the means, which the Court found inappropriate because they compromised individual freedoms and liberty too much. A very intriguing additional example can be found in *Shelton v. Tucker* (1960).[17] There, the Supreme Court declared unconstitutional an Arkansas statute requiring every teacher, as a condition of employment in a state-supported school or college, to file "annually an affidavit listing without limitation every organization to which he has belonged or regularly contributed within the preceding five years." The state's purpose in seeking this information was somewhat unclear. The act was based on the desire "to provide assistance in the administration and financing of the public schools" and to help resolve problems involved in responding to the Supreme Court's school desegregation decisions. There was no stated desire to fire teachers based on their organizational affiliations, and it appears that only refusal to submit the affidavit would be clear cause for action against the employee. In other words, on the face of it at least, all the state wanted was to know to which organizations its teachers belonged. On the other hand, there was some reason to believe that teachers belonging to the NAACP might be victimized as a result of the regulation. Although it recognized that the state had a legitimate interest in promoting the fitness and competence of its teachers, the Court found that the act placed too much of a strain on the right to freedom of association which, in the Court's words, "lies at the foundation of a free society." This was because the "breadth" of abridgment of constitutional rights "must be viewed in the light of less drastic means for achieving the same basic purpose." Less drastic and more appropriate means, in this case, for promoting competence and fitness could have been to ask certain teachers or even all teachers about *certain* of their organizational affiliations, or about the number of organizations to which they belonged. But to ask *every* teacher about *every* organization was simply too great an impairment of teachers' freedom of association.

The *Shelton* case is pertinent because it illustrates three constitutional principles relating to freedom and liberty that serve as constraints on public administrative action:

1. *Chilling effect.* Although the regulation involved did not prohibit or punish association, it had the tendency to deter the free exercise of the

right to association. This was particularly true because the statute did not prohibit public disclosure and placed heavy "pressure upon a teacher to avoid any ties which might displease those who control his professional destiny. . . ." In other words, the teacher's ardor for freedom of association would be "chilled."

2. *Overbreadth*. As noted above, a regulation that abridges or chills one's exercise of constitutional rights must be narrowly drawn so that it does not unnecessarily infringe upon legitimate activity. A regulation is overly broad if, in the process of legitimately constraining some activities, it gratuitously infringes on others protected by the Constitution. In *Shelton*, for example, if the state were concerned that some of its teachers belonged to so many organizations that they did not have enough time left to devote to the proper performance of their professional duties, it could have simply inquired about the number of associations with which the teachers were affiliated. If the state were concerned about membership in certain organizations, it could have asked directly about those, although it would need a strong governmental interest for doing so. Its scheme, however, had the tendency to deter membership in legitimate organizations for fear of public disclosure or reprisal by the state's educational system.

3. *The least restrictive alternative*. Overbreadth deters the exercise of legitimate rights on which the government has no compelling need or reason to place restrictions. The least restrictive alternative principle accepts the state's legitimate need to deal with an area of behavior, but requires that the state do so in the fashion that constitutes the least practicable infringement on protected rights. In other words, in *Shelton*, could the state have found a means of promoting competence and fitness that was less of an invasion of constitutionally protected freedom of association? From the traditional managerial perspective, the answer is "yes, but"—it could prove to be expensive, inefficient, and time-consuming. For instance, one alternative that would be very much less restrictive would have been to identify teachers whose competence and fitness were marginal, and then inquire of those teachers only whether they had extensive organizational affiliations that were diverting their attention from their professional performance. To do so, however, would require elaborate administrative means of measuring fitness and competence and hearings or investigations to ascertain the amount of time and nature of commitment a teacher devoted to his or her organizational memberships. From a managerial perspective, it was more satisfactory to achieve this in reverse: find the organizations to which every teacher belongs, and then identify teachers whose performance might be improved if they abandoned some of their affiliations.

The principles of "chilling effect," "overbreadth," and "least restrictive alternative" have emerged in a great number of cases involving the constitutionality of public administrative action. Consequently, it is important to emphasize that for the public administrator who seeks to adhere to constitutional values, they are guides rather than barriers to effective action. They do not prohibit the attainment of legitimate ends through public administrative action. Rather, they stand for the general view that freedom and liberty are so valuable that they should not be compromised more than is absolutely necessary to accomplish such an end.

Concerns with chilling effects, overbreadth, and the least restrictive alternative are part of the general structure of substantive constitutional rights, such as freedom of speech, assembly, and exercise of religion. Saying that rights have a structure is intended to convey the idea that there are a series of "if-then" statements one ordinarily asks about government practices that are challenged on constitutional grounds. Further, although judges and justices come and go, and they disagree with one another as to whether specific practices are constitutional or not, they all tend to apply the same structure when analyzing the cases before them.

The typical structure of substantive constitutional rights is presented in Box 11–3. The initial question is whether a governmental practice infringes on an individual's constitutional rights, even indirectly, as in the case of chilling effects. If not, of course, there is no violation of the Constitution. If so, however, the next question is whether the practice tightly serves any government interest. Overbreadth is of concern here because it prohibits more than

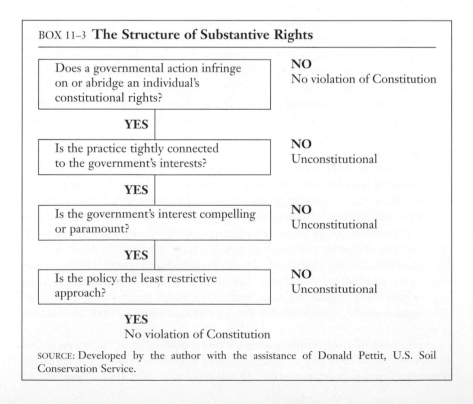

BOX 11–3 **The Structure of Substantive Rights**

Does a governmental action infringe on or abridge an individual's constitutional rights?

NO
No violation of Constitution

YES

Is the practice tightly connected to the government's interests?

NO
Unconstitutional

YES

Is the government's interest compelling or paramount?

NO
Unconstitutional

YES

Is the policy the least restrictive approach?

NO
Unconstitutional

YES
No violation of Constitution

SOURCE: Developed by the author with the assistance of Donald Pettit, U.S. Soil Conservation Service.

is necessary to serve the government's interests in a rational way. If the practice does not serve a governmental interest, then the infringement on rights is gratuitous and therefore unconstitutional. If it does serve such interests, it may still be unconstitutional unless it serves one that is compelling, or of the utmost importance to the political system (such as national security). Even then, the practice will be considered unconstitutional if it is not the least restrictive way of achieving the government's compelling interest. For public administrators, it is important to remember that, in most circumstances, efficiency, economy, and administrative convenience, as important as they are managerially, are not considered compelling interests by the courts.

Property Rights

Property, like liberty, is highly valued by the Constitution. In fact, the due process clauses of the Fifth and Fourteenth Amendments rank life, liberty, and property alongside one another and afford them all protection from arbitrary, invidious, or capricious governmental encroachment. Like liberty, property has frequently been considered anterior to the formation of the constitutional government. Property and property rights existed prior to 1789 and the adoption of the Constitution is not typically seen as infringing on them. On the contrary, the Constitution is generally viewed as affording them governmental protection. In the past, political theorists sometimes considered "liberty" and "property" as almost interchangeable or codeterminate. For example, James Madison once wrote that property exists not only in land and possessions but also in opinions, religious principles, and general liberty.[18] Moreover, he viewed property as an important factor in the development of individual personality and political preferences. As in the case of liberty, though, property rights are not absolute: Private property can be taken for public use, although just compensation should be provided. Similarly, searches and seizures of personal property can be undertaken by government, but only after a warrant is issued or the circumstances are such that there is constitutionally sufficient reason for them.

Historically, public administration has from time to time encroached upon established property rights, as in the case of zoning regulations that control the use of property so severely that they "take" it from the owners. In 1994, the Supreme Court established a new framework for the "takings clause" that raises concerns for public administrators, especially those in local and state governments. *Dolan v. City of Tigard*[19] involved what had come to be a typical way of getting private actors to produce public goods. Florence Dolan wanted to expand her plumbing and electrical supply store and its parking lot. Pursuant to its interests in controlling flooding and traffic congestion, the city offered Dolan the necessary building permit on condition that she dedicate about 10 percent of her property to a pedestrian/bicycle pathway. She was not offered compensation for the dedication. The Supreme Court held that a condition constitutes an unconstitutional taking unless it can pass a two-part test. First, there must be a nexus (or connection) between a legitimate governmental interest and the conditions imposed on the property owner. Second, there must be "rough proportionality" between the dedication required and the impact of the proposed changes in the owner's use of the property. The Court put the burden on the government to make the latter calculation quantitatively on an individualized, case-by-case basis—something the city had failed to do in this instance. Box 11–4 presents the general structure of the takings clause in such cases.

During the 1960s and 1970s, the idea took hold that governmental benefits (or largess), such as welfare payments, occupational licenses, and public housing, should be considered a form of "new property" and afforded constitutional protection.[20] This was a revolutionary development with major ramifications for public administration. Perhaps no case made this clearer than *Goldberg v. Kelly* (1970).[21] The issue was whether New York City could terminate welfare benefits to an individual without first affording him or her a full evidentiary hearing. The city did provide seven days' prior notice and an opportunity to respond in writing. For a majority on the Supreme Court, however, more due process was required. In the course of its opinion, the Court observed that "it may be realistic today to regard welfare entitlements as more like 'property' than a 'gratuity.' Much of the existing wealth in this country takes the form of rights that do not fall within the traditional common-law concepts of property." The emergence of this "new property" interpretation is made clear by Justice Black's vigorous dissent: "The Court . . . in effect says

BOX 11–4 **The Structure of Property Owner's Land Use Rights Under the "Takings Clause"**

Does a governmental action have implications for an owner's use of property?	**NO** No violation of Constitution
YES	
Is there an essential nexus between the permit condition and a legitimate governmental interest?	**NO** Unconstitutional
YES	
Is there a rough proportionality between the harm caused by the new land use and the benefit obtained by the condition?	**NO** Unconstitutional, unless compensated

YES
No violation of Constitution

SOURCE: Developed by the author with the assistance of Lisa Pollisar and Kristen Spencer.

that the failure of the government to pay a promised charitable installment to an individual deprives that individual of *his own property*, in violation of the Due Process Clause of the Fourteenth Amendment. It somewhat strains credulity to say that the government's promise of charity to an individual is property belonging to that individual when the government denies that the individual is honestly entitled to receive such a payment." Black went on to observe that "the procedure required today as a matter of constitutional law finds no precedent in our legal system."

The current constitutional concept that governmental benefits or largess, including much of public employment, are a form of "new property" to be afforded constitutional protection is an example of how the Constitution can be adapted to changing circumstances. The more dependent individuals became on the largess of the administrative or welfare state, the more they needed protection from arbitrary, invidious, or capricious treatment by it. By considering largess to be a form of property, the individual who receives or is entitled to it has a constitutional right to procedural due process if the government seeks to withhold it. From any managerial perspective, due process is an expensive, ineffective, and inefficient means of organizing and implementing public administration. Nevertheless, due process is now required in a wide range of administrative actions dealing with the distribution of benefits or largess.

Procedural Due Process

As noted many times throughout this text, procedural due process is fundamental to the legal approach to public administration. It is also a constitutional value of great importance. Procedural due process seeks to assure fundamental fairness when the government is taking action that will injure the life, liberty, or property interests of a specific individual.

The Supreme Court has said that due process is "an elusive concept. Its exact boundaries are undefinable, and its content varies according to specific factual contexts."[22] But, like substantive rights and the takings clause procedural due process has a structure (see Box 11–5). It requires a balance of three concerns: the individual interests at stake, such as traditional property or new property; the likelihood, relative to other possible procedures, that the procedure used will result in errors; and the government's financial and administrative interests in using the procedure. An underlying presumption of this structure is that there is a tradeoff between procedures that reduce errors and costs to the government. In other words, it is assumed that more elaborate procedures will be both more accurate and more costly. As the individual interests at stake become more substantial, due process is less tolerant of error and less sensitive to costs. To take the extreme example, the procedures used in capital punishment cases should leave the least possible room for error, regardless of cost. In cases involving a short disciplinary suspension from a civil service job, by contrast, far less exacting procedures can be used because the harm to the individual is limited and reversible (through back pay, for instance).

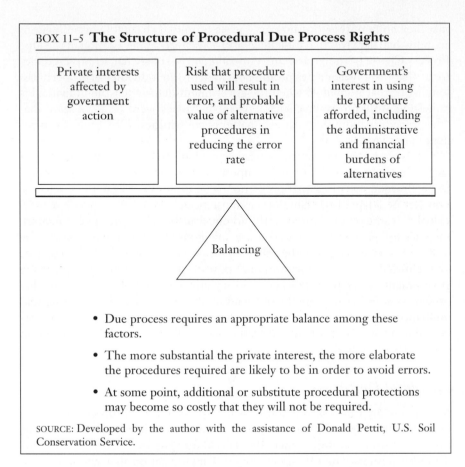

BOX 11–5 **The Structure of Procedural Due Process Rights**

| Private interests affected by government action | Risk that procedure used will result in error, and probable value of alternative procedures in reducing the error rate | Government's interest in using the procedure afforded, including the administrative and financial burdens of alternatives |

Balancing

- Due process requires an appropriate balance among these factors.

- The more substantial the private interest, the more elaborate the procedures required are likely to be in order to avoid errors.

- At some point, additional or substitute procedural protections may become so costly that they will not be required.

SOURCE: Developed by the author with the assistance of Donald Pettit, U.S. Soil Conservation Service.

Despite its flexibility, several constitutional principles of due process are reasonably well settled in the context of ordinary public administration:

1. The individual whose interests are likely to be injured by the governmental denial or cutoff of benefits, such as welfare, social security, public school attendance, or public employment, is entitled to advance *notice* of the proposed action.
2. The individual will have a chance to *respond* in writing or orally.
3. Depending on the nature of the action, the individual may have a right to a full-fledged *administrative hearing* prior to governmental implementation of the proposed action, as in the termination of welfare benefits.
4. The individual generally has a right to a posttermination hearing, if no prior hearing is afforded.
5. Depending on the interests at stake, the individual may have the right to *confrontation and cross-examination*, to be represented by an *attorney* (at least, at one's own expense), and to present *witnesses* on one's behalf before an *impartial governmental decision maker*, such as an administrative

law judge or hearing examiner. In some instances, due process may require that the hearing be open to the press and public. It is important to remember that the purpose of a hearing is to reduce the likelihood of an erroneous decision harming an individual's protected liberty or property interests. If all the pertinent information is agreed on and/or there is no controversy, a hearing may not be required.[23]

The constitutional principle that procedural due process of some degree applies to deprivations of the "new property" has been a major factor in the "judicialization" of much of public administration. Welfare and public housing agencies, the Social Security Administration, occupational licensing boards, and many other types of agencies have had to revamp their administrative procedures to accommodate this constitutional value. Public personnel administration has also been deeply affected by it (see Chapter 5). Moreover, accommodating due process has been expensive and sometimes inefficient and ineffective as a means of reducing fraud, preventing the distribution of benefits to individuals who are legally ineligible to receive them, and removing unfit public employees. The Supreme Court has not been oblivious to the administrative costs but, on the whole, has sought to protect individuals from harm through arbitrary, capricious, invidious, or patently unfair administrative actions.

Equal Protection

The Fourteenth Amendment provides that no state shall "deny to any person within its jurisdiction the equal protection of the laws." It has been held that *equal protection* is within the meaning of the "liberty" protected in the Fifth Amendment and therefore applies to the federal government as well.[24] The original purpose of the Fourteenth Amendment's equal protection clause was, at least, to protect freed slaves and African-Americans generally in the South. Whether those who drafted it expected more is now a moot point. Today, constitutional values and principles dictate broad application of the clause. An elaborate structure for determining what is required has been developed (see Box 11–6).

Classifications   It is often desirable or necessary in matters of public policy to classify people according to economic, social, demographic, or other characteristics. For instance, taxpayers may be classified by the amount of income they earn; individuals may be classified by age, veteran status, education, and geographic residence, citizenship, or alienage. They can also be classified by race, color, religion, gender, or national origin (ethnicity). Over the years, the Supreme Court has developed a "three-tier" approach to dealing with classifications of individuals. Some classifications are called "suspect" because, on their face, they appear to be used to deny individuals equal protection of the law or to discriminate against them. When a classification is suspect, the burden of proof is on the government to demonstrate that the categorization

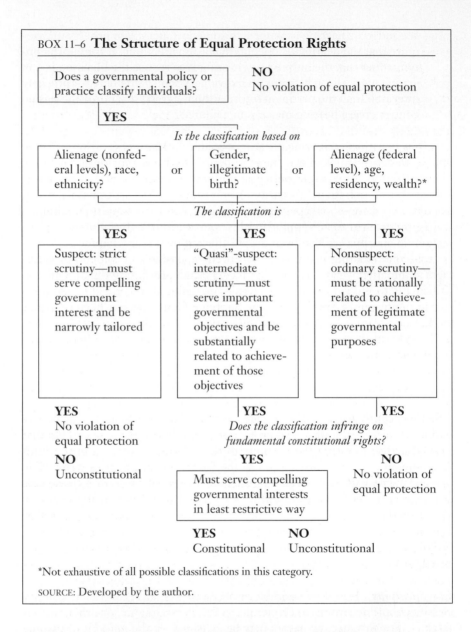

BOX 11–6 **The Structure of Equal Protection Rights**

Does a governmental policy or practice classify individuals?

NO
No violation of equal protection

YES

Is the classification based on

| Alienage (nonfederal levels), race, ethnicity? | or | Gender, illegitimate birth? | or | Alienage (federal level), age, residency, wealth?* |

The classification is

YES | **YES** | **YES**

Suspect: strict scrutiny—must serve compelling government interest and be narrowly tailored

"Quasi"-suspect: intermediate scrutiny—must serve important governmental objectives and be substantially related to achievement of those objectives

Nonsuspect: ordinary scrutiny—must be rationally related to achievement of legitimate governmental purposes

YES
No violation of equal protection

NO
Unconstitutional

YES
Does the classification infringe on fundamental constitutional rights?

YES

Must serve compelling governmental interests in least restrictive way

YES
Constitutional

NO
Unconstitutional

YES
NO
No violation of equal protection

*Not exhaustive of all possible classifications in this category.

SOURCE: Developed by the author.

serves a compelling state interest in a narrowly tailored fashion. This is difficult although possible to do. The courts will apply very "strict scrutiny" to the government's rationale in order to assure that the classification is fully appropriate. Under strict scrutiny the judiciary extends very little deference to administrative or other governmental claims. Narrow tailoring is similar to the concept of the least restrictive alternative. It requires that the governmental practice not be overly invasive of equal protection rights. At present, classifications based on race and ethnicity are suspect. This is true even if they are intended to help a group, as in the case of affirmative action. State and local governmental classifications based on citizenship are also generally suspect.

By contrast, some classifications, such as those based on age, wealth, or residency, are "nonsuspect" (or "ordinary"). There is no reason to believe they violate the purpose of the equal protection clause. Such classifications are found in a very wide array of public policies, including laws prohibiting the sale of alcoholic beverages to those who have not reached the age of 21, or providing reduced tuition at state universities for bona fide state residents. These classifications are subject to routine judicial scrutiny and are valid if they serve a legitimate governmental purpose in a rational way. The burden of persuasion typically falls on those challenging such classifications. Federal classifications based on citizenship are not treated as suspect because the Constitution specifically provides Congress with broad powers regarding naturalization (Article I, section 8).

Gender-based classifications fall in between the suspect and nonsuspect categories. They trigger intermediate scrutiny and must be substantially related to the achievement of important governmental objectives. At an earlier time, legislation treating women and men differently was common. Often the purpose was allegedly to "protect" women, but the result was to place barriers in the path of their employment, property rights, full citizenship, and educational and other opportunities. Society is now far more cognizant of unequal treatment of women, and the courts have begun to take a deeper look at gender-based classifications. In particular, the courts have "invalidated statutes employing gender as an inaccurate proxy for other, more germane bases of classification."[25] Eventually, such classifications may be considered just as suspect as those based on race, and require a compelling state interest and be subject to strict scrutiny and narrow tailoring.

Discriminatory Purpose   Many governmental regulations do not actually establish explicit classifications, but they tend to have a harsher impact on one social group than another. For example, the Supreme Court speculated that this may be true of "a whole range of tax, welfare, public service, regulatory, and licensing statutes that may be more burdensome to the poor and to the average black than to the more affluent white."[26] Such regulations are not considered in violation of equal protection unless a discriminatory purpose can be shown. In the Court's words, "Our cases have not embraced the proposition that a law or other official act, without regard to whether it reflects a racially discriminatory purpose, is unconstitutional *solely* because it has a racially disproportionate impact."[27] Rather, a purpose to discriminate must be present if the regulation is to be found in violation of equal protection. Such a purpose does not have to be "express or appear on the face of the statute" and it "may often be inferred from the totality of the relevant facts, including the fact . . . that the law bears more heavily on one race than another."[28] In short, the disproportionately harsh impact of a regulation on members of one racial or other social group is not enough to demonstrate a violation of equal protection. This was made evident in *Personnel Administrator* of *Massachusetts v. Feeney* (1979), in which the Supreme Court found that a veteran preference system in state employment strongly favored males over females but did not actually establish a gender-based classification either overtly or covertly, and was not intended to discriminate against women.[29] Consequently, the preference was not considered unconstitutional.

Classifications and Fundamental Rights   When a classification is used in a way that treads on fundamental constitutional rights, it will be subject to strict scrutiny and to the compelling governmental interest and least restrictive alternative tests. For instance, in *Shaprio v. Thompson* (1969),[30] the Supreme Court concluded that state (and District of Columbia) regulations requiring new residents to wait at least a year before applying for welfare benefits infringed on indigents' constitutional right to "travel interstate." Because the governments involved could not meet the requirement of demonstrating a compelling interest for using the residency classifications, the Court held that they were unconstitutional.

Equal Protection's Normative Philosophy   In terms of public administration, there is more to the equal protection clause than may be immediately apparent. The constitutional values and principles of equal protection tend to establish a different kind of "rationality" than that inherent in either the traditional managerial or political approaches to public administration. This was perhaps best illustrated by the case of *Craig v. Boren* (1976).[31] In an effort to promote traffic safety, Oklahoma adopted a statute that prohibited the sale of "3.2 percent" beer to males under the age of 21. Females could purchase it at the age of 18 and over. The state's rationale was that statistical evidence indicated that males in the 18-to-20 age bracket were more prone than females of the same age to be involved in alcohol-related driving offenses. These statistics were not overwhelmingly convincing—one survey found that of all those arrested in Oklahoma for driving while intoxicated, 0.18 percent of the group were females aged 18 to 20, whereas 2 percent of the group were males in the same age bracket. Nevertheless, this finding seemed to support what was taken to be common knowledge: namely, that males of this age were more of a threat on the road than their female cohorts. From a traditional managerial perspective, therefore, the regulation appeared sensible. It would be more expensive, inefficient, and less effective to arrest intoxicated 18- to 20-year-old males for driving offenses than simply to seek to reduce the likelihood that they would be driving while drunk at all by making it more difficult for them to obtain the 3.2 percent beer. Similarly, the political perspective supported the notion of aggregating all the males of this age into a group, and then addressing the circumstances of the group as a whole through legislation. From both perspectives the regulation was considered in the public interest because it promoted the public safety, especially that of the 18- to 20-year-old males.

In assessing the regulation from the perspectives of constitutional values and principles, the Supreme Court reached a startlingly different conclusion.

In a key paragraph, the Court's majority opinion attacked both the traditional managerial and political approaches: "Proving broad sociological propositions by statistics is dubious business, and one that inevitably is in tension with the normative philosophy that underlies the Equal Protection Clause. Suffice to say that the showing offered by the [state] does not satisfy us that sex represents a legitimate, accurate proxy for the regulation of drinking and driving." Here we see two very important constitutional principles at work. First, "sociological propositions" that create or are derived from social classifications, such as male/female or black/white, are disfavored by the equal protection clause because they inherently tend to suggest that public policy should treat different social groups differently. In other words, they suggest that different opportunities should be afforded to or different restrictions imposed on distinct social groups. Ideally, the principle of the equal protection clause is that no such classifications should be made in the public sector because the classifications themselves are too broad to guarantee equal protection to each and every individual within them. Justice Stevens made this point in a concurring opinion in *Craig* when he protested against the unfairness of treating all 18- to 20-year-old males "as inferior to their female counterparts." Certainly, there must be some males in that age group who could handle both 3.2 percent beer and driving. Moreover, some males of that age do not have driver's licenses and do not drive. Why should 18-year-old female drivers be afforded the right to buy 3.2 percent beer while it is denied to 20-year-old male nondrivers? The latter are clearly less threatening to traffic safety than the former.

The second constitutional principle evident in the Court's opinion is that the legislative or administrative classifications based on social groups must at least be accurate proxies for the regulation of the behavior with which the state is concerned. In particular, relying on stereotypes as the basis for such regulations is unacceptable under the equal protection clause. For example, it is not enough to assume that everybody knows teenage males in Oklahoma are wild "cowboys." If the state wants to treat them differently than teenage females, it has to demonstrate that the quality of being male is substantially related to the achievement of important public policy objectives. Here, then, is a place where solid policy analysis and constitutional law demand the same thing—an accurate understanding of the behavior of the target group. In fact, the Supreme Court suggested that such social classifications would have to rest on "predictive empirical relationships." Of course, even then, the classification could be unconstitutional if it were based on race or ethnicity and failed to serve a compelling state interest in the least restrictive way.

Thus, the constitutional values and principles associated with equal protection provide public administrators with a difficult challenge. In a nation with a heterogeneous population, such as the United States, the classification of social groups has long been deeply ingrained in the culture. Private individuals and public policy have traditionally used such classifications as proxies for knowing how to act and what to do. For instance, in *Baker v. City of*

St. Petersburg (1968), a police chief used the race of police officers as a proxy for being able to get along with citizens of the same race and to engage in efficient and effective police work.[32] In *U.S. v. Brignoni-Ponce*[33] (see Chapter 8), "looking Mexican" was taken as a proxy for the likelihood of being an illegal alien. Consequently, what the Supreme Court is saying in *Craig v. Boren* is nothing less than that the equal protection clause demands that we change our style of thinking. Classification by social group is viewed by the Constitution as inherently undesirable. What is the alternative?

Individuality

Constitutional values and principles prefer to look at individuals as individuals per se rather than as members of legislative classifications or categorical statistical groups. Class-action suits are entertained by the courts, but judges sometimes go to considerable pains to assure that such a class actually exists and that the individual or organization litigating the suit is truly a representative of it. Perhaps public sector mandatory maternity leave cases best illustrate the constitutional emphasis on individuality in the public administrative context.[34] School systems, acting on the basis of managerial values, sought to establish a systematic procedure for replacing pregnant schoolteachers. In particular, the schools wanted ample notice of when the teachers would no longer be able to fulfill their professional responsibilities. This would enable principals to plan ahead for the hiring of permanent substitutes or other replacements. Allowing the pregnant teacher to determine when she was no longer able to teach classes might provide too short notice to make adequate arrangements for the continuation of her classes. The regulations at issue in the cases reaching the Supreme Court required pregnancy leaves to begin in the fourth and fifth months of pregnancy. The Court found that these regulations infringed on the constitutionally protected Fourteenth Amendment liberty to make personal choices regarding matters of marriage and family. It also found the regulations to be irrational because if the fourth or fifth months of a teacher's pregnancy occurred toward the very end of the school year, then mandatory maternity leaves would actually disrupt the continuity of teaching, because many teachers would be medically able to continue well beyond that time. The infringement on liberty and the irrationality of the regulations, when coupled together, violated constitutional values and principles in the Court's view. Rather, it suggested, either mandatory leaves should commence very late in the term of a normal pregnancy (during the eighth month) or leaves should be based on an *individualized* medical determination of a pregnant teacher's ability to perform her professional responsibilities. In either event, of course, the school systems might not receive adequate notice of when the teacher's leave would begin, but the Court stressed the importance of treating the individual as an individual, rather than part of a group, in these circumstances. In short, in many cases, the constitutional value of individuality is likely to outweigh the administrative burdens it imposes.

Fourth Amendment Privacy Rights

The constitutional right to privacy is related to the value of individuality. The Fourth Amendment's protection against "unreasonable searches and seizures" enables individuals to have spheres into which the government cannot generally intrude. Like other constitutional rights, however, Fourth Amendment rights are not absolute. The protection is only against "unreasonable" searches and seizures, and what is reasonable has been subject to interpretations varying with the circumstances. For instance, the constitutional privacy protections public employees can claim in the workplace are more limited than those held by private citizens.[35] The broad structure of Fourth Amendment rights is diagrammed in Box 11–7.

Once it is determined that a governmental action has some implications for an individual's privacy, the key question is whether the individual had a reasonable expectation of privacy in the circumstances. Reasonable in this context means an expectation that society is prepared to support. If there is no such expectation, the individual's Fourth Amendment rights cannot be

BOX 11–7 **Structure of Fourth Amendment Privacy Rights**

Does a governmental action have implications for an individual's privacy rights under the Constitution?	**NO** No violation of Constitution
YES	
Does the individual have a reasonable expectation of privacy in the specific circumstances in which the action occurred?	**NO** No violation of Constitution
YES	
Did the government official engaging in the search have a warrant?	**YES** No violation of Constitution
NO	
Did the government official have probable cause or a reasonable basis for undertaking the search and for its scope?	**NO** Unconstitutional
YES	
Constitutionality will depend on the specific circumstances involved.	

SOURCE: Developed by the author with the assistance of Donald Pettit, U.S. Soil Conservation Service.

violated. For example, an individual cannot claim a reasonable expectation of privacy in the contents of a suitcase being brought through customs into the United States from abroad. Similarly, depending on a public employee's workplace practices, he or she may not be able to claim a reasonable expectation of privacy regarding the content of filing cabinets or even desk drawers. By contrast, many public employees not subject to security screening would probably be able to claim successfully a reasonable expectation of privacy in their briefcases.

Assuming the individual has a reasonable expectation of privacy, the government needs either a warrant or probable cause for undertaking a law enforcement search. In either case, the scope and objectives of the search must be clearly established. Simply snooping around someone's home or papers to see what turns up is unconstitutional. Warrants may also be required for administrative inspections, including those by the Occupational Health and Safety Administration,[36] but nonlaw enforcement searches are often subject to weaker requirements. For example, the Supreme Court has held that public employers and public schools have special needs that make warrants and probable cause impracticable. Searches in these contexts are generally governed by a standard of reasonableness in terms of inception and scope. However, the Supreme Court has upheld suspicionless urinalysis drug testing of some categories of public employees and of public school athletes.[37]

Equity

Equity is a final constitutional value that should be mentioned. It is generally thought of as "the power to dispense with the harsh rigor of general laws in particular cases."[38] In other words, where following the law to the letter would result in an obviously unfair or unreasonable resolution of a case, equity allows an exception to be made. Equity also enables the judiciary to develop *remedies* for breaches of constitutional rights, even though such remedies are not specifically provided for in any statutes. For example, the federal judiciary has ordered "forced busing" and taxation as means of desegregating school systems that unconstitutionally separated students by race.[39] It has also fashioned "quota" hiring and promotional systems to remedy racial discrimination in public personnel administration.[40] It has also mandated far-reaching prison and public mental health reforms.[41] Although the Constitution provides that the judicial power shall "extend to all cases, in law and equity," it is sometimes now contended that the judiciary has used its powers in equity to virtually transform the Constitution into "an omnibus piece of legislation."[42] Such criticism notwithstanding, public administrators should recognize that contemporary constitutional values are unlikely to tolerate harsh and unfair results in particular cases dictated by rigidly strict adherence to laws and precedents. Traditional, although not NPM, administrators may prefer to "go by the book" and avoid making exceptions, even when they seem appropriate. The Constitution, however, is less willing to do so. When combined, equity and the value and principles of procedural due process dictate procedures and substantive results of public administrative action that are considered fundamentally fair. This is true even if these procedures and results cause inefficiency and added expense, hamper effectiveness in some sense, or are politically unpopular.

State Action

With the exception of the Thirteenth Amendment, which prohibits slavery, the Constitution does not ordinarily apply to relationships among private parties. For instance, in the absence of civil rights legislation, private firms were free to (and did) discriminate based on race, sex, national origin, and religion. Constitutional equal protection, due process, free speech, privacy, and other rights are irrelevant to private relationships. However, when private parties engage in "state action," the Constitution may directly constrain their activity. Consequently, state action doctrine is of great importance to privatization, public-private partnerships, and hybrid arrangements such as quasi-governmental corporations.

State action refers to governmental action, whether at the federal, state, or local levels. Historically, the courts have sought to draw a dichotomy between governmental action and private conduct. But they have also recognized that public administration is not always so neatly packaged that one can find a bright line between governmental and nongovernmental activity. In the Supreme Court's words, the ". . . actions of private entities can sometimes be regarded as governmental action for constitutional purposes."[43] In general, state action will be present when (1) a private party engages in a public function; (2) the government is so deeply involved in the activity that it is responsible for the private party's conduct (e.g., public-private partnerships); and/or (3) the government has so authorized, approved, or encouraged the private party's activity that it bears responsibility for it (e.g., governmental control of contractors' decisions under some circumstances).[44] The main problem of state action doctrine is applying these imprecise and subjective standards to real-world administrative arrangements. The Supreme Court has admitted, "It is fair to say that 'our cases deciding when private action might be deemed that of the state have not been a model of consistency.'"[45] Nevertheless, some matters are clear.

First, the judiciary takes responsibility for determining what constitutes state action. In a case involving Amtrak (see Box 11–8), a hybrid federal corporation, the Supreme Court noted with emphasis that:

> . . . it is not for Congress to make the final determination of Amtrak's status as a government entity for purposes of determining the constitutional rights of citizens affected by its actions. If Amtrak is, by its very nature, what the Constitution regards as the Government, congressional pronouncement that it is not such can no more relieve it of its First Amendment restrictions than a similar pronouncement could exempt the Federal Bureau of Investigation from the Fourth Amendment. The Constitution constrains governmental action "by whatever instruments or in whatever modes that action may be taken."[46]

BOX 11–8 **When Is a Nongovernmental Entity a Governmental Entity?**

Michael Lebron contracted to rent the "Spectacular" billboard in Amtrak's Pennsylvania Station in New York City. The Spectacular is approximately 10 feet high and 103 feet long. It is curved and illuminated. Lebron wanted to create the following display:

> The work is a photomontage, accompanied by considerable text. Taking off on a widely circulated Coors beer advertisement which proclaims Coors to be the "Right Beer," Lebron's piece is captioned "Is it the Right's Beer Now?" It includes photographic images of convivial drinkers of Coors beer, juxtaposed with a Nicaraguan village scene in which peasants are menaced by a can of Coors that hurtles toward them, leaving behind a trail of fire, as if it were a missile. The accompanying text, appearing on either end of the montage, criticizes the Coors family for its support of right-wing causes, particularly the contras in Nicaragua. Again taking off on Coors' advertising which uses the slogan of "Silver Bullet" for its beer cans, the text proclaims that Coors is "The Silver Bullet that aims The Far Right's political agenda at the heart of America."

Amtrak refused the display because its policy was not to allow "political advertising" on the Spectacular. Lebron sued.

When the case reached the Supreme Court, the key question was whether Amtrak was a governmental actor. If it was, then its refusal to display Lebron's photomontage would be governed by the First Amendment's guarantee of freedom of speech. If it were a private actor, the First Amendment would not apply. Amtrak argued that it is not a government entity. It pointed out that its authorizing act, the federal Rail Passenger Service Act of 1970, declares that Amtrak "will not be an agency or establishment of the United States Government." Amtrak also noted that two previous Supreme Court decisions dealing with commercial matters characterized it as a "nongovernmental entity." The Court of Appeals agreed that Amtrak was not part of the government.

Nevertheless, the Supreme Court had no trouble concluding that Amtrak was indeed "an agency or instrumentality of the United States for the purpose of individual rights guaranteed against the Government by the Constitution." In a paragraph that would remind modern reformers that performance-based organizations are nothing new, the Court noted:

> A remarkable feature of the heyday of . . . [federal] corporations, in the 1930's and 1940's, was that, even while they were praised for their status as "agencies separate and distinct, administratively and financially and legally, from the government itself, [which] has facilitated their adoption of commercial methods of accounting and financing, avoidance of political controls, and utilization of regular procedures of business management," it was fully acknowledged that they were a "device" of "government," and constituted "federal corporate agencies" apart from "regular government departments."

BOX 11–8 *Continued*

If this history were not enough, the Court noted that (1) "Amtrak was created by special statute, explicitly for the furtherance of federal government goals"; (2) "six of the corporation's eight externally named directors . . . are appointed directly by the President of the United States— four of them (including the Secretary of Transportation) with the advice and consent of the Senate"; and (3) "the Government exerts its control [over Amtrak] . . . as a policymaker."

Having determined that Amtrak is governmental and therefore subject to constitutional constraints, the Court remanded the case to the lower court to determine whether the railroad had violated Lebron's First Amendment rights to show his distaste for Coors.

SOURCE: *Lebron v. National Railroad Passenger Corporation*, 115 S. Ct. 961 (1995).

Second, governmental corporations, performance-based organizations, and many public-private arrangements will be subject to constitutional constraints, no matter how much adherents to the NPM or other approaches would like them to operate just like private sector businesses. As the Supreme Court put it: "It surely cannot be that government, state or federal, is able to evade the most solemn obligations imposed by the Constitution by simply resorting to the corporate form. . . ."[47] For example, in one case the Court held that a college ". . . which had been built and maintained pursuant to a privately erected trust, was nevertheless a governmental actor for constitutional purposes because it was operated and controlled by a board of state appointees, which was itself a state agency."[48]

Third, private contractors performing governmental functions can become state actors who are subject to constitutional constraints.[49] For instance, physicians under contract to provide medical care to prisoners are state actors, regardless of the fact that they are neither state employees nor at the prisons on a full-time basis. They are bound by constitutional interpretation of the Eighth Amendment, which gives prisoners a right to adequate medical treatment. What might be ordinary malpractice in private practice may constitute a constitutional infringement when prisoners are involved. The difference is significant, because violations of constitutional rights can trigger additional liabilities.

Fourth, when private parties engaged in state action violate individuals' constitutional rights they are potentially liable in civil suits for money damages.[50] For example, a physician under contract to a prison who is "deliberately indifferent" to a prisoner's medical needs, can be sued for violating the prisoner's Eighth Amendment rights. As the law now stands, a private individual involved in such a suit could be held liable even though he or she was acting in accordance with established laws or agency procedures that later turned out to be unconstitutional. Unlike public employees, private individuals cannot defend themselves in such suits on the basis that they could not reasonably have known their actions were unconstitutional.

Contemporary state action doctrine has very broad implications for public administration organized according to NPM principles. Deregulating agencies by turning them into performance-based, corporate-style organizations outside of normal civil service regulations will not relieve them of their constitutional obligations. Their employment and customer relationships will still be governed by constitutional due process, equal protection, privacy, and First Amendment rights. Similarly, public-private partnerships and privatization can carry constitutional responsibilities with them. Depending on their functions, private contractors engaged in state action can face substantial liabilities for abridging individuals' constitutional rights. If experience with NPM arrangements grows, there will certainly be an increasing number of lawsuits involving questions of state action. Their outcome could be of particular importance to privatization and public-private partnerships. Subjecting such arrangements to constitutional constraints and attendant liabilities would complicate them significantly.

SYNTHESIS: AN ONGOING PARTNERSHIP

Constitutional values and principles have often stood at odds with those of public administration. Today, however, both the judiciary and public managers are more frequently realizing that there is a need to develop an ongoing partnership.[51] More searching judicial review of administrative action and the development of far greater personal and local governmental liabilities for public administration that violates individuals' constitutional or legal rights have forced public administrators to be aware of and responsive to constitutional values and principles. As judges have become more involved in administrative activity themselves, through overseeing the management of public institutions, such as schools, mental health facilities, and prisons, they have recognized the worth of some public administrative values and the practical constraints of administrative action. It was once taken virtually for granted by judges that they could bring these institutions up to constitutional standards by issuing decrees or directly involving the court in their day-to-day management. In retrospect, most would probably now recognize that this assumption was too optimistic.[52] Their decrees and redesigns of public school systems have sometimes been frustrated by "white flight," or the withdrawal of white students from the school systems. Their orders for reforms of prison and mental health facilities have likewise foundered upon the very unmanageability of those institutions. Thus, after two decades or so of a relatively high degree of confrontation between public administrators and judges, both sides now have a greater appreciation of the values and perspectives of the other.

A remarkable feature of the American constitutional law is its adaptive quality. The Constitution is a living document. Drafted in the horse-and-buggy age, it has survived through the Industrial Revolution, the rise of the contemporary administrative state and the consequent transformation of governmental structure and role, and continues with us into the postindustrial era. There is little doubt that its values and principles will be more completely synthesized with those of public administration in the future. Public administrators and judges have no choice but to make their partnership work, and they have the means to do so—for it depends primarily on both exercising their powers of reason.

NOTES

1. *Immigration and Naturalization Service v. Chadha*, 462 U.S. 919 (1983).
2. Dwight Waldo, *The Administrative State*, 2d ed. (New York: Holmes and Meier, 1984), xviii.
3. Woodrow Wilson, "The Study of Administration," *Political Science Quarterly* 56 (December 1941): 481–506, at 484 (originally published in 1887).
4. Ibid., 504.
5. *Smith v. Wade*, 461 U.S. 31 (1983). See also *Gore v. BMW*, 116 S. Ct. 1589 (1996).
6. Constance Horner, "Remarks on FEI's [Federal Executive Institute's] 20th Anniversary Dinner," Charlottesville, Va., 14 October 1988, 14.
7. Jeffrey Segal and Harold Spaeth, *The Supreme Court and the Attitudinal Model* (New York: Cambridge University Press, 1993).
8. *Minersville School District v. Gobitis*, 310 U.S. 586 (1940); *West Virginia State Board of Education v. Barnette*, 319 U.S. 624 (1943).
9. *Federal Baseball Club v. National League*, 259 U.S. 200 (1922); *Toolsen v. New York Yankees*, 346 U.S. 356 (1953); *U.S. v. International Boxing Club*, 348 U.S. 236 (1955); *Radovich v. National Football League*, 352 U.S. 445 (1957); *Flood v. Kuhn*, 407 U.S. 258 (1972).
10. *Federalist Paper No. 51*, in Clinton Rossiter, ed., *The Federalist Papers* (New York: Mentor, 1961), 321–322.
11. *American Federation of Government Employees v. Phillips*, 358 F. Supp. 60 (1973).
12. Governor Richard Snelling of Vermont, quoted in *Burlington Free Press*, 24 July 1983.
13. Max Weber, *From Max Weber: Essays in Sociology*, trans. and ed. by H. H. Gerth and C. W. Mills (New York: Oxford University Press, 1958), chaps. 4 and 8.
14. *West Virginia State Board of Education v. Barnette*, 319 U.S. 624 (1943).
15. Weber, *Essays in Sociology*, 228.
16. *Keyishian v. Board of Regents*, 385 U.S. 589 (1967).
17. *Shelton v. Tucker*, 364 U.S. 479 (1960).
18. See John Rohr, *Ethics for Bureaucrats* (New York: Marcel Dekker, 1978), 213.
19. *Dolan v. City of Tigard*, 114 S. Ct. 2309 (1994). See also *First English Evangelical Lutheran Church of Glendale v. County of Los Angeles*, 482 U.S. 304 (1987); *Nollan v. California Coastal Commission*, 483 U.S. 825 (1987).
20. Charles Reich, "The New Property," *Yale Law Journal* 73 (1964): 733–787.
21. *Goldberg v. Kelly*, 397 U.S. 254 (1970).
22. *Hannah v. Larche*, 363 U.S. 420, 442 (1960).
23. *Codd v. Velger*, 429 U.S. 624 (1977).
24. *Bolling v. Sharpe*, 347 U.S. 497 (1954).
25. See *Craig v. Boren*, 429 U.S. 190, 198 (1976).
26. *Washington v. Davis*, 426 U.S. 229, 248 (1976).
27. Ibid., 239.

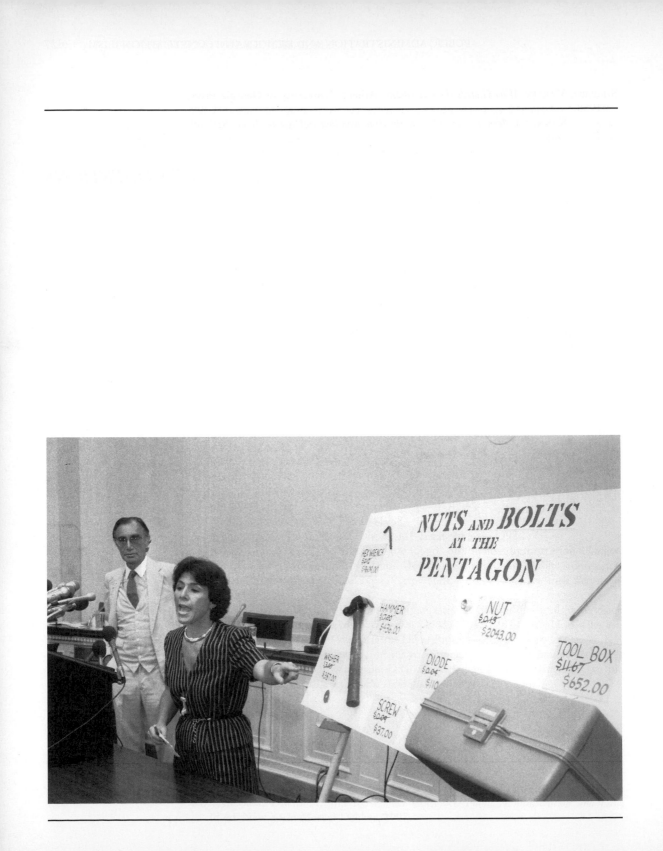

CHAPTER 12 | *Accountability and Ethics*

Public administrators may be seen as the "guardians" of the contemporary administrative state. This raises a very fundamental issue in political thought: "Who guards the guardians?" Public administrators must be held accountable because there are aspects of their jobs that can lead to misconception of the public interest, corruption, and even subversion. But there are also many aspects of public administration that make it difficult to attain a satisfactory level of accountability. This chapter will consider managerial, political, and legal perspectives on accountability and ethics. Ethics can be considered a form of self-accountability, or an "inner check" on public administrators' conduct. The various approaches are in many ways complementary to one another: The legal approach tends to favor the inner check; the traditional managerial approach, a check that is external to the individual but internal to the agency; and the political and new public management (NPM) approaches, a check that is external to the agency and exercised through outside oversight of some kind. Many consider a new sense of professionalism, including perhaps a "code of ethics," to be a sensible means of helping the "guardians" to guard themselves.

Public administration has become an important locus of political power and influence in the United States. Public administrators, sometimes individually, but generally collectively, play an active role in the formulation of public policies. They also have a great deal to do with the style, pace, and tone of the execution of those policies. Out of this set of conditions arises a fundamental problem. If public administrators are in fact the "permanent branch" of government, the guardians of the long-term public interest, and the keepers of the public trust, then who guards the guardians? Or as Frederick Mosher put the same question, "How does one square a permanent civil service—which neither the people by their vote nor their representatives by their appointments can replace—with the principle of government 'by the people'?"[1] To many concerned citizens and political authorities in nations throughout the world, this is the fundamental *political* issue presented by the development of the contemporary administrative state. However, it is also a central issue of modern management. As Victor Thompson noted, the increasing specialization and technical expertise of subordinate employees have created a severe imbalance between the formal hierarchical authority and responsibility of high-level administrators, on the one hand, and their actual intellectual capacity to manage their "staff," on the other.[2] That is one reason why the new public management (NPM) opposes hierarchy and favors employee empowerment. Accountability is also a legal matter. It concerns such questions as, "Who is liable for what?" and "What kinds of conduct are illegal?"

This chapter tackles the issue of ensuring that public administrators do not violate their public trust. It discusses traditional managerial, new public management, political, and legal perspectives on accountability and ethics. Ethics are considered an internal, personal check—a sense of personal responsibility; accountability is the process of applying external checks on public administrators. Because the accountability of public administrators is truly a worldwide concern, it is worth taking some time to consider precisely why public administrators might abuse their public trust and act in ways not considered by the citizenry and/or political authorities to be in the public interest.

WHY THE GUARDIANS NEED GUARDING

Although American public administration is generally considered exceptionally honest and able by world standards, one can point to three main types of factors that can impel public administrators to violate their public trust. One concerns misconception of the public interest; another, corruption; and the third, subversion.

Misconception of the Public Interest

There are several forces frequently at work in public administration that could lead civil servants to misconceive or misconstrue the public interest. First are the social forces. Public administrators, especially in the higher-level, more complex, and typically more politically influential jobs, may not constitute a social group that is representative of the nation's population as a whole. At the very least, they are likely to be disproportionately drawn from the ranks of the middle class.[3] They may come heavily from the upper class, as was true during the early years of the government. The social class basis of the civil service is important because it colors perceptions of how people live, what their problems are, and what they want and need. It also is an important element in the creation of individual and group values and norms of proper behavior. To a very considerable extent, one's world view is likely to be influenced by one's social attributes. As Seymour Lipset found, "The behavior of government bureaucrats varies with the nongovernmental social background and interest of those controlling the bureaucratic structure."[4] In this regard there are rarely neutral categories: one is born female or male; to one race or ethnicity or another; to a social class. Overall, in comparison to the nation's general population, public administrators in the United States are thought to be disproportionately middle class, and in the upper levels of public services, they are disproportionately white and male.[5]

A second factor that can lead public administrators to misconceive the public interest is an artifact of their specialization. Public administrators—like others who perform a highly specialized function—may eventually develop a narrow outlook concerning the public interest. They may tend to exaggerate the importance of what they do and downgrade the importance of what others do. They may also develop ways of thinking that make it difficult to understand alternative approaches or to recognize the dominance or even the legitimacy of competing values. There are many well-known instances of this in American life. Lawyers, for example, sometimes successfully defend individuals who they know are guilty of horrible crimes. Their rationale is that everyone is entitled to the best defense possible and that our system of justice cannot properly function otherwise. For the layperson, however, it may be somewhat more difficult to find a moral distinction between one who, for example, aids a child rapist to escape from the scene of the crime and the lawyer who uses the technical rules of evidence to get him off after an arrest has been made. Similarly, public health administrators, imbued with professional values emphasizing economy, have been known to authorize the routine nighttime drugging of patients to reduce staffing costs.[6] Although such practice is medically undesirable and potentially dangerous, it can be seen as desirable from narrow administrative perspectives concerned with cutting costs. Public administrators who deal with a particular type of client or population may eventually come to view them as truly representative of the population as a whole or of "human nature" in general. Police in urban settings are so accustomed to dealing with hard-core criminals, prostitutes, and sexual and other deviants that they may develop a distorted sense of the public. Boxes 12–1 and 12–2 present startling examples of agencies' misconceptions of the public interest and failure to act ethically.

These are familiar patterns that affect the thinking of individuals in some specialized job settings, including those in the civil service. They are augmented by various kinds of socialization at work. In bureaucracies, socializa-

BOX 12–1 **Misconstruing the Public Interest at the Atomic Energy Commission**

During the 1950s, the Atomic Energy Commission (AEC) conducted a number of nuclear tests in Nevada. The agency was aware of the dangers that radioactive fallout posed to those downwind from the test sites, mostly in Nevada and Utah. In some of the tests, the explosive devices were known to be "dirty," in the sense that the fallout would be especially heavy. Dirty weapons might have strategic military benefits, but they also had administrative ones. In 1957, the director of the AEC's division of biology and medicine explained that "if we continue to reduce the fraction [of radiation] we are willing to release, we eventually reach a cost of control [that] makes the operation prohibitive." In other words, there was a tradeoff between administrative economy and known danger to the public.

There was also a sense that the public was expendable. By 1955, the downwinders were becoming concerned about their exposure to radiation. But their apprehension was outweighed by the AEC's apprehension of the Soviet Union's nuclear threat. One commissioner said that "people have got to learn to live with the facts of life, and part of the facts of life are fallout." In another's view, "We must not let anything interfere with this series of tests—nothing."

Political scientist Howard Ball explains what followed:

> The next day, Feb. 24 [1955], another pinkish cloud appeared over Cedar City, Utah, and remained

there for several hours. The sky was hazy, and fallout dusted the ground. Local children, recounted a resident, "ate it, walked in it, breathed it. . . . You know how little kids love snow. They went out and would eat the 'snow.'"

Years later, large numbers of leukemia cases developed among the downwinders, many of whom had no histories of cancer in their families. In one family never previously affected by the disease, four teenagers died; in another, a man recounted the losses of a wife, niece, sister, sister-in-law, mother-in-law, uncle, grandmother, and two great-uncles to cancer.

Litigation was brought against the U.S. government, which denied responsibility for the sickness and death. Eventually, in 1984, a federal court found the government liable for some $2.7 million in damages. In so doing, the judge announced the following ethical principle:

> At the core of this case is a fundamental principle, a time-honored rule of law, an ethical rule, a moral tenet: The law imposes a duty on everyone to avoid acts in their nature dangerous to the lives of others.

It may seem obvious to almost everyone that at the very least the public interest required federal authorities to warn the downwinders not to let children eat the radioactive "snow." Nonetheless, the government appealed the verdict.

SOURCE: Based on Howard Ball, "Downwind from the Bomb," *New York Times Magazine*, 9 February 1986, 33 ff.

tion is often thought to be an important mechanism of inculcating values in employees and consequently influencing their on-the-job behavior. For instance, Anthony Downs notes that any administrative agency is apt to develop a **bureau ideology** that does the following:

1. emphasizes the positive benefits of the bureau's activities and deemphasizes their costs;
2. indicates that further expansion of the bureau's services would be desirable and any curtailment thereof would be undesirable;
3. emphasizes the benefits that the bureau provides for the society as a whole, rather than its services to particular "special interests";
4. stresses the high present level of the bureau's efficiency; [and]
5. emphasizes its achievements and future capabilities and ignores or minimizes its failures and inabilities.[7]

Moreover, in his view, these ideologies are imparted to the bureaucracy's key employees because "all officials exhibit relatively strong loyalty to the organization controlling their job security and promotion."[8] When taken together, administrative specialization and socialization can be important in coloring the public administrator's worldview. We are all accustomed to educators, military officials, and urban development, health, and other public administrators considering their functions to be the most crucial to the future welfare of society.

A close relationship with a particular clientele group or constituency is another factor that can lead public administrators to misconstrue the public interest. As noted in Chapter 2, the development of the American administrative state was partly an outgrowth of clientelism. Different economic interest and social groups sought the establishment of government agencies to promote their interests. Sometimes, however, this process has led the agency to confuse the interests of the clientele or constituency with the public interest and to act as an advocate of those interests. Public administrators in such agencies may mistakenly consider the interest groups with which they deal to be wholly representative of all individuals in the economic sectors or social groups involved. Joseph LaPalombara referred to this condition as a "clientela"[9] relationship in which "an interest group, for whatever reasons, succeeds in becoming in the eyes of a given administrative agency, the natural expression and representative of a given social sector which, in turn, constitutes the natural target or reference point for the activity of the administrative agency."[10] In the United States, relationships along these lines form the basis of mutually supportive relationships among interest groups, administrative bureaus, and legislative committees that may view the public interest with acute tunnel vision.

Corruption

Corruption can be defined as a betrayal of the public trust for reasons of private interest. By many accounts, corruption in public administration is

---

BOX 12–2 **And at the FBI**

Martin Luther King, Jr., has had the uncommon honor of having a public holiday created in his name. From that fact alone, it is wholly evident that he is to be publicly regarded as a national hero. Under the leadership of J. Edgar Hoover, however, the FBI reached a different conclusion. The agency viewed King's quest for racial justice, not as something in the public interest to which the nation should aspire, but rather as a subversive threat to it. The following text, from the "Report of the U.S. Senate Select Committee to Study Governmental Operations with Respect to Intelligence Activities (1975–1976)," shows how far off course an administrative agency can go.

From "late 1963" until his death in 1968, Martin Luther King, Jr. was the target of an intensive campaign by the Federal Bureau of Investigation to "neutralize" him as an effective civil rights leader. In the words of the man in charge of the FBI's "war" against Dr. King, "No holds were barred."

The FBI gathered information about Dr. King's plans and activities through an extensive surveillance program, employing nearly every intelligence-gathering technique at the Bureau's disposal in order to obtain information about the "private activities of Dr. King and his advisors" to use to "completely discredit" them.

The program to destroy Dr. King as the leader of the civil rights movement included efforts to discredit him with Executive branch officials, Congressional leaders, foreign heads of state, American ambassadors, churches, universities, and the press.

The FBI mailed Dr. King a tape recording made from microphones hidden in his hotel rooms which one agent testified was an attempt to destroy Dr. King's marriage.

---

virtually a worldwide phenomenon and a serious limitation on the ability of public administrative systems to accomplish some of the tasks assigned to them. To mention only a few examples, during the Vietnam War, forces in both North and South Vietnam publicly complained that "bureaucratic corruption" was hampering their efforts; during the Cold War, the "bash the bureaucrat" syndrome prevailed in both the Soviet Union and the United States, and examples of administrative corruption were ferreted out by the press and publicly denounced by officials; in many countries throughout the world, corruption in the form of bribery and the use of personal contacts has literally become institutionalized, and "baksheesh," "la mordida," "la bustarella," "speed money," "dash," and "protekzia" are considered as common a way of dealing with bureaucrats as filling out forms.* In the

---

*"Baksheesh," a "tip" or bribe in the Middle East; "la mordida," "the bite" in Latin America; "la bustarella," "the little envelope" in Italy; "speed money," used in India to expedite the processing of forms and requests; "dash," a tip or bribe in Western Africa; "protekzia," exploitation of personal contacts to achieve favorable treatment in Israel.

BOX 12–2 *Continued*

The tape recording was accompanied by a note which Dr. King and his advisors interpreted as threatening to release the tape recording unless Dr. King committed suicide.

The extraordinary nature of the campaign to discredit Dr. King is evident from two documents:

—At the August 1963 March on Washington, Dr. King told the country of his "dream" that:

all of God's children, black men and white men, Jews and Gentiles, Protestants and Catholics, will be able to join hands and sing in the words of the old Negro spiritual, "Free at last, free at last, thank God Almighty, I'm free at last."

The Bureau's Domestic Intelligence Division concluded that this "demagogic speech" established Dr. King as the "most dangerous and effective Negro leader in the country." Shortly afterwards, and within days after Dr. King was named "Man of the Year" by *Time* magazine, the FBI decided to "take him off his pedestal," "reduce him completely in influence," and select and promote its own candidate "to assume the leadership of the Negro people."

—In early 1968, Bureau headquarters explained to the field that Dr. King must be destroyed because he was seen as a potential "messiah" who could "unify and electrify" the "black nationalist movement." Indeed, to the FBI he was a potential threat because he might "abandon his supposed 'obedience' to white liberal doctrines (non-violence)." In short, a nonviolent man was to be secretly attacked and destroyed as insurance against abandoning non-violence.

SOURCE: See Eugene Lewis, *Public Entrepreneurship* (Bloomington: Indiana University Press, 1980), chap. 5, for a general discussion of this episode.

United States, the suffix "gate" has become part of the political lexicon, as in Watergate, Iran-Contragate, and Whitewatergate.

The main reason for the worldwide presence of public administrative corruption is that public administrators have something to allocate that other people want. As Michael Johnston explains:

The demand for government's rewards frequently exceeds the supply, and routine decision-making processes are lengthy, costly, and uncertain in their outcome. For these reasons, legally sanctioned decision-making processes constitute a "bottleneck" between what people want and what they get. The temptation to get around the bottleneck—to speed things up and make favorable decisions more probable—is built into this relationship between government and society. To get around the bottleneck, one must use political influence—and corruption, which by definition cuts across established and legitimate processes, is a most effective form of influence.[11]

Although the source of corruption is similar in all public administrative settings, precisely what is considered a betrayal of public trust and corrupt activity on the part of administrators varies among (and sometimes within) political cultures.[12]

Every country has norms and values that define the legitimacy of different kinds of **political exchanges.** Political exchanges can be thought of as quid pro quo relationships involving government and politics. For example, if a candidate for Congress says, "You vote for me and I'll reduce your taxes," it constitutes a political exchange. So does the plea to a traffic officer, "Let me go with a warning this time and I won't speed again." Trading votes and support for one another's positions in legislatures, in the drafting of political party platforms, and in the recruitment of party candidates for public office are all examples of political exchange. Obviously, no political system could operate without political exchanges of some kind. But not all kinds of political exchanges are considered legitimate in all societies. For example, in the United States a candidate for Congress may say, "Vote for me and I'll reduce your taxes," but if he or she says, "Vote for me and I'll give you $20," it becomes a crime. A public administrator may be requested to expedite a case involving congressional casework, but if the same case were speeded up because the private individual concerned paid the administrator to do so, it would be a criminal offense. One of the difficulties in understanding administrative corruption, therefore, lies in determining precisely which kinds of political exchanges are considered acceptable parts of political life.

In the United States, defining administrative corruption has largely involved a contest between the norms and values of two types of political cultures. One is the **boss-follower,** or **political-machine-based** culture. The other is generally referred to as the modern **civic culture.** These were represented in the epic contest over political ethics presented by the nineteenth-century civil service reform and the early twentieth-century Progressive movements, on the one hand, and political machines, on the other. In the machine-based political culture, political exchanges were generally between citizens and the boss or his agents and between the machine and businesses. Votes were traded for jobs and favors; money for licenses, franchises, and public works contracts. For the most part, these exchanges were not considered unacceptable, though sometimes they were termed "honest graft." Similarly, it was commonplace and acceptable for administrative officials to deviate from administrative rules or laws in minor ways to benefit supporters of the machine or friends. Public officials might also accept gifts from clients and others for the purpose of generating generalized goodwill. Public employees were expected to take part in electioneering and to contribute money to the political party in power. On election day, they would be expected to help "get out the vote" (among party loyalists), while being paid from the public treasury. Public officials might also legitimately profit from "insider" knowledge, as in the case of knowing in advance where a new road or building was to be located. In general, the purpose of politics in this system was not to accomplish any ideological or policy goals, but rather to make personal gain by trading political support and money for the granting of governmental largess.[13] (See Plunkitt's description of "honest graft" in Box 12–3).

BOX 12–3 **"Honest Graft"**

Everybody is talkin' these days about Tammany men growin' rich on graft, but nobody thinks of drawin' the distinction between honest graft and dishonest graft. There's all the difference in the world between the two. Yes, many of our men have grown rich in politics. I have myself. I've made a big fortune out of the game, and I'm gettin' richer every day, but I've not gone in for dishonest graft—blackmailin' gamblers, saloon-keepers, disorderly people, etc.—and neither has any of the men who have made big fortunes in politics.

There's an honest graft, and I'm an example of how it works. I might sum up the whole thing by sayin': "I seen my opportunities and I took 'em."

Just let me explain by examples. My party's in power in the city, and it's goin' to undertake a lot of public improvements. Well, I'm tipped off, say, that they're goin' to lay out a new park at a certain place.

I see my opportunity and I take it. I go to that place and I buy up all the land I can in the neighborhood. Then the board of this or that makes its plan public, and there is a rush to get my land, which nobody cared particular for before.

Ain't it perfectly honest to charge a good price and make a profit on my investment and foresight? Of course, it is. Well, that's honest graft.

SOURCE: From William L. Riordan, *Plunkitt of Tammany Hall* (New York: Knopf, 1948), 3–8.

The "civic culture" has a radically different outlook. Its essence is "community-regarding" in the sense of promoting public, rather than merely private, interests. It is also impersonal. Government is not looked on as a means of dispensing largess and favors. It is viewed as an organization capable of advancing the general welfare of the community. Rather than considering the "boss" as the protector of individuals' interests, the civic culture holds that this is the role of the state, as embodied in a written or unwritten constitution. In such a system trading votes for jobs is considered illegitimate. Offering money for licenses, franchises, and contracts is also considered corrupt. These benefits are to be allocated according to impersonal and community-regarding rules, such as contracts to the lowest competent bidder. Public administrators are forbidden to use their "inside" information for private gain, and conflict-of-interest laws are adopted to prevent them from so doing. They may also be prohibited from taking part in a wide range of partisan and electioneering activities. Rules are applied impersonally, without regard to partisanship, and bribery is strictly forbidden.[14] In fact, even offering a bribe may be illegal.

Part of the problem of identifying administrative corruption in the United States is a result of the coexistence of norms of each of these two political cultures. Political machines have dwindled, become fragmented, and are now much weaker than in the early part of the century. This has been an intended consequence of the civil service reform and Progressive movements. However, the norms, values, and some of the practices common to machines in the past still play a role in partisan politics. Some positions, those denoted "political executive," are still allocated on a partisan basis. Government largess is still used to manipulate votes, though its distribution in the form of "pork-barrel" projects is aimed at winning support from whole communities or states, rather than from specific individual beneficiaries only. Contracts for governmental supplies, ranging from pencils to very expensive military hardware, may be allocated, under political pressure, on a regional basis. But contemporary public administration is nonetheless imbued with the norms and values of the civic culture. It looks down upon the intrusion of partisan politics in administration as an unhealthy perversion of the need to be community-regarding and to operate in accordance with impersonal rules. Some very important legislation has been aimed at minimizing the extent to which such intrusions can occur. Political neutrality statutes and merit systems are leading examples.

Because public administrators are engaged in the allocation of governmental benefits, they are sometimes pulled or pushed in opposing directions by the machine-based and civic culture-based approaches to government. This is part of the tension sometimes found between political executives seeking to implement an electoral "mandate" of some kind and career public administrators who seemingly are intransigent in clinging to what they regard as established procedures for promoting community-regarding, impersonal administrative activity. The divergence between the machine-based and civic culture-based approaches is sometimes reflected in legislation. For instance, conflict-of-interest statutes may prohibit public administrators from quitting the public sector to work for private corporations with which they had official dealings. Yet there are no equivalent regulations on the future employment of members of Congress, and some have left the legislature to work for firms and lobbying organizations whose interests they previously promoted in an official capacity. Similarly, candidates for public office, including incumbents, may accept funding from political action committees (PACs), and may hold economic interests in firms with which the government deals. But public administrators are often under a very strict standard, requiring them to eliminate altogether even any *appearance* of impropriety or wrongdoing.[15]

Definitions of "corruption" vary with political cultures, but within any political or administrative system there will be several types of corruption. One useful way to organize thinking about corruption is to consider the mode of execution and the purpose of the corrupt activity.[16] Execution can involve a single individual or agency and be **unilateral** in the sense that it does not involve a direct exchange with another individual or corporate entity. For instance, an individual administrator may cover up his or her mistakes. So may a unit of an agency or even the agency as a whole. Individuals and agencies may also falsify data and records in order to make it look like they are doing a better job. In these examples, the purpose of the individual or agency is to retain, augment, or attain authority of some kind. But unilateral corruption can also be aimed at obtaining material benefits. Here, theft, embezzlement, and use of official resources for private gain would be leading examples.

Corruption can also be **transactional,** involving a direct exchange of some kind. Where concern is enhancing administrative authority, such behavior might take the form of extremely strong clientela relationships. In return for support from the clientele group, the individual administrator or agency grants it benefits that are not even arguably in the public interest. It was precisely because the potential for such perversions of the public interest is present that President Eisenhower once warned the nation about the possibility of the "military-industrial complex" extracting too much wealth from the society. Transactional corruption can also be for the purpose of obtaining material benefits. Bribery, extortion, kickbacks, and so forth are clear examples.

Subversion

Public administrators might also betray their public trust by engaging in subversion. This has been a serious fear many times in United States history, particularly in wartime. The clearest and most recent example occurred in the late 1940s and early 1950s, during the McCarthy era, in which there was pandemic fear of communism. Because the fear of subversion declined dramatically with the ebbing of the Cold War and its total demise in 1991, only a few points should be noted. One is that the fear of subversion was real, though actual instances were hard to find. For instance, the 1952 Republican party platform charged that the Democrats had "permitted communists and fellow travelers to serve in many key agencies and to infiltrate our American life."[17] Second, the potential for actual damage to the public interest from subversive civil servants is considerable. Third, in today's global competition, economic subversion is a growing concern.[18] Finally, although it is common to think of subversion in terms of efforts, instigated by foreign governments, to weaken or destroy the government, conscious subversion of administrative programs can occur for several reasons. For example, it can be the result of unilateral or transactional corruption for private gain. It can also be due to extreme discontent with one's position in the public service.

WHY IT IS DIFFICULT TO GUARD THE GUARDIANS

It is clear that public administrators should be held accountable for their actions, especially as there are such broad prospects for them to abuse their trust. However, finding satisfactory means of establishing accountability has been difficult in the United States and other countries. Several reasons for this are discussed below.

The Accretion of Special Expertise and Information   Public administrators are often expert at what they do. Outsiders are unable to match their knowledge or properly second-guess their decisions and activities. Public administrators also have information available to them that others have difficulty obtaining; it may be information that the administrators themselves decided to generate. This information is often the basis of decision making. Other information could lead one to make different decisions, but the initial decision as to what information to gather is frequently left up to the administrators (see Chapter 8). Because public administrators have such special expertise and access to information, at times it may be beyond the ability of those charged with oversight to hold the administrators accountable. There are also costs to obtaining information. The reporting requirements Congress imposes on agencies can impinge on administrators' ability to do other parts of their jobs.

The Advantage of Full-Time Status   For the most part, public administrators do their jobs on a full-time basis. Outsiders who would hold them accountable typically are engaged in other activities and cannot devote sufficient time to watching the public administrators. For instance, this is true of congressional oversight of administrative activities. Members of Congress have a great deal more to do than look over the shoulders of public administrators. Moreover, the incentives to engage in forceful oversight on a routine basis are often weak. Short of the scent of scandal, for Congress the net result is that most oversight activity is left up to the congressional staff. But because it is not an activity of high priority to their bosses (that is, members of Congress), there is a tendency to concentrate on other matters.

The Protective Nature of the Personnel System   Public personnel systems in the United States and elsewhere tend to afford public administrators a great deal of job security. Discipline and dismissal are possible, but cumbersome and difficult. Consequently, petty infractions, such as using public resources of limited value for private purposes, are likely to go unpunished. However, the cumulative impact of such infractions can be significant. If each federal employee used a dollar's worth of public property for private purposes, the total cost would be almost $3 million. Similarly, deviation from administrative rules or their misapplication may not be deemed worthy of discipline unless the consequences are severe and, possibly, public.

The "Law of Counter Control"   It takes bureaucracy to control bureaucracy. Anthony Downs has maintained that there is a "Law of Counter Control": "The greater the effort made by a sovereign or top-level official to control the behavior of subordinate officials, the greater the efforts made by those subordinates to evade or counteract such control."[19] But the greater the efforts in either direction, the more staff that are likely to be needed to try to secure accountability. The greater the number of staff, the more likely the effort to control one bureaucracy will result in another. For instance, to a large extent one could describe the history of expansion of the Executive Office of the President and Congress's creation of the Congressional Budget Office in 1974 as a counterforce to the executive's Office of Management and Budget in these terms.[20]

The Problem of Coordination   In the United States, the separation of powers complicates the quest for accountability. The president is charged with the faithful execution of the laws, but congressional involvement is necessary to create, fund, staff, and empower administrative agencies. Without coordination between the president and Congress, accountability is very difficult to obtain. But because both branches of government have different constituencies, roles, incentives, and interests, coordination is not a simple matter. There are times when one branch impedes the efforts of the other to hold public administrators accountable.

The Lack of Political Direction   Politics in the United States does not provide comprehensive political direction to public administrators. Political parties are fragmented and elections do not convey clear mandates. Undoubtedly, most public administrators would follow clear mandates, if they existed, but in their absence, political direction of public agencies is uncertain. This is exacerbated by the relatively short tenure of political executives, which is generally in the range of two to three years. Coupled with the protective nature of personnel systems, the absence of clear mandates and short tenure of political executives provide career public administrators little incentive to depart substantially from their views of the public interest and the interests of their agencies. Many political executives have complained bitterly about the difficulty of changing the directions of the career service.

The Fragmentation of Agency Structures and Functions   The structure of public agencies in the United States is often fragmented and missions are often overlapping. Fragmentation and overlapping responsibilities, addressed in Chapter 4, have their sources and benefits. However, they may make it difficult to pinpoint responsibility for any given administrative action. Agencies can be quite dexterous in obscuring and shifting the blame for even the clearest of agency failures.

The Large Size and Scope of Public Administration   On average, the federal government spends over $40,000 per second every second of the year. Some administrative departments and agencies have over 100,000 employees. The Department of Defense has at times employed more than a million civilians. The Postal Service employs more than 700,000. The *Federal Register* frequently tops 50,000 pages in length. In 1940, when the federal service was only about half its current size in terms of personnel, there were almost 19 million vouchers covering government expenditures.[21] Even with advances in computer technology, who can keep track of all these dollars, people, regulations, forms, and so forth? Unless there is some reason to suspect that public administrators or agencies have deviated from the public interest in some way, there is little possibility of using routine audits to find serious infractions. Rather, the scandal must break first—and by then it is too late to prevent whatever damage the infractions have caused.

"Third Party" Government   The contracting out or other "outsourcing" of governmental functions can make it difficult to determine who is responsible for what. To take a tragic private sector example, after the May 11, 1996, crash of a ValuJet plane in the Everglades that resulted in 110 deaths, the Federal Aviation Administration (FAA) admitted it had difficulty inspecting the airline's operations because so much of its maintenance was contracted out to "geographically diverse low bidders" throughout its flying region.[22] One expert noted, "There is no question that outsourcing maintenance increases the risk of miscommunication and greatly complicates the F.A.A.'s inspection task."[23] But what is true for the FAA and the airlines is also true for oversight and accountability within the government. Outsourcing requires careful monitoring and, in government, the monitoring will also have to be monitored. For instance, the General Accounting Office and congressional committees exercise oversight of how well the Department of Defense keeps tabs on the contractors that maintain its weapons systems.

These barriers to holding the "permanent" civil service accountable in a systematic fashion are so formidable that the formal theory of accountability in democracies is clearly at odds with the reality. In the formal theory,

> power emanates from the people and is to be exercised in trust for the people. Within the government each level of executive authority is accountable to the next, running on up to the President or the Cabinet. The executive authority as a whole is accountable to the Congress or Parliament, which is assisted in its surveillance of expenditures by an independent audit agency. Officials are required to submit themselves to periodic elections as a retrospective evaluation of their performances and to receive a new mandate from the people.[24]

However, as the authors of the above passage point out, perhaps inevitably, "accountability gets lost in the shuffle somewhere in the middle ranges of the bureaucracy."[25] How can we find and retrieve it?

PERSPECTIVES ON ACCOUNTABILITY AND ETHICS

The Traditional Managerial Perspective

The basic tenets of the traditional managerial approach to accountability and ethics are probably fairly well known to those who have had several dealings with public administrative organizations. As mentioned in Chapter 10, there has been a tendency for some managerially oriented norms to work their way into the cultural values of the American middle class. Specifically, however, in keeping with its emphasis on efficiency, economy, and effectiveness, the traditional managerial approach stresses the need for organizational unity as a means of establishing accountability and as a guide to ethics.

First, the traditional managerial approach emphasizes that authority and responsibility must be clearly assigned. Overlapping functions, which tend to obscure responsibility and consequently to frustrate accountability, should be reduced to a minimum. The lines of hierarchical authority should be clear and comprehensive. Ideally, they should culminate in a single position, rather than a commission of some kind. Plural agency heads are frowned upon because they can muddle the lines of authority and cloud issues of responsibility. They can also divide the loyalties of subordinates.

Second, this approach emphasizes the need for strict subordination, which is the other side of the coin of hierarchy. Underlings must strictly obey the directives and commands of superordinates. This is necessary for organizational effectiveness and accountability. An act of disobedience, termed insubordination, is a substantial offense against the organization, according to this view. It is often punishable by dismissal. Logically, this is viewed as necessary, for otherwise superordinates would be officially responsible for behavior that is beyond their control. Accordingly, under the traditional managerial approach a public administrator who is unwilling to follow orders is expected to leave his or her organization, either through transfer or resignation. As noted earlier, the traditional managerial approach finds street-level administration problematic because it is so difficult to supervise and control. Indeed, traditional management may go to considerable lengths to monitor street-level employees. In the summer of 1996, the Postal Service initiated a test to use Department of Defense reconnaissance satellites to keep track of postal trucks. The system has the potential to track 128 factors, including truck location, speed, and even if the driver has run a stop sign.[26]

Third, concern with strict subordination dictates a limited span of control. The span of control, it will be recalled, is the number of subordinates directly responsible to a superordinate. Orthodox public administrative theory paid a great deal of attention to determining the proper span of control. Discussions were oriented toward effective management, but concern with accountability was built into the concept. Just as plural leadership was considered inappropriate, too many subordinates per superordinate was also viewed as a problem.

Fourth, subordinates are encouraged to be loyal to the organization and to their superordinates. Loyalty is generated in several ways. One is through organizational socialization that attempts to inculcate the importance of the agency's mission and the need to work toward it with a high degree of unity. Another is through occupational specialization that makes it difficult for employees to find equivalent work elsewhere; firefighters are a good example of this. A third approach is to make the employees materially dependent upon the organization to a great extent. Aside from pay, pensions and conflict-of-interest regulations have an important role here. Sometimes pension plans create a strong incentive to remain with an organization. Conflict-of-interest regulations may seek to make the employee dependent, economically, on the organization. The employee may be required to divest himself or herself of economic assets that could create conflicting interests or loyalties. Attempting to "close the revolving door"—preventing public employees from taking private employment with firms they previously dealt with in their official capacities—is a related effort to make them dependent upon and loyal to their public employers. At the federal level in the United States, both traditional conflict-of-interest statutes and anti-revolving door regulations are currently comprehensive.[27]

Fifth, the traditional managerial approach relies on formal disciplinary systems to enforce accountability and subordination. These systems seek to identify breaches of proper conduct. As already noted, insubordination typically ranks high on the list of misbehavior. Other matters may range from very broad prohibitions on "immoral and notoriously disgraceful" conduct to specific considerations of misuse of agency authority or property. For example, using stationery with the agency's letterhead for personal purposes is sometimes considered a serious breach of ethics. It violates the concept of unity of authority within the agency, because it is unauthorized, and also suggests that government property is being misused for private purposes. John A. Rohr points out in *Ethics for Bureaucrats* that some agencies develop elaborate codes of conduct intended to impart a sense of what is to be considered ethical or unethical behavior.[28] Some of the examples he cites are drawn from the Department of Agriculture. They concern the use of office equipment (including telephones) for personal business, the use of government automobiles for personal purposes, and whether the agency can take action against employees who fail to pay personal debts. Rohr evaluates this approach as reducing ethical behavior to "staying out of trouble," and emphasizing "meticulous attention to trivial questions."[29] In fact, in his view, "These exercises provide a clear example of the worst aspects of the mentality that continues to dichotomize politics and administration."[30] For example, they are more concerned with a personal phone call than with whether the administrator engages in behavior that abridges someone's constitutional rights to due process (see Box 12–4).

The type of disciplinary system the traditional managerial approach prefers in enforcing these codes of conduct and organization norms is one that is simple and always under the control of the agency's own hierarchy. Otherwise unity and hierarchy are weakened—and these are the very goals of the codes of conduct in the first place. However, pressures for the fair treatment of employees have often led to collective bargaining agreements that seriously reduce managerial authority to discipline employees. In addition, the legal perspective's concern with protection of the constitutional rights of public employees has promoted both more elaborate adverse action hearing systems and judicial review of managerial disciplinary decisions and procedures.

Sixth, the traditional managerial perspective's concern with fiscal regularity and employee performance places emphasis on the use of internal audits. Audits can be a strong deterrent to corruption or other abuse of the public trust. Preaudits are effective in blocking the misuse of funds; postaudits create a deterrent to abuses and sometimes are performed by a unit within an organization, as the traditional managerial approach prefers. Other times, however, it is thought that an outside auditing body is more desirable, such as the General Accounting Office, which is an agency of Congress. At times, a compromise is adopted: the audit bureau is within the agency, but independent of its hierarchy.

BOX 12–4 General Services Administration's Code of Conduct: Some Examples

---

§ 105-735.210 Indebtedness.

GSA personnel shall pay their just financial obligations in a proper and timely manner, especially those imposed by law, such as Federal, State, or local taxes. For the purposes of this paragraph, a "just financial obligation" means one acknowledged by the employee, or reduced to judgment by a court. In a dispute between GSA personnel and an alleged creditor, GSA will not undertake to determine the validity or amount of a disputed debt.

§ 105-735.211 Gambling, betting, and lotteries.

GSA personnel shall not participate, while on property owned or leased by the Government or while on duty for GSA, in any gambling activity, including the operation of a gambling device, participating in a lottery or pool, participating in a game for money or property, or selling or purchasing a numbers slip or ticket, except as otherwise lawfully authorized.

§ 105-735.212 General conduct prejudicial to the Government.

GSA personnel shall not engage in criminal, infamous, dishonest, immoral, or notoriously disgraceful conduct prejudicial to the Government.

§ 105-735.213 Intermediaries.

In any relations with the public, GSA personnel shall not recommend or suggest the use of any non-Government person (individual, firm, corporation, or other entity) offering service as intermediary, consultant, agent, representative, attorney, expediter, or specialist for the purpose of assisting in any negotiations, transactions, or other business with GSA.

§ 105-733.214 Lending or borrowing money.

GSA personnel shall not lend money for profit to other GSA personnel or lend money for profit to any other person on Government premises. A supervisor shall not borrow money from a subordinate under any circumstances. This prohibition is not applicable to recognized employee credit unions or employee welfare plans.

§ 105-735.218 Purchase of real estate.

GSA personnel, whose official duties are in any way related to the acquisition or disposal of real estate or interests therein or to the maintenance or improvement of real estate, shall not, directly or indirectly, purchase any real estate or interest

---

Audits can be concerned with general fiscal matters of performance and management, or matters of reporting, such as the number of cases closed. Several federal agencies use "inspectors general" (IGs) as a kind of internal policing mechanism having authority to engage in investigations and audits in a broad range of circumstances (see Box 12–5). The IGs' ability to investigate financial matters was strengthened by the Chief Financial Officers Act of 1990. The act requires federal agencies to appoint chief financial officers (CFOs) to centralize financial management and adopt more standardized accounting practices. The CFOs prepare financial statements for administrative and legislative use.

BOX 12–4 *Continued*

---

therein except for occupancy as their personal residence unless a full disclosure of the proposed transaction is made in writing to the appropriate supervisor who shall consult with the Special Counsel to the Administrator for Ethics (regional counsel in a region), and the prior written approval of the appropriate supervisor is obtained. A copy of the approval shall be promptly furnished by the supervisor to the Special Counsel to the Administrator for Ethics. Surplus real property may not be purchased under any circumstances. (See § 105-735.217.)

§ 105-735.219 Use of intoxicants.

GSA personnel shall not use intoxicants habitually to excess (5 U.S.C. 7352). GSA personnel shall not use intoxicants on U.S. Government-owned or leased premises except upon occasions and on property as to which the Administrator or Regional Administrator has granted an exception in writing or, in the case of property occupied by another agency, except as authorized by the head of that agency in accordance with law.

§ 105-735.220 Use of Government vehicles.

GSA personnel shall not use or authorize the use of Government-owned or leased motor vehicles or aircraft for other than official purposes (31 U.S.C. 638(c)) and shall operate such vehicles or aircraft in strict compliance with all applicable laws.

§ 105-735.221 Use of official telephones.

GSA personnel shall not use Federal Telecommunications System or commercial telephone facilities for long-distance calls unless authorized to do so.

§ 105-735.222 Use of Government documents.

GSA personnel shall not knowingly, willfully and unlawfully conceal, remove, mutilate, falsify, or destroy any Government document or record (18 U.S.C. 2071).

SOURCE: Office of the Administrator, General Services Administration, "Revisions to GSA's Standards of Conduct Order," 29 November 1983 (Washington, D.C.: General Services Administration, 1983).

All these approaches are important in promoting accountability and ethics. They are all found in a vast array of contemporary public and private organizations in one form or another. Their main limitation, as Rohr points out, is their narrow focus. They are concerned with protecting managerial values more than protecting the public from a breach of trust in a more political sense.

The New Public Management

The NPM has a radically different view of accountability and ethics. It focuses almost exclusively on performance and results. It views the type of procedural safeguards on which the traditional managerial approach relies as obstacles to cost-effective government. It favors external oversight by legislatures that assesses performance, but opposes that which focuses on internal managerial matters, including spending, personnel administration, and organization. It advocates allowing employees to use agency credit cards for travel and the purchase of routine office supplies. It opposes controls and oversights imposed by central budget, procurement, and personnel agencies, such as the Office of Management and Budget, the General Services Administration, and the Office of Personnel Management. Accountability for results can also be enforced through market mechanisms and customers' judgments. However, viewing the public as customers, the NPM does not put much stock in traditional avenues for political participation, including elections and rule-making proceedings (not to mention legislative casework).

In the National Performance Review's (NPR) version of the NPM, ethics amount to achieving results with a high degree of customer satisfaction. The NPR discounts concern with corruption for two reasons. First, it assumes that the overwhelming number of public employees are good people. Its view is somewhat reminiscent of the contention by the eighteenth-century French Enlightenment philosopher, Jean Jacques Rousseau, that "Man is born free, and yet we see him everywhere in chains."[31] According to the NPR:

> . . . people—in government or out—are, for the most part, neither crooked nor stupid. Most people want to do the right thing, so long as the right thing makes sense. Perhaps the most important thing about the reinvention initiative, and its regulatory reform work in particular, is that it is based on a new assumption: that people are honest and that if you tell people what needs to be done, and let them get on with doing it, the chances are it will be done better—and more cheaply—than if you tell them how. Moreover, it values them as human beings.[32]

Treating honest and smart people as though they are crooked and stupid binds them in pointless and harmful red tape. As the NPR puts it, "This lack of trust in its own employees is one reason why doing almost anything in the government has always required a couple of dozen signatures: to be sure no one was cheating the taxpayer. Of course the process sometimes cost more than what was protected, but at least no one could be blamed if something went wrong."[33]

Second, given that most people are good, the cost of ferreting out and deterring corruption is too high in terms of the red tape such efforts create. In the NPR's words,

> . . . innovation, by its nature, requires deviation. Unfortunately, faced with so many controls, many employees have simply given up. They do everything by the book—whether it makes sense or not. They fill out forms that should never have been created, follow rules that should never have been imposed, and prepare reports that serve no purpose—and are often never even read. In the name of controlling waste, we have created paralyzing inefficiency.[34]

In short, the NPR seeks to replace many of the accountability and ethics controls imposed on public employees with a culture of trust:

BOX 12–5 **Federal Inspectors General**

As part of the overall civil service reforms of 1978 (see Chapter 5), Congress passed the Inspector General Act (Public Law 95-452). Among its provisions are the following:

Section 2: In order to create independent and objective units—

1. to conduct and supervise audits and investigations relating to programs and operations of the [agencies covered];

2. to provide leadership and coordination and recommend policies for activities designed (A) to promote economy, efficiency, and effectiveness in the administration of, and (B) to prevent and detect fraud and abuse in, such programs and operations; and

3. to provide a means for keeping the head of the establishment [agency] fully and currently informed about problems and deficiencies relating to the administration of such programs and operations and the necessity for progress of correction action;

. . . is hereby established in each of such establishments an office of Inspector General.

Section 5 (b): Semiannual reports of each Inspector General shall be furnished to the head of the establishment involved not later than April 30 and October 31 of each year and shall be transmitted by such to the appropriate committees or subcommittees of the Congress within thirty days after receipt of the report, together with a report by the head of the establishment containing any comments such head deems appropriate.

"IGs" are now used in a host of agencies, including the Departments of Agriculture, Commerce, Defense, Energy, Health and Human Services, Interior, Labor, State, and Transportation, as well as such independent establishments as the Environmental Protection Agency and the National Aeronautics and Space Administration.

There are approximately sixty IGs, about half of whom are appointed to larger agencies and departments by the president, with the advice and consent of the Senate. More than 10,000 employees work for IGs. In 1994, IG findings resulted in more than 14,000 successful civil and criminal actions and almost $2 billion in recovered funds. According to a congressional subcommittee, IG recommendations could have saved $24 billion in 1994.

Despite the IGs' successes, critics charge that they have a "gottcha" mentality and do not do enough to prevent mismanagement. The National Performance Review, in particular, claims that the IGs stifle employee creativity and willingness to rely on common sense.

SOURCES: Public Law 95-452; and Leigh Rivenbark, "Inspectors General Rapped," *Federal Times*, 14 August 1995, 15.

The essential ingredient in bringing about so great a people-led change—indeed, the essential ingredient of self-government—is trusting the people involved. In this case, that means government employees and the people they serve....

It's often said these days that the American people need to have more trust in the government. That's not all. If the reinvention initiative has taught the government anything (and it has taught it many things), it is that the government needs to have more trust in the American people—including its own employees. It needs to trust that when we say we need something, we're right. It needs to trust that when we say something needs fixing, it does. It needs to trust that when we're given a goal to reach, we'll reach it.

When we are not trusted, when nothing we say or do seems to make a difference, we feel powerless. Elections alone do not restore that power. The power that matters in a self-governing democracy is the power we can exercise "over-the-counter," on a daily basis, whenever we interact with our government, whenever we seek to make our needs known. Someone must be listening. Someone must act.[35]

This approach stands in remarkable contrast to the checks and balances so carefully crafted by the Constitution's Framers—as the NPR freely admits.[36] It not only views the potential for corruption as largely insignificant, it also asserts that agency and individual self-interest are inconsequential (although it embraces markets, in which all activity is assumed to be motivated by self-interest). Aside from the difficulties posed by accurately measuring performance, discussed in Chapter 8, the NPM's results orientation does not deal with the fundamental ethical problem of when ends may justify means. However, as the previous chapter explains, a great deal of American constitutional law centers on ends-means issues: that is precisely what procedural due process and the compelling governmental interest and least restrictive alternative tests are all about. Not surprisingly, the political approach to public administrative accountability and ethics takes a very different view.

The Political Perspective

In contrast to the traditional managerial perspective, but in agreement with the NPM, the political approach emphasizes the need for developing mechanisms for accountability that are *external* to public administrative agencies. In the past, this was done primarily through political control of public personnel through patronage appointments. Nowadays, however, the political approach must rely on other means. Among some of the more familiar are the following.

General Legislative Oversight   Legislative oversight is exercised by members of the legislature, their staffs, and legislative agencies, such as the federal General Accounting Office and the Congressional Budget Office. Depending on the incentives facing the legislature, oversight can be a forceful means of promoting accountability of public administrators. The congressional Watergate hearings in the early 1970s and the Iran-Contra hearings in 1986–1987 presented spectacular examples of the use of legislative oversight to hold the executive branch accountable. Generally speaking, though, legislatures are more likely to exercise careful oversight when crises develop than when operations seem to be running on a routine basis. This may change if legislatures begin to focus more systematically on program results, as the NPM urges. If the federal Government Performance and Results Act of 1993 works as planned, then agencies will regularly submit results-oriented reports to congressional (sub)committees. The Office of Government Ethics, an independent agency within the executive branch, assists the Senate in the process of confirming or rejecting presidential appointees to federal positions, especially in terms of financial disclosure. (See Box 12–6 for a brief review of the Office of Government Ethics.)

Budgetary Control   Historically, the "power of the purse" was considered an extremely important legislative check on the executive's "power of the sword." Although legislatures in the United States retain a great deal of the power of the purse, they tend to share the budgeting function with the executive to a very considerable extent. Nonetheless, they are apt to monitor agency spending in a variety of ways, including using overhead agencies such as the General Accounting Office, relying on CFO reports, and holding hearings. They also can become directly involved in agency decision making, which is sometimes denounced as "micromanagement." Despite the pejorative term, micromanagement does not always involve pork barrel forays. It can also concern major policy disputes.[37]

BOX 12–6 **The U.S. Office of Government Ethics**

The Ethics in Government Act of 1978 created an Office of Government Ethics (OGE) in the Office of Personnel Management. The Ethics Reform Act of 1989 strengthened the OGE, which is now an independent agency within the executive branch. The OGE is headed by a director, who holds a five-year term and is removable for cause only. There are designated agency ethics officials within each agency. The OGE is the federal government's central agency for ethics policy. Its mission includes

- Regulatory authority to establish rules regarding conflicts of interest, standards of conduct, postemployment, and financial disclosure

- Review of financial disclosure statements

- Education and training

- Guidance and interpretation of rules and laws

- Enforcement

- Evaluation

As of June 1996, the OGE employed eighty people. According to its current director, Stephen Potts, ethics education is a key priority.

Potts believes that one of the major difficulties in developing standards for ethical behavior is that whereas ideally rules should be intuitive, in practice there are so many facets to ethics that regulations are inevitably very complicated and legalistic.

SOURCES: See Stuart Gilman, "The U.S. Office of Government Ethics," *The Bureaucrat* (Spring 1991): 13–16. Potts discussed his priorities at a meeting of the Standing Panel of the Public Service, National Academy of Public Administration, Washington, D.C., 28 May 1991. Telephone interview with Stuart Gilman held on 7 June 1996.

Rotation in Office   The political approach has long stressed the need to rotate public administrators from office to office or in and out of the public service altogether. This is a matter of preventing misperception of the public interest because of too much specialization in one agency or function. In the 1840s and 1850s, rotation was through the spoils system, whereas today it is accomplished in a number of ways in modern public personnel systems. For instance, the creation of the Senior Executive Service in the federal civil service reform of 1978 was intended, in part, to enable top-level career civil servants to move from bureau to bureau or agency to agency in the hope that they would consequently develop a broader perspective on the public interest. The federal Intergovernmental Personnel Act authorized public administrators to move temporarily from positions in the federal government to the states and vice versa. Political executives are routinely rotated out of office when a new president or governor takes office, especially when there is a change in partisanship.

Representation and Public Participation   Just as rotation is aimed at reducing misconception of the public interest, encouraging pluralism within public administration can subject public administrators to a greater diversity of perspectives and interests. A socially representative public service is likely to be more diversified, in terms of values and political perspectives, than a homogeneous one. Allowing public participation and interest group representation in administrative processes further brings public administrators into contact with the views of the public, or at least segments of it. The Administrative Procedure Act of 1946, the Federal Advisory Committee Act of 1972, and the Civil Service Reform Act of 1978 all contain provisions, mentioned earlier in this book, that encourage representation and participation.

"Going Public"   The political perspective holds that it is proper and ethical for public employees to inform the public or its representatives, such as legislators, of misconduct by public administrators and of violations of the public trust or interest by agencies. In other words, they are expected to use their voices to protest administrative activities that they consider illegal and/or immoral. Public resignations and whistle-blowing are viewed as appropriate, and often highly moral, acts. Whistle-blowing is now statutorily protected at the federal level. In addition, the federal government has institutionalized a fraud, waste, and abuse "hot line," whereby employees or others can anonymously report instances of misconduct to the General Accounting Office for further investigation. Some of these hot line tips have resulted in the removal of public administrators from the federal service.[38] More important, though, is their deterrent effect. Where whistle-blowing and "hot lining" are regarded as virtuous activities, loyalty to the agency and superiors, in the managerial sense, is inevitably undermined. Agencies have sometimes issued "gag" orders to prevent employees from going public. But cover-ups are now more difficult, and individual acts of corruption are riskier. Today, federal employees who engage in whistle-blowing are afforded considerable statutory protection. These

protections reach beyond reporting mismanagement and fiscal abuse to speaking out on specific and substantial dangers to the public health or safety. Public employees at all levels of government also have some constitutional protections in speaking out on matters of public concern. One of the thornier issues in this area is when anonymous or secretive "leaks" to the press are appropriate. Sometimes the unauthorized disclosure of information can prematurely foreclose an agency's policy options or adversely affect the behavior of the public, as would be the case if someone in the Federal Deposit Insurance Corporation announced that a certain large bank was nearly insolvent.

"Sunshine"   The political perspective holds that open, public dealings are an important means of securing the accountability and proper conduct of public officials. Consequently, it has promoted a number of approaches to fostering "sunshine" in public administration. These range from the requirement that some hearings and meetings be open to the public to the Freedom of Information Act's creation of a right for members of the public to obtain many categories of federal administrative documents. At the federal level, freedom of information and open hearings provisions have been incorporated into the basic administrative law, the Administrative Procedure Act (originally enacted in 1946).

Conflict of Interest   The political approach agrees with the traditional managerial approach that conflicts of interest ought to be eliminated. It also holds that the "revolving door" should be watched carefully, though not sealed altogether, because it does make agencies more responsive to the economic interests with which they deal. The rationale here is less to bolster hierarchical authority within agencies than to eliminate the temptation to misuse positions of public trust for private gain.

The political approach to accountability emphasizes the need for external checks on public administrative conduct. Unlike the traditional managerial perspective, it is not content to allow the maintenance of accountability to be largely the purview of the administrative hierarchy itself. There has long been debate over how efficacious this approach can be. Max Weber maintained that outside (extra-agency) checks on public administration are inherently inadequate. Even if they functioned very well, they would militate against the maximization of the values of the traditional managerial perspective for efficiency, economy, and effectiveness. But relying exclusively on checks within agencies themselves has obvious limits. The world is too familiar with self-serving administrative action and corruption to expect the guardians alone to guard themselves. Moreover, both the political and traditional managerial approaches rely primarily on enforcement mechanisms that are *external to the individual.* This may seem inappropriate because "responsible conduct of administrative functions is not so much enforced as it is elicited."[39] In other words, the desire to engage in ethical behavior must spring, to a large extent, from within the individual public administrator. Similarly, the strongest system of accountability would be self-imposed.

From the perspectives of ethics as an inner, personal check on public administrators' conduct, the traditional managerial approach's emphasis on loyalty is regarded as being sound, but too narrow. John Rohr observes that it must be enlarged to encompass a broader sense of professionalism and to include dedication to **regime values.**[40] Combining these two concerns and adding some of the externally oriented approaches of the political perspective can provide the beginnings of a synthesis in terms of ethics and accountability in contemporary public administration. We will return to this prospect after mapping out the legal perspective, which stresses the concept of "regime values."

The Legal Perspective

We have noted at many points throughout this book how constitutional values and requirements can be at odds with the perspectives of the traditional managerial and political approaches to public administration. In response to this disjuncture, the federal judiciary has articulated a number of constitutional rights that are viewed as protections of individuals against certain administrative actions. Moreover, the judiciary has adjusted the standards of public administrators' liabilities for causing unconstitutional infringements of these rights. In the process, the courts have intentionally provided public administrators with a strong and *personally internalized incentive* to protect, or at least avoid abridging, the constitutional rights of the individuals upon whom they act in their official capacities. John Rohr notes that what the courts have done is tantamount to articulating a set of regime values to which public administrators should be accountable. Moreover, these regime values provide ethical guidance to public administrators.

More specifically, Rohr notes that the regime-values approach rests on three considerations: "(1) That ethical norms should be derived from the salient values of the regime; (2) That these values are normative *for bureaucrats* because they have taken an oath to uphold the regime; (3) That these values can be discovered in the public law of the regime."[41] To a very considerable extent, the regime values of the United States can be found in its constitutional law, and adherence to the values it articulates can be the internalized guide for public administrators, ethical behavior, and broad accountability. As noted in Chapter 11, some courts have even embraced the concept that public administrators have a right to *disobey* unconstitutional orders.

The legal approach to public administrative ethics also emphasizes the need for clear rules of conduct and enforcement mechanisms to assure compliance. Law is viewed as providing a minimal threshold for ethical administration. Behavior that fails to meet the threshold should be punished. An agency, such as the federal Office of Government Ethics, may be used to clarify and publicize standards. For matters potentially involving aggravated breaches of law, the legal approach may favor using independent counsels or special prosecutors to investigate and bring cases against government officials. In theory, independent counsels and special prosecutors are politically and administratively independent (as noted in the discussion of *Morrison v. Olson* in

Chapter 1). Their responsibility is to the rule of law. In practice, these functionaries sometimes appear to be partisan in their zeal to uncover embarrassing wrongdoing associated with a political party or a branch of government.

The focus of a great deal of ethics legislation and rules is on economic relationships. For instance, not only are blatant conflicts of interest outlawed, but the acceptance of hospitality, however harmless it may appear, is sometimes prohibited. Sometimes the effort to avoid appearances of impropriety can bump up against public administrators' constitutional rights. For instance, in *U.S. v. National Treasury Employees Union* (1995),[42] the Supreme Court found a First Amendment violation in regulations that prohibited federal employees below the GS-16 level from accepting honoraria for appearances, speeches, or writing articles. In the Court's view, the nexus between the ban and the government's interests in avoiding the appearance of improper conduct was too tenuous because "federal employees below Grade GS-16, [are] an immense class of workers with negligible power to confer favors on those who might pay to hear them speak or to read their articles."

The efficacy of ethics laws depends largely on their clarity and certainty of enforcement—two conditions that are often absent. In any event, mere compliance with the law, which is a prerequisite for ethical behavior, does not fully encompass ethics. For example, the law may contain loopholes that could be exploited by public administrators for their own gain. Although legal, the ensuing behavior would be considered unethical.

CONCLUSION: PERSONAL RESPONSIBILITY

In recent years, much of the American public administrative community has expressed considerable interest in questions of accountability and ethics. Although the managerial, political, and legal perspectives toward public administration do not have a common view of how best to promote accountability and ethics, there is some convergence. Personal responsibility has emerged as a common thread. In a book called *The Frontiers of Public Administration*, published in 1936, John M. Gaus called upon the individual civil servant to be responsible to an "inner check," derived from professional standards and ideals.[43] Today, that inner check is sometimes constitutionally required to avoid personal liability. Moreover, constitutional requirements have been augmented by a widely accepted, comprehensive code of ethics that can fruitfully inform an inner check. The code was formulated by the American Society for Public Administration (ASPA), a leading organization of concerned public administrators at all levels of government. It is printed in Box 12–7.

ASPA's ethical code is broad enough to encompass each of the perspectives toward public administration discussed throughout this book. It requires attention to NPM and constitutional concerns, as well as to those of the traditional managerial and political approaches. Understanding the different perspectives toward public administration and appreciating their breadth is a

BOX 12–7 **American Society for Public Administration Code of Ethics**

The American Society for Public Administration (ASPA) exists to advance the science, processes, and art of public administration. The Society affirms its responsibility to develop the spirit of professionalism within its membership, and to increase public awareness of ethical principles in public service by its example. To this end, we, the members of the Society, commit ourselves to the following principles:

I   Serve the Public Interest
Serve the public, beyond serving oneself.

ASPA members are committed to:

1. Exercise discretionary authority to promote the public interest.

2. Oppose all forms of discrimination and harassment, and promote affirmative action.

3. Recognize and support the public's right to know the public's business.

4. Involve citizens in policy decision-making.

5. Exercise compassion, benevolence, fairness and optimism.

6. Respond to the public in ways that are complete, clear, and easy to understand.

7. Assist citizens in their dealings with government.

8. Be prepared to make decisions that may not be popular.

II   Respect the Constitution and the Law
Respect, support, and study government constitutions and laws that define responsibilities of public agencies, employees, and all citizens.

ASPA members are committed to:

1. Understand and apply legislation and regulations relevant to their professional role.

2. Work to improve and change laws and policies that are counter-productive or obsolete.

3. Eliminate unlawful discrimination.

4. Prevent all forms of mismanagement of public funds by establishing and maintaining strong fiscal and management controls, and by supporting audits and investigative activities.

5. Respect and protect privileged information.

6. Encourage and facilitate legitimate dissent activities in government and protect the whistleblowing rights of public employees.

7. Promote constitutional principles of equality, fairness, representativeness, responsiveness and due process in protecting citizens' rights.

III   Demonstrate Personal Integrity
Demonstrate the highest standards in all activities to inspire public confidence and trust in public service.

ASPA members are committed to:

1. Maintain truthfulness and honesty and to not compromise them for advancement, honor, or personal gain.

BOX 12–7 *Continued*

2. Ensure that others receive credit for their work and contributions.

3. Zealously guard against conflict of interest or its appearance: e.g., nepotism, improper outside employment, misuse of public resources or the acceptance of gifts.

4. Respect superiors, subordinates, colleagues and the public.

5. Take responsibility for their own errors.

6. Conduct official acts without partisanship.

IV Promote Ethical Organizations

Strengthen organizational capabilities to apply ethics, efficiency and effectiveness in serving the public.

ASPA members are committed to:

1. Enhance organizational capacity for open communication, creativity, and dedication.

2. Subordinate institutional loyalties to the public good.

3. Establish procedures that promote ethical behavior and hold individuals and organizations accountable for their conduct.

4. Provide organization members with an administrative means for dissent, assurance of due process and safeguards against reprisal.

5. Promote merit principles that protect against arbitrary and capricious actions.

6. Promote organizational accountability through appropriate controls and procedures.

7. Encourage organizations to adopt, distribute, and periodically review a code of ethics as a living document.

V Strive for Professional Excellence

Strengthen individual capabilities and encourage the professional development of others.

ASPA members are committed to:

1. Provide support and encouragement to upgrade competence.

2. Accept as a personal duty the responsibility to keep up to date on emerging issues and potential problems.

3. Encourage others, throughout their careers, to participate in professional activities and associations.

4. Allocate time to meet with students and provide a bridge between classroom studies and the realities of public service.

Enforcement of the Code of Ethics shall be conducted in accordance with Article I, Section 4 of ASPA's Bylaws.

In 1981 the American Society for Public Administration's National Council adopted a set of moral principles. Three years later in 1984, the Council approved a Code of Ethics for ASPA members. In 1994 the Code was revised.

SOURCE: American Society for Public Administration, 1120 G Street NW Suite 700, Washington, D.C. 20005-3885.

prerequisite to recognizing the complexity of demands that public administrators face. But the hard work lies less in identifying their diverse ethical requirements than in integrating them in real-world, on-the-job situations. Here, there is no blueprint or formula. Nor can there be one. Knowing what to emphasize when, how to combine or prioritize disparate requirements, how to bridge and negotiate the separation of powers, and much, much more are all part of the art and craft of contemporary public administration. As the NPR contends, improving accountability and advancing ethics ultimately depend on the individual actions of public servants: "If the American people and our government—which, after all, is simply more American people—are to build trust in one another, it can only happen through thousands, even millions, of personal interactions....We have to do it ourselves, individually and through association with one another."[44] To the contention that such change can take a very long time, Vice President Gore would reply, "then there's no time to lose," we had better start now![45]

NOTES

1. Frederick Mosher, *Democracy and the Public Service* (New York: Oxford University Press, 1968), 5.
2. Victor Thompson, *Modern Organization* (New York: Knopf, 1961).
3. Samuel Krislov and David H. Rosenbloom, *Representative Bureaucracy and the American Political System* (New York: Praeger, 1981), esp. chap. 2.
4. Seymour M. Lipset, "Bureaucracy and Social Change," in *Reader in Bureaucracy*, ed. R. K. Merton et al. (Glencoe, Ill.: Free Press, 1952), 221–232, at 230.
5. Kenneth Meier, "Representative Bureaucracy: An Empirical Analysis," *American Political Science Review* 69 (June 1975): 526–542; David H. Rosenbloom, *Federal Equal Employment Opportunity* (New York: Praeger, 1977); V. Subramaniam, "Representative Bureaucracy: A Reassessment," *American Political Science Review* 61 (December 1967): 1010–1019.
6. *Heller v. Doe by Doe*, 113 S.Ct. 2637 (1993).
7. Anthony Downs, *Inside Bureaucracy* (Boston: Little, Brown, 1967), 279.
8. Ibid., 276.
9. Joseph LaPalombara, *Interest Groups in Italian Politics* (Princeton, N.J.: Princeton University Press, 1963).
10. Ibid., 262.
11. Michael Johnston, *Political Corruption and Public Policy in America* (Monterey, Calif.: Brooks/Cole, 1982), 3.
12. Arnold J. Heidenheimer, ed., *Political Corruption: Readings in Comparative Analysis* (New York: Holt, Rinehart and Winston, 1970).
13. For a concise discussion, see Edward Banfield and James Q. Wilson, *City Politics* (Cambridge, Mass.: Harvard University Press and the M.I.T. Press, 1963), chap 9.
14. Heidenheimer, *Political Corruption*, introduction.
15. Robert N. Roberts, "Lord, Protect Me from the Appearance of Wrongdoing," in *Public Personnel Policy: The Politics of Civil Service*, ed. David H. Rosenbloom (Port Washington, N.Y.: Associated Faculty Press, 1985), chap. 11.

16. See Johnston, *Political Corruption*, 11–12.
17. *New York Times*, 11 July 1952.
18. For a general discussion, see Martin Tolchin and Susan Tolchin, *Selling Our Security—The Erosion of America's Assets* (New York: Knopf, 1992).
19. Downs, *Inside Bureaucracy*, 262.
20. See David Nachmias and David H. Rosenbloom, *Bureaucratic Government, USA* (New York: St. Martin's Press, 1980), chap. 4.
21. Bruce Smith and James Carroll, eds., *Improving the Accountability and Performance of Government* (Washington, D.C.: Brookings Institution, 1982), 21.
22. Adam Bryant, "F.A.A. Struggles as Airlines Turn to Subcontracts," *New York Times*, 2 June 1996, 1, 26.
23. Ibid., 26.
24. Bruce Smith and D. Hague, *The Dilemma of Accountability in Modern Government* (New York: St. Martin's Press, 1971), 26–27.
25. Ibid.
26. Chet Bridger, "Carriers Plan More Protests," *Federal Times*, 3 June 1996, 10.
27. Carolyn Ban, "The Revolving Door: Have We Shut It Too Tightly?" (Paper delivered at the Annual Meeting of the American Political Science Association, Washington, D.C., 30 August–2 September 1984). See also Robert N. Roberts, "Conflict-of-Interest Regulation and the Federal Service: The Legacy of Civil Service Reform," in *Centenary Issues of the Pendleton Act of 1883*, ed. David H. Rosenbloom (New York: Marcel Dekker, 1982), chap. 7; and Robert Roberts and Marion Doss, Jr., "Public Service and Private Hospitality: A Case Study in Federal Conflict-of-Interest Reform," *Public Administration Review* 52 (May/June 1992): 260–270.
28. John A. Rohr, *Ethics for Bureaucrats* (New York: Marcel Dekker, 1978), 51–55.
29. Ibid., 54.
30. Ibid.
31. Jean Jacques Rousseau, *The Social Contract* (New York: Hafner, 1947 [originally published in 1762]), 5.
32. Al Gore, *Common Sense Government Works Better & Costs Less* (Washington, D.C.: Government Printing Office, 1995), 33.
33. Ibid.
34. Al Gore, *From Red Tape to Results: Creating a Government that Works Better & Costs Less* (Washington, D.C.: Government Printing Office, 1993), 3.
35. Gore, *Common Sense Government*, 93.
36. Ibid., 92.
37. Kenneth Mayer, "Policy Disputes as a Source of Congressional Controls: Congressional Micromanagement of the Department of Defense," *Public Administration Review* 53 (July/August 1993): 293–302.
38. *New York Times*, 30 September 1984.
39. Carl J. Friedrich, "Public Policy and the Nature of Administrative Responsibility," in *The Politics of the Federal Bureaucracy*, 2d ed., ed. Alan Altshuler and Norman Thomas (New York: Harper & Row, 1977), pp. 333–343, at 340.
40. Rohr, *Ethics for Bureaucrats*, esp. chap. 2.
41. Ibid., 59.
42. *U.S. v. National Treasury Employees Union*, 130 L. Ed. 2d 964 (1995).
43. Quoted in Friedrich, "Public Policy," 339.
44. Gore, *Common Sense Government*, 93.
45. Gore, *From Red Tape to Results*, iv.

ADDITIONAL READING

BOWMAN, JAMES, ED. *Ethical Frontiers in Public Management.* San Francisco: Jossey-Bass, 1991.

COOPER, TERRY, ED. *Handbook of Administrative Ethics.* New York: Marcel Dekker, 1994.

GREEN, RICHARD, AND KATHRYN DENHART, EDS., "Character Ethics in Public Administration," *International Journal of Public Administration*, vol. 17 (special Issue, 1994): 2137–2389.

HEIDENHEIMER, ARNOLD, MICHAEL JOHNSTON, AND VICTOR LeVINE. *Political Corruption.* New Brunswick, N.J.: Transaction, 1989.

ROHR, JOHN. *Ethics for Bureaucrats,* 2d ed. New York: Marcel Dekker, 1989.

STUDY QUESTIONS

1. Can you identify a case of public administration with which you are familiar where the official violated his or her public trust, in your view? If so, what seems to have been the cause? How was the breach of trust discovered, and how was the issue resolved? Do you believe the resolution was the best one possible?

2. How realistic do you think the notion of an "inner check" on administrators' conduct is?

3. Do you think public administrative corruption is a serious problem in the United States, relative to corruption among elected officials? If you see a disparity here, what might account for it? What can it teach us about accountability?

4. The National Performance Review (NPR) argues that, because most public employees are good and competent, comprehensive efforts to regulate conflicts of interest and other unethical behavior are not cost-effective. Do you agree or disagree with the NPR's underlying assumptions on these points? Why or why not?

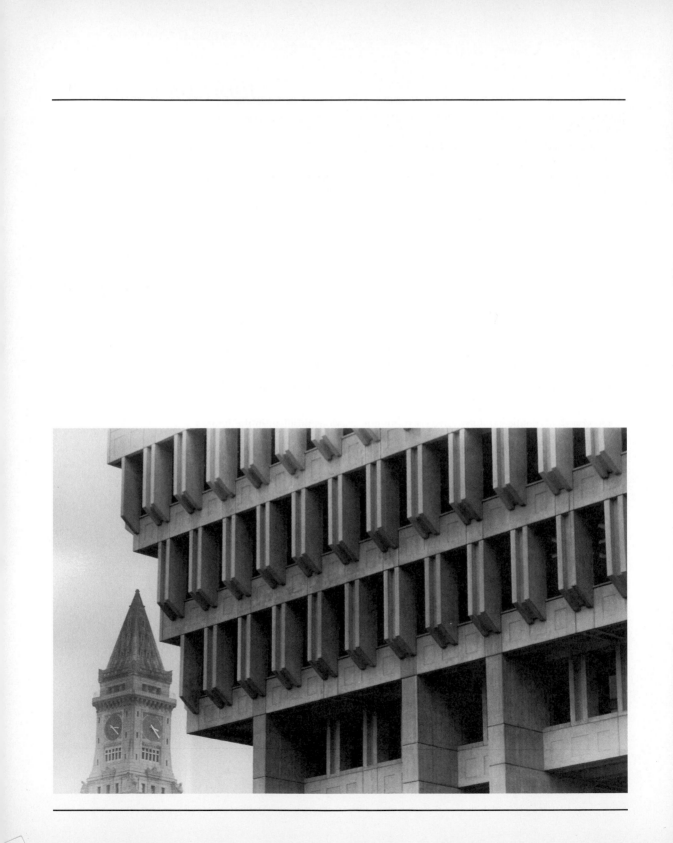

CHAPTER 13 | *The Future*

In the foreseeable future, public administration in the United States will be characterized by greater complexity, be subject to redefinition through politics, place increasing importance on law, emphasize performance, undergo disaggregation as an overall field of study and practice, witness decomposition of the civil service, redefine management, emphasize personal responsibility, and move toward a new administrative culture.

Today, public administration stands at a crossroads. It has stood there for a long time—a half-century has elapsed since the traditional managerial approach was convincingly attacked for being too limited in its vision of government. Ironically, the crossroads itself has become more complicated as new avenues have been brought to it. We have moved from a time when the traditional managerial approach dominated to the present in which the political and legal perspectives analyzed throughout this book broadly inform almost all public administrative activity. The new public management (NPM) has more recently joined the intersection of these earlier approaches, and whatever its staying power proves to be, it will certainly have many significant lasting impacts. The immediate problem of American public administrative practice and theory is to integrate or sort out the values, structural and procedural arrangements, and techniques associated with each of the perspectives. There is no map, which is one reason why we remain at the crossroads. Much of the task of moving ahead will fall on public administrators in the day-to-day performance of their jobs. Nevertheless, some generalizations about the future seem apt.

COMPLEXITY IS HERE TO STAY

Contemporary public administration is amazingly complex and it is becoming more complicated all the time. Public administrative activities range from trash collection to the exploration of outer space, from regulating the most developed postindustrial economies to helping some people move beyond the most rudimentary subsistence farming, from developing and using the most advanced biomedical technologies to the grinding task of going door to door at census time—and much, much more (recall Box 2-3). The essence of public administration is dealing with relationships among political, economic, social, ethical, organizational, managerial, legal, scientific, and technological values and systems at both microlevels and macrolevels. Public administrators bridge and coordinate the separation of powers and federalism, as well as the relationships between government, on the one side, and the economy and society on the other. Many work in an international arena as well. Boundaries are often blurred, and bright lines are likely to fade even more as governments rely increasingly on third parties to perform their work.

At the very least, public administrators need to be cognizant of all the approaches discussed throughout this book as they bear upon their jobs. Each perspective brings much to the crossroads. Although none is adequate on its own, each has a degree of internal coherence and enjoys substantial political and intellectual support. Where they agree with one another, the path is clear. But their disagreements are also instructive because they raise all the key issues facing today's public administration.

DOMINANT PUBLIC ADMINISTRATION
WILL BE DEFINED BY POLITICS

Historically, American public administration has always been defined by dominant political groups, parties, and/or coalitions.[1] From 1789 to 1828, federal administration was an extension of the elite who dominated national politics. The Jacksonian Revolution turned the federal service into the arm of the political parties. Building on the efforts of the nineteenth-century civil service reformers, the Progressives were able to institutionalize the politics-administration dichotomy and to base public administration on politically neutral, scientific, and technical expertise. Later, the New Deal placed federal administration under greater presidential control and made it more representative of and responsive to the clientele groups with which agencies dealt. Today, the National Performance Review (NPR) is an effort by "New Democrats" to show that government can be a cost-effective and responsive tool for intervening in the society and the economy. Given public concern with the cost of government, the alternative to making public administration "cost less and work better" is to eliminate many of its programs altogether.

The reality that politics has always defined dominant administrative practice in the United States is only thinly veiled by reformers' typical claims that their programs for change are apolitical. Like the civil service reformers more than a century ago, the NPR claims its reforms are intended to make the government more businesslike. And, like them, it ultimately admits that the big picture is political. For the reformers, it was a matter of changing the nation's political leadership; for the NPR, it is restoring the public's trust in government.[2] Administrative theory and practice are political theory and practice as well.[3] The successful advocacy of major administrative change in the United States has always been part of the overall program or vision of those in or gaining political power. Administrative ideas and techniques may be developed and implemented independently of politics—and they may be of great value—but the overall definition of what public administration should be is likely to continue to be politically determined.

Consequently, administrative doctrine and practice are not immutable. They have changed dramatically in the past, and they will probably change again in the future—perhaps as extensively as the NPR advocates. But how, if at all, will politics redefine public administration in the near future?

The NPM offers one strong prospect for change, as has been discussed throughout this book. Another possibility for politically inspired change should be mentioned as well. American government goes through periods when the strength of one institution grows relative to that of others. The New Deal presidency, institutionalized under the rubric of administrative reform, is a clear example. Today, Congress may be reasserting the powerful role that the Constitution designed for it. The 1994 Republican "Contract with America" fizzled along with Congress's effort to force its budget preferably disagree with White's assumption. Certainly, the federal government's highly developed separation of powers distinguishes its administration in important respects from that of local government under city managers. The vast array of activities in which administrators engage also detracts from the idea of a single process. Some administrators are generalists in program management; others specialize in functions such as personnel or budgeting; still others work in fields, including economics and engineering, that span both the public and private sectors. Intellectually, public administration has no single, coherent paradigm or conceptual framework. It has been suggested in several places throughout this book that one or more of the perspectives analyzed may be more applicable to different policy or program areas. There does not seem to be any compelling reason to treat overhead functions; sociotherapy; service; public utility, safety, and environmental regulation; and so forth as a single process.

DECOMPOSITION OF THE CIVIL SERVICE

Disaggregation promotes decomposition of the civil service. Two concepts that were central to traditional management are now disappearing. One is that any particular government, whether federal, state, or local, should act as a single, unified employer. The other is the concomitant idea of a unified civil service. The single employer concept was vital to the development of centralized public personnel systems with comprehensive position classification and pay schedules. A government, rather than its individual agencies, was the employer. Accordingly, the employee was a career civil servant rather than a worker for one agency or another. These concepts were stronger in the federal government than in most of the states, which traditionally had less well-developed administrative components, weaker central personnel agencies, and more limited merit systems. They have been seriously compromised to the point that one could question whether they are still operable.

First, the radical decentralization called for by the NPR and implemented by the U.S. Office of Personnel Management (OPM) places agencies in charge of their own personnel systems. They hire, train, and promote with little central oversight. For the most part, the famously comprehensive regulations of the *Federal Personnel Manual* are gone. Second, and relatedly, many agencies have gained exemption from the uniform body of law that regulates federal employment (that is, Title 5 of the U.S. Code). Whereas once perhaps 80 to 90 percent of all federal executive branch employees were subject to the same statutes and regulations, today, the number is closer to 50 percent. A large chunk of those who are exempt work for the corporatized Postal Service. But others are in regular executive agencies such as the Federal Aviation Administration and the Department of Veterans Affairs. When the federal government was viewed as a single employer, the House Post Office and Civil Service Committee and the Senate Governmental

Affairs Committee had subject matter jurisdiction for most civil service matters. They were part of a policy network that generally supported a strong, career-oriented civil service. In the future, as agency personnel practices are based on individual statutes tailored to their circumstances, jurisdiction will be dispersed among the various committees with oversight for those agencies and their programs.

Information technology also promotes decomposition. The "workplace" of the future may be no "place" at all. Telecommuting and computerization may redefine work sites as arenas "through which information circulates—information to which intellective effort is applied."[9] Finally, government will lose its distinctiveness as outsourcing blurs the boundaries between it and the private sector.

These changes may be highly beneficial. After all, the problems of the old "one size fits all" approach are well documented and real. However, they will also fundamentally alter the concept of civil service and will further fragment government.

THE CHANGING FACE OF MANAGEMENT

As its label suggests, the NPM is very much premised on the belief that, as a function, management must drastically change. From its perspective, the traditional view of management as voiced by Henry Mintzberg, a leading theorist, is quaintly archaic: "No job is more vital to our society than that of the manager. It is the manager who determines whether our social institutions serve us well or whether they squander our talents and resources."[10] To the contrary, the NPM claims that the empowered employees, entrepreneurs, and systems like total quality management (TQM) are vital to government performance. Traditional managers create bottlenecks, protect turf, and hoard information.

Whatever one's view of traditional management, information technology is already modifying the need for managers and their functions. Shoshana Zuboff has profitably studied the "informated" workplace ("informated" is as dramatic a change as was "automated," but it refers to computerization rather than mechanization).[11] She leaves no doubt that management is being reconceived. Traditional management changes or becomes obsolete when computers give employees access to a vast array of information; the capacity to communicate almost instantaneously with each other, clients, and customers; and the tools with which to redesign work processes. The computer can also replace the traditional role managers played in assuring employees were doing the work assigned to them. As Zuboff explains,

> The rigid separation of mental and material work characteristic of the industrial division of labor and vital to the preservation of a distinct managerial group (in the office as well as in the factory) becomes, not merely outmoded, but perilously dysfunctional. . . .

Under these circumstances, work organization requires a new division of learning to support a new division of labor. The traditional system of imperative control, which was designed to maximize the relationship between commands and obedience, depended upon restricted hierarchical access to knowledge and nurtured the belief that those who were excluded from the organization's explicit knowledge base were intrinsically less capable of learning what it had to offer. In contrast, an informated organization is structured to promote the possibility of useful learning among all members and thus presupposes relations of equality.[12]

Furthermore, as a whole, today's public employees are much better educated in problem solving than in the past. They are less dependent on management to show them how to do their jobs well. That is precisely why the NPM believes they should be empowered.

PERSONAL RESPONSIBILITY

There is currently broad agreement that public administrators should be held personally responsible for their actions. The NPR is explicit in emphasizing that empowered employees must be held accountable for results. Contemporary constitutional law is equally explicit in making public employees potentially personally liable for violating individuals' constitutional rights. Ethics law and rules demand that public employees personally avoid giving even the appearance of impropriety. Some aspects of environmental law impose criminal liability on public administrators, regardless of their hierarchical level, for illegal pollution.[13] External approaches to oversight and accountability are clearly being augmented by a sense that public employees must individually develop a sense of personal responsibility. The potential for administrators to do harm to other individuals, to communities, and to the environment are now so great that simply "going by the book" is inadequate. The culture in which "CYA" (cover your a[natomy]) would get one off the hook is no longer acceptable. Administration should not be "rule by nobody."[14] "The buck" currently stops almost everywhere, not just at the top of the hierarchy or formal chain of authority.

Personal responsibility sometimes requires behavior that traditionally was unacceptable and that remains uncomfortable. Statutes protecting whistle-blowers create a moral obligation to expose various kinds of maladministration, especially specific and immediate dangers to public health or safety. From a traditional perspective, whistle-blowing is insubordination and some whistle-blowers are still treated harshly. Yet, their responsibility is clear.[15] Similarly, there is a constitutional right and related obligation to disobey unconstitutional directives.[16]

If reliance on third-party government continues to grow, the demands for personal responsibility are likely to increase and even reach private individuals engaged in government work. The more attenuated the formal chains of accountability become as work is outsourced, the more the public may demand that specific individuals—not complex, inanimate systems—take responsibility for things gone wrong. The immense pressure put on the Federal Aviation Administration to dismiss individual officials after the tragic ValuJet crash in 1996 is an example.

A NEW ADMINISTRATIVE CULTURE

Whether or not public administration moves beyond its current crossroads, it is likely that a new **administrative culture** will emerge. Public administrators of the future will have to be at ease with complexity, law, and flexibility. They will be performance-oriented, have a strong service ethic, span boundaries, and be adroit at conflict avoidance and resolution. The public sector will increasingly "manage without managers," in Shan Martin's phrase.[17] Public administrators will be personally responsible for their actions. They will have to be comfortable with change, often rapid change. But some things will remain constant. Public administration will remain interesting, challenging, and a key to a better society and world. In 1926, Leonard White wrote that "administration has become, and will continue to be the heart of the problem of modern government."[18] More than half a century later, Dwight Waldo reiterated White's point in words that instruct and remind us of public administration's overarching importance:

> Whatever the future, excepting only oblivion—*no* future—public administration will have an important role in it. Public administration joins two major forces, government and administrative technology. Together they have been an integral part of the enterprise of civilization. They will not disappear unless and until civilization disappears, through decay or destruction, or through transformation into a new human condition.[19]

To improve public administration is to improve civilization. The NPR invites everybody to participate.

> We have to do it ourselves, individually and through association with one another. There are people in America who think that any individual who attempts to take responsibility for the common good is hopelessly naive. There are others who think such actions are dangerously radical. But we are a nation of hopelessly naive radicals—of people who will not give up the dream of a nation run by its own people.[20]

This book has provided the knowledge, information, and understanding necessary to join fruitfully in the effort to build a public administration that is appropriate for the twenty-first century. You can help create a better future by using it as a citizen, member of the general public, customer, coproducer of public goods and services, or public employee.

NOTES

1. David H. Rosenbloom, *Federal Service and the Constitution* (Ithaca, N.Y.: Cornell University Press, 1971).
2. Al Gore, *Common Sense Government Works Better & Costs Less* (Washington, D.C.: Government Printing Office, no date [1995]), 92–93.
3. This is an old lesson that is too often neglected. See the classic statement by Dwight Waldo in *The Administrative State* (New York: Ronald Press, 1948); second edition (New York: Holmes and Meier, 1984).
4. Leonard D. White, *Introduction to the Study of Public Administration* (New York: Macmillan, 1926), preface. Excerpts are published in Jay Shafritz and Albert Hyde, eds., *Classics of Public Administration*, 2d ed. (Chicago: Dorsey Press, 1987), 55–64.
5. David Rosenbloom and Rosemary O'Leary, *Public Administration and Law*, 2d ed. (New York: Marcel Dekker, 1997).
6. *Board of County Commissioners v. Umbehr*, 116 S.Ct. 2342 (1996); *O'Hare Truck Service v. City of Northlake*, 116 S.Ct. 2353 (1996).
7. Ibid. and *Dolan v. City of Tigard*, 114 S.Ct. 2309 (1994); *Gilleo v. City of Ladue*, 114 S.Ct. 2038 (1994); *Rosenberger v. Rector and Visitors of the University of Virginia*, 115 S.Ct. 2510 (1995); *J.E.B. v. Alabama ex rel T.B.*, 114 S.Ct. 419 (1994); *Adarand Constructors v. Peña*, 115 S.Ct. 2097 (1995), among others.
8. White, *Introduction to the Study of Public Administration*, preface.
9. Shoshana Zuboff, *In the Age of the Smart Machine* (New York: Basic Books, 1988), 395.
10. Quoted in Shan Martin, *Managing without Managers* (Beverly Hills, Calif.: Sage, 1983), 19.
11. Zuboff, *In the Age of the Smart Machine*.
12. Ibid., 393–394.
13. Rosenbloom and O'Leary, *Public Administration and Law*, chap. 3.
14. The phrase is Hannah Arendt's. See Owen Fiss, "The Bureaucratization of the Judiciary," *Yale Law Journal* 92 (1983): 1442–1468, for a discussion of its implications in the American context.
15. Marcia Miceli and Janet Near, *Blowing the Whistle* (New York: Lexington Books, 1992).
16. Robert Vaughn, "Public Employees and the Right to Disobey," *Hastings Law Journal* 29 (1977): 261–295.
17. Martin, *Managing without Managers*.
18. White, *Introduction to the Study of Administration*, preface.
19. Dwight Waldo, *The Enterprise of Public Administration* (Novato, Calif.: Chandler & Sharp, 1980), 189.
20. Gore, *Common Sense Government*, 93.

ADDITIONAL READING

CARNEVALE, DAVID. *Trustworthy Government*. San Francisco: Jossey-Bass, 1995.

LEVIN, MARTIN, AND MARY SANGER. *Making Government Work*. San Francisco: Jossey-Bass, 1994.

WALDO, DWIGHT. *The Enterprise of Public Administration*. Novato, Calif.: Chandler & Sharp, 1980.

ZUBOFF, SHOSHANA. *In the Age of the Smart Machine*. New York: Basic Books, 1988.

STUDY QUESTIONS

1. Do you agree or disagree that the predictions made in this chapter describe public administration's likely near-term future? Why? What additional ones would you add?

2. Based on your own values, what kind of public administrative future would you like to see, and what could you do to bring it about?

Glossary*

Administrative culture *(569)*   The set of shared values underlying administrative performance and the general structures and processes for achieving them.

Administrative decentralization *(104)* The delegation of administrative responsibility, authority, and discretion to administrative units having jurisdiction over at least one program or function in a subnational geographic territory.

Administrative law *(6)*   The regulatory law of public administration, consisting of statutes, constitutional requirements, executive orders, and other regulations that control administrative matters such as rule making, adjudication, enforcement, and handling of information.

Adversary proceeding *(441)*   The enforcement of statutes or regulatory rules by placing an agency or one party against another.

Advocacy administration *(196)*   An approach to administration in which those with authority act on behalf of the less powerful members of a community.

Affirmative action *(252)*   The use of goals and timetables for hiring and promotion of women and members of minority groups as part of an equal employment opportunity program.

Alienative involvement *(158)*   A type of involvement where individuals believe that although they would rather not be associated with an organization, they have no viable alternative.

Anomie *(461)*   A feeling of isolation and loss of control over one's life and environment.

Arbitration *(266)*   A means of resolving disputes; particularly, impasses reached in collective bargaining.

Assembled examinations *(232)*   A type of exam that requires that a test of some kind be taken.

Balanced budget amendment *(287)*   A proposed constitutional amendment requiring a balanced annual federal budget (except in emergency situations).

Bargaining units *(262)*   Groups of employees, often according to occupation, who have a legal right to select a bargaining agent (union) to negotiate working conditions on their behalf.

Boss-centered (leadership style) *(159)* A leadership style characterized by managerial control of the decision-making process.

Boss-follower (culture) *(536)*   A type of political culture that involves political exchanges between citizens and the political "boss" or his agents and between the machine and businesses. Also referred to as political-machine-based culture.

Bureau ideologies *(533)*   Beliefs developed in bureaucracies that tout their virtues.

Calculative involvement *(158)*   A type of organizational involvement where individuals calculate that participating in the organization serves some individual need.

Career SES appointments *(224)*   A type of SES appointment made in the federal bureaucracy.

Career reserved (SES position) *(224)*   A type of SES position limited to career appointees.

Case law *(347)*   The legal principles that can be derived by analyzing decisions in previous legal cases.

Casework *(75)*   Services rendered by members of Congress to constituents, generally aimed at resolving constituent difficulties with administrative agencies. Also referred to as constituency service.

Civic culture *(536)*   A type of political culture that emphasizes the community and promotion of the public interest over private interests.

Client-centered *(481)*   An approach to administration that seeks to create organizational structures and programmatic arrangements focusing on the clients' interests.

Client politics *(417)*   A type of politics that occurs when the benefits of a governmental policy or activity are concentrated, but the costs are widely distributed.

Clientele departments *(49)*   Departments that deal largely with, and often supply services to, a well-defined group of people with common economic interests, such as tobacco growers.

Codetermination *(261)*   A model of public personnel administration that involves joint policy making through collective bargaining.

Commission plan *(111)*   A form of municipal government in which a number of elected commissioners perform both legislative and executive functions. Each commissioner generally has executive responsibility for the operations of a specific department, such as transportation.

Comparability *(240)*   In terms of pay, it is the degree to which jobs in the public sector are compensated comparably to those in the private sector.

Comparable worth *(240)*   A concept that addresses the pay rates for different occupations by the same employer, especially where some occupations are predominantly staffed by women and others are staffed by men. The concept promotes equal pay for dissimilar jobs considered to be of equal value to the employer.

Concurrent validation *(234)*   A merit examination validation technique that administers an exam to those already employed and then seeks to determine the statistical relationship between their scores and their performance appraisals.

Conduct cases *(421)*   Regulatory or law enforcement actions taken in the belief that an individual or firm's conduct has been in violation of regulations.

Constraint agencies *(471)*   Agencies that directly regulate individual behavior.

Construct validation *(234)*   A merit examination validation technique that seeks to determine whether an exam ascertains the existence of "psychological constructs" of an examinee, such as "reliability."

Content validation *(234)*   A merit examination validation technique that seeks to establish whether the contents of an exam match the contents of a job.

Coproduction *(481)*   An approach to providing governmental services that involves service provision by both a governmental agency and a user.

Council-manager *(111)*   A form of municipal government comprised of an elected council with legislative authority and a manager, hired by the council, who serves as the chief executive officer of the jurisdiction.

Criterion-related *(234)*   An approach to merit examination validation that attempts to relate exam scores to on-the-job performance.

Cross subsidies *(414)*   A type of price regulation which results in one set of customers paying prices that are intended to subsidize another set of customers.

Decrementalism *(32)*   An approach to budgeting that cuts agencies' funding and/or programs in each successive budget period.

Deferrals *(297)*   An executive technique to control spending that delays the spending of appropriated funds.

Democratic organization *(195)*   An organization that integrates citizen and employee participation into its policy-making and decision-making processes.

Dillon's rule *(129)*   Court interpretation that local governments possess only those powers expressly allocated to them by the states.

Doctrine of privilege *(255)*   The constitutional doctrine considering public employment or largess to be a privilege rather than a right and, accordingly, allowing government to set virtually any conditions for it.

Eligibles register *(232)*   A tool used in selection decisions; simply a list of those who passed an examination, ranked in order of their scores.

Entitlements *(127)*   A government benefit required by law to be paid to eligible individuals, groups, or other governments.

Entrepreneurial politics *(418)*   A type of politics that occurs when the benefits of a governmental policy or activity are widely distributed, but the costs are concentrated.

Entrepreneurs (policy) *(418)*   Individuals who effectively represent groups and are not directly involved in legislative policy making.

Equal protection clause *(130)*   Clause in the Fourteenth Amendment to the Constitution requiring the states to afford equal protection of the laws to everyone within their jurisdictions.

Exclusive recognition (of a union) *(262)* The designation by a collective bargaining unit of a single union to bargain on behalf of all the employees in the unit.

Executive budget *(117)*   A budget prepared by the executive branch of a government that is submitted to the legislative branch for consideration.

Executive Office of the President (EOP) *(67)*   A federal organization created in 1939 to enable the president to exercise greater control over federal agencies. The EOP currently includes such key units as the White House Office, the Office of Management and Budget, and the National Security Council.

Ex parte *(192)*   One-sided contacts with agency decision makers when they are engaged in adjudication.

Expectancy theory *(164)*   Job motivation will depend upon the extent to which individuals expect that a certain activity will lead to some degree of satisfaction of their goals.

Experimental design *(366)*   A method of determining the impact of a policy that applies a policy to one group and not to another.

Expressive leaders *(160)*   Leaders who play a fundamental role in goal setting and in gaining adherence to the norms and objectives of an organization.

Externalities *(9)*   Costs or benefits not accounted for in a market exchange; these costs or benefits accrue to someone other than the buyer or seller.

Face validity *(234)*   A type of merit examination validation technique that seeks to address whether the exam appears reasonable on the surface.

Federalism *(100)*   A form of governmental organization that divides political authority between a central government and state or provincial governments.

Final offer arbitration *(266)*   The arbitrator or panel must choose the last offer of one side or the other, either in its entirety (whole package) or on each item (item by item).

Full faith and credit clause *(130)*   The clause in Article IV of the Constitution requiring states to recognize the legal acts of other states even though their policies and laws may differ.

General SES position *(224)*   A type of SES position open to any type of SES appointee.

Hiring freezes *(297)*   A technique used to control spending which prohibits the filling of vacant positions.

Human relations approach *(151)*   An approach to management that attempts to develop ways of making work in organizations more socially and psychologically acceptable to employees while at the same time enhancing or at least maintaining efficiency.

Human services integration *(475)*   An approach to administration that enables individuals seeking or requiring several services to apply to one office only.

Hygienes *(163)*   Environmental and contextual factors that have the capacity to make workers dissatisfied if they are inadequately met; however, they do not lead to job satisfaction in and of themselves.

Impact analysis *(366)*   A technique concerned with examining the extent to which a policy causes change in the intended direction.

Implementation evaluation *(372)*   A determination of whether the implementation or effect of a policy is appropriate.

Impoundment *(297)*   A technique used by governors and the president to control spending, which disallows an executive agency to spend the funds that have been allotted to it.

Income taxes *(281)*   Taxes levied on the earnings of individuals and corporations.

Incremental model *(338)*   An approach to decision making emphasizing small steps toward a general objective.

Incrementalism *(32)*   An approach to budgeting or decision making that focuses on limited changes in funding, programs, or policies.

Instrumental leadership *(160)*   A leadership style that involves maintenance of an organization in terms of securing the resources needed for its operation and assuring that they are distributed properly.

Interest group politics *(416)*   A type of politics that occurs when both the costs and benefits of a governmental policy or activity are narrowly concentrated.

Job performance *(233)*   The reality of how much work gets done.

Job proficiency *(233)*   The actual ability to perform the functions of a job.

Judicial activism *(77)*   The involvement of judges in public administrative and policy matters.

Judicialization *(33)*   The tendency for administrative processes to increasingly resemble courtroom procedures. Judicialization increases the role of legal values in agency decision making.

Keynesian approach *(284)*   An approach to fiscal policy which holds that governmental spending can be used to counteract the normal boom-and-bust tendencies of the business cycle.

Leadership *(153)*   The ability to influence people, to motivate them to serve a common purpose, and to fulfill the functions necessary for successful group action.

Limited emergency SES appointments *(224)*   A type of noncompetitive SES appointment that can last up to eighteen months.

Limited-term SES appointments *(224)* A type of noncompetitive SES appointment, which is nonrenewable and can last up to three years.

Line-item (budget) *(304)* A type of budget which requires that appropriations be linked to objects of expenditure.

Majoritarian politics *(416)* A type of politics that occurs when the costs and benefits of a governmental policy or activity are widely distributed.

Management by objectives (MBO) *(179)* A management technique that requires active participation by subordinates in goal setting.

Marginal costs *(375)* The additional cost of providing an additional unit of a good, service, or constraint.

Mayor-council (form of government) *(111)* A form of government in which an elected mayor serves primarily executive functions while a council performs both executive and legislative functions.

Mixed-scanning approach *(352)* An approach to decision making that attempts to combine incrementalism with the rational-comprehensive approach.

Moral involvement *(158)* A type of involvement in which individuals have a moral commitment to the goals and purposes of an organization.

Motivators *(163)* Factors that can produce greater job satisfaction.

Natural rights *(505)* Fundamental rights to freedom and liberty that exist independently of government; for instance, natural rights theory holds that all individuals have a right to reasonable self-defense.

Noncareer SES appointments *(224)* A type of SES appointment held by political appointees who assist top-level political executives of departments and agencies.

Ombudsman *(474)* Independent governmental agents who are empowered to investigate specific complaints by individuals alleging maladministration of some kind.

Operations management *(178)* A management approach that seeks to identify the specific operational responsibilities of government agencies and to design their organizations and work flows to maximize productivity.

Organization development *(182)* An approach for improving organization that assumes that organizations will be more effective at problem solving and coping with their environments when there is more trust, support, and cooperation among their members.

Overhead agencies *(55)* Administrative units, such as personnel agencies, that perform services for other agencies or are engaged in overseeing aspects of their operations.

Performance budget *(305)* A budget that relates performance levels to appropriations.

Pluralism *(31)* A distribution of political power characterized by dispersal among many groups, none of which can dominate others in all policy areas.

Police power *(107)* Governmental authority to regulate matters such as social behaviors, morals, health, public safety, and zoning.

Policy design *(372)* The choice of means to achieve a public policy's objectives.

Policy impact *(364)* The actual effects of policy outputs.

Policy output *(364)* The activities intended to achieve a policy objective.

Political exchanges *(536)* Quid pro quo relationships involving government and politics; for instance, receiving an administrative position in return for political campaign activity.

Political executives *(69)* Top executives appointed to positions in the Executive Office of the President and other agencies as a means for bringing presidential policy direction to the bureaucracy.

Political-machine-based culture *(536)* A type of political culture which involves political exchanges between citizens and the political "boss" or his agents and between the machine and businesses. Also referred to as boss-follower culture.

Pork barrel *(74)* The spending of federal funds in the home district of a member of Congress.

Position classification *(227)* The personnel management process of designing jobs, organizing them into useful managerial and career categories, and establishing their rates of pay.

Predictive validation *(234)* A method for assessing merit examination validation; it takes actual scores of examinees and associates them statistically with on-the-job performance at some later time.

Prefect *(105)* The head of an administrative district.

Preprogram-postprogram analysis *(369)* A method of determining policy impact by comparing the condition of the target population prior to program implementation and after program implementation.

Procedural due process *(35)* The value of fundamental fairness requiring procedures designed to protect individuals from malicious, arbitrary, erroneous, capricious, or unconstitutional deprivation of life, liberty, or property by the government.

Process analysis *(371)* A technique for assessing the ways in which a policy is being implemented.

Program budget *(305)* A budget that links funding to the achievement of agency purposes.

Property taxes *(282)* Taxes levied on the value of real estate.

Prospective adjudication *(344)* Future-oriented adjudication requesting a modification or change in a party's operations.

Public goods *(11)* Goods or services characterized by nonexcludability and nondivisibility. One person's consumption does not exclude another's and does not exhaust or significantly diminish the good. Also referred to as collective goods.

Quasi-experimental design *(369)* A method of determining policy impact that attempts to determine the impact of policies by contrasting performance among groups exposed to the policy and those not exposed while statistically controlling for confounding conditions.

Rescissions *(297)* An executive technique to control spending that terminates funds for an agency or a program.

Recruitment *(231)* The process of encouraging individuals to apply for positions.

Regime values *(553)* The core values of a political system, such as those embodied in a constitution.

Regulatory rachet *(429)* The tendency of regulatory agencies to add more and more regulations without deleting those that have become obsolete.

Repackaging *(301)* A strategy that seeks increased funding of existing programs by explaining them in terms that seem to fit new presidential priorities.

Representative bureaucracy *(184)* A concept holding that the social backgrounds and statuses of public administrators can affect their job performance and that the social composition of government agencies will affect their legitimacy.

Reprogramming *(298)* A device used to shift funds within agencies; funds are transferred between programs upon permission of relevant congressional committees.

Retrospective adjudication *(345)* Adjudication that involves an alleged past wrongdoing by an agency or party.

Sales taxes *(282)* Taxes levied on the sale of goods or services.

Scientific management *(149)*   A systematic management approach that aims to determine scientifically the most efficient way to perform a task. Also referred to as Taylorism.

Scope of bargaining *(262)*   The conditions of employment subject to negotiation between unions and employers.

Selection *(232)*   The process of choosing among applicants.

Situational factors *(233)*   Aspects of the work environment that can affect performance, such as noise levels.

Sovereignty *(12)*   Supreme political authority.

Span of control *(104)*   The extent of an administrator's responsibility, typically expressed in terms of the number of subordinates the administrator supervises.

Spoils system *(89)*   A system of awarding political supporters with government positions.

Strategic plans *(311)*   Used in decision making to respond to foreseeable environmental shifts through organizational and policy changes.

Street-level administrator *(34)*   Administrators who interact directly with the public in an unsupervised manner, such as police and social workers.

Structural cases *(422)*   Adjudicatory cases which are the result of patterns and broad practices that are deemed by the agency to be prohibited.

Subordinate-centered (leadership style) *(159)*   A leadership style that emphasizes subordinate participation in the decision-making process.

Sunset provisions *(315)*   A type of legislation that provides for the automatic termination of a program at some future date unless the program is reauthorized by statute at that time.

Sunshine laws *(392)*   Laws requiring that government agencies allow access by the public and the press to certain types of meetings and hearings.

Supply-side economics *(287)*   An approach to fiscal policy that entails a reduced government role in the economy.

Total quality management (TQM) *(179)*   A management philosophy that aims to build quality into an organization's products, rather than weed out defects through inspections and the like.

Transactional corruption *(539)*   A type of corruption that involves a direct exchange with another individual or entity.

Transfers (bugetary) *(298)*   A device used to shift funds within agencies; funds are transferred from one purpose to another.

Unassembled examinations *(232)*   A type of exam that merely requires the completion of forms.

Unilateral corruption *(538)*   A type of corruption that does not involve a direct exchange with another individual or entity.

Zero-base budgeting (ZBB) *(309)*   An approach to budgeting that requires annual justification of existing programs and activities.

Index

Abbott Laboratories v. Gardner (1967), 443, 445
Absolute immunity, doctrine of, 34
Accountability, 199, 245, 270, 529–557,
   568–569; in decision making, 339; difficulty
   of establishing, 539–542; implementation
   evaluation and, 392–393; legal approach, 529,
   553; managerial approach, 529, 542–549;
   National Performance Review and, 338; new
   public management and, 529, 545–549; political approach, 529, 549–553; in regulatory
   administration, 438; in Senior Executive Service, 225
Adams, John, 209, 210
Adams, John Quincy, 210
Adams, Walter, 55
Adarand Constructors v. Peña (1995), 223
Adjudication, 37–38, 189, 190, 192, 193, 195,
   197, 342, 344–348, 356, 455–456, 499; of
   discrimination cases, 251; prospective,
   344–345; by regulatory agencies, 421–422,
   441–442, 445, 446; retrospective, 345
Administrative Careers with America (ACWA)
   examination, 235
Administrative culture, 459–460, 569; boss-
   follower, 536–538; civic, 536–538
Administrative decentralization (*see* Decentral-
   ization)
Administrative discretion, 328, 337–338, 382,
   399, 423, 434, 435, 438–439, 443
Administrative Dispute Resolution Act (ADRA)
   (1990), 193, 446
Administrative law, 6, 33

Administrative law judges (ALJs), 33–34,
   192–193, 239–240, 244; neutrality of, 442
Administrative Procedure Act (APA) (1946),
   33, 54–55, 77, 88, 192, 341, 344, 346, 432,
   442, 551, 552, 564; interest groups and,
   482
Adversary procedure, 36, 189, 256, 345, 347; in
   regulatory administration, 441–442
Advisory Committee Act (1972), 480
Advisory committees, 85–86
Advocacy administration, 196–197
Affirmative action, 31, 169, 223, 248, 252, 327,
   372, 565
Agencies, alphabet, 409; budgets of, 292,
   296–297, 298–299, 311; client-centered,
   480–481; constraint, 471; cultures of, 328;
   customer service standards in, 384; regula-
   tory, 410
Agency shop, 267, 269
Agency theory, 196
Agriculture, U.S. Department of (USDA), 49,
   168, 187, 312, 391, 426, 486
Air Force, U.S., 180
Alien Act (1798), 123
Alienative involvement, 158
Allocational efficiency, 336
Alphabet agencies, 409
Alternative dispute resolution (ADR), 37,
   189–190, 193–194, 446
Alternative service delivery, 380–382
American administrative state, 46–59; authority
   and responsibility in, 59–64; Congress and,

American administrative state *(continued)*
73–77; individual in, 456–467; judicial
response to, 77, 80–85; legal origins of,
50–55; managerial origins of, 55–59; politi-
cal roots of, 47–50; president and, 65–69;
the public and, 454, 462; public depen-
dence on, 465–467; spending growth
and, 279
American Association of Retired Persons
(AARP), 439
American Fats and Oils Association, 428
American Federation of Government Employ-
ees, 500
*American Federation of Government Employees v.
Phillips* (1973), 499–500
American Management Association, 564
American Petroleum Institute, 349, 350
American Society for Public Administration
(ASPA), 554–556
Americans with Disabilities Act (1990),
249–252
Amtrak, 521–523
Anomie, 461
Anthony, Susan B., dollar, 391
Antitrust regulations, 55
Appalachian Regional Commission, 132
Appeals processes, 475
Appleby, Paul, 29, 183
Appropriations Committee, House, 294, 295;
Senate, 294
ARA, 380
Arbitration, 266
Armed Services Committee, House, 124
Army Corps of Engineers, 382
Arnold, R. Douglas, 75
Articles of Confederation, 129
Asimow, Michael, 92
Assembled examinations, 232–233
Assessment centers, 233
Atomic Energy Act (1946), 439
Atomic Energy Commission (AEC), 532
Attrition, 243
Audits, internal, 544–546
Authoritarian leadership, 158–159
Auto Safety Act (1966), 418
Autonomy, 186

Baker v. City of St. Petersburg (1968), 517–518
Balanced Budget Amendment, 287, 315
Ball, Howard, 532
Bardach, Eugene, 423, 435, 437
Bargaining units, 261–262
Barnard, Chester, 153, 158
Barzeley, Michael, 23
Bay of Pigs Invasion, 342
Behn, Robert, 348
Benchmarking, 23, 24, 239, 477
Bennis, Warren, 148
Benzene, in the work place, 348–352, 443
Bernstein, Marver, 417–418
Berry, Jeffrey, 87
Bicameralism, 394
Black, Hugo, 510–511
Blackmun, Harry, 103, 351
Bonfield, Arthur, 92
Border Patrol, U.S., 395
Boss-centered leadership, 159, 160
Boss-follower political culture, 536–538
Bounded rationality, 328
Bowsher v. Synar (1986), 38
Brandeis, Louis, 29, 392
Branti v. Finkel (1980), 91
Brennan, William, 91, 351
Broad banding, 230
Brock, James, 55
Brown, Jerry, 428
Brownlow Committee, 177
Bryan, William Jennings, 212–213
Budget cycle, 299
Budget Enforcement Act (1990), 289, 292, 295
Budgeting, 275–318; control function of, 550;
countercyclical fiscal policy, 284–287; federal
budgetary process, 288–302; glossary of
terms, 290–292; impact of judiciary on,
82–83; legal approach to, 38, 315–317; man-
agerial approach to, 20, 303–311, 313; new
public management approach to, 27,
303–304; political approach to, 32, 311–315;
size and growth in, 276–288; sources of revenue, 279–284; state, 118; in supply-side economics, 287–288; theories of, 302–317
Budgeting Impoundment and Control Act
(1974), 297–298

Bureau of the Budget, 288
Bureau ideologies, 533
Bureau of Labor Statistics, 240
Bureaucracy, 18, 19, 144–149, 220; conflict between democracy and, 463; conflict between society and, 456–461; human needs versus, 162–163; individual and, 456–461; politics of, 199; presidents and, 65–69; public attitudes toward, 467–474, 487; representative, 184, 247–248; rigidity of, 354; separation of powers and, 499; welfare, 380
Bureaucrat bashing, 470, 534
Burford, Anne Gorsuch, 428
Burger, Warren, 30, 350, 378, 499
Burnham, Walter Dean, 462–463
Bush, George, 66, 307
Bush v. Lucas (1983), 260

Calculative involvement, 158
Calhoun, John, 123
"Camel's nose" gimmick, 300–301
Campbell, Alan, 220
Capital budgets, 303
Capture theory, 417–418, 425, 439
Carbone v. Town of Clarkstown (1994), 108
Career appointments, 224
Career reserved positions, 224, 226
Caro, Robert, 157
Carson, Rachel, 414
Carter, Jimmy, 65, 67, 220, 311, 470
Case law, 347
Casework, 75–77, 393, 474, 536, 550, 565
Castro, Fidel, 342
Central Intelligence Agency (CIA), 392
Certified Color Manufacturers Association, 343
Charismatic authority, 154
Checks and balances, 111, 314, 499, 549
Cheney, Richard, 66
Chevron v. Natural Resources Defense Council (1984), 444
Chicago Teachers Union v. Hudson (1986), 268
Chief Financial Officers Act (1990), 545
Chilling effect, 506–507, 508
Circularity, 342
Citizen participation (*see* Participation)

Citizens to Preserve Overton Park v. Volpe (1971), 81, 443
Civic culture, 536–538
Civil Aeronautics Board (CAB), 62, 417, 425, 427, 435
Civil Rights Act (1964), 106, 222, 248, 496
Civil Service Act (1883), 212, 216–217, 219, 247–248
Civil Service Commission, U.S. (CSC), 59, 169, 172, 216, 217, 220, 224, 226, 327, 408
Civil Service Committee, House, 566–567
Civil service reform, 89, 212–226, 243–244
Civil Service Reform Act (1978), 29, 212, 219, 220–226, 236, 245, 248, 551
Civil suits, 260–261, 523
Civil War, 123
Clark, Tom C., 445
Classification Act (1949), 217
Classifications, 513–515, 516
Clayton Act (1914), 51, 414
Client-centered administration, 480–481, 485, 486
Client politics, 417–418
Clientala relationships, 533, 539
Clientele agencies, 49, 486
Clients, 454–455
Clinton, Bill, 288, 294, 300, 383, 392, 432, 433, 438
Closed-systems theory, 167
Coalition building, 312–313
Coalitions, legislative, 383
Codetermination, 261, 262
Cognitive approaches, legal, 37–38; managerial, 20; new public management, 26–27; political, 32
Cohen, Steven, 181
Cold War, 534
Collective bargaining, 222, 229, 236, 240, 247, 257, 261–269, 415, 544
Collective goods, 482
Commerce clause, 107–108
Commerce, U.S. Department of, 474, 486
Commission plan of governance, 111
Commissions, 190–191; regulatory, 53, 419–420, 426, 429, 433, 439, 499
Committee for Fair Pizza Labeling, 421

Common Cause, 88, 126, 130, 439, 482

Common law, 52

Communication, 155

Communist party, 504

Community action agencies (CAA), 480

Community action programs, 197–198

Comparability, 240

Comparable worth, 240, 241–243

Comparative studies, 149

Compensation, 238–243

Competitive examinations, 232–235, 248, 257

Complaint systems, 251

Compliance, with regulations, 430–4431

Computers, 355–356

Concurrent validation, 234

Conduct cases, 421

Confederal government, 101

Conflict-of-interest statutes, 538, 543–544, 552

Congress, U.S., 6, 13, 67, 125, 128, 563; administrative state and, 73–77, 462; and budgetary process, 285, 289, 294–299, 300–302, 311, 313, 500; budgets and, 287; and civil service reform, 220; and commerce clause, 107; committees and subcommittees of, 74, 186; interest groups and, 86; and legislative veto, 393–394; Occupational Safety and Health Administration and, 349–351; oversight by, 540; and personnel administration, 246–247; regulatory activities and, 420

Congressional Budget Office (CBO), 288, 289, 294, 540, 549, 564

Consensus building, 312–313, 334, 338–339, 340

Constitution, U.S., 6, 7, 8, 30, 49, 84, 102, 115, 131, 135, 209, 268, 394, 493–525; Article II, 298; Article IV, 102, 130; Article VI, 501; Bill of Rights, 106–107; diversity and, 503–504; due process in, 511–513; equal protection clause of, 130–131, 253, 513–518; equity and, 520–521; freedom and liberty and, 504–509; individuality and, 518–520; interstate commerce clause, 416; interstate relations and, 129; legitimacy and, 501–503; necessity of understanding, 494–498; Preamble, 47–48; property rights and, 509–511; state action and, 493, 494, 521–524; structure of, 498–501; amendments to: First, 85, 90, 91, 107, 244, 260, 347, 502, 504, 554; Fourth,

346, 519–520; Fifth, 509, 513, 565; Eighth, 523; Ninth, 505; Tenth, 102, 107, 108, 123; Eleventh, 394; Thirteenth, 8, 90; Fourteenth, 102, 104, 106–107, 244, 253, 257, 378, 498, 509, 513, 518; Fifteenth, 104; Seventeenth, 102

Constraint agencies, 471

Construct validation, 234, 375

Consumer Product Safety Commission (CPSC), 427

Consumer Reports, 435

Consumers Union, 88, 482

Content validation, 234

Continuing resolutions, 289, 290

Contract with America, 90, 287, 563

Coproduction, 381, 481–482

Corporate income tax, 279–282

Corruption, 380, 533–539, 565; in regulatory agencies, 427, 438; spoils system and, 211, 214; transactional, 539; unilateral, 538

Cosmetic, Toiletry and Fragrance Association, 343

Cost-benefit analysis, 307–308, 376; of regulation, 430–431, 433, 444–445

Cost-effectiveness, 375–377

Cost of living adjustments (COLAs), 302

Costs, passing on, 377–379, 475; of regulation, 424–425, 430

Council of Economic Advisers, 289, 294, 353

Council-manager form of government, 111–113

Council of State Governments, 126

Councils of Government, 135

Countercyclical fiscal policy, 284–287, 288, 303

Counties, 114

Courts, 6; federal, 8

Craig v. Boren (1976), 516–517, 518

Cramton, Roger, 82

Criterion-related validation, 234

Critical incidents appraisal, 238

Crosby, P., 170

Cross subsidies, 414, 478

Curtis, George William, 219–220

Customer service, standards of, 383, 384–385, 476–478, 485, 486

Customs Service, U.S., 382, 438

Cutbacks, of personnel, 243

Dahl, Robert, 445
Davidson, Roger, 31
Davis, Kenneth C., 190
Deason, Willard, 426
Debt ceilings, 301–302
Decentralization, 104–106, 178, 187, 313, 461, 566–567; responsiveness and, 391–392
Decision making, 323–357, 540; computers and information systems in, 355–356; incrementalism in, 346; legal approach, 38, 323, 344–348; managerial approach to, 20, 323, 324–338; new public management approach to, 27, 323, 335–338, 355; participation in, 389–390; political approach to, 32, 323, 338–344; rational-comprehensive model of, 328–329, 333–335; synthesis of approaches, 352–355
Declaration of Independence, 505
Declaratory Judgment Act, 443
Decrementalism, 32, 312
Defense, U.S. Department of (DOD), 49, 118, 120, 335, 541
Deferrals, 290, 297
Deficit spending, 284, 285, 314
Dehumanization, 18, 146, 147, 150–151, 152, 228–229; of clients, 460
Deming, W.E., 179, 180
Democracy, 195, 462–464, 477–478, 502
Democratic leadership, 159
Democratic organization, 195–198, 200
Democratic party, 212, 313
Demographic constituency interests, 390
Deregulation, 22, 55, 269, 270, 382, 409, 431, 445, 447, 524
Devolution, 461, 462, 464
Dillon's Rule, 129
Dimock, Marshall, 26, 33, 36
Direct participation, 479–480
Discretion, 337–338; administrative, 147, 328, 399, 423, 434, 435, 438–439, 443
Discrimination, 415, 515–516; adjudication of complaints, 251; administrative, 382
Dismissals, 256, 258–259
D.C. Federation of Civic Associations v. Volpe (1972), 192
Diversity, 503–504
Divided government, 67

Doctrine of absolute immunity, 83
Doctrine of privilege, 81, 255–256
Dolan v. City of Tigard (1994), 444, 509–510
Dolan, Florence, 509
Dormant commerce clause, 108
Douglas, Mary, 170–171
Douglas, William O., 392
Downs, Anthony, 165, 533, 540
Drew, Elizabeth, 308
Driving under the influence (DUI) laws, 390
Drucker, Peter, 372
Due process, 35, 128, 378, 510–511; procedural, 256, 395–396, 456, 511–513, 549; and regulatory administration, 442
Dukakis, Michael, 154
Dye, Thomas, 374

Eaton, Dorman B., 213, 216
Ecological model, 169
Economic Opportunity Act (1964), 480
Economics, individuals and, 464–467; of regulation, 425
Edible Oil Regulatory Reform Act (1995), 428
Effectiveness, of regulatory administration, 434, 437
Efficiency, allocational, 336; of bureaucracy, 19, 147; of collective bargaining, 262; in decision making, 333, 334, 340; of deterring corruption, 547; in era of "gentlemen," 210; of human relations approach, 151, 153; of incrementalism, 314; legal approach and, 35–36; of markets, 336; merit system and, 213; organizational, 198; in personnel administration, 231, 244, 257; of privatization, 270; of regulatory administration, 445; in scientific management, 150; of separation of powers, 500; in spoils system, 211; Supreme Court view of, 30; technical, 336
Eimicke, William, 181
Eisenhower, Dwight D., 539
Eligibles register, 232
Elrod v. Burns (1976), 91
Empathy, of leaders, 155
Employment Act (1946), 285
Employment participation, 195–196
Employment practices, regulation of, 415

Empowerment, 149, 198, 336–338, 356, 382–383, 457, 568
Energy, of leaders, 155
Energy, U.S. Department of, 335
Enforcement, of regulation, 437–439
Entitlements, 127–128, 295, 302
Entrepreneurial organizations, 336
Entrepreneurial politics, 418
Environmental impact statements, 415, 440, 444, 445
Environmental Protection Agency (EPA), 186, 424, 428, 474
Environmental regulation, 414, 445
Equal employment opportunity (EEO), 52–53, 213, 218, 222–223, 235, 248–252, 257, 259, 260, 329, 333, 334, 342, 427; adjudication of complaints, 347
Equal Employment Opportunity Act (1972), 242, 248
Equal Employment Opportunity Commission (EEOC), 59, 222–223, 253, 354, 415, 423
Equal Pay Act (1963), 240
Equal protection, 253–254, 513–518; implementation evaluation and, 394–395
Equal protection clause, 253
Equity, 282, 283, 339, 520
Estoppel, 396–398
Ethics, 529–557, 568; legal approach to, 529, 553; managerial approach to, 529, 542–549; new public management and, 529, 545–549; political approach to, 529, 549–553
Ethics in Government Act (1978), 7, 550
Ethics Reform Act (1989), 550
Etzioni, Amitai, 142, 151, 158, 159, 352
Examinations, 232–235, 248–249, 257
Exclusive recognition, 262
Executive budget, 117–118
Executive Office of the President (EOP), 67–69, 121, 288, 352–353, 392, 540
Executive privilege, 68
Expansion, bureaucratic, 157
Ex parte influences, insulation from, 191–192
Expectancy theory, 164
Expenditures (see Budgeting)
Experimental design, 366

Expertise, 148–149, 539
Expressive leaders, 160–161
Externalities, 9, 414

Face validity, 234
Fact-finding, 266
Fair Labor Standards Act, 52
Family-friendly workplaces, 226, 269
Federal Advisory Committee Act (1972), 29, 86, 389, 484, 551
Federal Aviation Administration (FAA), 182, 427, 434, 439, 542, 566, 569
Federal Bureau of Investigation (FBI), 155, 157, 171, 186, 534–535
Federal Communications Commission (FCC), 62, 190, 414, 420, 425–426, 439
Federal corporations, 121
Federal Council on Environmental Quality, 440
Federal Deposit Insurance Corporation (FDIC), 122, 434
Federal Election Commission, 244, 415
Federal Employees Pay Comparability Act (1990), 240
Federal Employment Information System, 385
Federal government, employees of, 46–47; public opinion of, 21; relations with state governments, 123–129; structure of, 118–122
Federal Labor Relations Authority (FLRA), 59, 222, 266–267
Federal Maritime Commission, 417, 425, 427, 429
Federal Quality Institute (FQI), 180
Federal Register, 541
Federal Reserve Act, 51
Federal Service Entrance Exam, 235
Federal Trade Commission (FTC), 190, 425, 442
Federal Trade Commission Act (1914), 51, 414, 416
FTC v. Sperry and Hutchinson (1972), 81, 443
Federalism, 8, 100–122, 123, 125, 369–370, 464; dual, 109, 126; interdependent models of, 109; juridical, 123; nation-centered, 109; regulatory, 415; state-centered, 109
Federalist Papers, 499, 503
Federalist party, 209

Fenwick, Millicent, 428
Final offer arbitration, 266
First English Evangelical Lutheran Church of Glendale v. County of Los Angeles (1987), 444
Fiscal policy, countercyclical, 284–287, 288, 303
Flat tax, 281, 284
Food and Drug Administration (FDA), 342, 343, 420, 423–424, 425, 427, 434, 435, 436, 443, 447
Food, Drug and Cosmetic Act (1960), 343, 436
Food stamps, 307
Forced choice appraisal, 238
Forced distribution appraisal, 238
Ford, Gerald, 90
Ford Motor Company, 476
Formal rulemaking, 54
Formalization, of decision making, 326–327
Franchising, 381
Freedom, 504–509; economic, 466
Freedom of Information Act (FOIA) (1966), 88, 364, 552
Freeman, Bill, 438
Friedman, Lawrence, 52
Friedman, Milton, 465–466
Fringe benefits, 242–243
Full faith and credit clause, 130, 131

Gaebler, Ted, 21, 22
Garcia v. San Antonio Metropolitan Transit Authority (1985), 108
Garfield, James, 216–217
Gaus, John M., 554
General Accounting Office (GAO), 58, 180, 393, 549, 550, 564
General positions, 224, 226
General Services Administration (GSA), 57–58, 545, 546–547
Globalization, 565
Goals, evaluation and, 383
"Going public," 551–552
Goldberg v. Kelly (1970), 510–511
Goodsell, Charles, 468–469, 471
Gore, Al, 22, 55, 177, 269, 288, 557
Gormley, William, 440
Goulder, Alvin, 459

Government Manual, 58
Government Performance and Results Act (GPRA) (1993), 77, 186, 307, 311, 313, 317, 318, 364–365, 383, 549–550, 564, 565
Government Printing Office (GPO), 58
Governmental Affairs Committee, Senate, 566–567
Governors, 116–118, 126
Grade creep, 229
Grants, 124, 381; block, 124; categorical, 124; formula, 125; matching, 125; project, 125; revenue sharing, 125
Great Society, 109, 128, 362
Grid regulations, 328, 330–332
Grievance arbitration, 266, 267
Grodzins, Morton, 126–127
Gross Domestic Product (GDP), 276–277, 287
Gulick, Luther, 20, 173

Hamilton, Alexander, 209
Hammond, Arthur, 314
Hampton, Robert, 169
Harley v. Schuylkill County (1979), 496
Hatch Acts (1939, 1940), 90, 244; revision of (1993), 244
Hawthorne effect, 152, 161, 438
Hayek, Friedrich, 467
Health, Education, and Welfare, U.S. Department of, (HEW), 146, 390–391
Health and Human Services, U.S. Department of (HHS), 146, 312, 343
Hearing examiners, 36, 239–240, 344, 400
Hearings, managerial perspective on, 374
Heckler v. Cheney (1985), 444
Henry, Gary, 472–473
Herzberg, Frederick, 163
Hierarchy, 326, 336
Hiring freezes, 297
Holmes, Oliver Wendell, 255
"Honest graft," 536, 537
Hoover Commission, 304
Hoover, J. Edgar, 155, 156–157, 534
Horner, Constance, 495, 497
Housing and Urban Development, U.S. Department of (HUD), 48
Human relations, 141, 151, 161, 162

Human resources management (*see* Personnel administration)

Human services integration, 135, 174, 176, 475, 477, 481

Hummel, Ralph, 18, 457

Hygiene factors, 163

Ideologies, bureau, 533

Immigration, 214–215

Immigration and Naturalization Service v. Chadha (1983), 30, 298, 393–394

Immunity, 260–261; of public administrators, 83–85

Impact analysis, 365–371

Impact assessments, 440–441

Impersonality, 327, 356, 460–461, 474, 475–476, 479, 503; of bureaucracy, 458

Implementation evaluation, 361, 372–400; legal perspective on, 393–398; managerial perspective on, 373–388; new public management and, 380–388; political perspective on, 389–393; utilzation of, 398–400

Implementation studies, 371–372

Impoundments, 291, 297–299

Inclusiveness, of regulation, 428–429; of rule-making, 435

Income taxes, 279, 281–282

Incompetence, 426–427

Incrementalism, 32, 312–315, 317; in decision making, 338, 346, 354, 356; precedental, 38

Independence of agencies, 190

Independent hearing examiners 192–193

Independent regulatory commissions (IRCs), 190

India-Pakistan War, 335

Individuals, constitutional view of, 518; in economic system, 464–467; in political system, 461–464; in society, 456–461

Industrial Union Department, AFL-CIO v. American Petroleum Institute (1980), 81, 349–351

Information systems, 355–356

Information technology, 567

Inspections, 383

Inspector General Act (1978), 548

Inspectors, 422–423

Inspectors general (IGs), 545, 548, 564

Institute of Shortening and Edible Oils, 428

Instrumental leadership, 160–161

Insubordination, 543

Interest arbitration, 266

Interest groups, 85–88; participation in, 482; public interest and, 533; regulatory administration and, 416–418; and state constitutions, 115

Intergovernmental Personnel Act, 551

Interior, U.S. Department of, 145, 180–181, 185, 333, 440

Internal Revenue Service (IRS), 181, 474

Interstate commerce clause, 416

Interstate Commerce Commission (ICC), 51, 190, 191, 409, 414, 417, 420, 425

Interstate relations, 129–132

Iran-Contra hearings, 549

Iron triangle, 87, 462

Jackson, Andrew, 89, 123, 210–211, 214, 563

Jackson, Robert H., 503

Jefferson, Thomas, 123, 209, 210, 297

Jehovah's Witnesses, 503

Job enlargement, 229

Job enrichment, 229

Job proficiency, versus job performance, 233

Job rotation, 229

Job security, 540

Job sharing, 243

Johnson, Andrew, 211

Johnson, Lyndon B., 109, 129, 307, 362, 426

Johnston, Michael, 535

Jones, James H., 367

Judgment, of leaders, 155

Judicial activism, 77

Judicial review, 54, 82, 346, 351, 408, 444, 483

Judicialization, 33–35, 483, 484, 513

Jurand, J., 179

Justice, U.S. Department of, Antitrust Division, 425

Kagan, Robert, 423, 435, 437

Kahn, Robert, 170

Kaplan, H. Roy, 183

Katz, Daniel, 170, 469, 471, 473

Katzenbach v. McClung (1964), 106

Kaufman, Herbert, 172, 187, 426
Kennedy, John F., 342
Keyishian v. Board of Regents (1967), 504, 506
Keynes, John Maynard, 285
Keynesian economics, 284–286
King, James, 59
King, Martin Luther, Jr., 534–535

Labor-management partnerships, 268–269
Labor, U.S. Department of, 486
Laissez-faire leadership, 159
La Palombara, Joseph, 533
Largess, 510–511, 538; public dependence on, 465–467
Law of Counter Control, 540
Leadership, 153; authoritarian, 159; boss-centered, 159, 160; democratic, 159; expressive, 160–161; instrumental, 160–161; laissez-faire, 159; subordinate-centered, 159–160
League of Women Voters, 88, 482
Least restrictive alternative, 507–508, 509, 516, 540
Lebron, Michael, 522
Lebron v. National Railroad Passenger Corporation (1995), 521–523
Legal approach, 33–38, 562, 564; to accountability, 529, 553; to budgeting, 315–317; to decision making, 344–348; to ethics, 553; to implementation evaluation, 393–398; to organization, 189–194; to personnel administration, 254–261; to the public, 482–483, 484, 485–486; to regulatory administration, 441–446
Legislative oversight, 393
Legislative Reorganization Act, 564
Legislative veto, 393–394
Legitimacy, 501–503
Lewis, Eugene, 155, 156–157
Liability, 83–85, 260–261, 346, 431–432, 483, 495, 524, 553, 554
Liberty, 504–509
Light, Paul, 72
Limited emergency appointments, 224
Limited-term appointments, 224
Lincoln, Abraham, 212
Line-item budgets, 304–305

Line-item veto, 72, 91, 298
Likert, Rensis, 182
Lipset, Seymour, 468, 531
Liston, Sonny, 466
Litigation, 455–456, 486
Little v. Streater (1981), 378
Lloyd-La Follette Act (1912), 216
Lobbyists, 85–88
Local governments, budgets of, 279, 281, 282–283, 284, 309, 317; public attitudes of services, 471–474; relationships among, 132–134
Locality pay, 240
Long, Norton, 184
Loyalty Review Board, 255
Loyalty-security programs, 246, 254
Lump sum budgets, 304

McCarthy, Joseph, 246
McCarthyism, 246, 539
McClelland, David, 164
Maccoby, Michael, 166–167
McConnell, Grant, 87
McGregor, Douglas, 182
McNamara, Robert, 306
Madison, James, 123, 177, 210, 498–499, 503, 509
Maine 200 experiment, 438–439, 447
Mainzer, Lewis, 197
Majoritarian politics, 416, 418
Management by objectives, 179
Managerial approach, 16–20, 498, 500, 517, 562; to accountability, 529, 542–549; to budgeting, 303–311, 313; to decision making, 324–338; diversity and, 503; and due process, 511; to ethics, 542–549; to implementation evaluation, 373–388; legitimacy and, 501, 502; to organization, 172–183; to personnel administration, 226–244; policy outputs and, 365; to the public, 474–478, 484–485; to regulatory activities, 434–439, 444–447
Mani, Bonnie, 181
Market-based organization, 198–200
Market failure, 416
Market forces, 10–12
Marriott, 380

Marshall, Thurgood, 351, 397
Martin, Shan, 569
Maslow, Abraham, 161–163
Maternity leave, 257, 518
Mayo, Elton, 152
Mayor-council form of government, 111
Meat Inspection Act, 51
Mediation, 266
Medicaid, 128, 280, 302
Medicare, 280, 300, 302
Meltzner, Arnold, 398–399
Merit systems, 89, 90, 212–219, 220, 327, 538;
    affirmative action and, 253; decision making
    and, 327–328; discriminatory aspects of, 249,
    257
Merit Systems Protection Board (MSPB), 59,
    192, 197, 220, 244, 249, 258, 259
Merton, Robert, 380
Miami-Dade County Metropolitan Govern-
    ment, 134
Micromanagement (*see also* Pork barrel alloca-
    tions and Casework), 75–77, 550, 565
Miles' law, 194, 362
Military-industrial complex, 539
Miller, Michelle, 471–472
Miller, Thomas, 471–472
Mintzberg, Henry, 567
Missouri v. Jenkins (1990, 1995), 38, 316
Misuse of funds, control of, 379–380
Mixed scanning, 323, 352
Model Cities Program, 389, 399, 480
Monitoring, of performance, 382–383
Monroe, James, 210
Moral involvement, 158
Morrill Act (1862), 124
Morrison v. Olson (1988), 7, 500–501
Moses, Robert, 155, 156–157
Mosher, Frederick, 462, 530
Motivation, 150, 152, 153, 161, 208
*Motor Vehicle Manufacturers Association v. State
    Farm Mutual Automobile Insurance Co.* (1983),
    81, 443
Moynihan, Daniel Patrick, 480
Multiple budgets, 288–289
Municipalities, 110–113
Myers v. United States (1926), 29

Nader, Ralph, 418, 439, 482
Narrow tailoring, 514, 515
National Aeronautics and Space Administration
    (NASA), 171–172
National Association for the Advancement of
    Colored People (NAACP), 506
National Cattlemen's Association, 391
National Commission on the Public Service, 72
National Environmental Policy Act (NEPA)
    (1969), 88, 440–441, 445, 482, 483
National Fish Meal and Oil Association, 428
National Food Processors Association, 343
National Highway Traffic Safety Administra-
    tion, 363, 443
National Labor Relations Act (1935), 417
National Labor Relations Board, 62, 222, 415,
    417, 478
National League of Cities, 126
National Milk Producers Federation, 421
National Performance Review (NPR), 22, 55,
    58–59, 66, 72–73, 180, 338, 565, 566, 568,
    569; and accountability and ethics, 545–549,
    557; and administrative discretion, 382; and
    budgeting, 288, 311; and decision making,
    335–338; and labor relations, 269; and
    market-based organization, 198; and
    performance-based organizations, 181;
    and performance measurement, 383; and per-
    sonnel administration, 208, 219, 224, 226,
    235, 238, 243, 297; and policy outputs, 365;
    and the public, 462, 463, 476–478; and regu-
    lation, 438
National Renderers Association, 428
National Security Council (NSC), 68, 294, 353
National Treasury Employees Union v. Von Raab
    (1989), 257
Natural rights, 505
Naturalization Act (1798), 123
Negative income tax, 366–368
Negotiated partnership, 382
Negotiated Rulemaking Act (NRMA) (1990),
    193, 446
Networks, 169
New Deal, 409, 563
New Deal Coalition, 313
"New Democrats," 288, 563

New England Regional Commission, 132
New federalism, 109
New property, 510–511, 513
New public management (NPM), 16, 20–27, 30, 49, 55, 57–58, 126, 134, 135, 141, 148, 149, 194, 494, 506, 530, 562, 565, 567; and accountability and ethics, 529, 545–549; and alternative dispute resolution and, 193; and budgeting, 303–304; and bureaucracy, 457; and decision making, 323, 335–338, 355; and diversity, 504; and implementation evaluation, 380–388; and labor relations, 268; and leadership, 161; and legitimacy, 501; and market-based organization, 198–99; and organization, 177; and personnel administration, 226–227, 230; and the public, 453, 454, 476–478, 484, 485; and regulatory activities, 400, 424, 437–439, 445, 446; and state action, 524; and total quality management, 180
New York Bureau of Municipal Research, 302
New York Department of Environmental Conservation, 198
New York State Department of Social Services, 456
Nice, David, 109
NIMBY syndrome, 441
Niskanen, William, 287
Nixon, Richard, 179, 297, 432
Nollan v. California Coastal Commission (1987), 444
Noncareer appointments, 224
Nonexperimental research design, 368–369
Nuclear Regulatory Commission, 434
Occupational Safety and Health Administration (OSHA), 348–351, 385, 415, 419, 421, 423, 425, 438, 443, 447, 520
Occupational Safety and Health Administration Act (1970), 62, 348, 351
O'Connor, Sandra Day, 108
Office of Economic Opportunity, 197, 368, 499–500
Office of Government Ethics, 550, 553
Office of Management and Budget (OMB), 58, 68, 270, 288, 289, 292, 294, 295, 311, 343, 365, 383, 432–433, 540, 547

Office of Personnel Management (OPM), 58–59, 192, 223–224, 225, 226, 235, 253, 258–259, 385, 476, 495, 547, 566
Oil Protection Act (1990), 428
Olney, Richard, 417
Ombudsmen, 474–475
Open-systems theory, 167–169
Operating budgets, 303
Operations management, 178–179
Oregon Benchmarks Program, 383
Organization, 141–200; contemporary approaches to, 164–172; contemporary managerial perspectives on, 177–183; definition of, 142; democratic, 195–198, 200; leadership and, 153; legal approach to, 189–194; managerial approach to, 172–183; market-based, 198–200; political approach to, 183–189
Organization theory, 142–143, 164, 177; evolutionary approach, 172; systems approach, 164, 167–170
Organizational culture, 170–172, 181, 182, 327–328
Organizational development, 182–183
Organizational humanism, 182–183
Osborne, David, 21, 22
Ott, Steven, 171
Outsourcing, 542
Overbreadth, 507–508, 509
Overhead agencies, 55, 57–59
Overhead policies, 399
Oversight, 73, 74; congressional, 540; external, 545; judicial, 483; legislative, 393, 549

Paine, Tom, 246
Paperwork Reduction Act (1980), 441
Parrish v. Civil Service Commission of County of Alameda (1967), 496
Participation, 197–198, 455; direct, 479–480; interest groups and, 482; political, decline in, 462–464, 479; in public administration, 478–482, 484, 486–487
Participative organization, 195–198, 200
Partnership councils, 268–269
Partnerships, negotiated, 382
Patent and Trademark Office, U.S., 182
Patronage, 89–90, 210, 213, 245

Pay, 238–243

Pay-as-you-go (PAYGO), 295, 297

Pay caps, 240

Pendleton Act (1883), 212, 216, 219, 247–248

Pensions, 242–243

Percent to maximum (PTM) method, 471–474

Performance agreements, 73

Performance appraisals, 225, 236–238

Performance-based organizations (PBOs), 181–182, 198–199, 335; constitutional constraints on, 523, 524

Performance budgets, 304, 305, 306

Performance measurement, 382–383, 386–388

Performance Review Board, 225

Perrow, Charles, 143, 169, 170, 196, 325–326

Person search, 232

Personal responsibility, 419, 554, 557, 568

Personnel administration, 169, 185, 207–270, 513, 566–567; accountability and, 540; collective bargaining and, 261–269; constitutional rights and, 255–260; cutbacks and, 243; in era of "gentlemen," 208–210; legal approach to, 254–261; liability and immunity in, 260–261; managerial approach to, 226–244; merit system of, 212–219; new public management and, 226–227, 230; pay system in, 238–243; performance appraisal in, 236–238; political approach to, 244–254; political neutrality in, 243–244; position classification in, 227–230; privatization and, 269–270; recruitment, selection, and promotion, 230–236; reform of, 216–226; regulation of, 415; representativeness in, 247–254; responsiveness in, 245–247; scientific management and, 150; in spoils system, 210–212

Personnel Administrator of Massachusetts v. Feeney (1979), 515–516

Pipeline expenditures, 299

Planning Programming Budgeting Systems (PPBS), 306–309, 311, 313, 317, 335

Pluralism, 31, 185–186, 551; in incremental decision making, 341

Poister, Theodore, 472–473

Policy analysis, 361, 362–372; utilization of, 398–400

Policy design, 372

Policy evaluation, 340

Policy impacts, 364, 365–371

Policy networks, 87

Policy outputs, 364–365

Political appointees, 426–427

Political approach, 27–32, 498, 500, 517, 562; to accountability, 529, 549–553; to budgeting, 311–315; to decision making, 338–344; diversity and, 504; to ethics, 549–553; to implementation evaluation, 389–393; legitimacy in, 501, 502; to organization, 183–189; to personnel administration, 244–254; to the public, 453, 478–480, 482, 484, 486; to regulatory activities, 439–441, 444–446

Political exchanges, 536

Political executives, 69–72, 538, 541, 551

Political-machine-based culture, 536–538

Political machines, 380

Political neutrality, 209, 216, 243, 420, 538; legitimacy and, 501

Political parties, 89–90; state governments and, 118

Politics, budgets and, 279, 283, 285, 311–315; client, 417–418; decision making and, 338–339; entrepreneurial, 418, 419; interest groups, 416–417, 418; majoritarian, 416, 418, 477; public participation in, 462–464, 478–482

Populists, 215

Pork barrel allocations, 74–75, 78, 79, 187, 279, 313, 538, 550, 565

POSDCORB, 173–174

Position classification, 227–230

Post Office Committee, House, 566–567

Postal Service, U.S., 49, 385, 472, 477, 478, 541, 543, 566

Potato Chip and Snack Food Association, 379

Potts, Stephen, 550

Powell, Lewis, 84, 91, 350

Power, coercive, 158; remunerative, 158

Prefectures, 105

Premise controls, 325–326

Preprogram-postprogram analysis, 369

Presentment clauses, 394

Prethus, Robert, 165

Privacy rights, 519–520

Private contractors, constitutional constraints on, 523

Privatization, 11, 12, 21, 269–270, 288, 462, 524, 564

Proactive cases, 421–422

Procedural due process (*see* Due process)

Process analysis, 371

Process measures, 374

Productivity, pay levels and, 239

Professional and Administrative Career Exam (PACE), 235

Program budgets, 305–309

Program evaluation, 355

Progressive movement, 89, 215, 535, 537, 563

Progressive tax, 281

Promotion of personnel, 235–236

Property rights, 509–511

Property taxes, 282–283, 284

Proposition 2½, 283

Proposition 13, 283

Prospective adjudication, 344

Public, 453–487; in the administrative state, 454, 456–467; evaluation of public adminis-trators by, 467–474, 487; interaction with public administration, 454–456; legal ap-proach to, 482–483, 484, 485–496; manager-ial approach to, 474–478, 484–485; new public management and, 453, 454, 476–478; political approach to, 453, 484, 486; synthesis of approaches, 483–487

Public administration, 3, 5, 6, 324, 362; defini-tion of, 4–5, 6; distinguished from private administration, 6–14; future of, 561–569; public participation in, 478–482; public per-ception of, 467–474, 487

Public choice, 10, 26–27, 134

Public choice theory, 102–104

Public Citizen Health Research Group, 343

Public employees, 59–64, 208; constitutional rights of, 255–260; job satisfaction of, 162–163; liability and immunity of, 260–261; rights of, 346–347; separation of powers and, 499; social class of, 531; socialization of, 531, 533; street-level administrators, 336–338; welfare bureaucracy and, 380

Public employment, 46–47

Public Employment Relations Boards (PERBs), 264, 266–267

Public goods, 11, 22, 454

Public Health Service, U.S. (PHS), 367, 481

Public interest, 9, 10, 88–89, 244, 334, 339, 354, 482, 506, 551; misconception of, 530–533; regulatory administration concern-ing, 439, 445

Public law litigation, 82–83

Public policy cycle, 12, 13

Public Works and Transportation Committee, 75

Pure Food and Drug Act (1906), 51, 413, 418

Pyhrr, Peter, 310, 311

Qualifications Review Board, 225

Quality circles, 196

Quality of work life (QWL) policies, 269

Quasi-experimental research design, 369–370

Quotas, 254

Rail Passenger Service Act (1970), 522

Rate-setting, 413–414, 446

Rational-comprehensive model of decision making, 328–329, 333–335, 338, 342, 350, 356

Rationality, bounded, 149, 328; of bureaucracy, 148

Reagan, Ronald, 65, 70, 109, 125, 135, 154, 287, 299, 433, 470

Real property taxes, 282–283, 284

Reasonableness, judicial assessment of, 442–444

Recruitment, 230, 231–232

Redford, Emmette, 462

Red scare, 80, 539

Red tape, 148, 199, 425–426

Reductions-in-force (RIFs), 225, 243, 247, 249

Regime values, 553

Regional councils, 135

Reg-neg, 446

Regressive tax, 281, 282, 283

Regulatory activities, 14–15, 51–55, 362–363, 381, 407–447, 463, 485; adjudication of, 350; agencies engaged in, 410–412; development and growth of, 408–419; federalism in, 126, 129–130; interest groups and, 86; legal

Regulatory activities *(continued)*
approach to, 400, 441, 444–446; managerial approach to, 434–439, 444–447; new public management and, 400, 424, 437–439, 445, 446; political approach to, 439–441, 444–446; problems in, 424–431; public attitudes toward, 470–471; structure and process, 419–424; supply-side economics and, 287; synthesis of approaches to, 444–447; takings, 444

Regulatory commissions, 119–121, 426, 429, 433, 439, 499

Regulatory federalism, 415

Regulatory Flexibility Act (1980), 441

Regulatory rachet, 429, 438

Rehnquist, William, 7, 107, 349, 351

Reich, Charles, 465, 466

Remedial law, 82–83

Reorganization, 188–189

Reorganization Act (1939), 177

Repackaging, 301

Reporting requirements, 540

Representation, 29, 30, 102, 184, 197, 223, 551; autonomy and, 186; budgetary process and, 314; budgeting and, 312; collective bargaining and, 262; decentralization and, 187; decision making and, 339, 340; in personnel administration, 209, 212, 219, 247–254; pluralism and, 185–196; of the poor, 480; in regulatory administration, 439–440

Representative bureaucracy, 184

Reprogramming, 298

Republican party, 209, 212, 217, 539, 563–564

Rescissions, 291, 297

Residency requirements, 327, 379

Responsiveness, budgetary process and, 314; collective bargaining and, 263; to constitutional values, 524; decision making and, 339, 340; implementation evaluation and, 390–392; in personnel administration, 245–247; regulation and, 400

Retrospective adjudication, 345

Revenues, sources of, 279–284

Revolving door, 86, 552

Riccucci, Norma, 157–158

Rickover, Hyman, 155, 156–157

Risk, intolerance of, 419

Roethlisberger, Fritz, 152

Rohr, John A., 544, 545, 553

Roosevelt, Franklin D., 80, 217, 313

Roosevelt, Theodore, 413

Rotation in office, 551

Rousseau, Jean Jacques, 545

Rulemaking, 54, 341, 346, 420, 432–433, 444, 482, 499

Rules, enforcement of, 434

Rutan v. Republican Party of Illinois (1990), 91

Sabol, Barbara, 461, 485

Safety net, 418

Sales taxes, 282

Santeria faith, 505

Savas, E.S., 380–382

Sayre, Wallace, 27

Scalia, Antonin, 7

Schmidt, Warren H., 159–160

Schneider, William, 468

Schultz, George, 67

Schurz, Carl, 213–214

Schweiker v. Hansen (1981), 397

Scientific management, 17, 18, 19, 141, 149–151, 161, 163, 229

Scope of bargaining, 262, 263

Scott, William, 169

Seat belts laws, 362–363, 370, 419, 431

Securities and Exchange Commission (SEC), 434

Sedition Act (1798), 123

Seidman, Harold, 31, 74, 185–186, 188–189, 328

Selection of personnel, 232–235

Self-regulation, 432, 437

Seminole Tribe of Florida v. Florida (1996), 394

Senate, U.S., 102

Senior Executive Service (SES), 70–71, 224–226, 227, 244, 245, 551

Separation of powers, 6, 8, 15, 29, 53, 62, 64, 77, 80, 93, 100, 111, 351, 394, 408, 429, 498–501, 566; accountability and, 541

Sequestration, 291, 295

Service activities, managerial approach to, 485

Service delivery, alternative, 380–382

Services, local government, 471–474
Sexual harassment, 249, 250, 251
Shapiro v. Thompson (1969), 379, 516
Shelton v. Tucker (1960), 506–507
Sherman Antitrust Act (1890), 51, 414, 416
Shipping Act (1916), 417
Simon, Herbert, 149, 176, 355
Sinclair, Upton, 413, 414
Site visits, 374
Situational approach to leadership, 158
Situational factors in job performance, 233
Situational view of leadership, 154
Socialization, 531, 533
Social Security, 280, 291, 302, 315
Social Security Administration, 397, 456, 477, 513
Social Security Disability Insurance (SSDI), 328, 330–332
Society, individual in, 456–461
Sociotherapeutic policies, 399–400
Sorensen, Theodore, 342
Sovereignty, 12–14, 100, 106, 135, 263, 462; state, 124, 261
Span of control, 104–105, 543
Special counsels, 197
Special districts, 114–115
Specialization, 334–335; decision making and, 324–326, 354
Spoils system, 13, 16, 89, 207, 210, 213–214, 216–217, 219, 243–244, 551
Standing, 483
State action, 493, 494, 521–524, 564
State, U.S. Department of, 335, 385
States, 115–118; budgets of, 279, 281, 282, 284, 298, 303, 309; federal relations with, 123–129; and mixes of federalism, 109–110
Steamboat Inspection Service, 408
Steck, Henry, 86
Stevens, John Paul, 350, 517
Stewart, Potter, 350
Stigler, George, 417
Strategic planning, 311, 353
Street-level administrators, 336–338, 373–374, 422, 486; public encounters with, 456
Strict scrutiny, 81, 253, 516
Strikes, 263–266

Structural cases, 422
Subordinate-centered leadership, 159–160
Substantive rights, 35, 508
Subversion, 539
Sunset provisions, 315, 364, 392
Sunshine laws, 392, 552
Supermajorities, 477–478, 502
Supply-side economics, 287–288
Supreme Court, 34, 52, 81, 130–131, 255, 268, 443, 444, 463, 497–498, 503, 506, 564–565; on affirmative action, 223, 254; and diversity, 504; on doctrine of privilege, 255–256; on due process, 510–511; and equal protection clause, 395, 515–516, 517; on immunity of public administrators, 83; on individuality, 518; on legislative veto, 393–394; on liability of public administrators, 84, 260; 495; on loyalty-security programs, 254; on maternity leave, 257; on patronage, 245, 254; on patronage dismissals, 90, 91, 212; on privacy rights, 520; on property rights, 509–510; on random drug testing, 257; on state action, 521–524
Surrogate market regulation, 414, 425, 431
Surveys, of encounters with public administrators, 469
Suspect classifications, 38, 513–515
Swiss, James, 180
System 4, 182
Systems theory, 164, 167–170

Takings, 444, 509, 565
Tannenbaun, Robert, 159–160
Tausky, Curt, 183
Taxation, 276, 279–284, 287, 468
Tax expenditures, 277, 278, 291–292, 381
Tax revolts, 565
Taylor, Frederick, 17, 149–151, 153, 172, 185, 229
Taylor Grazing Act (1934), 389, 439
Technical efficiency, 336
Tenure, 210–211, 216, 219, 541
Tenure of Office Act (1820), 211
Testing, 423–424
Theory X, 182, 183
Theory Y, 182, 183

Therapeutic services, 485

Third party government, 48–49, 126, 380, 542, 568

Thompson, James D., 170

Thompson, Victor, 148, 459, 530

Three hundred sixty degree evaluation, 238

Three Mile Island, 434

Total quality management (TQM), 179–181, 233, 236, 567

Townships, 112

Transfers, 298

Transportation, U.S. Department of, 426

Treasury, U.S. Department of, 288

Truman, Harry S., 66, 217

Tuskegee study, 366, 367

Unassembled examinations, 232–233

Unfunded mandates, 128

Uniform Commercial Code, 131–132

Unions, 229, 236, 247, 257, 262, 267

Union shop, 267

Unitary political systems, 100

United States v. *Brignoni-Ponce* (1975), 518

U.S. Canola Association, 428

U.S. Commission on Civil Rights, 340

United States v. Lopez (1995), 107–108

United States v. Maine et al. (1984), 103

United States v. National Treasury Employees Union (1995), 554

U.S. Term Limits v. Thornton (1995), 108, 394

Urwick, Lyndall, 20, 173

Validation techniques, 233–235

Values, of administrative culture, 460–461; regime, 553; social, 456–461

ValuJet, 427, 433, 434, 439, 542, 569

Vermont Yankee Nuclear Power Corporation v. Natural Resources Defense Council (1978), 444

Veteran preference, 247, 516

Veterans Affairs, U.S. Department of, 50, 301, 566

Vietnam War, 534

Volcker Commission, 72

Vouchers, 381

Wagner Act (1935), 417

Waldo, Dwight, 176–177, 494, 569

Wall Street Journal, 424–425, 426

Warwick, Donald, 51

Washington, George, 208

Watergate, 549

Wayne, Stephen, 68–69

Wealth, government control of, 465–467

Weber, Max, 18, 144, 146–149, 153, 154, 172, 173, 185, 457, 501, 503, 552

Weiss, Ted, 343

Welfare bureaucracy, 380

Welfare programs, 496, 510–511; flow chart for processing applicants, 178

Welfare state, 418

West Virginia State Board of Education v. Barnette (1943), 502–503, 504

Whig party, 211

Whistleblowing, 218, 222, 256–257, 383, 551–552, 568

White, Byron, 351

White, Leonard, 17, 20, 564, 565, 569

Wickard v. Fillburn (1942), 107

Wilcox, Herbert, 460

Wildavsky, Aaron, 314, 398

Wiley, Harvey, 418

Wilson, James Q., 49, 51–52, 416–418, 434

Wilson, Woodrow, 17, 20, 89, 214–215, 248, 363, 484, 487, 494–495

Wright, J. Skelley, 427

Wyatt v. Stickney (1971), 37

X efficiency, 336

Zero-Base Budgeting (ZBB), 309–311, 313, 315, 317, 335

Zone of Indifference, 153, 158

Zuboff, Shoshana, 356, 567